Betty Crocker's
PICTURE
COOK BOOK

REVISED AND ENLARGED

SECOND EDITION
(Third Printing)

Published by

McGraw-Hill Book Company, Inc.

NEW YORK   TORONTO   LONDON

HOME OF *Betty Crocker* SERVICE

Where Betty Crocker lives it's just like home—the furniture comfortable and charming—the colors bright and gay—the atmosphere pleasing and restful.

The office section beyond the curved mural depicting the serenity of country life is light and cheery. Walls and book shelves are painted a restful robin's egg blue. Through the wide view window straight ahead, you look into a bright yellow kitchen.

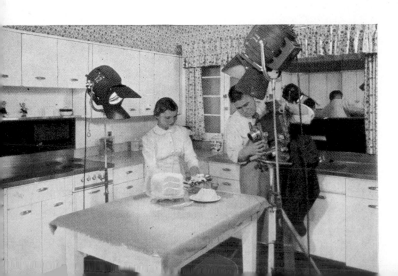

Kamera Kitchen

This has three complete working units, where foods to be photographed are "made up." Appropriate dishes and colorful fabrics to set them off are kept in the commodious cabinets. Wallpaper and matching draperies in a quaint sprigged calico pattern add charm.

Terrace Kitchen

This contains every known home-type convenience. General recipe testing, planned for taste tests at the Tasting Bar just outside, goes on here. And in this kitchen guest luncheons are prepared. Before entering, visitors find a homey welcome in a cozy grouping of Early American cherry furniture.

Kitchens of Tomorrow

In two of these, soft green walls, reproductions of old shutters, and copper accents are cool and restful. One kitchen is for important experimental baking, to develop new methods and new products for the future. The other is for daily products tests. In a third kitchen, of French Provincial design, new and glamorous recipes are created.

Early American Dining Room

In surprising contrast to the up-to-the-minute kitchens, this spacious room boasts mellow old panelling from a New England home of 1750. The wide fireplace with old-fashioned cooking utensils reveals how women used to labor. Antique chairs . . . a stretcher table . . . dough box . . . and old pewter and pressed glass convey the charm of oldtime peace.

Dear Friend,

Here are the secrets of good cooking—revealed in over 2,000 tested ways to prepare tasty, appetizing, nutritious meals for your family.

Now improved and revised, Betty Crocker's PICTURE COOK BOOK brings you a wealth of help with your meal-planning and preparation. Your hours in the kitchen will be fewer, lighter and more enjoyable with the aid of this *complete* guide to better, easier cooking.

More than 3,500,000 copies of the highly successful first edition were sold. Hundreds of thousands of homemakers wrote Betty Crocker saying how much it helped them achieve wonderful results in their kitchens. And now you hold in your hands an even more outstanding cook book!

New easy-to-follow recipes, many new drawings, pictures and color pages, stories about the origin of new recipes, and old favorites brought up to date add to the value of this handsome book. Expanded chapters on meats and main dishes, a special meal-planning section including everyday menus, holiday suggestions, favorite menus and dishes of celebrities, and timely information on freezing with the latest simplified methods give you a host of new ideas.

You can use with complete confidence all the recipes shown on the following pages. They represent the best of thousands Betty Crocker has offered in her many years of service. All have been tested and retested in representative homes throughout the country. Only those that passed this home testing with a top score for excellent results and eating enjoyment appear here. They include simple dishes for the beginner, everyday favorites and sophisticated triumphs for the expert.

No time, effort, experience or expense has been spared to make the Betty Crocker PICTURE COOK BOOK as useful, practical and interesting as possible. Its carefully planned features, plus its attractive, speedy-reference layout, make this book a basic essential for your kitchen. We hope it will bring you more fun in cooking and deeper joy in your homemaking.

Sincerely yours,
McGraw-Hill Book Company

SPECIAL HELPS

Planning your work
 To save precious time,
Pays dividends . . .
  Without costing a dime.

NOTE: *See tips, short cuts in every chapter.*

Keep a blackboard in your kitchen for grocery lists, menus, messages to your family, and reminders.

Save time . . . Insure sanitation

Rinse dishes with boiling water, leave on rack to dry. Wipe glasses, silver. Some prefer to wash dishes only once a day. Saves soap, time. Rinse and stack, then cover.

Plan ahead . . . meals for several days. Market only once or twice a week. Keep your meal patterns in mind.

Think ahead for efficiency

Right after using, **fill cooking pans with** hot water. Exception: use cold water for cereal, egg, milk dishes.

Keep spices on a tray or in a box. Lift out of cupboard all at one time.

One clean-up process instead of several

Before washing the breakfast dishes, do any necessary baking or advance meal preparation. Then wash all at once.

To boil potatoes in less time: remove a strip of skin from one side. Boil, then rest of skin peels off easily. *To bake potatoes* in half the time: boil first for 15 min.

Combine jobs to save time and energy

Bake cake or cookies while washing dishes or cooking dinner; peel potatoes while meat is browning; cook some foods to be served 2 or 3 times . . . beef for roast, hash, pie.

Do messy tasks, such as paring potatoes, on paper to be disposed of easily. Have a paper bag at working area for scraps.

Daily care saves time and equipment

Keep utensils and equipment in good working condition. Eliminate cleaning of broiler by placing aluminum foil under rack in broiler pan to catch drippings.

Easy and fun . . . have family "make their own" lunch or Sunday supper: take meat, cheese, leftovers from refrigerator; set out bread, relishes.

Bake and cook ahead

Prepare dishes for last-minute cooking. Bake and prepare large amount of foods at a time and freeze according to directions with freezer and on pp. 23-26.

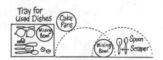

Learn good work habits. For example, assemble materials before starting to bake. Keep table cleared and cooking dishes washed as you go along.

Have logical and orderly arrangement in your kitchen

Establish convenient work centers . . . for clean-up (washing dishes, cleaning vegetables); for making salads; for baking; for serving, etc.

Keep all cleaning supplies and equipment in a basket and carry from room to room while cleaning.

SPECIAL HELPS

Make work easy.

If you're tired from overwork,
Household chores you're bound to shirk.
Read these pointers tried and true
And discover what to do.

Wear comfortable clothes and properly fitted shoes while working around the house.

For personal outlook

Eat proper food for health and vitality. Every morning before breakfast, comb hair, apply make-up, a dash of cologne, and perhaps some simple earrings. Does wonders for your morale.

Organize the family to cooperate. Train the children to help with different jobs. Very young children can set and clear the table. Older ones can cook.

Your mind can accomplish things while your hands are busy

Do head work while dusting, sweeping, washing dishes, paring potatoes, etc. Plan family recreation, the garden, etc.

Have sink, work table, counter tops, etc. at a height that is comfortable, to eliminate strain . . . if dishpan is too low, set it on a box.

Prevent unnecessary fatigue

Use a dust mop and a long-handled dust pan. Use self-wringing mop (no stooping).

If you feel tired, lie down on the floor on your back, put your hands above your head, close your eyes, and relax for 3 to 5 min.

Exercise, sunshine, fresh air are part of health

Get outdoors every day. Take a walk, do some gardening, take the children for an outing, or pay your neighbor a short visit.

If you have just a moment, sit down, put your feet up on a chair, close your eyes and just relax your muscles. Let your arms, hands, and head fall limp.

Good posture prevents fatigue

When standing, keep erect posture . . . do not slump or bend over tasks (poor posture is more tiring). Remember sitting uses much less energy than standing.

Alternate sitting down tasks and standing up tasks. Don't be on your feet too long at one time.

Check up on yourself

If after following all these rules for proper rest, exercise, diet, you are still tired and depressed, have a medical check-up and follow doctor's orders.

Harbor pleasant thoughts while working. It will make every task lighter and pleasanter.

Refresh your spirits

"Recreation" means "re-create" . . . for enthusiasm and courage. Garden, paint pictures, pursue any hobby, look through a magazine for home planning ideas, read a good book, or attend club meetings.

Notice humorous and interesting incidents to relate at dinnertime when family is together.

How to Get PERFECT Results from Recipes in this Book . . .

1 Read Recipe Carefully! Every word of it. And do be *sure* to see if there's anything to be purchased or done—like chopping nuts or melting chocolate before you start mixing.

2 Look at the Pictures! They give you "know how" you need for every step.

3 Turn on the Heat! If the cookies are to be baked immediately after mixing, see that the oven is heated to correct temperature.

4 Get Your Ingredients Together! Saves time and steps to have them all in one place.

5 Collect Utensils, Too! Gather together all you'll need . . . from the flour sifter to the baking pan.

6 Measure as Exactly as a Druggist follows a doctor's prescription! Two minutes spent measuring carefully may save you hours of grief.

7 Mix Carefully as Directed (cream or stir or beat or fold in, etc.). Follow every step exactly as described in the recipe and pictures.

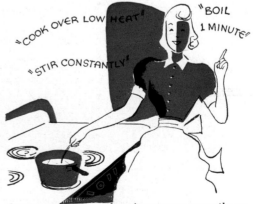

8 Bake or Cook or otherwise prepare correctly as the recipe indicates. Correct cooking or baking is necessary for complete success.

HOW TO MEASURE *to be Sure of Results . . .*

Use squares of paper when sifting, measuring, etc.

Cooking success is up to you!
If you'll take pains to measure true,
Use Standard cups and spoons all the way.
And then level off—it'll always pay!

Use straight-edged knife for "leveling off."

Liquid Measuring Cup . . . has rim above the 1-cup line.

Use for measuring any liquid ingredients.

Graduated Dry Measuring Cups . . . ¼, ⅓, ½, 1 cup.

Use for part-cups or whole cups of any dry ingredients or shortenings.

Measuring Spoons . . . ¼, ½, and 1 teaspoon, 1 tablespoon.

Use for less than ¼ cup of any ingredient.

FLOUR

1 Sift flour through large open sifter (to aerate it) onto square of paper before measuring.

2 Then spoon sifted flour lightly into a "dry" measuring cup . . . heaping it up.

3 Level off cup with straight-edged knife. Don't shake cup. This is important!

SUGAR

1 **White Granulated Sugar** needs sifting only if lumpy. Spoon lightly into "dry" measuring cup. Level it off with a straight-edged knife. Don't knock or tap cup.

2 **Brown Sugar.** If it's lumpy, put into airtight container. Place piece of moistened sponge on sugar. Remove sponge in 3 days. Replace cover. Pack into "dry" measuring cup until sugar holds its shape. Level off.

3 **Confectioners' Sugar.** Sift through flour sifter or press through sieve to remove lumps. Spoon lightly into "dry" measuring cup. Level off with straight-edged knife. Don't shake or knock cup.

HERE'S HOW WE MEASURE

Baking Powder, Soda, Salt, Cornstarch, Cream of Tartar, Spices, Etc.

Stir, then fill measuring spoon. Level off with straight-edged knife.

SHORTENING

Use graduated measuring cups. Have shortening at room temperature. Pack shortening firmly into measuring cup. Level off with straight-edged knife.

In measuring less than ¼ cup, use a tablespoon (hold fingers under bowl to prevent breaking it).

BUTTER

For approximate measure:
4 sticks (1 lb.) = 2 cups
1 stick (¼ lb.) = ½ cup
½ stick (⅛ lb.) = ¼ cup

EGGS

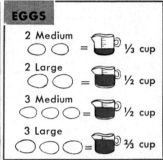

2 Medium = ⅓ cup
2 Large = ½ cup
3 Medium = ½ cup
3 Large = ⅔ cup

Size varies ... so measure eggs in most recipes. Do not use less or more than the amount specified in recipe.

LIQUIDS

Use "liquid" measuring cup to prevent spilling. Pour liquid into cup on table. Have measuring line at eye level.

MOLASSES OR SYRUP

Fill cup. It rounds up, so level off. Scrape out with rubber spatula.

DRIED FRUIT

Pack raisins, dates, figs., etc., lightly into measuring cup. Press gently to level off top.

NUTS AND COCONUT

Pack shredded coconut or shelled nuts lightly into measuring cup level with top.

SOFT BREAD CRUMBS

Pack lightly into measuring cup. Press gently until level with top.

SHREDDED OR GRATED CHEESE

Pack lightly into measuring cup until level with top.

FINE DRY BREAD CRUMBS

Spoon lightly into measuring cup. Level off. Don't shake cup.

MEANING OF TERMS

This page gives the meaning of terms in this book! It's here just to help you to be a Prize Cook!

SUGAR

Fine white granulated sugar, unless otherwise specified in recipe.

EGGS

Fresh eggs (*med. size*). Keep refrigerated to preserve good quality.

CHOCOLATE

Unsweetened baking chocolate. If sweet chocolate or bits or pieces are required, recipe will so state.

ALL-PURPOSE FLOUR

Gold Medal *"Kitchen-tested"* Enriched Flour—for all-purpose baking. *Recipes in this book, except those specifying Softasilk Cake Flour, have been perfected for Gold Medal only.*

CAKE FLOUR

Softasilk Cake Flour. It is specially milled from selected "soft" winter wheats to make exceptionally delicate, fine-textured cakes.

MILK

Fresh, sweet milk, unless otherwise indicated.

BUTTERMILK and SOUR MILK

May be used interchangeably. Too old milk has disagreeable flavor!

MOLASSES

Dark molasses . . . for rich flavor, dark color. Light molasses gives more delicate color and flavor.

SPICES and FLAVORINGS

High quality always, for flavor and dependability.

CREAM

This may be one of the following. The type is usually indicated.

Cultured	20% butterfat
Whipping	35% butterfat
Coffee	20% butterfat
Half and Half	12% butterfat

ROLLED OATS

Either quick-cooking or regular (uncooked).

MOIST SHREDDED COCONUT

Shredded coconut that's moist . . . either from a can or a package . . . or shredded from a fresh coconut.

BAKING POWDER

Any of the well known nationally distributed brands of double-action baking powder give good results with the recipes in this book.

COOKING (SALAD) OIL

Any fresh, mild-flavored salad oil of vegetable origin.

SHORTENING

Any fresh, mild-flavored solid fat . . . animal or vegetable, such as those at right. Butter is indicated in certain recipes for flavor.

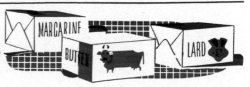

MEANING OF TERMS (cont.)

MUSTARD

Dry mustard: ground mustard seed in powdered form.

Prepared mustard: paste made of dry mustard blended with vinegar, sometimes specially seasoned.

CHEESE

American (Cheddar) cheese: "unaged" (green) or "aged;" the greener cheese is mild, the aged cheese sharper in flavor. It ranges from firm to crumbly in texture . . . from pale to deep yellow in color.

White cream cheese: of smooth creamy consistency. **Note:** 3-oz. and 8-oz. pkg.

PEPPERS

Black pepper: ground from whole peppercorns.

White pepper: from peppercorns with outer bark removed.

> **Paprika:** mildly pungent.
> **Red pepper:** sharper.
> **Cayenne:** hottest of all.

All ground from red pepper pods.

PLAIN GELATINS

Plain unflavored gelatin: each envelope contains 1 tbsp.

FLAVORED GELATINS

Gelatin with sugar, color, and flavoring added.

MUSHROOMS (2 forms)

Both should be sautéed in butter before using.

COFFEE

It is used in either liquid or powdered form. The type is indicated.

YEAST

The yeast used in recipes in this book is Dry yeast in granular form. You may prefer to use Fresh yeast.

One pkg. Dry yeast is equivalent to one 2/3-oz. or 3/5-oz. cake Fresh yeast.

Fresh yeast keeps about 2 weeks in the refrigerator. Dry yeast requires no refrigeration; it keeps fresh for weeks (*see expiration date on pkg.*).

MASHED POTATOES and POTATO WATER

Freshly mashed potatoes: no milk or seasoning added.

Potato water: in which potatoes have been boiled.

RYE FLOUR

Flour made from rye. Wheat flour is usually used with it to make bread light.

WHOLE WHEAT or GRAHAM FLOUR

The fine or coarsely ground kernels of wheat including bran, germ, and all.

CORN MEAL

The coarsely ground kernel of the corn (either white or yellow corn meal).

HERBS

Garden Fresh, Dried Crushed, Powdered: must be fresh, full-bodied. Keep in tightly covered jar in cold place. Replace when freshness is gone.

A DICTIONARY OF COOKING TERMS

Everyday and Special

A

à la king. Food served in rich cream sauce usually containing mushrooms, green pepper, pimiento—often flavored with sherry.

angelica. The candied leafstalk of a European herb . . . used in decorating cakes, candies, desserts, etc.

antipasto. Italian for assorted appetizers of fish, cold cuts, or vegetables.

aspic. A jelly made from concentrated vegetable, meat, or fish stock . . . with gelatin.

au beurre. With, or cooked in, butter.

au gratin. With a crust; usually fine bread crumbs. Sometimes with cheese.

B

baba. A French cake, made with a yeast dough, and usually flavored with rum or fruit juice.

bake. To cook by dry heat in oven.

barbecue. To roast meat on a rack over coals . . . basting it with highly seasoned sauce.

bar-le-duc. A jam originally made in Bar-le-duc, France, from currants and honey. The seeds were laboriously pushed out with a needle. Popularly made in the United States with the seeds left in.

baste. To moisten food while it is cooking (as meat while roasting) by spooning over it liquid or fat.

batter. A mixture of flour and liquid, or in combination with other ingredients . . . thin enough to pour.

beat. To mix with vigorous over-and-over motion with spoon, whip, or beater (to make smooth or incorporate air).

beurre noir. Browned butter sauce.

bisque. 1. A rich cream soup (usually from fish, vegetables, or game). 2. Or a frozen dessert, usually ice cream, with nuts in it.

blanch. 1. To skin fruit or nuts by immersing in boiling water (3 min.). 2. To whiten food by plunging into boiling water. French origin.

blend. To mix thoroughly.

boil. To cook in steaming liquid in which bubbles are breaking on surface.

bombe. A round or melon-shaped frozen dessert, combining frozen mixtures.

borsch. The Ukrainian national soup . . . made with beets or a variety of vegetables.

bouillabaisse. A French chowder of several varieties of fish and other ingredients.

bouillon. A clear meat broth.

braise. A method for cooking meat. See p. 309.

bread. To coat with flour, egg, and crumbs.

brioche. A slightly sweetened French breakfast yeast bun.

broil. To cook directly under heating unit or over fire.

brush. To spread thinly, as with a brush or with a crumpled paper.

C

café au lait. Coffee served with hot milk.

canapé. A tiny piece of fried or toasted bread topped with appetizers. See p. 65.

caramelize. To melt granulated sugar over med. heat to a golden brown syrup. (burnt sugar). See p. 29.

caviar. Prepared and salted roe (eggs) of the sturgeon and other large fish. Black or red, they are served as an appetizer.

chantilly. A dish in which whipped cream is one of the ingredients. Name derived from that of a castle north of Paris.

charlotte. A gelatin dessert containing flavored whipped cream, molded in a form lined with sponge cake strips or ladyfingers.

chill. To allow to become thoroughly cold.

chop. To cut in fine or coarse pieces with sharp knife or chopper.

chutney. A spicy, somewhat sweet relish, made from several fruits and vegetables. Originally from India.

coat. To cover with thin film as flour, fine crumbs, icing, sugar, or crushed nuts.

compote. 1. A stemmed dish. 2. A "stew" of fruits cooked slowly in syrup, during which fruits have retained their natural shape.

condensed milk. Whole milk commercially concentrated by evaporation, then sweetened.

condiment. Pungent substance such as catsup, chutney, mustard to make food more appetizing.

cool. Let stand at room temperature until no longer warm.

cracklings. The crisp residue of fat after the lard has been cooked out of it.

cream. To soften fat by rubbing it against the bowl with a spoon, or beating with mixer until it is light and fluffy (creamy).

creole. Highly seasoned food as prepared by the Creoles, descendants of early French and Spanish settlers of Louisiana.

croquette. A ball made of minced meat, rice, or the like, coated with egg and cracker crumbs and fried in deep fat.

croustade. A toast case.

crouton. See p. 30.

cube. To cut into solids of 6 equal square sides (usually ¼ to ½″ in size).

curry. A stew cooked or flavored with curry.

 cut in. To combine fat with dry ingredients using two knives, a fork, or pastry blender.

cutlet. A small piece of meat, cut from leg or ribs, for broiling or frying. Or mixture such as fish, shaped like a meat cutlet.

D

demitasse. The French for "half cup." A small cup for or of after-dinner coffee.

devil. To prepare with hot seasoning or sauce.

 dice. to cut into very small cubes (about ¼″).

dough. A mixture of flour and liquid in combination with other ingredients, thick enough to roll, knead, or drop off a spoon.

dredge. See "coat" (p. 12).

drippings. Fat and juice dripped from roasting meat.

E

éclair. Cream puff paste baked in oval shape filled with whipped cream or custard.

 en brochette. French term for cooked on a skewer.

entree. In formal dinners, a small "made" dish that is served as a separate course between the heavy courses. In informal meals, the chief dish of the main course . . . of meat, poultry, fish, or meat substitute.

evaporated milk. Whole milk from which 60% of its water has been evaporated.

F

filet mignon. Small, tender fillet, usually from beef tenderloin.

fillet. Long, thin, boneless strip of lean meat or fish—usually a choice cut.

flake. To break lightly into small pieces.

 fold in. To cut down through center of a batter with edge of spoon or spatula, bringing up close to bowl, then turning over, cutting down through again . . . turning bowl a quarter turn at same time. Repeat until ingredients are blended.

fondant. Sugar syrup cooked to the soft ball stage (234°), cooled, and kneaded to creaminess.

fondue. A light, fluffy baked food made with eggs, cheese, and milk and thickened with bread or cracker crumbs.

frappé. Diluted sweetened fruit juice, frozen to a mushy consistency.

French fry. To cook in hot fat deep enough to float the food.

fricassee. Properly, to cook by braising. For chicken it means stewing . . . the browning process may be omitted.

frizzle. To pan-fry until the edges curl.

fromage. French word for cheese.

frost. To cover with icing.

fry. To cook in hot fat.

G

garnish. To decorate with portions of colorful and contrasting food.

glacé. 1. Coated with a sugar syrup cooked to the "crack" stage. 2. Frozen.

glaze. To add luster to a food by coating with a syrup or jelly—then heating or chilling.

goulash. A thick Hungarian beef or veal stew flavored with vegetables and paprika.

grate. To rub against grater to shred food.

grind. To cut or crush in a food grinder.

grits. Hulled and coarsely ground corn or other grain.

gumbo. 1. West Indian plant, the okra, used to flavor and thicken. 2. A soup usually thickened with okra.

H

herb bouquet. Combination of herbs. See p. 56.

hollandaise. A sauce. See p. 402.

hors d'oeuvres. Variety of appetizers. See p. 64.

I

ice. 1. A frozen dessert. 2. To frost.

A DICTIONARY OF COOKING TERMS (cont.)

J

julienne. To cut food into match-like strips.

junket. A dessert of milk coagulated by rennet, sweetened, and flavored.

K

kisses. Small meringues.

knead. To work dough with a pressing motion accompanied by folding and stretching. See p. 106. Or to press dough with palms of hands ... alternately folding, and pushing, and stretching it. See p. 106.

L

lard. To insert strips of fat into or onto top of uncooked meat before roasting for flavor and moisture.

leek. Onion-like bulb, but smaller, more pungent than onion.

legumes. Vegetables which bear their fruit or seeds in pods, such as peas, beans, lentils.

lyonnaise. Seasoned with onions, parsley.

M

macaroons. Small cakes made from egg whites, sugar, and almond paste or powdered almonds.

macédoine. A mixture of fruits or vegetables.

maitre d'hotel. 1. A French term meaning "head steward or cook." 2. A sauce. See p. 338.

Marguerite. A salty cracker covered with a mixture of boiled frosting and nuts or coconut ... baked in the oven until browned.

marinade. An oil-acid mixture used to give flavor to meats or salads.

marinate. To let food stand in oil-acid mixture (usually French dressing) for added flavor.

meringue. A stiffly beaten mixture of egg whites and sugar (1) used to cover the top of a pie and usually browned in the oven, or (2) made in small cakes and baked.

mignon. 1. A French term meaning "favorite, delicate, darling." 2. A meltingly tender cut of boneless tenderloin beef.

mince. To chop or cut into very small pieces.

minestrone. Italian for thick vegetable soup.

mix. To combine ingredients, as by stirring.

mocha. A flavor from coffee infusion or a combination of coffee and chocolate.

monosodium glutamate (MSG). A white crystalline substance made from vegetable proteins. Enhances natural flavor of foods.

mousse. 1. A frozen dessert. See p. 256. 2. A certain hot dish of smooth texture. See pp. 275, 283.

P

pan-broil. To cook uncovered in ungreased or lightly greased hot skillet, pouring off grease as it accumulates.

pan-fry (sauté). To cook in small amount of fat in skillet.

parboil. To partially cook food in boiling water. The cooking is usually completed by another method.

parch. To brown with dry heat.

pare. To cut off outside covering as from apple or potato.

parfait. A frozen dessert. See p. 256.

pasteurize. To partially sterilize a liquid at a temperature (140 to 180°) which destroys bacteria (as for pasteurized milk).

paté de foie gras. Goose liver paste.

patty. A patty shell of puffed paste filled with a creamed mixture of chicken, fish, etc.

peel. To strip off outside covering as from orange, banana, or tomato.

petits fours. Little fancy iced cakes, made by cutting sheet cakes into special shapes (squares, diamonds, etc.). Frosting is poured on and decorations added.

pilau. Rice stewed with meat, poultry, or fish, spices, etc.

pit. To remove pits or seeds from fruit.

poach. To cook by surrounding with simmering (not boiling) water or other liquid, using care to retain shapes.

polenta. Italian for a corn meal or farina mush to which cheese is often added.

purée. 1. To press fruit or vegetables through a fine sieve. 2. A smooth, thick mixture made by rubbing cooked foods through a sieve.

R

ragout. A highly seasoned thick meat stew.

ramekin. An individual baking dish.

ravioli. Small shapes of Italian or noodle paste spread with a meat or vegetable filling folded over and poached in meat stock.

relish. A highly flavored food used with other foods to stimulate appetite.

render. To free fat from connective tissue over low heat.

rissole. A savory meat mixture enclosed in rich pastry and fried in deep fat.

roast. To cook by dry heat . . . usually in oven, sometimes in ashes, or on heated stones or metals.

roe. Eggs of fish. Roe Herring means herring with the eggs.

roll. 1. To place on a board and spread thin with a rolling pin. 2. A small shape made from a dough and baked.

roux. A cooked mixture of flour and butter used to thicken sauces.

S

salt. To season or cure with salt.

sauté. To brown or cook in small amount of fat in skillet.

scald. To heat to temperature just below boiling point.

scallion or shallot. A bulbless onion.

scallop. To bake in a baking dish food usually cut in pieces and mixed with a sauce.

 score. To cut narrow gashes part way through outer surface of food.

sear. To brown surface quickly.

sherbet. A water-ice with egg white added.

shortening. A fat suitable for baking.

shred. To tear or cut into small, but long narrow pieces.

sift. To pass through a sieve.

simmer. To cook in liquid just below boiling point on top of range.

skewer. 1. A long pin of wood or metal on which food is placed and held in shape while cooking. 2. To fasten meat with skewers to keep it in shape during cooking.

slice. To cut a thin, flat piece off and across something.

sliver. To cut or shred into long thin pieces.

soak. To immerse in liquid for a time.

soufflé. A delicate baked custard containing cheese, fruit, minced meat, or vegetables . . . made light by stiffly beaten egg whites.

sponge. A batter made with yeast in it.

steam. To cook in the steam which arises from a pan of boiling water or other liquid.

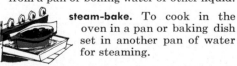 **steam-bake.** To cook in the oven in a pan or baking dish set in another pan of water for steaming.

steep. To extract flavor, colors, or other qualities from a substance by allowing it to stand in liquid just below the boiling point.

sterilize. To destroy microorganisms by boiling in water, by dry heat, or by steam.

stew. To cook slowly in a small amount of liquid for a long time.

stir. To mix, with a spoon, by rotary motion.

stock. The liquid in which meat, poultry, fish, or vegetables have been cooked.

T

tamale. A highly seasoned Mexican dish of ground meat, seasonings, cooked corn meal, beans, ripe olives, and fat, rolled in oiled cornhusks, steamed or boiled.

timbale. An unsweetened custard combined with minced vegetable, chicken, or fish, molded and baked.

 timbale case. A small shell fried on timbale iron.

toast. To brown by direct heat.

torte. A rich cake, usually made from crumbs, eggs, and nuts . . . or a meringue baked in the form of a cake. See p. 242.

tortilla. A thin round Mexican cake . . . made of corn meal and hot water and baked on a griddle. Mexican hot mixtures are often rolled in them.

toss. To lightly mix ingredients without mashing them.

truss. To tie a fowl or other meat so that it will hold its shape.

try out. To fry solid fat or fat meats, cut in small pieces, until fat is separated from membrane.

tutti-frutti. Mixed fruit.

U

until set. Until a liquid has become firm . . . often refers to a gelatin or custard mixture.

W

whip. To beat rapidly to produce expansion through the incorporation of air, as in egg whites, and whipping cream.

Z

zwieback. A kind of toasted biscuits or rusk.

COMMON FOOD EQUIVALENTS

(See bottom of page for nuts and dried fruits most frequently used in baking.)

	UNIT	APPROXIMATE MEASURE
Apples	1 lb.	3 medium (3 cups sliced)
Bananas	1 lb.	3 medium (2½ cups sliced)
Butter and Other Fats	1 lb.	2 cups
Cheese, American or Cheddar	1 lb.	4 cups grated
Cheese, Cottage	1 lb.	2 cups
Cheese, White Cream	3-oz. pkg	6 tbsp.
	½-lb. pkg	16 tbsp. (1 cup)
Chocolate, Unsweetened	½-lb. pkg	8 1-oz. squares
Coconut, Shredded	1 lb.	5 cups
Coffee, Ground	1 lb.	80 tbsp.
Cream, Whipping	1 pt.	2 cups (4 cups whipped)
Flour		
All-Purpose	1 lb.	4 cups (*sifted*)
Cake	1 lb.	4½ cups (*sifted*)
Whole Wheat	1 lb.	3½ cups
Rye	1 lb.	4½ to 5 cups
Lemon, Medium		
Juice	1	2 to 3 tbsp.
Rind, lightly grated	1	1½ to 3 tsp.
Marshmallows	¼ lb.	16
Orange, Medium		
Juice	1	⅓ to ½ cup
Rind, lightly grated	1	1 to 2 tbsp.
Sugar		
Granulated	1 lb.	2 cups
Brown	1 lb.	2¼ cups (firmly packed)
Confectioners'	1 lb.	3½ cups (*sifted*)
Powdered	1 lb.	2⅓ cups

EQUIVALENT WEIGHTS AND MEASURES

Nuts and Fruits Most Commonly Used

	NUTS IN SHELL	SHELLED NUTS
ALMONDS	1 lb. = 1 to 1¾ cups nutmeats	1 lb. = 3½ cups nutmeats
PECANS	1 lb. = 2¼ cups nutmeats	1 lb. = 4 cups nutmeats
PEANUTS	1 lb. = 2¼ cups nutmeats	1 lb. = 3 cups nutmeats
WALNUTS	1 lb. = 1⅔ cups nutmeats	1 lb. = 4 cups nutmeats

1 CUP WHOLE SHELLED NUTS = broken = cut-up = coarsely chopped = 1 cup minus 1 tbsp. = finely chopped = ⅞ CUP

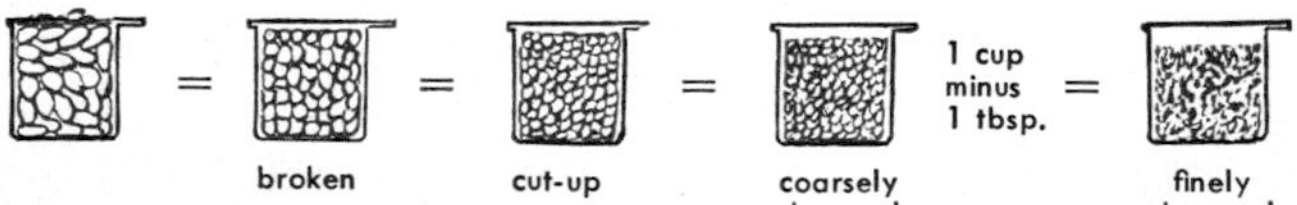

	WHOLE	PITTED	CUT-UP	FINELY CUT
DATES	1 lb. = 2¼ cups	2 cups	1¾ cups	1½ cups
PRUNES	1 lb. = 2⅓ cups	4 cups (cooked)	3 cups (cooked)	2⅞ cups (cooked)
FIGS	1 lb. = 2¾ cups	——	2⅔ cups	2½ cups
RAISINS	15-oz. pkg. = 3 cups	——	2¾ cups	2½ cups
CANDIED FRUIT	½ lb. = ——	——	1½ cups	——
CANDIED PEELS	½ lb. = ——	——	1½ cups	——

SUBSTITUTIONS FOR EMERGENCIES

It's best to use ingredients
The recipe recommends;
  But if you have to substitute,
This list solution lends.

For	Use
1 tbsp. cornstarch (for thickening)	2 tbsp. flour (approximately)
1 whole egg	2 egg yolks plus 1 tbsp. water (in cookies, etc.)
1 whole egg	2 egg yolks (in custards and such mixtures)
1 cup fresh sweet milk	½ cup evaporated milk plus ½ cup water
1 cup fresh sweet milk	powdered milk plus water (*directions on pkg.*)
1 cup fresh sweet milk	1 cup sour milk or buttermilk plus ½ tsp. soda (decrease baking powder 2 tsp.)
1 cup sour milk or buttermilk	1 tbsp. lemon juice or vinegar plus enough fresh sweet milk to make 1 cup
1 sq. unsweetened chocolate (1 oz.)	3 tbsp. cocoa plus ½ tsp. shortening
1 cup honey	¾ cup sugar plus ¼ cup liquid
1 cup canned tomatoes	about 1⅓ cups cut-up fresh tomatoes, simmered 10 min.

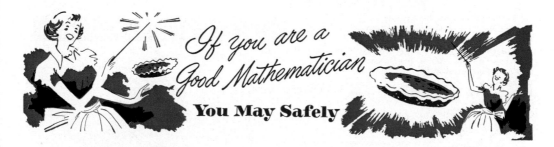

If you are a Good Mathematician **You May Safely**

REDUCE RECIPES

To make half a recipe:

Use exactly *one-half the amount of each ingredient.* (See Equivalents, p. 16, and How to Measure, p. 9, for help in dividing or multiplying ingredients.)

If the divided recipe calls for less than 1 egg, beat up a whole egg. Measure with a tablespoon. Divide. (Use egg that is left in scrambled eggs, sauces, etc.)

Baking pans used for half recipes of cakes, pies, etc. should measure about half the area of those for the whole recipe. Approximate baking time and oven temperature the same.

INCREASE RECIPES

To double a recipe:

Use exactly *twice the amount of each ingredient.* Add extra minute of beating for cakes.

If the increased recipe calls for uneven amounts of ingredients, it is a help to remember that

$\frac{2}{3}$ cup = $\frac{1}{2}$ cup plus $2\frac{2}{3}$ tbsp.
$\frac{5}{8}$ cup = $\frac{1}{2}$ cup plus 2 tbsp.
$\frac{7}{8}$ cup = $\frac{3}{4}$ cup plus 2 tbsp.

Use twice as many pans of the same size indicated for the original recipe or a pan double in area . . . so that the batter will be the same depth in the pan and same baking time and temperature may be maintained.

USEFUL KITCHEN UTENSILS A GUIDE FOR SELECTING

Just as every carpenter must have certain tools for building a house, every woman should have the right tools for the fine art of cooking. The size and needs of each household determine the kind and quantity that may be used for a number of purposes. Colorful utensils add a cheery note to the kitchen.

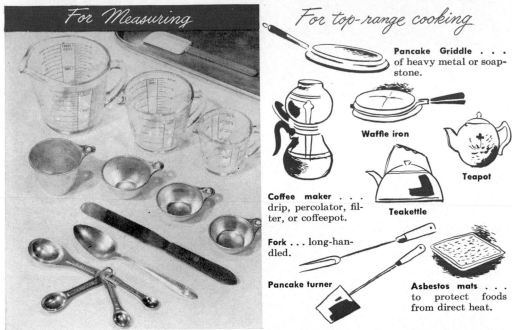

For Measuring

For top-range cooking

Pancake Griddle . . . of heavy metal or soapstone.

Waffle iron

Teapot

Coffee maker . . . drip, percolator, filter, or coffeepot.

Teakettle

Fork . . . long-handled.

Pancake turner

Asbestos mats . . . to protect foods from direct heat.

Set of standard measuring spoons.
Big spoon . . . for spooning into cup.
Straight-edge knife . . . for "leveling off."
Nest of measuring cups: for dry ingredients; **liquid measuring cup** with lip for liquids.
Pint and quart measures.
Utility tray.
Rubber spatula . . . to scrape out cups.

For top-range cooking

3 saucepans with close-fitting covers (2 to 4-qt. sizes).

2 lipped saucepans for heating liquids.

A double boiler (1½-qt. if you have only one).

A large kettle with steamer to fit . . . for steamed puddings, etc. Used without steamer for doughnuts, etc.

Deep fat frying basket . . . to fit into large kettle . . . for French fried potatoes, etc.

2 heavy skillets or frying pans with covers (one 9 to 10" diameter, one 6 to 7").

For Mixing

Kitchen fork and knife . . . for many uses.
Flat wire whip . . . beats more air into egg whites.
Pastry blender . . . for cutting in shortening.
Wooden spoon . . . for creaming, stirring sauces, etc.
Blending fork . . . for thorough mixing.
Rotary egg beater (sturdy) . . . for icings, etc.
Flour sifter (large open) containing a fine wire screen . . . sifting and aerating *white* flour.
Mixing bowls . . . a set of convenient sizes.

18

KITCHEN UTENSILS (cont.)

FOR FOOD PREPARATION

2 or 3 sharp **paring knives** . . . for paring, cutting vegetables, fruits, etc.

Vegetable parer with floating blade . . . for paring potatoes and other vegetables thinly.

Several **straight-edge knives.**

French pattern knife . . . for quickly mincing and cutting nuts, celery, green pepper, etc.

Bread knife with saw-tooth edge . . . for cutting breads, fruitcake, etc., neatly.

Long slicer . . . for evenly slicing roasts.

Limber **spatulas**—large and small . . . for removing cakes from pans, icing cakes, etc.

Grapefruit knife—with a curved blade . . . for cutting under grapefruit sections.

Small **ball cutter** . . . for cutting out melon balls, potato balls, butter balls.

Chopping bowl and knife . . . for chopping meat for hash, giblets for gravy, etc.

Ice crusher . . . to crush ice easily.

Apple corer . . . to remove apple cores.

Strawberry huller . . . for hulling strawberries, picking pin feathers from poultry, etc.

Sturdy pair of **kitchen scissors** . . . an essential for many uses.

Food choppers—with fine and coarse cutters . . . for grinding meats, vegetables, nuts, etc.

Several **tablespoons** . . . for general use.

Wire strainers—fine, coarse, and very fine . . . for straining foods, sieving them, etc.

Funnel . . . for filling jars and bottles.

Large spoon with holes or slots . . . for scooping food out of a liquid (as a poached egg).

Ladle—with long handle . . . for soups, jams.

Tongs . . . for lifting vegetables, meats, etc. out of liquid or pan.

Pastry brush . . . for greasing pans, brushing dough with melted butter, etc.

Potato ricer . . . for ricing potatoes or other vegetables, perhaps preliminary to mashing.

Potato masher—of solid wood or heavy wire . . . for mashing potatoes and other foods.

Set of graters . . . to grate food to different degrees . . . from very fine to coarse.

Lemon squeezer . . . for extracting juice from lemons, oranges, grapefruit.

Can opener. Jar opener. Bottle opener.

Corkscrew.

Molds—such as ring, melon, or fluted-shaped molds for puddings, salads, etc. Fancy shaped individual molds for single serving. (Custard and muffin cups may be used.)

Timer—with an alarm . . . to let you know when a dish has finished cooking.

Cutters of various shapes and sizes . . . for cookies, biscuits, doughnuts, etc.

Bread or pastry board . . . for kneading dough and rolling out cookies, pastry, etc. Also a canvas or heavy crash **cover** for the board.

Rolling pin—and, for a **cover,** a child's white ribbed cotton stocking with foot cut off.

Pastry set . . . a canvas or heavy crash cover for the board and a white jersey tube cover for the pin.

Colander (a perforated metal pan) . . . for straining coarse foods or puréeing vegetables.

FOR STORAGE

Canister set (cans for sugar, flour, etc.).

Bread box (if not part of cabinet).

Cake safe (if not part of cabinet).

Cooky jar.

Set of refrigerator dishes with covers.

Plastic refrigerator covers and bags.

Waxed paper, cheesecloth, rubber bands.

Aluminum foil.

FOR SINK AND CLEANING

Rubber scraper . . . for scraping dishes clean.

Dish pans . . . when sink not used for pan.

Rubber mats for drain boards.

Dish drainer.

Small scrub brush . . . **bottle brush** . . . **vegetable brush.**

Cellulose sponges . . . **dish cloths** . . . **dish mop.**

Pot holders . . . **dish towels.**

Paper towels with holder.

Sink strainer.

Waste basket.

Garbage can (if no incinerator or disposal).

Soap, steel wool, cleaning powder, etc.

KITCHEN UTENSILS (cont.)

Measure that Pan!

Do keep a ruler handy,
  To measure pans it's dandy.
Place the rule across the top,
  Right size pan prevents a flop!

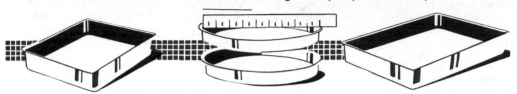

Square Pan 8″ square—2″ deep; 9″ square—1¾″ deep.

Round Layer Pans (2) at least 1½″ deep for 8″ pan; 1½″ deep for 9″ pan.

Oblong Pan . . . 13x9″ – 2″ deep.

Tube-center Pan 10″ diam.—4″ deep. 9″ diam.—3″ deep.

Pie Pans 1¼″ deep, measured from inside rim to inside rim, they measure 8 or 9″.

Bread Loaf Pan. 9x5″—3″ deep.

Cooky Sheet or Baking Sheet . . . without sides.

Ring Mold for puddings, breads, salads, etc.

Wire Rack for cooling cakes, cookies, breads, etc.

Oven Thermometer for checking oven temperature.

Jelly Roll Pan or Baking Sheet . . . with low sides. 15x10½″—1″ deep.

 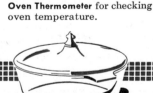 

Muffin Pan . . . large, medium, or small cups.

Baking dish with cover. Round, oval, square, or oblong 1-qt. 1½-qt., or 2-qt. size.

Individual Custard Cups . . . set in shallow pan to bake.

Fluted Pudding Mold . . . for steamed puddings, for breads, etc. 1 qt. (7″ diam.) or 2 qt. (8″ diam.).

Roasting Pan . . . with rack. In size suitable for family.

Round Pudding Mold (1 or 2 qt.) . . . for brown bread, plum puddings, and other steamed puddings.

STORING FOODS

SHORTENINGS

Keep *lard* and *butter* closely covered in refrigerator. Strain *drippings* directly into container and store in refrigerator.

MILK, CREAM, AND EGGS

Keep *milk* and *cream* covered, and *eggs* (unwashed until ready to use) near freezing unit in refrigerator.

CHEESE

Tightly cover *soft* cheese; wrap *hard cheese* in waxed paper; store covered in refrigerator. Grate left-over cheese; keep in covered jar.

SUGARS

Keep *granulated* and *confectioners' sugar* covered in dry place. Keep brown sugar in air-tight container. Hard brown sugar may be softened by placing on top of sugar in container any of the following: a slice of apple or orange on waxed paper (change fruit often to insure freshness), a crisp lettuce leaf, a damp cloth, a slice of fresh bread or a piece of moistened sponge. Remove any of these in 2 or 3 days and replace cover tightly.

FLOUR, CEREALS, CAKE MIXES, ETC.

Keep tightly covered in *cool*, dry place. Do not keep whole wheat or other coarse flours or cereals near white flour. (Damp flour may be dried by sifting before a heated open oven. Breakfast foods may be crisped by heating in oven.) For long keeping, store whole wheat, corn meal, and rye flours in tightly covered glass jars. In hot weather, place in refrigerator.

CAKES

After cake is cool, store it in a container with a tight cover; or invert a large bowl over the cake plate.

Fruitcake: First wrap cooled cake in waxed paper or aluminum foil. In old days, fruitcakes were wrapped in wine-dampened cloth to keep and mellow. Store in airtight container in cool place.

Cake with Cream Filling: Store in refrigerator until served.

BREADS

Keep cooled bread at room temperature in covered metal bread box ventilated with tiny air holes. Or keep in food compartment of refrigerator (here, it stales more quickly than in bread box but is less subject to mold).

PIES

Fruit Pies: Cover with waxed paper or transparent wrap and place on cupboard shelf at room temperature. Freshen by heating a few minutes in warm oven. Or cover with aluminum foil which may be left on when pie is heated in warm oven.

Cream, Custard, and Whipped Cream Pies: Always store in refrigerator both before and after serving.

COOKIES

Thin, Crisp Cookies: Store in can with loose cover.

Soft Cookies: Store in airtight container (a covered earthen jar or can with tight cover). Slices of apple or orange in jar help mellow and moisten cookies. Change fruit frequently.

STAPLE SUPPLIES

Keep tightly covered in cool, dry place. Replace herbs and spices as soon as they lose their freshness. After dried fruit package has been opened, wrap fruit in waxed paper, transparent wrap, or aluminum foil; or place in airtight jar.

NUTS AND COCONUT

Keep *shelled nuts* and *coconut* tightly covered in refrigerator. Renew softness of coconut by heating over hot water.

MARSHMALLOWS

Keep tightly sealed in bread box or glass jar. Soften by heating in damp bag in oven.

FRESH FRUIT

Keep *unripe fruit* at room temperature to ripen. Store *ripe fruit* (except pineapple, bananas) in cool place.

CUT LEMONS, ORANGES, MELONS

Place cut-side-down on plate or in covered container and store in refrigerator.

HULLED AND SWEETENED BERRIES AND SLICED PEACHES

Keep *fresh berries* wrapped in paper in refrigerator; wash and hull shortly before using. Keep leftover *hulled berries* in tightly covered glass jar in refrigerator.

PARSLEY, WATER-CRESS, LETTUCE

Keep washed *parsley* and *watercress* (with water shaken from them) in tightly covered jar in refrigerator. For storing *lettuce,* see "SALADS."

SALAD DRESSINGS

Cover tightly and keep at room temperature or in refrigerator (*not* coldest part). Never freeze!

CUT ONIONS AND GARLIC

Place cut-side-down in glass jar; cover tightly. Or wrap in aluminum foil. Cover, store in refrigerator.

CONDIMENTS, also SALAD OILS, SYRUPS, MOLASSES, ETC.

Keep tightly covered in refrigerator or kitchen cupboard.

CUSTARD MIXTURES

Very perishable. Cool, then cover, and store immediately in refrigerator **not more than 24 hr.** Never eat custard mixtures that have been kept overnight without careful refrigeration.

POTATOES, ONIONS, BEETS, CARROTS, OTHER ROOT VEGETABLES

Keep these in cool, dry, well ventilated place. Keep other vegetables in crisper in refrigerator.

COFFEE AND TEA

Keep tightly covered in cool, dry place. After opening, keep in refrigerator . . . and keep only week's supply on hand.

FREEZING FOODS

Use quality foods always.

Preserve quality by—

1 Proper handling before freezing.
2 Good packaging.
3 Storage at temperature no higher than 0° F.
4 Proper handling and cooking after removing from freezer.

Don't overestimate your needs.

A rapid turnover is important!

Make a STORAGE CHART to keep a record of what you put in your freezer, when you put it in, and the date by which the food should be removed.

WRAPPING MATERIALS

Good wrapping materials are moisture-vaporproof or resistant. For most solid foods, such as meat, cake, pie, and bread, use freezer weight paper such as aluminum foil, cellophane, pliofilm, or other transparent film. Polyethylene bags may be used for baked goods such as bread and cookies. To give form to shapeless plastic bags, put them in paper cartons, then fill and freeze.

Liquid-packed foods may be packaged in heavily waxed cartons, glass freezer jars, plastic or aluminum containers. Choose a size of container that holds enough for 1 meal; quart containers hold 4 to 6 servings; pints, 2 to 3. Use only containers with wide top openings so the food does not have to be thawed completely to remove it from the container. Some prepared foods like meat pies and casserole dishes may be frozen in the containers in which they were baked, ready for reheating at time of using.

Seal frozen food containers or packages with freezer locker tape, *not* general utility tape. Freezer locker tape may also be used as a label on hard-to-mark wrapping materials.

Label jars, cartons, and packages with china marking pencil or soft crayon, available at stationery stores.

HOW TO WRAP FOR FREEZING
Packaging with Freezer Sheet Material—the "Drugstore Wrap"

1 Place food in center of wrapping. Bring edges together evenly above food.

2 Fold edges over and over until fold is flat against the food. Press out air.

3 Fold inside edges; seal with freezer locker tape. Label plainly with contents and date.

Packaging in Rigid Container

Place food in container. Seal rigid food containers by adjusting the lids as required for the type of package used. Casseroles made of ovenproof material can be covered and then sealed with freezer tape. Label with contents and date.

Packaging in a Polyethylene Bag

Polyethylene bags are especially durable. They can be sealed by twisting the tops and securing with soft twine or rubber binders. Label with contents and date.

FREEZING BAKED FOODS

Fruit pies, mince pies, and chiffon pies freeze successfully. It is best *not* to freeze custard or meringue pies. Meringue toppings tend to toughen, shrink, separate, and stick to wrappers. Baked and unbaked pie shells and cooky crumb crusts may also be frozen.

Preparing Pies for Freezing

Both baked and unbaked pies may be frozen. Freeze either kind *unwrapped* just until frozen, keeping pie level. Before wrapping, place another pie plate over the top to protect the crust. Wrap and seal.

Baked pies should be cooled and frozen immediately.

Unbaked pies should be frozen as soon as they have been prepared. The top crust should not be slit before freezing. (This is to prevent evaporation of juices during freezing.) The lower crust may absorb juices and become a little soggy when baked. Deep dish pies may be frozen, eliminating the problem of a soggy bottom crust.

Freezing Pie Fillings

Save freezer space by freezing pie fillings to be defrosted and put into pie shells later. A pint frozen food container holds about the right amount for an 8″ pie.

Thawing Pies

Unbaked Pie: Remove wrapping. Make several slits in top crust of unbaked two-crust pie. Bake without thawing according to recipe, allowing 15 to 20 min. extra baking time.

Frozen Baked Pie: Heat in mod. oven (350°) until just warm. Do *not* reheat chiffon pie. Thaw in refrigerator about 3 hr. or at room temperature about 45 min.

Length of Storage

Storage time varies with the filling. Most pies may be kept frozen for 2 to 3 months.

Baked cakes freeze best! Although batters may be frozen, the quality of the cakes baked from them is usually not as satisfactory as that of cakes baked before being frozen.

Preparing Cake for Freezing

Wrap cake as soon as thoroughly cool. Freeze. Place in a metal container or heavy carton to protect cake from being crushed. Cakes do not freeze solid.

It is best not to frost and fill cakes before freezing. Fillings may make the cake a bit soggy, and it is difficult to wrap and defrost satisfactorily. If desired, however, cakes may be frosted with a confectioners' sugar or fudge frosting, frozen, and then wrapped.

Thawing Cake

Thaw cake in wrapping to prevent moisture from forming on the surface of the cake. A large cake thaws in 2 to 3 hr. at room temperature, a cake layer in about 1 hr., and cupcakes in about 30 min.

Length of Storage

Unfrosted cakes may be kept frozen for 2 to 3 months. Frosted cakes should be stored only 1 to 2 months. Fruitcakes may be stored for a longer period of time.

Freeze baked or unbaked! Both freeze well.

Cooky Dough

Shape dough for *refrigerator cookies*, wrap and freeze. When ready to use, remove from freezer, slice with sharp knife, place on baking sheet, and bake as directed in recipe.

Pack *drop or rolled cooky dough* in frozen food containers. When ready to bake, thaw dough until soft enough to handle.

Baked Cookies

Cool cookies after baking. Package in frozen food containers, cooky jars, or canisters with tight fitting covers. Seal and freeze. Thaw cookies in original containers. Cookies thaw in a very short time.

Length of Storage

Cooky dough and baked cookies may be stored at least 9 months.

FREEZING BAKED FOODS (cont.)

BREADS AND ROLLS Baked bread and rolls, properly wrapped and frozen, will be just as light and tender after freezing as they were before. Unbaked dough may be frozen, but bread and rolls made from it will probably be of poorer quality, because the frozen dough may lose some of its rising capacity.

Preparing Bread and Rolls for Freezing

Cool baked bread and rolls thoroughly. Then wrap, label, and freeze immediately.

Thawing Bread

Thaw bread in original wrapper at room temperature. Allow about 3 hr. to thaw a 1-lb. loaf of bread. Slices of frozen bread may be toasted in the toaster without thawing.

Thawing Rolls

Heat rolls in slow oven (275 to 300°) 10 to 15 min. Rolls may be defrosted in wrapper and then heated for serving.

Length of Storage

Baked bread and rolls may be stored in the freezer up to 3 months. *Bakery bread* may be stored in its original wrap for about 4 months, brown 'n serve rolls for 2 to 3 months.

BAKING POWDER BISCUITS Freeze baking powder biscuits, muffins, nut bread, pancakes, or waffles. It is best as with yeast breads, to freeze the baked product.

Preparation for Freezing

Bake according to recipe. When cool, wrap, label, and freeze immediately.

Thawing Quick Breads

When ready to serve, thaw in wrapping at room temperature or warm in slow oven (275 to 300°).

Frozen waffles need not be thawed. While still frozen, place in toaster to reheat. For serving *frozen pancakes*, place on broiler pan and heat under broiler.

Length of Storage

Quick breads, like yeast breads, may be stored frozen up to 3 months.

SANDWICHES Freeze sandwiches, sandwich spreads or fillings, or fancy party sandwiches. Follow these suggestions for fillings that freeze well.

Fillings to Freeze

Luncheon meats
Leftover sliced roast beef or roast pork
Baked ham
Sliced or minced chicken or turkey
Dried beef
Tuna or salmon
Sliced cheese or cheese spreads
Hard-cooked egg yolks
Peanut butter

Add sliced or chopped olives or pickles to any of these. Combine *very small amounts* of mayonnaise, salad dressing, cream cheese, or creamed butter for easy spreading.

It's Best Not to Freeze These!

Jelly, mayonnaise, and salad dressing (When used as a spread they soak into the bread, making it soggy.)
Hard-cooked egg whites
Lettuce, celery, tomatoes, carrots

Preparing Sandwiches for Freezing

Lunch sandwiches: Spread each slice of bread with softened butter, then fill. Wrap separately in freezer wrapping paper. Label; freeze. If desired, place a number of sandwiches together in a box.

Party sandwiches: Spread each slice of bread with softened butter. Then spread with filling; decorate. Place in box in layers with waxed paper between. Wrap; label; date. Rolled and ribbon sandwiches may be wrapped uncut and cut after defrosting.

Thawing Sandwiches

Thaw in original wrapping, 3 to 3½ hr. for lunch sandwiches, 1 to 2 hr. for party sandwiches. If not used immediately, hold in refrigerator.

Length of Storage

Sandwiches may be stored up to 3 weeks. Do not refreeze.

How convenient to be able to cook enough food when you have time so that you may freeze part of it for another day when you are busy with other things! Combination dishes, meat loaf, soups, and stews may all be stored this way. Just cook, cool, and freeze for future use!

COMBINATION DISHES

Preparing the Food for Freezing

Prepare the food according to the recipe, but undercook slightly. (If completely cooked before freezing, combination dishes develop a warmed-over flavor when heated.) If there is a crumb or cheese topping, leave it off until ready to heat for serving.

Quickly cool the food to stop the cooking. To hasten cooling, set covered pan in ice water. Stir occasionally, being careful not to mash or break up the food. Change water and supply more ice as needed until the food is completely cooled.

After cooling, package immediately. Pack solidly to avoid air spaces. Gravies and sauces packed with meats and vegetables help fill air spaces. Fill containers not quite full to allow for expansion of liquid during freezing. Seal, label, date. Freeze and store at 0° F. or colder. *Do not refreeze.*

If only a part of the recipe prepared is to be frozen, take that part from the saucepan before the food is completely cooked. Cool, package, and freeze immediately.

Heating for Serving

In oven: Put in baking pan, cover, and heat in mod. oven (350°). Ovenproof containers may be taken from freezer and placed immediately in oven to heat.

In saucepan: Place a small amount of butter or fat in saucepan, add frozen food. Heat over medium-low heat until completely thawed and heated through. Stir slightly with fork to break up food, but do not stir any more than absolutely necessary. *Do not overcook.*

Partially thawing the food in the refrigerator before heating may prevent scorching. Creamed dishes, stews, creamed soups, and dishes that scorch easily may be heated in a double boiler 20 to 30 min.

Length of Storage

Combination dishes may be frozen for 3 to 4 months. Storing them longer may cause them to lose their distinctive flavor. Differences in the quality of fat used greatly affect the length of time that many cooked foods may be stored.

SPECIAL SUGGESTIONS

SOUP: Make soup concentrates to save space. Freeze soup in freezer jars, leaving about 1" of head space at the top.

STEW: Slightly undercook stew. Add the vegetables when meat is nearly cooked. Meat should be tender but firm. Potatoes frozen in stew become mushy and grainy, so it is best to add them when reheating.

ROASTED MEATS: Trim leftover roasted meats such as beef, pork, ham, turkey, or chicken before freezing in order to save freezer space. Cover with gravy; freeze.

GRAVIES AND SAUCES: Although the fat may separate in gravies, it is usually recombined during heating. Dishes containing a large amount of milk may curdle or separate

during freezing, but this, too, usually recombines during heating.

MEAT LOAF: Meat loaf may be frozen cooked or uncooked.

POTATOES: Mashed potatoes and puffed potatoes in the half-shell freeze well. French fried potatoes freeze best when cut very thin. Use a good quality fat for frying. Candied sweet potatoes may also be frozen.

LEFTOVERS: Preparing an extra amount of food and freezing it immediately after preparation is a time-saving procedure. However, foods left over after the meal are likely to have a warmed over flavor if frozen and heated, because they have been completely cooked. Food should not be allowed to stand before freezing.

HOW TO PREPARE some special ingredients the quick, easy way.

MELTING CHOCOLATE

Place it on waxed paper set in bowl over boiling water. **or** Place it in a small bowl set in a wire strainer over boiling water. Remove melted chocolate from bowl or paper with rubber scraper.

PREPARING NUTS: Some foods look and taste their best if the nuts in them are in big chunks. In others, the nuts should be in smaller pieces. The recipes tell you just how.

Broken Nuts: It's quick and easy to break nuts with fingers into about ⅛″ chunks.

Cut-up Nuts: Cut with scissors (works better than knife) into about ¼″ pieces.

TOAST NUTS: to be sure they will taste fresh. Heat through in mod. oven (350°).

Coarsely Chopped Nuts: Chop with long, straight knife. Hold point against cutting board, chop crisply through spread-out nuts—swinging handle around in quarter circle.

Finely Chopped Nuts: Chop same as for Coarsely Chopped, but into finer pieces.

Blanched Nuts: Drop shelled nuts into boiling water. Let stand 2 to 5 min. (until skins are loosened). Pour off hot water, add some cold. Pinch each nut between thumb and finger to push off skins, and lay nuts on plate or paper toweling to dry.

Sliced or Slivered Nuts: First blanch . . . then cut with very sharp knife while nuts are moist and warm.
To brown blanched almonds, etc., spread in pan or on baking sheet. Heat in mod. oven until delicately browned. *Watch carefully.*

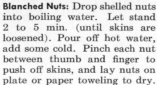

Ground Nuts: Use fine knife of food grinder for finely ground . . . coarse knife for coarsely ground. Nuts should be dry.

HOW TO PREPARE some special ingredients.

KNOW YOUR RAISINS

Seeded raisins are the large variety from which seeds have been removed. The sweetness released when they were slit open makes them sticky.

Seedless raisins are the small variety, both dark and light ... dried from seedless grapes. Cut them to get the full sweetness and flavor.

Plump seedless raisins by washing and spreading them out in a flat pan. Cover. Heat slowly in mod. oven (350°) until they puff up and wrinkles come out.

DATES / CANDIED FRUIT / GRATED RIND

Cut up dates and other sticky fruits with wet scissors. Dip scissors in water occasionally.

For cut-up citron or candied orange or lemon peel, cut *thin* slices into ¼" squares.

Rub washed fruit in short strokes across small area of grater. Grate only outermost colored rind.

FRESH COCONUT

Pierce 3 holes at one end. Drain out milk. Heat in mod. oven (350°) 30 min. Cool.

Break shell with hammer or chisel, remove. Break the meat in pieces. Pare off brown skin.

Grate or shred white meat. (Keep any not used, tightly covered, in refrigerator.)

PREPARING COCONUT

Snip through long shreds of coconut. The shorter shreds blend into doughs more evenly.

To tint coconut: Add food coloring to water. Let coconut soak in it until desired color. Drain; dry.

To toast coconut: Heat in shallow pan in mod. oven (350°) until golden brown, stirring frequently.

HOW TO PREPARE special ingredients.

CARAMELIZING SUGAR

Melt sugar in heavy pan over low heat, shaking pan as sugar melts.

Heat until melted to a golden brown syrup, stirring constantly.

Stir in hot water (amount recipe indicates). Be careful steam does not burn hand.

DISSOLVING GELATIN

Dissolve over hot water 1 tsp. unflavored gelatin softened in 1 tbsp. water.

KEEPING CREAM STIFF

Add gradually to 1 cup whipping cream just as it begins to stiffen. Beat until stiff.

WHIPPING CREAM

Beat chilled cream (30 to 35% butterfat) in chilled *deep* bowl with cold rotary beater until fluffy.

STUFFING DATES

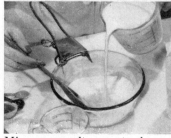

Fill pitted dates with nuts, Fondant (*p. 184*), cut-up marshmallows, or candied ginger. Roll in sugar.

SALTING NUTS

To 1 cup nuts in pan, add 1 tsp. salad oil. Stir. Brown in mod. oven, stir often. Drain. Salt.

SOURING MILK OR CREAM

Put 1 tbsp. vinegar or lemon juice into cup. Fill cup with sweet milk or cream. Let stand a few minutes.

PREPARING CREAM OR CUSTARD FILLING

Mix sugar, salt, cornstarch or flour. Gradually stir in liquid. Cook over low heat, stirring until mixture boils.

Boil 1 min., stirring constantly. Remove from heat. Stir a little of the hot mixture into the beaten eggs.

Blend into hot mixture. Boil 1 min. more, stirring. Remove from heat. Blend in butter and flavoring. Cool . . . stir occasionally.

29

HOW TO PREPARE bread for various uses.

SOFT BREAD CRUMBS.

With fork, pull day-old bread into crumbs. Or tear it into small pieces with fingers.

FINE DRY CRUMBS

Remove crusts from stale bread. Dry bread in slow oven. Crush. Or put through food grinder.

CUBES, CROUTONS

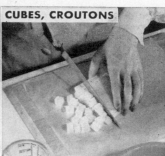

Trim and cut bread into cubes. For *croutons*, butter bread first, toast the buttered cubes in oven.

MELBA TOAST

Remove crusts from day-old bread. Slice thin (⅛″). Bake in slow oven until crisp, light brown (20 min.). Serve hot or cold.

BUTTERCUPS

Brush thinly sliced bread (crusts removed) with melted butter. Press into muffin cups. Toast in mod. oven (350°).

TOAST CASES

Cut bread 2″ thick. Remove crusts. Cut into squares or oblongs. Hollow out. Brush with melted butter. Toast in oven.

HOT BUTTERED FRENCH BREAD

Slice diagonally (thick, not through bottom crust). Spread soft butter on 1 side each slice (try garlic or chives in butter). Heat in mod. oven about 15 min.

BUTTERING THIN PARTY SANDWICHES

Spread softened butter on bread before cutting each slice.

TOASTED LOAF DE LUXE

Slice loaf, but not through bottom crust. Pour melted butter over slices, distributing evenly. Cover with paper bag. Heat in mod. oven 15 to 20 min. Serve hot.

CUTTING SANDWICH LOAF

Remove crusts from loaf of sandwich bread . . . leaving bottom crust until last. A long, very sharp knife is needed.

SLICING SANDWICH LOAF

For sandwich loaf or pinwheel sandwiches, slice into long layers of thickness desired. Lay each slice aside, keeping in order.

CLUB SANDWICH LOAF

Filling: chicken, lettuce, bacon, tomato. Cover with mild mayonnaise with chopped hard-cooked eggs in it.

HOW TO PREPARE some special ingredients.

FRESH MUSHROOMS

Wash mushrooms gently under cold running water. (Never soak.) Trim off spots.

Cut off stems. Use caps for baking, broiling. Mince stems, sauté for sauces and soups.

Slice whole mushrooms down through stems. Sauté in butter. Use for sauce, stuffing, etc.

CANNED MUSHROOMS

To sauté: add mushrooms and liquor to melted butter in hot pan. Cook till liquor is absorbed.

BROWNING FLOUR

Spread in thin layer in pan. Heat on range or in mod. oven, stirring until golden brown.

GRATING CHEESE

Firm cheese: rub over grater or shredder. **Soft cheese:** rub through coarse sieve.

CHOPPING OR MINCING ONION

Cut end slice from peeled onion. Discard. Cut exposed surface into tiny squares to any desired depth. Cut crosswise in thin slices.

ONION JUICE

Cut end slice from peeled onion. Discard. Squeeze out juice on lemon squeezer. Or scrape cut side of onion with back of knife.

DICING CELERY (or RHUBARB)

Place several stalks of cleaned celery together on board. Slash through all at once. Dice rhubarb stalks the same way.

PEELING A TOMATO

Hold over flame or heat 1 min.

Or place in boiling water 1 min. Then plunge into cold water.

Skin will slip off easily.

HOW TO PREPARE some special fruits for salads, desserts, appetizers.

CANDIED FRUIT GARNISH

Cut candied cherries and citron into shapes of flowers and leaves to decorate icings, etc.

PARING GRAPEFRUIT

Cut thin slice from top . . . then pare the grapefruit 'round and 'round like an apple.

GRAPEFRUIT SECTIONS

To section: cut along each dividing membrane. Lift out sections whole.

PINEAPPLE SLICES AND WEDGES

Cut off top of washed pineapple. Cut down length of pineapple in long, wide strokes to remove rind.

Cut "v"- shaped wedges full length on diagonal of "eyes." Then lift out wedges, and discard them.

Cut lengthwise in strips, remove cores . . . for salads. Or cut across in circles, remove cores, cut in wedges . . . for fruit cups.

PINEAPPLE BOAT

Cut in two lengthwise. Cut around edge with curved knife, remove fruit. Discard core.

MELON BALLS

Use a ball cutter or a rounded measuring spoon. Cut into melon with circular motion.

POMEGRANATE SEEDS

Cut washed pomegranate in two. Remove seeds with fork.

AVOCADO

Cut through avocado to seed . . . twist slightly to pull halves apart. If using only half, leave seed in other half. Wrap in foil to keep.

Run knife down center back of each half . . .cut through center of thin outer rind only. Pull off sections of skin.

Place avocado half on board. Slice as thick as desired. Drench slices with lemon or lime juice to prevent darkening.

~Well Planned Meals Bring~ Double Happiness

GOOD EATING brings happiness two ways. First, there is the joy and satisfaction of eating delicious, well prepared food. Then there's the buoyant health, vitality, and joy of living that comes from a wise choice of foods. Both are important to good nutrition.

Betty Crocker

WEDDING RECEPTION REFRESHMENTS

(1)   Fruit Punch (p. 74)
Dainty Open-faced Sandwiches
            Salted Nuts
Bride's Cake (p. 142) Groom's Cake (p. 167)

(2)   *Chicken Salad (p. 390)
    Olives   Radishes   Pickles
*Tiny Hot Buttered Rolls or Finger Sandwiches
      Ice Cream in Wedding Molds
Bride's Cake (p. 142) Groom's Cake (p. 167)
   Salted Nuts   Coffee   Bonbons

*Chicken à la King in Patty Shells may be
substituted for salad and breads.*

WEDDING RECEPTION BUFFET

Cold Sliced Roast Turkey, Beef, Baked Ham
Dainty Lettuce or Watercress Sandwiches
       Molded Fruit (p. 393) or
    Tomato Aspic (p. 394) Salad
Celery Hearts   Olives   Beet Pickles
       Bride's Cake (p. 142)
       *Groom's Cake (p. 167)
   Salted Nuts   Pastel Mints
Fruit Punch (p. 74)   Coffee

*Dark fruitcake, uniced. Guests take home
small pieces to dream on night of wedding.*

"Cooking comes from the heart as well as the hearth"—an adage.

Planning (paper and pencil for beginners) allows the necessary time for preparing food so it becomes an activity that is enjoyed rather than a "chore." Preparing food artistically (pleasing to the eye) and tastily (pleasing to the palate) can be as satisfying as the artist's creations on canvas.

HAVE A GOOD TIME PREPARING MEALS

Food prepared with a light heart and in a happy frame of mind is often the best food. Preparing the special foods that are favorites of those you love . . . making just a little effort to garnish the salad with a sprig of parsley, a bit of grated cheese, or a wild strawberry from the nearby meadow. This says "you cared enough to do the little extra things." This makes cooking pleasant and satisfying. Make the food look as pretty as it is good to eat.

TIME AND ENERGY LEFT FOR OTHER ACTIVITIES

Preliminary planning and preparation of the evening meal may be done right after breakfast . . . washing all the cooking dishes at one time. Then off to the golf course, the bridge table, or the sewing circle for relaxation and enjoyment. For those with freezers, the advance preparations may be even more successfully planned.

BEST USE OF LEFTOVERS AND FOOD ON HAND

A plan in advance for meals must be flexible enough to make good use of leftovers. Or plan to have leftovers, such as extra baked potatoes (so easy) for easy creamed potatoes the next day. When there are odds and ends of vegetables in the crisper, that's the signal to make a delicious soup or stew.

MONEY SAVED

Careful planning and avoiding waste of food can mean music lessons for little Sue, an occasional night out for recreation, or the new dress in the window. Planning includes economical-type buying of foods, arranging for their use in later meals, and avoiding unnecessary waste.

AMPLE TIME TO SHOP PLEASANTLY

Plan for one day a week, providing enough time to make a list of things needed, and enough time to shop without rushing. Go to the store during the less busy hours. Take the time to look around and become familiar with new products. If a neighbor comes along, don't be too busy to exchange a few pleasantries.

BETTER TASTING MEALS

With just a bit of extra effort the meals can become delicious rather than just something to eat. Add the herbs to the soup, the bit of lemon rind to the salad dressing, and plan to have the piping hot rolls come out of the oven at just the right time. Make a simple food, such as mashed potatoes, taste better with the right amount of seasoning, a pat of butter, and a sprinkling of paprika. And make sure hot foods are hot, cold foods are cold, when you serve them.

MORE HEALTHFUL MEALS

To be of complete nutritional value, food must be enjoyed. To stimulate the appetite, the food must be attractive and colorful. The food combinations for color, flavor, and texture contrasts should be selected from the Basic Foods (*p. 41*) to insure good health.

HAPPY FAMILY AND GUESTS

When the door is opened to welcome either family or guests, the homemaker with a plan has good food to serve, has had time for some interesting activity during the day, has a home that is tidy but with a lived-in look. She has a relaxed spirit. She welcomes those at the door with a happy smile and cheerful attitude. The spirit of warm hospitality and graciousness prevails. There is good food and good cheer for the gathering of the family and friends at mealtime.

CHECK YOUR DAILY MEAL PATTERN TO FIT

YOUR SITUATION: Is it an apartment, a house, or a cottage . . . with or without help? Must preliminary preparations be made because of activities away from home? What table accessories and dishes? Informal dining is a current trend; however, it does not mean the omitting of the little touches that add special charm and color. Do what is easy and natural for you, with the least amount of work. Let it be as simple or elaborate as your situation dictates. (*See Types of Table Service, p. 37.*)

YOUR COOKING SKILL: Stay within the realm of your ability to cook. Do not try unusual combinations for guests. When you entertain, choose foods that seem easy to you and will not create last minute problems. Try the new recipes on days you feel like experimenting and having special fun cooking . . . when there are no guests expected. Your family will enjoy the surprises and will give suggestions.

MONEY TO BE SPENT: Your food budget is the best guide for spending. The basic foods for good nutrition should come first. Buy less of the more expensive foods and more of the less expensive foods. The less expensive foods are often the most nutritious. Buy fresh fruits and vegetables in season . . . grow some of your own if possible, and take advantage of special sales.

A WELL PLANNED MEAL

Something soft and something crisp
  Should always go together,
And something hot with something cold
  No matter what the weather;
Something bland needs the complement
  Of something with tang and nip.
Follow these rules and all your meals
  Will have taste appeal and zip.

GUEST LIST: A congenial atmosphere must prevail if entertaining is to serve its purpose. The guest list must be chosen as carefully as you would choose the ingredients for a recipe. Combine the people that will "mix well." A surprise guest with some special talent or conversational skill can make a party more successful. Above all, the hostess must be able to enjoy her own party. The carefully prepared and executed plan, the short period of relaxation or rest before guests arrive, and a few special plans to liven the party—these can make entertaining a joy and satisfaction.

THE OCCASION: There is a birthday to be celebrated . . . there must be something special besides the birthday cake. Perhaps the favorite dinner menu of the birthday girl or boy. The holiday dinner will be for the whole family with everyone bringing part of the festive meal. Or will you prepare the entire meal? Have fun by making simple occasions special occasions. Light the candles and make party-like atmosphere for the family often.

RECIPES TO BE USED: For best results, follow tested recipes carefully. Save the recipes that you do especially well in a separate place . . . easy to find. Be on the alert for new recipe ideas to try, to add to the "active" recipe file. Use only the recipes you do well for guests.

GOOD NUTRITION: Check the list of foods in the Basic Foods (*p. 41*). Balance the meals for the whole day to insure good nutrition. Consider the special diet problems of the family or guests. These may be incorporated into satisfactory menus for all.

A FESTIVE HOLIDAY DINNER

Roast Turkey or Chicken

Bread Stuffing   Cranberry Sauce   Giblet Gravy

Lowell Inn Crescent Rolls   Tray of Crisp Relishes

Mashed Squash   Creamed Onions   Mashed Potatoes

Old-fashioned Mince Pie or Down East Pudding

SERVING ETIQUETTE AND TABLE SERVICE

HOW TO SERVE AND HOW TO REMOVE DISHES

Serve and remove all dishes at the left except beverages. Beverages are served and removed at the right. Table service should be done unobtrusively and quietly without interrupting conversations.

Who is served first?

Some prefer to serve the hostess first, so she may lead the way. Her plate is also removed first at the end of each course. Others serve the guest of honor first, continuing in order around the table.

When is the appetizer course placed on table?

For informal occasions, the appetizer course may be on the table when the guests are seated. For formal occasions, the appetizer course is served after the guests are seated, placed on the service plates, if they are used.

When are the service plates removed?

After the first course.

What should be removed before serving the dessert?

Everything except the centerpiece and the waterglasses or goblets. If necessary, remove crumbs with folded napkin and small plate. Dessert silver may then be put in place or served directly on dessert plates.

When is the coffee served?

It may be served with main course as well as dessert course at informal dinners or luncheons. At formal dinners, serve it last, either at the table or in living room. Small demitasse cups may be used.

TYPES OF TABLE SERVICE

English or Family Service

Most suitable for the average family. Food is served at table by host or hostess. Host serves meat and vegetables from serving dishes placed before him. Hostess serves dessert and coffee. Served plates are passed to the guests.

Compromise or Mixed Service

A combination of English and Russian service. The main course is usually served at the table; the soup, salad, and dessert Russian style, directly from the kitchen to guest.

In California it is popular to serve the salad as an appetizer. It is usually served in individual wooden bowls or abalone shells in place when guests are seated.

In summer, iced tea or coffee or a tall fruit beverage may be in place on the table before guests are seated.

---

formal dessert service —

At a formal dinner, finger bowls are brought in on dessert plates (small lace doily under bowl), with dessert fork on plate at left of bowl and dessert spoon at right. Each guest places finger bowl and doily aside, above plate at left, and places fork at left and spoon at right of plate.

Russian Service

More formal, not adaptable to servantless household. Host and hostess have no part in this service. Food is arranged on the individual plates in the kitchen and placed before each guest, or it is placed on platters in the kitchen and offered to each guest to help himself.

Mealtime Surprises

Be flexible! Make mealtime a real pleasure for the family!

Surprise them with a Sunday supper on trays in the living room or on the porch.

Pamper a house guest with Sunday breakfast in bed. Let the children plan a picnic supper. Or serve breakfast outdoors. Make mealtime a time of gay surprises!

TABLE SERVICE

IS YOUR TABLE ATTRACTIVE AT MEALTIME?

*Linen spotless? Silver and china shining? Glassware sparkling?
Table neat and orderly?*

TABLE LINENS

For formal dinners, use white, cream, or pastel-colored tablecloths of damask, linen, or organdy. For informal dinners, luncheons, and breakfasts, use place mats of linen, cotton, straw, plastic, or paper. If the china or glassware is colorless, select colored cloths.

Napkins: Choose napkins to harmonize with the cloth or place mats. The napkin, folded in square or rectangle, with open corner at lower right, is on the service plate unless the first course is in place—then it is to the left of the forks. If there is no service plate, the napkin may be in center of each cover.

PLACING OF CHINA AND GLASSWARE

Waterglass or Goblet: directly above point of knife. **Cups and Saucers:** at right of spoons, with handles to right. **Bread-and-Butter Plates:** directly above forks. (They are not usual at very formal dinners.) **Service Plates:** always used at formal dinners, often at informal dinners and luncheons, they are usually 10″ plates, attractive in design. Place them on table in center of each place 1″ from edge of table. Leave on table during appetizer and soup courses; remove just before placing main course plates.

A formal table needs fine porcelain, exquisite silverware, elegant cloths, and a centerpiece of distinction. An informal table uses earthenware, sturdier cloths and silverware, and a less pretentious centerpiece.

CENTERPIECE

The centerpiece should enhance but not obstruct the view of the diners. For formal dinners, it must be in the exact center. For an informal table, it may be placed on the unused side or end. The soft glow of candlelight lends a festive air to the evening meal. Candles should not be used for a daytime meal unless illumination is needed; then the curtains may be drawn and the candles lighted.

FLAT SILVER

Place silver 1″ from edge of table in straight line, with no more than 3 pieces on each side of plate . . . and place each piece in order of use, beginning at outside.

PLACING OF FLAT SILVER

Knives: at right of plate with sharp edge toward plate. **Butter-spreader:** across top of bread-and-butter plate. **Beverage and Soup Spoons:** at right of knives. Or beverage spoon on saucer; tiny after-dinner coffee spoon always on saucer. **Forks:** all but cocktail fork at left of plate, prongs up. Salad fork at left of dinner fork if salad is served as first course; to right, if served with main course. When salad accompanies main course, dinner fork may be used for both meat course and salad. Cocktail fork on appetizer plate or at extreme right. **Dessert Silver:** At informal meals, dessert silver may be on table at beginning of meal. For formal service, it is brought on with the dessert.

38

TEAS AND RECEPTIONS ("At Homes")

One of the easiest and loveliest ways in which to entertain.

Arrange the table with simple elegance, tea service at one end, coffee service at the other . . . with cups, plates, and spoons. (*See sketch below.*) Accompaniments for each should be nearby . . . the food placed conveniently for passing to guests who may stand or be seated. A hostess pours the tea or coffee. Guests may be invited to help themselves.

HOW TO SET THE TABLE FOR A TEA

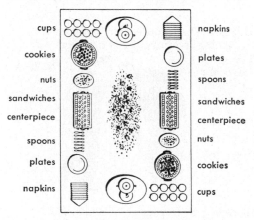

cups		napkins
cookies		plates
nuts		spoons
sandwiches		sandwiches
centerpiece		centerpiece
spoons		nuts
plates		cookies
napkins		cups

Tea or Coffee Menu

Tea. Coffee. Assorted Fancy Sandwiches. Little Cakes. Fancy Cookies or Wafers. Salted Nuts. Candies.

Reception Menu

Same as for a Tea (*above*) except that Fruit Punch served from a punch bowl is usually added (in which case tea is omitted).

BUFFET SUPPERS AND LUNCHEONS

One of the simplest and most delightful ways of entertaining.

The food, with the exception of the dessert, is all placed on the table at one time. The plates, silver, and napkins are so arranged as to make self-service easy. Guests love to help themselves . . . and immediately feel "at home" . . . thus an atmosphere of informal hospitality prevails. The food should be attractive, with dramatic garnishes.

HOW TO SET A TABLE FOR A BUFFET

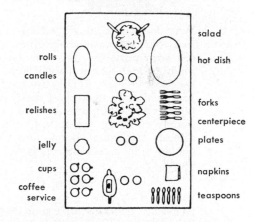

rolls		salad
candles		hot dish
relishes		forks
		centerpiece
jelly		plates
cups		napkins
coffee service		teaspoons

Buffet Luncheon or Supper Menu

Chicken à la King in Wild Rice Ring. Molded Gelatin Salad. Hot Buttered Rolls. Jelly. Watermelon Pickles. Ice Cream-filled Meringue Shells. Coffee.

SPECIAL OCCASION ENTERTAINING

See Index for special cookies, cakes, and breads to mark Holidays, Birthdays, and other festive occasions.

Table set for a smorgasbord in our Early American dining room

MEAL PLANNING

A MOTHER CAN GIVE HER FAMILY A PRICELESS GIFT

Why are some mothers tired all the time and some children fighting colds all winter? Probably because they don't eat the right things.

Food that abundantly nourishes can make the difference between a family that just lives and one that has enough and more of health and vigor. You probably know this if you and your family are eating the right foods; all of you have the extra vitality to meet health hazards, the extra enthusiasm to welcome challenges and opportunities.

Why does the kind of food make a difference? Because your body is in a constant state of building and replacing itself from the day you are born until the day you die. The only building and repair materials you have are the foods you eat. If they are good materials, your body can make and maintain resilient bones, good teeth, muscles that meet the demands of living, resistance to fatigue and disease, the extra bounce and vigor of the person who is always ready for what lies ahead.

Generally speaking, in a good diet there is a wide variety of foods. If your children enjoy all kinds of food, they are much more likely to

have a good diet than those whose tastes run to sweets or who "don't like meat" or "can't stand cooked vegetables." So if you give your children all kinds of food, well prepared and attractively served, so that they grow up enjoying all the wholesome foods, you are giving them a priceless gift—not only good nutrition and health but also the daily pleasure found in good eating.

Food can be grouped into types, according to the kind of nourishment they provide. On the following page is one way to group them. You can use it as a rough pattern in planning good nutrition and good eating for your family.

MEAL PLANNING

EACH DAY MEALS SHOULD INCLUDE FOODS FROM EACH OF THESE 7 GROUPS

Green and yellow vegetables

Dark green or bright yellow vegetables, fresh, frozen, or canned. One or more servings a day, sometimes served raw.

Necessary for normal growth, good skin condition, and to prevent night blindness.

Oranges, tomatoes, grapefruit

One or more servings a day of any one of the citrus fruits, tomatoes, raw cabbage, or salad greens.

Essential for healthy connective tissue, strong and elastic blood vessels, and to prevent bleeding gums.

Potatoes and other vegetables and fruits

Two or more servings a day (raw, dried, cooked, frozen, or canned).

Necessary for growth and normal function of body.

Milk and milk products

Milk may be skim or whole, dry or liquid, evaporated or condensed.

1½ pints to 1 quart of milk for each child. 1 pint a day for adults. Vitamin D milk is especially valuable for children and nursing or expectant mothers. Use for cooking to assure your family getting its quota.

Builds strong bones and teeth.

Meat, poultry, fish, and eggs

One serving of meat, poultry, or fish daily. Liver once a week. Occasionally dried beans or peas can be substituted for meat.

At least 3 or 4 eggs a week per person. Better to have an egg each day.

Normal rate of growth and repair of body.

Bread, flour, and cereals

Three or more servings a day. Whole-grain or enriched flour and restored or enriched cereals for minerals and vitamins.

Protein-rich foods are as a rule more expensive. Bread and cereals, less expensive, can also be depended upon for part of the daily protein needed—especially so when served with milk.

Energy and normal growth, healthy nervous system and skin, stimulate appetite.

Butter and fortified margarine

Use for a spread and in cooking. These fats contribute food values other than calories.

Promotes growth. Builds resistance to disease.

If your family's meals include all these kinds of foods every day as often as indicated in the pattern, you can be fairly sure they are being well nourished. If foods from one or more of the food groups are missing, you will do well to improve your food-planning and preparation to insure a well balanced, nutritious diet.

MEAL PLANNING

A GOOD BREAKFAST EVERY DAY FOR EVERYONE

Start everyone in your family off with fuel for the morning's activities. Breakfast can have as much variety as other meals.

> Fruit
> Cereal and milk
> Egg, meat, or cheese
> Bread and butter
> Milk or other beverage

Try combining such foods as the following in different ways:

Fruit	Egg or Meat	Bread and Cereal
Orange juice	Bacon and eggs	Buttered toast
Applesauce	Poached egg on toast	Cereal
Peaches	Scrambled eggs	Pancakes
Grapefruit sections	Creamed dried beef on toast	Cereal
Pears	French toast	Cereal
Mixed fruit	Fried egg in a frame	Cereal
Orange slices	Omelet	Coffee cake

LUNCH OR SUPPER IS THE "THIRD" MEAL

Lunch or supper should be a third well planned meal, lighter than dinner but well balanced and nutritious.

> Main Dish
> (meat, egg, or cheese)
> Vegetable or fruit
> Bread and butter
> Dessert
> Milk

These are easy foods that combine into a quick third meal:

Main Dish	Vegetable or fruit	Dessert
Welsh rarebit	Vegetable salad	Fruit and cooky
Omelet	Cole slaw	Pudding and cooky
Corned beef hash	Raw carrot strips	Hot cinnamon rolls
Egg salad	Buttered green beans	Ice cream and cooky
Salmon au gratin	Apple salad	Cake
Broiled cheese sandwiches	Creamed carrots	Cooky and fruit juice
Meat sandwich	Vegetable soup	Custard and brownie

DINNER IS AN IMPORTANT TIME OF DAY

Not only a place for good nutrition, dinner is one of the happiest times the family has together. *Good* food is important for family pleasure.

> Juice or soup
> Meat and potatoes
> Vegetables
> Salad
> Bread and butter
> Dessert
> Milk

These are some good dinner foods for a modern homemaker:

Meat	Potatoes	Vegetable	Salad	Dessert
Chuck roast	Mashed potatoes	Buttered carrots	Vegetable salad	Apple pie
Broiled hamburgers	Parsley potatoes	Corn-tomato casserole	Lettuce salad	Pineapple upside-down cake
Pork chops	Oven-fried potatoes	Broccoli	Apple salad	Gingerbread
Italian spaghetti	——	Buttered green beans	Cole slaw	Snow pudding
Liver and bacon	Scalloped potatoes	Harvard beets	Jellied carrot and pineapple	Ice cream and cake
Broiled halibut	French fried potatoes	Creamed peas	Fruit salad	Chocolate pie

Mother's Night Off: (Let one of the children take over as cook.)

Franks and beans	——	Carrot strips	Sliced tomato	Apple crisp cheese wedge

MENUS EVERYDAY BREAKFASTS

*Starred recipes are in this book. See general index.

Fruit	Main Dish	Cereal	Bread	Beverage	Something Special
Sliced Bananas and Top Milk	*Eggs Baked in Bacon Rings	Wheaties	*Country Breakfast Muffins	Coffee or Tea	Blueberries on bananas
Grapefruit Half	*Broiled Ham Slice	Oatmeal	*Quick Butterscotch Rolls	Coffee or Milk	Maraschino cherry and juice on grapefruit
Strawberries and Cream	*Waffles, Little Pork Sausages	Cheerios		Coffee or Tea	*Blueberry Waffles
Steamed Prunes	*Eggs in a Frame		Extra Toast	Breakfast Cocoa	Grated orange rind cooked with prunes
Orange Juice	*Scrambled Eggs with Ham	Trix	*Popovers	Coffee or Milk	Pour orange juice over orange sections for double flavor
Tomato Juice	*Delicate Fluffy Pancakes and Crisp Bacon			Coffee or Milk	Serve lemon wedge and Worcestershire sauce with tomato juice
Fruit Medley	*Jelly Omelet	Sugar Jets	*Cinnamon Coffee Cake	Breakfast Cocoa	Instead of one dried fruit, try medley of 2 or 3

EVERYDAY LUNCHES

Main Dish	Soup or Vegetable	Salad	Bread	Dessert	Something Special
*Crispy Browned Hash	Green Beans	Tomato Green Pepper Ring Salad	*Whole Wheat Bread	*Baked Apple	*Sour Cream Dressing
*Welsh Rarebit	*Potato Soup	Assorted Crisp Relishes	Toast Points		Sweet Pickles
*Southern Ham Shortcakes or Ham Sandwiches	Asparagus	*Molded Gelatin Salad		*Rhubarb Sauce Cookies	Extra biscuits for Bread
*Yankee Doodle Macaroni	*Easy Chicken Gumbo	*Grandma's Lettuce Salad	Hard Rolls	Peach Crisp	Green Tomato Relish
*Salmon Soufflé	Buttered Peas	Orange or Grapefruit Salad	Melba Toast	*Brownies	Dill Pickles
*Country Baked Limas	*Onion Soup au Gratin	Carrot Cabbage Salad	Rye Bread	*Tapioca Cream	
*Spanish Rice	Chopped Spinach	*Winter Salad Bowl	*Butter Dips	*Ice Cream Puffs	Orange Marmalade

*Starred recipes are in this book. See general index.

Meat or Main Dish	Potato or Alternate	Vegetable	Salad	Bread	Dessert	Something Special
*Roast Beef	*Browned Potatoes	New Peas in Cream	*Mixed Green Salad	*Dinner Rolls	*Fruit Ambrosia	*Yorkshire Pudding
*Fillet of Beef Tenderloin	*Baked French Potatoes	Brussels Sprouts Hollandaise	*Choice of Vegetable Salad	*Hot French Bread	*Crème Brulée	*Sautéed Mushroom Caps
*Broiled T-Bone or Club Steak	*Puffed Potatoes in Half Shell	*Broiled Tomatoes	*Best Tossed Salad	Crusty Rolls	*Apple Dumplings	*Maître D'Hôtel Butter
*Swiss Steak	Steamed Potatoes	Tomato (in the meat)	*Cabbage Salad	*Whole Wheat But- termilk Rolls	*Brown Betty	Mustard Pickles
*Pot Roast	Noodles	Buttered Carrots	*Winter Salad Bowl	*Pan Biscuits	*Prune Whip	Homemade Chili Sauce
*Old-fashioned Beef Stew	Potatoes (in stew)	Turnips, Carrots, Parsnips (in stew)	Lettuce, *Thousand Island Dressing	*Corn Bread	*Blueberry Pie	*Whipped Ice Cream
*Stuffed Flank Steak	Boiled Potatoes	*Golden Cabbage	*Complexion Salad	*Refrigerator Rolls	*Caramel Custard	Onion Gravy
*New England Boiled Dinner	Potatoes (with meat)	Onion, Carrots, Tur- nips (with meat)	Autumn Salad Bowl	*Anadama Bread	*Indian Pudding	Corn Relish
*Fluffy Meat Loaf	*Scalloped Potatoes	*Tangy Green Beans	*Grandma's Lettuce Salad	*Rich Egg Bread	*Fruit Sauce, *Ju- bilee Jumbles	Catsup
*Savory Meat Pie	(in the pie)	(in the pie)	Lettuce, *Green Goddess Dressing	*French Rolls	*Apple Crisp	*Cream of Spinach Soup
*Meat Croquettes	(rice in croquettes)	Green Beans	*Beet Salad Ring	*Whole Wheat Batter Bread	*Cherry Carnival	*Mushroom Sauce
*Texas Hash		*Fried Eggplant	*Waldorf Salad	*Whole Wheat Rolls	*Cherry Cobbler	Mustard Pickles
*Roast Pork	*Baked Sweet Potatoes	Buttered Cauliflower	*Orange-Grapefruit Salad	*Cloverleaf Rolls	*Ice Cream, Butter- scotch Sauce	*Tart Applesauce
*Stuffed Pork Tenderloin	*Shirred Potatoes	*Savory Baby Green Limas	*Tossed Green Salad	*French Rolls	*Ice Cream Bombe	*Apple Rings

MENUS EVERYDAY DINNERS

*Starred recipes are in this book. See general index.

Meat or Main Dish	Potato or Alternate	Vegetable	Salad	Bread	Dessert	Something Special
*Pork Chops Supreme	*Buffet Potatoes	Buttered Chopped Spinach	Lettuce, *Rancho Roquefort Dressing	*Mixed Batter Buns	*Velvet Crumb Cake Broiled Icing	Apple Jelly
*Spareribs and Sauerkraut	*Mashed Potatoes		*Waldorf Salad	*Whole Wheat Bread	*Old-fashioned Bread Pudding	*Hard Sauce
*Texas Barbecued Ribs	*Baked Potatoes	Buttered Whole Kernel Corn	*Cole Slaw	*Bran Pan Biscuits	*Cherry Pie	
*Baked Ham	*Potatoes au Gratin	Fresh Green Asparagus	*Molded Fruit Gelatin	*Pumpernickel	*Lemon Meringue Pie	*Horse-radish Sauce
*Broiled Ham Slice	*Puffed Potatoes in Half Shell	Buttered Green Limas	*Choice of Fruit Salad	*Swedish Limpa	Strawberry Sundae *Angel Food Cake	*Raisin Sauce
*Ham Loaf Superb	*Candied Sweet Potatoes	*Porcupine Cauliflower	Tokay Grape and Apple	*Herb Bread	*Orange Cake	*Easy Horse-radish Sauce
*Roast Leg of Lamb	*Parsleyed New Potatoes	*Glazed Carrots	*Lime Party Salad	*Butter Fluffs	*Portia's Pears	*Mint Sauce
*Lamb Chops	*Creamed New Potatoes	Buttered Peas	*Pineapple-Strawberry-Mint	*Jumbo Bread Sticks	*Angel Food Cake *Orange Sauce	Spring Onions and Radishes
*Braised Lamb Shanks	Potatoes (with meat)	Carrots and Celery (with meat)	Lettuce, *Thousand Island Dressing	*Whole Wheat Rolls	*Pineapple Upside-down Cake	Pickled Beets
*Irish Stew	Potatoes (in stew)	Carrots, Turnips (in stew)	*Tossed Green Salad	*Cloverleaf Rolls	*Strawberry Shortcake	Mint Jelly
*Lamb Curry	*Rice	Chopped Spinach	*Molded Garden Salads	*French Bread	*Apricot Wafer Pie	Chutney and Salted Peanuts
*Roast Veal	*Browned Potatoes	Asparagus, *Cashew Sauce	*Lime Party Salad	*Parkerhouse Rolls	*Silhouette Pudding	*Spiced Pears
*Veal Cutlets	*Mashed Potatoes	*Savory Beets	*Choice of Fruit Salad	*Butter Fluffs	*Butterscotch Pie	*Piquant Brown Sauce
*Veal Birds	*Escalloped Potatoes	Corn on Cob	*Sliced Cucumber and Tomato	*Lowell Inn Crescent Rolls	*Fruit Custard	Watermelon Pickles

*Starred recipes are in this book. See general index.

Meat or Main Dish	Potatoes or Alternate	Vegetable	Salad	Bread	Dessert	Something Special
*Veal Supreme	*Noodle Ring	*Chinese Celery	Bibb Lettuce, *Garlic French Dressing	Toasted *English Muffins	Fruit in Season	*Tomato Bouillon
*Veal Paprika	*Poppy Seed Noodles	Baby Green Limas	*Hartley Salad	*Bread Sticks	*Ice Cream Sundae Cake	Whole Tomato Soup
*Liver and Bacon	*Baked Potatoes	Mashed Squash	*Cabbage Salad	*White Bread	*Gingerbread Party Dessert	Dill Pickles
*Stuffed Veal Heart	*Mashed Potatoes	*Polish Beets	*Waldorf Salad	*Rye Bread	*Old-fashioned Creamy Rice Pudding	*Spicy Tomato Soup
*Oxtail Stew	Buttered Noodles	*Panned Cabbage	Raw Celery, Carrot Sticks	*Whole Wheat Bread	*Hot Fudge Pudding	Horse-radish
*Tongue	*Creamed Potatoes	Buttered Spinach	*Orange-Bermuda Onion Salad	*Anadama Bread	*Iowa Date Pudding	
*Roast Chicken or Turkey	*Mashed Potatoes *Stuffing	Broccoli	*24-Hour Salad	*Lowell Inn Crescents	*Lemon Ice *Sugar Cookies	Cranberry Relish
*Delmarvelous Broiled Chicken	Shoestring Potatoes	Buttered Beets	*Soufflé Salad	*Brown 'n Serve Rolls	Peach Halves, *Raspberry Sauce	*Crumb Sauce for Asparagus
*Fried Chicken	*Parsleyed New Potatoes	French Green Beans	*Garden Salad	*Herb Bread	*Strawberry Shortcake	Watermelon Pickles
*Chicken Fricassee	*Dumplings	*Mint-glazed Carrots	*Melon Salad	*French Rolls	*Baked Custard	
*Chicken Pie		Peas and Onions in Cream	*Molded Salad	*Dinner Rolls	*Baked Custard	Spiced Peaches
*Pressed Chicken	Potato Chips	Corn on Cob		*Brown 'n Serve Rolls	*Double Raspberry Shortcake	*Tomato-Cucumber Mayonnaise
*Chicken Pancakes Versailles		*French Green Beans Almondine	*Choice of Melon Salad	*Iris' Biscuits	*Pot de Crème au Chocolat	*Madrilene
*Scalloped Chicken Supreme	(rice in main dish)	New Peas	Grapefruit, *Ruby Red Dressing	*Madeline Island Rolls	*Angel Pie	*Dutch Poppy Seed Sauce

*Starred recipes are in this book. See general index.

Meat or Main Dish	Potatoes or Alternate	Vegetable	Salad	Bread	Dessert	Something Special
*Pheasant	*Wild Rice	*Braised Celery	*Orange-Bermuda Onion Salad	*Caraway Bread Sticks	*Cherries Jubilee	*Currant-Mint Sauce
*Venison	Scalloped Potatoes	Cauliflower	Green Salad	*Pumpernickel	*Hot Apple Pie	*Orange-Currant Sauce
*Roast Wild Duck	*Potatoes Anna	Mashed Rutabaga	*Grapefruit-Persimmon-Avocado Salad	Poppy Seed Rolls	*Fruit Pie	Lingonberries
*Lobster Thermidor	*French Fried Potatoes	*Chinese Celery	*Tossed Green Salad	*Sesame Seed French Rolls	*Ice Cream Bombe	*Coconut Kisses
*Crispy Fried Fish	Creamed Potatoes and Peas	Corn on Cob	*Fresh Spinach Salad	*Butter Fluff Rolls	*Lemon Chiffon Pie	*Tartar Sauce
*Fillets Almondine	*Parsleyed New Potatoes	Peas and New Onions in Cream	*Tomato-Cucumber Salad	*Corn Bread	*Fresh Rhubarb Pie	Lemon, Carrot Curls
*Codfish Balls		*Spinach Sprite	Sliced Tomatoes	Bread and Butter	*Strawberry and Rhubarb Sauce	*Egg Sauce
*Salmon Loaf	*Creamed Potatoes	Asparagus	*Grandma's Lettuce Salad	*Bran Pan Biscuits	*Lemon Cake Pudding	Sliced Cucumbers in Vinegar
*Broiled Lobster Tails	Shoestring Potatoes	Broccoli	*Western Way Salad	*Salt Sticks	*Fresh Fruit and Cheese	*Hollandaise Sauce
*Stuffed Green Peppers	Baked Squash	*Panned Cabbage	*Waldorf Salad	*Potato Refrigerator Rolls	*Hot Fudge Pudding	
*Savory Spaghetti		Buttered Zucchini	*Winter Salad Bowl	*Garlic-buttered French Bread	*Easy Lemon Cream	*Sugar Cookies
*Macaroni Loaf		Brussels Sprouts	*Tomatoes Vinaigrette	*Melba Toast or Rusks	*Southern Peach Skillet Pie	*Clear Consommé
*Cheese Soufflé		Asparagus	*Orange-Grapefruit Salad	*Whole Wheat Bread	*Down East Pudding	*Taffy Sauce
*Boston Baked Beans			*Cabbage Salad	*Brown Bread	*Baked Apples	Dill Pickles

AT THE WHITE HOUSE, WASHINGTON, D.C.

The year, 1956. President and Mrs. Dwight D. Eisenhower mention as one of their favorites a dinner menu that almost any American citizen can enjoy in his own home.

Broiled Sirloin Steak (p. 311)
Baked Potatoes   Green Beans
Green Salad with French Dressing
Apple Pie (p. 350) with Cheese
Coffee

AFTER THE CONCERT

Welsh Rarebit (p. 285)
or Grilled Cheese Sandwiches (p. 301)
Celery Hearts   Olives
Chocolate Cupcakes or Brownies (p. 204)
Bunches of Grapes, Sliced Fresh Pineapple,
or Broiled Grapefruit Halves (p. 62)
Coffee

MEMORIES OF THE AUSTRIAN TYROL

Risë Stevens, on the day of an operatic performance, enjoys a 4 o'clock dinner of a small steak, baked potato, light salad, and small dessert. But at other times, this star of the Metropolitan Opera often likes an evening meal built around a special dish she learned to prepare as a young American student in Europe.

Szegediner Gulyas (p. 277)
(sauerkraut with pork and veal)
Apple-Celery Salad   Rye Bread
Chocolate Vienna Torte (p. 243)

HAWAIIAN BUFFET LUNCHEON OR SUPPER

For table decorations, use lemon leaves, ferns, pineapple, bananas. Flowers (including lei for each guest) should be everywhere. Soft strains of Hawaiian music lend atmosphere.

Tropical Fruit Salad
(avocado sections, orange slices, whole
ripe olives . . . on bed of shredded lettuce)
with
Lime or Lemonade Dressing (p. 381)
Chicken Curry (p. 279)   Browned Rice (p. 290)
Toasted Whole Almonds
French-cut Green Beans
Sautéed Banana Quarters
Hawaiian Pineapple Cake (p. 143)

GLAMOUR SURROUNDS SIMPLE SUPPER OF A STAR

Helen Traubel, dear to music lovers all over America, serves a few well chosen dishes when she entertains informally.

Chicken En Casserole (p. 280)
Mixed Green Salad   Hard-crusted Rolls
Persian Melon
filled with
Raspberries, Cut-up Pineapple, Blueberries

ENTERTAINING IN HOLLYWOOD

Grace Kelly, winner of the Academy Award as the Best Moving Picture Actress of 1954, personally selected and sent us this menu as one of her favorites.

*Caviar Blinis
**Duck l'Orange   French-style Green Beans
***Hearts of Palm Salad Vinaigrette
Fruit   Cheese

*Caviar served on small buckwheat pancake with oil, lemon juice or vinegar, and various garnishes.
**Duck roasted with cut-up orange inside . . . served with an orange sauce.
***For Vinaigrette Dressing, see p. 379.

FROM SUNNY ITALY

To Marlon Brando, Academy Award Winner as the Best Moving Picture Actor of 1954, this menu recalls happy days in his Italian homeland.

Spaghetti with Meat Balls (p. 298)
Tossed Salad with Garlic French Dressing (p. 379)
Italian Bread Sticks
Bunches of Grapes

FASHION LUNCHEON

Climaxed with a dramatic dessert from Mr. John, celebrated designer of hats that women love.

Individual Cheese Soufflés (p. 284)
with Crabmeat Sauce (p. 398)
Asparagus Vinaigrette (p. 379)
Melba Toast (p. 30)
Mr. John's French Beret Pancake
Dessert (p. 251)
Coffee

HOLIDAY PARTIES 'ROUND THE YEAR

There's a special cooky (*p. 191*) or cake (*pp. 174–176*) for each of the most celebrated holidays . . . a special pie (*p. 339*) for many of them. The appropriate one will make a memory occasion out of the simplest family dinner or afternoon or evening gathering.

TO WELCOME THE NEW YEAR

A New Year's Buffet. Holiday Open House. Eggnog Party for the Holidays. See pp. 57, 67 for suggestions.

SCHOOLDAY REMEMBRANCE OF LINCOLN'S BIRTHDAY

One or several children in a schoolroom bring Lincoln Logs (*p. 191*) for all to enjoy with milk or a milk beverage (*p. 73*) at refreshment time.

ST. VALENTINE'S DAY DESSERT PARTY

Heart-shaped Meringue Torte (p. 252) or
Heart Party Cake (p. 175)
Salted Nuts   Coffee   Rosebud Mints

A SUPPER PARTY AT MOUNT VERNON

For George Washington's
birthday.

Old Virginia
Baked Ham
(p. 318)
Fried Oysters (p. 336) or
Stewed Chicken (p. 329)
Spoon Bread (p. 93)
Southern Biscuits (p. 83)   Sally Lunn (p. 125)
Damson Plum Preserves   Brandied Peaches
Old-time Sea Moss (same as Blanc Mange, p. 231)
Burnt Sugar Cake (p. 155)

EASTER BREAKFAST

Sliced Strawberries on Grapefruit Halves
Wheaties with Cream
Shirred Eggs in Bacon Rings (p. 266)
French Breakfast Puffs (p. 79)
Coffee

HAPPY EASTER DINNER

Frosted Fruit Juice (p. 63)
Baked Ham (p. 318)
(basted while baking
with currant jelly)
Glazed Sweet Potatoes
Buttered Asparagus
Molded Garden Salad (p. 393)
Herb Bread (p. 108)
Angel Pie (p. 252) or Lily Pons'
Fleur de Lily (p. 258)
Coffee

ST. PATRICK'S DAY IN THE EVENING

Let the musical background be songs of Old Erin, dreamy and gay, by Academy Award Winner Bing Crosby whose humor and versatility, both as singer and actor, have added happiness and inspiration to the lives of many.

Green-tinted Fruit Cup (p. 62) or Cream of
Spinach Soup (p. 417)
Pork Tenderloin (p. 316)
Puffed Potatoes in the Half Shell (p. 441)
Buttered Asparagus   Cloverleaf Rolls
Molded Lime Fruit Medley (p. 393)
Ice Cream with Crème de Menthe
Angel Food Cake (p. 157) with Green Icing
Coffee

DINNER AT MONTICELLO

This was a favorite menu of President Thomas Jefferson in his Blue Ridge Mountain home, a place famous for hospitality.

Baked Fish (p. 334)
Scalloped Potatoes with Onion (p. 441)
(potatoes and onion sliced paper-thin)
Green Asparagus with Hollandaise Sauce (p. 402)
Crème Brulée (p. 257)
Unfrosted Angel Food Cake

A TEA FOR MOTHER'S DAY

Remember a little corsage bouquet for each mother present.

Chicken Salad (p. 390) in Miniature
Cream Puffs (p. 241)
Roses in Snow Cake (p. 180)
(*featured each year by neighborhood bakers*)
Red and White Mint Wafers   Salted Nuts
Coffee   Tea

PROGRESSIVE DINNER FOR JULY FOURTH

Each course in a different home makes work light . . . fun for all.

Course 1: Fruit Plate or Melon Ball Cocktail (p. 62). Hot Cheese Puffs (p. 65).

Course 2: Fried Chicken (p. 328). Potato Salad (p. 389). Corn on the Cob (p. 433). Crisp Vegetable Relishes. Butter Dips (p. 83). Currant Jelly.

Course 3: Fresh Cherry Pie (p. 352). Or Ice Cream with Fresh Berries and Fourth of July Cupcakes (p. 174). Coffee.

EVERY DAY IS SOMEBODY'S BIRTHDAY

For the birthday cake, flower, and jewel of the month, see p. 176. In the home of Frances Kersteter, Minneapolis, the lighted birthday cake has always climaxed the favorite dinner menu of the birthday girl or boy.

HALLOWEEN REFRESHMENTS

(1) Cider and Doughnuts (p. 95).
(2) Pigs in Blankets (p. 84). Carrot Straws. Ripe Olives. Orange Sherbet. Chocolate Cupcakes with Orange Butter Icing (p. 177). (Jack O'Lantern faces traced on icing with melted chocolate.)

THANKSGIVING DINNER

See color picture and menu on p. 36. Also menus for Roast Chicken or Turkey (p. 47). **For Dessert:** Autumn Pumpkin Pie (p. 360), Pumpkin Chiffon Pie (p. 367), or Old-fashioned Mince Pie (p. 357) is a happy choice.

CHRISTMAS DINNER

See references for Thanksgiving Dinner above. **Finish** the festive meal with a flourish —with flame-wreathed English Plum Pudding (p. 239) or Down East Pudding (p. 238), White Christmas Pie (p. 368), Eggnog Chiffon Pie (p. 367), or Ice Cream and Sherbet with Christmas Candle Cupcakes (p. 175.)

CHRISTMAS EVE SUPPER

Oyster Stew (p. 418) or Cream of Tomato Soup
(p. 417)
Celery Hearts   Salty Crackers   Radish Roses
Molded Fruit Gelatin (Red) (p. 228)
Stollen (p. 120)   Holiday Cookies
Jule Kage (p. 122)
Coffee

A CHICKEN BARBECUE

Indoors or out.

Barbecued Chicken (p. 329)
Corn on the Cob   Best Tossed Salad (p. 383)
Hot Garlic-buttered French Bread (p. 105)
Strawberry or Peach Shortcake (p. 235) or
Fresh Fruit Pie or Ice Cream and Cake

A MOTHER GOOSE PARTY

Children are asked to come as some character from Mother Goose (Little Miss Muffet, Wee Willie Winkie, etc.). The mother of the child having the party, dressed as the Old Woman in the Shoe, welcomes the little guests as they arrive.

Creamed Chicken (p. 278)   Mashed Potatoes
Buttered Peas or Carrots
Lettuce Sandwiches
(cut in animal or flower shapes)
Ice Cream   Sponge Cake (pp. 164–165)
Cocoa

CAMPFIRE OR GIRL SCOUT COOK-OUT

*Pocket Stew
Buttered Split Hard Rolls
Whole Tomatoes
Walking Salad
(washed fresh fruit
in plastic bags)
Milk or Cocoa
Brownies

*Each one brings a pocketful of cleaned fresh vegetables and a few cubes of meat in a plastic bag. Combine all the pocketfuls in large kettle, cover with water, add cut-up onion, salt, pepper. Simmer until done over campfire.

PLATE DINNERS 'ROUND THE YEAR

See color picture on p. 422. Food is arranged on individual plates in kitchen, then placed before each guest. See Index for recipes.

Spring   Broiled Fish Fillet. Parsleyed New Potatoes. Peas and New Onions in Cream. Tomato-Cucumber Salad. **For Dessert:** Fresh Rhubarb Pie (p. 353).

Summer   Fried Chicken. Mashed Potatoes. Corn on the Cob. Zucchini. Pickled Peach. Celery Hearts. **For Dessert:** Strawberry Shortcake (p. 235).

Autumn   Broiled Ham Slice. Candied Sweet Potatoes. Green Beans with Cashew Nuts. Radish Roses and Raw Cauliflowerets on Watercress. **For Dessert:** Grape Pie (p. 354).

Winter   Broiled Porterhouse Steak. Puffed Potatoes in the Half-shell. Chinese Celery. Sautéed Onion Rings. Tomatoes Vinaigrette. **For Dessert:** Apple Crisp (p. 231).

51

FORMER FIRST LADY ENTERTAINS AT BRIDGE LUNCHEON

Mrs. Harry S. Truman finds that her guests enjoy this simple menu when she serves it in her Independence, Missouri home.

Chicken Salad (p. 390)
on tomato slices or in tomato cups
garnished with
watercress sprigs and olives
Hot Butter Dips (p. 83)
Frozen Lemon Pie (p. 258)
Coffee　　Tea

DINNER IN PARIS

As suggested by Christian Dior, renowned French designer of fashions for women.

Chilled Tomato Soup
*Turbot à la Cubaine　　Roast Chicken (p. 327)
French-style Green Beans (p. 427)
Green Salad (p. 382)　French Bread (p. 110)
Apricot Mousse (p. 256)　Assorted Cheeses
Demitasse

*Place flat fish, such as flounder, on bed of bread crumbs. Sprinkle with salt, pepper, cut-up pimiento and mushroom caps. Moisten thoroughly with white wine. Cover with buttered paper. Bake in mod. oven (350°) 30 min.

AFTER-THE-GAME SPECIAL

Scrambled Eggs　　Baby Sausages
Carrot Straws　　Corn Sticks　　Crisp Pickles
Marble Cake　　Coffee, Milk, or Other Beverage

"QUEEN'S PUDDING" FOR DESSERT

Ed Sullivan, of television and newspaper fame, recommends this as a perfect finish to a very simple, homey supper.

Broiled Lamb Chops (p. 319)
Buttered Garden Peas　Fluffy Mashed Potatoes
Tossed Green Salad
(if desired)
Ed Sullivan's Meringue Bread Pudding
("Queen's Pudding," p. 232)
Beverage

JIMMY DURANTE'S CHOICE

"This is what I like best for dinner," says the popular entertainer of stage and airways known as "the comedian with a heart."

Shrimp Cocktail (p. 62)
Tossed Salad with *Umbriago Dressing
Broiled Steak (p. 311)
Baked Potato with Sour Cream and Chives
Fresh Asparagus or Chopped Spinach
Fresh Fruit in Season
topped with Ice Cream or Sherbet
Tea

*Roquefort Dressing (p. 379) made "special" with olive oil, vinegar, Roquefort cheese, a little cream, lemon, English mustard, and Worcestershire sauce.

A CHINESE SUPPER

Chicken Almond
(p. 279) or Eggs Foo
Yung (p. 282) or
Chicken Chow Mein
(p. 279)
Poppy Seed Rolls
Tossed Green Salad
Orange Sherbet　Chinese Almond Cakes　Tea

ACCOMPANIMENT TO RECORDS

Teen-agers' choice.

Root Beer Floats
(Place ice cream in
bottom of tall glasses.
Fill glasses with root
beer.)
Hurry-up "Popcorn"
(p. 185)

FEATURING AN ITALIAN SPECIALTY

From the mother of Julius La Rosa, whose songs on television, stage, and radio bring enjoyment to many.

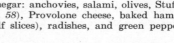

*Antipasto
Spaghetti with Meat Sauce
or Tomato Sauce
Spittini (p. 277)
Baked Potatoes　Green Salad
Fresh Fruit　　Demitasse

*Arrange on large platter and serve with oil and vinegar: anchovies, salami, olives, Stuffed Celery (p. 58), Provolone cheese, baked ham (rolled in half slices), radishes, and green pepper rings.

DESSERT MASTERPIECE OF FRENCH CHEF HIGHLIGHTS DINNER OF A DIVA

Named for her and created in her honor by Louis of The Ritz in Paris, Fleur de Lily is the choice of Metropolitan Opera Star, Lily Pons, as the perfect dessert for a favorite informal dinner.

Oyster or Clam Cocktail in Season (p. 62)
*Petites Marmites
**Galantine of Chicken
Wild Rice   Petits Pois Française
Endive and Avocado Salad, French Dressing
Lily Pons' Fleur de Lily (p. 258)
Demitasse

*A flavorful French soup (consommé with cooked cut-up vegetables added), served in individual casseroles or marmites. Garnish with thin slice of dry toast, sprinkle with grated Parmesan cheese, place under broiler until cheese melts.
**Jellied chicken, special French style.

FAMOUS VIOLINIST RECOMMENDS TWO VEGETABLE DINNERS

Yehudi Menuhin, gifted concert artist, whose violin music since childhood has charmed audiences throughout the world, sent us these suggestions for two delicious and satisfying dinners without meat.

1   *Creamed Mushrooms (p. 436)
in Ring of Wild Rice (pp. 291-292)
Crusty Whole Wheat Rolls or Bread (p. 108)
Fresh Fruit

*Use freshly ground whole wheat flour in making the sauce.

2 *Vegetable Melange   Beet Salad (p. 388)
Bread Pudding (p. 232)
(For this, Mr. Menuhin recommends bread made from fresh unpasteurized cream; date sugar; freshly grated nutmeg; walnuts and raisins soaked in orange juice.)

Vegetable Melange "In making this dish," says the world famous violinist, "all depends on the seasoning, care, and love with which it is done."

Sauté separately and gently in butter until lightly browned 1 lb. squash, sliced; 1 med. onion, sliced; 1 green pepper, in ½" pieces; ½ eggplant, sliced; 4 tomatoes, sliced. Mix lightly. Season with salt and pepper. Place in buttered baking dish. Top with bread crumbs and grated cheese. Dot with butter. Bake in mod. oven (350°) until vegetables are tender (not mushy), 20 to 25 min.

A MEXICAN SUPPER OR LUNCHEON

Macarones Con Jocoqui (p. 295)
Green Salad
Toasted Split Buns   Guacamole (p. 66)
Elena Zelayeta's Fresh Fruit Dessert (p. 257)

a simplified
SMORGASBORD

See picture on p. 39. A plain Swedish blue linen cloth makes a lovely background for the food on the buffet table. A chafing dish keeps meat balls cozy and warm. Use candles for lighting . . . baskets for breads . . . wooden bowls for salads . . . wooden platters for cheeses.

Tray of Relishes
(olives, pickles, stuffed celery, radishes)
Pickled Herring   Smoked Salmon
Baked Ham (p. 318)   Jellied Veal Loaf (p. 275)
Swedish Meat Balls
Trays of Breads
(Rye, Rye Crisp, Hot Rolls, Swedish Limpa)
Tray of Cheeses
Potato Salad   Garden Salad
Molded Fruit Salad   Cole Slaw
Lingonberry Sauce
Norwegian Blöte Kage (p. 248)   Coffee

HIS MOTHER'S SOUP SUPPER

 To Eddie Fisher, popular singing star of the entertainment world, this always brings fond memories of home.

Eddie Fisher's Lima Bean Soup (p. 414)
Radishes   Garlic Dill Pickles   Celery
Pumpernickel (p. 109)
Cheese Cake (p. 242) topped with Strawberries

ELECTION NIGHT "AT HOME"

In the rambling family mansion at Hyde Park one cold November night, Mrs. Franklin Delano Roosevelt welcomed neighbors to warm themselves before the crackling fire in the high-ceilinged drawing room. Then the guests stopped at the long, candlelit table in the spacious entrance hall where there were:

Chocolate Cake (pp. 148–152)
Coconut Cake (p. 139)
Sandwiches   Crackers and Cheese
Cider   Doughnuts (p. 95)   Coffee

GARNISHES To put over the menu.

IT'S THE FINISH THAT COUNTS

It may be only a ruffle of lettuce to set off a salad; a bunch of purple grapes for an accent note on a platter of roast chicken; a few tiny pimiento bells to add color to a bowl of oyster stew at Christmastime. Whatever the finishing touch, be sure to make it just as good to eat as it is to see. Best garnishes are simple, too.

Each should add contrast of shape, color, crispness, or flavor to the food it adorns. Notice the finishing touches suggested in many of our recipes . . . and shown in the color pictures in this book and in magazines. Take time to add that one little frill that can bring out color and appetite appeal of a special dish.

A Few Simple Examples

For FRUIT CUPS

Just before serving, top with:
- A whole berry
- A sprig of mint
- A dip of fruit ice or sherbet

Tint syrup a delicate color.
Set sherbet dish on decorative leaf.

For SOUPS

Just before serving, top with:
- A spoonful of salted whipped cream . . . minced parsley, chives, pimiento, etc. may be added
- A sprinkling of minced parsley, chives, watercress, fresh herbs
- Thin slice of lemon
- Vegetables julienne

For FISH

Surround fish on platter with:
- Lemon wedges or slices sprinkled with:
  - parsley   minced pimiento
  - paprika   minced green pepper
- Bright orange slices
- Grapefruit sections
- Thick slices of cucumber
- Tomato slices topped with thin slices of lemon and stuffed olive

For VEGETABLES

Combine contrasting colors:
- Red beets and green Brussels sprouts
- Yellow carrots and green peas

Combine contrasting shapes:
- Carrot strips and round peas
- Little round onions with slivered beans

Sprinkle grated cheese on white cauliflower
Sprinkle sieved hard-cooked eggs on:
- Asparagus   broccoli   spinach

All you have to do —

To make flower garnishes for meats: shape daffodils from carrot curls and slices cut like petals; turnips can be cut to form daffodils or calla lilies, etc.

For MEATS

Surround meat on platter with:
- Broiled fruits (p. 338)
- Pink cinnamon apples (with pork)
- Stuffed black prunes (with pork)
- Slices of orange decorated with watercress or parsley (with duck)
- Bunches of red, green, or purple grapes (with chicken)
- Molded cranberry cutouts on orange slices (with turkey and chicken)
- Canned pear halves filled with green mint jelly (with lamb)
- Spiced peach halves and watercress (with ham)
- Sautéed mushroom caps (with steak)
- French fried onion rings (with steak)
- Glazed onions and buttered carrot strips (with beef)
- Tiny scooped-out tomatoes filled with horse-radish (with pot roast)

For SALADS

Add gaily the last minute:
- Sprigs of watercress, mint, or parsley
- Thin strips of pimiento or green pepper
- Cream cheese balls . . . may be rolled in nuts or chives
- Prunes, dates, figs, or cherries stuffed with seasoned cream cheese or nuts

For DESSERTS

Top plain puddings with:
- Whole or sliced fresh berries . . . cherries
- Cubes of bright colored gelatin

Surround creamy or frozen desserts with:
- Bright colored fresh fruits or berries

Decorate dessert plates with:
- Clusters of berries or grapes
- Ivy or grape leaves
- A single fresh flower
- Ring of berries at base of sherbet dish

DRESS UP FOOD FOR EYE APPEAL

TOMATO FLOWER

Cut tomato into wedges, leaving base uncut. Press open slightly. (Fill with salad or other mixtures.)

FRINGED CUCUMBER SLICES

Cut off ends. Pare, if desired. Then pull sharp fork firmly down lengthwise surface. Repeat around cucumber. Slice thinly. Chill.

GREEN PEPPER RINGS

Slice firm green pepper thinly crosswise . . . cut out all white portions and remove seeds. Crisp in ice water.

CELERY STICKS WITH HEARTS

To include choice heart with each piece, slice through entire stalk from one end to the other.

CELERY CURLS

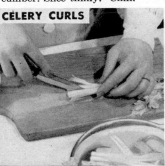

Cut into short lengths. Slit ends in narrow strips (can slit both ends). Ends will curl in ice water.

CARROT CURLS

Slice the length of scraped raw carrots paper-thin with slicer. Crisp in ice water until curled.

ONION RINGS

Slice Bermuda or Spanish onions thinly *crosswise* and separate into rings. Crisp in ice water.

CAULIFLOWERETS

Cut away green leaves and woody base of cauliflower. Wash and break head into tiny flowerets. Chill.

MINCED PARSLEY

Fold leaves of several stalks (washed). Hold together . . . cut fine with scissors.

MINCED GREEN PEPPER

Wash pepper. Cut out stem and seeds. Rinse with cold water. Cut into strips. Cut several strips held together into tiny pieces.

RADISH ROSES

Cut off root end, leave bit of stem, leaf. Cut *thin* petals from stem to root end around radish. Place in ice water to blossom.

LATTICED VEGETABLES

Use lattice cutter to cut attractive lattice slices and sticks from raw vegetables (carrots, potatoes, turnips, etc.).

MEANING OF TERMS

HERBS

Herb authorities claim there are six simple herbs basic to all seasoning.

Mint: For tea, iced drinks, ices, pea soup, cottage cheese, salads, salad dressings, meat broths, and potatoes.

Thyme: Common thyme (of the many varieties of this herb) is the general kitchen herb that glorifies such varying foods as soups, sauces, stuffings, cheeses, meats, hare, fish, and salad dressings. It is particularly delicious with tomatoes either in a salad or in cooked dishes.

Sage: Fresh sage is more satisfactory than dried. The gray pointed leaves should be added sparingly to beans, cottage cheese, salt fish, stews, duck, or geese. Although traditional in stuffing for turkey, herb authorities claim it is too strong for turkey or chicken. They recommend a blend of savory, thyme, and sweet basil for a more pleasing and subtle flavor.

Marjoram: Two kinds . . . sweet marjoram, one of the "big six," and wild marjoram, often called by its Spanish name, oregano. It is used in all Spanish and Mexican dishes, and is excellent with lamb or fresh mushrooms. The Italians call it the "mushroom herb." Sweet marjoram can be used successfully too in all of these. The Germans use sweet marjoram in making sausage and call it "Wurstkraut" . . . the sausage herb. Its general uses are in sauces, soups, salads, meats, stuffings, and fish.

Rosemary: Fragrant as a flower, this delightful herb gives subtlety to meat, poultry, sauces, greens, and stuffings. Some prefer it to garlic in a roast.

Basil: Adds distinction to soups, ragouts, salads, cottage cheese, meats, sauces, and fruit drinks.

ADDITIONAL HERBS FREQUENTLY USED

***Anise:** Seeds used in cookies, breads, cheese; the leaves used in salads.

Bay: Bay leaf for meats, soups, relishes, poultry, and stuffings.

***Caraway:** Seeds used in cookies, breads, sauerkraut, cream cheese, and over roasting pork.

Chervil: A salad herb par excellence. Combines well with other herbs. Good in soups, eggs, cheese, and some meats.

Chives: For potatoes, potato salads, omelettes, sauces, and cheese.

**Keep herb seeds in the refrigerator to prevent becoming rancid.*

Curry Powder: Not truly an herb, but a powdered combination of herbs and spices including green ginger, coriander seeds, cumin seeds, garlic, tumeric, chili, and peppercorns. Used with lamb and chicken.

Parsley: When used as a tasty, nutritious addition to sauces, soups, stews, meats.

Savory: Both leaves and flowers give flavor to poultry stuffings, salads, peas, pork, green beans, rice, horse-radish sauce.

Tarragon: Crumbled leaves are used sparingly in salads, soups, fish sauces, dressings, meats, stews, and sprinkled over fish.

Winter Savory: A milder herb, can be used in larger amounts. Good in fish dishes.

HERB BOUQUETS

The Herb Bouquet is the first thing Europeans throw into the soup, stew, casserole, or roasting pan to impart the subtle flavor average American cooking lacks.

Fines Herbes: French term for a combination of 3 or 4 herbs used to flavor certain dishes— such combinations as parsley, basil, and chives. They are mixed together, chopped fine, and tossed into the food just before serving. They are used in tartar sauce, cream soups, and cream cheeses. When used in omelettes, they are mixed with the eggs before cooking.

Bouquet Garni: French term for a tablespoon of powdered herbs (such as 2 sprigs parsley, 1 sprig marjoram, 2 sprigs thyme, and ½ bay leaf) tied in a muslin bag, and left in a roast or soup for the last hour of cooking, then removed. For canned soups, it should be left in for the entire cooking time. In cold foods, fruit juices, cocktails, or cottage cheese, it takes several hours to draw out the flavor.

Off to a good start

"Well begun is half done" is true when you serve appetizers before a meal! The entire atmosphere brightens when food appears. It may be the simplest fruit juice cocktail—for a tired husband just home from work . . . or it may be a tray of colorful canapés offered guests as soon as they arrive. Fatigue and formality vanish. Success of the meal or party is assured.

Betty Crocker

THERE'S ENDLESS VARIETY IN APPETIZERS . . . ALL MAY BE DRAMATIC

Some simple favorites from the many in this chapter are listed below.

FRUIT COCKTAILS (pp. 62–63)

Fruit Cup	Melon Ball Cocktail
Fruit Plate	Fruit Soup
Fruit Juice Cocktails	Cranberry Cocktail
Broiled Grapefruit	Spiced Cider

VEGETABLE COCKTAILS (p. 63)

Tomato Juice, Hot or Cold
Tomato Bouillon   Vegetable Cocktail

SEA FOOD COCKTAIL (p. 62)

HORS D'OEUVRES (p. 64)

Wedgies	Silver Dollar Hamburgers
Burning Bush	Bacon Wrap-arounds
Pastry Snails	Turkey, Ham Tempters
Dried Beef Rolls	Herring-Appleteaser

SIMPLE ACCOMPANIMENTS (p. 58)

SPREADS AND DIPS (p. 66)

Lobster Newburg Spread
Guacamole
Sardine Spread
Cheese-Anchovy Spread
Roquefort Cheese Dip
Deviled Ham-Cheese Dip
Garlic-Cheese Dip
Minced Clam-Cheese Dip
Hollywood Dunk

CANAPÉS (p. 65)

Deviled Ham	Hot Crabmeat Puffs
Tomato-and-Shrimp	Hot Cheese Puffs
Savory Mushroom	Miniature Pizzas
Hot Clam	

A SIMPLE COCKTAIL PARTY

Dunking Bowl
(see p. 66 for Spreads and Dips)
Potato Chips   Salty Crackers
Chilled Cooked Shrimp
Cocktail Sauce (p. 62)
Coffee   Soft Drinks or Other Beverages

For Holiday Open House: add Christmas cookies, red and green mint wafers, salted nuts.

A NEW YEAR'S BUFFET

Eggnog (p. 73) or Fruit Punch (p. 74)
Tray of Crackers   Bowl of Cheese Spread
Baked Ham (Sliced)   Roast Turkey (Sliced)
Buttered Thin Slices of
Rye, Whole Wheat, and White Breads
Olives   Celery   Radishes   Pickles
Potato Salad (p. 389)   Cranberry Jelly
New Year Clock Cookies (p. 191)

57

SIMPLE ACCOMPANIMENTS FOR COCKTAILS

Popcorn
Pretzel sticks
Olives, green or ripe

Toasted pumpkin,
sunflower, or
squash seeds

Chips—potato,
corn, cheese,
coconut

Salted nuts
Crackers of many
flavors, shapes

SAVORY CRACKERS

Spread crackers lightly with butter. Sprinkle with celery seeds, poppy seeds, sesame seeds, paprika, or any savory salt. Heat in mod. oven (350°) to crisp.

BUTTERED OR CHEESE KIX

Each taste calls for another.

Melt in heavy skillet ⅓ cup butter. Remove from heat. Stir in ⅓ cup grated Parmesan cheese, if desired. Add ¼ box KIX (4 cups). Sprinkle with ½ tsp. salt. Stir well.

GLOSSY OLIVES: Dip green or ripe olives in olive oil or other salad oil. For garlic flavor, add a cut clove of garlic and let stand an hour or more.

SEASONED POTATO CHIPS

Sprinkle potato chips with grated Parmesan cheese or garlic salt, onion salt, lemon juice, minced parsley or chives. Heat in mod. oven (350°).

CHEERIOS COCKTAIL SNACKS

There's enjoyment in variety.

Mix in shallow baking pan 1½ cups KIX, 1 cup CHEERIOS, 2 cups tiny cheese crackers, 2 cups pretzel sticks, and ½ lb. mixed nuts. Mix ¼ cup melted butter, ½ tsp. Worcestershire sauce, ¼ tsp. garlic salt, ¼ tsp. celery salt; and pour over mixture. Stir and salt lightly. Bake 1 hr. in slow oven (250°), stirring every 15 min. AMOUNT: 6 cups.

COLORFUL RELISHES FOR DECORATING APPETIZER TRAY

Among vegetables that add a gay touch are radish roses and accordions, raw cauliflowerets, carrot and turnip lilies, bouquets of parsley and watercress, celery and carrot curls and sticks, turnip sticks, tomato boats and flowers, cucumber sticks and petals. Keep vegetables crisp in ice water or refrigerator until serving time.

Bright and refreshing fruits add color and glamour. Among those frequently used are little bunches of grapes (green, blue, or red), pineapple sticks, melon balls, cherries, orange and lemon slices and sections, unhulled strawberries, others described below. Be sure fresh fruits are *fresh . . . and cold.*

CELERY TRUNKS (Stuffed Celery)

Fill matching stalks of celery with well seasoned cream cheese. Then fit stalks back together (the way they were grown). Tie with string and chill. When firm, slice ½" thick. The celery curls around the cheese in attractive form.

STUFFED CUCUMBER

Remove center from pared cucumber with apple corer. Stuff tightly with a firm cheese mixture. Chill. Slice ¼" thick.

GRAPE CLUSTERS (Lemon-glazed)

Dip little bunches of washed grapes into lemon juice, then sprinkle with sugar, and dry on wire cake rack.

FRUIT KABOBS

Slip onto a toothpick colorful pieces of fruit, such as pitted cherries, banana slices (which have been dipped in citrus fruit juice), pineapple wedges (edges dipped in paprika or minced parsley), melon balls or cubes, whole strawberries, seedless grapes.

For other fruit and vegetable garnishes for the appetizer tray, see pp. 54–55.

APPETIZERS

Appetizers are comparative newcomers in our American cuisine. Yet these "small portions of food or drink served before the first course of a meal," as the dictionary describes them, have been served in Europe for centuries. The custom seems to have started in Ancient Greece and Rome. In the days of their fabulous feasts, the Romans munched on chicory, endive, or celery, to excite hunger.

Later, nations of Europe picked up the custom and elaborated on it. They have passed on to us the elegance of Russian caviar, Italian anti-pasto, French hors d'oeuvres, and the Scandinavian smorgasbord with all its countless items.

During the rugged formative period of our country, hunger was the natural and best appetizer. But with the refinements of later years, we have wholeheartedly adopted European appetizers, and even added some innovations of our own. We serve them not only at formal dinners, but for informal hospitality like simple dinners, buffet suppers . . . even party refreshments.

It is "high style" to serve these tiny portions of food with beverages in the living room before a meal. The informality of moving around and helping themselves to the tidbits starts conversation and puts guests at ease. It's also a help to the hostess without a maid. While her guests are enjoying themselves, she can slip out and put the main course on the table.

Some appetizers—fruit cups, sea food cocktails, individual plates of hors d'oeuvres, etc.—are more conveniently served at the table. In this chapter, you will find the different types explained, and recipes for the most familiar and popular. We have featured those that are simplest to prepare. We hope they will make your entertaining easier and more fun.

APPETIZERS IN VARIETY

(1) Plate of Canapés (2) Platter of Hors d'Oeuvres (3) Roquefort Cheese Dip
(4) Cocktail Sauce (5) Cheese-anchovy Spread (6) Crabmeat Cocktail (7) Fruit Plate
(8) Cooked Fresh Shrimp (9) Celery Trunks (10) Shrimp Cocktail (11) Fruit Cup
(12) Simple Accompaniments (13) Cranberry Cocktail
(14) Frozen Fruit Cocktail (15) Tomato Juice (16) Vegetable Cocktail
(17) Fresh Strawberry Plate (18) Fruit Juice Cocktail

Fruits, sea foods, or vegetables usually make their appearance as appetizers in "cocktails." They are served in small individual dishes, such as sherbet glasses, or small cups sometimes set in a compote of crushed ice.

A highly seasoned cocktail sauce is poured over sea food or vegetables to add zest. Fruits are served in their own juice. The simplest form of cocktails are fruit or vegetable juices served in small fruit juice glasses. (*See picture, pp. 60–61.*)

FRUIT CUP

Fresh or whole frozen fruits are ideal because they are less sweet than canned fruit. Serve whole, halved, or cut in attractive sizes (not too small). Add lemon or lime juice for a refreshing tartness. To blend the flavors, prepare in advance and chill. Serve cold. Eat with spoon.

In Orange Cups: Serve any combination of fruit in hollowed-out orange halves. Garnish with watercress or mint.

Frozen Fruit Cocktail: Pour cold ginger ale over cut-up fruit and tiny sweet green grapes. Freeze to a mush. Serve in sherbet glasses.

FRUIT PLATE

Arrange attractively on leaves of lettuce, watercress, or endive on individual plates any colorful combination of fruits. Dark glossy prunes or dates stuffed with cream cheese add color accent; or top with a scoop of lemon, lime, or pineapple sherbet.

FRESH STRAWBERRY PLATE

Place large red strawberries (with green hulls and stems left on) in a ring around a mound of confectioners' sugar on individual plates. Dip berries into sugar and eat.

BROILED GRAPEFRUIT

Remove seeds from grapefruit halves. Cut around sections, remove center. Sprinkle with a bit of sugar (brown or maple). Broil slowly until heated (15 to 20 min.). Add a little maraschino cherry juice or sherry flavoring. Serve hot.

MELON BALL COCKTAIL

Scoop out balls of ripe watermelon, cantaloupe, and honeydew melon with ball cutter or $\frac{1}{2}$ tsp.-size measuring spoon. Fill glasses with melon balls and drip lemon or lime juice over them. Or use Aloha Sauce (*p. 222*). Chill and serve garnished with mint sprig.

For variation, try combining with other fruits, such as avocados, bananas, grapes, grapefruit, oranges, peaches, plums, pears, pineapple, raspberries, or strawberries.

OYSTERS ON THE HALF SHELL

Blue Point oysters are best. Wash the oysters in shells. Chill. Then open. Serve on deep halves of the shells. Arrange 5 to 7 on a plate of crushed ice. Place a tiny cup of cocktail sauce in the center and add a wedge of lemon.

SEA FOOD COCKTAIL

Use fresh sea food, frozen or canned.

For each serving, use 4 to 6 cleaned, cooked shrimp or $\frac{1}{4}$ cup flaked or pieces of cooked crabmeat or lobster. Season, add minced onion, finely diced celery. Or combine sea food with pieces of pineapple, grapefruit, or avocado. Serve ice cold in lettuce-lined sherbet glasses or shells . . . with Cocktail Sauce (*below*) and a garnish of lemon or seasoned mayonnaise.

COCKTAIL SAUCE

For sea food and vegetable cocktails.

Combine and chill thoroughly . . .
    $\frac{1}{2}$ cup chili sauce
    $\frac{1}{3}$ cup catsup
    2 to 4 tbsp. prepared horse-radish
    $1\frac{1}{2}$ tsp. Worcestershire sauce

NOTE: For a sharper sauce, add $\frac{1}{4}$ tsp. salt, 2 tbsp. lemon juice, dash of pepper, and a few drops Tabasco sauce.

SMOKED SALMON

Serve thin slices of it on plate garnished with lemon wedge and greens. Pass pepper grinder and cruet of olive oil.

The clever wife has a simple appetizing cocktail (cold in summer, hot in winter) ready for her weary husband when he comes home at night. Vegetable or fruit juices are at their best when two or three tart flavors are chilled and served ice cold in appropriate glasses.

TOMATO JUICE

Add a little salt, lemon juice, a few drops of Worcestershire sauce, and onion juice to tomato juice. Serve cold or hot.

TOMATO BOUILLON

Combine equal parts tomato juice and bouillon (dilute canned bouillon or use cubes with boiling water). Serve hot.

TOMATO-SAUERKRAUT JUICE

Combine 2 parts tomato juice and 1 part sauerkraut juice. Serve hot or cold.

TOMATO-CLAM JUICE

Combine equal parts clam juice and tomato juice; season to taste with onion, salt, and pepper. Serve hot.

APPETIZER SOUPS

Dissolve bouillon cubes as directed on container. Or dilute canned bouillon or consommé with water, as directed, and season to taste. Serve hot in bouillon cups. Garnish with minced parsley.

Recipes for jellied bouillon or consommé (good for hot weather) and other soups which can be served as appetizers are on p. 412.

FRUIT SOUP

From the Land of the Vikings.

    2 cups mixed dried fruit (12-oz. pkg.), such
        as currants, raisins, prunes, pears, apri-
        cots, peaches, apples
    3 cups water (half grape juice may be used)
    ½ lemon, sliced
    1 tbsp. tapioca
    ¼ tsp. salt
    ½ to ⅔ cup sugar
    1 stick cinnamon

Mix ingredients and cook, covered, until fruits are tender (about 30 to 40 min.). Serve either hot or cold.
AMOUNT: About 4 servings.

VEGETABLE COCKTAIL

Drain 4 cups cooked tomatoes, chop the tomato pulp finely and mix with . . .
    ¼ cup finely chopped celery
    ⅓ cup minced green pepper
    1 tbsp. grated onion
Add the tomato juice and . . .
    1 tbsp. grated horse-radish
    2 tbsp. sugar
    ¼ cup mild vinegar or lemon juice
    2 tsp. salt
    dash of red and black pepper
Chill several hours. Serve cold in sherbet glasses. Eat with spoon.
AMOUNT: 6 servings.

CRANBERRY COCKTAIL

Cook 2 cups cranberries in 3 cups water until skins pop; strain. Cook ½ cup sugar with juice until dissolved (about 2 min.). Chill and add a little lemon juice, half as much ginger ale, or unsweetened pineapple juice (to taste). Serve cold in glasses. *8 servings.*

SPICED CIDER

Simmer 2 qt. cider with 1 tsp. whole allspice, 1 stick cinnamon, and a few whole cloves for 15 min. Strain. If desired, just before serving, add ¼ cup lemon juice and 2 tbsp. orange juice. *10 servings.*

MINTED CITRUS JUICE

Combine equal parts lemon juice, orange juice, and water. Add 1 sprig of mint, crushed. Chill 2 hr. Serve cold.

All you have to do —

For fruit juice cocktails: combine two or three flavors to taste, such as pineapple, grape, and lime. For conveniency, use frozen fruit juice concentrates or canned juices. "Frost" with spoonful of fruit sherbet just before serving.

SERVE WITH GLAMOUR

For an elegant touch, try serving hot tomato juice in demitasse cups.
Cold soups will have an added sparkle if you serve them in clear glass sauce dishes.

Hors d'oeuvres are dainty finger foods, colorful and varied in size and shape, often exciting, too. Serve them on toothpicks stuck into a holder of wood, a grapefruit, apple, eggplant, pineapple, or bright red Edam cheese. Or serve hot ones from a chafing dish. Popular simple hors d'oeuvres are Deviled Eggs (*p. 265*), frankfurts (1″ pieces), sliced smoked salmon, lobster, smoked oysters, miniature hamburgers and meat balls, Vienna sausages, herring, and shrimp.

BURNING BUSH

Form seasoned softened cream cheese into balls. Roll in minced dried beef. (Balls may also be rolled in minced parsley, chives, or grated carrots for attractive color and flavor.)

WEDGIES

Spread 4 slices large bologna or minced ham with softened cream cheese seasoned with onion or chives and mustard. Place slices together (like a layer cake). Spread cheese over top and sides, decorate with sliced olives. Chill. Cut into wedges.

PASTRY SNAILS

Roll out Pastry (*p. 343*) thinly into an oblong. Spread with deviled ham (2¼-oz. can). Roll up as for jelly roll. Chill. Slice thin. Place on ungreased baking sheet. Bake in mod. hot oven (400°) until delicately browned (10 to 12 min.).

DRIED BEEF ROLLS

Spread slices of dried beef with softened cream cheese mixed with horse-radish to taste. Roll up, fasten with toothpicks, chill. Slice between picks to serve.

GREEN BALLS

Mix ½ cup grated Swiss cheese, ½ cup minced cooked ham, ½ tsp. prepared mustard, 1 egg yolk, ¼ tsp. salt, dash of pepper. Form into balls. Roll in minced chives or parsley.

All you have to do —

To serve hors d'oeuvres as a first course: arrange a few on individual plates to be eaten with a fork.

HOT

Hors d'oeuvres

A warm reception awaits hors d'oeuvres kept hot in a chafing dish.

SILVER DOLLAR HAMBURGERS, MEAT BALLS

Let guests help themselves to piping hot miniature hamburgers, meat balls (flattened), or sausages . . . and slip them into buttered split hot tiny Cocktail Buns (*p. 127*).

BACON WRAP-AROUNDS

Roll ½ strip bacon around any of the following: large stuffed green olive, cooked shrimp, raw oyster, pineapple chunk, Vienna sausage, or cooked mushroom. Broil or sauté 5 min. Serve hot from chafing dish.

TURKEY, HAM TEMPTERS

Place a hot plain or smoked turkey (chicken or pheasant) and/or baked ham on serving table . . . buttered thin small slices of rye, whole wheat, or pumpernickel bread and relishes nearby. Let guests make little open sandwiches with slices of turkey or ham, same size.

HERRING-APPLETEASER

Virginia Safford—newspaper columnist, delightful hostess, and connoisseur of good food—serves this as a "different" appetizer when friends gather at her lovely home in Cuernavaca, Mexico.

Place in shallow serving dish (such as glass pie plate) alternate layers of pieces of pickled herring, thinly sliced apple (pared), and Bermuda onion. Use skinless and boneless pickled herring soaked in wine, then drained. Season each layer with salt, pepper, and mustard. Sprinkle layers with capers and chives. Cover layers thinly with whipped thick sour cream. Chill. Serve coarse wheaty crackers with it.

Canapés, designed to be eaten gracefully from the fingers, are savory little morsels of food: a base covered with a favorite topping. They can be served for refreshments; or with cocktails in the living room to start a dinner off on a gay note.

Instead of serving an overwheiming variety of canapés and hors d'oeuvres, concentrate on one or two that are especially picture-pretty and delicious. Offer small cocktail napkins . . . small plates, too, if you choose, when serving.

TOAST BEDS FOR CANAPÉS

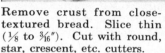

Remove crust from close-textured bread. Slice thin (⅛ to 3/16"). Cut with round, star, crescent, etc. cutters.

Toast *on one side only* by sautéing in a little butter in hot skillet over low heat until nicely browned.

About ½ hr. before serving, spread *untoasted side* lightly with mayonnaise, then with appetizer. Standing ruins them.

OTHER POPULAR CANAPÉ BASES: Bite-size crispy crackers. Toasted split English muffins and tiny yeast rolls. Melba toast.

Crisp, thin pastry in small shapes. Miniature cream puffs. Diminutive biscuits. Cucumber, zucchini, dill pickle slices.

SOME FAVORITE CANAPÉS
made from popular toppings and bases of your choice

DEVILED HAM CANAPÉS
Mash deviled ham with a little horse-radish, grated onion, and coarse black pepper to taste. Spread on canapé bases.

TOMATO-AND-SHRIMP CANAPÉS
Cut thin slice from small red tomato. Place slice on frill of lettuce on each toast bed. Center with dab of mayonnaise. Press in a shrimp.

SAVORY MUSHROOM CANAPÉS
Pan-fry finely chopped mushrooms with a little minced onion in butter. Season with garlic salt. Blend in 1 tbsp. flour and 1 tbsp. cream. Pile on bases. Keep warm in oven, if desired. Garnish with minced parsley or chives or watercress sprig.

HOT CRABMEAT PUFFS
A specialty at open house after the football games, at the home of Mrs. Harold Whittaker, Minneapolis, Minnesota.
Beat 2 egg whites until stiff. Fold in 1 cup mayonnaise and 1 cup flaked crabmeat (7-oz. can). Season, and pile on toast beds. Sprinkle with paprika. Broil 3 min. until puffy, lightly browned.

HOT CLAM CANAPÉS
A specialty of Helene Burton Kaplan, mother of four children, who efficiently combines an advertising job with homemaking.
Sauté finely chopped small onion and medium-sized green pepper in 3 tbsp. butter for 3 min. Add drained minced clams (7½-oz. can), ¼ lb. grated American cheese, ¼ cup catsup, 1 tbsp. Worcestershire sauce, 1 tbsp. cooking sherry, ⅛ tsp. cayenne. Cook until cheese melts. Serve hot over thin slice of dill pickle on buttered salty rye rounds. *8 to 10 servings.*

MINIATURE PIZZAS

They bring memories of sunny Italy.
On each toast bed round, place thin slice of tomato. Cover with onion ring, piece of anchovy, and ripe olive. Sprinkle with salt, pepper, and oregano or basil. Top with grated cheese. Broil until lightly browned.

HOT CHEESE PUFFS
Beat 2 egg whites until stiff. Beat in ½ tsp. baking powder, ¼ tsp. salt, ¼ tsp. paprika. Fold in 1 cup grated sharp cheese. Spread ¼" thick on toast beds. Broil until browned.

It's easy, informal, and fun for everyone if you place a lettuce-lined bowl or bowls (*see Decorative Bowls below*) of nippy spread or dip in the center of a tray with a suitable knife for spreading. Surround with crisp crackers, potato chips, corn or cheese chips, etc. Garnish tray with colorful relishes (*p. 58*), and place it on a convenient table for everyone to spread his own.

LOBSTER NEWBURG SPREAD

Melt ¼ cup butter, add 2 tbsp. flour, ½ tsp. salt, ¼ tsp. pepper, ¼ tsp. paprika, and a dash of cayenne. Stir in slowly ¾ cup milk and bring to a boil. Boil 1 min., stir a little into 1 egg yolk, then blend into mixture along with 1 cup flaked lobster (6-oz. can) and 1 tsp. lemon juice. Cool.

GUACAMOLE (Gwah-ka-mo-lay)

From Mexico.

Mix 1 cup mashed avocado (2 med.), 1 tbsp. lemon juice, 1 tsp. salt, and 1½ tsp. grated onion. Either chopped tomato, crumbled Roquefort cheese, curry powder, chili powder, Worcestershire sauce, or Tabasco sauce may be added.

SARDINE SPREAD

Drain oil from a 3¾-oz. can sardines and mash. Blend in 2 drops Tabasco sauce, 2 tsp. lemon juice, 2 tbsp. chili sauce, and 12 stuffed olives, chopped.

DECORATIVE BOWLS

Scooped-out tomatoes; pepper halves (seeds removed); sea shells, grapefruit, melon, and avocado shells — these are suitable for holding spreads and dips. And they make a colorful addition to the appetizer tray or table.

GREEN CHEESE BALL

"To have a delicious appetizer on hand for holiday entertaining," says Valentine Thorson of Minneapolis, "make a Green Cheese Ball. It's easy . . . and showy."

Soften equal amounts of sharp cheddar, cream, and Roquefort cheeses. Season well. Mix in chopped pecans and minced parsley. Form into a large ball. Roll in minced parsley and chopped nuts.

ROQUEFORT CHEESE DIP

To Beverly Steffen of our staff, a former "Alice in Dairyland" of Wisconsin, this and other cheese dips and spreads bring fond memories of her beautiful home state.

Mix 2 cups cottage cheese or 3 3-oz. pkg. cream cheese, ¼ lb. Roquefort cheese (4 oz.), 1 tbsp. grated onion, 1 tbsp. Worcestershire sauce, and enough mayonnaise or milk for a good dip consistency.

DEVILED HAM-CHEESE DIP

Mix 2 cups cottage cheese or 3 3-oz. pkg. cream cheese, ¼ cup horse-radish, 1 tbsp. grated onion, a 2¼-oz. can deviled ham, and mayonnaise or milk to make a good dip consistency. Chill.

GARLIC-CHEESE DIP

Mix 2 cups cottage cheese or 3 3-oz. pkg. cream cheese, 2 or 3 med. garlic cloves (crushed), 1 tsp. salt, ¼ cup chopped pickles or olives, and enough mayonnaise or milk for a good dip consistency. Chill.

CHEESE-ANCHOVY SPREAD

From Mrs. Ward H. Olmsted of Minneapolis, Minnesota, who says, "It's good and so easy."

Mix 3 3-oz. pkg. cream cheese softened with cream, anchovy paste to taste (about ½ tube), 1 tbsp. lemon juice, dash of cayenne, 1 tsp. Worcestershire sauce, 1 tsp. grated onion, ¼ bottle capers, ¼ tsp. paprika.

HOLLYWOOD DUNK

Combine ¼ cup deviled ham with ¼ cup horse-radish, 1 tbsp. grated onion, 2 tbsp. minced chives, and stiffly whipped cream to taste. (Whip about 1 cup cream.)

MINCED CLAM-CHEESE DIP

Mix a 7½-oz. can minced clams, drained, 2 3-oz. pkg. cream cheese, 1 tbsp. lemon juice, 1 tsp. Worcestershire sauce, ½ tsp. salt, ¼ tsp. flavor extender, and ⅛ tsp. ground pepper.

Favorite Beverages an Aid to Gracious Living

"Cups o' kindness" bring to mind the heart-warming sociability of friends over fragrant, steaming cups of coffee or tea. If the weather is warm, tall frosty glasses of chilled fruit juice take their part in pleasant hospitality.

Betty Crocker

SOME SUGGESTIONS FOR BEVERAGES TO SUIT YOUR MOOD, THE WEATHER, AND THE OCCASION

You'll find these and others in this chapter.

COFFEE (*pp. 70–71*)

Hot Coffee	Coffee for the Crowd
Iced Coffee	Coffee 'Round the
After-dinner	World
Coffee	Decaffeinated Coffee
(Demitasse)	

TEA (*p. 69*)

Hot Tea	Iced Tea
Spiced Tea	

EGG AND MILK DRINKS (*p. 73*)

Eggnogs	Milk Shakes
Ice Cream Sodas	

CHOCOLATE AND COCOA (*pp. 72–73*)

Hot Cocoa	Chocolate Malted Milk
Hot Chocolate	Chocolate Eggnog
Iced Chocolate	Chocolate Soda
South American	Chocolate Milk Shakes
Chocolate	

CHILLED FRUIT DRINKS (*p. 74*)

Lemonade and Variations

Party Punch	Raspberry Shrub

SERVING SUGGESTIONS (*p. 68*)

CONVENIENT AND PRECIOUS TIME-SAVERS (*p. 68*)

COME FOR COFFEE

Hot Coffee (*pp. 70–71*)
Sweet Rolls, Coffee Cake, Doughnuts,
Cookies, or Cake

LAWN OR PORCH PARTY

Lemon-Strawberry Punch (*p. 74*)
Assorted Dainty Tea Sandwiches
Angel Food Cake (*p. 157*)   Salted Nuts

HOME FROM SCHOOL

Let the children help themselves.
A Milk Drink (*p. 73*)
Bread   Butter   Peanut Butter   Jelly
Wagon Wheels (*p. 209*)

EGGNOG PARTY FOR THE HOLIDAYS

Eggnog (*p. 73*)
Thin Turkey Sandwiches   Sponge Cake Fingers
Salted Nuts   Coffee   Stuffed Dates

TWILIGHT HOUR ON CHRISTMAS DAY

Wassail Bowl (*p. 68*)
Thin Slices of Fruitcake (*p. 167*)
Salted Nuts   Christmas Cookies

SODA FOUNTAIN FOR CHILDREN'S PARTIES

Let each child choose his favorite flavor.
Ice Cream Sodas (*p. 73*)
(Chocolate, Fruit, Maple)

CONVENIENT AND PRECIOUS TIME-SAVERS

Follow directions given on each container.

Instant coffee
Frozen coffee
Instant tea
Instant cream (powdered concentrate)
Whole dry milk (powdered)
Non-fat dry milk

Malted milk powders, plain or chocolate
Ready-to-serve cocoa
Ready-to-serve eggnog
Frozen fruit juice concentrates
Frozen lemonade or orangeade concentrates
Fruit crystals

SERVING BEVERAGES

HOT TEA

A pitcher, small silver jug, or a second teapot with hot water should accompany the tea service, since some people like a milder flavored tea than others and can dilute it with hot water.

Offer milk, lemon, and sugar (either loaf or plain granulated). A small pitcher of lemon juice, thin lemon or orange slices which may be clove-studded, cinnamon candies, or honey are different accompaniments.

ICED TEA

Serve in tall glasses . . . with long handled spoons. Offer finely granulated sugar, lemon or orange wedges, mint sprigs.

GARNISHES FOR CHILLED FRUIT DRINKS IN GLASS OR PUNCH BOWL

Decorated Ice Cubes: Arrange in each section of refrigerator tray a berry, red cherry, piece of lemon or orange slice, or sprig of mint. Then fill with water and freeze as usual. Serve in fruit drinks.

Flavored Ice Cubes: Freeze fruit juices or sparkling beverages in ice cube trays. Serve in cold fruit drinks or sparkling beverages of contrasting flavors.

Other Garnishes: Thin slices of lemon, lime, or orange. Melon balls, strawberries, cherries, grapes. Scoops of lemon, lime, orange, or pineapple ice. Circle of leaves around base of bowl.

Glamorous Ice Ring for the Punch Bowl:

Fill ring mold with water, leaving ½" at top. Freeze. On top of frozen ring, arrange lemon slices and quarters, red and green maraschino cherries, and sprigs of mint or huckleberry. Fill to top with water. Freeze. Unmold; float on punch in punch bowl.

HOT COFFEE

Offer cream and sugar (loaf or plain granulated).

ICED COFFEE

Serve like Iced Tea, in tall glasses . . . with long handled spoons. Offer sugar and cream, as with hot coffee.

AFTER-DINNER COFFEE

Serve demitasse black and strong, or with sugar and cream, in small cups . . . with small spoons. Charming served in the living room after dinner, or at the dining table at the end of dinner.

HOT CHOCOLATE AND COCOA

Special chocolate cups are tall and narrow. Top each with whipped cream or a marshmallow. Or serve plain. Cinnamon or nutmeg may be sprinkled over the cream.

ICED CHOCOLATE

Serve like Iced Tea and Iced Coffee, in tall glasses . . . with long handled spoons. Top with whipped cream.

WASSAIL BOWL *for holiday entertaining*

Stud 3 oranges with whole cloves (about ½" apart), place in baking pan with a little water, and bake in slow mod. oven (325°) for 30 min. Heat 2 qt. cider with stick cinnamon to boiling. Add brandy or rum flavoring. Pour into punch bowl and float the baked oranges on top, using cinnamon sticks for stirring. *10 servings.*

Serving Note: Keep hot over low heat or heat in small batches as guests arrive.

The glamour of centuries surrounds tea. Serving and drinking it has long been a ceremony in both China and Japan. It made its debut in England in 1666 as "tay." The London coffee houses which first served it soon became "tea" shops. "There are few hours of life more agreeable than the hour dedicated to afternoon tea," wrote an American novelist on his visit to England.

Tea-drinking in this country had received a setback at the Boston Tea Party. However, in the earlier days it had been a popular custom in the American colonies. In New York, the Dutch housewife usually made several different kinds of tea in different teapots (pewter, china, and silver) to please the tastes of her guests. The tea table, teapot, sugar bowl or shaker, and strainer were the pride of the Dutch housewife. "Bite-and-stir" sugar boxes were special Dutch pieces. On one side was loaf sugar to nibble with the tea; and on the other, the granulated sugar to stir into the tea.

*THREE KINDS OF TEA

But over 3,000 varieties.

Black Tea: from India, Ceylon, Java, and Sumatra. The leaves are first fermented, then heated and dried.

Green Tea: from China and Japan. The leaves are not fermented. "Gunpowder" is a type of green tea.

Oolong Tea: from Formosa. The leaves are fermented only a short time.

Flower-scented teas have flower petals added. Jasmine is the most popular. Others are gardenia or yulan.

WHEN BUYING TEA REMEMBER

Orange Pekoe is not a kind of tea. It refers to the size of the tea leaf. "Pekoe" indicates a larger leaf than "orange" pekoe.
Tea bags of porous filter paper are a convenience for making 1 or 2 cups of tea. Each bag contains 1 tsp. tea . . . enough for 1 cup.
Buy tea in small amounts. It loses flavor in long storage. 1 lb. yields from 150 to 200 cups. Unless one serves a great deal of tea, ¼ lb. is enough to buy at a time.
Keep tea in an airtight container . . . away from spices . . . in a cool, dry place.

For tips on serving tea and for time-saving suggestions, see p. 68.

A GOOD CUP OF TEA . . . *Soothing, refreshing. Follow these simple rules for making:*

1. The Teapot Should be china, pottery, or heat-resistant glass. Keep spotlessly clean. Wash with soap and hot water after each using.

2. Scald Teapot Heat the teapot just before making tea by filling it with boiling water. Let it stand a few minutes. Then pour off water and put the tea leaves in the heated pot.

3. How Much Tea Allow 1 to 1½ tsp. tea for each cup of water.

ICED TEA

Strain freshly made *double strength* tea over ice in pitcher or in iced tea glasses. (Fill glasses with ice.)

4. Pour Fresh Boiling Water over Tea Leaves "Until the kettle boiling B, Filling the pot will spoil the T." It is important to have freshly drawn water boiling furiously when it is poured over the tea. "Take the teapot to the kettle, never the kettle to the pot."

5. Cover Pot and Let Tea Steep 3 to 5 min. will bring tea to desired strength. Then strain it into another heated pot or into cups. Tea becomes bitter if it steeps too long.

HOT SPICED TEA

Stud slices of lemon with cloves. Break cinnamon sticks into 1" pieces; place 1 piece in each cup before adding hot tea and lemon slice.

COFFEE BEVERAGES The All-American beverage.

Centuries ago in Abyssinia, a herdsman noticed his goats were unusually lively after eating the berries of a certain shrub. He took some of the berries to the abbot of a nearby monastery who dried and boiled them. He and his monks were delighted with the new black drink which they called "*,affia*" (the name of the shrub).

The use of coffee spread to Arabia, thence by caravan trade to India, Egypt, and Syria. By the seventeenth century, "coffeehouses" and clubs were flourishing in England and colonial America. The coffee shop was a gathering place for literary and business men who gossiped and discussed politics over their coffee cups.

Gradually the American people adopted the custom of drinking coffee at home. Now the art of making good coffee is an asset to successful homemaking.

SIX ESSENTIALS FOR A CUP OF GOOD COFFEE . . . easy to follow.

1. Fresh Coffee It loses flavor quickly when exposed to air. Keep it tightly covered and buy it often.

2. The Right Grind for the Coffee Maker "Drip" grind for glass vacuum makers and drip-olators. "Regular grind" or "steel cut" for percolators or for steeped (boiled) coffee.

3. A Clean Coffee Maker Wash with soap and water after each use. Stains in coffee pot can ruin the taste. Boiling water with soda in the pot removes stains. Follow directions for cleaning your type of coffee maker.

4. Start with Fresh Cold Water Not *hot* water from the tap or tea-kettle. Bring to a full rolling boil before putting the coffee container in the coffee maker.

5. Use Enough Coffee for Desired Strength
For *weak* coffee . . .
1 tbsp. to ¾ cup water;
For *medium* coffee . . .
2 tbsp. to ¾ cup water;
For *strong* coffee . . .
3 or 4 tbsp. to ¾ cup water.

6. Serve Coffee as soon as Possible If necessary to let it stand, remove grounds. Keep hot on asbestos pad over very low heat; or in pan of hot water. Cooled coffee loses flavor if reheated.

Caution For best results, brew coffee at full capacity of coffee maker.

Leftover Coffee If you want to use it, pour into glass jar. Cover. Keep in refrigerator. Reheat over low heat.

AFTER-DINNER COFFEE

Served in small after-dinner cups. It is called demitasse . . . French word for "half cup."

Make stronger than usual. Use 3 to 4 tbsp. coffee to ¾ cup water for each serving.

ICED COFFEE

Make coffee as usual, but use twice as much coffee. Pour over crushed ice in tall glasses.

For serving tips on coffee and for time-saving suggestions, see p. 68.

COFFEE FOR THE CROWD

For *40 cups* of coffee: mix 1 egg (shell and all) into 1 lb. coffee. Add 1 cup cold water. Tie coffee in cheesecloth bag large enough to allow room for coffee to swell. Measure 7 qt. cold water into large coffee pot. Immerse coffee bag in water, bring to boil. Remove pot from heat. Leave bag of coffee in water 3 to 4 min., remove and stir. Keep hot. If preferred, use boiling water to start, bring to boil. Stir. Remove from heat. Let stand 10 min. Remove coffee and serve.

MAKING COFFEE IN DIFFERENT TYPES OF COFFEE MAKERS

For "Six Essentials for a Cup of Good Coffee," see p. 70.

PERCOLATOR

Measure fresh cold water into the pot, and coffee (regular grind) into the basket. Let water boil until it has "perked" 5 to 10 min. for desired strength.

DRIPOLATOR

Measure coffee (drip grind) into filter section—vigorously boiling water into upper container. Cover. When water has dripped through coffee, remove upper section at once. Stir. Serve. If coffee *must* wait, keep hot on asbestos pad over *very low heat* or over hot water. Do not let coffee boil!

DECAFFEINATED COFFEE

This is coffee from which almost all the caffein has been removed.
The essentials for a good cup of it are the same as for regular coffee (*p. 70*) . . . and it is prepared in the same way.

OLD-FASHIONED COFFEEPOT

For steeped, commonly called "boiled" coffee.

Measure coffee (regular grind) and fresh cold water into pot. Place over heat. Stir. Bring just to boil. Stir again. Take off heat. Add dash of cold water. Strain. Serve.

"Boiled" Coffee with Egg: Stir ½ tbsp. beaten egg or egg white into about ⅓ cup coffee before adding the water.

VACUUM-TYPE

Measure fresh cold water into lower bowl. Fit top bowl on with filter adjusted. Put coffee (drip grind) in top. Place on heat. When water rises, lower heat. Stir once. Remove from heat in 1 min. When coffee is back in lower section, remove top, put on separate cover. Heat, and serve.

 COFFEE 'ROUND THE WORLD

ARABIA: Coffee is served black . . . with ground spices then added.

AUSTRALIA: Eggs, milk, syrup, and coffee are mixed to a foam; served cold.

CUBA: Ground coffee, milk, and cream are brewed together, strained, and served with sugar and whipped cream.

FRANCE: Coffee is served strong and black, laced with cognac. Or it is served as Café Au Lait in which equal amounts of coffee and milk are heated to scalding, then poured into the cup at the same time.

WARSAW: An aromatic mixture of coffee and whipped cream is served in tall glasses.

NEW ORLEANS: ⅓ cup milk, ⅓ cup heavy cream, and ⅓ cup black coffee are boiled together and served.

CAFÉ DIABLE: Strong black coffee is combined with cloves, cinnamon, sugar, grated orange rind, and flaming brandy.

TURKEY: Sugar is brewed with the coffee; served black.

UKRAINE: Pure chocolate, coffee, sugar, milk, and whipped cream are combined to make a rich drink.

VIENNA: Black coffee, usually demitasse, is served with whipped cream on top.

RUSSIA: Coffee is combined with cocoa in an unusual blend.

CHOCOLATE BEVERAGES Delicious and nourishing.

Cortez, the Spanish conquistador, was the first European to taste chocolate. Montezuma, the Aztec emperor of Mexico, gave a big feast and served "chocolatl" to his guests in a golden goblet. It was really a bitter mush, served stone cold. Cacao beans had been roasted and ground, then mixed with corn meal, vanilla, peppers, spices, and herbs. Cortez learned that the cacao beans were used as money among the Indians. He procured some.

Soon the Dutch, Italians, Austrians, and French were experimenting with these beans. In 1657, a notice in a London newspaper announced that a Frenchman in Bishopgate Street was offering an excellent West Indian drink, "jacolatte." Chocolate houses sprang up where society gathered afternoons to gossip and drink the new delicacy. Soon chocolate was being served by English colonists in America.

TYPES OF COCOA AND CHOCOLATE AVAILABLE TODAY

Unsweetened Chocolate: made from cocoa beans with no fat removed.

Semi-Sweet Chocolate: just enough sweetening added to give a partially sweet flavor. More cocoa butter is also added.

Cocoa: made from cocoa beans with varying amounts of cocoa butter removed.

Breakfast Cocoa: has a minimum of 22% cocoa fat.

Dutch Process Cocoa: made from special cocoa beans processed to make them more soluble.

For tips on serving cocoa and chocolate and for time-saving suggestions, see p. 68.

HOT COCOA

For each cup cocoa, mix ½ to 1 tbsp. sugar, 1 tbsp. cocoa, and ¼ cup water. Cook over *low* heat (boil about 1 min.), stirring constantly. Add ¾ cup milk. Heat until scalded, but do not boil. Add a pinch of salt (a drop of vanilla, too, if desired). Just before serving, beat with rotary beater. Serve hot. . . . poured over a marshmallow in each cup.

HOT CHOCOLATE

For 6 servings, heat over *low* heat 2 sq. unsweetened chocolate (2 oz.) and 1 cup water, stirring until chocolate melts. Add a pinch of salt and 3 to 4 tbsp. sugar. Boil 4 min., stirring. Then slowly stir in 3 cups milk. Heat until scalded. Do not boil. Just before serving, beat with rotary beater until smooth. Top with whipped cream. Serve hot.

SOUTH AMERICAN CHOCOLATE

Melt over hot water ½ lb. sweet cooking chocolate or a 7-oz. pkg. chocolate pieces. Add 1 cup strong hot coffee. Stir well and cook over *low* heat 1 min. Scald 6 cups milk (1½ qt.). Add to chocolate. Simmer until very hot. Beat with rotary beater until frothy on top. Set over hot water 10 min. to blend flavors. Just before serving, beat again with rotary beater. *8 servings.*

ICED CHOCOLATE

Make cocoa or chocolate your favorite way. Cool. Serve in glasses with chopped ice. Top with sweetened whipped cream.

MARTHA WASHINGTON'S COLONIAL CHOCOLATE

George Washington's favorite hot chocolate. From a radio friend who wrote, "It came from my cousin whose husband is a direct descendant of Martha Washington."

Mix to a smooth paste in saucepan . . .
    ¼ cup cocoa
    a little cold water
Stir in . . .
    2 cups water
    ⅓ cup sugar
    2 cups milk
Bring to boil and blend in . . .
    2 tbsp. cornstarch dissolved in a little cold milk
Boil 1 min. longer. Remove from heat and set in warm place.
Beat until light and foamy . . .
    1 egg with ½ cup hot water
Pour half of egg mixture into a pitcher.
Blend in . . .
    ½ tsp. vanilla

Add hot chocolate slowly. Pour remaining egg mixture over top. Serve at once.

AMOUNT: 6 servings.

EGGNOG (⚬ Recipe)

Beat together . . .
    1 egg, well beaten
    2 tbsp. sugar
Beat in . . .
    1 cup chilled rich milk
    *¼ tsp. vanilla
Serve cold in tall glass sprinkled lightly with . . .
    nutmeg

*1½ tbsp. sherry flavoring and 1 tbsp. either brandy or rum flavoring may be substituted for vanilla.

FRUIT EGGNOG

Make ⚬ recipe above—*except* use 2 tbsp. fruit or 1 tbsp. fruit juice (grape, orange, cherry juice, etc.) instead of vanilla and nutmeg.

CHOCOLATE EGGNOG

Make ⚬ recipe above—*except* omit sugar and blend in 2 tbsp. Chocolate Syrup (*at right*).

ORANGE EGGNOG

Mix thoroughly . . .
    1 egg, well beaten
    1 tbsp. lemon juice
    ½ cup orange juice
    1 tbsp. light corn syrup
Chill. Serve ice cold.
AMOUNT: 1 glass.

GRAPE JUICE WITH EGG

Appetite-tempter for convalescents.

Pour into a tall glass . . .
    3 tbsp. orange juice
    ½ cup grape juice
Add, stirring just enough to mix well. . .
    2 tsp. sugar
    dash of salt
    1 egg white, beaten stiff
AMOUNT: 1 tall glass.

MILK SHAKES

After-school treats for children, refreshing for invalids.

Have 1 cup milk thoroughly chilled. Shake or beat with fruit or other flavoring (*see below*) and ice cream, if desired, until well blended. Serve cold, topped with whipped cream and sprinkled with nutmeg, if desired.

Banana: Use ½ banana, mashed.

Strawberry: Use ¼ cup crushed sweetened strawberries.

Maple: Use 2 tbsp. maple syrup.

Chocolate: Use 1½ to 2 tbsp. Chocolate Syrup.

Chocolate Malted Milk: Beat 1 tbsp. malted milk powder into Chocolate Milk Shake.

Frosted Chocolate: Beat a small spoonful of ice cream into Chocolate Milk Shake.

CHOCOLATE SYRUP

Nice to keep on hand for beverages, desserts, and sauces.

Combine in saucepan . . .
    1 cup cocoa or 4 sq. unsweetened chocolate
        (4 oz.)
    2 cups sugar
    ¼ tsp. salt
Stir in . . .
    2 cups cold water
Simmer until smooth and thick (about 5 min.), stirring or beating with rotary beater.

Cool and add . . .
    1 tbsp. vanilla
Stir well. Pour into jar. Cover. Store in refrigerator.

ICE CREAM SODAS

For the make-believe soda fountain at home.

Place in tall glass . . .
    3 tbsp. Chocolate Syrup (see above)
        or maple syrup
        or ¼ cup crushed fruit mixed with 1 tsp. sugar

Fill glass ⅔ full with sparkling water. Add 1 scoop of ice cream; stir vigorously. Fill to top with sparkling water.

For convenient milk products to have on your shelf, see p. 68.

73

LEMONADE (ℐ Recipe) *As American as circus day . . . saves lemons, gives flavor.*

Combine in saucepan. . . . {
1 cup sugar
1 cup water
rind of 2 lemons, cut into pieces

Stir over *low* heat until
sugar is dissolved.
Boil about 1 min.
Strain; discard rind.
Cool.
Add. . . . . {
1 cup fresh or frozen lemon juice (5 to 6 lemons)
4 cups ice water (1 qt.)

Pour over ice in pitcher or tall glasses.

AMOUNT: 6 to 8 servings.

Minted Lemonade: Place bruised mint leaves in bottom of glasses before adding Lemonade (ℐ recipe above). Garnish each glass with a sprig of mint.

Pink Lemonade: Follow ℐ recipe above— and add a little grenadine syrup.

Limeade: Follow ℐ recipe above—*except* use lime juice instead of lemon juice. Add a little green food coloring, if desired.

QUICK LEMONADE

All you have to do—

To make lemonade quickly: squeeze lemons, add sugar and water to taste.

Orangeade: Follow ℐ recipe above—*except*, in place of lemon juice, use 2 cups orange juice and ¼ cup lemon juice.

For serving tips on chilled beverages and for time-saving suggestions, see p. 68.

RASPBERRY SHRUB

An old-time favorite from grandma's day.

Mix, cook together in saucepan 10 min. . . .
*3 pt. raspberries (washed and hulled)
1½ cups sugar
2 cups water
Strain and cool. Add . . .
1 cup fresh or frozen lemon juice
2 qt. water or sparkling water
Serve with crushed ice.

**If 5 to 10-oz. pkg. frozen berries (thawed) is used, omit sugar and water.*

AMOUNT: About 12 servings (2½ qt.).

ORANGE-CRANBERRY PUNCH

Make syrup by bringing to boil . . .
¼ cup sugar
¾ cup water
Cool and mix with . . .
6-oz. can frozen orange juice concentrate
2 cups cranberry juice
2 tbsp. lemon juice
Just before serving, add . . .
1 cup sparkling water
ice

Red food coloring may be added to give a bright color.

AMOUNT: 8 servings (1½ qt.).

LEMON-STRAWBERRY PUNCH

Pour into punch bowl . . .
three 6-oz. cans canned or frozen lemonade concentrate, diluted according to directions on can
Add and mix . . .
*1 pkg. frozen strawberries, thawed
Just before serving, add . . .
1 qt. ginger ale
ice

**If fresh berries are used, crush 1½ cups, add ½ cup sugar. Let stand ½ hr.*

AMOUNT: About 32 servings (about 1½ gal.).

PARTY PUNCH

Wonderful for large group affairs.

Make syrup by bringing to boil . . .
3 cups sugar
4 qt. water
Add . . .
1 qt. apple juice
2 qt. cranberry juice
1¼ cups fresh or frozen lemon juice
1 pt. orange juice
1 pt. strong black tea
Chill before serving.

AMOUNT: About 40 servings (2 gal.).

Breads·Quick and Hot
A Conversation Piece

Hot Quick Breads in their many delightful forms help tell the story of civilization. Notice the bits of history tucked into these pages and serve them up as table conversation. They'll make cooking, and eating, more fun.

Betty Crocker

THERE'S A QUICK BREAD FOR EVERY OCCASION
Some popular ones from this chapter are listed below.

PANCAKE OR WAFFLE SUPPER

Grapefruit or Melon Halves
(in cold weather, serve Broiled Grapefruit, p. 62)
Plenty of Hot Waffles (p. 89) or Pancakes (pp. 86–88)
Warm Maple Syrup
Crisp Bacon or Little Browned Sausages
Coffee

OF FIRST IMPORTANCE

The beauty of hot breads is in having them served piping hot.

Snuggle them in a napkin (just large enough to go around) in a serving dish to retain the heat. Then replenish from the oven.

HINTS AND QUICK TRICKS

• To avoid that last minute rush, measure all ingredients for muffins, biscuits, etc. ahead of time. Sift dry ingredients together. Then it takes only a jiffy to mix and pop into the oven.

• If dough is made up ahead of time, keep it in cold place until time to bake.

• Making square biscuits saves rerolling scraps. Also saves rolling out dough. Simply pat out on baking sheet. Cut in squares with sharp knife, or use ice cube divider from refrigerator tray.

• **FREEZING QUICK BREADS:** Quick Breads are at their best when first made. But you may freeze and reheat some leftovers satisfactorily as directed on p. 25.

• If muffins get done a little ahead of the meal, loosen them, tip them slightly in the pans, and keep them in the warm oven.

• When batter does not fill all the cups in the muffin pan, don't grease the muffin cups that are not to be filled. Wipe out the grease from unfilled cups before putting in oven so grease will not brown onto the pan.

• Muffins can be baked in paper baking cups set into ungreased muffin cups. Remove paper before serving.

• Serve second-day rolls, muffins, biscuits, or corn bread split, buttered, and toasted. Leftover waffles (unbuttered) become crisp again when heated in toaster or oven.

BEST SHORTCUT OF ALL
for 12 popular bakings

Just add liquid to Bisquick for Rolled Biscuits, Drop Biscuits, Fruit Shortcake, Dumplings.

Add only few extra ingredients for Waffles, Pancakes, Muffins, Coffee Cake, Cinnamon Rolls, Nut Bread.

PUFF PANCAKES

Cake-like griddle cakes with a delicate, lacy crust. And so quick and easy!

Beat with rotary beater until soft peaks form . . .
    2 eggs
Blend in . . .
    1 cup milk
Add . . .
    2⅓ cups Bisquick
    2 tbsp. sugar
Mix just until thoroughly dampened.
Fold in . . .
    ¼ cup cooking (salad) oil or other melted shortening

Spoon onto med. hot ungreased griddle. When puffed up and bubbles begin to break, turn and cook on other side. Serve with syrup . . . or as dessert with warm fruit, such as strawberries, and whipped cream.

AMOUNT: 15 to 20 pancakes.

CHIFFON WAFFLES

Luxuriously light and tender.

Follow recipe above for Puff Pancakes— *except* bake on heated waffle baker.

AMOUNT: 2 large or 6 small waffles.

PINEAPPLE STICKY BUNS

Buttery-rich, fruity upside-down rolls. Made deliciously in no time at all!

Mix . . .
    ¾ cup drained crushed pineapple
    ½ cup soft butter
    ½ cup brown sugar (packed)
    1 tsp. cinnamon

Divide mixture into 12 greased muffin cups. Make dough for Fruit Shortcake (*recipe on Bisquick pkg.*). Spoon over pineapple mixture in muffin cups. Bake. Invert on tray or rack immediately after baking to prevent sticking in pans.

TEMPERATURE: 425° (hot oven).
TIME: Bake 15 to 20 min.
AMOUNT: 12 buns.

HOMEMADE MAPLE SYRUP

Next best to the real thing.

Boil together slowly until consistency desired 1 cup granulated sugar, 1 cup brown sugar (packed), 1 cup water, stirring until sugars are dissolved. Maple flavoring may be added.

QUICK BREADS

May we introduce to you breads with a story? You see, the families of quick breads go way, way back into history. Our delicious American hot breads are the lineal descendants of the crude hearth cakes of primitive people. The famous "cakes" which King Alfred forgot to watch, as he sat in a peasant hut, were early ancestors of our present day quick breads. Others were the "bannocks o' barley" that Robert Burns wrote about. You will find that the bits of history given in these pages make interesting table conversation when you serve hot breads at your table.

These popular breads are classified as *quick* because they are made with quick-acting leavening—baking powder, or soda and sour milk, or steam, etc.—instead of the slower acting yeast. They include many different types of baked breads—biscuits, muffins, nut loaves, corn breads, etc. Some are cooked on a griddle—the pancakes, waffles, etc. Then there are those cooked by steam, such as dumplings and brown breads. And, last of all, the old favorites fried in deep fat—doughnuts and fritters. All of them can be made at the last minute and served piping hot and fresh from the oven, griddle, or kettle.

Our staff has found the easiest, quickest ways to make each and every type. You can now make most of these recipes by the one-bowl double-quick method.

Here are recipes for pancakes, waffles, or muffins for lovely leisurely breakfasts—popovers or nut breads for a luncheon to be long remembered! The scones and coffee cakes are ideal for the tea or coffee hour. And do try surprises like the butter dips and crunchy corn sticks for special dinners. There are delicious fruit breads for sandwiches and savory cheese biscuits just right for those important evening snacks. And they are quicker than ever to make!

POPOVERS

High hat muffins, popped so they are crusty shells, hollow inside.

Beat together with rotary beater just until smooth: 1 cup *sifted* GOLD MEDAL Flour, ½ tsp. salt, 1 cup milk, 2 eggs. Pour into well greased *deep* muffin cups (¾ full) or oven-glass cups (½ full). Bake in hot oven (425°) until golden brown, 40 to 45 min. Serve immediately. Makes 5 to 9 Popovers, depending on size of cup.

"LIGHT-AS-FEATHER" MUFFINS

One of the specialties of Mrs. K's Toll House, Silver Springs, Maryland, famous for its wonderful food and charming atmosphere.

Mix thoroughly . . .
    ¼ cup sugar
    ¼ cup soft shortening

Blend in . . .
    1 egg

Sift together . . .
    1 ¾ cups *sifted* SOFTASILK Flour
    4 tsp. baking powder
    ½ tsp. salt

Stir in alternately with . . .
    1 cup milk

Fill greased muffin cups ⅔ full. Bake until golden brown. Serve hot.

TEMPERATURE: 375° (quick mod. oven).

TIME: Bake 20 to 23 min.

AMOUNT: 14 to 16 small muffins.

OATMEAL MUFFINS

They're marvelous! So moist and rich.

Soak together for 1 hr. . . .
    1 cup rolled oats
    1 cup buttermilk or sour milk

Mix thoroughly . . .
    ⅓ cup soft shortening (part butter)
    ½ cup brown sugar (packed)
    1 egg

Sift together . . .
    1 cup *sifted* GOLD MEDAL Flour
    1 tsp. baking powder
    ½ tsp. soda
    1 tsp. salt

Stir into shortening mixture alternately with rolled oats and buttermilk.

Fill greased muffin cups ⅔ full. Bake until golden brown. Serve hot.

TEMPERATURE: 400° (mod. hot oven).

TIME: Bake 20 to 25 min.

AMOUNT: 12 med. muffins.

BEST BRAN MUFFINS

Follow recipe for Oatmeal Muffins above —*except* omit rolled oats. No soaking. Begin with mixing shortening, etc. *After* sifting together dry ingredients, mix with 3 cups bran (either fine or coarse), stir into shortening mixture alternately with the 1 cup buttermilk.

FRENCH BREAKFAST PUFFS

Like delicate, glorified doughnuts. Miss Esoline Beauregard of Fort Lauderdale, Florida, said, "Please try my mother's recipe."

Mix thoroughly . . .
    ⅓ cup soft shortening (part butter)
    ½ cup sugar
    1 egg

Sift together . . .
    1 ½ cups *sifted* GOLD MEDAL Flour
    1 ½ tsp. baking powder
    ½ tsp. salt
    ¼ tsp. nutmeg

Stir in alternately with . . .
    ½ cup milk

Fill greased muffin cups ⅔ full. Bake until golden brown. Immediately roll in . . .
    6 tbsp. butter, melted

then in mixture of . . .
    ½ cup sugar
    1 tsp. cinnamon

Serve hot.

TEMPERATURE: 350° (mod. oven).
TIME: Bake 20 to 25 min.
AMOUNT: 12 med. muffins.

COUNTRY BREAKFAST MUFFINS
(Sour Cream)

With that so good flavor and tenderness.

Beat until light . . .
    1 egg

Beat in . . .
    2 tbsp. sugar
    1 tbsp. soft shortening
    1 cup cultured sour cream

Sift together and stir in . . .
    1 ⅓ cups *sifted* GOLD MEDAL Flour
    1 tsp. baking powder
    ½ tsp. soda
    ½ tsp. salt

Fill greased muffin cups ⅔ full. Bake until golden brown. Serve hot.

TEMPERATURE: 400° (mod. hot oven).
TIME: Bake 20 to 25 min.
AMOUNT: 12 med. muffins.

All you have to do —

To serve muffins piping hot from the oven: mix and fill muffin cups ahead. Cover with waxed paper or aluminum foil. Let stand in refrigerator until about to serve, then bake. Or get ingredients all measured . . . . mix and bake at the last.

Off on the
right foot in
muffin-mixing:

First of all

Read through the recipe.

Preheat oven to 400° (mod. hot oven).

Assemble ingredients.

Assemble utensils and grease muffin cups.

Sift flour and measure all dry ingredients into sifter.

1 Beat egg slightly with fork. Stir in milk and oil or melted shortening.

2 Sift dry ingredients directly into the mixing bowl.

3 Stir just until flour is dampened. Batter should be lumpy. Do not overmix.

4 Fill well greased muffin cups ⅔ full. (Little paper cups or liners placed in muffin cups save greasing and washing pan.) Leave any unfilled cups ungreased.

5 Bake until golden brown. Loosen immediately with spatula. Serve warm. Muffins should have gently rounded tops that are pebbled rather than smooth.

MUFFINS (🔑 Recipe) *The name means "little muffs" . . . to warm the fingers.*

	Popular Muffins	Sweeter Muffins
Beat slightly with fork	1 egg	1 egg
Stir in	1 cup milk	½ cup
	¼ cup cooking (salad) oil or melted shortening	¼ cup
Sift together and add	2 cups *sifted* GOLD MEDAL Flour	1½ cups
	¼ cup sugar	½ cup
	3 tsp. baking powder	2 tsp.
	1 tsp. salt	½ tsp.

Stir *just* until flour is moistened. Batter should be lumpy. Do not overmix. Fill greased muffin cups ⅔ full.

TEMPERATURE: 400° (mod. hot oven).
TIME: Bake 20 to 25 min.
AMOUNT: 12 med. muffins.

WHOLE WHEAT MUFFINS (Graham Gems)

And they are gems!

Follow 🔑 recipe for Popular Muffins above—*except* use only 1 cup flour and 2 tsp. baking powder. Add 1 cup whole wheat (Graham) flour to the *sifted* dry ingredients *in the mixing bowl.*

SOUR MILK MUFFINS

Follow 🔑 recipe for Popular Muffins above—*except* use only 2 tsp. baking powder, and add ½ tsp. soda; substitute sour milk for sweet milk.

WHEATIES MUFFINS

An ideal hot bread for dinner.

Follow 🔑 recipe for Popular Muffins above—*except* use only 1 cup flour and ½ cup milk and carefully fold in 2 cups WHEATIES at the last.

PRUNE MUFFINS

Studded with the glossy dark fruit.

Follow 🔑 recipe for Popular Muffins above—*except* add ¼ cup brown sugar and ¼ tsp. nutmeg to flour mixture, and at the last, fold in ¾ cup cut-up well drained pitted cooked prunes.

SURPRISE MUFFINS

The secret's inside.

Follow 🔑 recipe for Popular Muffins above. Fill muffin cups half full of batter. Drop scant teaspoonful of jelly on center of batter. Add more batter to fill cup ⅔ full. Discovering the jelly inside the baked muffin is the surprise.

BLUEBERRY MUFFINS

Deliciously moist with luscious blue fruit.

Follow 🔑 recipe for Sweeter Muffins above—*except* at the last blend in carefully 1 cup well drained fresh blueberries. If canned berries are used, ¾ cup.

ORANGE-HONEY MUFFINS

Follow 🔑 recipe for Sweeter Muffins above—*except* use 2 eggs. Place in bottom of each well greased muffin cup 1 tsp. honey, then a thin slice of unpeeled orange, cut in quarters. Spoon batter on top. Serve orange slice up.

APPLE MUFFINS

A Sunday breakfast or supper treat.

Follow 🔑 recipe for Sweeter Muffins above—*except* sift ½ tsp. cinnamon with dry ingredients. Add 1 cup grated raw tart apple (unpared) with shortening. Bake 25 to 30 min. If desired, sprinkle top before baking with:

NUT-CRUNCH TOPPING

Mix ⅓ cup brown sugar (packed), ⅓ cup broken nuts, and ½ tsp. cinnamon.

MAPLE SYRUP MUFFINS

Follow 🔑 recipe for Popular Muffins above—*except* substitute ½ cup maple syrup for ½ cup of the milk.

DATE, FIG, OR RAISIN MUFFINS

Follow 🔑 recipe for Popular Muffins above—*except* add 1 cup finely cut-up dates or figs or raisins.

DO'S AND DON'TS WITH BISCUITS

First of all

Read through recipe.

Turn on oven so it will preheat to 450° (hot oven).

Assemble ingredients.

Assemble utensils.

Sift flour and measure all dry ingredients into sifter.

1 Sift dry ingredients into mixing bowl. Measure shortening and cut into flour mixture with pastry blender or blending fork until finely blended. The mixture should look like "meal."

2 Stir in almost all the milk. If dough does not seem pliable, add the rest. Use enough to make a soft, puffy dough easy to roll out. Too much milk makes dough sticky, not enough makes biscuits dry.

3 Round up on lightly floured cloth-covered board. Knead (fold dough over and press lightly with heel of hand about six times). Handle lightly. Too much handling makes biscuits tough.

4 Roll dough or pat out (with floured hand) ¼″ thick for thin, crusty biscuits . . . ½″ for thick, soft biscuits. "Southern" type biscuits are thin and rich; "Northern" type are thick, plainer biscuits.

5 Cut close together with floured biscuit cutter. For speed, cut in squares with knife. Fit leftover bits together. Do not reknead. Pat out dough, roll smooth, and cut as desired.

6 Place close together for biscuits with soft sides, an inch apart for biscuits with crusty sides, on ungreased baking sheet. If using pan with sides, invert pan; bake biscuits on bottom.

7 Bake in middle of oven. A heavy or shiny pan helps prevent overbrowning biscuits on bottom. Bake until golden brown. Serve immediately. Keep extras hot until needed.

BISCUITS (Recipe) *The daily bread of earlier days. (Served hot each meal of the day in the South.)*

Make either type desired.

	Typical Biscuits	Southern Biscuits
Sift together............................	2 cups *sifted* GOLD MEDAL Flour	2 cups
	3 tsp. baking powder	3 tsp.
	1 tsp. salt	1 tsp.
Cut in finely............................	¼ cup shortening	6 tbsp.
Stir in (to make soft dough)..............	¾ cup milk	⅔ cup

Round up on lightly floured cloth-covered board. Knead lightly (about 30 sec.). Roll or pat out about ½″ thick (only ¼″ thick for Southern biscuits). Cut. Place on ungreased baking sheet. Bake until golden brown. Serve piping hot with butter and also jelly, honey, syrup, etc.

TEMPERATURE: 450° (hot oven).
TIME: Bake 10 to 12 min.
AMOUNT: 20 1¾″ biscuits (1″ high).

For additional Southern biscuits, see Iris' Biscuits, p. 84.
For easy Stir-N-Roll Biscuits, see p. 85.

BUTTERMILK BISCUITS
Follow recipe above—*except*, in place of milk, use buttermilk. Use only 2 tsp. baking powder, and add ¼ tsp. soda.

BACON BISCUITS
Perfect with eggs.
Follow recipe above—*except* add ⅛ cup drained cooked bacon bits (about 4 strips) to flour and shortening mixture.

CHEESE BISCUITS
Golden and savory ... with salads.
Follow recipe above—*except* add ½ cup grated dry sharp American cheese to flour and shortening mixture.

CHIVES BISCUITS
A dash of green and taste supreme.
Follow recipe above—*except* add ¼ cup minced chives to flour mixture.

All you have to do

To save time and work: make Drop Biscuits.

HERB BISCUITS
Gourmets' delight ... with roast meats.
Follow recipe above—*except* add ¼ tsp. dry mustard, ½ tsp. dry sage, and 1¼ tsp. caraway seeds to flour mixture.

DROP BISCUITS
Follow recipe above—*except* increase milk to 1 cup. Drop from spoon on greased pan or into greased muffin cups.

ORANGE TEA BISCUITS
Follow recipe above—*except* add grated rind of 1 orange to dry ingredients. Before baking, press ½ cube of loaf sugar, dipped in orange juice, into top of each biscuit.

BUTTER DIPS
Mixed without shortening. Dipped and baked in real butter. Quick and easy as biscuits ... they taste like rolls. "I like to serve these golden-crusted biscuit bread sticks hot from the oven," says Mrs. Edwin W. Fierke, devoted homemaker and gracious hostess of Minneapolis. "They are a wonderful addition to any meal."

Melt in oven in 13x9″ oblong pan.. Remove pan as soon as butter is melted.	⅓ cup butter
Sift together..................	2¼ cups *sifted* GOLD MEDAL Flour
	1 tbsp. sugar
	3½ tsp. baking powder
	1½ tsp. salt
Add........................	1 cup milk

Stir slowly with fork until dough just clings together (about 30 strokes). Turn on well floured board. Roll over to coat with flour. Knead lightly about 10 times. Roll out ½″ thick into a rectangle, 12x8″. With floured knife, cut dough in half lengthwise, then crosswise into 16 strips. Dip each strip in butter on both sides and lay close together in two rows in pan. Bake until golden brown. Serve hot.

TEMPERATURE: 450° (hot oven).
TIME: Bake 15 to 20 min.
AMOUNT: 32 Butter Dips.

Cheese Butter Dips: Add ½ cup grated sharp American cheese to dry ingredients.

Garlic Butter Dips: Add ½ clove garlic, finely minced, to butter before melting.

Cinnamon Butter Dips: Sprinkle mixture of 2 tbsp. sugar and ½ tsp. cinnamon over Butter Dips before baking.

PIGS IN BLANKETS

The "pigs" are sausages wrapped in blankets of fluffy biscuit dough.

Follow ♪ recipe for Typical Biscuits (*p. 83*)—*except* roll dough only ¼″ thick. Cut into oblong pieces, 4x3″. Roll each piece around a wiener or frankfurter, letting tip show at each end. Seal well by pinching edge of dough into roll. Bake with sealed edge underneath, about 15 min. Serve hot with mustard, catsup, or relishes.

AMOUNT: 12 Pigs in Blankets.

TINY PIGS IN BLANKETS

These make excellent appetizers.

Follow recipe for Pigs in Blankets above —*except* roll dough thinner (⅛″). Cut into 2″ squares and wrap around tiny cooked Vienna sausages. Bake 10 min.

AMOUNT: 48 tiny rolls.

RING BISCUITS FOR SHORTCAKES

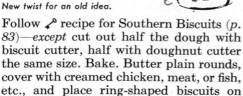

New twist for an old idea.

Follow ♪ recipe for Southern Biscuits (*p. 83*)—*except* cut out half the dough with biscuit cutter, half with doughnut cutter the same size. Bake. Butter plain rounds, cover with creamed chicken, meat, or fish, etc., and place ring-shaped biscuits on top. Garnish center with parsley or jelly.

HOT PIMIENTO CHEESE BISCUITS

Rich golden cheese melting on biscuits makes these special for snacks or salads.

Follow ♪ recipe for Typical Biscuits (*p. 83*). Place biscuits a little apart on lightly greased baking sheet. Melt over hot water soft-spreading pimiento cheese (6 to 8-oz. glass) with 2 tbsp. butter. Place a spoonful on each biscuit. Bake. The cheese will run down over it. Serve hot.

SCONES

A teatime favorite in the British Isles.

Follow ♪ recipe for Typical Biscuits (*p. 83*)—*except* add 2 tbsp. sugar to dry ingredients; use only ½ cup milk, and add 1 slightly beaten egg. Roll dough ¼″ thick. Cut into triangle and diamond shapes. Place slightly apart on baking sheet. Brush with milk and sprinkle with sugar. Bake.

QUICK CINNAMON ROLLS

Try these hot sweet rolls for breakfast, tea, or supper.

Follow ♪ recipe for Southern Biscuits (*p. 83*)—*except* roll dough ¼″ thick into rectangle, 16x7″. Spread with 2 tbsp. softened butter. Sprinkle with mixture of ¼ cup sugar and 1 tsp. cinnamon and with raisins, if desired. Roll up tightly as for jelly roll, beginning at the wide side. Seal well by pinching edge of dough into roll. Cut into 1″ slices. Place cut-side-down on greased baking sheet or in greased muffin cups. Bake in hot oven (425°) about 15 min. If desired, spread warm baked rolls with Quick White Icing (*p. 102*). Serve hot.

AMOUNT: 16 Cinnamon Rolls.

QUICK BUTTERSCOTCH ROLLS

Cinnamon rolls with a pecan-studded butterscotch glaze.

Follow recipe for Cinnamon Rolls above —*except* place the rolls in 16 especially prepared med. muffin cups (1 tsp. melted butter, 1 tsp. brown sugar, and 2 or 3 pecan halves in bottom of each). Bake. Serve hot, bottom-side-up.

PARTY PINWHEELS

Tempting with tea or salads.

Follow recipe for Cinnamon Rolls above —*except* spread dough with soft-spreading cheese or deviled ham or thick marmalade. A firm filling stays in the rolls. Bake in hot oven (450°) about 12 min.

from a Southern Cook Book—

IRIS' BISCUITS

"When I was a little girl," says Iris Davenport, famous food editor and culinary artist of the South, "biscuits were so important a part of the meal that they were usually made by the homemaker, no matter how many servants the family had."

Follow recipe for Southern Biscuits (*p. 83*) for method. But use: 2 cups *sifted* GOLD MEDAL Flour, 2 tsp. baking powder, ½ tsp. soda, 2 tsp. sugar, 1 tsp. salt, ⅓ cup shortening, ⅔ cup buttermilk. Roll dough a little less than ½″ thick. Cut with 1½″ cutter.

STIR-N-ROLL BISCUITS (✒ Recipe) *Especially rich, tender, and flaky within . . . with a wonderfully delicate, crispy crust on both top and bottom. Quick to make. No floury mess to clear up. So sure and easy!*

	Sweet Milk Biscuits	Buttermilk Biscuits
Sift together..........................	2 cups *sifted* GOLD MEDAL Flour	2 cups
	3 tsp. baking powder	2 tsp.
	1 tsp. salt	1 tsp.
		¼ tsp. soda
Pour into measuring cup (but don't stir together)..............	⅓ cup cooking (salad) oil	⅓ cup
	⅔ cup milk	⅔ cup buttermilk

Then pour all at once into the flour. Stir with a fork until mixture cleans sides of bowl and rounds up into a ball. For *rolled* or *patted* biscuits, smooth by kneading about ten times without additional flour. With the dough on waxed paper, press out ¼ to ½" thick with hands, or roll out between waxed papers.

Cut with unfloured biscuit cutter. Place on ungreased baking sheet. Bake until golden brown. Serve piping hot with butter and also jelly, honey, jam, syrup, etc.

TEMPERATURE: 475° (very hot oven).

TIME: Bake 10 to 12 min.

AMOUNT: 16 med. biscuits.

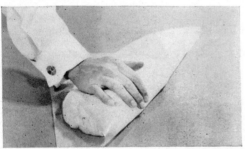

To knead easily: Turn dough onto a sheet of waxed paper; lift paper by one corner and fold dough over in half; press down firmly; pull back paper. Repeat with other corners of paper until dough looks smooth.

Pat or roll out dough ¼ to ½" thick between 2 sheets of waxed paper. Biscuits double in height during baking. Have dough ¼" thick for thin, crusty, "Southern" type biscuits . . . ½" thick for "Northern" type.

DROP BISCUITS

Follow ✒ recipe above—*except* omit kneading. Drop from spoon onto ungreased baking sheet.

BISCUIT WHIRLS

Follow ✒ recipe above—*except* roll dough into an oblong, 15x12". Remove top paper. Spread with 1 cup prepared mincemeat or ½ cup raspberry jam or prepared apple butter. Roll up beginning at wide side. Seal well by pinching edge of dough into roll. Cut into 12 to 15 slices, and place cut-side-up in lightly greased muffin cups. If desired, spread warm baked rolls with Quick White Icing (*p. 102*).

POCKETBOOK BISCUITS

Follow ✒ recipe above—*except* cut rounds with a 3" cutter. Fold over . . . or place about ½ tsp. red jelly in center before folding . . . then press edges together as tightly as possible. Bake.

JAM GEMS

Follow ✒ recipe above—*except* omit kneading. Fill greased muffin cups ⅔ full. Then make a small indentation in top of each muffin and fill with ½ tsp. raspberry jam. Bake. While warm, frost edges with Quick White Icing (*p. 102*).

AMOUNT: 9 med. or 12 small muffins.

One of the earliest forms of baking ... once called "hearth cakes" ... now known by many names. They vary from hearty buckwheat cakes to the delicate dessert cakes. But whatever the kind, the cakes should be light, tender, and uniformly golden brown. The Dutch settlers brought pancakes to America. Later, the Germans in Pennsylvania served pancakes for breakfast, supper, and noonday meals.

PEEKS AT PANCAKES

A *heavy griddle* is best for even browning of cakes (soapstone is ideal). *Modern* griddles require no greasing ... follow directions.

Heat griddle while mixing batter. To test, sprinkle with drops of water. If bubbles "skitter around," heat is just right, and cakes will brown immediately.

Pour batter from tip of *large* spoon (one pouring) or from pitcher, in pools a little apart (for perfectly round cakes). If it is necessary, grease griddle very lightly.

MAKE PANCAKES thick or thin, as desired. It is easy to adjust batter. Make thinner by adding a little liquid; make thicker by adding a little flour.

Turn pancakes as soon as they are puffed and full of bubbles, *but before they break* ... important for light cakes. Turn and brown on other side.

Keep pancakes hot for desserts, etc. by placing between folds of warm towel in warm oven. Or place pancakes separately on rack in very low oven with door ajar. (Don't stack them!)

OMELET PUFFS

Pancakes so airy and delicate they melt in your mouth.

Beat until thick and lemon-colored . . .

    4 egg yolks

Add . . .

    ¼ cup cold water
    ¼ cup GOLD MEDAL Flour
    ½ tsp. salt

Beat until smooth. Fold in . . .

    4 egg whites, stiffly beaten

Drop with large spoon on well greased hot griddle. Turn when lightly browned. Serve with Cheese or Mushroom Sauce.

FRENCH TOAST (6 slices)

Popular for breakfast or lunch.

Dip 6 slices stale bread into mixture of 2 beaten eggs, ¼ tsp. salt, ½ cup milk. Brown both sides in butter on hot griddle. Serve hot with maple syrup, jelly, honey, or sprinkling of confectioners' sugar.

OVEN FRENCH TOAST

A handy way to do many slices at one time.

Heat oven to 500° (very hot). Place dipped slices on greased baking sheet. Bake about 10 min., until browned. Serve hot as for French Toast above.

FAVORITE PANCAKES (✍ Recipe) *The good old-fashioned kind ... of sour milk.*

Heat griddle slowly while mixing batter.

Beat well.............................. 1 egg

Beat in...............................
- 1¼ cups buttermilk or sour milk
- 2 tbsp. soft shortening
- 1¼ cups *sifted* GOLD MEDAL Flour
- 1 tsp. sugar
- 1 tsp. baking powder
- ½ tsp. soda
- ½ tsp. salt

Beat with rotary beater until smooth.
Bake as directed on p. 86.

AMOUNT: 16   4″ pancakes.

WHEATIES PANCAKES

Follow ✍ recipe above—*except* fold in ½ cup WHEATIES at the last.

BLUEBERRY PANCAKES

Follow ✍ recipe above—*except* add ½ cup drained fresh or frozen berries to batter, folding in carefully at the last.

NUT PANCAKES

Follow ✍ recipe above—*except* add ¼ cup broken or chopped nuts to batter.

The French Colonists of Carolina and Louisiana used rice and hominy as the foundation for many breads and batter foods, such as pancakes. But both North and South claimed Buckwheat Cakes for their own.

SWEET MILK PANCAKES

Follow ✍ recipe above—*except* substitute sweet milk for buttermilk, add an extra ½ tsp. baking powder, and omit soda. For extra lightness, beat egg yolk, add milk, etc. Fold in stiffly beaten egg white.

SOUTHERN CORN CAKES

Follow ✍ recipe above—*except*, in place of the flour, use ¾ cup corn meal and only ¼ cup flour.

To make George Washington's Mother's Ferry Farm Sauce: heat together slowly over hot water 1 cup strained honey and ½ cup maple syrup. Remove from heat and blend in 1 tsp. cinnamon.

OLD-FASHIONED BUCKWHEAT CAKES *From Mary who cooked "with love." They bring memories of cozy comfort at the fireside of Hilda and Henry Maust, famous artist in Woodstock, New York ... who painted so many of our beautiful food pictures.*

Dissolve............................. 1 pkg. active dry yeast

  in................................. ½ cup warm water (not hot—110 to 115°)

Add................................. 2 cups cold water

Sift together and stir in.................
- 1 cup *sifted* GOLD MEDAL Flour
- 2 cups buckwheat flour
- 1½ tsp. salt

Beat vigorously until smooth. Cover, and place in refrigerator overnight. In morning, stir in...
- 1 tbsp. molasses
- ¼ cup butter, melted
- 1 tsp. soda dissolved in ½ cup hot water

Let stand at room temperature for 30 min. Bake as directed on p. 86.

AMOUNT: 36   4″ pancakes.

To use batter as a starter for another batch: Save out ... 1 cup of batter (before adding molasses, butter, soda). Add ... *1 cup cold water*, cover, and place in refrigerator until night before you wish to use it. Then, pour off water which has risen to top.

Blend in the amount of flours and salt as in original recipe. Add ... *2½ cups cold water*, cover, and let stand that night. In morning, stir in the molasses, butter, soda, and hot water as in original recipe. Let stand 30 min., and bake.

DELICATE FLUFFY PANCAKES

Most elegant pancakes you've ever tasted or that we've discovered in years of testing. From a wonderful cook, Mrs. Marian Bucholz of Los Angeles and Omaha.

Beat well with rotary beater . . .
    3 egg yolks
Beat in . . .
    1 ⅔ cups thick buttermilk
    1 tsp. soda
Sift together and beat in . . .
    1 ½ cups *sifted* GOLD MEDAL Flour
    1 tbsp. sugar
    1 tsp. baking powder
    ½ tsp. salt
Beat in . . .
    3 tbsp. soft butter
Gently fold in . . .
    3 egg whites, stiffly beaten
Bake as directed on p. 86.
AMOUNT: 16   4″ pancakes.

OATMEAL PANCAKES

From Mrs. Robert Rypinski of Pasadena, California, who says, "My two boys love them. They're not a bit rich, but they taste so delicious everyone raves about them."

Mix . . .
    1 ½ cups rolled oats
    2 cups buttermilk
Beat in . . .
    ½ cup *sifted* GOLD MEDAL Flour
    1 tsp. sugar
    1 tsp. soda
    1 tsp. salt
    2 eggs, beaten

NOTE: Rolled oats as manufactured these days do not require the soaking often required for old-fashioned oatmeal.

Bake as directed on p. 86. (This is a thin batter, right for oatmeal.)
AMOUNT: 12   4″ pancakes.

WAYS TO SERVE PANCAKES FOR DESSERT

Jelly Roll Pancakes: Thin cakes spread with jelly, rolled up, dusted with confectioners' sugar.

Colonial Cake Stack: Six plate-sized pancakes with butter, sugar, and cinnamon; or butter and jelly between. Sugar on top.

FRENCH PANCAKES

Thin but tender. From Betty Bucholz (Mrs. Arden Bucholz) of New York who, for years, contributed so much to our service.

Heat together in saucepan . . .
    1 cup milk
    2 tbsp. butter

When slightly cooled, beat in . . .
    2 eggs, beaten
    ½ cup *sifted* GOLD MEDAL Flour
    1 tsp. baking powder
    ½ tsp. salt

Beat until smooth. Bake (*see below*). Serve as dessert pancakes.

AMOUNT: 30   3″ pancakes.

All you have to do —

To bake thin pancakes easily: grease a 4 or 5″ skillet lightly. Heat, pour in batter to coat bottom. Tilt skillet to cover evenly. Cook 1 min. Loosen with spatula and "flip" onto heated griddle. Turn several times until a delicate brown.

SWEDISH PANCAKES
"Plättar" (Little Plates)

Follow recipe for French Pancakes. Bake small cakes (3″) on Swedish griddle (with indentations) *or* see below. Arrange a ring of 6 or 7 overlapping cakes on dessert plate; in center, a spoonful of lingonberries or jam, a fluff of whipped cream.

PANCAKES IN ORANGE SAUCE

Luscious! Idea brought from a resort by Mrs. Norman Mitchell of Minneapolis.

Heat thin pancakes in Orange Sauce: melt ⅓ cup butter, blend in 2 tbsp. sugar, ⅓ cup orange juice, and a dash of grated orange rind. Roll cakes around sweetened strawberries, if desired.

Crêpes Suzette are thin French pancakes heated in a special sauce of butter, sugar, grated orange peel, Cointreau, and brandy. The brandy is burned off, the cakes are rolled in the sauce. See recipe on p. 258.

The first waffle is said to have been made in 13th century England. A crusader wearing his armor accidentally sat in some freshly baked oat cakes. The cakes were flattened and bore deep imprints of the steel links. However, he spread butter on the cakes and ate them. His wife, delighted with the way butter stayed in the imprints from the armor, made him put it on once a week and sit on fresh oat cakes. They were called "waffres," meaning flat honeycomb-like cakes.

Dutch colonists brought their cherished "waffre" irons to America. They were long handled and very heavy to hold over an open fire.

HOW TO BAKE. Most waffle irons require no greasing after first tempering. Follow directions. Heat while mixing batter. If no automatic heat control, test by sprinkling grids with drops of water. If water "skitters around" before evaporating, iron is just right.

POUR batter from cup or pitcher into center of hot waffle iron. If batter is thick, spread to cover surface. Do not keep iron open longer than necessary. Bake until steaming stops. Lift off waffle carefully with fork. Serve hot with butter and syrup or other spreads.

Nut Waffles . . . special for supper

WAFFLES (⚡ Recipe) Crisp pancakes with tucks in them.

	Typical Waffles	Richer Waffles
Heat waffle iron while mixing batter.		
Beat well..........................	2 eggs	3 eggs
Beat in................................	2 cups buttermilk or sour milk	1½ cups
	1 tsp. soda	1 tsp.
	2 cups *sifted* GOLD MEDAL Flour	1¾ cups
	2 tsp. baking powder	2 tsp.
	½ tsp. salt	½ tsp.
	*6 tbsp. soft shortening	½ cup

Beat until smooth. This is a thin batter.
Bake in hot waffle iron.
*Fresh bacon fat is good in waffles.

AMOUNT: 8 waffles.

SWEET MILK WAFFLES
Follow either ⚡ recipe above—*except* omit soda and increase baking powder to 4 tsp.; substitute sweet milk for sour milk; and separate eggs. Beat egg whites until stiff and fold in last.

NUT WAFFLES
Follow either ⚡ recipe above. Sprinkle 2 tbsp. coarsely cut or broken toasted nuts over batter as soon as it has been poured into iron. Bake.

BLUEBERRY WAFFLES
Follow ⚡ recipe for Richer Waffles above. Sprinkle 2 tbsp. fresh berries or well drained canned berries over batter as soon as it has been poured into the iron. Bake.

CHEESE-AND-BACON WAFFLES
Follow ⚡ recipe for Typical Waffles above —*except* fold ½ cup grated American cheese into batter. Pour into iron. Lay short strip of bacon across batter. Bake.

89

SUPPER IN THE GARDEN

when good food and good company meet

Doughnuts	Boston Baked Beans
Steamed Brown Bread	Pigs in Blankets with Piccalilli
White Nut Loaf	Fresh Vegetable Relishes

KITCHEN BREAKFAST BUFFET

guests choose their favorites

Waffle   Orange Juice
Light-as-feather Muffins
Streusel-filled Coffee Cake   Canary Corn Sticks   Marmalade
Favorite Pancakes   Bacon and Sausages

The Indians taught the earliest colonists to parch corn and mix it with boiling water . . . and bake it in thin cakes. These were used by hunters and traders on their long journeys on foot over Indian trails; hence, the name "Journey Cake," later called "Johnny Cake." Almost as many different types of corn bread have been developed as there are different regions in our country. The South prefers white corn meal, the North yellow.

CLUES TO QUICK MIXING OF CORN BREADS

Beat egg. Beat in with rotary beater milk, dry ingredients, soft shortening (bacon fat is good). Beat just until smooth.

Generously butter 12 corn stick pans, *or* muffin cups, *or* a 9″ square pan. Heat in oven while mixing batter.

Pour batter into hot pans until *almost* full. If breads do not brown, brush with butter, put under broiler a minute.

	Canary Corn Sticks	**Corn Cake**	**Southern Corn Bread**
	From Ohio	*From Kentucky*	*From Arkansas*
Beat	1 egg	1 egg	2 eggs
	1½ cups buttermilk	1 cup plus 2 tbsp. milk	2 cups buttermilk
	½ tsp. soda		1 tsp. soda
	½ cup *sifted* GOLD MEDAL Flour	¼ cup *sifted* GOLD MEDAL Flour	
Beat in	1½ cups corn meal	1¼ cups corn meal	2 cups corn meal
	1 tsp. sugar	2 tbsp. sugar	
	3 tsp. baking powder	3 tsp. baking powder	
	1 tsp. salt	1 tsp. salt	1 tsp. salt
	¼ cup soft shortening	3 tbsp. soft shortening	

Pour or spoon into buttered hot square pan, muffin cups, or corn stick pans (*see above*). Bake just until set. Serve piping hot with butter. Cut corn breads (baked in square pan) into squares. Keep hot in pan until served.

TEMPERATURE: 450° (hot oven).

TIME: Bake 10 to 15 min. for corn sticks or muffins; 20 to 25 min. for corn bread.

AMOUNT: 12 muffins, corn sticks, or pieces.

BACON CORN BREAD

Follow recipe for Southern Corn Bread above—*except* add ⅓ cup diced crisply cooked bacon at the last, or lay short slices of partially cooked bacon on top of batter in pan (allow one piece to each serving). Bake.

PLANTATION SHORTCAKE

Serve Creamed Chicken over Corn Bread.

OLD-TIME JOHNNY CAKES

From Rhode Island . . . meal ground on stones.

Beat *1 egg.* Stir in *2 cups water-ground corn meal, 1 tsp. salt, 1¼ to 1½ cups milk* (to make thick batter). Drop spoonfuls of batter onto a well greased hot griddle and fry to a golden brown on each side. Stir batter occasionally to keep well mixed. Serve hot with butter.

AMOUNT: 12 Johnny Cakes.

Hoe Cake and Corn Pone were the first simple forms of corn bread in the South . . . simply corn meal mixed with water, salted, and baked. Hoe Cake was baked on a plank (or the cotton hoe) on hot embers. Pones were the "appones" of the Indians, shaped with the hands into small cakes, baked before the fire. Spoon Bread was evolved when an old-time Virginia cook put a dish of corn meal mush into the oven in the home of President James Monroe near Charlottesville.

BATTER BREAD

Soft and moist . . . custardy . . . delicious. Upholds the fame of Southern cookery. Traditional choice with roe herring.

Beat . . .
>1 egg

Beat in . . .
>¾ cup white corn meal
>½ tsp. soda
>½ tsp. salt
>1½ cups buttermilk

Pour into hot 1-qt. casserole or baking dish with 1 tbsp. butter melted in it. Bake just until set. Serve hot with butter or gravy.

TEMPERATURE: 400° (mod. hot oven).

TIME: Bake 20 to 25 min.

AMOUNT: 6 servings.

HUSH PUPPIES

Toothsome morsels from Florida hunters. When they sat around their camp fish-fries, their hunting dogs would whine for the good smelling food. The men tossed leftover corn patties to them calling, "Hush, puppies!" Satisfied, the dogs hushed. These crispy little corn cakes make a hit at Daytona Beach, Florida, served with fried shrimp and cole slaw.

Beat together . . .
>3 cups corn meal
>2 tsp. baking powder
>1½ tsp. salt
>1½ cups milk
>½ cup water

Blend in . . .
>1 egg, if desired
>1 onion, finely chopped, if desired

With hands, mold mixture into little cakes (about 1 tbsp. each) and fry in about 1" deep fat (375°), until well browned (1½ min. on each side). Drain on paper. Serve very hot.

AMOUNT: 2 doz.

SPOON BREAD

Light and souffle-like. Often served in place of potatoes with chicken and other meats. Mrs. Belle Tedford of Richmond, Virginia, a wonderful cook and friend, says that Virginians love it with fried tomatoes.

Pour . . .
>1½ cups boiling water

over . . .
>1 cup corn meal

Stir until cool to keep from lumping. Add . . .
>1 tbsp. butter
>3 egg yolks

Stir until egg is thoroughly blended.

Stir in . . .
>1 cup buttermilk or sour milk

Blend in . . .
>1 tsp. salt
>1 tsp. sugar
>1 tsp. baking powder
>¼ tsp. soda

Fold in . . .
>3 egg whites, beaten only enough to hold soft peaks

Pour into greased 2-qt. baking dish. Serve hot with butter.

TEMPERATURE: 375° (quick mod. oven).

TIME: Bake 45 to 50 min.

AMOUNT: 6 servings.

SOUTHERN CORN MUFFINS

From Mrs. Virginia McDonald who made her tea room at Gallatin, Missouri, the mecca for travelers from near and far.

Pour . . .
>1 cup boiling water

over . . .
>1 cup white corn meal

Beat in . . .
>½ cup milk
>½ tsp. salt
>2 tsp. baking powder
>1 tbsp. soft butter
>1 egg, well beaten

Pour into very *well* greased glass custard cups. Bake. Serve hot.

TEMPERATURE: 475° (very hot oven).

TIME: Bake 25 to 30 min.

AMOUNT: 9 med. muffins.

After Mixing Batter or Dough . . . melt fat for deep fat frying in a heavy kettle or deep fat fryer. Have fat 3 to 4″ deep. Heat to 390° (*a cube of bread browns in fat in 40 seconds*).

The fat cools some when foods are dropped in—it should be 370° to 380° while foods are frying. If fat is too hot, foods brown before they cook through. If too cool, they become grease-soaked.

DOUGHNUT DIPLOMACY

1 Turn part of dough onto floured cloth-covered board. Turn dough to lightly cover with flour. Roll out gently ⅛″ thick.

2 Let rest at least 20 min. Cut with floured sharp doughnut cutter. Take board close to kettle to transfer doughnuts easily.

3 Lift doughnuts on wide spatula, slide quickly into hot fat. Fry as many at a time as can be turned easily.

4 Turn doughnuts as they rise to surface and show a little color. Fry about 3 min. to completely brown on both sides. Lift from fat with long fork. Do not prick doughnuts. Drain over kettle, place on absorbent paper in warm place.

LAZY DAY DOUGHNUTS

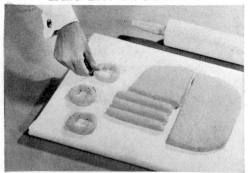

Roll out dough. Cut into strips, 4x½″, dipping knife in flour to prevent sticking. Twist each strip, press ends together to make circle.

Keep Fat to Use Again:
Clarify fat with raw potato in it (4 slices to 1 qt.). When fat bubbles, strain into jar or can through 2 or 3 thicknesses of cheesecloth, over wire strainer. (The potato absorbs flavors and collects sediment, the remainder settling to the bottom.) Keep in refrigerator in light-proof, tight, covered container.

Known in England in 1536 as "imported doughty cakes," doughnuts were brought to this country by Dutch and English settlers. Originally balls or nuts of yeast dough, the Yankees found a quicker way. Doughnuts were as popular with soldiers of the Revolutionary War as they were with the "doughboys" of World War I, and the G.I.'s of World War II. They are hearty and heartening.

FAVORITE DOUGHNUTS (✒ Recipe) *The best of old New England recipes.*

Beat thoroughly........................	4 egg yolks (or 2 whole eggs)
Beat in...............................	{ 1 cup sugar 2 tbsp. soft shortening
Stir in...............................	¾ cup thick buttermilk or sour milk
Sift together and stir in.................	3½ cups *sifted* GOLD MEDAL Flour 2 tsp. baking powder 1 tsp. soda ½ tsp. salt ¼ tsp. nutmeg ¼ tsp. cinnamon

See pictures on opposite page.

Turn onto generously floured board. Roll out ⅓" thick. Let rest 20 min. Cut with doughnut cutter. Fry in hot fat until brown. Drain on absorbent paper. Serve plain, sugared, or glazed.

NOTE: The amount and kind of spice may be varied to suit individual taste. 2 tsp. vanilla may be used in place of spices.
TEMPERATURE OF FAT: 370° to 380°.
AMOUNT: 2 doz. 3" doughnuts.

SWEET MILK DOUGHNUTS

Follow ✒ recipe above—*except* use sweet milk in place of sour milk; use 4 tsp. baking powder, and omit soda.

POTATO DOUGHNUTS

Tender and light, with delicious flavor.

No milk; when mashing potatoes, set aside 1 cup. Follow ✒ recipe above for method but use:

3 eggs
{ ¾ cup sugar
{ 3 tbsp. soft shortening
2¾ cups *sifted* GOLD MEDAL Flour
4 tsp. baking powder
1 tsp. salt
¼ tsp. nutmeg
1 tsp. mace

Stir in . . .
    1 cup mashed potato (unseasoned)

Chill dough 2 hr.
AMOUNT: 3 doz. 2½" doughnuts.

To Sugar Doughnuts: Just before serving, shake doughnuts one at a time in a paper bag with a little confectioners' or granulated sugar.

To Coat With Nuts and Sugar: Dip warm doughnuts into warm glaze (*see right*), then into mixture of ½ cup finely chopped nuts, ½ cup sugar, and 1 tsp. cinnamon.

GOLDEN PUFFS

Spicy-rich little doughnut balls. Exciting and different for "coffee and doughnuts" or afternoon tea.

Sift together . . .
    2 cups *sifted* GOLD MEDAL Flour
    ¼ cup sugar
    3 tsp. baking powder
    1 tsp. salt
    1 tsp. nutmeg or mace

Add . . .
    ¼ cup cooking (salad) oil
    ¾ cup milk
    1 egg

Stir with fork until thoroughly mixed. Drop with a teaspoon (too large puffs will not cook through) into hot fat (375°). Fry until golden brown (about 3 min.). Drain. Roll warm puffs in cinnamon-sugar mixture, or glaze puffs (*recipe below*).
AMOUNT: 2½ doz. puffs.

To Glaze Doughnuts:

Add ⅓ cup boiling water gradually to 1 cup confectioners' sugar. Mix well. Dip warm doughnuts into the warm glaze.

FRITTERS (✐ Recipe) *Patties or balls of batter-covered fruit or vegetables, fried in deep fat . . . served as a meat accompaniment.*

Prepare *Fritter Batter* (to bind together fruit or vegetables):

Beat.................................. 2 eggs

Stir in................................ ½ cup milk

Sift together and beat in................ { 1 cup *sifted* GOLD MEDAL Flour
1 tsp. baking powder
1 tsp. salt

Beat in.............................. 1 tsp. melted fat or cooking (salad) oil

Cut up fruit or vegetables (*see below*). Add to or dip in Fritter Batter. Drop into hot deep fat and fry until brown. Drain and serve hot with syrup or gravy.

TEMPERATURE OF FAT: 375°.

AMOUNT: 12 to 15 small fritters.

CORN FRITTERS

Follow ✐ recipe above—*except* add 1 cup grated-off-cob cooked corn or drained canned whole kernel corn to Fritter Batter. Drop by spoonfuls into hot fat.

APPLE OR BANANA FRITTERS

Follow ✐ recipe above, dipping apple slices (crosswise) or banana quarters into Fritter Batter. Drop into hot fat.

FRENCH FRIED ONIONS

Follow ✐ recipe above, dipping rings of *mild* onions (sliced ¼″ thick) into Fritter Batter. Drop rings into hot fat.

FRENCH FRITTERS (Creole Beignets)

A French delicacy from New Orleans . . . fresh fruits coated with a thin, crisp covering—served for dessert.

Sprinkle cut-up fruits (figs, pears, orange, pineapple, or apple slices) with sugar and grated lemon rind. Let stand 2 to 3 hr. Drain and dip into Thin Fritter Batter (*below*). Fry in deep fat at 375°. Drain and serve hot with confectioners' sugar or a sweet syrup or sauce.

THIN FRITTER BATTER

Beat together with rotary beater . . .
2 egg yolks
⅔ cup milk
1 cup *sifted* GOLD MEDAL Flour
½ tsp. salt
1 tbsp. butter, melted
2 tbsp. lemon juice

Fold in . . .
2 egg whites, stiffly beaten

CHICKEN, MEAT, OR FISH FRIED WITH BATTER

Dip pieces of cooked meat, fish, frog legs, or chicken into Fritter Batter (*above*) and fry in deep fat until golden brown.

FRENCH FRIED BREAD

Dip slices of bread into Fritter Batter and fry in deep fat until brown.

TIMBALE CASES AND ROSETTES

Cases are for creamed meat, fish, or vegetables. Rosettes are for dessert or tea . . . sprinkle with confectioners' sugar.

Sift together . . .
½ cup *sifted* GOLD MEDAL Flour
1 tbsp. sugar
½ tsp. salt

Mix and stir in . . .
½ cup water or milk
1 egg, slightly beaten
1 tbsp. cooking (salad) oil

Strain mixture. Heat timbale or rosette iron in hot fat (400°) 3″ deep in small saucepan. Tap off excess fat on absorbent paper. Dip into batter until ⅔ covered. Immerse in hot fat. Fry until delicately browned. Remove, tip upside down to drain. Push off case. Stir batter each time before dipping in iron.

AMOUNT: 18 timbale cases or rosettes.

All you have to do —

If rosettes don't come off iron: fry a little longer. If not crisp, fry a little slower.

DUMPLINGS (⟋ Recipe) *Puffs as light as thistledown . . . with flavorful stews, they bring renown. Cooking half time uncovered is the newest and best method.*

Sift together..........................	1½ cups *sifted* GOLD MEDAL Flour 2 tsp. baking powder ¾ tsp. salt
Cut in.................................	3 tbsp. shortening
Stir in only until blended................	¾ cup milk

Drop by spoonfuls *onto* chicken or meat in boiling meat stock (not in liquid). Cook slowly 10 min. with kettle uncovered, and 10 min. tightly covered. To prevent soggy dumplings, do not use self-basting cover.

Remove dumplings and meat to hot platter Keep hot while making gravy. Pour part of gravy around them. Serve the remainder separately.
Interesting variations at left below.

PARSLEY OR CHIVES OR HERB DUMPLINGS

Follow ⟋ recipe above—*except* add 3 tbsp. minced parsley or chives, or ¼ to ½ tsp. dried herbs (such as sage, celery salt or thyme) to sifted dry ingredients.

CHEESE DUMPLINGS

Follow ⟋ recipe above—*except* add ¼ cup grated sharp cheese to sifted dry ingredients.

All you have to do —

To make dough for Dumplings drop from the spoon easily:
(1) Dip spoon into the broth each time before taking dough.
(2) Use rubber scraper to slip dough off the spoon.

EGG DUMPLINGS

Especially delicious with chicken stew.

Sift together into bowl . . .
1 cup *sifted* GOLD MEDAL Flour
1½ tsp. baking powder
½ tsp. salt

Stir in until thoroughly blended . . .
2 tbsp. cooking (salad) oil
1 egg
¼ cup plus 2 tbsp. milk
2 tbsp. minced parsley

Cook as for Dumplings (*above*).

STEAMED BROWN BREAD

Of old—was always served with baked beans.

Mix . . .
1 cup rye flour or *sifted*
GOLD MEDAL Flour
1 cup corn meal
1 cup whole wheat flour
2 tsp. soda
1 tsp. salt
Stir in . . .
¾ cup molasses
2 cups sour milk or buttermilk

Beat well. Fill greased molds ⅔ full (using two 1-lb. coffee cans or one 7″ tube-center mold). Lay waxed paper over the top. Steam 3 hr. (For method, *see Steamed Puddings, pp. 238–239.*) Serve piping hot with butter.

STEAMING TIPS

If you don't have a steamer, improvise one with large kettle. Place mold above water line by placing it on rack set on cups, etc.

Cover steamer tightly. Do not lift cover until end of steaming unless water must be added, then quickly add boiling water.

CAUTION: Do not use a double boiler as a steamer unless recipe calls for it. It does not allow the steam to circulate completely around the mold of bread or pudding.

ORANGE-NUT LOAF (✗ Recipe) *Makes moist, tasty sandwiches for luncheons and lunch boxes.*

Mix thoroughly.	¾ cup sugar 2 tbsp. soft shortening 1 egg
Stir in.	¾ cup milk ¾ cup orange juice 4 tsp. grated orange rind
Sift together and stir in.	3 cups *sifted* GOLD MEDAL Flour 3½ tsp. baking powder 1 tsp. salt
Blend in.	¾ cup chopped nuts

Pour into well greased 9x5x3″ loaf pan. Let stand 20 min. before baking. Bake until toothpick stuck into center comes out clean. (Crack in top is characteristic.)
TEMPERATURE: 350° (mod. oven).
TIME: Bake about 70 min.

All you have to do — To *prevent crumbling when slicing fruit and nut loaves:* cool them first, then slice with a thin, sharp knife.

BANANA-NUT LOAF

Follow ✗ recipe above — *except* omit orange juice and rind. Increase sugar to 1 cup and add 1 cup mashed bananas with the milk.

WHITE NUT LOAF

Follow ✗ recipe above — *except* omit orange juice and rind. Increase milk to 1½ cups.

APRICOT-NUT LOAF

Follow ✗ recipe above—*except* increase sugar to 1 cup. Add 1 cup finely chopped dried apricots with the nuts.

MAPLE-NUT LOAF

Sift together into bowl . . .
    2½ cups sifted GOLD MEDAL Flour
    1 cup sugar
    3 tsp. baking powder
    ½ tsp. salt

Add . . .
    1 egg, well beaten
    1 cup milk
    ¾ tsp. maple flavoring

Mix only until dry ingredients are moistened.

Stir in . . .
    1 cup coarsely chopped nuts

Pour into well greased 9x5x3″ loaf pan. Let stand 20 min. before baking.
TEMPERATURE: 350° (mod. oven).
TIME: Bake 1 hr.

FIG- OR DATE-NUT LOAF

Follow ✗ recipe above — *except* omit orange juice and rind. Use brown sugar in place of granulated sugar. Increase milk to 1½ cups. Add ¾ cup chopped dates or figs with the nuts. Increase baking time about 10 min.

PRUNE-NUT LOAF

Follow ✗ recipe above — *except* omit orange juice and rind. For liquid, use ¼ cup milk, ¾ cup prune juice, and 1 cup *well drained* chopped pitted cooked prunes.

DATE-AND-NUT LOAF

Extra moist, delicious. Served by Mrs. Jack Bruce of Winnetka, Illinois, at a buffet supper.

Pour 1½ cups boiling water over . . .
    1½ cups cut-up dates

Let cool.

Mix thoroughly . . .
    ½ cup brown sugar (packed)
    1 tbsp. soft shortening
    1 egg

Stir in . . .
    the dates and water

Sift together and stir in . . .
    2¼ cups *sifted* GOLD MEDAL Flour
    1 tsp. soda
    ½ tsp. salt

Blend in . . .
    1 cup broken nuts

Pour into well greased 9x5x3″ loaf pan. Let stand 20 min. before baking.
TEMPERATURE: 350° (mod. oven).
TIME: Bake 60 to 70 min.

PRIZE COFFEE CAKE (🎵 Recipe) *The foundation costume for many delightful changes to fit every occasion.*

Mix thoroughly. . . . .
- ¾ cup sugar
- ¼ cup soft shortening
- 1 egg

Stir in. . . . .
- ½ cup milk

Sift together and stir in. . . . .
- 1½ cups *sifted* GOLD MEDAL Flour
- 2 tsp. baking powder
- ½ tsp. salt

Spread batter in greased and floured 9″ square pan. Sprinkle with desired topping (*see below*). Bake until toothpick stuck into center of cake comes out clean. Serve warm, fresh from the oven.

TEMPERATURE: 375° (quick mod. oven).

TIME: Bake 25 to 35 min.

AMOUNT: 9   3″ squares.

CINNAMON COFFEE CAKE

Tempting, spicy, delicious. Brought from Isle Royal by Esther Scarborough (now Mrs. Edgar Chapman) of Minneapolis.

Follow 🎵 recipe above—*except* sprinkle top with a mixture of ½ cup brown sugar (packed) and 1½ tsp. cinnamon.

STREUSEL-FILLED COFFEE CAKE

The rich cinnamony mixture both in the middle and on the top makes elegant eating.

Follow 🎵 recipe above—*except* spread only half the batter in pan. Sprinkle with half the Streusel Mixture (*below*). Add the remaining batter, and sprinkle remaining Streusel over top.

STREUSEL MIXTURE

Mix . . .
- ½ cup brown sugar (packed)
- 2 tbsp. flour
- 2 tsp. cinnamon
- 2 tbsp. butter, melted
- ½ cup chopped nuts

HOLIDAY COFFEE CAKE

Gay and colorful with Christmas fruit.

Follow 🎵 recipe above—*except* sprinkle top with mixture of ⅓ cup moist cut-up candied fruit, ½ tsp. cinnamon, and 3 tbsp. sugar.

QUICK APPLE CAKE

Follow 🎵 recipe above—*except* arrange apple slices in fancy design on top of batter, pressing them slightly into batter, then sprinkle top with 1 tsp. cinnamon mixed with 2 tbsp. sugar. For Christmas, use red cinnamon candies.

BLUEBERRY BUCKLE

The best of old-time Blueberry Teacakes. Wonderful for summertime Sunday breakfast. Makes a luscious, fruity, homey dessert. "We enjoy it especially during the month of August when fresh blueberries are so plentiful in our vicinity," says Mrs. Homer Dowdy of Flint, Michigan.

Follow 🎵 recipe above—*except* use 2 cups flour and carefully blend in at the last 2 cups well drained blueberries. Sprinkle top with:

CRUMB MIXTURE

Mix . . .
- ½ cup sugar
- ⅓ cup *sifted* GOLD MEDAL Flour
- ½ tsp. cinnamon
- ¼ cup soft butter

Bake 45 to 50 min.

ORANGE COFFEE CAKE

Refreshing orange flavor, always a favorite.

Follow 🎵 recipe above—*except* use orange juice for half of the milk, and add 1½ tsp. grated orange rind. Sprinkle top with Crumb Mixture (*given just above*), adding to it 1½ tsp. grated orange rind.

MARMALADE COFFEE CAKE

Follow 🎵 recipe above—*except* spread top with *Marmalade Mixture:* ½ cup brown sugar (packed), ½ cup *sifted* GOLD MEDAL Flour, 2 tbsp. butter, 1 tbsp. cream, ½ cup orange marmalade. (Topping melts down through the cake during baking.)

PINEAPPLE COFFEE CAKE

Follow 🎵 recipe above—*except* spread top with *Pineapple Mixture:* 2 tbsp. softened butter, 2 tbsp. honey, and ½ cup well drained crushed pineapple.

99

BUTTERQUICK COFFEE CAKE
(✧ Recipe)

Tender and light . . . with crunchy topping. Delicately butter flavored.

Sift together . . .
>2 cups *sifted* GOLD MEDAL Flour
>1 cup sugar
>3 tsp. baking powder
>1 tsp. salt

Add . . .
>⅓ cup soft butter
>1 egg
>1 cup milk

Beat hard 2 min. Pour into greased 9″ square pan. Cover with Crunchy Topping (*below*). Bake. Serve warm.

TEMPERATURE: 350° (mod. oven).

TIME: Bake 35 to 40 min.

CRUNCHY TOPPING

Mix with fork 2 tbsp. soft butter, ¼ cup brown sugar (packed), 2 tbsp. flour, 1 tsp. cinnamon, ½ cup coconut or chopped nuts.

SUGAR-NUT SQUARES

Follow ✧ recipe above—*except* pour into 13x9″ oblong pan, omit Crunchy Topping, and sprinkle before baking with mixture of ½ cup sugar, 1 tsp. cinnamon, and ¼ cup chopped nuts. Bake about 25 min.

LEMON-GLAZED GEMS

Festive looking. Little work. And so good. "I like to have them ready to serve warm from the oven when our relatives from Rochester arrive for the week end after a long drive," says Mrs. Roy Overland of Minneapolis. "Perfect with coffee!" is always the general exclamation.

Follow ✧ recipe above—*except* omit Crunchy Topping, fill greased muffin cups ⅔ full, and bake in mod. hot oven (400°) 15 to 20 min. While still warm, frost tops with Lemon Glaze (*below*).

AMOUNT: 18 med. gems.

LEMON GLAZE

Mix 1 cup *sifted* confectioners' sugar, 1 tsp. lemon juice, ½ tsp. grated lemon rind, 2 tbsp. milk.

QUICK INDIVIDUAL COFFEE CAKES

Brush cut-out Biscuits (*p. 83 or 85*) with melted butter; sprinkle with mixture of cinnamon and sugar. Bake in hot oven (450°) 10 to 12 min.

EVELYN'S CRANBERRY-ORANGE BREAD

Mrs. Richard Kranz, busy modern young mother of three little boys, still has time for gracious hospitality. This fruity, attractive bread is a favorite of hers to serve when neighbors drop in for morning or afternoon coffee.

Sift together . . .
>2 cups *sifted* GOLD MEDAL Flour
>1½ tsp. baking powder
>½ tsp. soda
>½ tsp. salt
>1 cup sugar

Mix in thoroughly . . .
>2 tbsp. shortening
>grated rind and juice of 1 orange plus water to make ¾ cup
>1 egg, beaten

Fold in . . .
>1 cup raw cranberries, cut in halves

Pour into greased 9x5x3″ loaf pan. Bake until toothpick stuck into center comes out clean.

TEMPERATURE: 350° (mod. oven).

TIME: Bake 1 hr.

SUGARLOAF COFFEE CAKE

Made with the old-fashioned combination of buttermilk, raisins, and spices.

Sift together into bowl . . .
>2½ cups *sifted* GOLD MEDAL Flour
>1¼ cups sugar
>3½ tsp. baking powder
>1 tsp. salt
>1 tsp. cinnamon
>1 tsp. nutmeg
>½ tsp. cloves
>½ tsp. allspice

Cut in fine . . .
>¾ cup shortening

Set aside 1 cup of this mixture for topping. To remainder, add . . .
>1 cup raisins

Mix and stir in *just until* dry ingredients are moistened . . .
>1 cup sweet milk or buttermilk
>1 egg, beaten

Pour into greased 9″ square pan. Sprinkle the 1 cup reserved mixture over top of batter. Bake. Serve warm.

TEMPERATURE: 375° (quick mod. oven).

TIME: Bake 40 to 45 min.

Bread - the Symbol of Hope, Home, and Hospitality

Yeast breads give our loved ones cheer . . .
Happiness all through the year.

~~~~ Betty Crocker ~~~~

THERE'S A BREAD FOR EVERY OCCASION
Below are listed a few suggestions from the many in this chapter.

EVENING REFRESHMENTS
Party Sandwich Loaf (p. 105)
Celery Hearts   Green Olives
Pastel-tinted Ice Cream Balls
Dainty Cake Fingers
Salted Nuts   Fondant Mints
Coffee

QUICK WHITE ICING

for rolls and coffee cakes

Sift a little confectioners' sugar into bowl . . . moisten with cream or milk to spreading consistency. Add flavoring. Spread over slightly warm breads.

Coffee cakes to be used later are best frosted after reheating, just before serving.

DOUBLE OR HALF THE RECIPE?

to make more or fewer loaves

Double: Take 2 times each ingredient except yeast. Not necessary to increase yeast more than 1½ times. If recipe to be doubled calls for 2 pkg. yeast, use only 3 pkg. if recipe is doubled.

Half: Take ½ of each ingredient except yeast (not very practical to divide package or cake of yeast).

SAVE TIME

To reduce rising time about 1 hr.: add 1 extra pkg. of yeast. Extra yeast does not make yeasty taste. Yeasty taste results from doughs being too warm during rising or rising too long.

REHEATING BUNS AND ROLLS

Place in paper bag. Sprinkle bag with water. Heat in mod. hot oven (400°). Or heat slowly in a bun warmer or heavy covered aluminum saucepan with a piece of aluminum foil in bottom. *Time:* Heat 10 min.

DOUBLE-QUICK BREADS

No kneading-no shaping-type coffee cake and rolls: see p. 124. To make breads with electric mixer, see p. 128.

BREAD PUDDING

Use dried odds and ends of coffee cakes for making delicious bread puddings (*p. 232*). The raisins, spices, and frosting add a flavor that is something special.

FREEZING BAKED BREAD AND ROLLS

Spend a day making your favorite breads. Let cool thoroughly; wrap immediately with perfect seal. *See* p. 25 for freezing directions. If wrapped in aluminum foil, reheat without unwrapping, to serve.

BREADS BROWN TOO RAPIDLY?

Place brown wrapping paper over breads during last part of baking if browning seems too rapid.

BROWN 'N SERVE TRICKS

Buy plain Brown 'N Serve Rolls at your grocer's. Before baking, spread with butter, sprinkle with a cinnamon-sugar mixture or a Streusel Topping (*p. 116*). Or frost with Quick White Icing (*above*).

GIVE THE BIRDS A TREAT

A feeding box, often best away from the house, offers a way of using leftover bread and gives delight to the family.

DRY SKIM MILK IN BREAD

Add the dry milk with first half of flour in mixing period. 3 tbsp. nonfat dry milk to 1 cup water is the equivalent of 1 cup fresh milk.

SERVE SWEET BREADS AS DESSERT

Serve delicious hot sweet rolls and coffee cakes as a special treat for desserts and late evening snacks for company. Arrange breads in a pretty napkin in a basket or on a bread tray or plate.

SCISSORS FOR WARM BREAD

Cut warm coffee cakes and breads with a scissors or hot knife, to preserve the delicate texture of freshly baked breads.

KEEP BREAD FRESH

Place cooled bread in metal-covered box, ventilated with tiny air holes. Wrap coffee cakes in waxed paper, aluminum foil or transparent wrap. Wash bread box often. Dry and air thoroughly in sunshine when possible.

TO PREVENT MOLD

During the hot humid summer months, store wrapped bread in refrigerator. However, bread stales more rapidly stored in refrigerator than when stored at room temperature in bread box. Freezing is the only complete insurance against mold and for retention of complete freshness. Freezing will not freshen stale bread.

YEAST BREADS

Bread has influenced history more than any other food. It has played an important role in the rise and fall of civilizations, and each nation has its own distinctive breads . . . developed to fit the customs and traditions of the land. The memory of a cozy kitchen filled with the warm fragrance of freshly baked bread *still* means home. It is unforgettable . . . the delight and satisfaction of that tantalizing yeasty aroma, the crunch of the golden crust as the knife cuts through, the full wheaty flavor of the buttered slice.

Today that warm fragrance of freshly baked bread comes from thousands of modern bakeries that turn out delicious and nutritious breads. And today's homemaker who wants to give her family the cozy comfort of freshly baked bread can make it much more easily and quickly than ever before. We have pictured and explained for you each special process in handling not only the new quick methods, but the standard method for making bread and sweet rolls. The new fast yeasts speed the rising and total time required.

Please notice the recipes of holiday breads from far-away lands. We have simplified and clarified the original recipes, yet kept the special flavor and deliciousness that characterize each one of them. When you make them and serve them, see if you don't sense the festivity and romance that have always surrounded these breads.

Handling yeast dough is more fun than any other "cooking." Members of our staff always feel this. You are dealing with something alive. The dough springs to life in silky smooth elasticity as you knead it. There's a deep centuries-old satisfaction in molding it into attractive shapes . . . watching the dough rise to a puffy lightness . . . then taking the beautifully browned breads from the oven. Best of all, there's the rich reward of seeing the beaming faces of the family as they enjoy these fruits of your homemaking.

WAYS WITH BREAD
before our Early American fireplace

Hot French Bread

Chicken à la King in Buttercups — Jumbo Bread Sticks

Skillet Bunburgers — Party Sandwich Loaf — Bun Boats

Individual English Pizzas

See color picture on opposite page.

HOT FRENCH BREAD

Use rye or Vienna bread, if preferred.

Slice bread diagonally, not quite through bottom crust. Spread with Garlic Butter or Seasoned Butter (*below*). Heat loaf until piping hot and crusty. Transfer in loaf shape to basket or bread tray with a napkin to help keep bread warm.

TEMPERATURE: 400° (mod. hot oven).

TIME: Heat about 15 min.

GARLIC BUTTER

Cream soft butter in a bowl rubbed with a cut clove of garlic. Or use garlic salt.

SEASONED BUTTER

Cream butter until soft and fluffy. Stir in desired seasonings:

minced parsley	pepper sauce
minced chives	curry
mustard	onion juice
horse-radish	grated cheese

JUMBO BREAD STICKS

Cut unsliced loaf of bread into "sticks" (about 5x1"). Melt butter in baking pan. Roll each stick in the melted butter, sprinkle with garlic salt, onion salt, celery salt, Parmesan cheese, sesame seeds, or poppy seeds, etc. Arrange on bottom of pan. Toast in quick mod. oven (375°) for 20 to 25 min., turning occasionally to brown all sides evenly. Serve hot.

SKILLET BUNBURGERS

Divide 1 lb. ground beef into 8 equal portions. Pat each into a round slightly larger than a round sandwich bun. Place in heated and lightly greased heavy skillet. Sprinkle with salt and pepper. Cook until browned on one side; turn over. Place cut side of top half of bun on top of beef patty; top with bottom half of bun, also cut side down. Cook in covered skillet over med. heat until patties are done and buns heated through. Remove from skillet with spatula. Serve immediately with potato chips and crisp relishes.

CHICKEN À LA KING IN BUTTERCUPS

Fill Buttercups (*p. 30*) with Chicken à la King (*p. 278*). Garnish with strip of pimiento and a sprig of parsley.

INDIVIDUAL ENGLISH PIZZAS

With crisp relishes or a tossed salad, they make a satisfying and "different" combination for supper, luncheon, or "after ten" refreshments.

Brush halves of English Muffins (*p. 125*) with olive oil or butter. Toast under broiler. Cover each with tomato slices, catsup, or tomato paste; onion rings; salami or pepperoni; and a few anchovies. Sprinkle with olive oil, salt, pepper, garlic salt, and oregano. Top with a slice of Mozzarella cheese or American cheese and a mushroom cap. Return to broiler until cheese melts and bubbles. Serve hot.

BUN BOATS

Garnish each with a sprig of parsley.

Hollow out oblong rolls, brush with melted butter. Heat in mod. hot oven (400°) until hot and crusty. Fill with Barbecued Hamburger (*p. 302*).

PARTY SANDWICH LOAF

Make ahead of time, store in refrigerator. Serve cold, garnished with lettuce, olives, radish roses, and pickle fans.

Remove crusts from loaf of sandwich bread, leaving bottom crust until last. Slice into 5 long slices. Prepare 4 fillings (*below*) by mixing ingredients with enough salad dressing to make easy to spread.

RED FILLING

4 slices boiled ham, minced
3 slices crisp bacon, crumbled
1 pimiento, minced

YELLOW FILLING

mashed yolks of 3 hard-cooked eggs, seasoned with salt and pepper

WHITE FILLING

half a 3-oz. pkg. cream cheese
½ cucumber, grated
2 tbsp. finely chopped ripe olives

GREEN FILLING

4 small sweet pickles, minced
6 sprigs watercress or parsley, minced

Butter each bread slice and spread with a filling in order given above; place one on top the other in the form of the whole loaf. Soften three 3-oz. pkg. cream cheese with cream and spread on outside of loaf as icing on a cake. Decorate with sliced stuffed olives and toasted almonds. Wrap in a damp cloth and chill in refrigerator 3 hr. or more. To serve, cut with a sharp knife into 1" slices.

WHITE BREAD (✒ Recipe) *So easy—so good!*
Warm mixing bowl with hot water in cold weather.

Measure into mixing bowl...............	
Add, stirring to dissolve.................	
Stir in................................	

To make more loaves of bread, see p. 102.

½ cup warm water (not hot—110 to 115°)
2 pkg. active dry yeast
1¾ cups lukewarm liquid (water, or potato water, or scalded milk)
half of 7 to 7¼ cups *sifted* GOLD MEDAL Flour
3 tbsp. sugar
1 tbsp. salt
2 tbsp. soft shortening

Beat with spoon until smooth and batter falls from spoon in "sheets." Using your hand, mix in enough remaining flour until dough cleans bowl. Turn onto lightly floured board. Cover; let rest 10 to 15 min.

Knead until smooth and blistered (about 10 min.). Round up in greased bowl; bring greased side up. Cover with cloth.

Let rise in warm place (85°) until double (about 1 hr.). Press 2 fingers into dough. It will leave indentation when dough is doubled. Punch down. Let rise again until almost double (about 30 min.).

Divide into 2 parts. Round up cover; let rest 10 min. Shape into loaves, let rise, and bake as shown in picture directions below and on p. 107.

TEMPERATURE: 425° (hot oven).
TIME: Bake 25 to 30 min.
AMOUNT: 2 loaves.

All you have to do —

To Make White Bread with compressed yeast: use ½ cup lukewarm water (80 to 85°) - not hot, not cold.

RAISIN, DATE, or NUT BREAD
Knead into the dough 1 cup raisins or coarsely cut-up dates or nuts.

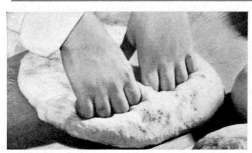

1 Flatten dough into oblong shape . . . the width about an inch longer than the length of the pan . . . the length about 12″. Then press out all air, as shown in picture above.

2 Fold dough in half lengthwise. Flatten to an oblong about 15″ long and 5″ wide. Press out air as in picture 1.

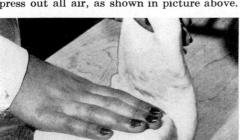

3 Fold in thirds by overlapping ends. Press out air, keeping width same as length of pan.

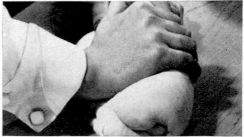

4 Fold toward you, ⅓ of the way at a time, sealing well with heel of hand.

5 Roll back and forth to tighten. Seal each end by pressing with edge of hands. Then smooth loaf lightly between hands to even.

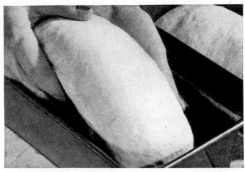

6 Place in 9x5x3″ greased loaf pan sealed edge down. Grease top. Cover, let rise until sides of dough reach top of pan and center is well rounded (50 to 60 min.).

7 Test gently with finger. A slight indentation shows loaves are ready to bake. Be careful that loaves do not rise too much.

8 Place the pans in center of hot oven (425°) . . . not touching each other or sides of oven.

9 Bake 25 to 30 min. To test the loaf, tap crust . . . it will sound hollow. If it doesn't, bake it a few minutes more.

10 Immediately remove bread from pans. Place on wire cooling racks or across top edges of the bread pans. Do not place in direct draft, or crust will crack.

All you have to do —

For a **Soft, Bright, Tender Crust:** brush loaves with soft butter or other shortening after removing them from pan. Cover with towel for a few minutes to soften crust.

For a **Crisp Crust:** do not grease loaves. Do not cover. Keep out of draft to prevent cracking.

For a **Highly Glazed Crust:** before baking, brush loaves with an egg yolk wash (1 egg yolk plus 2 tbsp. water).

107

RICH EGG BREAD (✎ Recipe)

Yellow-rich and tender. And it makes such good toast.

Measure into mixing bowl . . .
 ½ cup warm water (not hot—110 to 115°)

Add, stirring to dissolve . . .
 2 pkg. active dry yeast

Stir in . . .
 1½ cups lukewarm milk
 ¼ cup sugar
 1 tbsp. salt
 3 eggs
 ¼ cup soft butter
 half of 7¼ to 7½ cups *sifted* GOLD MEDAL
  Flour

Mix with spoon until smooth. Add enough remaining flour to handle easily; mix with hand. Turn onto lightly floured board; knead; let rise; and shape into 3 loaves as in directions for White Bread (*pp. 106–107*). Bake until a rich brown.

TEMPERATURE: 425° (hot oven).

TIME: Bake 25 to 30 min.

AMOUNT: 3 loaves.

JEWISH CHALLAH BRAID

Simplified version of the picturesque festival bread. Sprinkle with sesame or poppy seeds, if desired.

Follow ✎ recipe above—*except*, when ready to shape, divide dough into 3 equal parts. Roll each into a strand 14″ long. Place on greased baking sheet. Braid the 3 strands as in top picture directions (*p. 120*). Brush with butter. Cover with damp cloth; let rise until double (40 to 50 min.). Brush with Egg Yolk Glaze (*p. 111*).

NEW ENGLAND RAISIN BREAD

An old stand-by made for special occasions, such as Town Meeting Day and Fourth of July, in New England.

Follow ✎ recipe above—*except* mix in 2 cups raisins. Before baking, brush loaves with melted butter, then sprinkle them with sugar.

108

HERB BREAD

A Duncan Hines' favorite. Savory accompaniment to baked ham, roast lamb, or roast or fried chicken.

Measure into mixing bowl . . .
 ¼ cup warm water (not hot—110 to 115°)

Add, stirring to dissolve . . .
 1 pkg. active dry yeast

Stir in . . .
 ¾ cup lukewarm milk
 2 tbsp. sugar
 1½ tsp. salt
 1 egg
 ½ tsp. nutmeg
 1 tsp. sage
 2 tsp. caraway seeds
 2 tbsp. soft shortening
 half of 3 to 3¾ cups *sifted* GOLD MEDAL
  Flour

Stir with spoon until smooth. Add enough remaining flour to handle easily. Mix with hand. Turn onto lightly floured board; knead, let rise and shape as for White Bread (*pp. 106–107*). Let rise in pan until almost double (about 1 hr.). Bake until dark brown.

TEMPERATURE: 375° (quick mod. oven).

TIME: Bake 45 to 50 min.

AMOUNT: 1 loaf.

WHOLE WHEAT (Graham) BREAD

Moist and flavorful.

Measure into mixing bowl . . .
 ½ cup warm water (not hot—110 to 115°)

Add, stirring to dissolve . . .
 2 pkg. active dry yeast

Stir in . . .
 1 cup lukewarm milk
 1 tbsp. sugar
 2 tsp. salt
 ¼ cup molasses

Mix in with spoon . . .
 1 tbsp. soft shortening
 2 cups *sifted* GOLD MEDAL Flour

Mix in with hand . . .
 3 cups whole wheat flour

Turn onto lightly floured board; knead; let rise; and shape as for White Bread (*pp. 106–107*). Place in 2 greased loaf pans, 8½x4½x2¾″. Let rise until almost double (1 hr.).

TEMPERATURE: 400° (mod. hot oven).

TIME: Bake 30 to 35 min.

AMOUNT: 2 loaves.

Perfect for serve-yourself midnight snacks and buffet suppers. Cold ham, sharp cheese, and pickles enhance the flavors of these breads. Mrs. Donald F. Peterson (formerly Bernice Anderson of our staff) likes to serve Swedish Limpa on a shiny copper tray.

	Swedish Limpa	Pumpernickel
Measure into mixing bowl..............	1½ cups warm water (not hot—110 to 115°)	1½ cups
Add, stirring to dissolve................	2 pkg. active dry yeast	3 pkg.
	¼ cup molasses	½ cup
	⅓ cup sugar	
Stir in...............................	1 tbsp. salt	4 tsp.
	finely grated rind of 1 to 2 oranges	1 to 3 tbsp. caraway seeds
Mix in with spoon until smooth...........	2½ cups *sifted* rye flour	2¾ cups
	2 tbsp. soft shortening	2 tbsp.
Mix in with hand...................... (enough to handle easily)	2½ to 3 cups *sifted* GOLD MEDAL Flour	3½ to 4 cups

Turn onto lightly floured board; knead, and let rise as for White Bread (*p. 106*). Shape into 2 round, slightly flattened loaves. Place on opposite corners of greased baking sheet (sprinkled with corn meal, if desired). Cover with damp cloth. Let rise about 1 hr. Bake until brown.

TEMPERATURE: 375° (quick mod. oven).
TIME: Bake 30 to 35 min.
AMOUNT: 2 loaves.

ANADAMA BREAD

The name comes from a New England fisherman whose lazy wife always served him corn meal mush and molasses. One day, tired of the same corn meal mush for dinner, he mixed it with flour and yeast and baked it as bread, saying: "Anna damn her."

Bring to boil in saucepan................	1½ cups water
	1 tsp. salt
Stir in...............................	⅓ cup yellow corn meal
Return to boiling point, stirring constantly. Pour into large mixing bowl.	
Stir in............................... Cool to lukewarm.	⅓ cup molasses
	1½ tbsp. shortening
Dissolve.............................	1 pkg. active dry yeast
in.................................	¼ cup warm water (not hot—110 to 115°)
Add to lukewarm corn meal mixture. Mix well. Mix in half of........................	4 to 4¼ cups *sifted* GOLD MEDAL Flour

Add enough remaining flour to handle easily; mix with hand (dough will be sticky). Turn onto lightly floured board; knead, and let rise until double (1½ hr.). Punch down, place dough in greased 9x5x 3″ loaf pan and pat into a loaf shape. Let rise until almost double (about 1 hr.).

Brush top with melted butter. Sprinkle with a little corn meal and salt. Bake until a rich brown.

TEMPERATURE: 375° (quick mod. oven).
TIME: Bake 40 to 45 min.
AMOUNT: 1 loaf.

To Reheat Bread: see p. 102.

To Freeze Bread: see p. 25.

FRENCH BREAD

Crusty and delicious outside; open-textured and soft inside. It is an old-time custom in France for the baker's wife, as dawn creeps over the horizon, to peddle through the streets the results of her husband's nocturnal labor. This she does from an apron tied about her waist, or from a pushcart on two wheels. The typical French Bread is a pole-like loaf three to four feet long which people can carry home under their arm.

Follow ✓ recipe for White Bread (*p. 106*), but use:

  1¼ cups warm water (not hot—110 to 115°)
  1 pkg. active dry yeast
  1½ tsp. salt
  3 tbsp. soft shortening
  4 cups *sifted* GOLD MEDAL Flour

When dough is ready for shaping, shape according to the picture directions.

TEMPERATURE: 375° (quick mod. oven).

TIME: Bake 20 min.; then remove from oven and brush with Egg White Glaze (*below*). Bake 25 min. more.

1 Roll into 15x10″ oblong. Roll up tightly toward you . . . beginning with wide side. Seal edges by pinching together.

2 With a hand on each end, roll gently back and forth to lengthen loaf and taper ends. Place it diagonally on lightly greased corn meal-sprinkled baking sheet.

3 Make ¼″ slashes in dough at 2″ intervals or 1 slash lengthwise. Brush top with cold water. Let stand uncovered about 1½ hr. Brush again, and bake.

FRENCH ROLLS (Hard-crusted)

Crusty, crunchy . . . like French Bread.

Follow ✓ recipe above—*except*, after rising, divide dough into 16 equal parts. Form each into an oblong bun slightly tapered at ends or shape into a round bun. Place 2½″ apart on lightly greased and corn meal-sprinkled baking sheet.

With scissors, snip round buns in half, then in quarters, cutting through almost to bottom of rolls. Brush with water. Let rise uncovered 30 to 45 min. Brush with water again, or if desired use Egg White Glaze (*at right above*) with a sprinkling of sesame or poppy seeds. Bake until golden brown and crusty.

TEMPERATURE: 425° (hot oven).

TIME: Bake 10 min. Brush and bake 10 to 15 min. more.

AMOUNT: 16 rolls.

EGG WHITE GLAZE

Mix 1 unbeaten egg white and 2 tbsp. water. Brush over breads just before baking for shiny, light finish.

SALTY BREAD STICKS (Pane Bastone)

Crispy, dry, salty . . . serve with Italian foods.

Shape French Bread dough (*above*) into 20 8″ pencil lengths. Place on lightly greased and corn meal-sprinkled baking sheet. Brush with Egg White Glaze (*above*). Sprinkle with salt. Let rise until double (about 30 min.). Bake until crisp and delicately browned.

TEMPERATURE: 425° (hot oven).

TIME: Bake 20 to 25 min.

AMOUNT: 20 bread sticks.

LOWELL INN CRESCENT ROLLS *These tender, rich, golden brown crescents have been made famous by Nell and Arthur Palmer of beautiful Lowell Inn, "Mount Vernon of the West," at Stillwater, Minnesota.*

To Freeze Rolls: see p. 25.

To Reheat Rolls: see p. 102.

Measure into mixing bowl . . .
  ¾ cup warm water (not hot—110 to 115°)
Add, stirring to dissolve . . .
  2 pkg. active dry yeast
Stir in . . .
  ½ cup sugar
  1 tsp. salt
  2 eggs
  ½ cup soft shortening (part butter)
  half of 4 cups *sifted* GOLD MEDAL Flour

Add rest of flour; mix until smooth. Scrape dough from sides of bowl, cover with damp cloth. Let rise until double (about 1½ hr.). Divide into 2 parts. Shape as Crescents or Butterhorns (*p. 115*). Cover, let rise until double (1 hr.). Brush with butter, sprinkle with celery seeds, if desired. Bake until a rich golden brown.

TEMPERATURE: 400° (mod. hot oven).
TIME: Bake 12 to 15 min.
AMOUNT: 32 rolls.

FROSTED CRESCENTS

Make same as Lowell Inn Crescent Rolls above—*except* brush circle of dough with soft butter; sprinkle with cinnamon and sugar, or spread with jam. After baking, dribble Quick White Icing (*p. 102*) over tops. Sprinkle with nuts.

QUICK BUTTERMILK ROLLS

So fluffy and light!

Measure into mixing bowl . . .
  ¼ cup warm water (not hot—110 to 115°)
Add, stirring to dissolve . . .
  1 pkg. active dry yeast
Stir in . . .
  ¾ cup lukewarm buttermilk
  ¼ tsp. soda
  1 tsp. sugar
  1 tsp. salt
  3 tbsp. soft shortening
  half of 2½ cups *sifted* GOLD MEDAL Flour

Add rest of flour; mix with hand. Turn onto lightly floured board. Knead until smooth and elastic. Shape into crescents or any of the desired shapes (*p. 115*). Let rise until double (about 1½ hr.). Bake until golden brown.

TEMPERATURE: 400° (mod. hot oven).
TIME: Bake 15 to 20 min.
AMOUNT: 1½ doz. rolls.

WHOLE WHEAT BUTTERMILK ROLLS

Make same as Quick Buttermilk Rolls above—*except* substitute whole wheat flour for half of the white flour.

EGG YOLK GLAZE

Mix with fork 1 egg yolk and 2 tbsp. cold water. Brush over breads just before baking for shiny golden brown finish.

BRAN PAN BISCUITS

Flavorful, light, and crusty. Mrs. Agnes Bassett, well known cateress of Minneapolis, Minnesota, and formerly associated with us, has often made these for very special luncheons in our beautiful Early American dining room.

Measure into mixing bowl . . .
  1 cup warm water (not hot—110 to 115°)
Add, stirring to dissolve . . .
  1 pkg. active dry yeast
Stir in . . .
  ¼ cup brown sugar (packed)
  1½ tsp. salt
  ½ cup whole bran or rolled oats
  1 egg
  3 tbsp. soft shortening
Stir with spoon until smooth.
Add just until easy to handle . . .
  3½ to 3¾ cups *sifted* GOLD MEDAL Flour

Mix with hand. Place greased-side-up in greased bowl. Cover with damp cloth and set to rise in warm place (85°) until double (1½ hr.). Shape into Old-fashioned Biscuits (*p. 114*). Flour or grease fingers while shaping as dough is sticky. Cover and let rise until double (45 min.). Bake until brown.

TEMPERATURE: 375° (quick mod. oven).
TIME: Bake 20 to 25 min.
AMOUNT: 2 doz. biscuits.

RIBBON LOAF

Cinnamon, sugar, and butter make attractive ribbon effect.

Use ½ White Bread dough (*p. 106*) or ⅓ Rich Egg Bread dough (*p. 108*). After dough rises, roll out into oblong, 15x12".

Brush with melted butter and sprinkle with mixture of ...
> ½ cup sugar
> 2 tsp. cinnamon

Fold over in thirds to make a strip, 15x4". Cut dough into 20 equal parts. Stand on end close together in 2 rows in a greased 8 or 9" square pan.
Cover and let rise in warm place until double (about 1 hr.). Bake until browned. Cover with paper the last 10 min. of baking if loaf browns too quickly.

TEMPERATURE: 425° (hot oven).
TIME: Bake 25 to 30 min.
AMOUNT: 1 loaf.

ROUND SANDWICH LOAF

It looks like a Paul Bunyan Hamburger Bun. Slice and serve. Or make it into a sandwich loaf (see below).

Use ½ White Bread dough (*p. 106*) or ⅓ Rich Egg Bread dough (*p. 108*).

After dough rises, shape into a round, slightly flattened loaf. Place on greased baking sheet or in 9" round pan. Cover, let rise in warm place until double (about 1 hr.). Bake until golden brown. Cool and store until next day before slicing.

TEMPERATURE: 425° (hot oven).
TIME: Bake 25 to 30 min.
AMOUNT: 1 loaf.

All you have to do —

To make a sandwich loaf: slice round loaf crosswise into thirds. Butter each layer, spread with Ham Filling (*p. 105*) on one and Egg Filling (*p. 105*) on the other. Wrap loaf in damp cloth, refrigerate overnight. Let come to room temperature before serving. Or brush with butter and reheat in mod. oven (350°) about 10 min. Serve in wedge-shaped pieces.

OATMEAL MOLASSES BREAD

Moist, delicious, and crusty! Made without kneading.

Stir together in mixing bowl ...
> 1½ cups boiling water
> 1 cup rolled oats
> ⅓ cup shortening
> ½ cup light molasses
> 1 tbsp. salt

Cool to lukewarm.
Combine, stirring to dissolve ...
> 2 pkg. active dry yeast
> ½ cup warm water (not hot—110 to 115°)

Stir into lukewarm oatmeal mixture. Mix well.
Add ...
> 2 eggs
> 5½ cups *sifted* GOLD MEDAL Flour

Mix thoroughly. Cover; let stand 15 min. Place dough in 2 greased 9x5x3" loaf pans and pat into a loaf shape. Let rise in warm place (85°) until double (1½ hr.). Bake until brown.

TEMPERATURE: 350° (mod. oven).
TIME: Bake 1 hr.
AMOUNT: 2 loaves.

COTTAGE BREAD (Baked in a Casserole)

Old-time favorite. Deliciously moist. Somewhat coarser than many of the modern breads.

Measure into mixing bowl ...
> 2¾ cups warm water (not hot—110 to 115°)

Add, stirring to dissolve ...
> 2 pkg. active dry yeast

Stir in ...
> 3 tbsp. sugar
> 1 tbsp. salt
> 2 tbsp. soft shortening
> half of 6½ cups *sifted* GOLD MEDAL Flour

Beat 2 min. until smooth. Mix in rest of flour thoroughly. Cover, let rise in warm place (85°) until double (30 min.). Beat batter down for ½ min. Pour half into greased 9x5x3" loaf pan, half into 1½-qt. baking dish. Let rise (20 to 30 min.). Brush with melted shortening. Bake until brown.

TEMPERATURE: 375° (quick mod. oven).
TIME: Bake 40 to 50 min.
AMOUNT: 2 loaves.

TRADITIONAL HOLIDAY BREADS

Kulich

Bohemian Braid

Stollen

Jule Kage

SWEET ROLL DOUGH (⚯ Recipe)

The basic magic dough to create glamorous coffee cakes, such as Swedish Tea Ring and Stollen, as well as dinner and luncheon rolls in many interesting shapes. Bake more than you need so you can either share with your neighbors or freeze the breads for later use.

Measure into mixing bowl................ ½ cup warm water (not hot—110 to 115°)

Add, stirring to dissolve................. 2 pkg. active dry yeast

Stir in....................................
- 1½ cups lukewarm milk
- ½ cup sugar
- 2 tsp. salt
- 2 eggs
- ½ cup soft shortening
- half of 7 to 7½ cups *sifted* GOLD MEDAL Flour

> For excellent eating and keeping quality, keep doughs as soft as possible, almost sticky . . . just so you're able to handle them.

Mix with spoon until smooth. Add enough remaining flour to handle easily; mix with hand. Turn onto lightly floured board; knead until smooth and elastic (about 5 min.). Round up in greased bowl, greased side up. Cover with damp cloth. Let rise in warm place (85°) until double (about 1½ hr.). Punch down; let rise again until almost double (about 30 min.). Divide dough for desired rolls and coffee cakes. Shape, let rise, bake according to directions on following pages.

AMOUNT: 1 large coffee cake and 1½ to 2 doz. rolls.

SWEET ROLL DOUGH WITH COMPRESSED YEAST

Follow ⚯ recipe above—*except* use 2 pkg. moist compressed yeast. Use ½ cup lukewarm water (80 to 85°—not hot, not cold when tested on wrist).

RICHER SWEET DOUGH

Follow ⚯ recipe above—*except* use only ½ cup milk, 1 tsp. salt and 4½ to 5 cups flour.

To Make Double-quick Yeast Rolls and Coffee Cakes: see p. 124.

ROLLS OF ALL SHAPES

Follow ⚯ recipe above. Shape dough as desired . . . just follow sketches and directions below and on opposite page (*p. 115*). Let rise until light (15 to 20 min.). Bake on lightly greased pan. Serve piping hot.

TEMPERATURE: 400° (mod. hot oven).

TIME: Bake 12 to 15 min.

DINNER ROLLS

Roll dough into cylindrical shapes with tapered ends and place on pan.

OLD-FASHIONED BISCUITS

Form dough into balls ⅓ size desired. Place close together in a greased round pan.

PARKERHOUSE ROLLS

Roll dough ¼″ thick. Cut with biscuit cutter. Brush with melted butter. Make crease across each. Fold so top half slightly overlaps. Press edges together at crease. Place close together on pan.

CLOVERLEAF ROLLS

Form bits of dough into balls about 1″ in diameter. Place 3 balls in each greased muffin cup. Brush with butter for flavor.

To use egg yolks in these doughs: use 2 yolks plus 1 tbsp. water in place of 1 whole egg.

QUICK FOUR LEAF CLOVER ROLLS

Place 2″ ball of dough in each greased muffin cup. With scissors, cut each ball of dough in half, then in quarters.

ANOTHER ROLL-SHAPING TRICK

Roll out dough ¼″ thick. Cut with doughnut cutter. Brush lightly with butter. Place 3 centers in greased muffin cups for clover leaf rolls. Shape the cut circles into twists.

For all the twisted shapes, roll dough into an oblong 12″ wide and a little less than ½″ thick. Spread with soft butter. Fold ½ of dough over the other half. Cut into strips ½″ wide and 6″ long.

FIGURE 8's

Hold one end of strip in one hand and twist the other end ... stretching it slightly until the two ends when brought together on greased baking sheet will form a figure 8.

CLOTHESPIN CRULLERS

Wrap strip around greased clothespin so edges barely touch. When baked, twist clothespin and pull out. May be filled with jelly or one of Fruit Fillings (*p. 118*).

TWISTS

Same as Figure 8's, but give strip additional twist just before placing it on baking sheet.

KNOTS

Twist and tie each strip into a knot. Press ends down on greased baking sheet.

SNAILS

Twist and hold one end of the strip down on baking sheet. Wind strip around and around. Tuck end underneath.

TOAD-IN-HOLE (Turk's Cap)

Twist and tie each strip with a knot in one end of strip. Then pull the longer end through center of knot.

BUTTERFLY ROLLS

Roll dough only ⅛″ thick into an oblong 6″ wide. Spread with soft butter, and roll up like jelly roll. Cut into 2″ pieces. Make a deep impression with narrow wooden handle in middle of each roll (to resemble butterfly).

BUTTER FLUFFS (Fan Tans)

Roll dough ⅛″ thick into oblong 9″ wide. Spread with soft butter. Cut into 6 long strips 1½″ wide. Stack 6 strips evenly, one on top of other. Cut into 1″ pieces. Place cut-side-down in greased muffin cups.

CRESCENTS (Butterhorns)

Roll dough scarcely ¼″ thick into a 12″ circle. Spread with soft butter. Cut into 16 pie-shaped pieces. Beginning at rounded edge, roll up. Place on pan, point underneath.

SALT STICKS

Roll dough very thin into oblong 8″ wide. Cut into 4″ squares. Starting at a corner, roll each square diagonally to opposite corner. Round the ends. Brush with egg yolk and sprinkle with coarse salt.

CINNAMON ROLLS (✂ Recipe) *Pinwheel rolls with fragrant cinnamon-sugar butter.*

Use ½ Sweet Roll Dough (*p. 114.*). After dough rises:

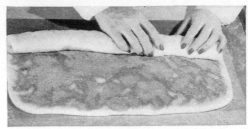

1 Roll dough into oblong, 15x9". Spread with 2 tbsp. softened butter and sprinkle with ½ cup sugar and 2 tsp. cinnamon.

2 Roll up tightly, beginning at wide side. Seal well by pinching edges of roll together. Stretch roll slightly to even.

Cover and let rise until double in bulk (35 to 40 min.). Bake until golden brown. While slightly warm, frost with Quick White Icing (*p. 102*).

3 Cut roll into 1" slices. Place a little apart in greased 13x9" pan or 18 greased muffin cups.

TEMPERATURE: 375° (quick mod. oven).

TIME: Bake 25 to 30 min.

AMOUNT: 1½ doz. rolls.

BUTTERSCOTCH ROLLS

Cinnamon Rolls with butterscotch-pecan glaze.

Make Cinnamon Rolls as above—*except* place cut slices in baking pan coated with . . .

 ⅓ cup butter, melted
 ½ cup brown sugar (packed)
 1 tbsp. corn syrup or water
 ½ cup pecan halves

Bake. Immediately turn upside down on a large tray. Let pan stay over rolls a minute so butterscotch runs down over them.

FROSTED ORANGE ROLLS

"Luscious!" says Margaret Doyle Stevening (Mrs. Oliver H. Stevening), who was in charge of our first test kitchen.

Make Cinnamon Rolls as above—*except* spread dough with ½ Creamy Orange Frosting (*below*). Let rise. Bake. Remove from pan. Spread with rest of frosting.

CREAMY ORANGE FROSTING

Mix until smooth: 3 tbsp. soft butter, 1 tbsp. grated orange rind, 2 tbsp. orange juice, 1½ cups *sifted* confectioners' sugar.

STREUSEL TOPPING

Rub together until crumbly: ⅓ cup GOLD MEDAL Flour, ⅓ cup sugar, 3 tbsp. butter.

HUNGARIAN COFFEE CAKE

Nut encrusted rolls—baked as a cake.

Use ½ Sweet Roll Dough (*p. 114*). After dough rises, cut into pieces size of walnuts.

Form into balls. Roll each ball in . . .
 ½ cup melted butter (total amount)

Then roll in mixture of . . .
 ¾ cup sugar
 1 tsp. cinnamon
 ½ cup finely chopped nuts

Place 1 layer of balls so they barely touch in well greased 9" tube pan (without removable bottom . . . or line with waxed paper). Sprinkle with a few raisins. Add another layer of balls, sprinkle with raisins. Let rise 45 min. Bake in quick mod. oven (375°) 35 to 40 min. Loosen from pan. Invert pan so butter-sugar mixture runs down over cake. Break apart with 2 forks.

STREUSEL COFFEE CAKE

Fluffy coffee cake with crumbly topping.

Use ¼ Sweet Roll Dough (*p. 114*). After dough rises, pat out to fit into greased round layer pan. Sprinkle Streusel Topping (*at left*) over dough. Cover. Let rise until double in bulk (about 30 min.). Bake in mod. hot oven (400°) 25 to 30 min. Serve warm.

SWEDISH TEA RING
Spectacular, but easy to make. People used to "OH and AH!" as Elsa Wallin Louis of our staff made it at our demonstrations and cooking schools. As Mrs. John Louis of Minneapolis, she still makes it for her family and friends.

Follow ✍ recipe for Cinnamon Rolls (*p. 116*)—*except* sprinkle dough with ½ cup raisins in addition to sugar (granulated or brown) and cinnamon.

1 Roll up as for Cinnamon Rolls. Then place sealed-edge-down in ring on lightly greased baking sheet. Pinch ends together.

Frost while warm with Quick White Icing (*p. 102*) and decorate with nuts and cherries. Serve warm.

2 With scissors, make cuts ⅔ of the way through the ring at 1" intervals. Turn each section on its side. Let rise, and bake as for Cinnamon Rolls (*p. 116*).

TEMPERATURE: 375° (quick mod. oven).
TIME: Bake 25 to 30 min.

CINNAMON KUCHEN

"This brings memories of happy school days and afternoon coffee at Heidelberg University when I studied there one summer," says Mrs. Norris C. Jones of Minneapolis.

Use ¼ Sweet Roll Dough (*p. 114*). After dough rises, pat into greased 9" square or round pan.
Spread top of dough with . . .
   1 tbsp. melted butter
Sprinkle with mixture of . . .
   ¼ cup sugar
   ¼ tsp. cinnamon
Let rise until double (25 to 30 min.). Bake until well browned. Serve warm.
TEMPERATURE: 400° (mod. hot oven).
TIME: Bake 25 to 30 min.

APFEL KUCHEN

"Just like my mother used to make," says Dr. F. A. Collatz of our company.

Follow recipe for Cinnamon Kuchen (*above*)—*except* arrange thin overlapping apple slices over dough; sprinkle with sugar-cinnamon mixture. Cover first 10 min. of baking. **For Christmas:** sprinkle little red cinnamon candies over top before baking.

POTECA (Po-teet-za)

A traditional bread baked by the Slavs in the south of Yugoslavia. For them no holiday, wedding, christening, or gathering is complete without Poteca.

Use ½ Sweet Roll Dough (*p. 114*).

After dough rises, place dough on large floured cloth and roll out almost paper-thin into an oblong, 30x20". Spread Walnut Filling (*below*) over dough, bringing it to edges. Starting at the wide side of the oblong, lift cloth and let dough roll up like a jelly roll. Seal well by pinching edges into dough. Place in greased 13x9" oblong pan or on a greased baking sheet in snail shape. Let rise until almost double (1 hr.). Bake until brown.

TEMPERATURE: 325° (slow mod. oven).
TIME: Bake 40 to 45 min.

WALNUT FILLING
Mix . . .
   ¼ cup soft butter
   ½ cup brown sugar (packed)
   1 egg

Stir in . . .
   ¼ cup milk
   ½ tsp. vanilla
   ½ tsp. lemon flavoring

Blend in . . .
   2 cups walnuts, finely ground (not chopped)

KOLACHE ("Ko-latch-ee") No other nation offers anything quite like these intriguing little fruit buns from Czechoslovakia. Introduced to us by a former staff member, Mary Lapic, now Mrs. Joseph Boucher of Hopkins, Minnesota. They come in three shapes and with a choice of different fillings.

Follow ✒ recipe for Sweet Roll Dough (*p. 114*)—*except*, with first addition of flour, add . . .

> ½ tsp. mace
> 1 tsp. grated lemon rind

Prepare any of the Fruit Fillings below. After dough rises, shape dough into balls or ovals or squares and fill (*see pictures*). Let rise on greased baking sheet or in muffin cups until not quite double (30 to 40 min.). Brush with Egg Yolk Glaze (*p. 111*), if desired. Bake until brown.
TEMPERATURE: 400° (mod. hot oven).
TIME: Bake 12 to 15 min.
AMOUNT: About 3 doz. buns.

1 Shape dough into 1½" balls. With thumb, make large enough depression to hold 1 heaping teaspoonful of fruit filling (*below*).

2 Roll balls of dough into ovals ⅛" thick. Place a spoonful of filling on half of each. Fold other half over. Pinch edges together well.

3 Roll dough ⅛" thick. Cut into 3" squares. Place a spoonful of desired filling on each. Fold corners to center, pinch together tightly.

FRUIT FILLINGS FOR KOLACHE
Each filling below is enough for ½ of dough.

CINNAMON-APPLE FILLING

Cook in saucepan until soft . . .
> 4 small apples, peeled and cut up
> 3 tbsp. cinnamon candies
> ⅓ cup water

Drain and press pulp through sieve.

POPPY SEED-FRUIT FILLING

Mix . . .
> 24 cooked prunes or apricots, mashed
> ½ tsp. cinnamon
> ¼ cup sugar
> 2 tbsp. poppy seeds

DATE, FIG, RAISIN, OR PRUNE FILLING: see page 216.

GERMAN FRUIT BUNS Gladis Schmidt of our staff says, "These are what we often served with afternoon coffee in our family home in Dundee, Minnesota."

Make Kolache as in picture 2 above—*except*, before baking, sprinkle tops with Streusel Topping (*p. 116*).

RAISED DOUGHNUTS (✒ Recipe)

Brown and crusty . . . best served warm. New Englanders make them for breakfast and serve them with cheese.

Use ½ Sweet Roll Dough (*p. 114*). After dough rises, roll out dough ⅓″ thick. Cut with floured 3″ doughnut cutter. Let rise on board until very light (30 to 45 min.). Leave uncovered so a crust will form on the dough. Drop into deep hot fat (375°) . . . see directions and pictures (*p. 94*). Drain on absorbent paper. For sugared doughnuts: place in bag with granulated sugar, and shake.

AMOUNT: 1½ to 2 doz. doughnuts.

YEAST FRITTERS

Delicious with chicken or ham.

Measure into mixing bowl . . .
   ½ cup warm water (not hot—110 to 115°)

Add, stirring to dissolve . . .
   1 pkg. active dry yeast

Stir in . . .
   2 tbsp. sugar
   ½ tsp. salt
   1 tbsp. shortening
   1 egg
   1½ cups sifted GOLD MEDAL Flour

Stir to mix well (1 min.).

Blend in . . .
   1½ cups chopped apple
    or 1 cup drained whole kernel corn

Cover and let rise in warm place (85°) until double (35 to 40 min.). Heat fat to 375°. Stir down batter. Drop by teaspoonfuls into hot fat and fry until golden brown, 2 to 5 min., turning only once. Drain on absorbent paper. Serve hot with hot syrup or as an accompaniment to baked or fried ham or chicken.

AMOUNT: 2 doz. fritters.

BISMARCKS

Puffy, jelly-filled, crusty, brown balls.

Follow ✒ recipe for Raised Doughnuts above—*except* roll dough ½″ thick. Cut rounds with a floured 3″ cooky cutter. Fry as for Raised Doughnuts. When cool, cut a *short* slit in the side of each fried ball through the center. Thrust a teaspoonful of jelly into the center and close tightly. Roll in sugar or glaze. Serve fresh.

To Glaze Doughnuts: see p. 95.

NANTUCKET DO-NUTS

Sometimes called "fried men," "frogs," or "jolly boys."

Pinch off small irregular pieces of raised bread or sweet dough and drop into hot fat as for doughnuts. They bubble and puff up into all sorts of interesting shapes and often look like little brown men or like frogs. Dip quickly into molasses (thinned with a little hot water), or in maple syrup, or honey. Drain. May also be sprinkled with sugar.

CRULLERS

Old Dutch term for twisted dough.

Follow ✒ recipe above—*except* shape into Twists and Slit Squares. Fry as for Raised Doughnuts.

Twists: Roll dough ½″ thick. Cut in strips ¾″ wide, 10″ long. Shape into twists or figure 8's and drop into hot fat. Fry.

Slit Squares: Roll out dough ¼″ thick. Cut in 2″ squares. Make 4 slits in each. Then lift by picking up alternate strips between fingers and thumb. Drop into hot fat. Fry.

STOLLEN (⚲ Recipe) Mrs. Allan B. Wilson (formerly Mary Madison of our staff) likes to bake this for friends at Christmas. See color picture, p. 113.

Follow ⚲ recipe for Sweet Roll Dough (p. 114)—except, with first addition of flour, add . . .

> 1 cup cut-up blanched almonds
> ½ cup each cut-up citron and
>   candied cherries
> 2 cups raisins
> 2 tbsp. grated lemon rind

After dough rises, divide dough into 2 parts. Roll or pat out each dough into an oval about 12x8″. Spread with soft butter. Fold in two the long way. Form into a crescent. Press folded edge firmly so it won't spring open (see right above). Place on greased baking sheets. Brush tops with butter. Let rise until double (35 to 45 min.). Bake until golden brown. Frost

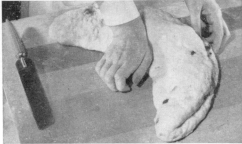

while warm with Quick White Icing (p. 102). Decorate with blanched almond halves, pieces of citron, and halves of candied cherries to simulate poinsettias.
TEMPERATURE: 375° (quick mod. oven).
TIME: Bake 30 to 35 min.
AMOUNT: 2 Stollen.

BOHEMIAN BRAID

A fruity, nutty, braided elegance for holidays. See color picture, p. 113.

Follow ⚲ recipe for Sweet Roll Dough (p. 114)—except, with first addition of flour, add . . .

> 2 tsp. grated lemon rind
> ¼ tsp. mace
> 1 cup raisins
> 1 cup chopped blanched almonds

After dough rises, divide dough into 2 portions to make 2 braids. Divide each portion into 4 equal parts. Shape 3 of the parts into strands 14″ long. Place them on lightly greased baking sheet. Braid loosely as shown in picture at right, fastening strands at one end, then tucking under.

Divide remaining portion of dough into 3 parts and shape into 3 strands each 12″ long. Make another braid and place second braid on top of the large braid, as in picture directions at right. Repeat for the other braid.

Cover and let rise until double (45 to 60 min.). Brush with Egg Yolk Glaze (p. 111), if desired. Bake until rich golden brown. Ice while warm with Quick White Icing (p. 102).
TEMPERATURE: 350° (mod. oven).
TIME: Bake 30 to 40 min.
AMOUNT: 2 large braids.

For a Special Holiday Touch: Decorate with candied cherries and pecan halves (see color picture, p. 113).

BREAD-TRAY STOLLEN
pictured on p. 113
Follow ⚲ recipe above—except divide dough into 4 parts to make 4 small Stollen. To serve, cut without separating slices, spread butter between, place on oblong bread plate.

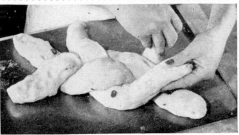

1 Braid gently and loosely. Do not stretch. Fasten ends; tuck under securely.

2 Place second braid on top. Seal braid ends by pressing firmly together and then tucking under.

All you have to do —

So braids will be even: elongate dough and divide it evenly.

KULICH *A delicate, sweet, fruity bread rising above tops of cans in mushroom or mosque-like shapes . . . characteristic of old Russia's holiday breads. Perfected by Bernadine Landsberg, formerly of our staff. See color picture, p. 113.*

Follow ✗ recipe for Sweet Roll Dough (*p. 114*)—*except*, with first addition of flour, add . . .

{ 1 cup raisins
½ cup chopped blanched almonds
1 tsp. vanilla

After dough rises, divide into 3 portions. Round up into 3 well rounded bun-like shapes. Place in 3 well greased 1-lb. tin cans. Pat tops of dough even. (Cans will be ½ full.) Cover. Let rise until double (30 to 40 min.). Place on baking sheet. Bake until well browned. Remove from cans. Cool slightly, ice, decorate.

NOTE: The tiny colored decorating candies used for tops of Kulich can be bought at most grocery stores. They are called 100's and 1000's.

TEMPERATURE: 375° (quick mod. oven).

TIME: Bake 35 to 40 min.

AMOUNT: 3 loaves.

To Decorate Kulich

While still warm, drizzle over the tops . . . allowing it to drip over the sides . . .

Confectioners' Sugar Icing

Mix ½ cup sifted confectioners' sugar, ½ tbsp. warm water, ½ tsp. lemon juice, and a bit of grated rind.

Sprinkle tiny colored decorating candies over the icing.

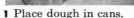

1 Place dough in cans.   **2** Iced and decorated.

HOT CROSS BUNS *Served in England in the pre-Christian era in honor of the Goddess of Spring. Later, the cross was placed on the bun in a missionary spirit.*

Measure into mixing bowl	½ cup warm water (not hot—110 to 115°)
Add, stirring to dissolve	2 pkg. active dry yeast
	½ cup lukewarm milk
	¾ cup unseasoned mashed potatoes
	½ cup sugar
	1¼ tsp. salt
Stir in until smooth	½ cup butter
	2 eggs
	1 cup raisins
	1 tsp. cinnamon
	¼ tsp. nutmeg
	half of 4½ cups sifted GOLD MEDAL Flour

Add enough remaining flour to handle easily; mix with hand. Turn onto lightly

floured board. Knead until smooth. Let rise until double (about 1½ hr.). Punch down and divide in two. Shape each part into 16 buns. Place in 2 greased 9″ round or square pans or 2″ apart on greased baking sheet. Let rise until double (30 min.). Brush with Egg Yolk Glaze (*p. 111*). Bake. Cool slightly; then make cross on top of each bun with Quick White Icing (*p. 102*).

TEMPERATURE: 375° (quick mod. oven).

TIME: Bake 20 to 25 min.

AMOUNT: 32 buns.

CHRISTMAS TREE BREAD

Something the children can make.

Use ½ Sweet Roll Dough (*p. 114*). After dough rises, divide dough in two (one for each tree). Form each into 17 1½" balls. Arrange on slightly greased baking sheet in a 5, 4, 3, 2, 1 pattern and with 2 balls rolled together for the trunk. Let rise until double (20 to 30 min.). Bake until golden brown. Decorate with Quick White Icing (*p. 102*), candied fruits, and decorating candies (including silver dragées).

TEMPERATURE: 350° (mod. oven).

TIME: Bake 15 to 20 min.

AMOUNT: 2 large trees.

JULE KAGE

A Christmas bread found on the table in Norway for a "Glad Jule." See color picture, p. 113.

Measure into mixing bowl . . .
    ¼ cup warm water (not hot—110 to 115°)

Add, stirring to dissolve . . .
    1 pkg. active dry yeast

Stir in . . .
    ¾ cup lukewarm milk
    ½ cup sugar
    ½ tsp. salt
    ½ tsp. powdered cardamom
    1 egg
    2 tbsp. shortening
    1 cup candied fruit
    1 cup raisins
    half of 3¼ to 3½ cups *sifted* GOLD MEDAL
        Flour

Mix with spoon until smooth.

Add rest of flour until easy to handle. Mix with hand. Turn onto lightly floured board; knead until smooth and elastic. Round up in greased bowl; cover and let rise until double (about 1½ hr.). Punch down; let rise again (about 45 min.). Shape into round loaf; place in greased 8 or 9" round pan. Cover, let rise (45 min.), brush with Egg Yolk Glaze (*p. 111*). Bake until brown.

TEMPERATURE: 350° (mod. oven).

TIME: Bake 30 to 40 min.

AMOUNT: 1 loaf.

Christmas Tree Bread

LUCIA BUNS (Saffron Buns)

Since long ago, Lucia Day, December 13, has marked the opening of the Christmas season for many of Swedish descent.

In Sweden, the ceremony is very pretty. Early in the starlit morning, young girls dressed in white, wearing holly crowns set with lighted candles, wake their parents and serve them saffron buns and cups of steaming coffee. Then they proceed around to neighbors and friends.

Follow ♪ recipe for Sweet Roll Dough (*p. 114*)—*except* add saffron (1 tsp. powdered cooking saffron to 2 tbsp. boiling water) to the first group of ingredients.

Mix, knead, and let rise as in directions for Sweet Roll Dough. To shape, roll out ¼" thick. Cut in strips, 4x½". Cross 2 strips to make an "X." Then curl each end out and in to form a broken "8." Press 4 raisins into each bun and brush with egg yolk to make a crispy, golden glaze. Let rise 15 to 20 min. Bake until golden brown. While warm, dribble with Quick White Icing (*p. 102*).

TEMPERATURE: 400° (mod. hot oven).

TIME: Bake 10 to 12 min.

AMOUNT: 4 doz. buns.

BREAD AS YOU LIKE IT

French Bread	Cottage Bread
Anadama Bread	New England Raisin Bread
Rich Egg Bread	Oatmeal Molasses Bread
Swedish Limpa	

DOUBLE-QUICK COFFEE BREAD (✒ Recipe)

One bowl for everything. Thorough beating takes the place of kneading. No rolling or cutting of dough. These breads are fluffier, have thinner crusts, and are more cake-like than kneaded breads. Delicious served warm.

Measure into mixing bowl . . .
    ¾ cup warm water (not hot—110 to 115°)
Add, stirring to dissolve . . .
    1 pkg. active dry yeast
Stir in . . .
    ¼ cup sugar
    1 tsp. salt
    half of 2¼ cups *sifted* GOLD MEDAL Flour
Beat 2 min., or until mixture sheets off spoon.
Add and beat until smooth . . .
    1 egg
    ¼ cup soft shortening or butter
    remaining flour

1 Batter sheets off the spoon after 2 min. of mixing.

2 Drop small spoonfuls of dough over entire bottom of pan.

Drop small spoonfuls over entire bottom of greased 8 or 9″ sq. pan, 10″ skillet, 9″ ring mold, or 16 to 20 greased med. muffin cups. Choose your favorite topping or upside-down variation (*below*). Cover, let rise in warm place until double (about 1 hr. for coffee cake; about 20 min. for buns). Bake until golden brown. Immediately turn out to avoid sticking.

TEMPERATURE: 375° (quick mod. oven).
TIME: Bake 30 to 35 min. for coffee cake, 15 to 20 min. for buns.
AMOUNT: 1 coffee cake *or* 16 to 20 buns.

BUTTERSCOTCH PECAN BUNS

Follow ✒ recipe above—*except* first prepare pan as follows:

Melt in pan . . .
    ⅓ cup butter
Mix in . . .
    ½ cup brown sugar (packed)
    1 tbsp. corn syrup
    ½ cup pecans
    candied cherries, if desired

Cool to lukewarm before spooning dough over mixture in pan.

BROWNED BUTTER-ALMOND BUNS

Follow ✒ recipe above—*except* first prepare pan as follows:

Melt in pan . . .
    ⅓ cup butter
Mix in . . .
    ½ cup slivered blanched almonds
Heat, stirring, until butter foams up and almonds are a light golden brown.
Cool to warm. Mix in . . .
    2 tbsp. corn syrup
    ½ cup sugar
    ½ tsp. almond flavoring
Spoon dough over mixture in pan.

WILLIAMSBURG BUNS

A colonial favorite from Old Virginia.

Follow ✒ recipe above—*except* sift with the flour . . .
    ½ tsp. mace
    ½ tsp. nutmeg
If desired, blend in with the egg . . .
    1 tbsp. sherry flavoring

TUTTI-FRUTTI COFFEE CAKE

Follow ✒ recipe above—*except* add with the egg . . .
    ½ cup candied fruit
    ¼ cup chopped nuts

Spoon dough into pan. When baked, ice with Quick White Icing (*p. 102*). Decorate with candied fruits and nuts.

SALLY LUNN

Came to America from Bath, England, home of Sally Lunn. The distinctive feature is the shape . . . baked in a tube pan. The texture is fluffy, porous, and sponge-like. Serve hot in wedges with butter . . . or serve when a day old, toasted and buttered.

Measure into mixing bowl . . .
  ½ cup warm water (not hot—110 to 115°)

Add, stirring to dissolve . . .
  2 pkg. active dry yeast

Stir in . . .
  1½ cups lukewarm milk
  2 tbsp. sugar
  1½ tsp. salt
  2 eggs
  ¼ cup soft shortening
  5½ cups *sifted* GOLD MEDAL Flour

Beat until smooth (100 strokes). Cover and let rise until very light (1 hr.). Beat down and pour into greased 10″ tube pan. Let rise to within 1″ of top of pan (45 min.). Bake until golden brown and crusty.

TEMPERATURE: 350° (mod. oven).

TIME: Bake 45 to 50 min.

AMOUNT: 16 servings.

SOUR CREAM TWISTS

A prize-winning recipe. It came to us from a wonderful cook in Ohio.

Measure into mixing bowl . . .
  ¼ cup warm water (not hot—110 to 115°)

Add, stirring to dissolve . . .
  1 pkg. active dry yeast

Stir in . . .
  ¾ cup lukewarm sour cream
  3 tbsp. sugar
  ⅛ tsp. soda
  1 tsp. salt
  1 large egg
  2 tbsp. soft shortening
  3 cups *sifted* GOLD MEDAL Flour

Turn dough onto lightly floured board and fold over several times until smooth. Roll into an oblong, 24x6″. Proceed as in picture directions at right. Then cover, let rise until double (1 hr.). Bake until golden brown. While warm, frost with Quick White Icing (*p. 102*). Delicious garnished with fresh strawberry halves.

TEMPERATURE: 375° (quick mod. oven).

TIME: Bake 12 to 15 min.

AMOUNT: 2 doz. twists.

ENGLISH MUFFINS

Serve split, toasted, and buttered . . . with marmalade.

Measure into mixing bowl . . .
  1 cup warm water (not hot—110 to 115°)

Add, stirring to dissolve . . .
  1 pkg. active dry yeast

Stir in . . .
  1 tsp. sugar
  2 tsp. salt
  ¼ cup soft shortening
  3 cups *sifted* GOLD MEDAL Flour

Mix until well blended and dough is soft. Roll out ¼″ thick on floured board. Cut into 3½″ circles. Place on corn meal-sprinkled baking sheet. Sprinkle muffins with corn meal. Let rise in warm place (85°) until double (1 hr.). Bake on medium-hot ungreased griddle or grill baker about 7 min. on each side. Split cooled muffins. Toast, butter, and serve warm.

AMOUNT: 10 to 12 muffins.

All you have to do—

To sour sweet cream: measure 1 tbsp. vinegar or strained lemon juice into measuring cup. Fill cup with sweet cream.

1 Spread with 2 tbsp. soft butter. Sprinkle half of dough with a mixture of ⅓ cup brown sugar and 1 tsp. cinnamon. Fold other half over. Cut into 24 strips 1″ wide.

2 Hold strip at both ends and twist in opposite directions. Place on greased baking sheet 2″ apart.

3 Press both ends of twist to baking sheet. Cover and let rise until light . . . 1 hr.

125

What Doughs Can I Keep in the Refrigerator?

Almost any dough except plain bread dough. Those made with at least ¼ cup sugar and milk, keep about 3 days. Doughs made with water keep about 5 days. (Temperature in refrigerator should be 50° or lower.)

When Is the Dough Put in the Refrigerator?

Immediately after mixing. Or it may be allowed to rise once, punched down, and then put into the refrigerator. Then it must be punched down occasionally as it rises.

How Should I Prepare the Dough?

Grease top of dough well and cover with waxed paper or refrigerator cover; then with a damp cloth. Keep cloth damp.

Must I Bake All the Dough at Once?

No, cut off only as much as needed for number of rolls or amounts of coffee cakes. Then return remainder of dough to refrigerator.

How Long to Let Rise Before Baking?

Until doubled (1½ to 2 hr.). The time will vary with coldness of dough, size of rolls, etc.

POTATO REFRIGERATOR ROLLS (⚭ Recipe) *Rich and sweet.*

Measure into mixing bowl...............	1½ cups warm water (not hot—110 to 115°)
Add, stirring to dissolve.................	1 pkg. active dry yeast
Stir in....................................	⅔ cup sugar 1½ tsp. salt ⅔ cup soft shortening 2 eggs 1 cup lukewarm mashed potatoes
Mix in with hand until dough is easy to handle............................	7 to 7½ cups *sifted* GOLD MEDAL Flour

Turn onto lightly floured board. Knead until smooth and elastic. Place greased-side-up in greased bowl. Cover with damp cloth; place in refrigerator (*see above*). About 2 hr. before baking, shape dough into rolls, coffee cakes, etc. (*see pp. 114–* *116*). Cover and let rise until double (1½ to 2 hr.). Bake according to directions for each type.

TEMPERATURE: 400° (mod. hot oven).
TIME: Bake 12 to 15 min.
AMOUNT: 4 doz. med. rolls.

EASY REFRIGERATOR ROLLS

No kneading. Fresh rolls every night.

Mix and handle dough as in ⚭ recipe above—*except do not knead*. Use these ingredients:

2 cups warm water (not hot—110 to 115°)

2 pkg. active dry yeast

½ cup sugar
2 tsp. salt
¼ cup soft shortening
1 egg

6½ to 7 cups *sifted* GOLD MEDAL Flour

CARAWAY BREAD STICKS

Delicious as salad or soup accompaniment.

Mix and handle dough as in ⚭ recipe above—*except do not knead*. Use these ingredients:

1 cup warm water (not hot—110 to 115°)

1 pkg. active dry yeast

1 tbsp. sugar
1½ tsp. salt
½ tsp. nutmeg
1 tsp. leaf sage, crumbled
2 tsp. caraway seeds
¼ cup soft shortening
1 egg

3 to 3¼ cups *sifted* GOLD MEDAL Flour

Beat vigorously. Cover and refrigerate at least 2 hr. or overnight before forming into sticks. Divide the chilled dough into 3 doz. small pieces. Roll into 8″ pencil-like strips and place 1″ apart on greased baking sheet. Let rise and bake as in ⚭ recipe above.

AMOUNT: 3 doz. bread sticks.

COCKTAIL BUNS

"These are just right for Silver Dollar Hamburgers or Meat Balls (p. 64) . . . to serve with beverages when I entertain," says Mildred Berg of our staff. "I like to keep a supply near the chafing dish. The miniature shapes fascinate my guests."

Use ½ dough for Potato Refrigerator or Easy Refrigerator Rolls (*p. 126*) or ½ Sweet Roll Dough (*p.114*). Shape into tiny balls (¾ to 1″). Dip tops in Egg Yolk Glaze (*p. 111*); then dip in sesame or poppy seeds, if desired. Place 1″ apart on greased baking sheet. Flatten gently. Let rise until double. Bake until golden brown. Brush with butter.

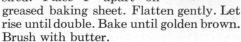

TEMPERATURE: 400° (mod. hot oven).

TIME: Bake 8 to 10 min.

AMOUNT: About 7 doz. buns.

SURPRISE TREATS

Each little bun has a surprise center.

Use ¼ Sweet Roll Dough (*p. 114*) or dough for Potato Refrigerator Rolls or Easy Refrigerator Rolls (*p. 126*). Wrap a small piece of dough around a cherry, a nut, raisins, dates, figs, candied fruit, etc. Place in 9″ greased layer pan. Before baking, brush with Egg White Glaze (*p. 110*). Sprinkle with sugar and nuts. Let rise until double. Bake until golden brown.

TEMPERATURE: 375° (quick mod. oven).

TIME: Bake 20 to 25 min.

AMOUNT: 1½ doz. rolls.

MINCEMEAT OR JAM DANDIES

Just bursting with goodness!

Use ⅓ Sweet Roll Dough (*p. 114*) or dough for Potato Refrigerator Rolls or Easy Refrigerator Rolls (*p. 126*). Roll out dough into oblong, 18x9″. Cut into 3″ squares. Place 1 tbsp. prepared mincemeat or jam on each. Bring corners of square to center; fasten with toothpick. Place in 18 greased muffin cups. Brush with melted butter; sprinkle with cinnamon and sugar mixture. Let rise until double. Bake until brown.

TEMPERATURE: 375° (quick mod. oven).

TIME: Bake 15 to 20 min.

AMOUNT: 1½ doz. rolls.

NUT COILS

Frosted nut-crusted twists.

Use ½ Sweet Roll Dough (*p. 114*) or dough for Potato Refrigerator Rolls or Easy Refrigerator Rolls (*p. 126*). Roll out dough into oblong 20x14″.

Spread with . . .

   ¼ cup soft butter
   ½ cup finely chopped nuts

Fold the ends of dough over in thirds . . . making an oblong of dough with 3 layers. Cut with sharp knife into 24 strips, ½″ wide. Twist the strips and wind into a "coil" shape on greased baking sheet. Let rise until double. Bake until brown. Frost with Quick White Icing (*p. 102*).

TEMPERATURE: 425° (hot oven).

TIME: Bake 10 to 12 min.

AMOUNT: 24 nut coils.

MADELINE ISLAND ROLLS

From that happy vacation land on one of the Apostle Islands in Lake Superior. Mrs. Thomas Vennum, of delightful Chateau Madeleine there, says, "These rolls are favorites with our guests. Serve whole . . . each pulls off his own roll."

Use ½ Sweet Roll Dough (*p. 114*) or dough for Potato Refrigerator Rolls or Easy Refrigerator Rolls (*p. 126*). Shape dough into 1½″ balls, roll in melted butter, and place in greased 10″ tube pan . . . making 2 layers of balls. Let rise until double (about 60 min.). Bake until golden brown. Remove from pan. Cool slightly. Pour over top Quick White Icing (*p. 102*) with rum flavoring added.

TEMPERATURE: 375° (quick mod. oven).

TIME: Bake 35 to 40 min.

PICNIC BUNS

Quick for the picnic!

Use ½ Sweet Roll Dough (*p. 114*) or dough for Potato Refrigerator Rolls or Easy Refrigerator Rolls (*p. 126*). Divide in 2 parts. Roll each into a 7½″ square, ½″ thick. Cut into 9 buns, each 2½″ square. Place on greased baking sheet. Let rise until double. Bake until brown.

TEMPERATURE: 400° (mod. hot oven).

TIME: Bake 12 to 15 min.

AMOUNT: 1½ doz. buns.

MIXER BATTER BUNS (Recipe)

So light and good . . . so easy to make!

Measure into mixer bowl . . .
    1 ¼ cups warm water (not hot—110 to 115°)

Add, stirring to dissolve . . .
    2 pkg. active dry yeast

Add . . .
    ¼ cup sugar
    1 tsp. salt
    ½ cup soft shortening
    2 eggs
    2 cups *sifted* GOLD MEDAL Flour

Combine with the mixer on low speed. Beat 2 min. on medium speed, guiding batter into beaters with rubber scraper.

Add . . .
    1 ¼ cups *sifted* GOLD MEDAL Flour

Beat with rubber scraper until smooth. Spoon into greased muffin cups a scant ½ full. Let rise in warm place (85°) until batter reaches top of muffin cups (30 to 40 min.). Bake until golden brown. Serve warm.

TEMPERATURE: 375° (quick mod. oven).

TIME: Bake 18 to 20 min.

AMOUNT: About 2 ½ doz. buns.

CINNAMON BUTTER BUNS

"Marvelous!" say friends of Mrs. P. J. Braheney as she passes these at afternoon coffee in the patio of her California home.

Follow recipe above—*except,* after baking, roll buns in melted butter and then in a mixture of ½ cup sugar and 1 tsp. cinnamon.

CARAMEL BALLS

Another name for them might be "Hurry-up Butterscotch Rolls."

Follow recipe above—*except* prepare muffin cups by mixing 1 tsp. soft butter, 2 tsp. brown sugar, and ¼ tsp. water in each. Arrange 3 walnut or pecan halves on mixture in bottom of each cup.

ORANGE BLOSSOMS

Butter-rich . . . with an orange flavor. "Delightful addition to luncheon or afternoon tea," says Mrs. John M. Henry (formerly Margaret O'Keefe of our staff).

Follow recipe above—*except* prepare muffin cups by spooning cooled Orange Syrup *(below)* into each.

ORANGE SYRUP

Bring to boil . . .
    ½ cup sugar
    ¼ cup undiluted frozen (or fresh) orange juice
    ¼ cup butter
    ¼ cup light corn syrup

ALMOND PUFFS

Follow recipe above—*except,* before baking, sprinkle with mixture of ¼ cup sugar, ½ tsp. cinnamon, ¼ cup slivered almonds.

CORN MEAL BUNS

Tender, crusty, yellow-rich.

Follow recipe at left above—*except* add 1 cup yellow corn meal with the first addition of flour. Omit ¼ cup of the flour.

WHOLE WHEAT BATTER BREAD

Moist and delicious, open-textured. Requires no kneading. Just pour the batter into the pan.

Measure into large mixing bowl . . .
    2 ½ cups warm water (not hot—110 to 115°)

Add, stirring to dissolve . . .
    2 pkg. active dry yeast

Mix on a paper . . .
    2 cups *unsifted* whole wheat flour
    4 cups *sifted* GOLD MEDAL Flour
    4 tsp. salt

Add ½ flour mixture and . . .
    ¼ cup soft shortening
    ¼ cup honey or brown sugar

Beat on medium speed 2 min., guiding batter into beaters with rubber scraper. Add remaining flour mixture and blend in with rubber scraper or spoon until smooth (1 to 1 ½ min.). Scrape down batter from sides of bowl. Cover with waxed paper and let rise in warm place (85°) until double (about 30 min.). Stir down batter by beating about 25 strokes. Divide batter into 2 greased 9x5x3″ loaf pans. Let rise until edges of batter reach top of pans (about 40 min.). Bake until brown.

TEMPERATURE: 375° (quick mod. oven).

TIME: Bake 40 to 50 min.

AMOUNT: 2 loaves.

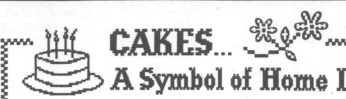

CAKES...
A Symbol of Home Life

From the beautiful cake for the announcement party—to the triumphantly towering wedding cake—and children's birthday cakes, blazing with candles—to the proud cake celebrating the silver or golden wedding—cakes play an important role in the most significant moments in our lives.

Betty Crocker

THERE'S A CAKE FOR EVERY OCCASION

To help you make a choice, a few from this chapter are listed below.

CAKES FROM A BOX

They save you time and work. Yet even when you start with a package you end with a cake you made yourself. Your grocer has a mix to correspond with almost every recipe on the following pages ... Angel Food, spice, devils food, yellow, white, marble ... all the favorites and variations are easy.

Here are some new ways to use Betty Crocker mixes.

SPECIAL-DAY CAKES

For Junior's Birthday

From 2 pkg. Betty Crocker White Cake Mix, bake a 3-layer cake and 12 cupcakes for centerpiece and place cards. Decorate cake and line edge of plate with candles stuck in gumdrops. Write children's names on cupcakes and set one at each place with ribbons leading to the cake centerpiece. Serve the cake for dessert and let each little guest take a cupcake place card home. ➡

Carnival Angel Food

A rainbow of delicate colors with a subtle cherry-almond flavor. Make cake using Betty Crocker Confetti Angel Food Mix. Ice with Cherry Butter Frosting (*p. 152*) and decorate with vari-colored candies.

HOW TO BAKE ODD-SHAPED CAKES

| Lamb | Bell | Christmas Tree | Star | Heart |

Fill odd-shaped pans:

⅔ full for Creaming Method cakes
½ full for Double-quick Method cakes

Betty Crocker Cake Mixes are best for these pans—or butter-type cake made by the Simplified Creaming or Double-quick Method.

HOW TO MEASURE CAPACITY OF AN ODD-SHAPED PAN: Fill pan with water. Measure the water. To fill odd-shaped pan ½ full: Use ½ that amount of batter.

FAVORITES FOR ANY DAY

With a Cake Mix

ORANGE SPICE CAKE

Into Betty Crocker Honey Spice Cake Mix, fold grated rind of 2 oranges (2 tbsp.). Frost with Orange Butter Icing (*p. 177*).

CREOLE BELLE CAKE

Into Betty Crocker Chocolate Devils Food Cake Mix, stir 1 tsp. cinnamon, ½ tsp. nutmeg, ¼ tsp. cloves before adding liquid. Frost with Chocolate Butter Icing (*p. 177*).

With Bisquick

VELVET CRUMB CAKE

Easy and quick, yet as rich and tender as grandmother's butter cake. It also doubles as delicate berry shortcake or delicious dessert with a whipped cream topping.

Heat oven to 350° (mod.). Grease and flour 8″ square pan. Mix 1⅓ cups Bisquick, ¾ cup sugar, 3 tbsp. soft shortening, 1 egg, ¼ cup milk. Beat vigorously 1 min. Stir in gradually ½ cup milk, 1 tsp. vanilla. Beat ½ min. Pour into pan. Bake 35 to 40 min. Top with Broiled Icing (*p. 179*).

HOW TO CUT A 2-LAYER BEAUTY TO GET MORE PIECES AND DAINTIER ONES: Use a thin, sharp knife. Insert the point of knife into the cake ... keeping the point down and handle up, slice ... pulling the knife toward you. If frosting sticks, dip knife in hot water.

Cut around cake in a circle half way to the center. Cut pieces from outer circle. Cut pieces from inner circle. Makes 38 pieces. } or { Cut cake in 4 quarters. Then cut each quarter into slices. The 2 pieces closest to the middle of cake may be cut in half. 32 pieces.

CAKES

We now proclaim you a member of the Society of Cake Artists! And do hereby vest in you all the skills, knowledge, and secrets of the "gentle art" of cakemaking. Your part is only to heed the directions herein.

For centuries, cakemaking changed very little. The 16th century Spice Cake, the 18th century Nun's Cake, even the rich Pound Cake of our colonial days required long hours of labor. Old "receipts" read . . . "take half a peck of fine wheat-flower . . . three pounds of refined sugar . . . dry them by the fire . . . take four pounds of butter, beat it with a cool hand, then beat thirty-five eggs," etc. Later recipes called for smaller amounts but the method of mixing was essentially the same.

More recently our staff introduced a cake method to homemakers—a stream-lined method based on precision timing and modern ingredients. It uses only one bowl . . . saves the creaming of shortening and sugar, the separate beating of eggs. It has been given different names, but we call it our *Double-quick Method*. We have now adapted most of our favorite cakes to it. But knowing that some of you still like to make cakes the old way, we give you the creaming method too, simplified.

The first really new cake of the century is Chiffon Cake—new in taste, new in texture, new in eating quality. It combines the best qualities of both angel food and butter cakes . . . but it, too, is made an entirely new way.

Cakes from every land have come to America . . . but none so glamorous as the typically American concoction of richly tender layers, crowned with luscious, creamy icing. Meals are more satisfying, special occasions more festive, with one of these delicious cake creations.

THIS IS THE WAY to mix a "butter" cake by the DOUBLE-QUICK METHOD.

First: follow the five steps at the top of opposite page.

In addition, be extra sure you do the following:

1 Use hydrogenated shortening.

2 Use only the size pans called for in the recipe.

3 If you are using an electric mixer, guide the batter into the beaters with a rubber scraper so that all the batter will be beaten sufficiently.

4 If you have no mixer, beat vigorously with spoon. The more you beat, the better the cake.

5 Use the exact ingredients called for.

6 Have your oven checked regularly for accuracy by your local utility com-

Double-quick Method of Mixing

1 Sift flour before measuring. Then sift together directly into mixing bowl all the dry ingredients—flour, sugar, baking powder and/or soda, salt. If cocoa is used, sift it in with the flour, unless otherwise specified.

2 Add softened shortening and ⅔ of the liquid. Measure flavoring into liquid. *When using all-purpose flour (GOLD MEDAL), the batter is somewhat heavier so add all the liquid at once.*

3 Beat on med. speed (middle of dial) 2 min., scraping bowl constantly to guide batter into beaters. Or beat vigorously with spoon 2 min. (150 strokes per min.), stopping to rest occasionally.

4 Add remaining liquid and unbeaten eggs, egg whites, or egg yolks. Beat 2 min. more, scraping bowl frequently.

See "CAKES TO MAKE YOU FAMOUS," p. 170.

135

5 Divide batter evenly into prepared pans. (Batter made by Double-quick Method is thin.) Stagger layers as in picture above— away from oven walls and slightly apart. Rack should be at middle of oven.

6 When minimum baking time is up, test cakes made with cake flour by lightly touching middle of cake. If no imprint remains, cake is done. Cakes made with all-purpose flour require longer baking time.

Extra test for doneness: stick toothpick into center. If it comes out clean, cake is done.

7 Remove from oven. Let stand in pans 10 min. Turn out on towel or paper towel as shown above by putting (1) towel over cake, (2) inverted wire cooling rack over towel. Then turn whole thing upside down.

8 Next, place another inverted wire cooling rack on bottom of cake and turn the whole thing over. The cake will then be right side up on cooling rack . . . where air can circulate around it.

9 When cake is cool, spread frosting or filling between the layers (placing bottoms together) almost to outer edge. Then ice sides of the cake first. See "HOW TO FROST A LAYER CAKE," p. 172.

10 Spread frosting on top last . . . swirling it just to the built-up edge. (Bringing the icing up high on the sides is the secret of a nicely shaped cake which does not have sloping edges.)

PICK THE PROPER PAN When baking fine layers, loaves, any type cakes, choose the size pan the recipe states.

Use the size pan called for in the recipe.

Too *Big* a pan. Cake is pale, flat, and shrunken.

Too *Little* or too *Shallow* a pan. Cake bulges over and loses contour. Layer pans should be 1½″ deep, square and oblong pans 2″ deep.

Just the *Right* size pan. Good contour, easy to frost.

The pan material is also important.

Shiny aluminum or tin pans distribute heat evenly and give a delicate golden brown crust to the cake.

If you are baking in heat-proof glass pans, reduce the oven temperature 25° and use same baking time called for in recipe.

HOW TO PREPARE PANS so that cakes are easy to remove.

Grease bottom and sides of pans thoroughly—using about ½ tbsp. shortening in each layer pan.

Dust the greased pans with flour until well coated on bottom and sides. Shake out excess flour.

Line pans for fruitcake with aluminum foil or brown paper to keep cakes from getting too brown. (Leave "ears.")

HOW TO BAKE CUPCAKES

Fill cups:
> ⅔ full for Creaming Method cupcakes
> ½ full for Double-quick Method cupcakes
> ⅞ full for Chiffon cupcakes

Cupcakes have nicely rounded tops and hold their shape best if baked in paper cups or liners placed in muffin cups. Saves greasing and washing pan.

TEMPERATURE: 400° (mod. hot oven).

TIME: Bake 18 to 20 min.

AMOUNT: 1½ to 2 doz. cupcakes from recipe calling for 2¼ cups flour.

HOW TO BAKE ODD-SHAPED CAKES See p. 130.

EGG WHITE **CAKES** Perfect . . . made with cake flour and 3, 4, or 5 egg whites.

DOUBLE-QUICK METHOD

SILVER WHITE CAKE (4-EGG WHITE) (✗ Recipe) *High, fluffy, showy. Delicately flavored.*

Reminiscent of White Mountain Cake, the rage of the Gay Nineties and the first popular "white" cake to be created. Originally it was baked in four layers, frosted and filled with white coconut icing, and served on a high glass cake stand.

Grease generously and flour . . . .
   2 8 or 9" layer pans
      or 13x9" oblong pan

Sift together into bowl . . . .
  2¼ cups *sifted* SOFTASILK Flour
  1½ cups sugar
  3½ tsp. baking powder
  1 tsp. salt

Add . . . .
  ½ cup soft shortening
  ⅔ cup milk
  1 tsp. flavoring

Beat 2 min.

Add . . . .
  another ⅓ cup milk
  4 egg whites (½ to ⅔ cup), unbeaten

Beat 2 more min.

Pour into prepared pans. Bake until cake tests done. Cool. Finish with desired filling and icing. Elegant with lemon or orange filling (*p. 182*) and a cooked white icing sprinkled with coconut (*p. 139*).

TEMPERATURE: 350° (mod. oven).

TIME: Bake layers 30 to 35 min., oblong 35 to 40 min.

3-EGG WHITE CAKE

A little less cake for a small family.

Grease and flour 2 8" layer pans *or* 13x9" oblong pan. Follow ✗ recipe above for method. But use:

  2¼ cups *sifted* SOFTASILK Flour
  1⅓ cups sugar
  2½ tsp. baking powder
  ½ tsp. salt

  ½ cup soft shortening
  ⅔ cup milk
  1½ tsp. vanilla

  another ⅓ cup milk
  3 egg whites (⅜ cup), unbeaten

TEMPERATURE: 350° (mod. oven).

TIME: Bake layers 30 to 35 min., oblong about 35 min.

MIRACLE MARBLE CAKE

Rich chocolate and dainty white . . . in intriguing marbled effect. "Guests at my home exclaim over it especially when I serve fingers of it with pink strawberry ice cream on white milk glass plates," says N. Faye Woodward of Lawrence, Kansas.

Follow ✗ recipe above. Pour ⅔ of batter into pans. To remaining batter add 1 sq. unsweetened chocolate (1 oz.), melted, mixed with ¼ tsp. soda and 2 tbsp. warm water. Pour here and there over white batter. Cut through batter with knife several times for marbled effect. Bake. Cool. Frost with chocolate icing.

5-EGG WHITE CAKE

To serve a large group.

Follow ✗ recipe above for method . . . use 2 9" layer pans *or* 13x9" oblong pan. But use:

  2¾ cups *sifted* SOFTASILK Flour
  1¾ cups sugar
  4½ tsp. baking powder
  1 tsp. salt

  ⅔ cup soft shortening
  ¾ cup milk
  2 tsp. flavoring

  another ½ cup milk
  5 egg whites (⅔ cup), unbeaten

NEW MARASCHINO CAKE

A lovely pink variation . . . cherry flavored and studded.

Follow ✗ recipe above for method. But use:

  2¼ cups *sifted* SOFTASILK Flour
  1⅓ cups sugar
  3 tsp. baking powder
  1 tsp. salt
  ½ cup soft shortening
  ¼ cup maraschino cherry juice (5-oz. bottle)
  16 maraschino cherries, cut in eighths
  ½ cup chopped nuts
  ½ cup milk
  4 egg whites (½ cup), unbeaten

Finish with cooked white frosting made with cherry juice in place of water. Decorate with red stemmed cherries.

EXQUISITE COCONUT CAKE

Layers of Silver White Cake or Golden Layer Cake ... with Clear Lemon
or Orange Filling between the layers and White Mountain Frosting
sprinkled with snowy coconut over top and sides.

EGG WHITE CAKES Made with cake flour . . . and 4 egg whites.

FLUFFY WHITE CAKE (✒ Recipe) *Old-time favorite. Luscious to eat.*

Grease generously and flour..............	2 8 or 9" layer pans or 13x9" oblong pan
Cream together until fluffy...............	½ cup soft shortening (half butter) 1½ cups sugar
Sift together.........................	2½ cups *sifted* SOFTASILK Flour 2½ tsp. baking powder 1 tsp. salt
Mix in alternately with .... (Use low speed on mixer.)	1 cup milk 1½ tsp. flavoring
Fold in.............................	4 egg whites (½ cup), stiffly beaten

Pour into prepared pans. Bake. Cool. For a special treat, finish with Date Cream Filling (*p. 182*) and a butter icing (*p. 177*).

TEMPERATURE: 350° (mod. oven).
TIME: Bake layers 30 to 35 min., oblong 35 to 45 min.

LADY BALTIMORE CAKE

A Christmas delicacy made famous long ago by cooks of the plantation mansions of South Carolina and Maryland.

Bake ✒ recipe above in layers. Spread both cooled layers with Fruit-Nut Filling (*below*). Cover each with a thin layer of White Icing (*below*). Put layers together. Then cover top and sides with the remaining icing.

LADY BALTIMORE WHITE ICING

Mix and boil to 242° (or until an 8" thread spins from spoon) . . .
    1½ cups sugar
    1 tsp. light corn syrup
    ⅔ cup water
Pour slowly, beating constantly, into . . .
    2 egg whites (¼ cup), beaten stiff
Add . . .
    1 tsp. vanilla
Continue beating until mixture is fluffy and will hold its shape.

LADY BALTIMORE FRUIT-NUT FILLING

Take about ⅓ of icing (*above*) and mix in . . .
    ⅓ cup raisins, cut fine
    ⅓ cup figs, cut in strips
    ½ cup chopped walnuts

PEPPERMINT CANDY CAKE

Follow ✒ recipe above—*except* fold ⅓ cup finely crushed peppermint stick candy into batter. Ice with Pink Mountain Frosting (*p. 180*). Sprinkle with crushed peppermint stick candy.

COCONUT CREAM CAKE

A specialty of Mrs. James F. Mason of Los Gatos, California, the most hospitable and gracious of homemakers.

Bake ✒ recipe above in layers. Make Cream Filling (*p. 182*). Add about ½ cup coconut to ⅓ of the filling and spread between cooled layers. Coat top and sides thinly with remaining filling. Sprinkle generously with coconut (about 1½ cups).

PINK AZALEA CAKE

Dainty pink and white creation that makes you feel the beauty of springtime in Virginia with all the pink azaleas in bloom. Soft, pink cake layer between two of white. Fluffy pink icing over top and sides.

Follow recipe for any of the Egg White Cakes, preparing 2 or 3 pans for 2 thick or 3 thinner layers. Tint batter for one layer a delicate pink. Bake. Cool. Into ½ of White Mountain Frosting (*p. 180*), fold cut-up maraschino cherries or strawberries and nuts. Put layers together with filling. Tint remaining frosting pink and frost top and sides of cake.

SNOWFLAKE CAKE (↗ Recipe) *Full volumed ... deliciously moist eating quality.*

Grease and flour......................	2 8 or 9" layer pans or 13x9" oblong pan
Sift together into bowl..................	2 cups plus 2 tbsp. *sifted* GOLD MEDAL Flour 1½ cups sugar 3½ tsp. baking powder 1 tsp. salt
Add.................................	½ cup soft shortening 1 cup milk 1 tsp. flavoring
Beat 2 min.	
Add.................................	4 egg whites (½ to ⅔ cup), unbeaten
Beat 2 more min.	

Pour into prepared pans. Bake until cake tests done. Cool. Delicious with lemon filling (*p. 182*) and a white icing with a touch of lemon rind added for flavoring.

TEMPERATURE: 350° (mod. oven).

TIME: Bake layers 35 to 40 min., oblong 40 to 45 min.

CHOCOLATE CHIP CAKE

There are little surprise chunks of rich chocolate all through the white layers.

Follow ↗ recipe above—*except* fold in carefully ½ cup finely chopped sweet or semi-sweet chocolate. Bake. Finish cooled cake with a fudgy frosting or with a glossy white icing decorated with curls of chocolate.

All you have to do—

To make chocolate curls: barely warm a bar of chocolate (*do not melt*). With a razor blade or peeler, take off thin shavings from back or sides of chocolate. (They curl up.)

NEW MARASCHINO CHERRY CAKE

Pink and light ... with refreshing pieces of cherries and crunchy nuts to add goodness.

Follow method in ↗ recipe above. But use:

2 cups plus 2 tbsp. *sifted* GOLD MEDAL Flour
1⅓ cups sugar
3 tsp. baking powder
1 tsp. salt

½ cup soft shortening
¼ cup maraschino cherry juice (5-oz. bottle)
16 maraschino cherries, cut in eighths
½ cup milk

4 egg whites (½ to ⅔ cup), unbeaten
½ cup chopped nuts

Frost with white icing tinted a pastel pink with maraschino cherry juice.

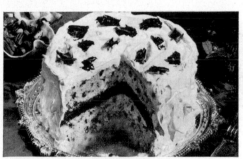

Chocolate Chip Cake

RIBBON BON BON CAKE

Alternate layers of white cake, lemon-flavored, and beige cake, enticingly spiced. Lemon Spice Icing.

Follow ↗ recipe above—*except* use ½ tsp. lemon flavoring instead of vanilla. Pour half of batter into one of the prepared layer pans. To remaining batter add:

½ tsp. cinnamon
¼ tsp. nutmeg
¼ tsp. cloves
1 tbsp. molasses

Stir well and pour into the other pan. Bake. Cool. Split into 4 layers. Ice with:

LEMON SPICE ICING

Beat in bowl until smooth and fluffy ...
3 cups *sifted* confectioners' sugar
4 egg yolks
⅓ cup soft shortening (part butter)
¼ tsp. cinnamon
⅛ tsp. *each* cloves and nutmeg
grated rind of 1 lemon
2 tbsp. lemon juice

141

We used to call it the "Bride's Cake" ... that ethereal structure of white tender cake all iced and decorated with snowy frosting. The dark fruitcake which maidens put under their pillows to dream on is traditional wedding cake. But nowadays it's the Bride's Cake that is the "Wedding Cake," and the fruitcake is the "Groom's Cake." It is sometimes given to guests in small white boxes to take home.

GET READY

Mix the cake in two batches ... following, for each batch, directions below for "MAKE THE CAKE."

Each tier will consist of two identical layers (12″, 9″, 6″).

Use recipe for Silver White Cake (*p. 138*) as basis for amount of ingredients.

Assemble ingredients for making two double recipes. Use half almond, half vanilla flavoring.

Grease generously and flour 3 round layer pans: one 12″, one 9″, one 6″ in diameter ... at least 1½″ deep.

MAKE THE CAKE

Mix batter for one double recipe *each time*, beating 2½ min. each mixing time. Pour a little over half of batter (4½ cups) into 12″ pan and place in center of oven, allowing plenty of space for cake to rise. Test for doneness by inserting a toothpick in center of cake. Cool in pan.

Pour remaining batter into 9″ and 6″ pans (6″ pan requires about 1¼ cups batter). Refrigerate these layers until 12″ cake is baked. Then place 9″ layer near rear of oven and 6″ layer near front.

TEMPERATURE: 350° (mod. oven).
TIME: Bake 12″ layer 30 to 40 min.,
9″ layer 30 to 35 min.,
6″ layer 25 to 30 min.

For second layers, repeat above process.

MAKE THE FROSTING

While cake is still slightly warm, spread each layer with thin coating of Butter Icing (*p. 177*) (to prevent crumbs getting into final frosting and help keep moist and fresh). *Do not* put layers together.

Choose an appropriate permanent foundation such as a mirror, crystal or silver cake plate, or a heavy, round cardboard covered with lace paper doilies.

Make 4 times recipe for Butter Icing (*p. 177*), using 2 tbsp. vanilla and ¾ tsp. almond flavoring. Ice 12″ layers as for regular layer cake. Lay 9″ cardboard circle on top. Set 9″ layer on cardboard. Frost 9″ layers as for layer cake. Lay 6″ cardboard circle on top. Follow same directions for 6″ layers.

DECORATE THE CAKE

Pipe icing (delicately tinted, if desired) around base of each layer and elsewhere as desired. Little icing flowers and other decorations appropriate for a wedding cake are available in stores. A small vase, all iced, with a few perfect rosebuds in it, or a miniature bride and groom, may be placed on top of cake.

SERVE THE CAKE

The bride cuts the first piece and shares it with the groom. Then someone else cuts pieces for the guests. After the first few pieces are cut from the outer bottom layer so as not to destroy its appearance, the cake may be removed to the kitchen and the layers cut individually and served to the wedding guests.

DOUBLE-QUICK METHOD

An excellent use for leftover egg yolks. CAKES EGG YOLK

NEW GOLD CAKE (⚷ Recipe) Soft ... and rich yellow.

Grease generously and flour . . . .
2 8" layer pans
or 13x9" oblong pan

Sift together . . . .
2 cups *sifted* SOFTASILK Flour
or 1¾ cups *sifted* GOLD MEDAL Flour
1⅓ cups sugar
3 tsp. baking powder
1 tsp. salt

Add . . . .
Beat 2 min.
⅓ cup soft shortening
*⅔ cup milk
½ tsp. lemon flavoring
½ tsp. vanilla

Add . . . .
Beat 2 more min.
another ⅓ cup milk
4 egg yolks (⅓ cup), unbeaten

Pour into prepared pans. Bake. Cool. Ice as desired. Especially delicious with a fruity icing, such as Strawberry Butter Icing (*p. 177*) or Lemon or Orange Butter Icing (*p. 177*).

TEMPERATURE: 350° (mod. oven).

TIME: Bake layers 30 to 35 min., oblong 35 to 40 min.

If using GOLD MEDAL Flour, add all milk at once.

LORD BALTIMORE CAKE

Named for one of the wealthiest gentlemen who first colonized America ... George Calvert, Lord Baltimore.

Make ⚷ recipe above in layers. Spread both cooled layers with Fruit-Nut Filling (*below*). Cover with a thin layer of Pink Frosting (*below*). Put layers together. Then cover top and sides with the Pink Frosting.

LORD BALTIMORE PINK FROSTING

Mix and boil to 242° (or until 8" thread spins from spoon) . . .

1½ cups sugar
⅓ cup water
⅓ cup maraschino cherry juice
1 tsp. light corn syrup

Pour slowly, beating constantly, into . . .

2 egg whites (¼ cup), beaten stiff

Add . . .

½ tsp. lemon flavoring
1 tsp. grated orange rind

Continue beating until mixture is fluffy and will hold its shape.

LORD BALTIMORE FRUIT-NUT FILLING

Into about ⅓ of Pink Frosting above, mix . . . ¼ cup *each*

macaroon crumbs, dried and toasted
pecans, cut up and toasted
almonds, blanched, cut up, and toasted
maraschino cherries, chopped

HAWAIIAN PINEAPPLE CAKE

Gold and white beauty perfected by Irene Anderson of our staff. Use 2 yolks and 1 whole egg in the cake and save the other 2 whites for the icing.

Follow ⚷ recipe above and bake in layers—*except* use 2 egg yolks and 1 whole egg in place of 4 egg yolks.

Put cooled layers together with Pineapple Filling (*p. 182*) . . . spreading about ½ cup over center of top layer. Frost sides and a 1½" border on top with a fluffy white icing.

It is as elegant to eat as it is beautiful to look at.

143

WHOLE EGG CAKES High, fluffy, fine textured . . . made with 2 eggs . . . cake flour.

DOUBLE-QUICK METHOD

GOLDEN LAYER CAKE (⚲ Recipe) Versatile with its many variations.

Grease and flour	2 8 or 9" layer pans or 13x9" oblong pan
Sift together into bowl	2¼ cups sifted SOFTASILK Flour 1½ cups sugar 3 tsp. baking powder 1 tsp. salt
Add	½ cup soft shortening ⅔ cup milk 1½ tsp. flavoring
Beat 2 min.	
Add	another ⅓ cup milk 2 eggs (⅓ to ½ cup)
Beat 2 more min.	

Pour into prepared pans. Bake until cake tests done. Cool. Finish with filling or frosting as desired. The oblong cake is ideal finished with Broiled Icing or Choc-O-Nut Topping (p. 179) or with Pink Mountain Frosting (p. 180) sprinkled with crushed peppermint stick candy.

TEMPERATURE: 350° (mod. oven).
TIME: Bake layers 30 to 35 min.,
oblong 40 to 45 min.

FRESH ORANGE CAKE

Soft, tender, refreshing. Gladys Mason of our company, a food artist and a true Californian, makes this cake deliciously with oranges from her native state.

Follow ⚲ recipe above—*except* use 2 tsp. baking powder and ¼ tsp. soda in place of 3 tsp. baking powder. Use ¼ cup orange juice and ¾ cup milk or water for the liquid. For flavoring, add grated rind of 1 orange (about 1 tsp.). If baked in layers, use Clear Orange Filling (p. 182) between layers and White Mountain Frosting (p. 180) on top and sides.

MAPLE SYRUP CAKE

Modern version of an old Vermont recipe sent to us by Marian Burnes of Montpelier. This originally was a recipe from her great-grandmother's cook book.

Follow ⚲ recipe above—*except* substitute 1 cup maple syrup for 1 cup of the sugar (use only ½ cup sugar). Decrease milk to ½ cup. Add the syrup with it. Omit the 1 tsp. flavoring. Blend in ½ cup cut-up butternuts (or other nuts). Bake. Cool. Frost with Maple Butter Icing (p. 147) or Maple Syrup Icing (below).

MAPLE SYRUP ICING

Boil 1¼ cups maple syrup to firm ball stage (242°) and beat gradually into 2 stiffly beaten egg whites.

ALLEGRETTI CAKE

Named after a famous candy shop in New York.

Bake Golden Layer Cake (*above*). Cool. Ice with White Mountain Frosting (p. 180). Melt over hot water 1 sq. unsweetened chocolate (1 oz.) with ¼ tsp. shortening. Using a teaspoon, drip chocolate around top edge of iced cake, letting chocolate run down sides in uneven lines.

DAFFODIL (JONQUIL) CAKE

As pretty as its name.
Make Fresh Orange Cake (*at left above*). Cool. Spread Clear Orange Filling (p. 182) between layers and over top of cake. Frost sides with a cooked white frosting (tinted yellow) and pull frosting up over filling in the shape of daffodil petals.

BUTTERSCOTCH CAKE

Follow ⚲ recipe above—*except* use brown sugar in place of white. Bake oblong 35 to 40 min. Delicious iced with a fluffy white icing or creamy Easy Penuche Icing (p. 181).

STARLIGHT CAKE (✗ Recipe) *Of all cakes baked in homes, this undoubtedly is made most often.*

Grease and flour...................... 2 8 or 9" layer pans
or 13x9" oblong pan

Sift together......................... {
2 cups plus 2 tbsp. *sifted* GOLD MEDAL Flour
1½ cups sugar
3½ tsp. baking powder
1 tsp. salt
}

Add............................... {
½ cup soft shortening
1 cup milk
1 tsp. flavoring
}

Beat 2 min.
Add............................... 3 eggs (½ to ⅔ cup)
Beat 2 more min.

Pour into prepared pans. Bake until cake tests done. Cool and ice as desired.

TEMPERATURE: 350° (mod. oven).

TIME: Bake 8" layers 35 to 40 min.,
9" layers 30 to 35 min.,
oblong 45 to 50 min.

GOLDEN DATE CAKE

A light-colored date cake, moist and delicious . . . with refreshing orange icing. Kathryn Lambert Boehm (Mrs. Frank L. Boehm), wonderful homemaker and delightful hostess of Los Angeles, says, "This is a household favorite with us."

Use 9" layer pans or 13x9" oblong pan. Follow ✗ recipe above—*except* add in first beating 1 cup pitted dates, cut up fine after measuring. Fold in ½ cup coarsely chopped nuts at the end. Bake layers 35 to 40 min., oblong 45 to 50 min. Frost with Orange Butter Icing (*p. 177*).

BUTTERSCOTCH SUNDAE CAKE

Follow method in ✗ recipe above. But use:

{
2¼ cups *sifted* GOLD MEDAL Flour
3 tsp. baking powder
1 tsp. salt
}
{
1¾ cups brown sugar (packed)
½ cup soft shortening
1 cup milk
1 tsp. vanilla
}
2 eggs (½ to ⅔ cup)

Frost with a cooked white icing. Decorate with Butterscotch Glaze (*at right*).

KITCHENETTE CAKE

A small 1-egg cake that keeps and carries well. "This is just the right size for my sister and me," says Olga Stege of our staff. "We frost it with Coconut Icing and cut it in squares . . . right in the pan . . . taking out just the number of pieces we want to serve each time."

Grease and flour a 9" square pan. Follow method in ✗ recipe above. But use:

{
1⅓ cups *sifted* GOLD MEDAL Flour
1 cup sugar
2 tsp. baking powder
½ tsp. salt
}
{
⅓ cup soft shortening
⅔ cup milk
1 tsp. flavoring
}
1 egg (¼ to ⅓ cup)

TEMPERATURE: 350° (mod. oven).

TIME: Bake 30 to 35 min.

BUTTERSCOTCH GLAZE

Measure into saucepan . . .
¼ cup brown sugar (packed)
3 tbsp. butter
2 tbsp. water

Bring to a full rolling boil, stirring constantly. Then boil vigorously without stirring 1½ min. Remove from heat and immediately dribble with a teaspoon around top edge of cake. Glaze will run over sides in uneven lines. Or make a small groove around edge of cake after it has been frosted, using back of teaspoon. Dribble glaze in the groove and over the edge. This makes it look more like a Butterscotch Sundae.

145

ONE-EGG CAKES
Simply delicious . . . with only 1 egg . . . and using cake flour.

ONE-EGG CAKE (⚲ Recipe) *Light, tender, rich, and moist. Developed especially for use when eggs are scarce. But delicious any time.*

Grease and flour.	2 8" layer pans or 9" square pan
Sift together.	{ 2 cups *sifted* SOFTASILK Flour 1¼ cups sugar 2½ tsp. baking powder 1 tsp. salt
Add. . . . . Beat 2 min.	{ ⅓ cup soft shortening ⅔ cup milk 1 tsp. vanilla
Add. . . . . Beat 2 more min.	{ another ⅓ cup milk 1 egg (¼ cup)

Pour into prepared pans. Bake until cake tests done. Cool. Frost with your favorite icing. The square cake is ideal for finishing with an easy broiled topping, ice cream, or fruit and whipped cream.

TEMPERATURE: 350° (mod. oven).

TIME: Bake layers about 30 min., square 30 to 35 min.

MARBLE ONE-EGG CAKE
Follow ⚲ recipe above—*except* pour half of batter into another bowl and add a mixture of 1 sq. unsweetened chocolate (1 oz.), melted, ¼ tsp. soda, and 2 tbsp. water. Beat ½ minute. Spoon chocolate and white batters alternately into prepared pan or pans. Run knife through to give marbled effect. Frost with a chocolate icing.

SPICE ONE-EGG CAKE
Follow ⚲ recipe above—*except* sift ½ tsp. cinnamon and ¼ tsp. *each* cloves, allspice, nutmeg with dry ingredients. Frost with Easy Penuche Icing (*p. 181*).

BIT O' CHOCOLATE ONE-EGG CAKE
Enticing bits of grated chocolate all the way through.

Follow ⚲ recipe above—*except* fold 2 sq. unsweetened chocolate (2 oz.), grated med. coarse, into the batter.

DINETTE CAKE
Small . . . and good.

Grease and flour 9" square pan. Follow ⚲ recipe above for method. But use:

{ 1½ cups *sifted* SOFTASILK Flour
1 cup sugar
2 tsp. baking powder
½ tsp. salt
⅓ cup soft shortening
⅔ cup milk
1 tsp. flavoring
1 egg (¼ to ⅓ cup)

ORANGE ONE-EGG CAKE
"We often enjoy this with coffee in our patio—in the shade of our own orange tree," says Mrs. Arthur Hennessy, charming hostess of Alhambra, California.

Follow ⚲ recipe above—*except* add ¼ tsp. soda with dry ingredients. In place of 1 cup milk, use ¼ cup fresh or diluted frozen orange juice and ¾ cup milk. Omit vanilla. Beat in 1 tsp. grated orange rind with the egg. Spread Clear Orange Filling (*p. 182*) between layers and Orange Butter Icing (*p. 177*) over top and sides of cake.

BANANA ONE-EGG CAKE
Follow ⚲ recipe above—*except* reduce baking powder to 1 tsp. and add 1 tsp. soda with the dry ingredients. Use ½ cup buttermilk or sour milk and 1 cup mashed ripe bananas in place of the sweet milk. Add all at once in first beating time. Finish cooled cake with sweetened whipped cream covered with banana slices.

SIMPLIFIED CREAMING METHOD

Old-fashioned yellow cakes ... richly flavorful. CAKES BUTTER

BONNIE BUTTER CAKE (⚘ Recipe) *A fluffy yellow cake made with butter.*

Grease and flour......................	2 9" layer pans
	or 13x9" oblong pan
Cream together until fluffy...............	⅔ cup soft butter
(Beat 5 min. high speed on mixer or by hand.)	1¾ cups sugar
	2 eggs (⅓ to ½ cup)
	1½ tsp. vanilla
Sift together.........................	3 cups *sifted* SOFTASILK Flour
	or 2¾ cups *sifted* GOLD MEDAL Flour
	2½ tsp. baking powder
	1 tsp. salt
Mix in alternately with...................	1¼ cups milk
(Use low speed on mixer.)	

Pour into prepared pans. Bake. Cool. Frost as desired. Delicious iced with a fluffy white icing sprinkled with coconut, or Strawberry Butter Icing (*p. 177*).

TEMPERATURE: 350° (mod. oven).

TIME: Bake layers 35 to 40 min., oblong 45 to 50 min.

NEW BUTTERCUP CAKE

The interesting flavor combination of this cake was sent to us by Mrs. C. Breeden of St. Louis, Missouri.

Follow method in ⚘ recipe above. But use:

⅔ cup soft shortening (half butter)
1¾ cups sugar
2 eggs (⅓ to ½ cup)
¾ tsp. vanilla
½ tsp. lemon flavoring
¼ tsp. almond flavoring

3 cups *sifted* SOFTASILK Flour
1¼ tsp. baking powder
½ tsp. soda
1 tsp. salt

1¼ cups buttermilk

Ice cooled cake with a fluffy white frosting. Decorate with grated orange or lemon rind to resemble border of buttercups.

TEMPERATURE: 350° (mod. oven).

TIME: Bake layers 35 to 40 min., oblong 50 to 55 min.

WALNUT BONNIE BUTTER CAKE

Delicious nut-enriched version. A favorite of a famous Kentuckian and screen star, Irene Dunne.

Follow ⚘ recipe above—*except* fold in 1 cup chopped nuts just before pouring batter into pans. Delicious finished with Browned Butter Icing (*p. 177*) or Maple Butter Icing (*below*).

MAPLE BUTTER ICING

Blend ...

⅓ cup soft butter
3 cups *sifted* confectioners' sugar

Stir in ...

½ cup maple syrup

ORANGE BONNIE BUTTER CAKE

It has a delicate butter-orange flavor.

Follow ⚘ recipe above—*except* add 2 tsp. grated orange rind in place of vanilla. Spread Clear Orange Filling (*p. 182*) between layers, Orange Butter Icing (*p. 177*) over top and sides of cake.

MARBLE BONNIE BUTTER CAKE

Follow ⚘ recipe above—*except* pour only ⅔ of batter into pans. Beat into remaining batter for about 30 seconds a mixture of 1 sq. unsweetened chocolate (1 oz.), melted, 2 tbsp. warm water, 1 tbsp. sugar, ¼ tsp. soda. Pour here and there over light batter. Cut through batter with knife several times for marbled effect.

NEW FUDGE CAKE (✎ Recipe) 4 squares of chocolate. *Dark, delectable, fudge-like. See color picture on p. 149 (opposite).*

	For Large Cake	Small Cake
Grease and flour.....................	2 8 or 9" layer pans or 13x9" oblong pan	9" square pan
Sift together into bowl.................	1¾ cups *sifted* GOLD MEDAL Flour	1¼ cups
	2 cups sugar	1⅓ cups
	2 tsp. baking powder	1¼ tsp.
	¼ tsp. soda	¼ tsp.
	1 tsp. salt	½ tsp.
Add................................	¼ cup soft shortening	3 tbsp.
Beat 2 min.	1½ cups milk	1 cup
	1 tsp. vanilla	½ tsp.
Add	2 eggs (⅓ to ½ cup)	1 egg (¼ to ⅓ cup)
Beat 2 more min.	4 sq. unsweetened chocolate (4 oz.), melted	3 sq. (3 oz.)
Stir in.............................	1 cup chopped nuts	⅔ cup

Pour into prepared pans. Batter will be thin in first stage. Bake until cake tests done. Cool. Ice with a fudge frosting.

TEMPERATURE: 350° (mod. oven).
TIME: Bake layers 35 to 40 min.,
        oblong 40 to 45 min.,
        square 35 to 40 min.

CHOCOLATE JOY CAKE

3 squares of chocolate. *A family favorite from Mrs. Samuel C. Gale, wife of our own vice president.*
Grease and flour . . .
    2 8 or 9" layer pans
       or 13x9" oblong pan
Stir until thick . . .
    ½ cup boiling water
    3 sq. unsweetened chocolate (3 oz.), melted
Cool.
Cream together until fluffy . . .
(Beat 5 min. high speed on mixer or by hand.)
    ½ cup soft shortening
    1⅔ cups sugar
    3 eggs (½ to ⅔ cup)
    cooled chocolate mixture
Sift together . . .
    2¼ cups *sifted* SOFTASILK Flour
       or 2 cups plus 2 tbsp. *sifted*
       GOLD MEDAL Flour
    2¼ tsp. baking powder
    ¼ tsp. soda
    1 tsp. salt
Mix in alternately with . . .
(Use low speed on mixer.)
    1 cup buttermilk
Beat just until smooth.
Pour into prepared pans. Bake. Cool. Finish with a chocolate or fudge icing. Trim with sliced Brazil nuts.
TEMPERATURE: 350° (mod. oven).
TIME: Bake layers 30 to 40 min.,
        oblong about 45 min.

BROWN BEAUTY CAKE

2 squares of chocolate. *Very rich and fudgy . . . with a slightly red color.*
Grease and flour . . .
    8" square pan
Stir until chocolate melts . . .
    2 sq. unsweetened chocolate (2 oz.), cut up
    ½ cup boiling water
Cool.
Sift together and stir into above mixture . . .
    1 cup *sifted* SOFTASILK Flour
    1 cup sugar
    ¼ tsp. baking powder
    ½ tsp. soda
    ½ tsp. salt
Add . . .
    ¼ cup soft shortening
Beat 1 min.
Add . . .
    ¼ cup buttermilk or sour milk
    ½ tsp. vanilla
    1 egg
Beat 1 more min.
Pour into prepared pan. Bake until cake tests done. Cool. Ice with a cooked white marshmallow or chocolate fudge frosting.
TEMPERATURE: 350° (mod. oven).
TIME: Bake 35 to 40 min.

CHOCOLATE CHERRY CAKE

Follow recipe above—*except* add ¼ tsp. almond flavoring and 10 maraschino cherries, chopped and drained.

CHOCOLATE CAKE AS YOU LOVE IT
New Fudge Cake with Minute Fudge Frosting
Real Red Devils Food Cake with Satiny Beige Frosting
Black Midnight Cake with White Mountain Frosting, Fudge Sundae Sauce

DEVILS FOOD CAKES Modern and old-time favorites.

POPULAR CHOCOLATE CAKE (✎ Recipe) Moist and fluffy . . . with a rich brown color. Made with
chocolate and either buttermilk or sweet milk.

	For Large Cake	Small Cake
Grease and flour......................	2 9" layer pans or 13x9" oblong pan	2 8" layer pans
Cream together until fluffy............... (Beat 5 min. high speed on mixer or by hand.)	⅔ cup soft shortening 1½ cups sugar 3 eggs (½ to ⅔ cup)	½ cup 1¼ cups 2 eggs (⅓ to ½ cup)
Blend in............................	2½ sq. unsweetened chocolate (2½ oz.), melted	2 sq. (2 oz.)
Sift together........................	2¼ cups sifted SOFTASILK Flour 1 tsp. soda 1 tsp. salt	1¾ cups ¾ tsp. 1 tsp.
Mix in alternately with................. (Use low speed on mixer.)	1¼ cups buttermilk or sweet milk	1 cup

Pour into prepared pans. Bake until cake tests done. Cool. Finish with Chocolate Butter Icing (*p. 177*) or Easy Chocomint Icing (*below*).

TEMPERATURE: 350° (mod. oven).

TIME: Bake layers 30 to 35 min., oblong 40 to 45 min.

EASY CHOCOMINT ICING

A bit sticky, but elegant to eat.

Use about 12 large chocolate-covered peppermint cream patties for frosting for 13 x9" oblong cake, 8 for 9" square. The minute cake comes out of oven, place chocolate peppermints over top. As they melt, spread quickly.

Place chocolates on hot cake. Then begin to spread.

And complete spreading to cover cake.

CHOCOLATE PECAN CAKE

Perfected from one in the old Williamsburg Cook Book. Its unusual, rich, pecan flavor characterizes the sumptuousness and abundance of the best early Virginia cookery. Made with brown sugar, cocoa, and sour whipping cream.

Grease and flour 2 9" layer pans *or* 13x9" oblong pan. Follow method in ✎ recipe above. But use:

½ cup soft shortening
2 cups brown sugar (packed)
2 large eggs (½ cup)
1½ tsp. vanilla
3 tbsp. cocoa mixed with
   ⅔ cup water
2¼ cups *sifted* SOFTASILK Flour
1 tsp. soda
1 tsp. salt
⅔ cup sour whipping cream
   (30 to 35% butterfat)
⅔ cup pecans, cut up

Pour into prepared pans. Bake. Cool. Frost with Brown Beauty Icing (*p. 178*).

All you have to do —

To keep cocoa cakes brown on the outside: grease and "cocoa" the pans instead of grease and "flour."

REAL RED DEVILS FOOD CAKE (♪ Recipe) *A rich, moist cake ... made with cocoa. Developed by Lorraine Kilgren of our staff. See color picture, p. 149.*

Grease and flour . . . . 2 8 or 9″ layer pans
or 13x9″ oblong pan

Sift together into bowl . . . .
- 1 ¾ cups *sifted* SOFTASILK Flour
- 1 ½ cups sugar
- 1 ¼ tsp. soda
- 1 tsp. salt
- ⅓ cup cocoa

Add . . . .
- ½ cup soft shortening
- ⅔ cup milk

Beat 2 min.

Add . . . .
- another ⅓ cup milk
- 2 eggs (⅓ to ½ cup)
- 1 tsp. vanilla

Beat 2 more min.

Pour into prepared pans. Bake until cake tests done. Cool. Finish with White Mountain or Satiny Beige Frosting (*p. 180*) or with Chocolate Butter Icing (*p. 177*).

TEMPERATURE: 350° (mod. oven).

TIME: Bake 8″ layers 35 to 40 min.,
9″ layers 30 to 35 min.,
oblong 45 to 50 min.

RED DEVILS FOOD CAKE

A 3-egg devils food cake made with cocoa. Long a favorite with homemakers.

Grease and flour . . .
2 8 or 9″ layer pans
or 13x9″ oblong pan

Sift together into bowl . . .
- 1 ⅔ cups *sifted* GOLD MEDAL Flour
- 1 ½ cups sugar
- 1 ¼ tsp. soda
- 1 tsp. salt
- ½ cup cocoa

Add . . .
- ½ cup soft shortening
- 1 cup milk
- 1 tsp. vanilla

Beat 2 min.

Add . . .
- 3 eggs (½ to ⅔ cup)

Beat 2 more min.

Pour into prepared pans. Bake until cake tests done. Cool. Frost with Brown Beauty Icing (*p. 178*) or White Mountain Frosting (*p. 180*).

TIME: Bake 8″ layers 35 to 40 min.,
9″ layers 30 to 35 min.,
oblong about 45 min.

All you have to do –

To get a rich red devils food cake: use a recipe calling for sweet milk and soda. Pop your cake into the oven quickly.

MARDI GRAS CAKE

Makes you think of New Orleans and its traditional and gay Mardi Gras season.

A fluffy, spicy devils food developed by Mabel Martin of our staff.

Make either of the cakes on this page in layers, but sift 1 tsp. cloves with the dry ingredients. Spread White Mountain Frosting (*p. 180*) between cooled layers and over top and sides. Decorate the icing by dipping the tip of a teaspoon into melted chocolate and making indentations in the shape of circles here and there over the entire surface.

151

SPECIAL CHOCOLATE CAKES Dusky beauties you'll like.

BLACK MIDNIGHT CAKE (✧ Recipe)

Margaret Norrdin of our staff says this cake is the "best ever" ... "especially when creamy fudge-frosted." This cake is made with cocoa and water. See color picture, p. 149.

Grease and flour......................	2 9" layer pans or 13x9" oblong pan
Cream together until fluffy............... (Beat 5 min. high speed on mixer or by hand.)	⅔ cup soft shortening 1⅔ cups sugar 3 eggs (½ to ⅔ cup)
Sift together.........................	2¼ cups *sifted* SOFTASILK Flour ⅔ cup cocoa ¼ tsp. baking powder 1¼ tsp. soda 1 tsp. salt
Mix in alternately with................... (Use low speed on mixer.)	1⅓ cups water 1 tsp. vanilla

Pour into prepared pans. Bake until cake tests done. Cool. For a striking color contrast, spread a snowy white frosting, such as White Mountain (*p. 180*), between layers and over top and sides of cake.

TEMPERATURE: 350° (mod. oven).

TIME: Bake layers about 35 min., oblong 40 to 45 min.

COCOA CREAM CAKE

Follow ✧ recipe above for Black Midnight Cake in layers. When cake is cool, split each layer crosswise into two layers. For perfect cutting, use a long, thin, sharp knife.

Spread sweetened whipped cream (1½ to 2 cups) between layers. Frost top and sides with Milk Chocolate Icing (*at right above*). Cake will keep in refrigerator 2 or 3 days.

They'll all take Cocoa Cream Cake.

MILK CHOCOLATE ICING

Melt together . . .
 ⅓ cup shortening
 ½ cup cocoa

Stir in . . .
 3 cups *sifted* confectioners' sugar
 ½ cup hot scalded milk
 1 tsp. vanilla

Place pan in ice water, beat until consistency to spread (3 to 5 min.).

CHERRY-FROSTED CHOCOLATE CAKE

"I like any cake . . . just so it's chocolate," says Winona Kennedy (Mrs. James G. Kennedy). "But this one is extra special. We bake it in an oblong pan to take on picnics when I'm visiting at my old home on Long Island."

Make Black Midnight Cake (*above*) or any favorite chocolate cake. Cool. Frost with Cherry Butter Icing (*below*). Decorate with drained maraschino cherry halves.

CHERRY BUTTER ICING

Blend together . . .
 ⅓ cup soft butter
 3 cups *sifted* confectioners' sugar

Stir in until smooth . . .
 about ¼ cup maraschino cherry juice

PEPOMINT CHOCOLATE CAKE

Follow ✧ recipe above for Black Midnight Cake—*except* fold into batter ¼ tsp. peppermint flavoring. Ice with a chocolate or white icing . . . sprinkle with crushed peppermint stick candy.

DOUBLE-QUICK METHOD

The shortening is rich sweet or sour cream. CAKES CREAM

SWEET CREAM CAKE (✗ Recipe) *Easy and quick to make. Different, too!*

Grease and flour......................	2 8 or 9" layer pans or 13x9" oblong pan
Sift together and set aside...............	{ 2⅓ cups *sifted* SOFTASILK Flour or 2¼ cups *sifted* GOLD MEDAL Flour 3 tsp. baking powder 1 tsp. salt
Beat until very thick in small mixer bowl (about 5 min.)....................	3 eggs (½ to ⅔ cup)
Beat in gradually.....................	1⅓ cups sugar
Transfer egg-sugar mixture into large mixing bowl.	
Stir in flour mixture alternately with........	{ 1⅓ cups whipping cream (30 to 35% *butterfat*) 1½ tsp. vanilla

Pour into prepared pans. Bake until cake tests done. Cool. Finish with sweetened whipped cream or desired icing. Or, for a tempting sugary topping, sprinkle sugar and cinnamon over top of cake 3 min. before removing from oven.

TEMPERATURE: 350° (mod. oven).

TIME: Bake layers 25 to 30 min., oblong about 40 min.

SPICE CREAM CAKE

Follow ✗ recipe above—*except* add 3 tsp. cinnamon, 1½ tsp. cloves, and 1½ tsp. allspice to dry ingredients before sifting. Frost with Creamy White Icing (*p. 179*) with ½ cup chopped raisins, dates, or figs and ½ cup nuts added to it. Delicious, too, with Easy Penuche Icing (*p. 181*).

WHIPPED CREAM CAKE

"Iced with chocolate frosting and served with fruit gelatin, this is a favorite in our farm home," says Mrs. Lee Christopher of Jackson, Minnesota.

Grease and flour 2 8 or 9" layer pans *or* 13x9" oblong pan.

Whip until stiff . . .
> 1½ cups whipping cream
> (30 to 35% *butterfat*)

Fold in . . .
> 3 eggs (½ to ⅔ cup), well beaten
> 1½ tsp. vanilla

Sift together . . .
> 2¼ cups *sifted* SOFTASILK Flour
> 1½ cups sugar
> 2 tsp. baking powder
> ½ tsp. salt

Fold in gently with a wire whip.

Pour into prepared pans. Bake until cake tests done. Cool. Serve uniced, with sugar topping as in Sweet Cream Cake (*above*), or with any desired icing.

TEMPERATURE: 350° (mod. oven).

TIME: Bake layers 30 to 35 min., oblong 35 to 40 min.

SOUR CREAM CAKE

Mrs. George Holm of Cuba, North Dakota, says, "What is better with afternoon coffee on the farm . . . or anywhere else . . . than Sour Cream Spice Cake frosted with Easy Penuche Icing?" (See recipe below.)

Grease and flour 9" square pan. Follow method in ✗ recipe above. But use:

> { 1½ cups *sifted* GOLD MEDAL Flour
1 tsp. baking powder
½ tsp. soda
½ tsp. salt

> 2 eggs (⅓ to ½ cup)
1 cup sugar

> { 1 cup sour whipping cream
(30 to 35% *butterfat*)
1 tsp. vanilla
¼ tsp. lemon flavoring

TEMPERATURE: 350° (mod. oven).

TIME: Bake 35 to 40 min.

All you have to do —

To make a Sour Cream Spice Cake: add 1¼ tsp. cinnamon, ¾ tsp. cloves, ¾ tsp. allspice with the dry ingredients when making Sour Cream Cake (*above*). Delicious with Easy Penuche Icing (*p. 181*) or White Fudge Frosting (*p. 181*).

SOUR CREAM CUPCAKES

Follow recipe above and fold in at the last about ½ cup *each* chopped nuts and raisins. Fill greased muffin cups about ⅔ full. Bake in mod. oven (400°) 18 to 20 min.

SPICE CAKES New ways with old-time favorites.

BUTTERMILK SPICE CAKE (✿ Recipe) *A buttermilk-brown sugar cake with a spicy flavor.*

Grease and flour......................
2 9" layer pans
   or 13x9" oblong pan

Sift together into bowl...................
2¼ cups *sifted* SOFTASILK Flour
   or 2 cups plus 2 tbsp. *sifted* GOLD MEDAL Flour
1 cup sugar
1 tsp. baking powder
¾ tsp. soda
1 tsp. salt
¾ tsp. cloves
¾ tsp. cinnamon

Add................................
¾ cup brown sugar (packed)
½ cup soft shortening
1 cup buttermilk

Beat 2 min.
Add................................
3 eggs (½ to ⅔ cup)

Beat 2 more min.

Pour into prepared pans. Bake until cake tests done. Cool. Frost with Easy Penuche Icing (*p. 181*).

TEMPERATURE: 350° (mod. oven).
TIME: Bake layers 35 to 40 min.,
      oblong 45 to 50 min.

APPLESAUCE CAKE

The old-time quilting bee favorite.

First, make thick, unsweetened applesauce (*below*). Grease and flour 13x9" oblong pan. Use method as given in ✿ recipe above—*except* stir in walnuts and raisins at the last. But use:

2¾ cups *sifted* SOFTASILK Flour
   or 2½ cups *sifted* GOLD MEDAL Flour
2 cups sugar
¼ tsp. baking powder
1½ tsp. soda
1½ tsp. salt
¾ tsp. cinnamon
½ tsp. cloves
½ tsp. allspice

½ cup soft shortening
½ cup water
1½ cups unsweetened applesauce

2 eggs (⅓ to ½ cup)

½ cup chopped walnuts
1 cup raisins, cut up

TEMPERATURE: 350° (mod. oven).

TIME: Bake 45 to 50 min.

All you have to do —

To make 1½ cups unsweetened applesauce: wash, quarter, and core 6 to 8 tart apples. Add ¼ cup water. Cover and cook to a mush, stirring occasionally. Press through a sieve or food mill.

All you have to do —

For a Chrysanthemum Cake: make a Burnt Sugar or Spice Cake in layers. Frost with Creamy Burnt Sugar Icing (*p. 155*) or Easy Penuche Icing (*p. 181*). Place clusters of garden chrysanthemums around outside edge of cake plate.

AN AUTUMN DESSERT PARTY: Chrysanthemum Cake, Salted Almonds, Coffee.

TEMPTATION SPICE CAKE

A delicate spice cake made with sweet milk.

Grease and flour 2 8 or 9" layer pans *or* 13x9" oblong pan. Follow method in ✿ recipe above. But use:

2 cups *sifted* GOLD MEDAL Flour
1⅓ cups sugar
3½ tsp. baking powder
1 tsp. salt
1 tsp. cinnamon
½ tsp. nutmeg
¼ tsp. cloves

½ cup soft shortening
1 cup milk
1 tsp. vanilla

3 eggs (½ to ⅔ cup)

TEMPERATURE: 350° (mod. oven).

TIME: Bake 8" layers 35 to 40 min.,
      9" layers 30 to 35 min.,
      oblong 40 to 45 min.

DOUBLE-QUICK METHOD

Old favorites in double-quick time. CAKES SPECIAL FLAVOR

BURNT SUGAR CAKE *Caramel flavor in the cake . . . caramel flavor in the icing. The real old-time, caramel-rich variety of cake that always has been first choice at church suppers.*

Grease and flour......................	2 8 or 9″ layer pans or 13x9″ oblong pan
To make syrup: First, *caramelize the sugar (see p. 29).* Melt in *heavy* skillet over low heat until clear and med. brown, shaking pan gently to keep from burning........................	½ cup sugar
Remove from heat. Add *slowly*, stirring constantly............	½ cup boiling water
Stir over *low* heat until lumps are dissolved. Measure, add water to make............ Cool.	1 cup liquid
Sift together into bowl..................	2¼ cups *sifted* SOFTASILK Flour 1 cup sugar 3 tsp. baking powder 1 tsp. salt
Add................................. Beat 2 min.	½ cup soft shortening ⅔ cup *cooled* caramel-water mixture
Add................................. Beat 2 more min.	remaining ⅓ cup *cooled* caramel-water mixture 2 eggs (⅓ to ½ cup) 1 tsp. vanilla, if desired

Pour into prepared pans. Bake until cake tests done. Cool. Finish with Creamy Burnt Sugar Icing (*below*).

TEMPERATURE: 350° (mod. oven).

TIME: Bake 8″ layers 30 to 35 min.,
      9″ layers 25 to 30 min.,
      oblong 35 to 40 min.

CREAMY BURNT SUGAR ICING

First, make another caramel-water mixture following directions in recipe above.

Caramelize . . .
   ½ cup sugar
Add . . .
   ¼ cup boiling water
Do not add any more water.
Melt in saucepan . . .
   ½ cup shortening (part butter)
Remove from heat and add . . .
   2½ tbsp. SOFTASILK Flour
   ¼ tsp. salt
Stir in slowly . . .
   caramel-water mixture
Bring to boil, stirring constantly. Boil 1 min. If mixture curdles, do not be alarmed. Remove from heat. Beat in alternately . . .
   3 cups *sifted* confectioners' sugar
   about 3 tbsp. water
Set saucepan in bowl of cold water. Beat until consistency to spread. Stir in . . .
   ½ tsp. vanilla

If it becomes too thick to spread, add a little water.

PEANUT BUTTER CAKE

Grease and flour . . .
   2 9″ layer pans
      or 13x9″ oblong pan
Sift together into bowl . . .
   2¼ cups *sifted* SOFTASILK Flour
   1½ cups sugar
   3 tsp. baking powder
   1 tsp. salt
Add . . .
   ⅓ cup soft shortening
   ⅓ cup chunk-style peanut butter
   ⅔ cup milk
Beat 2 min.
Add . . .
   another ⅓ cup milk
   2 eggs (⅓ to ½ cup)
Beat 2 more min.

Pour into prepared pans. Bake. Cool. Finish with Peanut Butter Broiled Icing (*p. 179*) for oblong or Peanut Butter Icing (*p. 181*) for layers.

TEMPERATURE: 350° (mod. oven).

TIME: Bake layers 30 to 35 min.,
      oblong about 40 min.

155

ANGEL FOOD CAKES How our "angels" get their wings.

Read recipe
Preheat oven
Assemble ingredients
Collect utensils
Sift flour, measure sugar

Separate eggs while cold
Beat whites at room
temperature
Beat eggs with wire whip
for highest volume

2 Sift (3 times) part of sugar with flour. Measure egg whites into *large* bowl. Add cream of tartar and salt.

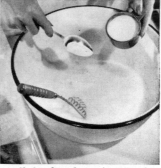

1 Separate eggs while cold. Drain off each white into saucedish. Drop yolks into cup. Pour whites into measuring cup. Bring to room temperature (70°).

3 Beat whites until frothy, beat in remaining sugar (2 tbsp. at time), beating 10 sec. after each addition. (Med. speed on mixer.)

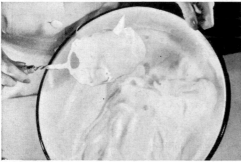

4 Continue beating until meringue is very *firm* and holds stiff *straight* peaks when wire whip is pulled up. (Use high speed on mixer.) Fold in flavorings.

5 Sift flour-sugar mixture (3 tbsp. at a time) over meringue. Cut and fold in gently, with wire whip or spatula, until flour-sugar mixture disappears each time.

7 Push and level batter gently against tube and sides to prevent large holes.

6 Carefully push batter with rubber scraper into deep tube pan.

8 Bake until no imprint remains when finger lightly touches top of cake. Invert immediately on funnel. Let hang until cold.

ANGEL FOOD CAKE (⚗ Recipe)

So tender ... light as air ... fluffy as a cloud. But very stiff beating of the egg whites is required. Mrs. William Lilliquist (we know her as "Aunt Nannie") of Minneapolis, who loves Angel Foods above all other cakes and makes perfect ones, still prefers to beat the egg whites on a large turkey platter, using a wire whip.

	Angel Food Supreme	Angel Food De Luxe
Set out but do not grease	10x4″ tube pan	10x4″ tube pan

Measure and sift together 3 times..........	1 cup *sifted* SOFTASILK Flour
	¾ cup plus 2 tbsp. sugar
	   (granulated)
		1 cup
		1½ cups (sifted
		   confectioners')

Measure into large mixing bowl	1½ cups egg whites (12) 1½ tsp. cream of tartar ¼ tsp. salt	1½ cups (12) 1½ tsp. ¼ tsp.

Beat with wire whip or electric mixer until foamy.
Gradually add, 2 tbsp. at a time..........
	¾ cup sugar
	   (granulated)
		1 cup
		   (granulated)

Continue beating until meringue holds stiff peaks. Fold in........................	1½ tsp. vanilla ½ tsp. almond flavoring	1½ tsp. ½ tsp.
Sift gradually	flour-sugar mixture	
over	the meringue	

Fold in gently just until the flour-sugar mixture disappears. Push batter into ungreased tube pan. Gently cut through batter with a knife. Bake until top springs back when lightly touched. Invert on a funnel. Let hang until cold.

TEMPERATURE: 375° (quick mod. oven).

TIME: Bake 30 to 35 min.

CHOCOLATE ANGEL FOOD

Follow ⚗ recipe for Angel Food De Luxe above—*except* substitute ¼ cup cocoa for ¼ cup of the flour (sift together 3 times). Omit almond flavoring.

GOLD-SILVER ANGEL FOOD

Follow ⚗ recipe for Angel Food De Luxe above—*except* omit flavoring. Divide batter into 2 parts. Into 1 part, fold 4 well beaten egg yolks and 1 tsp. lemon flavoring. Fold 1 tsp. vanilla into other part. Drop by spoonfuls into pan, alternating white and yellow batter. Cut around through batter with knife 5 or 6 times.

ALMOND CREAM ANGEL FOOD

Made for one of our early ads by Esther Bierman, then on our staff, now Mrs. John Simon of Portland, Oregon.

For this and other special Angel Food Desserts, see pp. 246–247.

STRAWBERRY GLAZE

Perfect to spread thinly over angel food, sponge, chiffon cakes. Let drip irregularly down the sides.

Mix thoroughly 2 cups *sifted* confectioners' sugar, dash of salt, 2 tsp. lemon juice, 2 to 4 tbsp. crushed strawberries.

COCONUT ANGEL FOOD

"For birthdays, I sometimes frost it with a yellow icing, add lighted yellow candles, and encircle it with a wreath of green leaves," says Mrs. Glenn M. Lewis of Knollwood, Hopkins, Minnesota, an authority on home beautification.

Follow either ⚗ recipe above—*except* fold in (in 2 additions) 1 cup shredded coconut.

CHERRY ANGEL FOOD CAKE

Follow ⚗ recipe for Angel Food De Luxe above—*except*, at the last, fold in ½ cup chopped maraschino cherries drained on paper towel.

LOVELIGHT YELLOW CHIFFON CAKE (🖋 Recipe)
Delicate and feathery light. The name was inspired by the comments of our home testers . . . many of whom said, "My husband is especially fond of this cake. It's just the kind he loves best!"

Grease and flour......................
> 2 8 or 9x1½" layer pans
> or 13x9" oblong pan

Sift together into bowl..................
> 2¼ cups *sifted* SOFTASILK Flour
> 1 cup sugar
> 3 tsp. baking powder
> 1 tsp. salt

Add...............................
> ⅓ cup cooking (salad) oil or soft butter
> ½ cup milk
> 1½ tsp. flavoring

Beat 1 min.

Add...............................
> another ½ cup milk
> 2 egg yolks

Beat 1 more min.

Fold in very stiff meringue of.............
> 2 egg whites
> ½ cup sugar

Pour into prepared pans. Bake until cake tests done. Cool. Frost with a fluffy white icing and sprinkle with coconut.

TEMPERATURE: 350° (mod. oven).
TIME: Bake 8" layers 30 to 35 min.,
9" layers 25 to 30 min.,
oblong 40 to 45 min.

LOVELIGHT CHOCOLATE CHIP CHIFFON CAKE

Follow 🖋 recipe above—*except* fold in 2 sq. unsweetened chocolate (2 oz.), grated med. fine. Add after meringue.

LOVELIGHT SPICE CHIFFON CAKE

Prepare pans and bake as in 🖋 recipe above.

Sift together into bowl . . .
> 2¼ cups *sifted* SOFTASILK Flour
> 1 tsp. baking powder
> ¾ tsp. soda
> 1 tsp. salt
> ¾ tsp. *each* nutmeg, cloves, and cinnamon

Add . . .
> 1 cup brown sugar (packed)
> ⅓ cup cooking (salad) oil
> ⅔ cup buttermilk

Beat 1 min.

Add . . .
> another ⅓ cup buttermilk
> 2 egg yolks

Beat 1 more min.

Fold in very stiff meringue of . . .
> 2 egg whites
> ½ cup sugar

When cool, ice with Browned Butter Icing (*p. 177*) or a cooked white icing.

LOVELIGHT LEMON CHIFFON CAKE

Follow 🖋 recipe above—*except* add 1 tsp. grated lemon rind with the vanilla. Spread Egyptian Filling (*p. 182*) between cooled layers, a white icing over top and sides.

LOVELIGHT BANANA CHIFFON CAKE

Prepare pans and bake as in 🖋 recipe above.

Sift together into bowl . . .
> 2 cups *sifted* SOFTASILK Flour
> 1 cup sugar
> 1 tsp. baking powder
> 1 tsp. soda
> 1 tsp. salt

Add . . .
> ⅓ cup cooking (salad) oil
> 1 cup mashed, very ripe bananas
> ⅓ cup buttermilk or sour milk
> 1 tsp. vanilla

Beat 1 min.

Add . . .
> another ⅓ cup buttermilk
> 2 egg yolks

Beat 1 more min.

Fold in very stiff meringue of . . .
> 2 egg whites
> ⅓ cup sugar

Fold in gently . . .
> ½ cup chopped nuts, if desired

Ice cooled cake with Browned Butter Icing (*p. 177*) or a cooked white icing.

LOVELIGHT CHOCOLATE CHIFFON CAKE (✗ Recipe)

Grease and flour.	2 8 or 9x1½" layer pans or 13x9" oblong pan
Sift together into bowl.	1¾ cups *sifted* SOFTASILK Flour 1 cup sugar ¾ tsp. soda 1 tsp. salt
Add. . . . . Beat 1 min.	⅓ cup cooking (salad) oil ½ cup buttermilk
Add.	another ½ cup buttermilk 2 egg yolks 2 sq. unsweetened chocolate (2 oz.), melted
Beat 1 more min. Fold in very stiff meringue of.	2 egg whites ½ cup sugar

Pour into prepared pans. Bake until cake tests done. Cool. Frost with White Mountain Frosting (*p.180*) or Cocoa Fluff Topping (*below*).

TEMPERATURE: 350° (mod. oven).

TIME: Bake 8" layers 30 to 35 min., 9" layers 25 to 30 min., oblong 40 to 45 min.

LOVELIGHT CHOCOLATE CREAM CAKE

Follow ✗ recipe above. When cool, split each layer crosswise into 2 layers. Spread Cocoa Fluff Topping (*below*) between layers and over top and sides of cake.

COCOA FLUFF TOPPING

Mix in chilled bowl . . .

2 cups chilled whipping cream
1 cup *sifted* confectioners' sugar
½ cup cocoa
dash of salt

Beat until stiff.

LOVELIGHT CHOCOLATE CHIFFON CUPCAKES

Follow ✗ recipe above and pour batter into 24 greased or paper-lined med. muffin cups (fill ⅔ full). Bake. Cool. Frost with White Mountain Frosting (*p. 180*) or Cocoa Fluff Topping (*above*).

TEMPERATURE: 400° (mod. hot oven).

TIME: Bake 18 to 20 min.

HOW TO QUICK-FROST CUPCAKES

Twirl the cupcake right in the frosting bowl.

Lovelight Chocolate Cream Cake

LOVELIGHT PEANUT BUTTER CHIFFON CAKE

Follow ✗ recipe above for method—*except* add brown sugar and peanut butter with oil and first addition of milk.

2¼ cups *sifted* SOFTASILK Flour
3 tsp. baking powder
¼ tsp. soda
1 tsp. salt

1 cup brown sugar (packed)
⅓ cup chunk-style peanut butter
⅓ cup cooking (salad) oil
½ cup milk

2 egg yolks
another ¾ cup milk

2 egg whites
½ cup granulated sugar

Finish with Peanut Butter Icing (*p. 181*).

159

CHIFFON CAKE
topped with Sweetened Whipped Cream and Fresh Berries

CHIFFON CAKE
finished with Strawberry Butter Icing

Read recipe   Assemble ingredients

Collect utensils   Preheat oven

Sift flour and measure ingredients

2 Beat with spoon until smooth.

1 Sift flour, sugar, baking powder, salt into mixing bowl. Make a "well," then add in order: oil, egg yolks, water, lemon rind, and flavoring.

3 Beat egg whites and cream of tartar in large bowl until they hold *very stiff* peaks. Do not underbeat. A dry rubber scraper drawn through them leaves a clean path.

4 Pour egg yolk mixture in thin stream over entire surface of egg whites, gently cutting and folding in with rubber spatula.

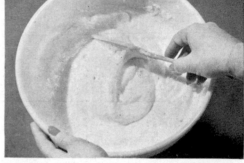

5 Fold gently ... bringing scraper across *bottom* of bowl, up the side and over. Turn bowl and continue until completely blended.

6 Pour into ungreased pan. Bake until surface springs back when lightly touched. Invert pan immediately on funnel. Let hang until cold. To remove, loosen with a spatula. Turn pan over and hit edge sharply on table.

7 Frost and trim cake as desired. This is the Peppermint Chip Chiffon (*p. 163*) with a cooked white frosting and crushed peppermint stick candy sprinkled over it. Chiffon cakes are also delicious unfrosted.

161

CHIFFON CAKE (⌀ Recipe)

CHIFFON CAKE (⌀ Recipe) Light as angel food, rich as butter cake. "It's the first thing I think of when planning a party," says Dorothy Quinn (Mrs. Fred J. Quinn) of Tajunga, California. "It's so easy to make, everyone likes it, and it can be served in so many glamorous ways."

	Large Cake	Small Cake
Set out but do not grease...............	10x4" tube pan or 13x9" oblong pan	9" tube pan or 9x5x3" loaf or 8 or 9" square pan
Sift together into bowl..................	2¼ cups *sifted* SOFTASILK or 2 cups *sifted* GOLD MEDAL Flour	1 cup plus 2 tbsp. or 1 cup
	1½ cups sugar	¾ cup
	3 tsp. baking powder	1½ tsp.
	1 tsp. salt	½ tsp.
Make a "well" and add in order..........	½ cup cooking (salad) oil	¼ cup
	5 egg yolks, unbeaten (if you use SOFTASILK) or 7 egg yolks, unbeaten (if you use GOLD MEDAL Flour)	2 yolks or 3 yolks
	¾ cup cold water	¼ cup plus 2 tbsp.
	2 tsp. vanilla	1 tsp.
Beat with spoon until smooth.	2 tsp. grated lemon rind	1 tsp.
Then measure into large mixing bowl.......	1 cup egg whites (7 or 8)	½ cup (4)
	½ tsp. cream of tartar	¼ tsp.

Beat until whites form very stiff peaks. Pour egg yolk mixture gradually over beaten whites, gently folding with rubber scraper just until blended. Pour into ungreased pan. Bake until top springs back when lightly touched. Invert on funnel. Let hang until cold.

TEMPERATURE AND TIME:
Bake 10" tube at 325° for 55 min., then at 350° for 10 to 15 min.
Bake 9" tube at 325° for 50 to 55 min.
Bake oblong cake at 350° for 45 to 50 min.
Bake loaf cake at 325° for 50 to 55 min.
Bake square cake at 350° for 30 to 35 min.

MAPLE PECAN CHIFFON

Elegant with Maple Butter Icing (p. 147).

Follow ⌀ recipe for Large Cake above—*except* omit vanilla and lemon rind. Sift only ¾ cup white sugar with the dry ingredients. Add ¾ cup brown sugar (packed, no lumps) to the sifted dry ingredients. Use 2 tsp. maple flavoring. Gently fold in at the last 1 cup very finely chopped pecans.

BUTTERSCOTCH CHIFFON

A sun-tanned favorite.

Follow ⌀ recipe for Large Cake above—*except* omit sugar and lemon rind. Add 2 cups brown sugar (packed) to sifted ingredients. Finish with Easy Penuche Icing (*p. 181*).

CHOCOLATE CHIP CHIFFON

Delicious chips all through.

Follow ⌀ recipe for Large Cake above—*except* increase sugar to 1¾ cups and omit rind. At the last, sprinkle over batter and fold in carefully with a few strokes 3 sq. unsweetened or sweet chocolate (3 oz.), shaved. Frost with Chocolate Butter Icing (*p. 177*).

SPICE CHIFFON

Finish with Browned Butter Icing (p. 177).

Follow ⌀ recipe for Large Cake above—*except* omit vanilla and lemon rind. Add to the dry ingredients 1 tsp. cinnamon, ½ tsp. *each* nutmeg, allspice, and cloves. 2 tbsp. caraway seeds may be added.

ORANGE CHIFFON Delicate and refreshing.

Follow ⌀ recipe for Large Cake above—*except* omit vanilla and lemon rind. Add 3 tbsp. grated orange rind. Finish with Orange Butter Icing (*p. 177*).

BIT O' WALNUT CHIFFON

Follow ♪ recipe for Large Cake, p. 162 —*except* omit rind. At the last, sprinkle over batter . . . gently folding in with a few strokes . . . 1 cup very finely chopped walnuts. (If black walnut flavor is desired, use black walnuts or ½ tsp. black walnut flavoring in place of vanilla.) Frost top and sides with Browned Butter Icing (*p. 177*) with toasted walnut halves.

HOLIDAY FRUIT CHIFFON

Follow ♪ recipe for Large Cake, p. 162 —*except* add ½ tsp. cinnamon to dry ingredients. At the last, sprinkle over batter . . . gently folding in with a few strokes . . . ¾ cup very finely cut-up candied cherries, ½ cup very finely chopped pecans, ¼ cup very finely cut-up citron.

MAHOGANY CHIFFON

Combine and let cool . . .
    ¾ cup boiling water
    ½ cup cocoa
Sift together into bowl . . .
    1¾ cups *sifted* SOFTASILK Flour
    1¾ cups sugar
    1½ tsp. soda
    1 tsp. salt
Make a "well" and add . . .
    ½ cup cooking (salad) oil
    7 unbeaten egg yolks (med.)
    the cooled cocoa mixture
    2 tsp. vanilla
Beat until smooth. Then measure into large mixing bowl and beat until very stiff . . .
    1 cup egg whites (7 or 8)
    ½ tsp. cream of tartar
To finish, see directions for Banana Chiffon beginning "Pour egg yolk mixture." Ice with Brown Beauty Icing (*p. 178*).

PEPPERMINT CHIP CHIFFON

Follow ♪ recipe for Large Cake, p. 162 —*except* omit lemon rind and use 1 tsp. peppermint flavoring in place of the vanilla. At the last, sprinkle over batter . . . gently folding in with a few strokes to give marbled effect . . . ½ tsp. red food coloring. To frost, see picture on p. 161.

CHERRY-NUT CHIFFON

Use a 10″ tube pan. Follow ♪ recipe for Large Cake, p. 162—*except* omit rind, use only 1 tsp. vanilla. Use ¼ cup maraschino cherry juice and ½ cup water for the liquid. At the last, sprinkle over batter . . . and fold in with a few strokes . . . ½ cup *each* very finely chopped nuts and finely chopped maraschino cherries, well drained. Bake at 325° for 65 to 70 min.

To cool a square or oblong cake . . . rest edges of pan on two other inverted pans.

When cold, loosen with spatula. Invert pan, hit sharply on table. Cake drops out.

BANANA CHIFFON

Sift together into bowl . . .
    2¼ cups *sifted* SOFTASILK Flour
    1½ cups sugar
    3 tsp. baking powder
    1 tsp. salt
Make a "well" and add . . .
    ½ cup cooking (salad) oil
    5 egg yolks, unbeaten
    ⅓ cup cold water
    1 cup mashed ripe bananas
    1 tsp. vanilla
Beat until smooth. Then measure into large mixing bowl and beat till very stiff . . .
    1 cup egg whites (7 or 8)
    ½ tsp. cream of tartar

Pour egg yolk mixture in thin stream over entire surface of egg whites, gently cutting and folding in with rubber spatula until completely blended. Pour into ungreased 10″ tube pan. Bake until cake tests done. Invert. Let hang until cold.
TEMPERATURE: 325° (slow mod. oven).
TIME: Bake 65 to 70 min.

FLUFFY SPONGE CAKE *A lovely, high, light sponge cake—easy for the amateur.*

Have ready but do not grease...........	10x4″ tube pan
Sift together and set aside...............	1½ cups *sifted* SOFTASILK Flour or 1½ cups *sifted* GOLD MEDAL Flour 1 tsp. baking powder ½ tsp. salt
Beat in small mixer bowl until very thick and lemon-colored.....................	6 egg yolks (about ½ cup)
Pour beaten yolks into large bowl and beat in gradually......................	1½ cups sugar
Beat dry ingredients in alternately (slowly . . . on low speed) with	⅓ cup cold water 2 tsp. vanilla 1 tsp. lemon flavoring 1 tsp. grated lemon rind, if desired
In large bowl, beat until stiff.............	6 egg whites (¾ cup) ½ tsp. cream of tartar

Gradually and gently fold egg yolk mixture into beaten whites. Pour into *ungreased* pan. Bake until top springs back when lightly touched. Turn pan upside down with tube over neck of funnel or bottle. Cool. Remove from pan.

TEMPERATURE: 325° (slow mod. oven).

TIME: Bake 60 to 65 min.

EGG YOLK SPONGE CAKE *Light and fluffy. Especially good with berries. And a wonderful way in which to use extra egg yolks.*

	For Large Cake	Small Cake
Grease and flour.....................	2 8 or 9″ layer pans or 13x9″ oblong pan	8 or 9″ layer pan or 8″ square pan
Sift together and set aside...............	1½ cups *sifted* SOFTASILK Flour 2 tsp. baking powder ½ tsp. salt	¾ cup 1 tsp. ¼ tsp.
Beat in small mixer bowl until very thick and lemon-colored.....................	6 egg yolks (½ cup)	3 (¼ cup)
Beat in gradually.....................	1 cup sugar	½ cup
(For large cake, pour egg-sugar mixture into large bowl.)		
Blend in slowly . . . on low speed.........	½ cup boiling water 2 tsp. vanilla 1 tsp. lemon flavoring	¼ cup 1 tsp. ½ tsp.

Quickly blend in dry ingredients. Pour immediately into prepared pans. Bake until top springs back when lightly touched. Let cool upright in pans 8 to 10 min., then remove.

TEMPERATURE: 350° (mod. oven).

TIME: Bake oblong about 30 min., layers and square about 25 min.

HOT WATER SPONGE CAKE
Light and fluffy. "Elegant with sweetened whipped cream and berries, peaches, or bananas," says Mrs. Parker Wagner of Richland, Washington, whose husband asks for this often.

Grease and flour.	9" square pan
Sift together and set aside.	⎧ 1¼ cups *sifted* SOFTASILK Flour ⎨ 1½ tsp. baking powder ⎩ ½ tsp. salt
Beat in small mixer bowl until very thick and lemon-colored.	3 eggs (½ to ⅔ cup)
Pour beaten eggs into large mixer bowl and beat in gradually.	¾ cup sugar
Blend in slowly . . . on low speed.	⎧ ⅓ cup hot water ⎨ 1 tsp. vanilla ⎩ ½ tsp. lemon flavoring
Quickly and thoroughly blend in the dry ingredients.	

Pour into prepared pan and put in oven *immediately*. Bake until cake tests done. Cool.

TEMPERATURE: 350° (mod. oven).

TIME: Bake 25 to 30 min.

JELLY ROLL JAMBOREE
Tired of jellies and jams? Try these Fillings (p. 182).

Clear Orange	Pineapple
Clear Lemon	Chocolate Cream

To use these special fillings in a jelly roll . . . roll up a plain Jelly Roll (*opposite*) right after baking. Let cool. Unroll. Spread with cooled filling and reroll.

STRAWBERRY CREAM ROLL
Less than an hour before serving, unroll Jelly Roll (*opposite*). Spread with about 1 cup Sweetened Whipped Cream (*p. 222*). Sprinkle with 2 cups sliced fresh strawberries. Reroll. Chill. Serve in thick slices.

JELLY ROLL

Lots of fun to make and serve. See "how to roll" in picture at left below.

Grease a 15½x10½" jelly roll pan and line bottom with greased brown paper or with aluminum foil.

Sift together and set aside . . .
> 1 cup *sifted* SOFTASILK Flour
> > or 1 cup *sifted* GOLD MEDAL Flour
> 1 tsp. baking powder
> ¼ tsp. salt

Beat in small mixer bowl until very thick and lemon-colored . . .
> 3 large eggs (⅔ cup)

Pour beaten eggs into large bowl.
Gradually beat in . . .
> 1 cup sugar

Blend in . . . on low speed . . .
> ⅓ cup water
> 1 tsp. vanilla

Slowly mix in dry ingredients . . . on low speed . . . just until batter is smooth. Pour into prepared pan. Bake until top springs back when lightly touched. Loosen edges and immediately turn upside down on a towel sprinkled with confectioners' sugar. Carefully remove paper. Trim off any stiff edges. While cake is still hot, roll cake and towel from narrow end. Cool on wire rack. Unroll cake, remove towel. Spread with soft (not syrupy) jelly or filling. Roll again. If desired, sprinkle with confectioners' sugar. Cut in 1" slices.

TEMPERATURE: 375° (quick mod. oven).

TIME: Bake 12 to 15 min.

BANANA-NUT CAKE *Wonderfully tender. Delicate flavor of ripe bananas.*

Grease and flour...................... 2 9" layer pans
                                or 13x9" oblong pan

Sift together.........................
- 2½ cups *sifted* SOFTASILK Flour
- 1⅔ cups sugar
- 1¼ tsp. baking powder
- 1¼ tsp. soda
- 1 tsp. salt

Add................................
- ⅔ cup soft shortening
- ⅓ cup buttermilk
- 1¼ cups mashed ripe bananas (about 3)

Beat 2 min.

Add................................
- 3 eggs (½ to ⅔ cup)
- another ⅓ cup buttermilk

Beat 2 more min.

Fold in............................. ⅔ cup finely chopped nuts

Pour into prepared pans. Bake until cake tests done. Cool. Finish with Butter Icing (*p. 177*) or "frost" with whipped cream . . . decorate with sliced bananas.

TEMPERATURE: 350° (mod. oven).

TIME: Bake layers about 35 min., oblong 45 to 50 min.

USE RIPE BANANAS

Bananas should be medium yellow with brown spots on the skins, but firm inside. Green tipped bananas aren't ripe.

RAISIN-NUT CAKE

Rich cake with the unusual flavor that buttermilk gives. Modern version of an 18th century recipe . . . when cakes with raisins or currants were favorites.

Grease and flour . . .
- 2 9" layer pans or 13x9" oblong pan

Sift together . . .
- 2 cups plus 2 tbsp. *sifted* GOLD MEDAL Flour
- 1 cup sugar
- 1 tsp. baking powder
- ¾ tsp. soda
- 1 tsp. salt

Add . . .
- ¾ cup brown sugar (packed)
- ½ cup soft shortening
- 1 cup buttermilk

Beat 2 min.

Add . . .
- 3 eggs (½ to ⅔ cup)

Beat 2 more min.

Fold in . . .
- ½ cup cut-up nuts
- ½ cup cut-up raisins

Pour into prepared pans. Bake until cake tests done. Cool. Frost with Easy Penuche Icing (*p. 181*) or White Fudge Frosting (*p. 181*).

TEMPERATURE: 350° (mod. oven).

TIME: Bake layers 35 to 40 min., oblong 45 to 50 min.

DATE-AND-NUT CAKE

Deliciously moist and fruity. Many like it unfrosted. But a penuche icing makes a perfect finish.

Grease and flour . . .
- 9" square pan

Pour . . .
- 1 cup hot water

over . . .
- 6½-oz. pkg. dates, finely cut (about 1¼ cups)

Let stand until cool.

Cream together until fluffy . . .
(Beat 5 min. high speed on mixer or by hand.)
- ¼ cup soft shortening
- 1 cup sugar
- 1 egg
- 1 tsp. vanilla

Sift together . . .
- 1⅔ cups *sifted* GOLD MEDAL Flour or 1¾ cups *sifted* SOFTASILK Flour
- 1 tsp. soda
- ½ tsp. salt

Mix in alternately with . . .
(Use low speed on mixer.)
- date-water mixture

Stir in . . .
- ½ cup chopped nuts

Pour into prepared pan. Bake. Cool. Frost with Easy Penuche Icing (*p. 181*).

TEMPERATURE: 350° (mod. oven).

TIME: Bake 40 to 45 min.

First, prepare fruits: slice finely and cut up (¼ to ½") citron, orange, and lemon peel. Cut other candied fruits larger. "Plump up" seedless raisins and currants (*see p. 28*): leave whole. Heat nuts and cut them up coarsely. When measuring raisins, cut-up candied peel, candied cherries, etc., remember that:

½ lb. = 1½ cups
¼ lb. = ¾ cup

FRUITCAKE (✍ Recipe for Basic Batter)

Line with heavy wrapping paper and grease.	2 9x5x3" loaf pans or 10x4" tube pan
Cream together until fluffy...............	{ 1 cup soft shortening { 2 cups brown sugar (packed)
Beat in............................	4 large eggs (1 cup)
Sift together........................	{ 3 cups *sifted* GOLD MEDAL Flour { 1 tsp. baking powder { 1 tsp. salt { spices as given in recipes below
Stir in alternately with.................	1 cup liquid (as given in recipes below)
Blend in...........................	candied fruit, nuts, etc.

Fill prepared pans almost full. Bake (cover with paper the last hr.) until toothpick stuck in the center comes out clean. Cool. Wrap in waxed paper or aluminum foil. In old days, fruitcakes were wrapped in wine-dampened cloth to keep and mellow. Store in airtight container in *cool* place. To glaze, see p. 179.

NOTE: For small cakes, use any small can or pudding mold.

TEMPERATURE: 300° (slow oven).

TIME: Bake loaf cakes 2½ to 3 hr.,
tube cake 3½ to 4 hr.,
small cakes about 1½ hr.

GOLDEN FRUITCAKE
A holiday tradition in the home of Mae Chesnut, formerly of our staff.

Follow ✍ recipe above and add 1 tsp. cinnamon to dry ingredients. For liquid, use ½ cup milk and ½ cup light jelly. Add 1 tsp. vanilla.

Blend in . . .
1 lb. white raisins
½ lb. citron
¼ lb. *each* candied cherries and pineapple
¼ lb. *each* candied orange and lemon peel
½ lb. nuts

HOLIDAY FRUITCAKE
From our good friend Jessie De Both (Mrs. Carl Dreutzer) of New York City.

Follow ✍ recipe above—*except* use 6 eggs.

Add to dry ingredients:
1 tsp. *each* cinnamon and nutmeg
½ tsp. *each* mace and cloves
½ tsp. soda
Increase liquid . . . using ¾ cup strong coffee, ½ cup tart jelly, and ½ cup molasses.
Blend in . . .
1 lb. seedless raisins
½ lb. *each* currants and dates
1 lb. mixed candied fruits
½ lb. nuts
grated rind and juice of 1 orange, 1 lemon

DARK FRUITCAKE
Less fruit—least expensive.

Follow ✍ recipe above. Add to the dry ingredients:
1 tsp. *each* cinnamon and mace
½ tsp. *each* nutmeg and allspice
¼ tsp. cloves
For liquid, use ½ cup fruit juice and ½ cup dark jelly beaten with fork.
Blend in . . .
1½ lb. seedless raisins
½ lb. *each* currants, citron, and nuts

WHITE FRUITCAKE
Christmastime choice of the Old South.

Follow ✍ recipe above for method—*except* bake in slow oven (275°) 2½ to 3 hr. But use:
{ 1½ cups soft shortening
{ 1½ cups sugar
{ 2¼ cups unbeaten eggs (about 9)
{ 3 cups *sifted* GOLD MEDAL Flour
{ 1½ tsp. baking powder
{ ¾ tsp. salt
{ ⅔ cup orange juice
{ 1 lb. *each* white raisins and candied cherries
{ ¾ lb. candied pineapple
{ ¼ lb. *each* candied citron and orange peel
{ ½ lb. *each* coconut (2 4-oz. cans or 3½
{ cups), blanched almonds, and pecans

LOAF O' GOLD CAKE (✍ Recipe) Modification of the original Pound Cake . . . in which one pound of each ingredient was used. With the modern ingredients, the cake recipe also had to be changed. Since the batter is very stiff, an electric mixer is a great help.

Grease and line with paper . . . . 9x5x3" loaf pan (see p. 137)

Sift together into bowl . . . .
- 2¼ cups *sifted* SOFTASILK Flour
  or 1¾ cups *sifted* GOLD MEDAL Flour
- 1 cup sugar
- 2 tsp. baking powder
- 1 tsp. salt

Add . . . .
- ½ cup soft shortening (half butter)
- 1 tsp. vanilla
- 5 egg yolks (⅜ cup), unbeaten
- *½ cup milk

Beat 2 min.
Add . . . . *another ¼ cup milk
Beat 2 more min.

Spoon batter into prepared pan. Bake. Cool and finish with Orange Glaze (*at right below*).

If GOLD MEDAL Flour is used, add the entire ¾ cup milk at once.

TEMPERATURE: 350° (mod. oven).
TIME: Bake 60 to 70 min.

CHOCOLATE CHIP LOAF CAKE

Delicious new flavor for pound cake.

Follow ✍ recipe above—*except*, after mixing, fold in 2 sq. unsweetened chocolate (2 oz.), coarsely grated, and ½ cup chopped nuts.

PECAN LOAF CAKE

A lovely white pound-like cake with nuts all the way through it.

Grease and line with paper . . .
    9x5x3" loaf pan (see p. 137)

Sift together into bowl . . .
    2 cups *sifted* SOFTASILK Flour
    1¼ cups sugar
    1½ tsp. baking powder
    1 tsp. salt

Add . . .
    ½ cup soft shortening
    ½ cup milk
    1 tsp. vanilla

Beat 2 min.

Add . . .
    4 egg whites (½ to ⅔ cup)

Beat 2 more min.

Fold in . . .
    ½ cup chopped pecans (toasted, if desired)

Pour into prepared pan. Arrange pecan halves on top of batter, if desired. Bake. Lift out of pan and cool.

TEMPERATURE: 350° (mod. oven).
TIME: Bake 60 to 65 min.

ORANGE GLAZE

Very thin. It soaks into the warm cake, making it moist and giving it an orange flavor.

Mix . . .
    ½ cup orange juice
    ½ tsp. grated orange rind
    1 cup *sifted* confectioners' sugar

Let stand on top of oven while baking cake, stirring occasionally. When cake is baked, remove from pan and punch holes on top surface with a fork. Pour the warm glaze, a little at a time, over the top.

Punch holes in cake with fork.

Dribble warm glaze over the top.

ESKIMO IGLOO CAKE

Bake any layer cake you wish—white, yellow, chocolate, etc. Make 1½ times White Mountain Frosting (*p. 180*). Prepare a special chocolate mixture by melting together over hot water 1 sq. unsweetened chocolate (1 oz.) and ¼ tsp. shortening.

How to decorate cake:

Cut each layer in half. Spread icing on one side of all halves except one. Set halves side by side on their cut edges with icing between to form a long rounded cake which makes the igloo. Frost the semicircular top and ends with the remaining icing. To make ice blocks on igloo, mark icing into squares by dripping melted chocolate mixture from end of teaspoon.

How to cut cake:

Cut crosswise in half, then cut from either flat end of cake to center. This gives flat slices of cake with icing on the top and on the sides.

FIELD DAISY CAKE

Very appropriate for summer.

Bake any chocolate cake you wish in layers. Frost with Chocolate Butter Icing (*p. 177*).

How to decorate cake:

Snip top half of 6 marshmallows into 6 sections, cutting about ¾ of way through marshmallows. Spread sections gently, pinching to resemble petals. Arrange on top of frosted cake. In center of each flower, place small yellow gumdrop. At sides of each flower, place green gumdrop leaves or pieces of citron cut to resemble leaves.

A DAY-AT-THE-ZOO CAKE

Bake any cake you wish as long as recipe calls for a 13x9″ pan. Then make 1½ times the recipe for White Mountain Frosting (*p. 180*) or Butter Icing (*p. 177*). Tint orange or green with food coloring

How to decorate cake:

Frost cake, making icing on top about ¼″ thick. Decorate by spacing animal crackers about 1″ apart around top of cake, pressing crackers gently into icing to hold upright. Form a rectangle in center of oblong cake by setting candles into icing. Decorate sides of cake by pressing additional animal crackers flat against icing. If desired, dip animal crackers in 2 sq. unsweetened chocolate (2 oz.) melted with ½ tsp. shortening. Let dry on a wire rack.

FUDGE SUNDAE CAKE

The sauce may be passed at the table.

Cover top of 8 or 9″ square chocolate cake with a fluffy white frosting. Pour Fudge Sundae Sauce (*below*) over frosting to cover it . . . letting it drip down sides.

FUDGE SUNDAE SAUCE

Combine in saucepan and stir over low heat until smooth and creamy . . .

6-oz. pkg. semi-sweet chocolate pieces
2 tbsp. light corn syrup
3 tbsp. cream
1 tbsp. butter

169

DO IT YOURSELF

Yes, you can easily be famous in your community for your always-perfect cakes. You don't have to be a born cook. It's easy to make a perfect cake if you have good ingredients, the right recipe, and follow it exactly.

Every one of our recipes has been tested in home kitchens as well as in our own Betty Crocker kitchens.

TO MAKE THAT PERFECT CAKE, FOLLOW THESE RULES

1 USE HIGH QUALITY INGREDIENTS—always those called for. Substitutes may give you a failure instead of a triumph.

Flour is the foundation of your cake, so the right kind and amount is essential. In some types of cakes we use cake flour (Softasilk), in others all-purpose flour (Gold Medal), while in a few cakes either will be successful. For the best results, be sure to use the kind of flour called for in the recipe.

Sugar means granulated white sugar, either cane or beet. When brown or confectioners' sugar is intended, it is specified in the recipe. These different sugars are not interchangeable because they vary in composition.

Baking Powder means double-action baking powder such as Calumet, Clabber Girl, Davis' OK, KC. If you use single-action baking powder such as Royal, Schilling, Rumford, Dr. Price, Jewel Tea, and Davis' Phosphate, sprinkle it over batter during last minute of beating when making Double-quick cakes. Then finish beating and bake immediately.

Eggs should be measured if the recipe directs it. Adding that "extra" egg does not make a cake better and may mean a failure.

Liquids vary. Use the kind called for. Buttermilk and sour milk are interchangeable.

Shortenings are very important. They often indicate the method used in making the cake. Hydrogenated shortenings such as Crisco, Spry, Snowdrift, should always be used in Double-quick cakes. Part butter (don't use more than half) will add the flavor so rich

and delicious in white and yellow cakes. Oil or melted shortening should be used only when the recipe calls for it.

Chocolate means unsweetened chocolate. It is not interchangeable with cocoa in cakes. Some of our recipes use one and some use the other.

2 CHOOSE YOUR METHOD WISELY

In making cakes with shortening, you will want to use the method that suits your taste, your time, and your equipment.

Creaming Method is the old familiar time-honored way of making cake—the kind you may want to make when you have both time and inclination. The creaming method can be done by hand or by mixer.

Double-quick Method was developed primarily for the mixer and is a simpler, quicker way to make a light, fine-grained cake. Double-quick cakes may also be made by hand. Be sure to count actual beating time or strokes.

3 USE ACCURATE MEASUREMENTS

A cake recipe, like a druggist's prescription, is a delicately balanced formula. Level measurements in standard measuring cups and spoons are essential.

4 WATCH THE BAKING TIME CAREFULLY

Underbaking will cause a cake to sink— Sponge, Angel Food, or Chiffon Cakes may fall out of the pan.

Overbaking dries out a cake and causes shrinkage.

If your oven seems to bake too fast or too slow, you should have it checked by the local utility company.

5 STORE YOUR CAKE PROPERLY

After the cake is cool, store it in a container with a tight cover; or invert a large bowl over the cake plate.

Frostings Dress the Cake

A BUTTER ICING is like a favorite cotton dress ... simple and easy to put on ... cooked white frostings like a perky street ensemble ... and the extra touches of tinted coconut, toasted nuts, or allegretti are the gay accessories that make a costume "special." Your family will enjoy your "dressed-up" cakes the more because they look so pretty.

Betty Crocker

THERE'S A FROSTING FOR EVERY CAKE

Below are listed a few suggestions from the many in this chapter.

Homemade Candy Brings Compliments

Homemade candies, an old-fashioned art,
Assemble your ingredients and then, just start.

Below are listed recipes for some of the many treats you will find in this chapter.

BE SURE WITH A THERMOMETER!

For best results with cooked frostings, use a "candy" thermometer. Follow the cold water tests given in each recipe, if you don't have a thermometer. Give one as a gift to the next bride.

EASY-TO-MAKE DECORATING TUBE

See p. 188.

QUICKEST-EVER FROSTINGS

Easy to make with the Betty Crocker Instant Frosting Mixes, such as Chocolate Fudge, Chocolate Malt, Peanut Creme, and Angel Fluff. Just follow the simple directions on the package.

HOW TO FROST A 2-LAYER CAKE: Frost as soon as thoroughly cool. Brush away crumbs.

Place layer upside down on plate. Spread with filling or frosting. Let stand until set.

Place remaining layer right side up on top of filling. Frost top and sides with spatula.

Spread lightly and make attractive swirls, ridges, with outer ridge to shape up cake.

JIFFY CAKE FILLINGS

Prepare quick pudding mixes according to directions on package. The uncooked instant type is not satisfactory for this.

TO MAKE CHOCOLATE CURLS

Barely warm a bar of chocolate (do not melt). With razor blade, take off thin shavings from back side of bar . . . they curl up.

DO NOT BEAT . . . JUST STIR

This is the best rule for uncooked frostings high in shortening. To hasten thickening, place bowl in ice water. To regain gloss, add a few drops of hot water.

A "GIVE-AWAY" CAKE

Cut a cardboard several inches larger than the cake. Cover with foil. Frost and decorate cake on foil-covered cardboard. Garden flowers or fruits in season placed around the base make the cake special. A transparent wrap over entire cake with a pretty ribbon bow completes the gift.

EGG WHITES WON'T WAIT

Beaten egg whites break down if left standing too long waiting for the syrup to cook for a cooked white frosting or divinity candy.

# CANDY CARNIVAL

FANCY FUDGE FAVORITES

Fold quartered marshmallows and whole salted peanuts into beaten fudge. Pour into pan. When set, cut into squares.

DELICIOUS NUT CLUSTERS

Melt 6-oz. pkg. semi-sweet chocolate bits with 1 tbsp. butter. Fold in ¾ to 1 cup nuts. Drop onto waxed paper.

"TRUFFLES"

Drop small spoonfuls of Chocolate, Opera, or Penuche Fudge into chopped nuts, grated chocolate, or shredded coconut, etc. Roll to cover surface entirely.

EASY NUT ROLL

Turn out cooled fudge onto buttered waxed paper. Knead or fold over several times. Shape into 12″ roll. Place on waxed paper covered with cut-up nuts. Roll up in the paper. Chill. Slice.

DID THE FUDGE SUGAR?

Do not despair! Just add a bit of hot water or cream and return to boiling point. Then cool to lukewarm, and beat.

RIBBON FUDGE

Make Old-fashioned Chocolate Fudge (p. 183). When set, pour over it beaten Opera Fudge (p. 184). Let set. Then cut through both layers into squares. *36 layered 1½″ squares.*

CROWNING THE CAKE WITH GLORY

Directions on p. 172 (*opposite*).

NEW YEAR CALENDAR CAKE

Bake a favorite cake in 13x9″ oblong pan. Ice with a white frosting. Tint some of frosting with food coloring, and add a little extra confectioners' sugar. With decorating tube, mark January and year across top; mark off squares for days of month; initial days of week. Make simple scalloped edge; or press on colored flat mints for interesting effect.

LINCOLN'S LOG CAKE

Bake Chocolate Roll (*p. 249*) (*color picture on p. 253*). Run point of knife lengthwise in frosting to simulate bark. Sift cocoa lightly over top or sprinkle with a few chocolate decorating candies. Decorate with candied or maraschino cherries and cut-up gumdrops shaped into leaves.

WASHINGTON'S BIRTHDAY CAKE

Frost New Maraschino Cake (*p. 138*) with a white icing and trim with clusters of stemmed cherries. Use strips of green gumdrops or citron for leaves, and angelica for stems.

BLARNEY STONES

Frost 3x1″ oblongs of Sponge or Chiffon Cake with Butter Icing (*p. 177*). Roll in chopped peanuts. Serve each on green shamrock paper cut-out placed on lace paper doily.

EASTER BUNNY CAKE

Bake a white or yellow cake in layers. Cut one cooled layer in half to make 2 half circles. Put halves together with white frosting or whipped cream. Stand upright on cut edge. With sharp knife, cut a notch in edge to indicate the rabbit's head. Save cut-out piece for the tail. Secure with toothpick. Frost rabbit with remaining icing and cover generously with coconut. Cut ears of folded white paper; color inside pink with crayon. Use pink candies for eyes and nose. Coconut tinted green or paper grass and a few Easter eggs form an attractive nest around the bunny.

MAYPOLE CAKE

Bake Angel Food or Chiffon Cake in 10″ tube pan. Cover with pale green frosting. Sprinkle with green tinted coconut and a few tiny flowers or buds. In the center, place a candle or candlestick . . . winding it with two pastel colored ribbons with bow on top. Tie 12 sugar cubes with tiny ribbon to reach from edge of cake to top of "pole." Place sugar cubes around edge of cake. Greens and flowers at base of cake will make an attractive setting.

JUNE BRIDE SHOWER CAKE

Bake 2 Angel Food Cakes. Cool and remove from pans. Trim slice from side of each cake. Place cakes, flat sides together, on large serving tray (18x12″) or foil-covered heavy cardboard. Cover with a fluffy white frosting. Sprinkle with silver dragées. Smilax or huckleberry and sweetheart roses around the base enhance this beautiful cake.

DRUM CAKE

Bake a 2-layer cake. Frost with a white icing; sprinkle lightly with blue decorating sugar. Place strips of red stick gumdrops or pieces of candy sticks and white lifesaver-type candies on sides to simulate a drum. Lifesaver-type candies may be placed along top edge for candleholders if used for a birthday cake. Top cake with a pair of drumsticks of 2 candy sticks, crossed, with a hard candy ball at the end of each stick. Miniature flags stuck into gumdrops may be arranged on plate around edge of cake.

FOURTH OF JULY PICNIC CAKES

Frost cupcakes with a white frosting, top each with a tiny flag sticker fastened to a toothpick.

MOTHER'S DAY CAKE

Tuck red and white carnations into smilax or other greens around base of cake.

Bake a white cake in layers. Split each layer to make 4 layers in all. Spread between layers and frost sides with . . .

LEMON CREAM FILLING

Prepare and cool . . .
   Clear Lemon Filling (p. 182)
Whip . . .
   2 cups whipping cream
(Reserve 1 cup of the whipped cream for top of cake.)
Fold rest of whipped cream into . . .
   Clear Lemon Filling

Spread the 1 cup whipped cream over top of cake. Sprinkle sides of cake with finely shredded coconut. Refrigerate several hours.

GIFT PACKAGE CAKE

"To Dad on Father's Day."

Bake father's favorite cake in 9x5x3" or 10x5x3" pan, such as the Chocolate Chip Loaf Cake (*p. 168*). Place on oblong tray or plate. Ice with a chocolate frosting. Make white or pastel frosting ribbon tie, with bow design, on top. Use as table centerpiece with other wrapped small gifts surrounding it.

HEART PARTY CAKE

For the "Sweet Sixteen Party," Valentine's Day, a birthday, many other occasions. Maxine Utke (Mrs. Chester H. Utke), formerly of our staff, likes this cake on her Valentine birthday.

Bake New Maraschino Cherry Cake (*p. 141*) or a white cake delicately tinted pink in heart-shaped layer pans; or bake in round layer pans (then cut heart-shaped layers). Frost with a white icing tinted pink. Dot with rosebuds or forget-me-nots. Or sprinkle silver dragées over top and sides of cake.

FLOWER BASKET CUPCAKES

Decoration, favor, place card, dessert.

Bake cupcakes in heavy paper baking cups. Top with a white frosting. Cut small paper doily crisscross in center so it will slip over bottom for a ruffly edge at top of each cupcake. Attach pipe cleaner handles, tinted with vegetable coloring, with a tiny flower attached. Small name cards may be added.

FOOTBALL CAKE

Make a hit with the gang after the game.

Bake a chocolate cake in 13x9" oblong pan. Place on large tray or foil-covered cardboard. Cover top and sides with chocolate frosting. Sprinkle top with green decorating sugar. Make white lines with white sugar or frosting. Goal posts may be stick candy. Place a tiny toy football in center. Or make one by shaping a piece of apple or banana, then covering with melted chocolate.

HALLOWEEN PUMPKIN CAKE

Bake large Orange Chiffon Cake (*p. 162*). Place cake top-side-up on serving plate. With spatula cover sides, top, and inside center hole with a fluffy white frosting tinted orange (pumpkin color) with yellow and red food coloring. (Color about ¼ cup with green for the stem.) Smooth frosting in deep curves from top to bottom to resemble pumpkin. Make grooves in pumpkin by using tip of spatula, starting at bottom and going up to center. For the pumpkin stem, insert peeled banana in hole in center of cake. Use pieces of another banana as wedge to hold it firmly in place. Spread stem with the green tinted frosting. Serve the same day, removing the stem for cutting.

AUTUMN SYMPHONY CAKE

To grace the table for fall festivities.

Bake a spice cake (*p. 154*) in layers. Frost cake (on a stemmed cake plate) with a penuche frosting. Or use a white frosting tinted a delicate yellow. Tuck bronze mums around base of cake and 3 on top. Place plate with frosted cake on a large round plate or Lazy Susan. Arrange cluster of sugared green grapes and purple grapes, unshelled walnuts, and colored fall leaves on outer edge of Lazy Susan.

CHRISTMAS CANDLE CUPCAKES

They thrill the children—grownups, too.

Frost cupcakes with a fluffy white frosting. Place red candle in center of each cupcake, and decorate with small sprays of holly. Cut the red berries out of candied cherries and the leaves from citron.

Every day is someone's birthday.

January
Carnation — Garnet

A favorite cake with white frosting, moist snowy white coconut, 2 or 3 fresh red carnations on top.

February
Primrose — Amethyst

The birthday child's best liked cake with white frosting trimmed with cherries, cinnamon hearts, or peppermint candy.

March
Violet — Bloodstone

A cake baked in a tube pan (Angel, Sponge, or Chiffon) with delicately tinted icing and a bunch of fresh violets in a glass vase in the center hole.

April
Easter Lily — Diamond

The chosen cake baked in layers spread with luscious filling. Frost top and sides with a soft white frosting. Make little tinted swirls of frosting for candle holders.

May
Lily of the Valley — Emerald

A favorite cake frosted with a dark icing. Tie up tiny bouquets of lilies of the valley with emerald green ribbon and place around cake.

June
Rose — Moonstone

The special oblong cake with cooked white frosting—fresh strawberries folded in. Trim with whole berries (hulls left on) for color.

What month is your birth date?
What star shines on you?
Here are jewels and flowers
and birthday cakes, too!

July
Sweet Pea — Pearl

Frost a selected cake. Tie up little bunches of sweet peas with satin ribbon. Place around the cake and give to women guests.

August
Gladiolus — Sardonyx

Three layers of cake with filling and soft icing and individual flowers of assorted gladioli attractively arranged around base of cake.

September
Morning Glory — Sapphire

Cut layer cake in two. Place rounded edges together (butterfly fashion). Trim with white icing . . . sprinkle with blue sugar. Serve on blue plate. (Appropriate for twins' birthdays, too.)

October
Dahlia — Opal

The birthday child's favorite with Satiny Beige Frosting (p. 180) or Easy Penuche Icing (p. 181), toasted pecans, and flaming red dahlias or autumn leaves around base.

November
Chrysanthemum — Topaz

A rich white layer cake with lemon filling between layers and over the top. Ice entire cake with a white cooked frosting. Sprinkle with grated lemon and orange rind.

December
Holly — Turquoise

Trim a white frosted cake (using pastry tube) with gay red musical notes and "Happy Birthday." Place red candles in red holders. Sprigs of holly are appropriate.

Happy birthday to you!

A revolving musical cake plate that plays "Happy Birthday to You" adds to the joy of the birthday.

BUTTER ICING (⚲ Recipe) *For extra richness, add 1 egg yolk.*

Blend together . . . .
{ ⅓ cup soft butter
{ 3 cups *sifted* confectioners' sugar

Stir in until smooth . . . .
{ about 3 tbsp. cream
{ 1½ tsp. vanilla

AMOUNT: For 2 8 or 9″ layers
or 13x9″ oblong.

CHOCOLATE BUTTER ICING
Follow ⚲ recipe above—*except* stir 3 sq. unsweetened chocolate (3 oz.), melted, into blended mixture.

MOCHA BUTTER ICING
Follow ⚲ recipe above—*except* omit cream and vanilla, and blend in 2 tsp. powdered instant coffee dissolved in 2 tbsp. hot water. Stir in a few drops water if too thick.

BROWNED BUTTER ICING
Follow ⚲ recipe above—*except* brown butter in saucepan over med. heat until a delicate brown. Blend with sugar.

BUTTER DECORATING ICING
Tint as desired. Use vegetable shortening instead of butter for a very white icing.
Cream together thoroughly . . .
 ½ cup soft butter
 6 cups *sifted* confectioners' sugar
 ¼ cup cream
Add, beating until smooth and fluffy . . .
 4 egg whites, stiffly beaten
 1 tbsp. vanilla
AMOUNT: For 1 large special-occasion cake.

RICH ALMOND FROSTING
For top of 9″ square cake, 13x9″ oblong cake, or especially nice on angel food cake.
Mix thoroughly . . .
 ½ cup soft butter
 1¾ cups *sifted* confectioners' sugar
 1 unbeaten egg yolk
 ½ tsp. almond flavoring
 4 tsp. milk
Stir over ice water until thick enough to spread.

ORANGE (or LEMON) BUTTER ICING
Follow ⚲ recipe above—*except* omit vanilla, and in place of the cream, use orange (or lemon) juice. Blend in 1½ tbsp. grated rind for extra flavor.

PINEAPPLE BUTTER ICING
Follow ⚲ recipe above—*except* omit cream and vanilla. Stir in ⅓ cup well drained crushed pineapple.

STRAWBERRY BUTTER ICING
Follow ⚲ recipe above—*except* omit cream and vanilla. Stir in 3 to 4 tbsp. crushed fresh or frozen strawberries.

AS YOU LIKE IT FROSTING
To suit three different tastes.

Divide ⚲ recipe above into 3 parts. Into first part, blend 1 sq. unsweetened chocolate (1 oz.), melted. Into second part, blend grated rind of 1 orange. Tint orange with red and yellow food coloring. Leave third part plain.

Mark cake into thirds, and frost each third with one of the icings. Sprinkle chopped nuts over plain (white) section.

QUICK-AS-A-WINK CHOCOLATE FROSTING *Made with semi-sweet chocolate.*

Combine in saucepan . . . .
{ 6-oz. pkg. semi-sweet chocolate pieces
{ 2 tbsp. butter
{ 3 tbsp. milk

Stir over low heat until chocolate is *just* melted.
Remove from heat. Stir in . . . .   1 cup *sifted* confectioners' sugar
Beat until smooth, glossy, and easy to spread.   (If not glossy, stir in a few drops of hot
AMOUNT: For 8 or 9″ square.   water.)

For hobnail effect, twist tip of spoon in the icing.

BROWN BEAUTY ICING

Much like a cooked fudge frosting ... soft, dark, glossy, and moist.

Blend in mixing bowl ...
    1⅓ cups *sifted* confectioners' sugar
    ¼ cup soft shortening
    ¼ cup milk
    3 sq. unsweetened chocolate (3 oz.), melted
    1 tsp. vanilla
Add ...
    1 whole egg (or 3 egg yolks)

Beat with rotary beater *just* until frosting is smooth. Place bowl in ice water and *stir* until frosting is thick enough to spread. If frosting becomes too thick, dip bowl in hot water for a few seconds and stir to desired consistency.

AMOUNT: For 2 8 or 9″ layers
          or 13x9″ oblong.

GLOSSY CHOCOLATE ICING

Tastes like a cooked fudge frosting. Very dark and chocolatey. No eggs.

Melt together over hot water ...
    3 tbsp. shortening
    3 sq. unsweetened chocolate (3 oz.)
Blend in ...
    2 cups *sifted* confectioners' sugar
    ¼ tsp. salt
    ⅓ cup milk
    1 tsp. vanilla

Stir until smooth. Place bowl in ice water and continue stirring until thick enough to spread. Stir in ½ cup chopped nuts, if desired.

AMOUNT: For 2 8 or 9″ layers
          or 13x9″ oblong.

THIN CHOCOLATE ICING

For Boston Cream Pie, Cream Puffs, and such.

Melt together over hot water ...
    1 sq. unsweetened chocolate (1 oz.)
    1 tsp. butter
Remove from over hot water.
Blend in ...
    1 cup *sifted* confectioners' sugar
    2 tbsp. boiling water

Beat *only* until smooth but *not* stiff.

GLAMOROUS NUT TOPPING

Spread frosting between layers and on sides of layer cake. Stir cut-up pecans or walnuts into remaining frosting for top of the cake.

CREAMY COCOA ICING (⚖ Recipe)

A favorite dark icing using cocoa.

Sift together ...
    2⅔ cups *sifted* confectioners' sugar
    ⅓ cup cocoa
Add ...
    ⅓ cup soft butter
    3 to 4 tbsp. milk

Stir until well blended.

AMOUNT: For 2 8 or 9″ layers
          or 13x9″ oblong.

COCOA-MOCHA ICING

A spice cake takes this frosting treatment nicely.

Follow ⚖ recipe above—*except* use only 3 tbsp. cocoa. Dissolve 1 tbsp. powdered instant coffee in 2 tbsp. hot water and use in place of the milk.

COCOA-PEANUT BUTTER ICING

For peanut lovers. Try this on white cookies.

Follow ⚖ recipe above—*except* use chunk-style peanut butter in place of the butter. Use ¼ to ⅓ cup milk.

ROCKY ROAD FROSTING

"Candy on top of cake. And mmmm is it good!" says Shirley Busta of our staff.

Make any one of the chocolate icings on this page and blend in ...
    1 cup quartered marshmallows
    ½ cup salted peanuts

BROWN SUGAR MERINGUE

Especially delicious on a spice cake.

A few minutes before cake is removed from oven, beat until frothy . . .

    2 egg whites (¼ cup)

Gradually beat in until stiff . . .

    1 cup brown sugar (packed)
    1 tbsp. lemon juice

Spread on hot cake immediately.

Sprinkle with . . .

    ½ cup nuts, cut up

Bake 8 to 10 min. at 400° (mod. hot oven) to brown meringue.

CHOC-O-NUT TOPPING

Some in the middle; some on the top.

Mix . . .

    2 cups coconut, cut up
    ⅓ cup water
    ½ cup semi-sweet chocolate pieces, melted

Pour ½ of cake batter into prepared pan. Sprinkle with ½ of choc-o-nut mixture. Add remaining batter. Bake. As soon as cake is done, sprinkle with remaining choc-o-nut mixture.

CREAMY WHITE ICING

Never sugary, never grainy. S-m-o-o-t-h.

Melt in saucepan . . .

    ½ cup shortening (part butter)

Remove from heat. Blend in . . .

    2½ tbsp. flour
    ¼ tsp. salt

Stir in slowly . . .

    ½ cup milk

Bring to boil, stirring constantly.

Boil 1 min. Remove from heat. Stir in . . .

    about 3 cups *sifted* confectioners' sugar
    ½ tsp. vanilla

Stir until thick enough to spread. (Place pan in ice water while stirring to set the icing.)

CREAMY RAISIN OR NUT

Add about ½ cup cut-up raisins or nuts.

CREAMY ORANGE OR LEMON

Omit vanilla. In place of the milk, use orange or lemon juice. Add 1½ extra tbsp. flour. Add grated orange or lemon rind for extra flavor.

CREAMY FUDGE

Reduce shortening to ¼ cup. Add 2 sq. unsweetened chocolate (2 oz.), melted, after the sugar.

CREAMY BROWNED BUTTER

Use all butter. Brown it first. (*See p. 177.*)

BROILED ICING

Bubbles and browns under the broiler. Wonderful on Butterscotch Cake, Spice Cake, and Hot Water Sponge Cake.

Mix . . .

    ⅓ cup soft butter
    ⅔ cup brown sugar (packed)
    ¼ cup rich cream
    ½ cup nuts, cut up

Spread over top of warm cake. Place low under broiler until mixture browns. For extra goodness, add 1 cup moist shredded coconut.

PEANUT BUTTER BROILED ICING

Mix . . .

    ⅔ cup brown sugar (packed)
    ¼ cup soft butter
    ¼ cup cream
    ¼ cup peanut butter

Stir in . . .

    1 cup peanuts, chopped

Spread on warm cake, place low under broiler until mixture browns slightly.

FRUITCAKE GLAZE

A shiny finish for fruitcakes—not sticky.

Combine and bring just to a rolling boil . . .

    ½ cup light corn syrup
    ¼ cup water

Remove from heat. Cool to lukewarm. Pour over cold cake before or after storing.

Fruitcakes are usually decorated *after* storing. Dip underside of candied fruits in cooked white frosting or sugar-water syrup and press lightly into top surface. For candied fruit decorations, see p. 32.

WHIPPED CREAM TOPPINGS AND FILLINGS

Sweetened Whipped Cream (*p. 222*).
Fruited whipped creams (*pp. 247-248*).
Cocoa Fluff Filling and Topping (*p. 246*).

WHITE MOUNTAIN FROSTING
(✒ Recipe)

Soft, never grainy, spreads easily.

Mix in saucepan . . .
   ½ cup sugar
   2 tbsp. water
   ¼ cup light corn syrup

Cover saucepan, bring to rolling boil.

Remove cover and cook to 242° or until syrup spins a 6 to 8″ thread. Just before syrup is ready, beat until stiff enough to hold a point . . .
   2 egg whites (¼ cup)

Pour hot syrup very slowly in a thin stream into the beaten egg whites. Continue to beat until frosting holds peaks.

Blend in . . .
   1 tsp. vanilla

When spreading on cake, make pretty swirls with spatula.

AMOUNT: For 2 8 or 9″ layers
           or 13x9″ oblong.

PINK MOUNTAIN FROSTING

Follow ✒ recipe above—*except* use 2 tbsp. maraschino cherry juice in place of water.

LEMON FROSTING

Follow ✒ recipe above—*except*, in place of vanilla, use 1 tbsp. lemon juice and fold in a little grated lemon rind.

CHOCOLATE REVEL FROSTING

Follow ✒ recipe above. At the very last, fold in 1 sq. unsweetened chocolate (1 oz.), *coarsely grated*, or ½ cup semi-sweet chocolate pieces.

MARSHMALLOW FROSTING

Follow ✒ recipe above. At the last, fold in 6 to 8 quartered soft marshmallows.

ROSES IN SNOW CAKE

A favorite for Mother's Day.

Cover top and sides of a rich white cake with cooked white frosting. Sprinkle lavishly with moist shredded coconut. Lay 2 or 3 fresh red roses on the top.

Boil syrup until it spins a 6 to 8″ thread (242°).

Pour very slowly into stiffly beaten egg whites. Continue beating until frosting holds its shape.

COMFORT FROSTING

Divinity type.

Follow ✒ recipe at left above for method. But use:
   1½ cups sugar
   1 tbsp. light corn syrup
   ½ cup water
   2 egg whites (¼ cup)
   1 tsp. vanilla

PINEAPPLE FROSTING

Follow ✒ recipe at left above—*except*, at the last, fold in ½ cup *well drained*, crushed pineapple and 1 tsp. grated lemon rind. Omit vanilla.

TUTTI-FRUTTI FROSTING

Follow ✒ recipe at left above. At the very last, fold in nuts, candied cherries, dates, and raisins (all chopped).

SATINY BEIGE FROSTING

Follow ✒ recipe at left above—*except* use brown sugar in place of granulated. Use only ½ tsp. vanilla.

PEPPERMINT FROSTING

Follow ✒ recipe at left above—*except* fold in, after beating, ½ tsp. peppermint flavoring or ⅓ cup coarsely crushed peppermint stick candy.

GUEST'S NAME CAKE

The cake with the personal touch.

Bake Jelly Roll (*p. 165*). Roll up in towel to cool. Unroll and spread with whipped cream. Roll up and ice with chocolate frosting. Write names of guests with Easy Decorating Icing (*p. 188*) across roll (name will be on each slice). Store in refrigerator until serving time. Cut slices between names and serve on a round of ice cream.

DOUBLE-BOILER FROSTING
(7-Minute) (✒ Recipe)

	2 8 or 9″ layers	For 13x9″ oblong

Combine in top of double boiler . . .

2 egg whites (¼ cup)	1 (2 tbsp.)
1½ cups sugar	¾ cup
¼ tsp. cream of tartar or	⅛ tsp.
1 tbsp. light corn syrup	or 1½ tsp.
⅓ cup water	3 tbsp.

Place over boiling water and beat with rotary beater until mixture stands in stiff peaks. Scrape bottom and sides of pan occasionally. Fold in . . .

1 tsp. vanilla	½ tsp.

STRAWBERRY ICING

Follow ✒ recipe above—*except* use juice from frozen or fresh strawberries in place of the water.

LEMON BUTTER FLUFF ICING

Made with cream cheese. So delicious on angel food, sponge, and chiffon cakes. Enough for 1 large cake.

Combine and beat until light and fluffy . . .

3-oz. pkg. cream cheese (room temperature)
2 tbsp. cream
½ cup soft butter (¼ lb.)
4 cups *sifted* confectioners' sugar
1 tbsp. lemon juice
2 to 3 tsp. grated lemon rind
1 tsp. vanilla

MINUTE FUDGE FROSTING (✒ Recipe)

Quick. Sure. Creamy.

Mix in saucepan . . .

2 cups sugar
¼ cup light corn syrup
½ cup milk
½ cup shortening
2 sq. unsweetened chocolate (2 oz.), cut up
¼ tsp. salt

Stir over low heat until chocolate and shortening melt. Bring to a full rolling boil, stirring constantly. Boil 1 min. (220°). Remove from heat and beat until lukewarm (120°). Stir in . . .

1 tsp. vanilla

Continue beating until a smooth spreading consistency.

AMOUNT: For 2 8 or 9″ layers
or 13x9″ oblong.

MINUTE PENUCHE FROSTING

Follow ✒ recipe above—*except* use brown sugar in place of granulated. Omit corn syrup and chocolate.

PRIZE FUDGE FROSTING (✒ Recipe)

> When fudge-type frostings become too *thick* to spread, add a little cream as needed. When too *thin*, add *sifted* confectioners' sugar.

Mix in saucepan . . .

1½ cups sugar
½ cup water
1 tbsp. light corn syrup
1 tbsp. butter
2 sq. unsweetened chocolate (2 oz.), cut up

Cover and cook slowly until mixture boils. Remove cover and cook without stirring until a little dropped into cold water forms a soft ball (234°). Remove from heat; let stand until cool. Add . . .

1 tsp. vanilla

Beat until thick enough to spread.

AMOUNT: For 9″ square or 13x9″ oblong.

WHITE FUDGE FROSTING

Delicious on spice and chocolate cakes.

Follow ✒ recipe above—*except* omit the chocolate and use sour cream or rich milk in place of water. Fold in cut-up seedless raisins, if desired.

PEANUT BUTTER ICING

Glossy and creamy. Especially good on Peanut Butter Cake (p. 155).

Stir together until creamy . . .

¼ cup chunk-style peanut butter
3 cups *sifted* confectioners' sugar
¼ to ⅓ cup milk

AMOUNT: For 2 8 or 9″ layers
or 13x9″ oblong.

EASY PENUCHE ICING

Perfect on date, spice, whole egg, or chocolate cakes.

Melt in saucepan . . .

½ cup butter

Stir in . . .

1 cup brown sugar (packed)

Boil and stir over low heat 2 min.

Stir in . . .

¼ cup milk

Bring to boil, stirring constantly. Cool to lukewarm (120°). Gradually stir in . . .

1¾ to 2 cups *sifted* confectioners' sugar

Place pan in ice water and stir until thick enough to spread.

AMOUNT: For 2 8 or 9″ layers
or 13x9″ oblong.

CREAM FILLING (✎ Recipe)

So smooth and rich.

Mix in saucepan . . .
- ¼ cup sugar
- 1 tbsp. cornstarch
- ¼ tsp. salt

Stir in gradually . . .
- 1 cup milk

Bring to boil over med. heat, stirring constantly. Boil 1 min. Remove from heat. Stir at least half of hot mixture into . . .
- 1 egg yolk, slightly beaten

Blend into remaining mixture.
Boil 1 min. more. Remove from heat.
Blend in . . .
- 1 tbsp. butter
- 1 tsp. vanilla

Cool, stirring occasionally.

ALMOND CREAM FILLING

Follow ✎ recipe above—*except* use only ½ tsp. vanilla and add ¼ tsp. almond flavoring. Cool. Add ½ cup toasted chopped blanched almonds.

DATE OR FIG CREAM FILLING

Follow ✎ recipe above—*except* fold in ½ cup cut-up dates or figs and ½ cup toasted nuts (almonds, walnuts, pecans, or peanuts).

CHOCOLATE CREAM FILLING

Follow ✎ recipe above for method. Use:

¼ cup cocoa may be used in place of chocolate. Blend in with dry ingredients.

- ½ cup sugar
- 1 tbsp. cornstarch
- ¼ tsp. salt
- 1 sq. unsweetened chocolate (1 oz.), cut up
- 1 cup milk
- 1 egg yolk, slightly beaten
- 1 tbsp. butter
- ½ tsp. vanilla

EGYPTIAN FILLING

Custard type . . . enhanced with raisins and nuts.

Mix in saucepan . . .
- ⅔ cup sugar
- 2 egg yolks
- ⅔ cup cream (20%)
- 1 cup seedless raisins

Cook over low heat, stirring constantly, until slightly thickened (5 to 6 min.). Remove from heat. Add . . .
- ½ tsp. vanilla
- ½ cup chopped pecans

Cool thoroughly.

CLEAR LEMON FILLING (✎ Recipe)

Wonderfully tart and delicious.

Mix in saucepan . . .
- ¾ cup sugar
- 3 tbsp. cornstarch
- ¼ tsp. salt

Stir in gradually . . .
- ¾ cup water

Bring to boil over direct heat, stirring constantly. Boil 1 min. Remove from heat. Stir in . . .
- 1 tbsp. butter
- 2 tbsp. grated lemon rind

Add gradually . . .
- ⅓ cup lemon juice

Cool thoroughly.

RICH LEMON FILLING

Use the leftover egg whites in frosting.

Follow ✎ recipe above—*except*, after mixture has boiled 1 min., stir half of hot mixture into . . .

- 2 egg yolks, slightly beaten

Blend into remaining mixture. Boil 1 min. more. Remove from heat and add the butter, lemon rind, and juice.

CLEAR ORANGE FILLING

Refreshing. Full orange flavor.

Follow ✎ recipe above for method. Use:

Frozen reconstituted orange juice may be used.

- 1 cup sugar
- ¼ cup cornstarch
- ½ tsp. salt
- 1 cup orange juice
- 2 tbsp. butter
- 2 tbsp. grated orange rind
- 2 tbsp. lemon juice

PINEAPPLE FILLING

Follow ✎ recipe above for method. Use:

- ½ cup sugar
- 3 tbsp. cornstarch
- ½ tsp. salt
- ¾ cup pineapple juice
- about 1 cup crushed pineapple, well drained
- 1 tbsp. butter
- 1 tsp. lemon juice

Cool thoroughly.

TEEN-AGE SPECIAL

Combine in large home kitchen or amusement room.......................... special friends
favorite records
conversation
candy-making

"Stir gently" until well blended.
"Turn out" on a Friday night.
Let stand until "set" but not "chilled."
Serve often.

OLD-FASHIONED CHOCOLATE FUDGE (✐ Recipe)

Recalls to many their first cooking experience.

Combine in saucepan . . .
  2 cups sugar
  ⅔ cup milk
  2 sq. unsweetened chocolate (2 oz.)
      or ⅓ cup cocoa
  2 tbsp. light corn syrup
  ¼ tsp. salt

Stir over med. heat until chocolate melts and sugar dissolves. Cook to 234° or until a little dropped in cold water forms a soft ball. Stir occasionally. Remove from heat.

Add . . .
  2 tbsp. butter

Cool to lukewarm *without stirring.* Add . . .
  1 tsp. vanilla

Beat until thick and no longer glossy. Quickly stir in . . .
  ½ cup nuts

Pour into buttered 8 or 9″ square pan. When set, cut into squares.

AMOUNT: 36 (1½″) pieces.

PENUCHE

"Oh, how I love it!" exclaims Mrs. J. A. O'Gordon of St. Louis Park, Minnesota, as she passes Penuche in her antique silver bonbon dish.

Combine in saucepan . . .
  2 cups brown sugar (packed)
  1 cup sugar
  1 cup cream (20%)
  2 tbsp. light corn syrup
  ¼ tsp. salt

Stir over med. heat to dissolve sugar. Cook to 234° or until a little dropped in cold water forms a soft ball. Stir occasionally. Remove from heat.

Add . . .
  2 tbsp. butter

Let stand *without stirring* until bottom of pan is lukewarm (120°).

Add . . .
  1 tsp. vanilla
Beat until creamy.
Mix in . . .
  ½ cup chopped nuts

Pour into greased 8 or 9″ square pan. Cut into squares.

AMOUNT: 36 (1½″) pieces.

DIVINITY *Jan Korslund of our staff says: "This never-fail Divinity was often made Sunday afternoons in our farm home in Iowa. Black walnuts gathered from the tree in our yard made it extra delicious."*

Place in saucepan over low heat.......... { 4 cups sugar
1 cup light corn syrup
¾ cup water

Stir until sugar is dissolved; then cook without stirring to 255° (a little dropped into cold water forms a hard ball). Remove from heat and pour, beating constantly, in a fine stream into.............................. 3 egg whites, stiffly beaten

Continue beating until mixture holds its shape and loses its gloss. Add................. { 1 tsp. vanilla
1 cup broken nuts

Drop quickly from tip of spoon onto waxed paper in individual peaks . . . or spread in a buttered pan and cut into 1″ squares when firm.

AMOUNT: 8 doz. pieces.

TOFFEE FUDGE

Crispy toffee squares ... chocolate-coated tops. Mrs. H. E. Roy, well known in the musical circles of Minneapolis, Minnesota, makes this often for her family and friends.

Sprinkle on bottom of greased 9″ square pan ...
    1 cup pecans, chopped
Combine in saucepan ...
    ¾ cup brown sugar (packed)
    ½ cup butter
Bring to boil, stirring constantly, for 7 min. Remove from heat, and spread over nuts. Sprinkle over top ...
    ½ cup semi-sweet chocolate pieces
        or pieces of 4½-oz. milk chocolate bar

Cover pan so heat will melt chocolate. Spread evenly over top. Cut in squares while warm. Refrigerate to set.
AMOUNT: 36 1½″ pieces.

OPERA FUDGE

Follow recipe for Old-fashioned Chocolate Fudge (*p. 183*)—*except* omit the chocolate or cocoa.

CREAM CARAMELS

Chewy. Creamy-rich.
Sprinkle on bottom of buttered 8″ square pan ...
    ½ cup chopped nuts
Mix in saucepan ...
    2 cups sugar
    ¾ cup light corn syrup
    ½ cup butter
    1 cup cream (20%)
Bring to boil over low heat, stirring constantly. Then stir in gradually ...
    1 more cup cream

Continue to stir as mixture thickens, and cook to 250° or until a little dropped in cold water forms a hard ball. Remove from heat and pour over nuts in pan. When cold, cut into squares.
AMOUNT: 5 doz. caramels.

UNCOOKED FONDANT

Ideal for party candy variations.
Combine in mixing bowl ...
    1 egg white
    2 cups *sifted* confectioners' sugar
    2 tsp. butter
    ½ tsp. vanilla

Mix until creamy. Tint as desired with few drops of food coloring. Drop small spoonfuls onto waxed paper. Decorate with nuts, candied fruits, or silver dragées. Let stand to become firm.

QUICK CHOCOLATE FUDGE

Creamy and smooth ... always.
Place in mixing bowl ...
    1 cup semi-sweet chocolate pieces (6 oz.)
    4½-oz. milk chocolate bar, broken in pieces
    ⅔ cup marshmallow creme
    1 tbsp. butter
    1⅓ cups chopped nuts
Combine in saucepan ...
    ⅔ cup undiluted evaporated milk
    1½ cups sugar

Bring to boil over med. heat. Boil 5 min. or to 225°, stirring constantly. Remove from heat and pour over ingredients in bowl. Stir until chocolate melts and mixture is smooth. Pour into ungreased 9″ square pan. Cool, and cut into squares.
AMOUNT: 36 1½″ pieces.

ENGLISH ALMOND TOFFEE

Buttery-rich and brittle.
Combine in saucepan ...
    ⅔ cup butter
    ½ cup sugar
    ⅓ cup water
    ½ tsp. salt

Cook over low heat, stirring constantly until it boils. Cook without stirring to 236° or until a little dropped in cold water forms soft ball.
Add ...
    ⅔ cup blanched almonds
Continue cooking to 290° (soft crack stage), stirring constantly. Remove from heat. Mixture changes to a deep caramel color.
Stir in ...
    ¼ tsp. soda
Turn out onto greased baking sheet; spread to ¼″ thickness.
Immediately spread with ...
    ½ cup semi-sweet chocolate pieces
        or two ⅞-oz. milk chocolate bars
Spread chocolate over top as it melts.
Sprinkle with ...
    ½ cup chopped pecans
Cool. Break into pieces.

MINT WAFERS

Follow recipe for Uncooked Fondant at left—*except* use 2½ cups confectioners' sugar. Substitute peppermint flavoring for the vanilla. Tint in shades of delicate yellow, pink, and green. Knead with hands. Shape into 1″ balls; place on waxed paper and flatten with tines of a fork.

POPPED CORN

1 cup unpopped corn makes about 5 cups popped corn.

After popping, mix in melted butter or salad oil as desired; sprinkle with salt.

HURRY-UP "POPCORN"

Preferred by many.

Melt in heavy skillet . . .
2 to 4 tbsp. butter

Add . . .
4 cups KIX, CHEERIOS,
SUGAR JETS, or TRIX

½ tsp. salt
Stir over med. heat 5 min.

CARAMEL POPCORN

Have ready in large bowl . . .
3 qt. popped corn, KIX, CHEERIOS, SUGAR
JETS, or TRIX

Measure into saucepan . . .
1 cup sugar

Stir over low heat until melted and golden brown.

Stir in carefully . . .
¾ cup hot water
½ cup brown sugar (packed)

Cook to 238° or until a little dropped into cold water forms a soft ball. Pour over popped corn or other cereal. Mix gently to coat well. Press into balls or spread out to cool so that pieces separate.

EASY CARAMEL CORN

No syrup to cook . . . just dissolve caramels.

Stir over hot water until smooth . . .
½ lb. caramels (28)
2 tbsp. hot water

Pour over . . .
5 cups popped corn, KIX, CHEERIOS, SUGAR
JETS, or TRIX

Mix gently until blended. Drop by spoonfuls onto waxed paper.

AMOUNT: About 3 doz.

WHEATIES TING-A-LINGS

Melt over hot water . . .
2 6-oz. pkg. semi-sweet chocolate pieces

Cool at room temperature.

Mix in gently . . .
4 cups WHEATIES

Drop by tablespoonfuls onto waxed paper. Place in refrigerator to set (2 hr.).

AMOUNT: 42 clusters.

POPCORN BALLS (🦴 Recipe)

Make into interesting shapes for kiddies.

Have ready in large bowl . . .
7 cups popped corn, KIX, CHEERIOS, SUGAR
JETS, or TRIX

Mix in saucepan . . .
1 cup sugar
⅓ cup water
⅓ cup light corn syrup
1 tsp. salt
¼ cup butter

Cook to 250° or until a few drops form a hard ball when dropped into cold water. Remove from heat. Stir in . . .
1 tsp. vanilla

Pour in thin stream over the popped corn or other cereal, stirring constantly to mix well. Shape, with buttered hands, into balls or any of the shapes below.

AMOUNT: 12 to 15 large balls.

EASTER BUNNIES

Follow 🦴 recipe above—*except* form into bunny shapes. Shape slices of marshmallow for the ears, half marshmallow for the tail, and use pipe cleaners for the whiskers.

JACK-O-LANTERNS

Just the thing for "tricks or treats."

Follow 🦴 recipe above—*except* add a little red and yellow food coloring for an orange-colored syrup, and form into pumpkin shapes. Use small gumdrops for eyes and nose; corn candy for the teeth; a green gumdrop or jelly bean for the stem.

JET COMETS

These make a hit with Brownies and Cub Scouts.

Have ready in large bowl . . .
5 cups SUGAR JETS or TRIX

Mix in saucepan . . .
6-oz. pkg. semi-sweet chocolate pieces
½ cup peanut butter

Stir over low heat until chocolate is melted. Pour mixture over cereal stirring gently. Drop onto waxed paper into jet shapes. Insert small paper wings at sides cut from colored paper to resemble jets. Chill at least 2 hr. or overnight to set.

AMOUNT: 60 comets.

MARSHMALLOW BARS (⚘ Recipe)

Melt over hot water . . .
    ⅓ cup butter
    ½ lb. marshmallows (32)

Stir occasionally.

Measure into large greased bowl . . .
    5 cups KIX, CHEERIOS, SUGAR JETS, or TRIX

Stir gently to coat well. Pack into greased 9″ square pan. Cool. Cut into 3x1″ bars.
AMOUNT: 27 bars.

PEANUT BUTTER-MARSHMALLOW BARS

Follow ⚘ recipe above—*except* add ½ cup peanut butter to the butter and marshmallow mixture over hot water.

KIDDIE KONES

Serve ice cream in them for special treats.

Follow ⚘ recipe above—*except* pack, with greased hands, into 12 greased custard cups, leaving centers hollow. Cool thoroughly. Remove from cups before filling with ice cream.

CHRISTMAS TREES

For delightful favors at Christmastime.

Follow ⚘ recipe above—*except* pack lightly into 12 greased paper cone drinking cups. Insert wooden skewer in each to form trunk of tree. When cool, gently remove paper cups. Roll in fine colored candies or colored sugar. Push ends of skewers into large gumdrops or thick slices of apple so trees will stand upright.

LOLLIPOPS

Follow ⚘ recipe above—*except* press firmly into 2″ balls. Roll in crushed peppermint stick candy. Place ball on end of a peppermint stick or wooden skewer. Let stand to become firm.

AMOUNT: 2 doz. Lollipops.

WREATHS

Follow ⚘ recipe above—*except* press into greased 3½″ ring molds. Attach bright red bow; dot with cinnamon candies. Let stand to become firm.

AMOUNT: 10 Wreaths.

BIRDS' NESTS

Attractive place card favors for a child's party.

Make WHEATIES Ting-a-Lings (*p. 185*)—*except* hollow center of each slightly with back of spoon. When cool, fill with green tinted coconut and tiny jelly beans.

AMOUNT: 42 small nests.

GOLDEN BARS

So good, they'll vanish like magic!

Mix in large greased bowl . . .
    4 cups CHEERIOS
    1 cup salted peanuts
    1 cup coconut

Mix in saucepan . . .
    1 cup sugar
    ½ cup light corn syrup
    1 cup cream (20%)

Cook over low heat, stirring occasionally, to 236° or until a little dropped in cold water forms a soft ball. Remove from heat. Pour syrup mixture over CHEERIOS mixture. Mix well. Turn out into buttered 9″ square pan. With hand protected with waxed paper, pat out mixture evenly in pan. Cool. Cut into 2x1″ bars.

AMOUNT: 32 bars.

ELSIE'S NOUGAT BARS

From Elsie Martinson Allison whose children love them.

Melt over hot water . . .
    3 tbsp. butter
    ½ lb. marshmallows

Remove from heat. Fold in . . .
    4 cups KIX (or CHEERIOS)
    ¼ cup coarsely chopped nuts
    ½ cup moist shredded coconut
    ½ tsp. salt

Turn into buttered 8″ square pan. With hand protected by piece of waxed paper, pat out mixture evenly in pan. Pour over top 4-oz. sweet or semi-sweet chocolate, melted . . . spreading it in thin layer with rubber scraper or spatula. Chill until set (45 to 60 min.). Cut into 2x1″ bars.

AMOUNT: 32 bars.

A Full Cooky Jar Makes a Home "Homey"

Some of the sweetest memories of Home are bound up with Mother's Cooky Jar. Long after the spicy fragrance of her ginger cookies baking has faded into the years ... the thought of that ample cooky jar on the shelf will bring back vividly the old-time peace ... and comfort ... and security of Home.

Betty Crocker

THERE'S A COOKY FOR EVERY OCCASION

Below are listed a few suggestions from the many in this chapter.

COOKIES IN NO TIME
warm and fresh from the oven

REFRIGERATE THE DOUGH

Make up your favorite cooky dough and keep it chilled and covered in the refrigerator. Then just before or as soon as guests drop in, pop the cookies into the oven and put on the coffeepot.

or you may

FREEZE THE DOUGH to bake later

Wrap as directed on pp. 23–24. Store in freezer (up to 9 months). If shaped before freezing, dough need not be thawed before baking.

or you may

FREEZE COOKIES already baked

Cool cookies. Wrap as directed on pp. 23–24. Store in freezer (up to 6 months). Thaw with wrapping intact.

QUICK PARTY COOKIES

Use ready-made cookies from your neighborhood baker or grocer. Ice them with Easy-Creamy Icing (below) and decorate as you choose or as suggested on pp. 191, 213.

children love
PLACE CARD COOKIES

Write names on cookies with melted chocolate (using toothpick) or Easy-Creamy Decorating Icing (below) (using pastry tube or paper funnel).

lightning-quick
GINGER COOKIES
and BROWNIES

Easier than ever to make with Betty Crocker Gingerbread Mix and Betty Crocker Brownie Mix. Just follow simple directions on pkg.

OTHER DELICIOUS COOKIES
in a hurry

Spice. Chocolate Chip. Other varieties. All easily made from Betty Crocker Cake Mixes and Bisquick.

EASY-CREAMY ICING
Smooth-spreading.   Delicious.   Quick.

Blend 1 cup *sifted* confectioners' sugar, ¼ tsp. salt, ½ tsp. vanilla or other flavoring (lemon, almond, or peppermint, etc.), and liquid to make easy to spread (about 1 tbsp. water or 1½ tbsp. cream). Tint if desired with a few drops of food coloring. Spread on cookies with spatula or pastry brush.

EASY-CREAMY DECORATING ICING

Make same as Easy-Creamy Icing (above) —except use less liquid . . . only enough to make icing easy to force through pastry tube—yet hold its shape (about ¾ tbsp. water or 1 tbsp. cream). Pile into pastry tube and squeeze onto cookies in desired design.

All you have to do —

To make a paper funnel for use with decorating icing: cut off a tiny corner of an envelope. An excellent substitute for a pastry tube.

COOKIES

Won't you come into our kitchen and join us in our "Cooky Shines?" That used to mean tea parties, but it's what we call our sessions of cooky baking. We have lots of fun trying out all the delicious cookies that come to us from many lands. I'd like to show you the cookies most popular with staff members and friends who have shared their favorite recipes with us. You'll see many varieties in the color pictures on the next pages.

They're ever so easy to make! For we've worked out a new simplified method—a *double-quick* method! Takes less than half the usual mixing time! Would you like to know the secret? Then turn to the step-by-step pictures following. Could anything be easier? There's no laborious creaming, no separate beating of eggs, only one bowl!

Now turn to the recipe pages. You'll find all the little pointers you would notice if you were right in our kitchen. There's a brand-new feature which I think will be a big help to you. We tell how to judge when the cookies are done. We've tried to include all the hints, shortcuts, and tricks that save you time and work so you can delight your family with new treats each week.

Cookies bring such a big reward in cheer and satisfaction! They make hospitality so easy! And they're fun to share with friends and neighbors, near or far away. A little of your love, remember, goes with every gift you bake.

New Year Clock

Shamrock

Lincoln Log

Easter Flower

HOLIDAY COOKIES 'ROUND THE YEAR
For those special days at home, at school, or at play.
Directions on p. 191.

Valentine Heart

Halloween Cooky With Face

Washington Cherry Cooky

Christmas Star

 # A Year of Holiday Cookies

Other suggestions on p. 213.

NEW YEAR CLOCKS

Roll Light Dough for Merry Christmas Cookies (*p. 213*) ¼" thick. Cut into 2½" rounds. Bake. Cool. Frost with Easy-Creamy Icing (*p. 188*) (for faces). Mark hours and hands pointing to five minutes of twelve with melted chocolate (using toothpick for outlining).

LINCOLN LOGS

Cut chocolate-frosted Brownies (*p. 204*) in bars about 3x¾". Draw prongs of fork through icing down length of each to make it resemble a log. Decorate with star made of silver dragées or with a tiny silk or paper flag.

VALENTINE HEARTS

Roll dough for Ethel's Sugar Cookies (*p. 208*) or Butter Cookies (*p. 209*) ¹⁄₁₆" thick. Cut in heart shapes. Bake. Cool. Frost with pink-tinted Easy-Creamy Icing (*p. 188*). Sprinkle with lacy coconut or edge with silver dragées or tiny hearts.

WASHINGTON CHERRY COOKIES

Make Fruit-and/or-Nut Drops (*p. 196*) . . . using 1 cup candied cherries cut in halves for the fruit (no nuts). Cool. Frost with Easy-Creamy Icing (*p. 188*) or Marie's Chocolate Icing (*p. 204*). Decorate with bunches of cherries . . . cutting small red cherries from candied or maraschino cherries, stems and leaves from citron or green gumdrops.

SHAMROCKS FOR ST. PATRICK'S DAY

Roll dough for Ethel's Sugar Cookies (*p. 208*) or Butter Cookies (*p. 209*) ⅛" thick. Cut in shamrock shapes with club-shaped cutter. Bake. Cool. Frost with Easy-Creamy Icing (*p. 188*) tinted pale green. Center with deeper green candy shamrock or other St. Patrick's Day symbol.

EASTER FLOWERS

Tint dough for Ethel's Sugar Cookies (*p. 208*) or Butter Cookies (*p. 209*) pastel shades of pink, green, or yellow with a few drops of food coloring. Roll out ¹⁄₁₆" thick. Cut with little scalloped cutters for petal effect. Sprinkle with tinted sugar to match the dough before baking. Bits of candied orange peel or yellow gumdrops may be used for stamen centers.

HALLOWEEN COOKIES WITH FACES

Roll dough for Gingies (*p. 210*) ½" thick. Cut into 2½" rounds. Bake. Cool. Cover with orange-tinted Easy-Creamy Icing (*p. 188*). Make faces with melted chocolate (using toothpick for outlining).

CHRISTMAS STARS

Roll Light Dough for Merry Christmas Cookies (*p. 213*) ¼" thick. Cut in star shapes. Bake. Cool. Cover with Easy-Creamy Icing (*p. 188*). Sprinkle with sky blue sugar.

For Special Occasions

PATTERN COOKIES   DECORATED COOKIES

Cut in fancy shapes or decorated in a festive way, delicious cookies take on a party air. You will find it fun to use your own ingenuity in designing cookies appropriate to any occasion and color scheme.

PATTERNS

Star, heart, bell, diamond, animal, flower, and many other shapes are available in aluminum, tin, or plastic cutters in housewares departments.

Or you can have cutters of your own design made up by a local tinsmith.

Lacking either commercial cutters or specially made ones, you can still create any desired patterns or designs by cutting them out of cardboard, greasing or dusting them with flour, then laying them on the dough and cutting around them with a sharp knife.

ICINGS

Easy-Creamy Icing for frosting cookies. Recipe on p. 188.

Easy Decorating Icing for use with pastry tube or paper cornucopia. Recipe on p. 188.

Before You Start

Read through the recipe
Get together the ingredients
Collect the utensils
Heat up the oven
Measure the ingredients

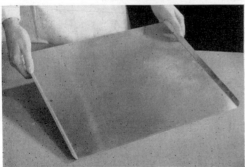

1 Select baking sheets or pans as indicated in each recipe. They should be *shiny* and bright for delicately browned crusts . . . and at least 1″ narrower and shorter than oven to let heat circulate around them.

Standard Sizes of Baking Sheets

14x10″   15½x12″   17x14″

2 If pan with sides is used for baking sheet, turn it upside down and bake cookies on the bottom . . . (insures even browning). Grease cool pans as indicated in recipes . . . with *unsalted* shortening.

3 Mix thoroughly the *softened* shortening, sugar, and eggs—also any molasses, syrup, or melted chocolate in the recipe.

4 Stir in the liquid and flavoring. (A few recipes indicate that liquid and flour mixture should be added alternately.)

5 Sift together and stir in the flour, salt, and leavening (baking powder *or* cream of tartar and soda)—also any spices in the recipe. Then, mix in any fruit or nuts.

6 Chill dough (covered), if indicated in recipe, to make it easy to handle. Then shape dough as directed in the recipe. Place on or in prepared pans.

7 Bake. If baking one sheet or pan at a time, place rack in center of oven; if two, place racks to divide oven into thirds. If cooky tops do not brown properly, move to higher rack last few minutes.

8 Look at cookies when minimum baking time is up. As soon as they are done (according to recipe), remove from oven. With a wide spatula, slip off baking sheet or out of pan onto wire rack to cool (as recipe directs).

Keep Them Perfect

Store cooled cookies properly to keep top eating quality.

Keep crisp, thin cookies in can with loose cover.

Keep soft cookies in airtight container (a covered earthen jar or a can with tight cover). Slices of apple or orange in jar help mellow and moisten cookies. Change fruit frequently.

HOW TO MAKE DROP COOKIES (preliminary steps on pp. 192–193)

1 Drop dough by rounded or heaping tea-spoonfuls, depending on size of cookies desired. With another teaspoon, push dough onto baking sheet . . . being careful to peak up the dough.

2 Make filled cookies easily by dropping filling on mounds of dough on baking sheet . . . then covering filling with a little more of the dough.

BROWN SUGAR DROPS (⚲ Recipe) Soft, chewy. Wonderful brown sugar flavor.

Mix thoroughly.	1 cup soft shortening 2 cups brown sugar (packed) 2 eggs
Stir in.	½ cup sour milk or buttermilk or water
Sift together and stir in.	3½ cups *sifted* GOLD MEDAL Flour 1 tsp. soda 1 tsp. salt

Chill at least 1 hour. Drop rounded tea-spoonfuls about 2″ apart on lightly greased baking sheet. Bake until set . . . just until, when touched lightly with finger, almost no imprint remains.

TEMPERATURE: 400° (mod. hot oven).

TIME: Bake 8 to 10 min.

AMOUNT: About 6 doz. 2½″ cookies.

HOLIDAY FRUIT COOKIES

Elegant. Richly studded with fruits and nuts. Butterscotch-flavored. Perfect for your loveliest hospitality.

Follow ⚲ recipe above—*except* mix into the dough 1½ cups broken pecans, 2 cups candied cherries, cut in halves, and 2 cups cut-up dates. Place a pecan half on each cooky. Make these rich cookies smaller . . . only 2″.

SALTED PEANUT COOKIES

These tempting peanut crunches are always a favorite both with children and grownups.

Follow ⚲ recipe above—*except*, in place of the 3½ cups flour, stir in 2 cups *sifted* flour, 2 cups rolled oats, 1 cup WHEATIES, 1 cup coarsely chopped salted peanuts (without husks). Bake until brown, 12 to 14 min.

EASY FILLED COOKIES

Mrs. Edwin Korslund of Eagle Grove, Iowa, gave us this idea for making filled cookies the quickest way. See picture 2 above.

Follow ⚲ recipe above—*except* place ½ tsp. Date Filling (p. 216) on each tea-spoonful dough. Cover with ½ tsp. dough. Bake until lightly browned, 10 to 12 min.

JEWELLED COOKIES

Glowing with gems of spicy gumdrops (red and green for Christmas holidays).

Follow ⚲ recipe above—*except* mix into the dough 4 cups cut-up gumdrops.

HERMITS

Spicy, fruity, satisfying. Contributed by Mrs. William G. Dorr, who worked with us in our test kitchen one summer. She says they were always first choice with her little girls.

Mix thoroughly . . . .
- 1 cup soft shortening
- 2 cups brown sugar (packed)
- 2 eggs

Stir in . . . .
- ½ cup cold coffee

Sift together and stir in . . . .
- 3½ cups *sifted* GOLD MEDAL Flour
- 1 tsp. soda
- 1 tsp. salt
- 1 tsp. nutmeg
- 1 tsp. cinnamon

Mix in . . . .
- 2½ cups halved seeded raisins
- 1¼ cups broken nuts

Chill at least 1 hour. Drop rounded teaspoonfuls about 2″ apart on lightly greased baking sheet. Bake until set . . . just until, when touched lightly with finger, almost no imprint remains.

TEMPERATURE: 400° (mod. hot oven).

TIME: Bake 8 to 10 min.

AMOUNT: About 6 doz. 2½″ cookies.

OATMEAL FRUIT-NUT DROP COOKIES

Deliciously moist and rich. A treasured heirloom recipe from the charming "Mennonite Community Cookbook" by Mary Emma Showalter, who says of her Mennonite grandmothers, "They taught me by example the worth of good cooking."

Mix thoroughly . . .
- 1 cup soft shortening
- 1½ cups sugar
- 2 eggs

Stir in . . .
- ½ cup sour milk or buttermilk

Sift together and stir in . . .
- 1¾ cups *sifted* GOLD MEDAL Flour
- 1 tsp. soda
- 1 tsp. baking powder
- ½ tsp. salt
- 1 tsp. cinnamon

Stir in . . .
- 2 cups rolled oats
- 1 cup cut-up raisins or dates
- ½ cup cut-up nuts

Drop rounded teaspoonfuls 2″ apart on ungreased baking sheet. Bake until lightly browned.

TEMPERATURE: 400° (mod. hot oven).

TIME: Bake 8 to 10 min.

AMOUNT: About 5½ doz. cookies.

All you have to do — to plump seedless raisins

Wash them and spread out in flat pan. Cover pan; heat slowly in mod. oven.
To get full flavor, cut raisins in two with scissors after plumping.

WHEATIES DROP COOKIES

Treats for young champions. Whole wheat flakes add extra flavor and goodness to these spicy drops.

Mix thoroughly . . .
- 1 cup soft shortening
- 1 cup sugar
- 2 eggs

Stir in . . .
- 1 cup sour milk

Sift together and stir in . . .
- 2 cups *sifted* GOLD MEDAL Flour
- ½ tsp. soda
- ½ tsp. salt
- 1 tsp. cinnamon
- ½ tsp. nutmeg
- ½ tsp. cloves

Stir in . . .
- ¾ cup coarsely chopped nuts
- 1 cup cut-up raisins

Fold in . . .
- 3 cups WHEATIES

Chill dough. Drop by teaspoonfuls about 2″ apart on lightly greased baking sheet. Bake until, when touched lightly with finger, no imprint remains.

TEMPERATURE: 400° (mod. hot oven).

TIME: Bake 10 to 12 min.

AMOUNT: About 5 doz. 2½″ cookies.

JUBILEE JUMBLES (✐ Recipe) Soft, tender, creamy-rich.

Especially chosen to commemorate the seventy-fifth anniversary of the naming of GOLD MEDAL Flour. It happened in 1880 at the International Millers' Exhibition in Cincinnati, Ohio, when the flour previously known as Washburn's Superlative was awarded the medal of gold.

Mix thoroughly . . . .
- ½ cup soft shortening
- 1 cup brown sugar (packed)
- ½ cup granulated sugar
- 2 eggs

Stir in . . . .
- 1 cup cultured sour cream or undiluted evaporated milk
- 1 tsp. vanilla

Sift together and stir in . . . .
- 2¾ cups *sifted* GOLD MEDAL Flour
- ½ tsp. soda
- 1 tsp. salt

Chill dough if soft. Drop rounded table-spoonfuls about 2" apart on greased baking sheet. Bake just until, when touched lightly with finger, almost no imprint remains.

TEMPERATURE: 375° (quick mod. oven).

TIME: Bake about 10 min.

AMOUNT: About 4 doz. 2½" cookies.

BUTTERSCOTCH COOKIES WITH BROWNED BUTTER GLAZE

Really delectable, especially with the unusual buttery icing. Mrs. R. C. Karstad of Nicollet, Minnesota, won a prize on them.

Follow ✐ recipe above—*except* use brown sugar in place of granulated sugar. Mix into the dough ⅔ cup cut-up nuts. Spread cooled cookies with

BROWNED BUTTER GLAZE

Melt ¼ cup butter until golden brown. Blend in 1 cup *sifted* confectioners' sugar and ½ tsp. vanilla. Stir in 1 to 2 tbsp. hot water until icing spreads smoothly.

AMOUNT: Icing for about 30 cookies.

COCONUT CREAM DROPS

Follow ✐ recipe above—*except* mix into the dough 1 cup moist shredded coconut.

to sour sweet cream

Use freshly soured cream for good flavor. Buy it from the dairy. Or sour it yourself by measuring 1 tbsp. vinegar or lemon juice into cup . . . then filling cup with sweet cream.

All you have to do—

To give iced cookies a professional air: place the same amount of icing (1 tsp.) on center of each. Then, with a spatula, spread the icing with circular motion in pretty swirls.

CHOCOLATE CREAM DROPS

Follow ✐ recipe above—*except* stir into shortening mixture 2 sq. unsweetened chocolate (2 oz.), melted. Mix into the dough 1 cup cut-up nuts. Frost cooled cookies if desired with Marie's Chocolate Icing (*p. 204*) or peppermint-flavored Easy-Creamy Icing (*p. 188*).

Chocolate-Cherry Drops: Mix into the dough 2 cups candied or maraschino cherries, cut in halves.

Holiday Chocolate Drops: Mix into the dough ⅔ cup *each* cut-up dates and candied or maraschino cherries, cut in halves. Place a pecan half on each cooky.

FRUIT-AND/OR-NUT DROPS

Follow ✐ recipe above—*except* sift with dry ingredients 1 tsp. cinnamon, ½ tsp. cloves, ¼ tsp. nutmeg. Mix into the dough 1 cup cut-up dates (or raisins) and 1 cup cut-up nuts . . . or 2 cups of either.

NOTE: The spices may be omitted.

CHOCOLATE CHIP COOKIES *Glamourous, crunchy, rich with chocolate bits and nuts.*

Also known as "Toll House" Cookies . . . from Kenneth and Ruth Wakefield's charming New England Toll House on the outskirts of Whitman, Massachusetts. These cookies were first introduced to American homemakers in 1939 through our series of radio talks on "Famous Foods from Famous Eating Places."

Mix thoroughly . . . .
- ⅔ cup soft shortening (part butter)
- ½ cup granulated sugar
- ½ cup brown sugar (packed)
- 1 egg
- 1 tsp. vanilla

Sift together and stir in . . . .
- *1½ cups *sifted* GOLD MEDAL Flour
- ½ tsp. soda
- ½ tsp. salt

Stir in . . . .
- ½ cup cut-up nuts
- 6-oz. pkg. semi-sweet chocolate pieces (about 1¼ cups)

*For a softer, more rounded cooky, use 1¾ cups sifted flour.

Drop rounded teaspoonfuls about 2″ apart on ungreased baking sheet. Bake until delicately browned . . . cookies should still be soft. Cool slightly before removing from baking sheet.

TEMPERATURE: 375° (quick mod. oven).

TIME: Bake 8 to 10 min.

AMOUNT: 4 to 5 doz. 2″ cookies.

OLD-TIME CINNAMON JUMBLES

Made with buttermilk . . . delicately soft and cake-like. "So easy . . . that making them is a thrill for the girls in the Home Economics classes each year," according to Miss Sarah M. Knight of Buffalo, New York. And even her little sixth-graders report making them with great success in their own homes!

Mix thoroughly . . .
- ½ cup soft shortening (part butter)
- 1 cup sugar
- 1 egg

Stir in . . .
- ¾ cup buttermilk
- 1 tsp. vanilla

Sift together and stir in . . .
- 2 cups *sifted* GOLD MEDAL Flour
- ½ tsp. soda
- ½ tsp. salt

Chill dough. Drop rounded teaspoonfuls about 2″ apart on lightly greased baking sheet. Sprinkle with mixture of sugar and cinnamon (¼ cup sugar and 1 tsp. cinnamon). Bake until set but not brown.

TEMPERATURE: 400° (mod. hot oven).

TIME: Bake 8 to 10 min.

AMOUNT: About 4 doz. 2″ cookies.

STIR-N-DROP SUGAR COOKIES

Just stir, then drop—makes these cookies easy. They're delicately flavored and crispy.

Beat with fork until well blended . . .
- 2 eggs

Stir in . . .
- ⅔ cup cooking (salad) oil
- 2 tsp. vanilla
- 1 tsp. grated lemon rind

Blend in until mixture thickens . . .
- ¾ cup sugar

Sift together and stir in . . .
- 2 cups *sifted* GOLD MEDAL Flour
- 2 tsp. baking powder
- ½ tsp. salt

Drop by teaspoonfuls about 2″ apart on ungreased baking sheet. Flatten with greased bottom of glass dipped in sugar. Bake until a delicate brown. Remove immediately from baking sheet.

TEMPERATURE: 400° (mod. hot oven).

TIME: Bake 8 to 10 min.

AMOUNT: About 3 doz. 3″ cookies.

197

GINGER CREAMS *Fluffy ginger cakes . . . topped with creamy white icing.*

They bring memories of a real farm home near Owatonna, Minnesota, where children trooped to the cooky jar after chores were done. Mildred Bennett (now Mrs. Axel Anderson), who was honored one year as national 4-H girl, brought us this recipe when she was a member of our staff.

Mix thoroughly . . . .
- ¼ cup soft shortening
- ½ cup sugar
- 1 small egg
- ½ cup molasses

Stir in . . . .
- ½ cup water

Sift together and stir in . . . .
- 2 cups *sifted* GOLD MEDAL Flour
- ½ tsp. soda
- ½ tsp. salt
- 1 tsp. ginger
- ½ tsp. nutmeg
- ½ tsp. cloves
- ½ tsp. cinnamon

Chill dough. Drop rounded teaspoonfuls about 2″ apart on lightly greased baking sheet. Bake until set . . . just until, when touched lightly with finger, almost no imprint remains. While slightly warm, frost with lemon or vanilla-flavored Easy-Creamy Icing (*p. 188*).

TEMPERATURE: 400° (mod. hot oven).

TIME: Bake 7 to 8 min.

AMOUNT: About 4 doz. 2″ cookies.

GOLDEN CARROT COOKIES

Refreshingly flavorful . . . deliciously moist. Mrs. Henry Thoeny, noted for her gracious hospitality, often serves these cookies with coffee in her Glencoe, Minnesota home when friends drop in.

Mix thoroughly . . .
- 1 cup soft shortening (part butter)
- ¾ cup sugar
- 1 cup mashed cooked carrots
- 2 eggs

Sift together and stir in . . .
- 2 cups *sifted* GOLD MEDAL Flour
- 2 tsp. baking powder
- ½ tsp. salt
- ¾ cup shredded coconut

Drop about 2″ apart on lightly greased baking sheet. Bake until, when touched lightly with finger, almost no imprint remains. Frost cooled cookies with Orange Butter Icing (*p. 177*).

TEMPERATURE: 400° (mod. hot oven).

TIME: Bake 8 to 10 min.

AMOUNT: About 4 doz. 2″ cookies.

To save scrubbing browned grease from baking sheet or pan: grease (with unsalted shortening) only spots where you will drop or place the cooky dough.

COCOA DROP COOKIES

So chocolatey, soft, and tender.

Mix thoroughly . . .
- ½ cup soft shortening (part butter)
- 1 cup sugar
- 1 egg

Stir in . . .
- ¾ cup buttermilk or sour milk
- 1 tsp. vanilla

Sift together and stir in . . .
- 1¾ cups *sifted* GOLD MEDAL Flour
- ½ tsp. soda
- ½ tsp. salt
- ½ cup cocoa

Mix in, if desired . . .
- 1 cup cut-up nuts or raisins

Chill at least 1 hour. Drop rounded teaspoonfuls about 2″ apart on lightly greased baking sheet. Bake just until, when touched lightly with finger, almost no imprint remains. Frost cooled cookies if desired with Browned Butter Glaze (*p. 196*) or Marie's Chocolate Icing (*p. 204*) and sprinkle with chopped nuts or chocolate shot.

TEMPERATURE: 400° (mod. hot oven).

TIME: Bake 8 to 10 min.

AMOUNT: About 3½ doz. 2½″ cookies.

COCONUT KISSES (⚷ Recipe) *Moist, chewy, macaroon-like.*

Beat until frothy........................	½ cup egg whites
Gradually beat in......................	1¼ cups sugar
Continue beating with rotary beater or mixer until very stiff and glossy.	
Stir in...............................	¼ tsp. salt ½ tsp. vanilla 2½ cups moist shredded coconut

Drop heaping teaspoonfuls 2″ apart on un-greased wrapping paper on baking sheet. Bake until set and delicately browned.

CHOCOLATE-COCONUT KISSES

Follow ⚷ recipe above—*except* stir into the batter 2 sq. unsweetened chocolate (2 oz.), melted and slightly cooled.

NUT KISSES

Follow ⚷ recipe above—*except*, in place of coconut, use 2 cups finely chopped nuts. Use hazelnuts, pecans, walnuts, blanched almonds, roasted peanuts (without husks).

TEMPERATURE: 325° (slow mod. oven).

TIME: Bake about 20 min.

AMOUNT: About 3 doz. kisses.

EASILY REMOVE KISSES FROM PAPER

Lift off paper, lay wet towel on hot baking sheet. Place paper of Kisses on towel, let stand 1 min. Steam will loosen Kisses. Slip off with spatula.

WHEATIES-COCONUT KISSES

Follow ⚷ recipe above—*except*, in place of 2½ cups coconut, use 2 cups WHEATIES and 1 cup coconut. Bake 12 to 15 min.

SWEDISH MACAROON TEACAKES

They look like tiny tarts. The rich cooky-type crust and the delicious macaroony filling are baked together.

Cream together thoroughly . . .
    1 cup soft butter
    ½ cup sugar
Beat in . . .
    1 egg
    1 tsp. vanilla
Stir in . . .
    2 cups *sifted* SOFTASILK Flour or GOLD
        MEDAL Flour

Drop a rounded teaspoonful of batter into each greased tiny muffin cup . . . pressing batter over bottom and up around sides (a coating ¼″ thick . . . leaving center hollow). Chill. Fill each hollow with

ALMOND MACAROON FILLING

Beat until light and foamy . . .
    2 eggs
Gradually beat in until well blended . . .
    ½ cup sugar
Mix in . . .
    1¼ cups blanched almonds, finely ground
    ½ tsp. almond flavoring

Bake until delicately browned and set.

TEMPERATURE: 325° (slow mod. oven).

TIME: Bake 25 to 30 min.

AMOUNT: 2 doz. teacakes.

PINEAPPLE COOKIES

"These are my children's favorite cookies!" says Mrs. Frank Parauka of Grand Rapids, Michigan, who sent us the recipe. The delightful pineapple flavor and macaroon-like top add to their appeal.

Mix thoroughly . . .
    1 cup soft shortening
    1½ cups sugar
    1 egg
Stir in . . .
    9-oz. can crushed pineapple with juice
        (1 cup)
Sift together and stir in . . .
    3½ cups *sifted* GOLD MEDAL Flour
    1 tsp. soda
    ½ tsp. salt
    ¼ tsp. nutmeg
Mix in . . .
    ½ cup chopped nuts

Chill at least 1 hour. Drop rounded teaspoonfuls about 2″ apart on lightly greased baking sheet. Bake until, when touched lightly with finger, no imprint remains.

TEMPERATURE: 400° (mod. hot oven).

TIME: Bake 8 to 10 min.

AMOUNT: About 5 doz. cookies.

HOW TO MAKE REFRIGERATOR COOKIES (preliminary steps on pp. 192–193)

1 Press and mold dough with hands into a long roll, even and smooth, and as big around as you want your cookies to be. Wrap in waxed paper . . . twisting ends to hold the roll in shape. Or press into a waxed cardboard carton (butter or ice cream carton) or can (baking powder or frozen fruit juice, etc.).

2 Chill roll of dough until it is firm enough to slice easily. To speed up chilling, place in freezing compartment of refrigerator. Slice with a thin knife, very sharp, to insure neat slices with uncrumbled edges. Wrap and return unused dough to refrigerator so it can remain stiff.

REFRIGERATOR COOKIES (⌀ Recipe) Melt-in-the-mouth, rich, and crispy.

Mix thoroughly . . . .
{
1 cup soft shortening
½ cup sugar
½ cup brown sugar (packed)
2 eggs
}

Sift together and stir in . . . .
{
2¾ cups *sifted* GOLD MEDAL Flour
½ tsp. soda
1 tsp. salt
*2 to 3 tsp. cinnamon
}

*Or use 1½ tsp. vanilla (add with eggs).

Mix thoroughly with hands. Press and mold into a long smooth roll about 2½" in diameter. Wrap in waxed paper, and chill until stiff (several hours or overnight). With a thin, sharp knife, cut in thin slices ⅛ to 1/16" thick. Place slices a little apart on ungreased baking sheet. Bake until lightly browned.

TEMPERATURE: 400° (mod. hot oven).
TIME: Bake 6 to 8 min.
AMOUNT: About 6 doz. 2½" cookies.

NUT REFRIGERATOR COOKIES

Nut-lovers really go for these cookies.

Follow ⌀ recipe above—*except* mix into dough ½ cup cut-up blanched almonds *or* black walnuts *or* other nuts.

DATE-NUT REFRIGERATOR COOKIES

Follow ⌀ recipe above—using both cinnamon and vanilla. Mix into dough ½ cup finely chopped nuts and ½ cup finely cut dates.

ORANGE-ALMOND REFRIGERATOR COOKIES

Follow ⌀ recipe above—*except* omit cinnamon. Stir 1 tbsp. grated orange rind into shortening mixture. Mix into dough ½ cup cut-up blanched almonds.

CHOCOLATE REFRIGERATOR COOKIES

Follow ⌀ recipe above—*except* omit the cinnamon. Blend 2 sq. unsweetened chocolate (2 oz.), melted and cooled, into the shortening mixture.

All you have to do—

For Variety in Design: make 2 rolls of dough of contrasting colors: one Refrigerator (plain), one Chocolate Refrigerator. Or make only plain Refrigerator dough, divide it in two, tint half a pastel color. STRIPED FANCIES: After chilling, cut rolls in half lengthwise. Press together cut surfaces of contrasting halves. Wrap. Chill. Slice. Bake. PINWHEELS: Roll out the 2 doughs and proceed as directed for Chocolate Pinwheels (*p. 208*).

RING AROUND THE COOKIES

Decorative edges give a gay appearance to these buttery-rich shortbread-type refrigerator cookies.

Mix thoroughly . . . .
> 1 cup soft shortening (part butter)
> 1 cup *sifted* confectioners' sugar
> 2 tsp. vanilla

Mix in thoroughly . . . .
> 1¼ cups *sifted* GOLD MEDAL Flour
> ½ tsp. salt
> 1 cup rolled oats

Shape into 2 rolls 1½″ in diameter. Coat by rolling in chocolate shot, grated semi-sweet chocolate, chopped nuts, shredded coconut, or chopped candied fruit. Wrap in waxed paper, and chill until stiff (several hours or overnight). Cut into ¼″ slices. Place a little apart on ungreased baking sheet. Bake until lightly browned.

TEMPERATURE: 375° (quick mod. oven).

TIME: Bake 10 to 12 min.

AMOUNT: 4 doz. 1½″ cookies.

GINGER REFRIGERATOR COOKIES

Gingery favorites in jig-time!

Mix thoroughly . . .
> 1 cup soft shortening
> 1 cup sugar
> 2 eggs
> ½ cup dark molasses

Sift together and stir in . . .
> 4½ cups *sifted* GOLD MEDAL Flour
> 1 tsp. soda
> 1 tsp. salt
> 1 tbsp. ginger (3 tsp.)

Mix thoroughly with hands. Press and mold into a long, smooth roll about 2½″ in diameter. Wrap in waxed paper, and chill until stiff (several hours or overnight). With thin, sharp knife, cut in thin slices ⅛ to ¹⁄₁₆″ thick. Place slices a little apart on ungreased baking sheet. Bake until lightly browned.

TEMPERATURE: 400° (mod. hot oven).

TIME: Bake 8 to 10 min.

AMOUNT: About 9 doz. 2½″ cookies.

NEW NORTHLAND COOKIES

Crunchy, flavorful shortening-savers.

Languid days on the St. Lawrence; the pink, rocky cliffs and blue icebergs of Labrador; and afternoon tea on deck. Such are the memories these cookies bring to Ruth G. Anderson of our staff who brought back the recipe after a cruise to the Northland.

Mix thoroughly . . .
> ½ cup soft shortening (part butter)
> 1 cup brown sugar (packed)

Stir in . . .
> ¼ cup cold water

Sift together and stir in . . .
> 1¾ cups *sifted* GOLD MEDAL Flour
> 1 tsp. soda
> ½ tsp. salt
> ½ tsp. cinnamon

Mix in . . .
> ½ cup cut-up blanched almonds

Mix thoroughly with hands. Press and mold into a long smooth roll about 2½″ in diameter. Wrap in waxed paper, and chill until stiff (several hours or overnight). With thin, sharp knife, cut in thin slices ⅛ to ¹⁄₁₆″ thick. Place slices a little apart on ungreased baking sheet. Bake until lightly browned. Remove from pan immediately.

TEMPERATURE: 400° (mod. hot oven).

TIME: Bake 6 to 8 min.

AMOUNT: About 4 doz. 2½″ cookies.

BON BON COOKIES

PETTICOAT TAILS *Richly delicate and dainty.*

This recipe was brought from France to Scotland by Mary, Queen of Scots. The French name "Petits Gateaux Tailles" means—"little cakes cut off." But the name came to be pronounced as it sounded to the Scotch and English—"Petticoat Tails."

Mix thoroughly...................

{ 1 cup soft butter
1 cup *sifted* confectioners' sugar
1 tsp. flavoring (vanilla, almond, wintergreen, or rose)

Sift together and stir in.................

{ 2½ cups *sifted* GOLD MEDAL Flour
¼ tsp. salt

Mix thoroughly with hands. Press and mold into a long, smooth roll about 2″ in diameter. Wrap in waxed paper, and chill until stiff (several hours or overnight). With thin, sharp knife, cut in thin slices ⅛ to ¹⁄₁₆″ thick. Place slices a little apart on ungreased baking sheet. Bake until lightly browned.

TEMPERATURE: 400° (mod. hot oven).

TIME: Bake 8 to 10 min.

AMOUNT: About 6 doz. 2″ cookies.

OATMEAL REFRIGERATOR COOKIES *Nice and chewy, with a molasses-lemon tang.*

Voted the best oatmeal cooky ever tasted ... when sent to our Recipe Contest by Mrs. J. A. Gmeinder of St. Paul, Minnesota. The distinguishing molasses-lemon flavor was an idea from Mrs. Richard Nugent, Brooklyn, New York.

Mix thoroughly....................

{ ½ cup soft shortening
½ cup sugar
½ cup brown sugar (packed)
1 egg
1½ tsp. grated lemon rind
1½ tbsp. molasses
½ tsp. vanilla

Sift together and stir in....................

{ 1 cup *sifted* GOLD MEDAL Flour
½ tsp. soda
½ tsp. salt

Mix in.............................. 1½ cups rolled oats

Mix thoroughly with hands. Press and mold into a long, smooth roll about 2½″ in diameter. Wrap in waxed paper, and chill until stiff (several hours). With thin, sharp knife, cut in thin slices ⅛ to ¹⁄₁₆″ thick. Place slices a little apart on ungreased baking sheet. Bake until lightly browned.

TEMPERATURE: 400° (mod. hot oven).

TIME: Bake 8 to 10 min.

AMOUNT: About 4 doz. 2½″ cookies.

PRETTY FOR PARTIES

All you have to do—

To make Petticoat Tails match your color scheme: tint the dough with a few drops of red food coloring and use rose flavoring for a pink party. Use wintergreen flavoring and a few drops of green coloring for a green party.

HOW TO MAKE BAR COOKIES (preliminary steps on pp. 192–193)

1 Spread dough in greased pan and bake as directed.

2 Cut into squares or bars when slightly cool.

3 Remove from the pan with a wide spatula.

BROWNIES (✿ Recipe) *Chewy, fudgy squares . . . everyone loves them!*

Melt together over hot water..............	2 sq. unsweetened chocolate (2 oz.) ⅓ cup shortening
Beat in............................	1 cup sugar 2 eggs
Sift together and stir in..................	¾ cup *sifted* GOLD MEDAL Flour ½ tsp. baking powder ½ tsp. salt
Mix in.............................	½ cup broken nuts

Spread in well greased 8″ square pan. Bake until top has dull crust. A slight imprint will be left when top is touched lightly with finger. Cool slightly . . . then cut into squares.

TEMPERATURE: 350° (mod. oven).

TIME: Bake 30 to 35 min.

AMOUNT: 16 2″ squares.

FROSTED BROWNIES

Star of Marie Watson's delightful parties in her Minneapolis home.

Follow ✿ recipe above—cool, then spread before cutting with pink tinted, peppermint-flavored Easy-Creamy Icing (*p. 188*) or

MARIE'S CHOCOLATE ICING

Melt over hot water 1 tbsp. butter and 1 sq. unsweetened chocolate (1 oz.). Blend in 1½ tbsp. warm water. Stir and beat in about 1 cup *sifted* confectioners' sugar (until icing will spread easily).

DAINTY TEA BROWNIES

Picturesque . . . very thin. A highlight of the silver teas at a Minneapolis church.

Follow ✿ recipe above—*except* chop nuts *finely* and spread dough in *two* well greased 13x9″ oblong pans. Sprinkle with ¾ cup blanched and finely sliced green pistachio nuts. Bake 7 to 8 min. Cut immediately into squares or diamonds. Remove from pan while warm.

BUTTERSCOTCH BROWNIES

Rich, brown sugar flavor. These chewy squares, adored by Helen Hansen, an executive secretary of General Mills, keep deliciously soft for days in a tightly covered jar.

Melt over low heat . . .
   ¼ cup butter or other shortening
Remove from heat. Stir in until blended . . .
   1 cup light brown sugar (packed)
Cool. Stir in . . .
   1 egg
Sift together and stir in . . .
   ¾ cup *sifted* GOLD MEDAL Flour
   1 tsp. baking powder
   ½ tsp. salt
Stir in . . .
   ½ tsp. vanilla
   ½ cup coarsely chopped walnuts

Spread in well greased 8″ square pan. Bake until, when touched lightly with finger, only a slight imprint remains. Don't overbake! Cut into bars while still warm.

TEMPERATURE: 350° (mod. oven).

TIME: Bake 25 min.

AMOUNT: 1½ doz. 1x2½″ bars.

TOFFEE-NUT BARS (𝒫 Recipe) *Almond-coconut topping on melt-in-the-mouth crust.*

BOTTOM LAYER

Mix thoroughly........................{ ½ cup soft shortening (half butter)
½ cup brown sugar (packed)

Stir in............................. 1 cup *sifted* GOLD MEDAL Flour

Press and flatten with hand to cover bottom of ungreased 13x9″ oblong pan. Bake 10 min. Then spread with

TEMPERATURE: 350° (mod. oven).
TIME: Bake 10 min.

ALMOND-COCONUT TOPPING

Beat well........................... 2 eggs

Stir in.............................{ 1 cup brown sugar (packed)
1 tsp. vanilla

Mix and stir in........................{ 2 tbsp. GOLD MEDAL Flour
1 tsp. baking powder
½ tsp. salt

Mix in.............................{ 1 cup moist shredded coconut
1 cup cut-up almonds (or other nuts)

Return to oven and bake 25 min. more until topping is golden brown. Cool slightly . . . then cut into bars.

TEMPERATURE: 350° (mod. oven).
TIME: Bake 25 min.
AMOUNT: About 2½ doz. 1x3″ bars.

HAZELNUT BARS *Crusty, macaroon-like.*

Old-time German party cookies that keep beautifully.

Beat in top of double boiler until stiff . . .
2 large egg whites

Beat in gradually . . .
1 cup sugar

Fold in . . .
1 tbsp. GOLD MEDAL Flour

Cook over boiling water 3 min., stirring constantly.

Remove from over hot water.

Blend in . . .
1 tsp. vanilla
1½ cups coarsely ground unblanched filberts (*hazelnuts*)

Spread dough smoothly ¼″ thick in ungreased paper-lined 13x9″ oblong pan. With fingers, pat top gently with warm water. Bake until top looks dull. While warm, cut into bars 1½x2″. Cool slightly, then turn paper over (bars and all). Dampen entire surface with cold water. When water penetrates paper, bars are easily removed. If desired, place two bars together with a butter icing between (*see Browned Butter Glaze, p. 196*).

TEMPERATURE: 350° (mod. oven).
TIME: Bake 15 to 20 min.
AMOUNT: 32 single bars, 1½x2″.

JELL-MERINGUE-FILBERT BARS

Specialty of Mrs. George Ludcke, Jr. (formerly Jeanette Campbell of our staff).

Follow 𝒫 recipe above for Bottom Layer —*except* use *sifted* confectioners' sugar in place of brown, and stir 2 egg yolks into the sugar and shortening mixture. Bake. Spread with ½ to ¾ cup softened jelly (currant, raspberry, or grape), then with

MERINGUE-FILBERT TOPPING

Beat until stiff . . .
2 egg whites

Beat in gradually . . .
½ cup sugar
¼ tsp. cinnamon

Fold in . . .
1 cup ground filberts (unblanched)

Return to oven and bake 25 min. more until topping is golden brown. Cool slightly . . . then cut into bars.

The fluffy meringue-filbert topping is piled on top of softened jelly spread over the crust.

FILLED BAR COOKIES (✐ Recipe)

First, prepare desired filling (*see below*), and cool.

FOR CRUST

Mix thoroughly . . . .
- ¾ cup soft shortening (part butter)
- 1 cup brown sugar (packed)

Sift together and stir in . . . .
- 1¾ cups *sifted* GOLD MEDAL Flour
- ½ tsp. soda
- 1 tsp. salt

Stir in . . . . 1½ cups rolled oats

Mix thoroughly. Place one-half of this crumb mixture in greased 13x9″ oblong pan. Press and flatten with hands to cover bottom of pan. Spread with cooled filling. Cover with remaining crumb mixture . . . patting lightly.   Bake until lightly browned. While warm, cut into bars and remove from pan.

TEMPERATURE: 400° (mod. hot oven).
TIME: Bake 25 to 30 min.
AMOUNT: About 2½ doz. 1½x2″ bars.

DATE BARS (Matrimonial Cake)

These cookies won the first prize at the famous Minnesota State Fair one year . . . for Mrs. C. Arlt of St. Paul.

Follow ✐ recipe above using

DATE FILLING

Mix in saucepan . . .
- 3 cups cut-up dates
- ¼ cup sugar
- 1½ cups water

Cook over low heat, stirring constantly, until thickened (about 10 min.). Cool.

Date Bars . . . perfect pals for good hot coffee or tea

DATE-APRICOT BARS

Follow ✐ recipe above using

DATE-APRICOT FILLING

Mix in saucepan . . .
- 1 cup cut-up dates
- 2 cups mashed cooked dried apricots (drained)
- ½ cup sugar
- 2 tbsp. of the apricot juice

Cook over low heat, stirring constantly, until thickened (about 5 min.). Cool.

CHRISTMAS MINCEMEAT BARS

Sophie Kerr and June Platt, writers and gourmets of note, include a similar recipe for these wonderful holiday cookies in their fascinating book, "The Best I Ever Ate."

Mix thoroughly . . .
- 1 tbsp. soft butter
- 1½ cups brown sugar (packed)
- 2 eggs
- 2 tbsp. molasses
- 1 tsp. vanilla

Sift together and stir in . . .
- 2 cups *sifted* GOLD MEDAL Flour
- ½ tsp. salt
- ½ tsp. soda
- 1 tsp. cinnamon
- 1 tsp. cloves

Stir in . . .
- 3 tbsp. hot water

Then stir in . . .
- ¼ cup almonds, sliced
- ¼ cup seedless raisins (cut in two)
- 9-oz. pkg. mincemeat, broken up with fork

Spread thin in 2 greased 13x9″ oblong pans. (Dough puffs and fills in any holes as it bakes.) Bake until, when touched lightly with finger, no imprint remains.

Spread immediately with mixture of . . .
- 1½ cups *sifted* confectioners' sugar
- about 3 tbsp. hot milk
- ½ tsp. vanilla
- ½ tsp. almond flavoring

Cut into squares or diamonds.

TEMPERATURE: 400° (mod. hot oven).
TIME: Bake 12 to 15 min.
AMOUNT: 6 doz. 1½x2″ cookies.

DATE-AND-NUT SQUARES

Chewy, rich flavored. Much like the Bishop's Bread served to circuit-riding preachers in days of Early America.

Beat until foamy . . .

    2 eggs

Beat in . . .

    ½ cup sugar
    ½ tsp. vanilla

Sift together and stir in . . .

    ½ cup *sifted* GOLD MEDAL Flour
    ½ tsp. baking powder
    ½ tsp. salt

Mix in . . .

    1 cup cut-up walnuts
    2 cups finely cut-up dates

Spread in well greased 8″ square pan. Bake until top has dull crust. Cut into squares, cool, remove from pan.

TEMPERATURE: 325° (slow mod. oven).

TIME: Bake 25 to 30 min.

AMOUNT: 16 2″ squares.

To sugar confection-like Date-and-Nut Squares *(above)* . . . dip in confectioners' sugar and shake.

SNICKERDOODLES

Mrs. Ronald Anfinson (formerly Pat Roth of our staff) said, "It's one of my happy childhood memories. My mother would be baking when we came home from school and we would have these crunchy, crinkly-topped, spicy rounds hot out of the oven with a glass of milk."

Mix thoroughly . . .

    1 cup soft shortening (part butter)
    1½ cups sugar
    2 eggs

Sift together and stir in . . .

    2¾ cups *sifted* GOLD MEDAL Flour
    2 tsp. cream of tartar
    1 tsp. soda
    ¼ tsp. salt

Roll into balls the size of small walnuts. Roll in mixture of 2 tbsp. sugar and 2 tsp. cinnamon. Place 2″ apart on ungreased baking sheet. Bake until lightly browned . . . but still soft. (These cookies puff up at first . . . then flatten out.)

TEMPERATURE: 400° (mod. hot oven).

TIME: Bake 8 to 10 min.

AMOUNT: About 5 doz. 2″ cookies.

CINNAMON COFFEE BARS

Cake or cooky bars . . . "So quick and easy to make for a last minute dessert!" says Ramona Gerhard Sutton of Los Angeles, California, an accomplished cook as well as a most gifted musician.

Cream together thoroughly . . .

    ¼ cup soft shortening
    1 cup brown sugar (packed)
    1 egg

Stir in . . .

    ½ cup hot coffee

Sift together and stir in . . .

    1½ cups *sifted* GOLD MEDAL Flour
    1 tsp. baking powder
    ¼ tsp. soda
    ¼ tsp. salt
    ½ tsp. cinnamon

Blend in . . .

    ½ cup seedless raisins
    ¼ cup chopped nuts

Spread in greased 13x9″ oblong pan. Bake. Cut into bars. Frost while warm with thin coating of Easy-Creamy Icing (*p. 188*).

TEMPERATURE: 350° (mod. oven).

TIME: Bake 18 to 20 min.

AMOUNT: 2 doz. 1½x3″ bars.

MOLASSES CRINKLES

Thick, chewy, with crackled, sugary tops.

When served at Mrs. Fred Fredell's in St. Paul, Minnesota, they were so delicious I begged the recipe. Thanks to her, thousands of homes have enjoyed these spicy cookies.

Mix thoroughly . . .

    ¾ cup soft shortening
    1 cup brown sugar (packed)
    1 egg
    ¼ cup molasses

Sift together and stir in . . .

    2¼ cups *sifted* GOLD MEDAL Flour
    2 tsp. soda
    ¼ tsp. salt
    ½ tsp. cloves
    1 tsp. cinnamon
    1 tsp. ginger

Chill dough. Roll into balls the size of large walnuts. Dip tops in sugar. Place, sugared-side-up, 3″ apart on greased baking sheet. Sprinkle each cooky with 2 or 3 drops of water to produce a crackled surface. Bake just until set but not hard.

TEMPERATURE: 375° (quick mod. oven).

TIME: Bake 10 to 12 min.

AMOUNT: About 4 doz. 2½″ cookies.

HOW TO MAKE ROLLED COOKIES (preliminary steps on pp. 192–193)

1 To prevent "sticking," slip a canvas cover over board, and stockinet over rolling pin. Rub flour into the covers.

2 Roll lightly, small amount dough at a time . . . keeping the rest chilled. Roll very thin for crisp cookies.

3 Cut as many cookies from each rolling as possible. Dip cooky cutter in flour, then shake it and cut.

Short Cut: instead of rolling it, drop dough and flatten with glass. See page 218.

ETHEL'S SUGAR COOKIES (♪ Recipe) Crispy, thin, flavorful.

"Perfect with lemonade on a hot summer day," says Mrs. J. H. Wolfe of Iowa City, Iowa, who gave us the recipe. "And at Christmastime they are traditional in our home . . . cut in fancy shapes and decorated with gay icings and tiny candies."

Mix thoroughly . . . .
- ¾ cup soft shortening (part butter)
- 1 cup sugar
- 2 eggs
- ½ tsp. flavoring (vanilla or lemon or a combination of the two)

Sift together and stir in . . . .
- 2½ cups *sifted* GOLD MEDAL Flour
- 1 tsp. baking powder
- 1 tsp. salt

Chill at least 1 hour. Roll out ⅛" thick. Cut into desired shapes. Place on ungreased baking sheet. Sprinkle with sugar, if desired. Bake until delicately golden.

TEMPERATURE: 400° (mod. hot oven).

TIME: Bake 6 to 8 min.

AMOUNT: About 4 doz. 3" cookies.

LEMON SUGAR COOKIES

Follow ♪ recipe above—*except*, in place of flavoring, use 2 tsp. grated lemon rind and 1 tsp. lemon juice.

FILLED SUGAR COOKIES

Follow ♪ recipe above—*except* put together in pairs before baking with 1 tsp. Date, Fig, or Raisin Filling (*p. 216*) or a solid chocolate mint wafer between. Press edges together with tines of fork.

CARAWAY COOKIES

Follow ♪ recipe above—*except* omit flavoring, sift ½ tsp. nutmeg with the dry ingredients, and mix 1 tsp. caraway seeds into the dough.

CHOCOLATE PINWHEELS

Fascinating whirls of dark and light . . . an unusual taste delight.

Follow ♪ recipe above. Divide dough into 2 equal parts. Into 1 part, blend 2 sq. unsweetened chocolate (2 oz.), melted and cooled. Chill. Roll out white dough 9x12". Roll out chocolate dough same size and lay on top of white dough. Roll the double layer of dough gently until ³⁄₁₆" thick. Roll up tightly, beginning at wide side, into a roll 12" long and 2" in diameter. Chill. Slice ⅛" thick. Place slices a little apart on lightly greased baking sheet. Bake.

NUT SUGAR COOKIES

Follow ♪ recipe above—*except* mix into the dough 1 cup finely chopped nuts.

WAGON WHEELS

Large, flat, chewy, inexpensive molasses cookies . . . intriguingly flavored with spices. Almost as old as America itself. In early days, travellers by covered wagon carried them west across the country in their journey to new homes.

Mix well . . . .
{ ½ cup soft shortening
{ 1 cup sugar

Stir in . . . .
{ 1 cup dark molasses
{ ½ cup water

Sift together and stir in . . . .
{ 4 cups *sifted* GOLD MEDAL Flour
{ 1 tsp. soda
{ 1½ tsp. salt
{ 1½ tsp. ginger
{ ½ tsp. cloves
{ ½ tsp. nutmeg
{ ¼ tsp. allspice

Chill dough several hours or overnight. Roll out ¼″ thick. Cut into 3″ circles. Sprinkle with sugar. Place on well greased baking sheet. Press a large raisin into center of each. Bake until, when touched lightly with finger, almost no imprint remains. Leave on baking sheet a few min. before removing to prevent breaking.

If desired, make "spokes" of Easy Decorating Icing (*p. 188*) radiating out from centers of cooled cookies.

TEMPERATURE: 375° (quick mod. oven).

TIME: Bake 10 to 12 min.

AMOUNT: 2½ doz. 3″ cookies.

BUTTER COOKIES

Crisp, with the true buttery flavor, but not too sweet. Dainty and perfect for party occasions. To shape with a cooky press, see p. 217.

Mix thoroughly . . .
   1 cup soft butter
   ½ cup sugar
   1 egg

Stir in . . .
   3 tsp. flavoring (vanilla, lemon, almond, etc.)

Sift together and stir in . . .
   3 cups *sifted* GOLD MEDAL Flour
   ½ tsp. baking powder

Chill dough. Roll very thin (1/16″). Cut into desired shapes. Place on ungreased baking sheet. Press blanched almond or pecan half into top of each cooky. If glazed cooky is desired, brush mixture of 1 egg yolk and 2 tbsp. water over top of cookies before baking. Bake until delicately browned.

TEMPERATURE: 425° (hot oven).

TIME: Bake 5 to 7 min.

AMOUNT: About 7 doz. 2″ cookies.

CREAMY BUTTER FILLING

Blend together ¼ cup soft butter, ¾ cup *sifted* confectioners' sugar, 1 egg yolk, 1 tsp. vanilla.

CREAM WAFERS (Pariserwafier)

Buttery rich, creamy white little cookies . . . wonderful for teas. The Parisian recipe came to the United States via Sweden. Mrs. G. C. Olson of Lake Minnetonka, Minnesota, brought it with her when she came to this country as a bride.

Mix thoroughly . . .
   1 cup soft butter
   ⅓ cup thick cream (35%)
   2 cups *sifted* GOLD MEDAL Flour

Chill at least 1 hour. Roll out ⅛″ thick. Cut into 1½″ rounds. Transfer to waxed paper heavily sprinkled with sugar . . . turning rounds with spatula to coat both sides with sugar. Place on ungreased baking sheet. Prick in about 4 places with fork. Bake until slightly puffy but not brown. Put each two cooled cookies together with Creamy Butter Filling (*at left below*).

TEMPERATURE: 375° (quick mod. oven).

TIME: Bake 7 to 9 min.

AMOUNT: About 5 doz. 1½″ double cookies.

GINGIES (⚡ Recipe) Soft and puffy . . . true old-fashioned ginger cookies.

A happy tradition at the famous Girard College, Philadelphia, Pennsylvania. The boys hoard them . . . old grads long for them.

Mix thoroughly . . . .
- ⅓ cup soft shortening
- 1 cup brown sugar (packed)
- 1½ cups dark molasses

Stir in . . . .
⅔ cup cold water

Sift together and stir in . . . .
- 6 cups *sifted* GOLD MEDAL Flour
- 2 tsp. soda
- 1 tsp. salt
- 1 tsp. allspice
- 1 tsp. ginger
- 1 tsp. cloves
- 1 tsp. cinnamon

Chill dough. Roll out very thick (½″). Cut with 2½″ round cutter. Place far apart on lightly greased baking sheet. Bake until, when touched lightly with finger, no imprint remains.

TEMPERATURE: 350° (mod. oven).

TIME: Bake about 15 min.

AMOUNT: 2⅔ doz. fat, puffy 2½″ cookies.

FROSTED GINGIES

Follow ⚡ recipe above—and frost when cool with Easy-Creamy Icing (*p. 188*).

All you have to do —

To make a Cooky Lollipop: spread Easy-Creamy Icing (*p. 188*) on a baked round cooky. Place a colored drinking straw or wooden stick across the middle . . . letting one end extend several inches beyond edge of cooky. Place a second cooky of same size on top . . . pressing down slightly.

GINGERBREAD BOYS

Make holidays gayer than ever.

Follow ⚡ recipe above—*except* mix in 1 more cup *sifted* GOLD MEDAL Flour. Chill dough. Roll out very thick (½″). Grease cardboard gingerbread boy pattern, place on the dough, and cut around it with a sharp knife. Or use a gingerbread boy cutter. With a pancake turner, carefully transfer gingerbread boys to lightly greased baking sheet. Press raisins into dough for eyes, nose, mouth, and shoe and cuff buttons. Use bits of candied cherries or red gumdrops for coat buttons; strips of citron for tie. Bake. Cool slightly, then carefully remove from baking sheet. With Easy Decorating Icing (*p. 188*), make outlines for collar, cuffs, belt, and shoes.

AMOUNT: About 12 Gingerbread Boys.

STONE JAR MOLASSES COOKIES Crisp and brown . . . without a bit of sugar.

Heat to boiling point . . . .
1 cup molasses
Remove from heat.

Stir in . . . .
- ½ cup shortening
- 1 tsp. soda

Sift together and stir in . . . .
- 2¼ cups *sifted* GOLD MEDAL Flour
- 1¾ tsp. baking powder
- 1 tsp. salt
- 1½ tsp. ginger

Chill dough. Roll out very thin (1⁄16″). Cut into desired shapes. Place on lightly greased baking sheet. Bake until set. (Overbaking gives a bitter taste.)

TEMPERATURE: 350° (mod. oven).

TIME: Bake 5 to 7 min.

AMOUNT: About 6 doz. 2½″ cookies.

PATTERN FOR GINGERBREAD BOY

Trace on tissue paper. Then cut pattern from cardboard. Place greased or floured pattern on dough. Cut around it with a sharp knife.

Other cooky patterns can be made in same way from other designs. See p. 191.

To make "dancing" Gingerbread Boys... bend the legs and arms into "action" positions when you place them on baking sheet (as shown in small figures below).

GOOD TRAVELERS

Jubilee Jumbles. Holiday Fruit Cookies. Hermits. Chocolate Cream Drops. Ginger Creams. Golden Carrot Cookies. Pineapple Cookies. Brownies. Toffee Nut Bars. Date-Nut Squares. Wagon Wheels. Gingies. Lebkuchen. Nurnberger.

COOKIES FROM HOME

Packing Cookies Successfully For Mailing

1 Choose cookies that will travel well. See suggestions at right above.

2 Select heavy box, line with waxed paper. Use plenty of filler (crushed wrapping or tissue paper, or unbuttered popcorn or Cheerios).

3 Wrap each cooky separately . . . in waxed paper. Or place cookies back-to-back in pairs . . . then wrap each pair.

4 Pad bottom of box with filler. Fit wrapped cookies into box closely, in layers.

5 Use filler between layers to prevent crushing of cookies.

6 Cover with paper doily, add card, and pad top with crushed paper. Pack tightly so contents will not shake around.

7 Wrap box tightly with heavy paper and cord. Address plainly with permanent ink . . . covering address with cellophane tape or colorless nail polish. Mark the box plainly: "PERISHABLE."

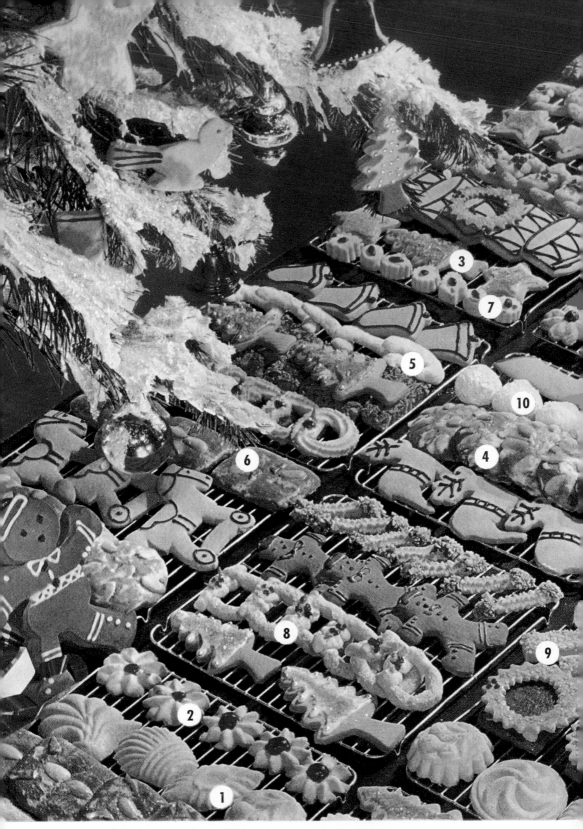

COOKIES FOR CHRISTMAS

(1) Sandbakelser (2) Spritz (3) Merry Christmas Cookies (4) Nurnberger
(5) Almond Crescents (6) Lebkuchen (7) Scotch Shortbread (8) Berliner Kränze
(9) Finska Kakor (10) Russian Tea Cakes

MERRY CHRISTMAS COOKIES (✐ Recipe) *Soft, cushiony cookies, dark or light.*

LIGHT DOUGH . . . *For bells, stockings, stars, wreaths, etc.*

Mix thoroughly . . . .
{
⅓ cup soft shortening
⅓ cup sugar
1 egg
⅔ cup honey
1 tsp. lemon flavoring
}

Sift together and stir in . . . .
{
2¾ cups *sifted* GOLD MEDAL Flour
1 tsp. soda
1 tsp. salt
}

Chill dough. Roll out thick (¼″). Cut into desired shapes. Place 1″ apart on lightly greased baking sheet. Bake until, when touched lightly with finger, no imprint remains. When cool, ice and decorate as desired.

TEMPERATURE: 375° (quick mod. oven).

TIME: Bake 8 to 10 min.

AMOUNT: About 5 doz. 2½″ cookies.

DARK DOUGH

For animal shapes, toy shapes, and boy and girl figures.

Follow recipe for Gingies (*p. 210*) or Wagon Wheels (*p. 209*).

TO HANG ON CHRISTMAS TREE
Just loop a piece of green string and press ends into the dough at the top of each cooky before baking. Bake with string-side *down* on pan.

TO DECORATE
Use recipe for Easy Decorating Icing (p. 188). For decorating ideas, see pp. 188, 190, 191, 212. Sugar in coarse granules for decorating is available at bakery supply houses.

WREATHS

Cut with scalloped cutter . . . using smaller cutter for center. Cover with white icing. Sprinkle with green sugar and decorate with clusters of berries made of red icing—leaves of green icing—to give the realistic effect of holly wreaths.

BELLS

Outline with red icing. Make clapper of red icing. (A favorite with children.)

STOCKINGS

Sprinkle colored sugar on toes and heels before baking. Or mark heels and toes of baked cookies with icing of some contrasting color.

SANTA CLAUS

Outline with red icing. Fill bag with tiny colored candies or silver dragées. Paint boots with melted chocolate.

CHRISTMAS TREES

Spread with white icing . . . then sprinkle with green sugar. Decorate with silver dragées and tiny colored candies.

TOYS

(Drum, car, jack-in-the-box, etc.): Outline shapes with white or colored icing.

ANIMALS

(Reindeer, camel, dog, kitten, etc.): Pipe icing on animals to give effect of bridles, blankets, etc.

BOYS AND GIRLS

Pipe figures with an icing to give desired effects: eyes, noses, buttons, etc.

LEBKUCHEN (♪ Recipe) *The famous old-time German Christmas Honey Cakes.*

Mrs. Moritz Wismer of Britton, South Dakota, remembers that her great-grandmother, Wilhelmina Lutz Haish, said of them: "No Christmas celebration in the whole Black Forest region was ever complete without them."

Mix and bring to a boil.................	½ cup honey
	½ cup molasses
Cool thoroughly.	¾ cup brown sugar (packed)
Stir in........	1 egg
	1 tbsp. lemon juice
	1 tsp. grated lemon rind
	2¾ cups *sifted* GOLD MEDAL Flour
	½ tsp. soda
Sift together and stir in............	1 tsp. cinnamon
	1 tsp. cloves
	1 tsp. allspice
	1 tsp. nutmeg
Mix in........................	⅓ cup cut-up citron
	⅓ cup chopped nuts

Chill dough overnight. Roll small amount at a time, keeping rest chilled. Roll out ¼″ thick and cut into oblongs, 1½x2½″. Place 1″ apart on greased baking sheet. Bake until, when touched lightly, no imprint remains. While cookies bake, make Glazing Icing (*recipe below*). Brush it over cookies the minute they are out of oven. Then quickly remove from baking sheet. Cool and store to mellow.

TEMPERATURE: 400° (mod. hot oven).

TIME: Bake 10 to 12 min.

AMOUNT: About 6 doz. 2x3″ cookies.

GLAZING ICING

Boil together 1 cup sugar and ½ cup water until first indication of a thread appears (230°). Remove from heat. Stir in ¼ cup confectioners' sugar and brush hot icing thinly over cookies. (*When icing gets sugary, reheat slightly, adding a little water until clear again.*)

NURNBERGER

Round, light-colored honey cakes from the famed old City of Toys.

Follow ♪ recipe above—*except*, in place of honey and molasses, use 1 cup honey; and reduce spices (using ¼ tsp. cloves, ½ tsp. allspice, and ½ tsp. nutmeg . . . with 1 tsp. cinnamon).
Roll out the *chilled* dough ¼″ thick. Cut into 2″ rounds. Place on greased baking sheet. With fingers, round up cookies a bit toward center. Press in blanched almond halves around the edge like petals of a daisy. Use a round piece of citron for each center. Bake just until set. *Immediately* brush with Glazing Icing (*above*). Remove from baking sheet. Cool, and store to mellow.

AMOUNT: About 6 doz. 2½″ cookies.

TO "MELLOW" COOKIES

. . . store in an airtight container for a few days. Add a cut orange or apple . . . changing it frequently to insure freshness.

MORAVIAN GINGER COOKIES

Crisp, spicy, paper-thin.

From that former Austrian crownland which became part of Czechoslovakia in 1918. Previously, Moravians had settled in the United States in Pennsylvania and North Carolina, founding Bethlehem, Pennsylvania, on Christmas Eve, 1741.

Mix thoroughly . . .
   3 tbsp. soft shortening
   2 tbsp. brown sugar
   ⅓ cup molasses

Sift together and stir in . . .
   1¼ cups *sifted* GOLD MEDAL Flour
   ½ tsp. salt
   ¼ tsp. soda
   ¼ tsp. *each* cinnamon, ginger, cloves
   dash *each* of nutmeg and allspice

Work with hands until well blended. Cover and chill about 4 hours. (Dough does not hold together until thoroughly chilled.) Roll out paper-thin, a little at a time. Cut in desired shapes. Place on greased baking sheet. Bake until lightly browned. When cool, frost thinly, if desired, with Easy-Creamy Icing (*p. 188*).

TEMPERATURE: 375° (quick mod. oven).

TIME: Bake 5 to 6 min.

AMOUNT: About 5 doz. 2″ cookies.

SCOTCH SHORTBREAD

Old-time delicacy from Scotland . . . crisp, thick, buttery. Allene Moe of our staff likes to divide the dough and tint it in assorted pastel colors with a few drops of food coloring before chilling it.

Mix thoroughly.......................... { 1 cup soft butter
½ cup sugar

Stir in............................... 2½ cups *sifted* GOLD MEDAL Flour

Mix thoroughly with hands. Chill dough. Roll out ⅓ to ½" thick. Cut into fancy shapes (small leaves, ovals, squares, etc.). Flute edges, if desired, by pinching between fingers as for pie crust. Place on ungreased baking sheet. Bake. (The tops do not brown during baking . . . nor does shape of the cookies change.)

TEMPERATURE: 300° (slow oven).

TIME: Bake 20 to 25 min.

AMOUNT: About 2 doz. 1x1½" cookies.

FINSKA KAKOR (Finnish Cakes)

Nut-studded butter strips from Finland.

Mix thoroughly . . .
¾ cup soft butter
¼ cup sugar
1 tsp. almond flavoring
Stir in . . .
2 cups *sifted* GOLD MEDAL Flour

Mix thoroughly with hands. Chill dough. Roll out ¼" thick. Cut into strips 2½" long and ¾" wide. Brush tops lightly with 1 egg white, slightly beaten. Sprinkle with mixture of 1 tbsp. sugar and ⅓ cup finely chopped blanched almonds. Carefully transfer (several strips at a time) to ungreased baking sheet. Bake just until cookies begin to turn a very delicate golden brown.

TEMPERATURE: 350° (mod. oven).

TIME: Bake 17 to 20 min.

AMOUNT: About 4 doz. 2½x¾" cookies.

The ring of sleigh bells fills the air as everyone races to church on Christmas Day in Finland.

SANDBAKELSER (Sand Tarts)

Fragile almond-flavored shells of Swedish origin, made in copper molds of varied designs.

Put through fine knife of food grinder twice . . .
*⅓ cup blanched almonds
*4 unblanched almonds
Mix in thoroughly . . .
¾ cup soft butter
¾ cup sugar
1 small egg white, unbeaten
Stir in . . .
1¾ cups *sifted* GOLD MEDAL Flour

In place of the almonds, you may use 1 tsp. vanilla and 1 tsp. almond flavoring.

Chill dough. Press dough *into* Sandbakels molds (or tiny fluted tart forms) to coat inside. Place on ungreased baking sheet. Bake until very delicately browned. Tap molds on table to loosen cookies and turn them out of the molds.

TEMPERATURE: 350° (mod. oven).

TIME: Bake 12 to 15 min.

AMOUNT: About 3 doz. cookies.

FILLED COOKY TURNOVERS (⚭ Recipe) *Tender, creamy-white . . . holding luscious fillings.*

See p. 194 for Easy Filled Cookies.
See p. 208 for Filled Sugar Cookies.

Mix thoroughly............................	½ cup soft shortening 1 cup sugar 2 eggs
Stir in..............................	2 tbsp. thick cream 1 tsp. vanilla
Sift together and stir in..................	2½ cups *sifted* GOLD MEDAL Flour ¼ tsp. soda ½ tsp. salt

Chill dough. Roll very thin (⅟₁₆"). Cut 3" rounds or squares. Place on lightly greased baking sheet. Place a rounded teaspoonful of desired cooled filling (*see at right below*) on each. Fold over like a turnover, pressing edges together with floured tines of a fork or tip of finger. Bake until delicately browned.

TEMPERATURE: 400° (mod. hot oven).
TIME: Bake 8 to 10 min.
AMOUNT: About 6 doz. 3" cookies.

FILLED COOKIES IN FANCY SHAPES

Follow ⚭ recipe above—but cut dough with scalloped round cooky cutter or with heart, diamond, or 2½" cutter of any desired shape, cutting 2 alike for each filled cooky. To give a decorative effect, cut the center out of the top cooky with a tiny cutter of heart, star, or scalloped round shape. Place the bottom pieces on lightly greased baking sheet. Spread desired filling (*see right*) on each . . . spreading up to edge. Cover with the top pieces. Press edges together.
AMOUNT: 4 doz. 2½" filled cookies.

Spread filling almost to the edges . . . when making filled cookies. To keep the filling in, press edges of filled cookies together with the fingers or with floured tines of a fork.

DATE, FIG, RAISIN, OR PRUNE FILLING

Cook together slowly, stirring constantly until thickened . . .
    2 cups dates, figs, or raisins, finely cut up, or
      2 cups mashed cooked prunes (2⅔ cups uncooked)
    ¾ cup sugar
    ¾ cup water
Add, if desired . . .
    ½ cup chopped nuts
Cool.
AMOUNT: Filling for about 5 doz. cookies.

Clean sticky fruits from your food grinder quickly and easily by running a few small pieces of dry bread through it.

PINEAPPLE FILLING

Mix in saucepan . . .
    1 cup sugar
    ¼ cup GOLD MEDAL Flour
Stir in . . .
    1½ cups well drained crushed pineapple (no. 2 can)
    ¼ cup lemon juice
    3 tbsp. butter
    ¼ tsp. nutmeg
    ¾ cup pineapple juice

Cook slowly, stirring constantly, until thickened (5 to 10 min.). Cool.
AMOUNT: Filling for 4 doz. cookies.

HOW TO MAKE COOKIES WITH A PRESS

Use a dough rich in shortening, such as that for Butter Cookies (*p. 209*), Spritz, and Almond Wreaths (*below*). If very warm, chill the dough. But keep it pliable. (It crumbles if too cold.) Force dough through cooky press (or pastry tube), following manufacturer's directions, onto ungreased baking sheet.

SPRITZ (⚲ Recipe) ("Spurted out of a press") *Crisp, fragile, buttery-tasting curlicues.*

Mix thoroughly . . . .
- 1 cup soft butter
- ⅔ cup sugar
- 3 egg yolks
- 1 tsp. flavoring (almond or vanilla) or ¼ cup grated almonds

Work in with the hands . . . . 2½ cups *sifted* GOLD MEDAL Flour

Force the dough through cooky press onto ungreased baking sheet in letter S's, rosettes, fluted bars, or other desired shapes. Bake until set . . . but not brown.

TEMPERATURE: 400° (mod. hot oven).

TIME: Bake 7 to 10 min.

AMOUNT: About 6 doz. cookies.

CHOCOLATE SPRITZ

Follow ⚲ recipe above—*except* blend into the shortening mixture 2 sq. unsweetened chocolate (2 oz.), melted.

Have baking sheet cold before forcing cooky dough through press onto it. If sheet is not cold, the fat in the dough will melt and the cookies will pull away from the sheet when the press is lifted.

BUTTER COOKIES

Follow recipe for Butter Cookies on p. 209. Force pliable dough through cooky press onto ungreased baking sheet in form of flowers, wreaths, or any desired shapes.

Dough for press cookies may be rolled out and cut into desired shapes. For wreaths, cut with scalloped cooky cutter . . . then cut out center with a smaller sized cutter.

ALMOND WREATHS

Beautiful almond-topped garlands.

Mix thoroughly . . .
- 1 cup soft shortening (mostly butter)
- ¾ cup *sifted* confectioners' sugar
- 2 egg yolks
- 1 egg white
- 1 tsp. vanilla
- ¼ tsp. salt

Work in with the hands . . .
- 2 cups *sifted* GOLD MEDAL Flour

Force the dough through cooky press onto ungreased baking sheet in shape of wreaths. Brush wreaths with slightly beaten egg white. Sprinkle with mixture of 2 tbsp. sugar, ¼ tsp. cinnamon, and ¼ cup very finely chopped blanched almonds. Bake until set but not brown.

TEMPERATURE: 350° (mod. oven).

TIME: Bake 8 to 10 min.

AMOUNT: About 6 doz. cookies.

TO DECORATE

Press bits of red or green candied cherry into top of wreaths to simulate a bow.

HOW TO MAKE MOLDED COOKIES (preliminary steps on pp. 192–193)

1 With hands, roll dough into balls or into long, pencil-thick rolls, as indicated in recipe.

2 Flatten balls of dough with bottom of a glass dipped in flour (or with a damp cloth around it), or with a fork—crisscross (see bottom of page).

3 Cut pencil-thick strips . . . and shape as directed . . . as for Almond Crescents (p. 219) or Berliner Kränze (p. 220).

DATE-OATMEAL COOKIES Like soft, old-fashioned rolled cookies . . . enriched with dates.

Mix thoroughly. . . . .
- ¾ cup soft shortening (half butter)
- 1 cup brown sugar (packed)
- 2 eggs
- 3 tbsp. milk
- 1 tsp. vanilla

Sift together and stir in. . . . .
- 2 cups *sifted* GOLD MEDAL Flour
- ¾ tsp. soda
- 1 tsp. salt

Stir in. . . . .
- 2 cups rolled oats
- 1½ cups cut-up dates
- ¾ cup chopped nuts, if desired

Chill dough. Roll into balls size of large walnuts. Place 3″ apart on lightly greased baking sheet. Flatten (to ¼″) with bottom of glass dipped in flour. Bake until lightly browned.

TEMPERATURE: 375° (quick mod. oven).

TIME: Bake 10 to 12 min.

AMOUNT: About 4 doz. 2½″ cookies.

PEANUT BUTTER COOKIES (⚡ Recipe) Crunchy rounds. Perfect for the Children's Hour.

Mix thoroughly . . . .
- ½ cup soft shortening (half butter)
- ½ cup peanut butter
- ½ cup sugar
- ½ cup brown sugar (packed)
- 1 egg

Sift together and stir in. . . . .
- 1¼ cups *sifted* GOLD MEDAL Flour
- ½ tsp. baking powder
- ¾ tsp. soda
- ¼ tsp. salt

Chill dough. Roll into balls size of large walnuts. Place 3″ apart on lightly greased baking sheet. Flatten with fork dipped in flour . . . crisscross. Bake until set . . . but not hard.

TEMPERATURE: 375° (quick mod. oven).

TIME: Bake 10 to 12 min.

AMOUNT: About 3 doz. 2½″ cookies.

HONEY PEANUT BUTTER COOKIES

Follow ⚡ recipe above—*except* use only ¼ cup shortening, and in place of brown sugar use ½ cup honey.

Flattening balls of dough with fork.

THUMBPRINT COOKIES *Nut-rich . . . the thumb dents filled with sparkling jelly.*

We are as delighted with this quaint addition to our cooky collection, from Ken MacKenzie, as is the collector of old glass when a friend presents her with some early thumbprint goblets.

Mix thoroughly . . . . {
½ cup soft shortening (half butter)
¼ cup brown sugar (packed)
1 egg yolk
½ tsp. vanilla

Sift together and stir in . . . . {
1 cup *sifted* GOLD MEDAL Flour
¼ tsp. salt

Roll into 1" balls. Dip in slightly beaten egg whites. Roll in finely chopped nuts (¾ cup). Place about 1" apart on ungreased baking sheet and press thumb into center of each. Bake until set. Cool. Place in thumbprints a bit of chopped candied fruit, sparkling jelly, or tinted confectioners' sugar icing.

TEMPERATURE: 375° (quick mod. oven).
TIME: Bake 10 to 12 min.
AMOUNT: About 2 doz. 1½" cookies.

BON BON COOKIES

Fascinating. Beautiful. Delicious. Bake them as cookies. Eat them as candies. They're full of surprises inside and out. And easy as 1-2-3. Created by a true westerner, Mrs. Joseph J. Wallace, high in her Rocky Mountain home near Whitehall, Montana. (See color picture, p. 202.)

Mix thoroughly . . .
½ cup soft butter
¾ cup *sifted* confectioners' sugar
1 tbsp. vanilla
food coloring, if desired
Mix in with hand . . .
1½ cups *sifted* GOLD MEDAL Flour
⅛ tsp. salt

If dough is dry, add 1 or 2 tbsp. cream. Wrap level tbsp. dough around filling (a candied or well drained maraschino cherry, pitted date, gumdrop, or ½ tsp. of mixture of 1 sq. unsweetened chocolate, melted, and ½ cup shredded coconut). Place 1" apart on ungreased baking sheet. Bake until set but not brown. Dip tops of warm cookies in Icing (*at right above*). Decorate with chopped nuts, coconut, candied fruit, chocolate pieces, etc.

Chocolate Dough: Blend in 1 sq. unsweetened chocolate (1 oz.), melted.

Penuche Dough: Use ½ cup brown sugar (packed) in place of confectioners' sugar.

TEMPERATURE: 350° (mod. oven).
TIME: Bake 12 to 15 min.
AMOUNT: 1½ to 2 doz. cookies.

> Let your ingenuity be your guide in varying the taste and beauty of Bon Bon Cookies in many fascinating ways.

The perfect gift—Bon Bon Cookies

BON BON COOKIES ICING

Mix . . .
1 cup *sifted* confectioners' sugar
2 tbsp. cream
1 tsp. vanilla
food coloring, if desired

For Chocolate Icing: Add 1 sq. unsweetened chocolate (1 oz.), melted, and use ¼ cup cream.

ALMOND CRESCENTS

Richly delicate, buttery. Party favorites.

Mix thoroughly . . .
1 cup soft shortening (half butter)
⅓ cup sugar
⅔ cup ground blanched almonds
Sift together and work in . . .
1⅔ cups *sifted* GOLD MEDAL Flour
¼ tsp. salt

Chill dough. Roll with hands pencil-thick. Cut in 2½" lengths. Form into crescents on ungreased baking sheet. Bake until set . . . not brown. Cool on pan. While slightly warm, carefully dip in 1 cup confectioners' sugar and 1 tsp. cinnamon, mixed.

TEMPERATURE: 325° (slow mod. oven).
TIME: Bake 14 to 16 min.
AMOUNT: About 5 doz. 2½" cookies.

219

RUSSIAN TEACAKES *Crunchy, sugared, nut-filled snowballs.*

This favorite with men came to us from a man. Carl Burkland, an eastern radio executive, often makes them himself at Christmastime.

Mix thoroughly . . . .
{ 1 cup soft butter
½ cup *sifted* confectioners' sugar
1 tsp. vanilla

Sift together and stir in . . . .
{ 2¼ cups *sifted* GOLD MEDAL Flour
¼ tsp. salt

Mix in . . . .
¾ cup finely chopped nuts

Chill dough. Roll into 1″ balls. Place on ungreased baking sheet (cookies do not spread). Bake until set, but not brown. While still warm, roll in confectioners' sugar. Cool. Roll in sugar again.

TEMPERATURE: 400° (mod. hot oven).

TIME: Bake 10 to 12 min.

AMOUNT: About 4 doz. 1″ cookies.

CANADIAN HONEY DROPS

These soft brown sugar cookies look just like children's Yo-Yos when put together in pairs with apricot jam between. Mrs. W. G. Oliver of Winnipeg, Manitoba, mother of Margaret Oliver of our Canadian office in Toronto, sent us this treasured recipe.

Mix thoroughly . . .
1 cup soft shortening (part butter)
1 cup brown sugar (packed)
2 eggs

Stir in . . .
⅓ cup honey
1 tsp. vanilla

Sift together and stir in . . .
3½ cups *sifted* GOLD MEDAL Flour
2 tsp. soda

Chill until firm . . . several hours or overnight. Roll into balls size of larger walnuts. Place on ungreased baking sheet. Bake until, when lightly touched with finger, almost no imprint remains. When slightly cooled, put together in pairs with apricot or other jam between.

TEMPERATURE: 350° (mod. oven).

TIME: Bake 10 to 12 min.

AMOUNT: 3 doz. double 2″ cookies.

BUTTER FINGERS

Nut-flavored, rich, buttery party cookies.

Follow recipe for Almond Crescents (*p. 219*)—except, in place of almonds, use black walnuts or other nuts, *chopped*. Cut into finger lengths and bake. While still warm, roll in confectioners' sugar. Cool, and roll in the sugar again.

BERLINER KRÄNZE (Berlin Wreaths)

Delicious and buttery, these gay little wreaths are made each holiday season in Norway.

Mix thoroughly . . .
1½ cups soft shortening (half butter)
1 cup sugar
2 tsp. grated orange rind
2 eggs

Stir in . . .
4 cups *sifted* GOLD MEDAL Flour

Chill dough. Break off small pieces and roll to pencil size about 6″ long and ¼″ thick. Form each piece into a circle, bringing one end over and through in a single knot. (*See sketch below.*) Leave ½″ end on each side. Place on ungreased baking sheet. Brush tops with *meringue* (made by beating 1 egg white until stiff, gradually beating in 2 tbsp. sugar). Press bits of red candied cherries on center of knot for holly berries. Add little jagged leaves cut out of green citron. Bake until set . . . but not brown.

TEMPERATURE: 400° (mod. hot oven).

TIME: Bake 10 to 12 min.

AMOUNT: About 6 doz. 2″ cookies.

All you have to do —

To shape a Berliner Kränz: form a circle and bring one end over and through.

If rich dough splits apart or seems crumbly, let it get slightly warm or work in a few drops of liquid until the dough sticks together.

Desserts.... The Grand Finale

We look forward to dessert. It is like the last act of a play . . . the happy ending we've anticipated from the first. This may be a gorgeous fanfare of triumph, or a homey, heart-satisfying scene. In the same way the dessert, in keeping with the meal preceding it, can be dramatic and spectacular, or a cozy old-time favorite beloved by generations.

Betty Crocker

THERE'S A DESSERT FOR EVERY OCCASION
Below are listed a few suggestions from the many in this chapter.

COME FOR DESSERT
At 2 in the afternoon or 8 in the evening.

It's a charming custom, and one that's easy on the hostess, to ask your guests for dessert only. Use your prettiest linen, china, and silver. Choose a glamorous dessert from the many in this chapter. Among impressive ones, are those listed under "For Entertaining" or "For Holidays" at left. With the dessert, serve coffee . . . and, if you wish, salted nuts and pastel mints to accent your color scheme.

ICE CREAM BALLS

Place scoops or balls of ice cream, ices, and sherbets in a variety of flavors and colors on cold baking sheet. Put uncovered in food freezer. When solid, wrap and store in freezer.

ALOHA SAUCE

For fruit cocktails. Especially delicious and refreshing on melon balls.

Mix thoroughly 2 tbsp. *each* strained lemon juice, orange juice, and lime juice; ⅓ cup water; and ⅔ cup sugar. Chill.

DAISY FLOAT

Tuck a daisy or other flower in season into ends of each sipper for a child's party. Fill glasses ⅔ full with Chocolate Milk or Fruit Milk Shake (*p. 73*). Drop scoop of vanilla or chocolate ice cream into each glass. Serve immediately.

COLORFUL GELATIN EASTER EGGS

Save egg shells where only the tip was broken away when egg was removed. Fill thoroughly dried shells with fruit-flavored gelatin in different colors. Set in muffin cups to chill until gelatin is firm. Break away shells. Serve in little nests of coconut on large chop plate.

FROSTED GRAPES

Pick over and wash grapes, dividing into small bunches. Sprinkle with sugar. Place in defrosting (not freezing) tray of refrigerator 1 hr.

CRÈME BRULÉE . . . In Haste

Place cultured sour cream in shallow pan. Sprinkle with brown sugar. Broil until bubbly. Serve over fruit.

QUICK BAKED ALASKA

Buy the small round individual sponge-type shortcake bases from your grocer or baker to make Baked Alaskas (*p. 245*) in record time.

ICE CREAM SUNDAE CAKES

Bake your favorite Betty Crocker Cake Mix in 9" layers or 13x9" oblong pan. Cut in wedges or squares and top with scoop of ice cream. Serve fresh fruit or a chocolate or butterscotch sauce over each serving. Frost the remaining cake or freeze (*p. 24*) to have on hand for later use.

WHIPPED ICE CREAM

Whip ice cream with electric mixer at med. speed or with wooden spoon until softened and smooth. Do not melt. Spoon the whipped ice cream over cake, pie, or dessert. Top with crushed raspberries or strawberries or other fruit.

VARIETY WITH ICE CREAM

Into 1 qt. vanilla ice cream (homemade or commercial), blend special flavor ingredients (*p. 254*). Work quickly to prevent melting. Replace in freezer or freeze in tray until firm again.

HURRY-UP COBBLERS, SHORTCAKES

See Bisquick pkg. Use canned berry pie fillings available at your grocer's.

QUICK TAPIOCA OR RICE PUDDINGS

Prepare as directed on pkg.

ICE CREAM SHAKES

Combine 1 part fresh fruit with 2 parts vanilla ice cream and a few drops lemon juice. Beat until smooth in blender or mixer. Serve in small glasses or cups with colored straws.

WHIPPED GELATIN

For a frothy appearance, when gelatin is partially set, beat with rotary beater until light. (A stiffly beaten egg white may be folded in.) Mold and chill. Serve with cold Speedy Custard Sauce (*below*).

SWEETENED WHIPPED CREAM

For topping Angel Food, Chiffon, Sponge cakes . . . and cream and fruit pies.

Chill deep bowl and beater.

Then place in bowl and beat together until stiff . . .

1 cup chilled whipping cream (35 or 40%)
¼ cup *sifted* confectioners' sugar
flavoring, if desired

SPEEDY CUSTARD SAUCE

Use vanilla pudding mix and add 1½ times the amount of milk the recipe on package calls for. This is never-fail.

FRUITED CREAM FILLING AND FROSTING: See p. 247.

COCOA FLUFF TOPPING: See p. 246.

ORANGE FLUFF FILLING AND TOPPING: See p. 245.

WHIPPED CREAM FRUIT FILLINGS: See p. 248.

DESSERTS

Dessert originally meant food served after the table had been cleared or "deserted" of everything else . . . even the cloth removed. We find accounts of grand dinners served in the early days of our country describing the polished mahogany tables with candles in tall silver candelabra casting a mellow glow over the guests enjoying a "dessert" of fresh fruit. In Europe, "dessert" still means fruit served at the end of the meal. However, for them, this fruit course follows a "sweet" . . . that is, a pudding, pastry, soufflé, or an elaborate torte creation. We Americans have simply promoted the "sweet" to the place of honor at the end of the meal.

European visitors in our country are amazed at the array of "sweets" Americans have to choose from. In addition to those we have adopted from other nations, British steamed puddings, German and Austrian tortes, French meringues, and Italian soufflés, we have developed our own special favorites, including ice creams and our fruit shortcakes and cobblers.

This wide variety of truly delightful desserts makes it difficult to choose a selection for one chapter. It would have been easier to fill a whole cook book with dessert recipes. We have tried, however, to give you dessert favorites of each type. You will find some that are suitable for holiday dinners and parties . . . others for simple family meals where consideration must be given to what the children may eat. Then there are the elaborate distinctly party desserts for buffet suppers or dessert luncheons. Of course we have made it a point to include homey, old-time favorites, too!

With all these at your fingertips, we hope you will have fun serving desserts that will bring each meal to a satisfying and delightful finish.

FLAMING PEACH JUBILEE DESSERT

Bake your favorite spice cake in layers. Cool. Put together and top with sweetened whipped cream. Arrange drained peach halves over cake. Center each with sugar lump soaked in lemon extract. Light sugar lumps . . . bring to table flaming!

FRESH FRUIT AND CHEESE

The easiest of all desserts.

A bowl heaped with colorful fruit washed, dried, and chilled—a variety to choose from . . . is both decorative and tempting. Cheese and crisp unsweetened crackers are natural affinities, or crisp rich cookies are pleasant accompaniments. Serving can be very simple: just an individual dessert plate, a suitable knife for cutting fruit and spreading soft cheese. Finger bowls are correct to save linens from stubborn fruit stains, but nowadays paper napkins are often used with fruit.

INFORMAL COMPANY DESSERT TRAY

Guests will be thrilled with this charming Hospitality Tray, an idea from Marye Dahnke of Kraft Foods Company.

Arrange sections of fresh cored (but not peeled) pears petal-fashion on lettuce or grape leaves. Surround with cored (but not peeled) apple rings. On outer edge of tray place alternate wedges of American Camembert and American Roquefort or Bleu cheeses.

Fruits are used in place of crackers: pears with American Roquefort or Bleu cheese, and apples with American Camembert.

SALADS SERVED AS DESSERTS

See "SALADS" for many delightful fruit combinations.

FRESH FRUIT DESSERTS IN SEASON

Combinations always popular.

- Honeydew melon with lime or lemon, and garnish of mint leaves.
- Cantaloupe filled with ice cream.
- Peaches and raspberries, plain or with ice cream.
- Brandy-flavored cherries and ice cream.
- Strawberries, raspberries, blackberries, or blueberries with cream.
- Sliced peaches and cream.
- Sliced bananas with raspberries or sliced strawberries, topped with a mound of ice cream, or with whipped cream or sour cream sprinkled with brown sugar.
- Orange slices in orange juice. Orange Ice added.
- Grapefruit halves, either chilled or Broiled (*p. 62*), centered with cherries.

CHEESE AND FRUIT PARTNERS ... *with bread or cracker accompaniment.*

- Concord grapes. Smoked, French Brie, Gouda, Edam, or Swiss cheese. Salty crackers.
- Red apples. Camembert, Liederkranz, or New York cheese. Gingersnaps. Nuts.
- Fresh Pears. Bar-le-duc (currant preserves). Cream cheese. Buttered hot tiny baking powder biscuits or salty crackers.

Fresh strawberries (with hulls) around a mound of cream cheese sweetened with confectioners' sugar, a hint of rum flavoring. Dip strawberries into cheese mixture.

- Tokay grapes. Mild brick or Cheddar cheese. Thin slices of buttered Pumpernickel (*p. 109*).

Gouda or Edam cheese (cut in wedges almost to bottom but left intact). Circles of onion and garlic-flavored cheese, melon wedges, small green grapes, Bing cherries with stems. Assorted crackers.

- Green Gage or other plums (Italian prunes) stewed with strips of candied ginger, served chilled with Brie or other soft sharp cheese. Crackers.
- Wedges of unhulled fresh pineapple, Camembert, Liederkranz, or sharp New York cheese. Whole wheat crackers.
- Tart plums and sugared blue grapes. Thin slices buttered caraway rye bread. Camembert, Roquefort, or Bleu cheese.

FRUIT AMBROSIA

Make it with any fruit you have on hand.

Sprinkle fruit (such as orange slices, bananas, unpared red apples, pineapple) with confectioners' sugar. Chill. Just before serving, top with plain or toasted coconut, salted peanuts or almonds, or maraschino cherries.

SOUTHERN AMBROSIA

Pile shredded fresh coconut with orange slices into sherbet glasses.

MEXICAN AMBROSIA

Heap snowy shredded coconut over slice of fresh or drained canned pineapple on each dessert plate.

BAKED APPLES

Choose baking-type apples such as Roman Beauty, Jonathan, Wealthy, or Greening.

Wash and core apples. Either pare upper half of apples or slit around center. Place in baking dish; fill center of each apple with 1 to 2 tbsp. granulated or brown sugar, 1 tsp. butter, and ⅛ tsp. cinnamon. Cover bottom of pan with water about ¼″ deep. Bake uncovered until tender when pierced with fork (time varies with apple size and variety). Baste syrup over apples occasionally while baking.

TEMPERATURE: 375° (quick mod. oven).

TIME: Bake about 45 min.

BUTTER-GLAZED APPLES

Serve warm or cold with cream or ice cream. Or offer as an accompaniment to pork.

Melt in large skillet . . .
    2 tbsp. butter
Add . . .
    1 qt. sliced, cored, washed apples (4 med.)
Sprinkle with . . .
    ½ cup granulated or brown sugar
    1 tsp. cinnamon

Cover skillet, cook over low heat for 10 min. Remove cover. Cook over med. heat, stirring frequently, until apples are glazed, tender, and slightly transparent.

AMOUNT: 4 to 6 servings.

COOKED FRESH FRUIT ("SAUCE")

Easy, popular everyday dessert . . . served with a cooky or piece of cake.

Wash, pare, core, cut up or leave whole . . .
    1 qt. fresh, firm fruit (apples, peaches, pears, plums, cherries)

Bring to boil in saucepan . . .
    1 cup sugar
    1 cup water

Add prepared fruit. Simmer until tender and slightly transparent. Cool.

COOKED DRIED FRUIT ("SAUCE")

Prunes, apricots, apples, pears, peaches, figs.

Packaged Dried Fruit: follow cooking directions on pkg. **Bulk Dried Fruit:** wash, soak in cold water until plump, simmer in same water until tender (30 to 45 min.), then sweeten to taste.

OLD-FASHIONED APPLESAUCE

Especially good with Greenings, Wealthies, Baldwins, Jonathans, or Winesaps.

Wash, pare, if desired, quarter, and core apples. Add water about ½″ deep in pan; cover, and simmer until tender. Sweeten to taste (about ¼ cup sugar to 4 med. apples), and again bring to boil. If desired, press through sieve or colander. Season with cinnamon.

RHUBARB SAUCE (♪ Recipe)

"A Spring tonic," said our grandmothers. "And it is so pretty if it's pink."

Wash and cut rhubarb in 1″ pieces (*p. 32*). Use 1 cup sugar for 4 cups rhubarb. Cook as for Old-fashioned Applesauce above— *except* omit cinnamon.

RHUBARB-STRAWBERRY SAUCE

Follow ♪ recipe above—*except* use 3 parts rhubarb to 1 of strawberries.

to poach fruit

Cook it gently (a single layer) just until tender in a thin sugar-and-water syrup of 1½ cups sugar and ¾ cup water. Do not stir. Dip syrup over fruit to glaze.

TAPIOCA CREAM (🖊 Recipe)

The fluffy type.

Mix in saucepan . . .
    2 egg yolks, slightly beaten
    2 cups milk
    2 tbsp. sugar
    2 tbsp. quick-cooking tapioca
    ¼ tsp. salt

Cook over low heat, stirring constantly, until mixture boils. Remove from heat. Cool. Stir in . . .
    1 tsp. vanilla

Fold in Meringue (method on p. 362) made with . . .
    2 egg whites
    ¼ cup sugar

Spoon into dessert dishes. Serve with cream or with grape, raspberry, or other fruit juice.

AMOUNT: 6 servings.

ORANGE TAPIOCA CREAM

Follow 🖊 recipe above—*except* add 1 tbsp. grated orange rind with the 2 tbsp. sugar. In place of vanilla, use 1 tbsp. lemon juice. Garnish with orange sections.

PEANUT BRITTLE TAPIOCA CREAM

Follow 🖊 recipe above—*except* fold in at the last ¼ cup crushed peanut brittle.

CHOCOLATE TAPIOCA CREAM

Follow 🖊 recipe above—*except* fold in at the last semi-sweet chocolate pieces.

PINEAPPLE TAPIOCA CREAM

Follow 🖊 recipe above—*except* reduce milk to 1½ cups and omit vanilla. Add no. 1 flat can undrained crushed pineapple (1 cup) before cooking.

FRUIT TAPIOCA CREAM

Follow 🖊 recipe above—*except* fold in at the last drained fresh, frozen, or canned fruit or berries.

FRUIT SOUP (Frukt Suppa)

Serve as a dessert. A. Herbert Nelson, Minneapolis, Minnesota, says that as a child in his home in Willmar, Minnesota, his mother served it once each day and twice on Sundays.

See recipe on p. 63. Popular also as a first course appetizer. And no smorgasbord is complete without it.

OLD-FASHIONED CREAMY RICE PUDDING

Requests come to us often for this recipe.

Combine in top of double boiler . . .
    ½ cup uncooked rice (not instant-type)
    ½ tsp. salt
    ¼ cup sugar
    ¼ tsp. cinnamon or nutmeg
    2½ cups milk
    ½ cup seedless raisins, if desired

Cook covered over boiling water until rice is tender and milk is almost absorbed (1 hr.), stirring frequently. Serve warm with cream or a soft custard.

AMOUNT: 6 to 8 servings.

INSTANT RICE PUDDING

Make it in a hurry; it's good, too!

Combine in saucepan . . .
    1 cup uncooked instant-type rice
    1½ cups milk
    3 or 4 tbsp. sugar
    ½ tsp. salt
    ¼ tsp. cinnamon or nutmeg
    ¼ cup seedless raisins, if desired

Bring to a full rolling boil, stirring constantly. Remove from heat. Cover and let stand 12 to 15 min., stirring occasionally. Serve warm with cream.

AMOUNT: 4 servings.

GLORIFIED RICE

Margret Christopher of our staff says: "To me, this is the perfect dessert."

Mix . . .
    1 cup cold Boiled Rice (p. 290)
    ½ cup sugar
    1½ cups crushed pineapple, drained
    ½ tsp. vanilla
    1 cup whipping cream, whipped
    8 marshmallows, cut up

Chill very thoroughly before serving.

AMOUNT: 6 to 8 servings.

MOLDED FRUIT GELATIN (⚲ Recipe)

An old standby . . . a favorite for everyday meals, buffets, smorgasbords, and church bazaars.

Prepare according to pkg. directions . . .
    1 pkg. fruit-flavored gelatin
        (Use juice from canned or frozen fruit for some of liquid, if desired.)

Cool until mixture begins to thicken.

Then stir in . . .
    1 tbsp. lemon juice ⎫ if desired
    1 tsp. grated lemon rind ⎬
    1 to 2 cups drained cut-up fruit (fresh or canned)

Pour into 1-qt. mold or 6 individual molds. Chill until set. Unmold. Serve with cream, whipped cream, or a soft custard (*p. 230*).
AMOUNT: 6 servings.

MELON GRAPE ROYAL

Bring to boil . . .
    1 cup grape juice

Pour over, stirring to dissolve . . .
    2 pkg. lemon-flavored gelatin

Add another 2 cups grape juice. Pour into 1-qt. ring mold. Chill until firm. Unmold on serving plate and fill center with 3 cups assorted melon balls. Garnish with grape or mint leaves.
AMOUNT: 6 to 8 servings.

FRUIT-FILLED HONEYDEW

"Serve these pretty slices on dessert plates and garnish with at least 6 unstemmed Bing cherries," says Mrs. William E. Bjerke, Jr., Mason City, Iowa.

Prepare according to pkg. directions . . .
    1 pkg. lime-flavored gelatin

Chill until partially set. Slice off one end of a peeled honeydew melon and scoop out seeds and fiber. At the other end, cut off just enough so melon will stand firmly upright. Turn upside down on absorbent paper to drain.

Fold into partially set gelatin . . .
    2 cups little sweet green grapes

Fill cavity of melon with lime-grape mixture. Cover with waxed paper and refrigerate until gelatin is firm. (The remaining mixture can be chilled in custard cups or individual molds.) Cut into 1" slices just before serving.
AMOUNT: 6 to 8 servings.

SUMMER FRUIT COMPOTE

A colorful variety of fruits held together by soft gelatin. Enjoyed at Ann Mulholland's home in Santa Barbara, California.

Follow ⚲ recipe at left—*except* use 4 cups mixed *fresh* fruits (strawberries, cherries, green grapes, melon balls, sliced peaches, etc.) and add 2 tbsp. Cointreau or sherry flavoring. Serve in a large compote.

STRAWBERRY BAVARIAN CREAM (⚲ Recipe)

"Perfect," says Mrs. J. Hollingsworth Senseni, Webster Groves, Missouri. "Made-in-advance chilled desserts are my specialty during the heat of summer."

Thaw and drain juice from 10-oz. pkg. frozen strawberries. Prepare according to pkg. directions . . .
    1 pkg. strawberry-flavored gelatin
        (Use 1 cup boiling water and strawberry juice with cold water to make 1 cup.)

Chill until almost firm.

Whip until stiff . . .
    1 cup whipping cream

Beat gelatin until foamy. Fold together whipped cream, whipped gelatin, and drained strawberries (½ cup). Spoon into 1-qt. mold or 6 to 8 individual molds. Chill until firm. Unmold. Garnish with fresh unhulled strawberries or other fruits. Top with whipped cream or a soft custard (*p. 230*), if desired.
AMOUNT: 6 to 8 servings.

RASPBERRY BAVARIAN CREAM

Follow ⚲ recipe above—*except* use raspberry-flavored gelatin and frozen raspberries.

PINEAPPLE BAVARIAN CREAM

Follow ⚲ recipe above—*except* use lemon-flavored gelatin and a no. 1 flat can of crushed pineapple instead of frozen fruit.

FRESH STRAWBERRY OR RASPBERRY BAVARIAN CREAM

See Strawberry or Raspberry Chiffon Pie (*p. 366*). Mold and serve filling as above.

LIME, LEMON, OR ORANGE BAVARIAN CREAM

See Lemon Chiffon Pie and variations (*p. 366*). Mold and serve filling as above.

Bavarian, Velvet, or Spanish Cream . . . names applied to smooth, creamy, molded desserts of gelatin and milk made delicate with whipped cream or fluffy egg whites.

CRÈME VANILLE (Vanilla Bavarian Cream) (🖋 Recipe) As elegant as its French name.

Blend thoroughly in saucepan. . . . .

> ½ cup sugar
> 1 envelope unflavored gelatin (1 tbsp.)
> ¼ tsp. salt
> 2¼ cups milk
> 4 egg yolks, slightly beaten

Cook over med. heat, stirring constantly, just until mixture comes to a boil. Place pan in cold water; cool until mixture mounds slightly when dropped from a spoon. Fold in . . . .

> 1 cup whipping cream, whipped stiff
> 1 tsp. vanilla

Pour into buttered 1-qt. mold. Chill until firm (about 4 hr.). Unmold on large serving dish. Garnish with Sweetened Whipped Cream (*p. 222*) and fresh fruit, such as strawberries, raspberries, or sliced peaches. AMOUNT: 8 servings.

MOCHA BAVARIAN CREAM

Follow 🖋 recipe above—*except* add 3 tbsp. powdered instant coffee to mixture before cooking. Garnish with whipped cream, sprinkle with toasted slivered almonds or crushed peanut brittle.

> ### TO UNMOLD GELATIN DESSERTS
> Cut around edge of mold. Let air in at side, shaking gently to loosen gelatin mixture. Place serving plate on top, invert mold . . . then lift off. If gelatin mixture sticks, dip mold quickly into hot water . . . gelatin will slip out easily.

CHOCOLATE MARSHMALLOW CREAM
Lovely, fluffy pudding.

Blend thoroughly in saucepan . . .
> ½ cup sugar
> 1 envelope unflavored gelatin (1 tbsp.)
> 2¼ cups milk
> 1 sq. unsweetened chocolate (1 oz.)

Cook over med. heat, stirring constantly, just until mixture comes to a boil. Place pan in cold water; cool until mixture mounds slightly when dropped from a spoon.

Stir in . . .
> ¼ lb. marshmallows (11 to 16), cut up
> ¼ cup ground nuts, if desired

Fold in . . .
> 2 egg whites, stiffly beaten
> 1 cup whipping cream, whipped stiff

Chill 4 hr. Serve in sherbet glasses.

AMOUNT: 8 servings.

CHOCOLATE BAVARIAN CREAM

Follow 🖋 recipe above—*except* add ½ cup semi-sweet chocolate pieces to mixture before cooking. Remove from heat. Stir until chocolate pieces are entirely or partially melted.

PEPPERMINT CREAM

Serve in sherbet glasses with Frosted Brownies (*p. 204*). Or use as filling for Chocolate Peppermint Dream (*p. 258*). Garnish with sprig of fresh mint.

Melt together over hot water . . .
> 24 marshmallows
> ½ cup milk

Remove from heat. Cool slightly; then stir in . . .
> 3 drops peppermint flavoring
> 1 tsp. vanilla
> ⅛ tsp. salt
> few drops green or red food coloring

Cool until mixture mounds slightly when dropped from spoon. Fold in . . .
> 1 cup whipping cream, whipped stiff

ORANGE OR PINEAPPLE MARSHMALLOW CREAM

Afternoon-out dessert contributed by Mrs. Earl Gammons of Washington, D. C.

Heat in saucepan over low heat . . .
> 1 cup orange juice (with pulp)
>   or 1 cup crushed pineapple
> ¼ lb. marshmallows (11 to 16), cut up
> ½ tbsp. lemon juice (with pineapple only)

Stir until marshmallows are dissolved. Remove from heat. Cool. When partially set, fold in . . .
> ½ cup whipping cream, whipped stiff

Chill 4 hr. Serve in sherbet glasses. Garnish with fresh fruit or berries.

AMOUNT: 4 servings.

BAKED CUSTARD

Beat slightly to mix . . .
> 2 eggs (or 4 egg yolks)
> 1/3 cup sugar
> 1/4 tsp. salt

Scald (crinkly film forms on top) . . .
> 2 cups milk

Stir into egg mixture. Add . . .
> 1/2 tsp. vanilla, if desired

Pour into 6 custard cups or a 1½-qt. baking dish and set in pan of hot water (1″ deep). Sprinkle a little nutmeg over top. Bake just until silver knife inserted 1″ from edge comes out clean (soft center sets as it stands). Immediately remove from heat. Serve cool or chilled in same cups on dessert plates, or unmold and serve. Pass grape or other fruit juice to pour over, if desired.

TEMPERATURE: 350° (mod. oven).
TIME: Bake 45 to 50 min.
AMOUNT: 6 servings.

BAKED CARAMEL CUSTARD

A hotel on the Bay of Naples served it on a silver platter under a glistening cover of spun caramelized sugar.

Caramelize 1/2 cup sugar (*p. 29*). Pour a little into each custard cup. Move cups about so that caramel will coat sides. When caramel is hard, fill cups with custard (follow recipe above for Baked Custard—*except* add 1 more egg). When unmolded, melted caramel runs down sides forming a sauce.

POT DE CRÈME AU CHOCOLAT

An elegant chocolate custard cream from France.

Melt over hot water . . .
> 1/4 lb. German sweet chocolate

Gradually stir in until smooth . . .
> 1 tbsp. sugar
> 1/2 cup cream

Remove from heat; slowly blend into . . .
> 2 egg yolks, slightly beaten
> 1/2 tsp. vanilla

Pour into small individual dessert dishes or demitasse cups (use little after dinner coffee spoons with these). Chill. Serve with garnish of whipped cream.

AMOUNT: 4 servings.

SOFT CUSTARD

Delicate pudding or sauce to dress up other desserts.

Scald in top of double boiler over direct heat . . .
> 1 1/2 cups milk

Beat in small bowl . . .
> 4 egg yolks
> (or 2 whole eggs)

Blend in . . .
> 1/4 cup sugar
> 1/4 tsp. salt

Gradually stir in scalded milk. Return to double boiler. Cook over simmering (not boiling) water, stirring constantly. When custard coats silver spoon (thin coating), remove from heat. Cool quickly. If custard should start to curdle, beat vigorously at once with rotary beater until smooth. Blend in 1 tsp. vanilla. Serve in sherbet glasses topped with whipped cream; or use as a sauce over fruit, cake, or other desserts.

AMOUNT: 6 servings.

EASY CUSTARD SAUCE

No cooking over hot water required.

Make Rich Custard Filling (*p. 241*)—then thin to desired consistency with milk (1 1/2 to 2 cups).
AMOUNT: 1 qt.

FRUIT CUSTARD

Robert S. Bryant, prominent orchid grower of Clear Springs, Hopkins, Minnesota, says "Orchids to you!" when Mrs. Bryant makes this with fresh raspberries from their own bushes.

Make either Soft Custard or Easy Custard Sauce above—*except* pour over cut-up fresh fruit (bananas, orange sections, strawberries, raspberries, halved small green or seeded Tokay grapes) in individual dessert dishes or serving dish.

FLOATING ISLAND

Grandma called it "float," a company dessert presented in tall glass compote.

Make Soft Custard above—*except* make a meringue of 2 egg whites and 1/4 cup sugar. Drop this meringue as "islands" on hot custard in serving dish. Chill before serving.

INDIAN PUDDING

The Puritan women learned to make it from the Indians. In New England, it always shared the old brick oven with baked beans.

Mix in saucepan . . .
    ¼ cup corn meal (Indian Meal)
    1 cup water
    1 tsp. salt
    2 cups milk

Bring to boil, stirring constantly. Boil 10 min. Blend in a mixture of . . .
    1 egg, well beaten
    ¼ cup sugar
    ½ cup light molasses
    1 tbsp. butter
    1 tsp. cinnamon
    ½ tsp. ginger

Pour into buttered 1½-qt. baking dish. Bake ½ hr. then stir in . . .
    1 cup milk
Bake 1½ hr. more.
TEMPERATURE: 325° (slow mod. oven).
TIME: Bake 2 hr. (total).
AMOUNT: 6 servings.

APPLE CRISP (Apple Crumble) (🦴 Recipe)

Phyllis Berg (Mrs. Herbert A. Berg), St. Paul, Minnesota, known for the many "goodies" she serves to friends and neighbors, likes to substitute 1 cup graham cracker crumbs for the flour and oatmeal in this recipe.

Place in greased 8″ square pan . . .
    4 cups sliced, pared, cored baking apples
        (about 4 med.)
Blend until crumbly; then spread over apples . . .
    ⅔ to ¾ cup brown sugar (packed)
    ½ cup *sifted* GOLD MEDAL Flour
    ½ cup rolled oats
    ¾ tsp. cinnamon
    ¾ tsp. nutmeg
    ⅓ cup soft butter

Bake until apples are tender and topping is golden brown. Serve warm with cream, Whipped Ice Cream (*p. 222*), or Hard Sauce (*p. 405*).
TEMPERATURE: 375° (quick mod. oven).
TIME: Bake 30 to 35 min.
AMOUNT: 6 to 8 servings.

BROWN BETTY

"It's my favorite dessert!" says Marge Eggan. "And my cousins in Norway loved it when I made it for them from this recipe when I was there last summer."

Follow 🦴 recipe above—*except* place alternate layers of the sliced apples and crumb mixture in pan. Pour ¼ cup water over the top.

BLANC MANGE (Cornstarch Pudding) (🦴 Recipe)

The French name for "White Food."

Mix in saucepan . . .
    ⅓ cup sugar
    3 tbsp. cornstarch
    ¼ tsp. salt
Stir in gradually . . .
    2¼ cups milk

Cook over med. heat, stirring constantly, until mixture boils. Boil 1 min. Remove from heat. Blend in . . .
    1½ tsp. vanilla

Chill. Serve in sherbet glasses topped with fresh fruit, grape or other fruit juice, or whipped cream. Delicious, too, served warm topped with vanilla ice cream.
AMOUNT: 4 to 6 servings.

MACAROON BLANC MANGE

Follow 🦴 recipe above—*except*, at the last, fold in ½ cup whipping cream, whipped, and ½ cup macaroon crumbs.

CHOCOLATE BLANC MANGE
(Chocolate Pudding)

Follow 🦴 recipe above—*except* increase sugar to ⅔ cup. Add 2 sq. unsweetened chocolate (2 oz.), cut up, or ⅓ cup cocoa with the sugar.

STOUFFER'S BAKED PRUNE WHIP

A first choice dessert among guests at the famous Stouffer restaurants.

Beat together with rotary beater until stiff enough to hold shape (about 5 min.) . . .
    1 cup cooled cut-up prunes (cooked, drained, pitted)
    3 egg whites
    ⅓ cup sugar
    ¼ tsp. salt
Fold in, if desired . . .
    1 tbsp. lemon juice
    ¼ cup pecans, chopped

Pour into 1½-qt. baking dish. Set in pan of hot water (1″ deep). Bake until puffed and a thin coating has formed over the top. Serve with Sweetened Whipped Cream (*p. 222*) or a soft custard (*p. 230*).
TEMPERATURE: 350° (mod. oven).
TIME: Bake 30 to 35 min.
AMOUNT: 6 servings.

UNBAKED PRUNE WHIP

Make Prune Whip (above)—*except* do not bake. Fold in or serve garnished with Sweetened Whipped Cream (*p. 222*).

ED SULLIVAN'S MERINGUE BREAD PUDDING

Rich and delicate. Sometimes called "Queen's Pudding." The famous and popular newspaper columnist and television master of ceremonies gave us this recipe as one of his favorites.

Place in ungreased 1½-qt. baking dish . . . . .   2 cups fine dry bread crumbs (p. 30)

Blend in . . . .
3 cups scalded milk
1 whole egg plus 2 egg yolks, slightly beaten
⅓ cup sugar
1 tsp. vanilla

Sprinkle with nutmeg. Place baking dish in pan of hot water (1" deep). Bake until silver knife inserted 1" from edge comes out clean. Remove from oven. Spoon thin layer of currant jelly over pudding. Cover with a Meringue (*method on p. 362*) made of 2 egg whites and ¼ cup sugar. Return to oven and bake about 15 min., until meringue is browned. Cool 20 to 30 min. before serving.

TEMPERATURE: 350° (mod. oven).
TIME: Bake about 1 hr. and 15 min.
AMOUNT: 6 to 8 servings.

OLD-FASHIONED BREAD PUDDING
(⚷ Recipe) *Rich, crusty, raisin-filled.*

Place in 1½-qt. baking dish . . .
3 cups soft bread crumbs (p. 30)
(use 4 cups for firmer pudding)
Blend in . . .
2 cups milk, scalded with ¼ cup butter
½ cup sugar
2 eggs, slightly beaten
¼ tsp. salt
1 tsp. cinnamon or nutmeg
½ cup seedless raisins

Place baking dish in pan of hot water (1" deep). Bake until silver knife inserted 1" from edge comes out clean. Serve warm, with or without hard sauce or cream.

TEMPERATURE: 350° (mod. oven).
TIME: Bake 40 to 45 min.
AMOUNT: 6 servings.

CHOCOLATE BREAD PUDDING
Follow ⚷ recipe for Old-fashioned Bread Pudding—*except* use ½ cup semi-sweet chocolate pieces instead of raisins. Omit the spices.

BUTTERSCOTCH BREAD PUDDING
Follow ⚷ recipe for Old-fashioned Bread Pudding—*except* use brown sugar instead of granulated sugar.

DATE-AND-NUT BREAD PUDDING
Follow ⚷ recipe for Old-fashioned Bread Pudding—*except* use ½ cup chopped dates and ¼ cup broken nuts instead of the raisins.

DANISH APPLE PUDDING
Tart apple flavor blended with rich buttery bread crumbs and whipped cream. Easy to do. Loretta Bonde (Mrs. H. S. Bonde) of our staff brought us this recipe from her grandmother. Ole Risom, New York art director, says this brings fond memories of his Danish homeland.

Sauté gently until evenly browned . . .
1½ cups fine Zwieback crumbs or fine dry bread crumbs in . . .
⅓ cup butter
Line greased 8" square pan with half of crumb mixture. Mix . . .
2 cups applesauce (no. 303 can)
¼ tsp. salt
1 tbsp. lemon juice
½ tsp. cinnamon

Pour half of this mixture over crumbs; then cover with rest of crumbs and remaining applesauce. Top with Sweetened Whipped Cream (½ *recipe on p. 222*).

Chill several hours. Serve in squares decorated with bits of red jelly, if desired.
AMOUNT: 6 to 8 servings.

COTTAGE PUDDING (🦴 Recipe) *Fluffy, delicious, easy to make.*

Sift together into bowl...................
- 1 ¾ cups *sifted* GOLD MEDAL Flour
- 2 tsp. baking powder
- ½ tsp. salt

Add...............................
- ¼ cup soft shortening
- ¾ cup sugar
- 1 egg
- ¾ cup milk
- 1 tsp. vanilla

Beat until smooth. Pour into greased and floured 9″ square pan. Bake. Cut into 3″ squares. Serve warm with hot Vanilla, Lemon, Nutmeg, or Chocolate Sauce (*below*).

TEMPERATURE: 350° (mod. oven).

TIME: Bake 25 to 30 min.

AMOUNT: 9 servings.

VANILLA, LEMON, OR NUTMEG SAUCE

Mix in saucepan . . .
- 1 cup sugar
- 2 tbsp. cornstarch

Stir in gradually . . .
- 2 cups water

Boil 1 min., stirring constantly. Stir in . . .
- ¼ cup butter
- 2 tsp. vanilla or 2 tsp. lemon juice with 1 tbsp. grated lemon rind or 2 tsp. grated nutmeg

CHOCOLATE SAUCE: See p. 404.

CINNAMON FLUFF

Mrs. Mary Putnam of Pine Bluff, Arkansas, describes her prize-winning dessert as "more delicate than cake."

Mix thoroughly . . .
- ½ cup soft shortening
- ⅔ cup sugar
- 2 eggs

Sift together . . .
- 1 ½ cups *sifted* GOLD MEDAL Flour
- 2 tbsp. cinnamon
- 1 tsp. baking powder
- 1 tsp. soda
- ½ tsp. salt

Stir in alternately with . . .
- 1 cup sour milk

Pour into greased and floured 9″ square pan. Rub together ½ cup sugar, 1 tbsp. butter, 1 tbsp. cinnamon, and sprinkle over batter. Bake. Serve with cinnamon-flavored whipped cream or Lemon Sauce (*above*).

TEMPERATURE: 325° (slow mod. oven).

TIME: Bake 40 to 45 min.

AMOUNT: 9 servings.

CHERRY CARNIVAL

Rich, luscious cherry favorite from Mrs. Jessie Smith of Galesburg, Illinois.

Follow 🦴 recipe above—*except* increase sugar to 1 cup, omit vanilla. Blend in 2 cups cut-up well drained pitted sour cherries (no. 2 can, save juice) and ½ cup cut-up nuts. Bake 30 to 40 min. Serve hot with hot

CLEAR RED SAUCE

Mix in saucepan . . .
- ½ cup sugar
- 2 tbsp. cornstarch

Stir in gradually . . .
- 1 cup water
- ¾ cup juice from cherries or raspberries

Boil 1 min., stirring constantly. Stir in . . .
- ¼ tsp. almond flavoring
- few drops red food coloring, if desired

IOWA DATE PUDDING

Virginia Van Nostrand, formerly of our staff, finds this soft, rich combination of dates and nuts under a crusty meringue-like top a dessert to be served often.

Beat until light and fluffy . . .
- 3 eggs

Beat in thoroughly . . .
- 1 cup sugar

Sift together and stir in . . .
- ¼ cup GOLD MEDAL Flour
- 1 tsp. baking powder
- ¼ tsp. salt

Stir in . . .
- 2 ½ cups chopped dates (1 lb.)
- 1 cup broken nuts

Pour into greased 9″ square pan. Bake until golden brown. Serve warm with whipped cream.

TEMPERATURE: 350° (mod. oven).

TIME: Bake 25 to 30 min.

AMOUNT: 9 to 12 servings.

FAVORITE OLD-TIME PUDDINGS
on a red fringed tablecloth with great-grandmother's china

English Plum Pudding with Hard Sauce   Strawberry Shortcake

Squares of Favorite Gingerbread   Sauce   White Plum Duff   Fruit Cobbler

STRAWBERRY OR RASPBERRY SHORTCAKE (✗ Recipe)

See color picture opposite. The good old-time American dessert . . . still first choice. Frozen and fresh berries make a superb combination. Use 1 qt. in all.

Sift together into bowl . . .

2 cups *sifted* GOLD MEDAL Flour
2 tbsp. sugar
3 tsp. baking powder
1 tsp. salt

Cut in fine with pastry blender . .
⅓ cup shortening

Stir in, just until blended . . .
1 cup milk

Spread dough in 2 greased 8″ layer pans. Dot with butter. Bake until med. brown. Place one layer on serving plate upside down; cover with sweetened berries; top with other layer, right side up; cover with more berries. Serve warm with plain or whipped cream. Or serve Raspberry Shortcake with Raspberry Sauce (*p. 405*). Garnish with whole berries.

TEMPERATURE: 450° (hot oven).
TIME: Bake 12 to 15 min.
AMOUNT: 6 to 8 servings.

> For a less crusty shortcake, spread all the dough in one 8″ layer pan. Bake until med. brown, 15 to 20 min. Split crosswise while hot. Spread with butter, if desired. Fill and top with sweetened berries, as above.

preparing fresh berries

See p. 352. Then add sugar and let stand at room temperature for about an hour.

INDIVIDUAL SHORTCAKES

Make Rich Biscuits (*p. 83*). Break apart while hot. Spread with butter. Place bottom half on dessert dish, spoon over sweetened berries. Top with other half, *cut side up*, then with more berries. Serve with plain or whipped cream.

PEACH SHORTCAKE

Mrs. Homer Westbrook and Mrs. Hugh Smith, delightful hostesses of the Old South, serve this often during fresh peach season in their Atlanta, Georgia, home.

Follow ✗ recipe above—*except* use 1 qt. sliced fresh peaches, sweetened.

CAKE-TYPE SHORTCAKE

See Sponge Cakes (*pp. 164–165*).

CANNED FRUIT COBBLER (✗ Recipe)

"Cobble up" means to put together in a hurry. For the fruit, use cherries, peaches, apricots, or blackberries, etc.

Mix in saucepan . . .
½ cup sugar
1 tbsp. cornstarch

Stir in gradually . . .
2½ cups canned fruit or berries and juice (no. 2 can)

Bring to boil and boil 1 min., stirring constantly. Pour into 1½-qt. baking dish and dot with butter. Sprinkle with cinnamon. Sift together . . .

1 cup *sifted* GOLD MEDAL Flour
1 tbsp. sugar
1½ tsp. baking powder
½ tsp. salt

Cut in with pastry blender or 2 knives until mixture looks like "meal" . . .
3 tbsp. shortening

Stir in . . .
½ cup milk

Drop by spoonfuls onto hot fruit or berries. Bake until golden brown. Serve warm with juice and cream.

TEMPERATURE: 400° (mod. hot oven).
TIME: Bake 25 to 30 min.
AMOUNT: 6 to 8 servings.

FRESH FRUIT COBBLER

Follow ✗ recipe above—*except*, in place of canned fruit or berries, use 3 cups fresh fruit with any juice there might be, mixed with ⅔ to 1 cup sugar, 1 tbsp. cornstarch, and 1 cup water.

SOUTHERN PEACH SKILLET PIE

The recipe for this luscious, homey dessert was given us by a gracious, charming educator, Miss Wylle B. McNeal.

Make ½ Southern Biscuit dough (*p. 83*) —*except* roll or pat out dough ¼″ thick. Place in heavy 8″ skillet, allowing some of dough to hang over edge.

Top with . . .
6 fresh peaches, peeled and sliced

Mix . . .
½ cup sugar
½ tsp. salt
¼ tsp. cinnamon
1½ tbsp. soft butter

Sprinkle over fruit.

Fold hanging dough toward center, leaving a little space uncovered. Bake.

TEMPERATURE: 425° (hot oven).
TIME: Bake 25 min.
AMOUNT: 6 servings.

PINEAPPLE UPSIDE-DOWN CAKE (✗ Recipe) *Sometimes called "skillet cake." Handsome dessert to serve at table.*

First, prepare the pan:

Melt ⅓ cup butter in heavy 10″ skillet or 9″ square pan. Sprinkle ½ cup brown sugar (packed) evenly over butter. Arrange drained pineapple (no. 2 can) (crushed may be used if well drained) in attractive pattern on the butter-sugar coating. Decorate with pecan halves and cherries, if desired.

Then make Cake Batter to finish:

Make Cake Batter (*see right*) and pour over fruit. Bake until toothpick stuck into center of cake comes out clean. Immediately turn upside down on serving plate. Leave pan over cake a few minutes. Brown sugar mixture will run down over cake. Serve warm with whipped cream and Pineapple Sauce (*below*).

TEMPERATURE: 350° (mod. oven).
TIME: Bake 40 to 50 min.

CAKE BATTER

Sift together . . .
  1½ cups *sifted* SOFTASILK Flour
      or 1⅓ cups *sifted* GOLD MEDAL Flour
  1 cup sugar
  2 tsp. baking powder
  ½ tsp. salt

Add . . .
  ⅓ cup soft shortening
  ⅔ cup milk
  1 tsp. vanilla
  ½ tsp. lemon flavoring, if desired

Beat 2 min.

Add . . .
  1 egg (¼ to ⅓ cup)

Beat 2 more min.

CHECKERBOARD UPSIDE-DOWN CAKE

Prunes and apricots, checkerboard style.

Follow ✗ recipe above—*except* arrange drained cooked apricot halves and pitted cooked prunes in checkerboard fashion in prepared pan.

SPONGE-TYPE UPSIDE-DOWN CAKES

Follow ✗ recipe above—*except* use small recipe of Egg Yolk Sponge Cake (*p. 164*) for Cake Batter.

APRICOT UPSIDE-DOWN CAKE

Follow ✗ recipe above—*except* use drained apricot halves instead of pineapple and serve with Apricot Sauce (*below*).

PINEAPPLE OR APRICOT SAUCE

Mix in saucepan . . .
  ⅓ cup brown sugar (packed)
  1 tbsp. cornstarch

Stir in . . .
  1 cup pineapple or apricot juice from drained fruit (add water if necessary to make 1 cup)

Bring to boil. Boil 1 min. over med. heat, stirring constantly. Remove from heat. Add . . .
  2 tbsp. butter
  ½ tsp. lemon juice

Serve warm over each serving.

LEMON CAKE PUDDING (✧ Recipe) *Delicate cake and refreshing lemon sauce in one pudding.*

Sift together into mixing bowl . . . .
- ¼ cup *sifted* GOLD MEDAL Flour
- 1 cup sugar
- ¼ tsp. salt

Stir in . . . .
- 1½ tsp. grated lemon rind (1 lemon)
- ¼ cup lemon juice
- 2 egg yolks, well beaten
- 1 cup milk

Fold in . . . .
- 2 egg whites, stiffly beaten

Pour into 1-qt. baking dish (6½") or 6 custard cups. Set in pan of hot water (1" deep). Bake. Serve warm or cold, with or without whipped cream.

TEMPERATURE: 350° (mod. oven).

TIME: Bake 50 min.

AMOUNT: 6 servings.

LIME CAKE PUDDING

Follow ✧ recipe above—*except*, in place of lemon, use lime juice and rind.

ORANGE CAKE PUDDING

Follow ✧ recipe above—*except*, in place of lemon, use orange juice and rind.

PINEAPPLE CAKE PUDDING

Follow ✧ recipe above—*except* reduce sugar to ½ cup, use only ½ cup milk, only 1 tbsp. lemon juice. Add ¼ cup drained crushed pineapple and ¼ cup pineapple juice.

For a refreshing warm weather dessert: serve these puddings cold.

LAST-MINUTE DATE RAPTURES

Delicate, luscious with fruit . . . fresh from the oven . . . they really are raptures.

Sift together into bowl . . .
- 1 cup *sifted* GOLD MEDAL Flour
- ½ tsp. baking powder
- ½ tsp. soda
- ½ tsp. salt

Add . . .
- ¼ cup soft shortening
- ½ cup sugar
- 1 egg
- ⅓ cup buttermilk or sour milk
- 1 tbsp. grated orange rind

Beat until smooth.

Blend in . . .
- 1 cup cut-up dates

Pour into greased muffin cups (⅔ full). Bake.

TEMPERATURE: 350° (mod. oven).

TIME: Bake 25 to 30 min.

AMOUNT: 6 servings.

Serve hot. Pour over them

SWEETENED ORANGE JUICE

Mix . . .
- ¾ cup strained orange juice
- ¼ cup sugar

No cooking; the juice soaks into cakes.

All you have to do –

To keep pudding sauce hot until time to serve: let stand over hot water.

HOT FUDGE PUDDING

We are grateful to Mrs. Oswin Keifer of Bostwick, Nebraska, for this rich tasting chocolate dessert . . . easy to make, inexpensive. The sauce forms as pudding bakes.

Sift together into bowl . . .
- 1 cup *sifted* GOLD MEDAL Flour
- 2 tsp. baking powder
- ¼ tsp. salt
- ¾ cup sugar
- 2 tbsp. cocoa

Stir in . . .
- ½ cup milk
- 2 tbsp. shortening, melted

Blend in . . .
- 1 cup chopped nuts

Spread in 9" square pan.

Sprinkle with mixture of . . .
- 1 cup brown sugar (packed)
- ¼ cup cocoa

Pour over entire batter . . .
- 1¾ cups hot water

Bake. During baking, cake mixture rises to top and chocolate sauce settles to bottom. Invert squares of pudding on dessert plates. Dip sauce from pan over each. Or the entire pudding can be inverted in a deep serving platter. Serve warm, with or without whipped cream.

TEMPERATURE: 350° (mod. oven).

TIME: Bake 45 min.

AMOUNT: 9 servings.

(1) A steamer with holes in the bottom, and a tight fitting cover to hold in steam. (2) A deep kettle that holds water to last through the entire steaming, or a deep well cooker with wire frame to hold pudding mold.

(1) Tube center mold allows steam to quickly reach center of pudding. (2) Turk's head mold with spiral fluting. (3) Round can (coffee can, etc.) or bowl. (4) Individual molds, custard cups, or jelly glasses.

HOW TO STEAM

1 Pour pudding batter into generously greased molds . . . filling them ½ to ⅔ full. This allows room for expansion of batter.

2 Place in steamer. Tie waxed paper loosely over mold to prevent steam which collects on cover dropping on pudding.

3 Remove from steamer after prescribed time. Remove waxed paper. Place pudding in oven 1 min. to dry the top slightly.

4 Loosen pudding at one side to let in air. Turn out on hot serving dish. The flaming pudding of old had heated brandy over it. A lighted match touched off the brandy.

5 The new way is to soak lumps of sugar in lemon or orange extract, place around pudding. Touch match to one lump and the pudding is encircled with bright flames.

DOWN EAST PUDDING

Made with cranberries or raisins. An inspiration from Cape Cod.

Combine and let stand for a few minutes . . .
   1 cup boiling water
   1 cup cut-up cranberries (or raisins)
   2 tbsp. shortening
Beat together; add to above mixture . . .
   1 egg
   ½ cup sugar
   ½ cup molasses
Sift together and stir in . . .
   1½ cups *sifted* GOLD MEDAL Flour
   1 tsp. *each* salt and soda

Pour into well greased 1-qt. mold (⅔ full). Steam. Serve piping hot with Taffy Sauce (*p. 405*).

TIME: Steam 2 hr.

AMOUNT: 8 servings.

PLUM DUFF (Dark)

Moist, fruity, yet delicate and light. From Mrs. E. A. Parker of San Francisco, California, who really knows elegant food.

Beat well . . .
   2 eggs
Blend in . . .
   1 cup brown sugar (packed)
   ½ cup shortening, melted
   2 cups well drained cut-up pitted cooked
      prunes
Sift together and stir in . . .
   1 cup *sifted* GOLD MEDAL Flour
   ½ tsp. salt
   1 tsp. soda

Pour into well greased 1-qt. mold. Steam. Serve hot with Creamy Sauce (*p. 239*).

TIME: Steam 1 hr.

AMOUNT: 8 servings.

An old Yorkshire tradition: "In as many homes as you eat plum pudding in the 12 days following Christmas, so many happy months will you have during the year."

Thrifty colonial homemakers evolved new variations. Modern methods and equipment have made puddings lighter, fluffier, and more delicious.

ENGLISH PLUM PUDDING

We think it's the best of all the real English recipes for plum pudding.

Sift together . . .
- 1 cup *sifted* GOLD MEDAL Flour
- 1 tsp. soda
- 1 tsp. salt
- 1 tsp. cinnamon
- ¼ tsp. nutmeg
- ¾ tsp. mace

Mix in . . .
- 1½ cups finely cut raisins (½ lb.)
- 1½ cups currants (½ lb.), plumped
- ¾ cup finely cut citron (¼ lb.)
- ¾ cup finely cut candied orange and lemon peel
- ½ cup chopped walnuts
- 1½ cups coarse soft bread crumbs (p. 30)

Mix and blend in . . .
- 2 cups ground suet (½ lb.)
- 1 cup brown sugar (packed)
- 3 eggs, beaten
- ⅓ cup currant jelly
- ¼ cup fruit juice (old recipes called for brandy or sherry)

Pour into a well greased 2-qt. mold (or 2 1-qt. molds). Steam. Serve piping hot with Hard Sauce (p. 405).

TIME: Steam 6 hr.

AMOUNT: 16 servings.

WHITE PLUM DUFF See color picture on p. 234.

It's dramatically black and white . . . dark prunes contrasting sharply with the white batter.

Cook in 2 cups water . . .
- ½ lb. prunes (1 cup cooked)

Drain, reserving juice for sauce. Pit prunes.

Sift together into bowl . . .
- 1 cup *sifted* GOLD MEDAL Flour
- 1½ tsp. baking powder
- ½ tsp. salt

Add . . .
- ¼ cup soft shortening
- ½ cup sugar
- 1 egg
- ½ cup milk
- 1 tsp. vanilla

Beat with rotary beater or spoon until smooth. Grease *generously* a 1-qt. mold.

STEAMED CHOCOLATE PUDDING

Many were tried, this one chosen . . . the recipe was brought in by Dorothy Elliott of our staff.

Beat well with rotary beater . . .
- 1 egg
- 1 cup sugar
- 2 tbsp. soft butter
- 2 sq. unsweetened chocolate (2 oz.), melted

Sift together . . .
- 1¾ cups *sifted* GOLD MEDAL Flour
- 1 tsp. salt
- ¼ tsp. cream of tartar
- ¼ tsp. soda

Beat in alternately with . . .
- 1 cup milk

Pour into greased 1-qt. mold. Steam. Serve hot with Creamy Sauce (*below*).

TIME: Steam 2 hr.

AMOUNT: 8 servings.

CREAMY SAUCE

Beat 1 egg until foamy. Blend in ⅓ cup melted butter, 1½ cups *sifted* confectioners' sugar, and 1 tsp. vanilla. Fold in 1 cup whipping cream, whipped stiff.

Place 1 cup well drained cooked prune halves, shiny-side-down, on bottom and sides of mold. Pour in batter. Cover with aluminum foil or waxed paper tied over top. Steam. Serve hot with hot Prune Sauce (*below*).

TIME: Steam 2 hr.

AMOUNT: 6 servings.

PRUNE SAUCE

Mix in saucepan . . .
- 1½ tbsp. cornstarch
- ⅓ cup sugar
- 1 cup prune juice
- 1 tbsp. lemon juice or mild vinegar

Boil 1 min., stirring constantly.

Remove from heat. Blend in . . .
- 1 tbsp. butter
- dash of nutmeg

Early American colonists made gingerbread much as we do today. When Lafayette returned to America in 1784, he went to Fredricksburg to visit George Washington's mother. She served him mint julep with "spiced gingerbrede." Her recipe included "West India molasses," a "wine glass of brandy," and "the juice and rind of orange" in addition to the usual ingredients.

FAVORITE GINGERBREAD (ℓ Recipe)
Deliciously rich, black, and moist. Grandma knew it as "Fort Atkinson Gingerbread" in the popular old brown covered GOLD MEDAL Cook Book that was a treasure trove for brides in the 1870's.

Mix thoroughly........................
- ½ cup soft shortening
- 2 tbsp. sugar
- 1 egg

Blend in.............................
- 1 cup dark New Orleans molasses
- 1 cup boiling water

Sift together and stir in.................
(beating until smooth)
- 2¼ cups *sifted* GOLD MEDAL Flour
- 1 tsp. soda
- ½ tsp. salt
- 1 tsp. ginger
- 1 tsp. cinnamon

Pour into well greased and floured 9″ square pan. Bake. Cut into 3″ squares in pan. Keep hot and serve piping hot with Sweetened Whipped Cream (*p. 222*), or with applesauce, chocolate sauce, or any of the toppings given below.

TEMPERATURE: 325° (slow mod. oven).

TIME: Bake 45 to 50 min.

AMOUNT: 9 servings.

GINGERBREAD WITH APRICOT GLAZE

Mix 2½ cups cooked apricots with juice (no. 2 can), 1 cup sugar, ⅓ cup boiling water. Boil until thick like jam. Cool. Cover top of hot gingerbread with slices of banana. Pour apricot glaze over all.

HADDON HALL GINGERBREAD

"Ideal for 'dessert and coffee' party," says Ruth Sweat, Pasadena, California, once in charge of our test kitchens.

Soften cream cheese with a little cream. Beat until fluffy. Split each serving of hot gingerbread, spoon cheese between layers. Top with more cheese. Serve with Old-fashioned Lemon Sauce (*p. 405*).

GINGERBREAD PARTY DESSERT

Madelon Mitchel of Hollywood says: "I often enjoy being served this in the home of a good friend."

Bake ℓ recipe above in square pan. Top squares of hot gingerbread with vanilla ice cream, Orange Cream Cheese Topping (*at right*), and canned whole or halved peeled apricots.

GINGERBREAD RING WITH APPLESAUCE

Glamour with old-time taste appeal.

Follow ℓ recipe above—*except* bake in greased and floured 9″ ring mold. Serve hot with bowl of fresh applesauce in center, whipped cream or ice cream for topping.

ORANGE CREAM CHEESE TOPPING

Blend until smooth . . .
- two 3-oz. pkg. cream cheese
- 1¼ cups *sifted* confectioners' sugar
- 3 tbsp. orange juice
- 1 tsp. lemon juice

CREAM PUFFS (✐ Recipe) *French-born delicacy . . . crisp, hollow.*

Heat to a rolling boil in saucepan . . .
  1 cup water
  ½ cup butter
Stir in all at once . . .
  1 cup *sifted* GOLD MEDAL Flour
Stir vigorously over low heat until mixture leaves the pan and forms into a ball (about 1 min.). Remove from heat.
Beat in thoroughly, 1 at a time . . .
  4 eggs

Beat mixture until smooth and velvety. Drop from spoon onto ungreased baking sheet (*see pictures below*). Bake until dry. Allow to cool slowly.

TEMPERATURE: 400° (mod. hot oven).
TIME: Bake 45 to 50 min.
AMOUNT: 8 large puffs.

1 Stir constantly until mixture leaves the pan and forms a ball. Beat in the eggs, 1 at a time. Beat until velvety.

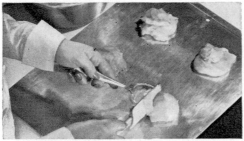

2 Drop from spoon onto baking sheet forming 8 mounds 3″ apart. Bake until puffed, golden brown, and dry. Allow to cool slowly, away from drafts.

3 Cut off tops with sharp knife. Scoop out any filaments of soft dough. Fill with Sweetened Whipped Cream (*p. 222*). Replace tops. Dust with confectioners' sugar. Serve cold.

CHOCOLATE ÉCLAIRS

Follow ✐ recipe above—*except* put dough through pastry tube, or shape with spatula into 12 fingers 4″ long and 1″ wide. Fill with Rich Custard Filling (*at right*). Frost with Thin Chocolate Icing (*p. 178*).
AMOUNT: 12 éclairs.

FRUIT-FILLED CREAM PUFFS

Fold stiffly whipped cream into sweetened cut-up fresh fruit (strawberries, raspberries, sweet cherries, peaches, etc.). Use ¾ cup fruit, ¼ cup sugar, ¾ cup whipping cream. Fill Cream Puffs with mixture.

PETITS CHOUX (Midget Puffs)

Three on a plate . . . a dessert of distinction.

Follow ✐ recipe above—*except* make 18 tiny puffs the size of a walnut. Bake 30 min. Fill with Rich Custard Filling (*at right above*). Frost with Thin Chocolate Icing (*p. 178*).

CUSTARD-FILLED PUFFS

Fill Cream Puffs with

RICH CUSTARD FILLING

Mix in saucepan . . .
  ½ cup sugar
  ½ tsp. salt
  ⅓ cup GOLD MEDAL Flour
Stir in . . .
  2 cups milk
Cook over med. heat, stirring until it boils. Boil 1 min. Remove from heat. Stir a little over half of this mixture into . . .
  4 egg yolks (or 2 eggs), beaten
Blend into hot mixture in saucepan. Bring *just* to boiling point. Cool and blend in . . .
  2 tsp. vanilla or other flavoring

ICE CREAM PUFFS

Fill Cream Puffs with ice cream. Serve with appropriate sauce: chocolate sauce with peppermint ice cream, butterscotch sauce with burnt almond ice cream.

Torte is the old German name for a special type of rich dessert . . . compact and flat rather than high and fluffy. Made light with eggs, the bread crumbs or ground nuts take the place of flour.

DATE AND NUT TORTE

Beat thoroughly . . .
 4 eggs
Beat in gradually . . .
 1 cup sugar
Mix and stir in . . .
 1 cup fine dry bread crumbs (p. 30)
 1 tsp. baking powder
Stir in . . .
 2 cups finely cut pitted dates
 1 cup cut-up walnuts

Spread in well greased 9″ square pan. Bake until set. Cut in oblongs, 3x2″. Serve cool with whipped cream or ice cream.
TEMPERATURE: 350° (mod. oven).
TIME: Bake 35 min.
AMOUNT: 12 servings.

BLITZ TORTE (Lightning Cake)

Beautiful . . . the meringue top encrusted with sugar and toasted almonds.

Mix thoroughly . . .
 ½ cup soft shortening
 ¾ cup sifted confectioners' sugar
Beat in . . .
 4 egg yolks, well beaten
Sift together and stir in . . .
 1 cup sifted GOLD MEDAL Flour
 1 tsp. baking powder
 ¼ tsp. salt
Stir in . . .
 3 tbsp. milk

Spread batter in 2 greased and floured round 8″ layer pans.

For meringue, beat until frothy . . .
 4 egg whites
Beat in gradually . . .
 1 cup sugar (half confectioners')
Beat until stiff and glossy.
Spread half of meringue over batter in each pan. Sprinkle each with half of . . .
 ½ cup shaved blanched almonds
 2 tbsp. sugar

Bake until cake tests done and meringue is set. Cool. Then remove from pans. Place one layer on serving plate *meringue-side-up.* Spread with Rich Custard Filling (*p. 241*). Place other layer on top *meringue-side-up.* If desired, pipe with Sweetened Whipped Cream (*p. 222*).
TEMPERATURE: 325° (slow mod. oven).
TIME: Bake 35 to 40 min.
AMOUNT: 12 servings.

CHEESE CAKE (Torte)

Elegant . . . yet practical. Best served the day it's baked.

Butter an 8 or 9″ spring-form pan or a 9″ layer pan (with an aluminum foil strip above rim for added height). Dust bottom and sides with Crumb Mixture for Cheese Cake (*below*).

Beat until thick and lemon-colored . . .
 5 eggs
Beat in gradually . . .
 1 cup sugar
Add, beating until thick and smooth . . .
 ¾ lb. cottage cheese (12 oz.)
 ¾ lb. cream cheese (12 oz.)
Stir in . . .
 grated rind and juice of 1 lemon
Pour into crumb-lined pan. Bake in mod. oven (350°) for 1 hr. or until set. Remove from oven.
Spread over top . . .
 1 cup thick sour cream (cultured)
 ⅓ cup toasted slivered blanched almonds
  (sprinkled over top)

Return to hot oven (450°) 5 min. Cool. Serve with fruit sauce (strawberry or raspberry) or fresh peach or pear halves.
AMOUNT: 12 to 16 servings.

CRUMB MIXTURE FOR CHEESE CAKE
Mix ½ cup fine Zwieback crumbs, fine dry bread crumbs, or fine dry graham cracker crumbs, 1 tbsp. sugar, ¼ tsp. cinnamon, ¼ tsp. nutmeg.

STRAWBERRY MERINGUE TORTE

Luscious! The meringue is the crust. Introduced by Gladys Black, University of Omaha, at a Home Economics dinner.

Beat until frothy . . .
 3 egg whites
 ½ tsp. baking powder
Beat in gradually until whites are stiff . . .
 1 cup sugar
Fold in . . .
 10 sq. (2″) soda crackers, rolled fine
 ½ cup cut-up pecans

Spread in well buttered 9″ pie pan. Bake in slow oven (300°) 30 min. Cool. Fill with 1 qt. unsweetened strawberries and top with sweetened whipped cream (whip ½ cup cream). Chill several hours.

CHOCOLATE VIENNA TORTE (♪ Recipe)

Easy to make . . . like a chocolate chip sponge cake.

Beat in small mixer bowl until thick and lemon-colored..........................	6 egg yolks
Beat in................................	½ cup sugar
Sift together and stir in.................	¾ cup *sifted* GOLD MEDAL Flour 1 tsp. baking powder 1 tsp. salt
Beat until frothy.......................	6 egg whites ½ tsp. cream of tartar
Beat in gradually......................	another ½ cup sugar
Beat until very stiff and glossy.	
Gently fold in.........................	¾ cup grated unsweetened chocolate 1 tsp. vanilla

Carefully fold in egg yolk mixture. Pour into 2 9″ round layer pans lined with greased paper. Bake until, when touched lightly with finger, no imprint remains. Turn out of pans and immediately remove paper. Cool. Put together and top with Sweetened Whipped Cream (*p. 222*) or Whipped Cream Filling (*below*). Garnish with flakes of dark chocolate.

TEMPERATURE: 350° (mod. oven).
TIME: Bake 25 to 30 min.
AMOUNT: 16 servings.

WHIPPED CREAM FILLING: Soften 1 tsp. unflavored gelatin in 1 tbsp. water. Dissolve over hot water. Whip 1 cup whipping cream and ¼ cup confectioners' sugar until it begins to thicken. Gradually add dissolved gelatin. Beat until stiff. Add 1 tsp. flavoring.

CARAMEL ALMOND VIENNA TORTE

Caramelize ¾ cup sugar (*p. 29*). Add and cook, stirring until lumps are dissolved, ½ cup hot water.

Follow ♪ recipe above—*except* stir 2 tbsp. of caramel mixture into egg yolk mixture. Instead of chocolate, fold ¾ cup finely chopped toasted almonds into egg white mixture. Put cooled layers together with Sweetened Whipped Cream (*p. 222*) or Whipped Cream Filling (*above*). Cover with

CARAMEL TOPPING

Add to caramel syrup in skillet . . .
½ cup sugar
¼ cup butter
¼ tsp. salt
½ cup milk

Stir until smooth. Cook over med. heat, stirring occasionally, to soft ball stage, 234°. Add . . .
¼ cup cream

Cook again to 234°. When partially cool (no stirring), pour over top of torte letting it drip down sides here and there.

PECAN OR BRAZIL NUT TORTE (♪ Recipe)

Rich, nutty, flat . . . not cake-like. Found on a very old plantation along the Bayou Teche of Louisiana by Mrs. T. M. Dupes of Tescott, Kansas.

Beat in small mixer bowl until thick . . .
6 egg yolks
Beat in gradually . . .
¾ cup sugar
Mix . . .
2 tbsp. flour
2 tsp. baking powder
¼ tsp. salt
Blend into . . .
3 cups *finely* chopped pecans or Brazil nuts
Beat until frothy . . .
6 egg whites
Beat in gradually . . .
another ¾ cup sugar

Beat until stiff and glossy. Carefully fold in egg yolk mixture, then the nut mixture. Pour into 2 9″ round layer pans lined with greased paper. Bake until, when touched lightly with finger, no imprint remains. Turn out of pans and immediately remove paper. Cool. Spread Whipped Cream Filling (*at left above*) between layers and over top and sides. Pipe with Sweetened Whipped Cream (*p. 222*). Garnish with chocolate curls and nuts.

TEMPERATURE: 350° (mod. oven).
TIME: Bake 25 to 30 min.
AMOUNT: 16 servings.

BAKED ALASKA

A dessert of beauty . . . and mystery.

BAKED ALASKA (✦ Recipe) See color
picture opposite. Ice cream on cake, covered with meringue, then baked in the oven! Mrs. George Cammack of
Minneapolis says that her guests just gasp at the beauty
of this mysterious dessert when she serves it on an antique silver-edged pink china cake plate.

Use 9″ round layer of Egg Yolk Sponge
Cake (p. 164). Pack about 2 qt. strawberry ice cream in round bowl (about 1″
smaller around than layer of cake) and
place in freezing compartment of refrigerator until serving time.

Shortly before serving, make a

> ### SPECIAL MERINGUE
> Beat 6 large egg whites with ½ tsp.
> cream of tartar until frothy. Beat in
> gradually 1 cup sugar. Continue beating
> until meringue is stiff and glossy.

Place cooled layer of cake on a board on a
baking sheet. Loosen ice cream from bowl
with spatula. Invert bowl over cake. Remove bowl. Cover cake and ice cream
completely with Special Meringue (*above*),
sealing meringue to board for a complete
seal. (This is the secret so ice cream will
not melt in oven.) Place in very hot oven
(500°) for 3 to 5 min. (just until meringue
is delicately browned). Slip the dessert
onto serving platter, board and all, if
board is small. Serve at once.
AMOUNT: 12 to 16 servings.

BRICK ALASKA
Follow ✦ recipe above—*except* use any
desired cake cut 1″ larger around than a
pt. brick of ice cream. Use only ½ Special
Meringue (*above*).

Chocolate Brick Alaska: Use chocolate
cake, either vanilla or chocolate ice cream.
Sprinkle meringue before baking with
slivered almonds and shaved chocolate.

Brownie Brick Alaska: Use Brownies (cut
sheet the correct size), peppermint ice
cream.

INDIVIDUAL ALASKAS
Follow ✦ recipe above—*except*, for cake
base, cut rounds of cake 1″ larger around
than ice cream round. Cut slice of round
carton-packed ice cream to top each
cake slice. Use only ½ Special Meringue
(*above*).

ORANGE ALMOND DELIGHT
Split a 10″ Sponge Cake (p. 164) or Orange
Chiffon Cake (p. 162) into 2 or 3 layers.
Put layers together and frost with

ORANGE FLUFF FILLING AND
TOPPING (Russian Sauce)

Mix well in top of double boiler . . .
  3 or 4 egg yolks
  ½ cup sugar
  ⅓ to ½ cup orange juice (1 large orange)
Cook over hot water, stirring constantly, until it
thickens (about 15 min.). Stir in . . .
  1 tbsp. grated orange rind
Cool. Fold in . . .
  1 cup whipping cream, whipped stiff
  ½ cup toasted chopped blanched almonds
    or fresh grated coconut

FRENCH RIBBON CAKE
Split a loaf of Chiffon Cake (p. 162)
into 4 layers. Put layers together and
frost cake with

> ### CHOCOLATE FILLING AND FROSTING
> Cream together ¾ cup soft butter and
> 1 cup *sifted* confectioners' sugar. Beat in
> 3 egg yolks, one at a time, and 3 sq. un-
> sweetened chocolate (3 oz.), melted.
> Fold in 3 egg whites, beaten stiff.

Sprinkle sides of frosted cake with chopped
nuts or decorate edge with blanched almond halves stuck into frosting. Chill in
refrigerator several hours.
AMOUNT: 10 servings.

BOSTON CREAM PIE
Make a one-egg cake (p. 146) in one
9″ square pan. Split into 2 thin layers.
Put together with cooled Cream Filling
(p. 182). Spread Thin Chocolate Icing
(p. 178) over top. Serve like pie.

WASHINGTON PIE
From Civil War days when Washington, D. C. housewives
could not get lard for pies. They made plain cakes, split
and filled them with jelly from their cellars. Ever since, they
have been called "Washington Pies."

Make Egg Yolk Sponge Cake (p. 164) in
a layer pan or use 1 layer of Lovelight
Yellow Chiffon Cake (p. 158). Cool. Split
into 2 layers. Put together with jelly.
Sprinkle confectioners' sugar on top.

HOW TO FILL ANGEL FOOD CAKES: First make a 10" Angel Food (see p. 157). Then read recipes on p. 247 and prepare the desired filling and frosting.

1 Place a 10" Angel Food Cake upside down on plate or waxed paper. Slice entire top from cake about 1" down. Lift off top and lay to one side.

2 Cut down into the cake 1" from outer edge, and 1" from middle hole, leaving a substantial "wall" of cake about 1" thick, and a 1" base at the bottom.

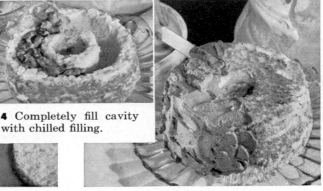

4 Completely fill cavity with chilled filling.

3 Remove center with a curved knife or spoon, being careful to leave a "wall" of cake at bottom 1" thick. Place on serving plate.

5 Replace top of cake and press gently. Cover top and sides with the remaining chilled cream mixture.

ANGEL FOOD WALDORF

Crunchy nuts in luscious creamy chocolate.

Prepare Angel Food Cake as above. Make Cocoa Fluff Filling and Topping (*below*).

Into half of mixture, fold . . .
    ⅓ cup cut-up toasted almonds

Use this to fill cake cavity. Replace top of cake and spread remaining cream mixture on top and sides of cake.

Sprinkle with . . .
    ⅓ cup shaved toasted almonds

Chill until set (3 or more hours).

COCOA FLUFF FILLING AND TOPPING

Mix in chilled bowl, then beat until stiff . . .
    3 cups chilled whipping cream
    1½ cups *sifted* confectioners' sugar
    ¾ cup cocoa
    ¼ tsp. salt

6 Decorate appropriately (*see recipes*) and chill until well set (4 hr. or more). Cut into generous pieces. 12 to 16 servings.

All you have to do —

To get the greatest volume when whipping cream: chill cream, bowl, and beater together.

Make Angel Food Cake (*p. 157*) for any of the
party desserts below. 16 to 18 servings.

APRICOT ICE CREAM-FILLED ANGEL FOOD

*Most picturesque, delicious, and unusual. From Adair
McRae Roberts, remembered as a gifted musician.*

Prepare Angel Food Cake for filling (*p.
246*). But first make the Apricot Purée
and Apricot Ice Cream for the filling.

APRICOT PURÉE

Simmer until apricots are soft (about 30 min.) . . .
    ¾ lb. dried apricots
    2 cups water

Press through sieve; stir in . . .
    ¼ cup sugar

Cool.

APRICOT ICE CREAM

Into 1 qt. vanilla ice cream, blend 1 cup
cold Apricot Purée (work quickly). Place
in refrigerator tray and freeze again until
firm but not hard (about 1 hr.).

Fill cake cavity with Apricot Ice Cream.
Replace top of cake. Spread remaining
Apricot Purée over top and sides.

Spread 1 cup whipping cream, whipped
stiff and sweetened, over the apricot
coating. Arrange 6 fresh apricot halves
round-side-up, around base. Add a few
fresh green leaves. *Serve immediately.*

ANGEL FOOD À LA RUSSE

Serve large pieces of Angel Food Cake
topped with Orange Fluff Topping (Russian Sauce) (*p. 245*).

ALMOND CREAM ANGEL FOOD

Split 10″ Angel Food into 2 or 3 layers.
Put layers together with Almond Cream
Filling (*p. 182*). Frost cake with a cooked
white icing. Decorate with daisies of
toasted blanched almond halves for petals
—with rounds of orange rind for centers.

LUSCIOUS CHOCOLATE ALMOND DESSERT

*Served at lovely dinner parties by Louise Strong Cosgrove
of Minneapolis, Minnesota.*

Split Chocolate Angel Food De Luxe (*p.
157*) into 2 or 3 layers. Put layers together
with Almond Cream Filling (*p. 182*) and
frost with White Mountain Frosting (*p.
180*). Cover with chocolate allegretti
coating (*p. 144*).

ANGEL FOOD DELIGHT

Choice of an epicure, Judge Leslie L. Anderson, Minneapolis, Minnesota.

Prepare Angel Food Cake for filling (*p.
246*). Fill cake cavity with

FRUITED CREAM FILLING AND FROSTING

Whip together until stiff . . .
    3 cups whipping cream
    ⅓ cup confectioners' sugar

Fold into a little less than half the cream . . .
    ¾ cup crushed pineapple, well drained
    1 cup fresh strawberries, cut in halves
    6 marshmallows, cut in quarters

Replace top of cake and spread remaining
cream on top and sides. Chill 4 to 8 hr.

CHOCOLATE PEPPERMINT ANGEL FOOD

*Delectable, and truly beautiful . . . served on a high, light
blue Daisy and Button cake plate in the charming foothills
home of George and Florence Mehl, Altadena, California.*

Make pink-tinted, peppermint-flavored
Angel Food. Split into 2 or 3 layers. Put
layers together and frost with Cocoa Fluff
Topping and Filling (*p. 246*).

ICE CREAM SANDWICHES

Place ice cream (any flavor desired) between 2 slices Angel Food. Pour sauce (*p.
404*) or crushed fruit over. For 6, use 1 qt.
ice cream, 12 slices cake.

SINGED ANGEL WINGS

Brush cut sides of wedges of Angel Food
with melted butter. Lightly brown both
sides under broiler (1 min. each side).
Serve with Clear Orange Sauce (*p. 405*).

STRAWBERRY OR RASPBERRY ANGEL FOOD

Prepare Angel Food Cake for filling (*p.
246*). Prepare Strawberry or Raspberry
Bavarian Cream (*p. 228*)—*except* use 1½
cups whipping cream. After folding in
cream and fruit, chill 10 min. (until
slightly firm). Fill cake cavity and replace
top of cake. Frost with remaining mixture. Chill until set (about 4 hr.). Garnish
with whole fresh berries.

RAINBOW DESSERT (Blöte Kage)

RAINBOW DESSERT (Blöte Kage) See color picture on p. 253. A dazzling dessert with fillings of rainbow colors served at exclusive hotels in Norway. The Norwegian name Blöte Kage means Soft Cake. It was brought to us by Mrs. Gladys Petch, formerly of Oslo, Norway, now of New York, Radio Consultant to the Norwegian Information Services.

Cut a cooled large Sponge Cake (*p. 164*) or Chiffon Cake (*p. 162*) into four 1″ layers. Put layers together with 3 different fillings:

On bottom layer, spread *Pineapple Filling*.

Place second layer on top and spread with *Apricot Filling*.

Place third layer and spread with *Raspberry Filling*.

Add the fourth layer and cover top and sides of cake with remaining whipped cream. Sprinkle with green pistachio nuts (blanched and shaved). Chill 3 hr. before serving. Arrange apricot halves, rounded-side-out, around base of cake. Add a few green leaves. Serve.

WHIPPED CREAM FOR FILLING AND FROSTING

Whip until stiff 3 cups whipping cream and 6 tbsp. confectioners' sugar.

For *each* one of the 3 fillings, soften 2 tsp. gelatin in 1 tbsp. fruit juice. Dissolve over hot water. Stir into the fruit. Chill. When partially set, fold in 1 cup of the sweetened whipped cream (1 cup for each).

PINEAPPLE FILLING

Use 1 cup drained crushed pineapple (no. 1 can). Tint with green food coloring.

APRICOT FILLING

Use 1 cup mashed apricot pulp (sweet).

RASPBERRY FILLING

Use 1 cup thick raspberry jam.

NORWEGIAN CHARLOTTE

NORWEGIAN CHARLOTTE Chosen as a thrilling dessert from a set of Scandinavian recipes by our true Swedish blonde, Margaret Lindquist Remington, now of St. Joseph, Missouri.

To Prepare Cake:

Cut a large Chiffon Cake (*p. 162*) or Sponge Cake (*p. 164*) into 4 layers, each 1″ thick. With a sharp knife, enlarge the hole in center of the top 3 layers of cake so it is about 3″ across. *Do not cut through bottom layer.* Fill the small hole in bottom layer with a piece of the cut out cake. Fit it in tightly.

To Make Filling for Center of Cake:

Make Cream Filling (*p. 182*). Cool, then stir together with pieces of cake cut out of the top 3 layers until mixture is well blended. Whip 1 cup whipping cream until stiff and fold into custard-cake mixture. Chill.

To Make Filling for Layers of Cake:

Make an almond paste by blending together 1 cup ground blanched almonds, 1½ tsp. almond flavoring, and ½ tsp. green food coloring.

Make a Meringue (*for method, see p. 362*) by beating until stiff 4 egg whites and ¼ cup sugar. Divide meringue into 2 equal parts.

Almond Filling: into first part of meringue blend the almond paste and a little water, if necessary, to make easy to spread.

Coconut Filling: into second part of meringue, blend 1 cup moist shredded coconut.

To Finish Cake:

On bottom layer (but not over center), spread half of Almond Filling. Add next layer of cake and spread with Coconut Filling. Add third layer of cake and spread with rest of Almond Filling. Add the fourth layer. Fill center with chilled Cream Filling. Frost entire cake with

MERINGUE FROSTING

Beat until frothy . . .
> 4 egg whites (½ cup)
> ½ tsp. cream of tartar

Gradually beat in . . .
> 1 cup *sifted* confectioners' sugar

Beat until stiff and glossy.

CHOCOLATE DELIGHT

Chocolate-and-white marbled refrigerator dessert . . . bits of angel food layered with fluffy chocolate cream.

Melt over hot water . . .
> 6-oz. pkg. semi-sweet chocolate pieces

Cool slightly. Pour over and mix with . . .
> 4 eggs, very well beaten

Fold in . . .
> 1 cup whipping cream, whipped stiff
> 1 tsp. vanilla, if desired
> ¾ cup finely chopped nuts

Tear into small pieces . . .
> ½ large Angel Food Cake (p. 157)

Line 13x9″ oblong pan with half of cake pieces. Pour over half of the filling. Cover with remaining cake pieces and filling. Sprinkle with chopped nuts. Chill several hours. Cut in squares or oblongs.

AMOUNT: 10 to 12 servings.

REFRIGERATED CHEESE CAKE
(Unbaked Type)

For Cheese Cake (Baked Type), see p. 242.

Butter pan and dust with Crumb Mixture for Cheese Cake (*p. 242*) . . . reserving about ½ of crumbs for top.

Mix in saucepan . . .
> 2 envelopes unflavored gelatin (2 tbsp.)
> ¾ cup sugar
> ¼ tsp. salt

Beat together . . .
> 2 egg yolks
> 1 cup milk

Add gradually to mixture in saucepan.

Bring *just* to boil over med. heat, stirring constantly.

Remove from heat. Stir in . . .
> 1 tsp. grated lemon rind
> 1 tbsp. lemon juice
> 1 tsp. vanilla

Cool. Sieve into large mixing bowl . . .
> 3 cups cream-style cottage cheese (24 oz.)

Stir in cooled gelatin mixture. Chill, stirring occasionally, until mixture mounds slightly when dropped from spoon.

Fold in a Meringue (*see method on p. 362*) of . . .
> 2 egg whites
> ¼ cup sugar

Then fold in . . .
> 1 cup whipping cream, whipped stiff

Pour mixture into 8″ spring-form pan or 8 or 9″ square pan or 9x5x3″ loaf pan. Sprinkle with remaining Crumb Mixture. Chill until firm . . . at least 4 hr.

AMOUNT: 16 servings.

CHOCOLATE ROLL (Cherry Tree Log) *See color picture on p. 253. Glamorous on the buffet table. Delectable any time. "This has always been one of the best loved desserts in our home," says Mrs. William H. Lord of Foley, Minnesota. "Often we omit the icing and serve a chocolate sauce over the slices."*

Make Jelly Roll (*p. 165*)—*except* sift ¼ cup cocoa with the dry ingredients.

Unroll, removing towel. Fill with 1 cup Sweetened Whipped Cream (*p. 222*). Roll up carefully. Frost with Thin Chocolate Icing (*p. 178*). Chill thoroughly. To serve, cut in 1″ slices.

AMOUNT: 10 to 12 servings.

To make Lincoln's Log Cake: see p. 174.

PINEAPPLE REFRIGERATOR DESSERT

A rich combination of crushed pineapple and vanilla wafers, butter, cream, and whipped cream . . . refrigerated.

Crush vanilla wafers to make 1½ cups. Spread 1 cup crumbs in 8 or 9″ square pan.

Beat together until light and fluffy . . .
> ½ cup soft butter
> 1 cup *sifted* confectioners' sugar
> 1 egg (room temperature)

Spread mixture over crumbs. Whip until stiff . . .
> 1 cup whipping cream

Fold in . . .
> 1½ cups well drained crushed pineapple (no. 2 can)

Spread over butter mixture. Sprinkle top with remaining crumbs. Cover with waxed paper. Chill overnight. Cut in squares or oblongs to serve.

AMOUNT: 9 servings.

APRICOT WAFER PIE

Crushed chocolate wafers, apricots, and whipped cream combined. So good, too, with strawberries in place of apricots, according to Annette Calhoun (Mrs. James E. Calhoun) of our staff.

Crush chocolate wafers to make 1½ cups. Spread ½ of crumbs in 8″ square pan.

Beat together until light and fluffy . . .
> ½ cup soft butter
> 1 cup *sifted* confectioners' sugar
> 1 egg (room temperature)

Spread over crumbs in pan. Add . . .
> 1 cup sweetened apricot pulp (from cooked dried or drained canned apricots)

Spread over fruit . . .
> 1 cup whipping cream, whipped stiff

Sprinkle with remaining crumbs. Chill 12 hr. or longer. To serve, cut in squares.

AMOUNT: 9 servings.

SILHOUETTE PUDDING (✐ Recipe) Dramatic . . . delicious flavor combinations.

Use 30 *crisp, thick 3″ cookies*, such as Ginger or Chocolate Refrigerator Cookies (*pp. 200–201*). Whip 2 cups whipping cream stiff and sweeten with ¼ cup confectioners' sugar. Spread a spoonful on a cooky. Place another cooky on top . . . continue until there are 6 piles of 5 cookies with whipped cream between.

Lay piles crosswise on serving platter. Cover the roll evenly with remaining whipped cream. Chill at least 6 hr.

To decorate **Fudge Cream Roll** (made with chocolate cookies): garnish with walnut or pecan halves. Offer a chocolate sauce (*p. 404*).

For **Ginger Cream Roll** (made with ginger cookies): garnish with bits of candied ginger. A bit of clear apricot jam on top is delicious.

CHOCOLATE TOFFEE DESSERT
So rich . . serve just a small piece.

Roll fine with rolling pin . . .
    20 vanilla wafers (1 cup crumbs)

Cream together . . .
    ⅔ cup soft butter
    1⅓ cups sifted confectioners' sugar

Stir in . . .
    2 egg yolks
    *two 4-oz. bars German sweet chocolate, melted, or 1⅓ cups semi-sweet chocolate pieces, melted
    ⅔ cup chopped walnuts
    1 tsp. vanilla

Fold in . . .
    2 egg whites, stiffly beaten

*For a milder chocolate flavor, use 1 cup semi-sweet chocolate pieces, melted.

Sprinkle half of crumbs on bottom of 8″ square pan. Spread chocolate mixture over crumbs. Sprinkle remaining crumbs over top. Chill. Serve small squares topped with whipped cream on individual dessert plates.

AMOUNT: 9 to 12 servings.

All you have to do —

To use leftover cake and cookies: break them up and mix lightly into Soft Custard (*p. 230*) with a little whipped cream folded in. Chill.

VANILLA STRAWBERRY ROLL

Follow ✐ recipe above—using Vanilla Wafers. In place of whipped cream, use Strawberry Bavarian Cream (*p. 228*).

ENGLISH TRIFLE
Glamorous, elegant dessert from early days. Still one of the most served desserts in the British Isles and English colonies.

Make Rich Custard Filling (*p. 241*); then thin with ½ cup milk.

Cool. Then assemble:
    2 doz. ladyfingers
    ⅓ cup raspberry jam
    ⅓ cup sherry flavoring
    ½ cup macaroon or
        vanilla wafer crumbs

Split the ladyfingers into halves. Stand them upright, close together around edge of 8″ round serving dish. Stick remaining ladyfinger halves together with raspberry jam. Cover bottom of dish with a layer of these, sprinkle with half of sherry. Pour in half of cooled custard. Add half of crumbs.

Add another layer of filled ladyfingers. Sprinkle with remaining sherry flavoring. Add remaining custard and crumbs. Chill 4 hr. Decorate with sweetened whipped cream, blanched almonds, and bits of candied cherries and green citron.

AMOUNT: 12 servings.

MR. JOHN'S FRENCH BERET PANCAKE DESSERT

"Roll fluffy little pancakes with sugared Fraise des Bois (wild strawberries) or strawberry jam. Top jauntily with thick cream." The recipe for this delectable dessert came to us from Mr. John, of French Room hat fame.

Beat until stiff . . .
    2 egg whites
In separate bowl, mix . . .
    2 egg yolks
    ½ cup milk
Beat in until smooth . . .
    ¼ cup GOLD MEDAL
        Flour
    2 tsp. sugar
    2 tsp. butter, melted

Fold into egg whites. Heat buttered skillet. Use 2 tbsp. of batter for each pancake. Brown quickly on one side and turn to brown other side. Serve 3 rolled pancakes for each serving.

AMOUNT: 4 servings.

CHOCOLATE SOUFFLÉ

Rich chocolate-flavored dessert. Very delicate.

Melt in saucepan . . .
    ¼ cup butter
Blend in and cook until smooth and bubbly . . .
    ¼ cup *sifted* GOLD MEDAL Flour
    ¼ tsp. salt
Remove from heat and stir in . . .
    ¾ cup milk
    2 sq. unsweetened chocolate (2 oz.), cut up
Bring to boil. Boil 1 min., stirring constantly. Remove from heat.
Beat until thick and lemon-colored . . .
    3 egg yolks
Beat in gradually . . .
    ½ cup sugar
Then blend chocolate mixture into egg yolk mixture.
Beat until stiff . . .
    3 egg whites
    ¼ tsp. cream of tartar

Carefully fold in egg yolk-chocolate mixture. Pour into greased 2-qt. baking dish. Set in pan of hot water (1" deep). Bake until silver knife inserted in center comes out clean. Serve immediately on warm dessert plates. Top with whipped cream and toasted sliced almonds or one of steamed pudding sauces (*p. 405*).

TEMPERATURE: 350° (mod. oven).

TIME: Bake 45 to 50 min.

AMOUNT: 6 to 8 servings.

ORANGE SOUFFLÉ

"I'm crazy about it! I want it for my wedding supper!" says Beverly Prevey, Minneapolis, Minnesota.

Butter entire inside of top of 2-qt. double boiler . . . including inside of cover. Beat until frothy . . .
    3 egg whites (⅓ to ½ cup)
Add gradually . . .
    3 tbsp. sugar
    1 tsp. orange flavoring
Continue beating until mixture is stiff. Fold in . . .
    2 tbsp. cut-up orange marmalade

Cook in covered double boiler over boiling water 1 hr. Do not lift cover. Turn off heat, let stand until ready to serve (not more than ½ hr.). Turn out onto hot serving dish. Garnish with shaved almonds. Serve with Golden Eggnog (*p. 406*) or Clear Orange Sauce (*p. 405*).

AMOUNT: 6 servings.

SNOW PUDDING (Lemon Sponge)

"Is there anything more refreshing?" asks Mrs. William Fulton of Minneapolis. She often serves it in sparkling little Early American pressed glass saucedishes that are extra wide and deep . . . "so that plenty of Soft Custard can be poured over."

Mix in saucepan . . .
    ¾ cup sugar
    1 envelope unflavored gelatin (1 tbsp.)
    1¼ cups water
Cook just until boiling, stirring constantly. Blend in . . .
    ¼ cup lemon juice
    1 tbsp. grated lemon rind
Place pan in cold water and cool until mixture mounds when dropped from a spoon.
Beat until stiff . . .
    2 egg whites

Slowly blend gelatin into beaten egg whites using rotary beater. When blended, stir mixture with rubber spatula until it holds its shape. Spoon into dessert dishes or mold. Chill until firm. Serve with Soft Custard (*p. 230*) as sauce.

AMOUNT: 6 to 8 servings.

ICE CREAM BOMBE

Ice creams of different flavors in 1 pretty mold.

Line sides and bottom of a 2-qt. mold, such as a melon mold, with 1 qt. ice cream. Fill center with another 1 qt. ice cream or sherbet (contrasting color).

Cover with waxed paper. Freeze 3 to 4 hr. Unmold. Garnish with whipped cream and fresh fruit.

MERINGUE TORTE (♪ Recipe)

A charming Minneapolis hostess has a special way of serving meringues at her delightful luncheon parties. She bakes little rounding handles of meringue to use with individual meringue shells (baked on the same paper) . . . then fashions meringue baskets of ice cream and fruit for individual servings.

Beat together until frothy . . .
    3 egg whites
    ¼ tsp. cream of tartar

Gradually beat in, a little at a time . . .
    1 cup sugar

Beat until very stiff and glossy. Tint, if desired, with food coloring. Bake and cool (*see pictures*). Serve filled with ice cream topped with fresh berries or cut-up fruit, or chocolate or butterscotch sauce.

TEMPERATURE: 275° (very slow oven).

TIME: Bake 60 min. Turn off oven and leave in until cool.

AMOUNT: 8 to 10 servings.

1 Spread on heavy brown paper on baking sheet in 8 or 9" round, heart, or any desired shape. Or in 9" round layer pan with cutter.

2 For 8 individual meringue shells, drop ⅓ cup meringue for each on heavy brown paper on baking sheet. Shape, as above, with back of spoon.

3 Fill either large or individual meringue shells with ice cream and sweetened fruit or a sauce. If desired, top with Sweetened Whipped Cream (*p. 222*).

All you have to do —

To *make meringue shells of special shapes:* draw an outline of shape on brown paper on baking sheet. Spoon meringue mixture inside pencil outline.

Make Them in Advance

Meringue shells (cooled) may be loosely wrapped in waxed paper and stored in a cupboard for several days. (Do not place in airtight container.)

ANGEL PIE (Lemon Schaum Torte)

The perfect finish for a hearty meal.

Follow ♪ recipe above—*except* use 4 egg whites. See pictures above for shaping. Spread with cooled Lemon Torte Filling (*below*). Top with 1 cup whipping cream, stiffly whipped. Chill about 12 hr. before serving.

LEMON TORTE FILLING

Beat 4 egg yolks in small mixer bowl until thick and lemon-colored. Gradually beat in ½ cup sugar. Blend in ¼ cup lemon juice, 2 tbsp. grated lemon rind. Cook over hot water, stirring constantly, until thick (5 to 8 min.). Cool.

STRAWBERRY ANGEL PIE

"Our guests just love this dessert," says Mrs. L. Norwood Smith of charming Colonial Inn in St. Louis Park, Minnesota, a treasure house of rare and lovely antiques where delicious foods are served.

Make Angel Pie (*at left*)—*except*, in place of lemon filling, use Strawberry Cream Filling made by folding 1 cup sweetened mashed fresh strawberries into 2 cups whipping cream, whipped stiff. Heap into meringue shell. Serve immediately or store in refrigerator.

GLAMOROUS DESSERTS FOR ENTERTAINING

Pistachio Ice Cream with Cranberry
Ice and Coconut Balls

Rainbow Dessert (Blöte Kage)

Meringue Torte with Ice Cream
and Strawberries

Cherry Tree Log (Chocolate Roll)

Luxury-loving Romans of Julius Caesar's day knew a kind of ice cream ... snow from the high mountain passes, carried to Rome by fleet runners. There it was flavored with fruit juices and enjoyed as a rare delicacy.

Centuries later, "Cream Ice" was so well liked by Charles I of England, that he pensioned the French chef who made it for him.

Virginia cavaliers brought that idea to the new world. Generations later, Dolly Madison reversed the name and "Ice Cream" appeared on the White House menu.

FRENCH VANILLA ICE CREAM
(Recipe) For refrigerator.

The egg yolks make it a lovely yellow. Keep trays covered with waxed paper to help prevent crystals.

Set refrigerator control for fast freezing.
Blend in saucepan ...

> ½ cup sugar
> ¼ tsp. salt
> 1 cup milk
> 3 egg yolks, beaten

Cook over med. heat, stirring constantly, *just until* mixture comes to a boil. Cool. Add ...

> 1 tbsp. vanilla

Pour into refrigerator tray. Freeze until mixture is mushy and partly frozen (½ to 1 hr.). Whip until barely stiff ...

> 1 cup whipping cream

Empty partially frozen mixture into chilled bowl, beat until smooth. Fold in whipped cream. Pour into two refrigerator trays and freeze until firm, *stirring frequently and thoroughly*, during first hour of freezing. Freezing time will be 3 to 4 hr. AMOUNT: 6 to 8 servings (1 qt.).

MOCHA ICE CREAM

Follow recipe for either French Vanilla or Philadelphia Ice Cream above—*except* add 3 tbsp. powdered instant coffee to mixture in saucepan before cooking.

CHOCOLATE ICE CREAM

Follow recipe for either French Vanilla or Philadelphia Ice Cream above—*except* add ½ cup semi-sweet chocolate pieces to mixture in saucepan before cooking.

NESSELRODE PUDDING

A guest paid a New York hotel $20 for this recipe. Years later she gave it to a friend, the mother of Mae Chesnut, formerly of our staff.

Follow recipe for either French Vanilla or Philadelphia Ice Cream above—*except* add 2 tbsp. cocoa with the sugar. Before freezing, fold in ½ cup cut-up seedless raisins and ¼ cup chopped, toasted, blanched almonds.

FRENCH VANILLA ICE CREAM
For crank freezer.

Follow recipe at left—*except*, after custard has cooled, blend in vanilla and whipping cream without whipping. Freeze according to directions on freezer.

PHILADELPHIA ICE CREAM (Recipe)
For crank freezer only.

Smooth ... melts down to pure cream.

Mix ...

> 1 qt. whipping cream, scalded
> ¾ cup sugar

Cool. Blend in ...

> 1½ tbsp. vanilla
> ⅛ tsp. salt

Freeze as directed on freezer.

WHAT FLAVOR WILL YOU HAVE?

Just before freezing either French Vanilla or Philadelphia Ice Cream, blend in flavor ingredients: more than one, if desired.

FRESH PEACH, STRAWBERRY, OR RASPBERRY: 1½ cups mashed fruit, sweetened with ½ to ¾ cup sugar.

BANANA: 1½ cups mashed bananas, 1 tbsp. lemon juice, 2 tbsp. sugar. Omit vanilla.

PINEAPPLE: ½ cup drained crushed pineapple (no. 1 flat can).

ORANGE-ALMOND: ½ cup orange juice and pulp, 1 tsp. grated orange rind, ½ cup chopped blanched almonds.

PEPPERMINT: ½ cup crushed peppermint stick candy.

NUT BRITTLE: 1 cup crushed almond, pecan, or peanut brittle.

CHOCOLATE CHIP: 1 cup shaved or bits of semi-sweet chocolate.

PISTACHIO: ½ cup chopped pistachio nuts or almonds, ½ tsp. almond flavoring, and a few drops green food coloring.

BLACK WALNUT: ½ cup chopped black walnuts.

ORANGE SHERBET (🖋 Recipe)

Mix in saucepan . . .
   ¾ cup sugar
   1½ tsp. unflavored gelatin

Stir in gradually . . .
   2 tbsp. lemon juice
   ¾ cup orange juice and pulp
   2 tbsp. grated orange rind

Bring to boil. Cool. Stir in slowly . . .
   1 cup milk

Pour into refrigerator tray. Freeze to a mush (about 1 hr.). Beat in chilled bowl with rotary beater until creamy. Fold in . . .
   1 egg white, stiffly beaten

Return to tray. Freeze until firm (2 to 3 hr.), stirring occasionally.

AMOUNT: 6 to 8 servings.

PINEAPPLE SHERBET

Follow 🖋 recipe above—*except* add drained crushed pineapple in place of orange juice and rind.

STRAWBERRY OR RASPBERRY SHERBET

Follow 🖋 recipe above—*except* use crushed strawberries or raspberries in place of orange juice and rind.

LEMON SHERBET

Follow 🖋 recipe above—*except* increase sugar to 1 cup. Increase lemon juice to ⅓ cup. Omit orange juice and rind. Add 2 tsp. grated lemon rind.

ORANGE ICE

Follow 🖋 recipe above—*except* increase orange juice and pulp to 1 cup; and omit milk.

EASY LEMON CREAM

For a change, pour cream mixture into refrigerator tray lined with graham cracker or cooky crumbs. Sprinkle some on top. Serve in squares or triangles.

Whip until stiff . . .
   1 cup whipping cream

Fold in . . .
   15-oz. can sweetened condensed milk
   ⅓ cup lemon juice (2 lemons)

Pour into refrigerator tray. Cover with waxed paper. Freeze until firm.

AMOUNT: 6 servings.

PINEAPPLE ICE (🖋 Recipe)

Mix in saucepan . . .
   1 tsp. unflavored gelatin
   ¾ cup sugar

Stir in and bring to boil . . .
   1 cup water
   ¼ cup lemon juice
   1 cup crushed pineapple (no. 1 flat can), undrained

Cool. Pour into refrigerator tray; freeze to a mush. Beat in chilled bowl with rotary beater until fluffy. Fold in . . .
   1 egg white, stiffly beaten

Return to tray. Freeze until firm (2 to 3 hr.) stirring occasionally.

AMOUNT: 6 to 8 servings.

LEMON ICE

Follow 🖋 recipe for Pineapple Ice above —*except* omit pineapple and add 2 tsp. grated lemon rind.

With Frosted Grapes: Bess Plummer of Minneapolis unmolds lemon ice or sherbet onto serving dish. Around it, she arranges clusters of blue, green, and red grapes (*frosted, p. 222*). With a garnish of grape leaves, it is a delight for epicures. Creme de Menthe may be passed.

RASPBERRY OR STRAWBERRY ICE

Follow 🖋 recipe for Pineapple Ice above —*except* omit lemon juice and pineapple; and add 10-oz. pkg. frozen raspberries or strawberries, undrained.

CRANBERRY ICE

"No holiday dinner is complete without it!" says Dr. W. P. Duerre of Lake City, Minnesota. It's a wonderful accompaniment to turkey; also makes a colorful holiday dessert with pistachio ice cream (see color picture on p. 253). Serve in avocado halves for holiday appetizer.

Cook until skins are broken (about 10 min.) . . .
   1 qt. cranberries (4 cups)
   2 cups water

Rub through a fine sieve to make smooth pulp.

Stir in . . .
   2 cups sugar
   ¼ cup lemon juice (2 lemons)
   1 tsp. grated orange rind or ½ cup orange juice
   2 cups cold water (part raspberry juice may be used)

Pour into refrigerator tray. Freeze until firm (2 to 3 hr.), stirring 2 or 3 times.

AMOUNT: 8 servings.

"Mousse," French for moss or foam, describes its smooth, spongy quality. Parfait, meaning "perfect," is more creamy than ice cream. Marlows use marshmallows instead of gelatin.

CHRISTIAN DIOR'S APRICOT MOUSSE (Recipe)

Christian Dior, famous for design trends in women's fashions, sent us this recipe as a special favorite. The Dior treatment in this recipe is the addition of Kirsch, a cherry liqueur, for flavor.

Soften . . .
   1 tsp. unflavored gelatin
in . . .
   1 tbsp. liquid (fruit juice or water)
Dissolve over hot water. Stir into . . .
   1 cup sieved cooked apricots
Combine in chilled bowl . . .
   2 cups whipping cream
   ½ cup sifted confectioners' sugar
   ¼ tsp. salt
Whip until stiff.

Fold into apricot mixture. Turn into refrigerator tray, freeze until firm.
TIME: Freeze 3 to 4 hr.
AMOUNT: 6 servings (1 qt.).

STRAWBERRY OR RASPBERRY MOUSSE

Follow recipe above—*except* use slightly sweetened strawberries or raspberries, mashed, for the fruit pulp.

EASY CHOCOLATE MOUSSE

From Mrs. Lewis Washburn Child of Minneapolis, Minnesota, who gave us several fine frozen dessert recipes.

Follow recipe above—*except*, in place of fruit pulp, use canned chocolate syrup.

PEPPERMINT MOUSSE

Fold 1 cup crushed peppermint stick candy (crush in cloth bag) into 2 cups whipping cream, whipped stiff. Turn into refrigerator tray, freeze until firm.
AMOUNT: 6 servings.

FRUIT MARLOWS

Heat 1 cup fruit pulp and juice and 2 tbsp. lemon juice with ½ lb. marshmallows, cut up. Chill. Fold in 1 cup whipping cream, whipped stiff. Freeze in refrigerator tray.
AMOUNT: 6 servings.

CHERRY-NUT PARFAIT

Bring to boil in small saucepan . . .
   ½ cup sugar
   ¼ cup water
Continue cooking until a little dropped in cold water forms a firm ball (242°).
Pour over . . .
   2 egg whites, stiffly beaten
Beat until soft peaks form.
Fold in . . .
   1 cup whipping cream, whipped stiff
   1 tsp. vanilla
   ¼ cup drained cut-up maraschino cherries
   ½ cup chopped nuts

Pour into refrigerator tray or mold. Freeze until firm (3 to 4 hr.).
AMOUNT: 8 servings.

FRENCH VANILLA PARFAIT

A special favorite of Helen Friis-Hansen of Herlufsholm, Denmark, a graduate of Den Suhrske Husmoderskole. She spent a year with us as a member of our staff.

Whip until stiff . . .
   2 egg whites
Whip until stiff . . .
   1 cup whipping cream
Beat . . .
   2 egg yolks with ¼ cup sugar

Fold together egg whites, whipped cream, egg yolk mixture, and 2 tsp. vanilla. Pour into mold or refrigerator tray. Freeze until firm.
AMOUNT: 8 servings.

PISTACHIO PARFAIT

Make French Vanilla Parfait above—*except* add a few drops green food coloring, ¼ tsp. almond flavoring, and ½ cup chopped pistachio nuts before freezing.

FROZEN GRAPE CREAM

Serve in compote with a few blackberries or black raspberries sprinkled over the top.

Whip until stiff . . .
   1⅔ cups whipping cream
Fold in . . .
   two 6-oz. cans undiluted frozen grape juice (partially thawed)

Pour into 2 refrigerator trays. Freeze just until set (about 1 hr.). Empty into bowl. Beat with wooden spoon until smooth. Return to refrigerator trays. Freeze until firm.
AMOUNT: 8 to 10 servings.

CRÈME BRULÉE (Burned Cream)

We enjoyed it at a lovely luncheon given by a delightful hostess, Elizabeth Case, co-author of "Cook's Away." This elegant dish was a feature of the famous hospitality of Thomas Jefferson's Virginia home, "Monticello." He brought the recipe from France in 1790.

Beat until very thick . . .
　6 egg yolks
Gradually beat in . . .
　⅓ cup sugar
Scald in top of double boiler over direct heat . . .
　3 cups whipping cream

Pour scalded cream gradually into egg mixture. Return to double boiler and cook over hot water, stirring frequently, until mixture thickens (about 5 min.). Pour into heatproof serving dish. Cool.

Sprinkle top with . . .
　⅓ cup brown sugar (packed)

Place under hot broiler until sugar melts and forms glaze (about 1 min.). Chill. Serve with sweetened fresh strawberries, raspberries, or peaches; or green gage plums, or pears gently poached in syrup. The Crème Brulée is spooned over the fruit in individual dessert dishes.

AMOUNT: 8 to 10 servings.

ELENA ZELAYETA'S FRESH FRUIT DESSERT

From Elena Zelayeta of San Francisco, California, whose courageous spirit is an inspiration to us all.

Around a pile of melon balls, arrange clusters of Bing cherries (stems on) alternating with small bunches of green grapes. Border with sliced peeled peaches. Lay bananas (cut in half, then split in two) over peaches like spokes in a wheel. Garnish with strawberries and mint leaves. Serve with Fresh Raspberry Sauce (*below*) or thawed frozen raspberries—a swirl of cream cheese softened with milk spooned over each serving.

FRESH RASPBERRY SAUCE

Mix 1 pt. raspberries with ½ to 1 cup sugar. Let stand 2 hr. Put through sieve.

PEACH MELBA

From the peaches raised right outside her back door, Mrs. Arthur C. Burslie, The Dalles, Oregon, can hastily prepare this tempting concoction for family and guests.

Peel fresh peaches and poach halves in syrup (*see "to poach fruit," p. 226*). Chill. Place a peach half on a mound of vanilla ice cream. Add sweetened mashed raspberries, chilled.

ZABAGLIONE

A confection-like custard from Italy.

Beat in small mixer bowl until thick and lemon-colored . . .
　4 egg yolks
Beat in thoroughly . . .
　¼ cup sugar
　¼ tsp. salt
Blend in . .
　¼ cup sherry flavoring

Pour into top of double boiler and cook over hot water, stirring constantly, until thickened (5 min.). Cool. Serve hot or cold in sherbet or parfait glasses . . . or in demitasse cups. Or try it as a topping for fruit, ice cream, or cake (angel food, sponge, chiffon).

AMOUNT: 1 cup or 4 servings.

PEAR HELENE

First enjoyed at the luxurious Chateau Lake Louise in the Canadian Rockies.

Pare and core fresh pears. Poach halves in syrup (*see "to poach fruit," p. 226*). Chill. For each serving, arrange a pear half on a mound of vanilla ice cream in a deep dessert dish. If desired, sprinkle with crystallized violets. Pass Glossy Chocolate Sauce (*p. 404*) to pour over the ice cream and pear.

PORTIA'S PEARS

We first met this intriguing dessert at the home of Mrs. Chester MacMillan . . then of Murray Hill, Excelsior, Minnesota, now of Houston, Texas.

Use a whole canned pear (small) for each serving. Moisten cocoa (allow 1 tbsp. for each pear) with some of the pear juice. Fill center cavity of 1 half. Place 2 halves together, fasten with toothpick. Chill. Brush pears with pink coloring. Place in dessert dish on top of

　SUNSHINE SAUCE (Creamy Eggnog)
Whip together until stiff . . .
　1 cup whipping cream
　½ cup sifted confectioners' sugar
Blend in . . .
　2 egg yolks, very well beaten
　2 tbsp. brandy flavoring

257

CRÊPES SUZETTE

Original recipes call for Cointreau and brandy poured over the sauce in chafing dish after crepes are added ... then lighted before serving.

In Advance: Make Crepes (French Pancakes) (*p. 88*). Cool. Keep covered so crepes will not dry out.

At the Table: In chafing dish, melt ⅓ cup butter. Blend in 2 tbsp. sugar, ⅓ cup orange juice, a bit of grated orange rind. Turn crepes in the hot sauce, then fold them in halves or quarters. Place 3 or 4 on each dessert plate with some of the sauce spooned over.

LILY PONS' FLEUR DE LILY

Dainty, lily-shaped dessert. Created for the brilliant star of the Metropolitan Opera by Louis, fabulous chef of The Ritz in Paris.

Beat until frothy ...
    3 egg whites
Gradually beat in ...
    ½ cup sugar
Beat until stiff. Fold in ...
    ⅓ cup *sifted* GOLD MEDAL Flour
    ⅓ cup finely ground almonds
    ⅓ cup butter, melted and cooled
    1 tsp. vanilla

Use 2 tbsp. batter for each lily. Drop 2" apart on greased heavy baking sheet. Bake until lightly browned. Loosen immediately with spatula and form quickly into little cones. Seal by lapping edges. Cool. Fill with Sweetened Whipped Cream (*p. 222*) into which strawberries, cherries, or blueberries have been folded. Sprinkle with chopped pistachio nuts.

TEMPERATURE: 400° (mod. hot oven).

TIME: Bake 8 to 10 min.

AMOUNT: 10 to 12 lilies.

CHOCOLATE PEPPERMINT DREAM

Friends of Marie Anderson of our company have enjoyed this dessert as a delightful finish to her long-to-be-remembered dinners.

Make same as Bess Truman's Frozen Lemon Pie (*at right above*)—*except* use crisp chocolate cooky crumbs instead of graham cracker, and, in place of Lemon Cream Filling, use Peppermint Cream (*p. 229*).

BESS TRUMAN'S FROZEN LEMON PIE

A specialty of a gracious former White House hostess, Mrs. Harry S. Truman, whose husband's fascinating book, "The Truman Memoirs," is captivating the people of America.

Sprinkle well greased 9" pie pan with ...
    ¼ cup fine graham cracker crumbs
Pour in ...
    Lemon Cream Filling (*below*)
Sprinkle over top ...
    ¼ cup fine graham cracker crumbs

Chill or freeze to desired consistency.

AMOUNT: 6 to 8 servings.

LEMON CREAM FILLING

Beat until frothy ...
    3 egg whites
Gradually add ...
    ½ cup sugar
Beat until stiff and glossy.
Beat until thick and lemon-colored ...
    3 egg yolks
Fold into egg white mixture.
Mix and beat until stiff ...
    1 cup whipping cream
    2 to 3 tsp. grated lemon rind
    ¼ to ⅓ cup lemon juice

Fold into egg mixture.

CHERRIES JUBILEE

For a glamorous touch, Mrs. Ralph Teynor, Albany, Oregon, adds ½ cup brandy just before serving. Without stirring, she lights it with a match so the flaming cherries can be spooned over each serving.

Melt in chafing dish over direct heat ...
    ¾ cup currant jelly
Add ...
    no. 303 can pitted Bing cherries or 2
        cups fresh Bing cherries, poached
        (See "to poach fruit," p. 226.)
    1 tbsp. grated orange rind
    brandy flavoring (to taste)

Heat slowly to simmering, stirring occasionally. Serve hot over vanilla ice cream.

AMOUNT: 8 to 10 servings.

The Egg and You!

A fresh egg is a delicacy . . . not only in the morning but all 'round the clock. Eggs are so versatile, they can provide a tempting breakfast, a nourishing lunch, or a party supper. Every way you fix them, they have a different flavor. In fact, you'll find the egg and you can get together every day without boredom.

Betty Crocker

EGGS ARE APPROPRIATE ANY TIME OF DAY . . . ON ANY OCCASION

Below are listed a few suggestions from the many in this chapter.

WEIGHT-WATCHER'S LUNCHEON OR DINNER

Did you know that 1 egg contains 75 calories?

Salad of Hard-cooked Egg Slices, Cucumber Sticks, and Tomato Sections on Lettuce sprinkled with lemon juice and salt

Melba Toast (p. 30)

½ Grapefruit or 1 Orange

Buttermilk or Skim Milk

A COUNTRY DINNER

Eggs Baked on Corned Beef Hash (p. 266)

Baked Carrots   Baked Onions

Cabbage-Apple Salad (p. 388)

Pumpernickel (p. 109)

Pineapple Upside-down Cake (p. 236)

HAMPER PICNIC FOR ROADSIDE LUNCH

Jug of Coffee or Lemonade (p. 74)

Baked Ham Sandwiches

Cheese-Rye Sandwiches

Deviled Eggs   Whole Tomatoes

Cupcakes or Brownies (p. 204)   Fresh Fruit

ENTERTAINING AT BREAKFAST

Honeydew Melon Rings
filled with fresh or frozen berries

Eggs Benedict (p. 267)
(use toasted lower half of English Muffin, p. 125, for base of each)

Toasted English Muffins
(use toasted upper half of muffin for accompaniment)

Orange Marmalade   Coffee

KNOW YOUR EGGS!

Federal and state regulations for grading eggs vary. Find out what your state regulations mean. Different grades are found in all sizes of eggs. Eggs for the breakfast table should be strictly fresh (top grade) of any size you prefer. For cooking (in meat loaves, custards, etc.), you may use smaller eggs and of lower grade. For baking (especially cakes), use large eggs (2 oz.) or their equivalent.

IF YOU MEASURE EGGS

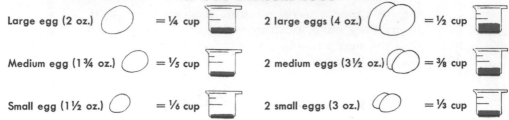

Large egg (2 oz.) = ¼ cup

2 large eggs (4 oz.) = ½ cup

Medium egg (1¾ oz.) = ⅕ cup

2 medium eggs (3½ oz.) = ⅜ cup

Small egg (1½ oz.) = ⅙ cup

2 small eggs (3 oz.) = ⅓ cup

Are they fresh?

"Their shells should look dull . . .
Not shiny or bright;
But it makes no difference
If they're brown or they're white."

A fresh egg sinks when placed in cold water. Inside, the yolk is firm and upstanding; the white thick.

Chances that you are getting fresh eggs are greater if you buy from a stock that is refrigerated.

KEEP THEM COOL!

Place eggs immediately in refrigerator—in the humidity-controlled section if you have one. (Do not freeze!)

TO SEPARATE YOLKS FROM WHITES

It's much easier if the eggs are cold (yolks are less apt to break).

LEFTOVER EGG YOLKS

See Index

Store yolks in a tightly covered jar in refrigerator.

Use 2 egg yolks for 1 whole egg in soft and baked custards, salad dressings, cream pie fillings, etc.

Use 2 egg yolks plus 1 tbsp. water for 1 whole egg in yeast doughs, cookies, etc.

For salads, sandwich fillings, garnishes, etc., hard cook yolks by simmering in hot water 10 minutes.

DON'T WASH EGGS!

The protective coating on the shell helps preserve them until ready to use. If eggs are dirty, wipe with a cloth, or rub off spots with a brush.

FOR HIGHEST VOLUME

Let egg whites stand at room temperature a while before beating.

LEFTOVER EGG WHITES

See Index

Egg whites keep for weeks if stored in a tightly covered jar in the refrigerator.

Use them in making angel food cakes, white butter cakes, icings, meringues, frozen desserts, fruit whips, etc.

EGGS

Remember how you used to chant the old "One, Two, Buckle My Shoe" rhymes? Generations of children have learned to count by them. Well, here are some rhymes to learn for *egg* wisdom:

One, two—they're good for you! Humpty Dumpty (alias The Egg) is a many-sided food! Remember—Humpty Dumpty's always on call, bursting with vitamins for us all—proteins and minerals, too, in his shell, what we all need to help keep us well.

Three, four—they taste like "more!" Nothing can match the wonderful flavor of fresh eggs properly cooked. For eggs that are delicate (done just *so*) . . . cook them over heat that's low!

Five, six—they're fun to fix! Eggs don't have to be "just eggs." The poached egg on a toasted English muffin with thinly sliced fried ham and hollandaise sauce becomes delicious "Eggs Benedict." Creamed eggs with a bright garnish of sieved hard-cooked egg yolks and parsley bouquets become "Eggs à la Goldenrod."

Seven, eight—they're mealtime bait! The recipes that follow are sure to lure the family to meals. And the pages will show you by word and picture tested methods to insure superbly cooked eggs and egg dishes in attractive variety for many a meal to come.

Nine, ten—here's how and when! There's more than one way to crack an egg . . . and cook it! There's a *best* way even to cook eggs in the shell. The pages that follow show you how to work egg wonders for many a day.

Eleven, twelve—dig and delve! Delve into the recipes and we feel sure you'll be inspired to try every one of them.

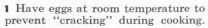

You like them soft to start the day,
But hard, they make a garnish gay.

1 Have eggs at room temperature to prevent "cracking" during cooking.

2 Start in cold or boiling water.

3 Cover eggs completely with water.

4 Choose large enough pan. Do not pile eggs on top of each other.

5 Time accurately, by clock or timer.

6 Cook at temperature below boiling.

Cold Water Start

Soft-cooked Eggs
2 to 4 min. *off the heat*

Hard-cooked Eggs
23 to 25 min. *off the heat*

1 Cover eggs in saucepan with cold water. Heat until water boils.

2 Remove from heat. Cover pan. Let stand *off heat* until eggs are cooked.

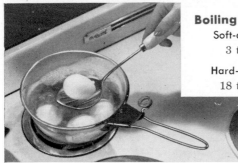

Boiling Water Start

Soft-cooked Eggs
3 to 5 min.

Hard-cooked Eggs
18 to 20 min.

1 Bring water to a boil in saucepan. With a spoon, carefully lower eggs into the water to prevent cracking the shell.

2 Reduce heat. Keep water simmering until eggs are cooked. (Turn eggs several times . . . helps keep yolks centered.)

Cool eggs under cold water. This makes eggs easier to handle, eases shelling hard-cooked eggs, and immediately stops the cooking (overcooking causes the yolks to become darkened). Cracking shells slightly before cooling makes eggs easier to peel.

CODDLED EGGS *Super-delicate.*

Follow directions for cooking eggs with Boiling Water Start above—*except* cover pan tightly, and remove from heat. Let stand until eggs are cooked.
Soft-coddled Eggs: 4 to 6 min. *off heat.*
Hard-coddled Eggs: 30 to 35 min. *off heat.*

MILK GLASS HEN KEEPS EGGS WARM AND COZY

IN THE SHELL...OR OUT!

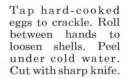

Crack egg sharply *at large end* when egg is to be eaten from shell, set in individual egg cup.

Crack egg sharply *in center* if to be turned into egg dish or cup.

Season with salt, pepper, and butter. "Use bone or ivory spoon," say the English.

Pull down top of egg slicer. Fine wires cut hard-cooked eggs. Use slices for gold-and-white garnish for salads, fish, etc.

Tap hard-cooked eggs to crackle. Roll between hands to loosen shells. Peel under cold water. Cut with sharp knife.

Press yolks and whites separately through coarse sieve. Use rows of white and yellow on canapés, to border meat loaves. Sprinkle over spinach, creamed eggs, etc.

EGGS À LA GOLDENROD

Pretty gold and white main dish ready for luncheon.

Creamed Eggs with whites and some of yolks in the Medium White Sauce,
poured over buttered toast . . . sieved yolks over top.

DEVILED EGGS (✎ Recipe) Mounds of savory yellow egg yolks in white frames. A stunning garnish and satisfying appetizer . . . food for picnics and parties.

Cut in halves . . . 6 hard-cooked eggs

Slip out yolks. Mash with fork.

Mix in . . . . . . ½ tsp. salt
　　　　　　¼ tsp. pepper
　　　　　　½ tsp. dry mustard
　　　　　　about 3 tbsp. salad dressing or vinegar or cream
　　　　　　　(enough to moisten)

Refill whites with egg yolk mixture, heaping it up lightly. Use with salads, cold meat platters, etc.

To Carry Deviled Eggs To Picnics

Fit two halves together, wrap in waxed paper (twisting the ends).

DEVILED EGGS DE LUXE

"Different" for appetizers, meat garnish, etc.

Follow ✎ recipe above—*except* add to egg yolks with the seasonings 2 tbsp. of any of the following: finely minced parsley, chives, celery, or pimientos. Refill whites with this egg yolk mixture.

STUFFED EGGS FOR SPECIAL DISHES

Follow ✎ recipe above—*except* add to mashed yolks 2 tbsp. minced cooked ham, crisp bacon, or frizzled dried beef; or flaked tuna, lobster, salmon, shrimp, or crabmeat; or mashed sardines or anchovies.

CREAMED EGGS (✎ Recipe) Offer endless possibilities for plain and fancy fare.

Make. . . . . *1 cup Medium White Sauce (p. 398)

Carefully fold in. 4 hard-cooked eggs, cut into quarters

Serve hot over hot buttered toast or biscuits, crisp chow mein noodles, or fluffy boiled rice; or in toast Buttercups (*p. 30*) or patty shells. Sprinkle with paprika and garnish with sprigs of parsley, crisp bacon, etc.

*QUICK VARIATION-DELICIOUS: Use seasoned canned cream of mushroom soup (undiluted) in place of Medium White Sauce.

CURRIED EGGS

Add ¼ tsp. curry powder with other seasonings when making Medium White Sauce for Creamed Eggs.

CREAMED EGG SPECIALS

For luncheons, suppers, and parties.

Add to Creamed Eggs about 1 cup of:
　flaked shrimp, salmon, crab, or tuna
　or diced cooked chicken or ham
　or frizzled dried beef
　or sautéed mushrooms and minced
　　　pimiento and green pepper

Deviled Egg plate ready for the party.

265

HOW TO FRY EGGS ... SUNNY-SIDE-UP

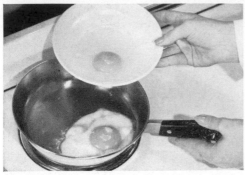

1 Heat a thin layer of butter or bacon fat in heavy skillet until moderately hot. Break eggs, one at a time, into saucer; slip into skillet. Immediately reduce heat to low.

2 Cook *slowly*, spooning fat over eggs until whites are set and a film forms over yolks (3 to 4 min.). Sprinkle with salt and pepper. Serve at once on warm plate.

FRIED EGGS ... OVER

Fry eggs (*see above*)—*except* turn eggs over quickly when whites are set. Cook until done as desired.

POACHED-FRIED EGGS
They have lovely pink tops.

Fry eggs (*see above*)—*except* use just enough fat to coat skillet. Immediately add ½ tsp. water or cream for each egg. Cover tightly. Cook to firmness desired (5 to 6 min.).

Delicious Combination

Egg fried in butter . . . served on fried tomato slice. Curry Sauce (*p. 398*).

BACON-OR-HAM AND EGGS

Fry bacon or ham in skillet; remove; keep warm. Then fry eggs in some of fat in pan. Serve immediately surrounded by hot bacon or ham, garnished with parsley, broiled peach or apricot halves, etc.

EGGS IN A FRAME
A Sunday evening treat.

Cut circle from slice of bread; then butter rest of slice generously on both sides. Place in hot buttered skillet over low heat. Drop an egg into center. Cook slowly until egg is set and underside of bread is brown. Turn. Brown on other side. Season with salt and pepper.

BAKED OR SHIRRED EGGS

Break each egg into a greased 3″ shallow baking dish. Dot with butter. Sprinkle with salt and pepper. Add 1 tbsp. cream or cultured sour cream, tomato juice, or undiluted cream of mushroom soup. Bake in mod. oven (350°) until set (15 to 20 min.). Serve hot in the dish as an individual serving . . . garnished with sprig of parsley or watercress.

EGGS BAKED ON
CORNED BEEF HASH

Spread warmed moist corned beef hash in well greased shallow baking dish. With bottom of custard cup, make deep hollows in hash. Dot each with butter and break an egg into it. Season with salt and pepper; cover with 1 tbsp. cream. Bake in mod. hot oven (400°) until eggs are set (15 to 20 min.). Serve immediately from the same dish.

EGGS BAKED IN BACON RINGS
Festive serving of Bacon and Eggs.

Follow directions opposite—*except* circle inside of each baking dish with a partially cooked bacon strip (not crisp) before breaking in egg.

A COOKY SHEET MAKES A HANDY TRAY on which to set a number of individual dishes during baking.

HOW TO POACH EGGS

1 Fill greased skillet with hot water to cover eggs by 1". Add salt (1 tsp. to 1 qt. water). Bring to boil; then reduce to simmering. Break each egg into a saucer and slip one at a time into the water. Slide egg toward side of pan to keep yolk in center. Cover pan. Cook below simmering 3 to 5 min.

2 Lift eggs from water, one at a time, with slotted turner. Drain. Season with salt and pepper. Serve at once on hot buttered toast, codfish cakes, ham-covered toast rounds, fried tomato slices, hot asparagus on toast, toasted split cornbread, or corned beef hash slices; or in nests of cooked garden spinach.

EGGS POACHED IN MILK

Poaching Eggs in Muffin Rings.

"My mother always prepared them this way for my sisters and brothers and me when we were children. And, until we were grown up, we didn't know that eggs could be poached in any other way," says James Fish, advertising executive of our company.

Poach eggs (*see above*)—*except* use milk in place of water. Pour the hot milk over eggs on the hot toast.

Poaching Eggs in Egg Poacher

EGGS À LA REINE

Fit for a queen's luncheon or supper.
Place rounds of toast in baking dish. Cover with sliced mushrooms sautéed in butter . . . then with poached eggs. Pour over all, hot Cheese Sauce (*p. 398*). Sprinkle with grated cheese. Place in quick mod. oven (375°) until cheese melts.

EGGS À LA LEE

As served in Old Virginia.
For each serving, cover hot toast round with thin slice of boiled ham. Top with hot poached egg. Pour hot Mushroom Sauce (*p. 398*) over all. Serve at once.

EGGS MORNAY

Place poached eggs in shallow baking dish. Cover with Sauce Mornay (*p. 399*). Sprinkle with grated Parmesan cheese. Brown under broiler. Serve at once.

POACHED EGGS ON HASH CAKES

They go together like ham 'n' eggs.
Prepare patties of hash. Top each with a poached egg. Serve hot with chili sauce.

EGGS POACHED IN A WHIRLPOOL

Stir simmering water in skillet briskly... slip egg into center of whirlpool. Cover pan. A number of eggs may be cooked at one time. Cut eggs apart.

EGGS BENEDICT

The original recipe was brought to Old New Orleans by the French.
For each serving, cover a round of split and toasted English Muffin (or toast) with a thin slice of fried ham (same size), or spread with deviled ham. Top each with a poached egg and cover with Hollandaise Sauce (*p. 402*). Serve at once.

SCRAMBLED EGGS (✗ Recipe) *Moist, tender, and golden. Delicious served on toast strips covered with anchovy paste, smoked salmon, deviled ham, crisp bacon, or creamed chicken.*

1 Place in bowl with egg 1 tbsp. milk or cream for each egg, a dash of salt, and pepper. Beat with fork. For gold-and-white effect, do not blend completely.

2 Heat butter or other fat (½ tbsp. for each egg) in mod. hot skillet. Pour in egg mixture and reduce heat to low. (Eggs should be scrambled slowly and gently.)

3 When mixture starts to set at bottom and sides, lift cooked portions with spatula, and turn gently so as to cook all portions evenly.

4 As soon as eggs are cooked through but are still moist and glossy (5 to 8 min.), quickly remove to hot platter and serve at once.

QUICK SCRAMBLED EGGS

Pour eggs directly into hot fat in skillet. Add salt and pepper to taste. Stir gently.

DELICATE SCRAMBLED EGGS

Made in double boiler without fat.

Follow ✗ recipe above—*except* cook in top of double boiler over simmering—not boiling—water, stirring occasionally, until eggs are thick and creamy.

SCRAMBLED EGGS WITH HERBS

Follow ✗ recipe above—*except* add minced *fresh* herbs (chives, parsley, tarragon, or chervil) to egg mixture.

All you have to do—

To *make Eggs à la Buckingham:* pour scrambled eggs (slightly underdone) over toast covered with Medium White Sauce (*p. 398*). Sprinkle with grated cheese. Put in oven to melt cheese.

SCRAMBLED EGGS WITH CHEESE

Follow ✗ recipe above—*except*, for each egg, add 1 tbsp. grated American cheese, ¼ tsp. minced onion to egg mixture. Tomato Sauce (*p. 283*) makes a tasty finish.

SCRAMBLED EGGS WITH MUSHROOMS

Follow ✗ recipe above—*except* first sauté sliced fresh or canned mushrooms (1 to 2 tbsp. for each egg) in the hot fat.

SCRAMBLED EGGS WITH DRIED BEEF OR HAM

Follow ✗ recipe above—*except* frizzle flaked pieces of dried beef or boiled ham in the hot fat before adding eggs. For something special, serve with hot Mushroom Sauce (*p. 398*).

FRENCH OMELET (✗ Recipe) *Creamy, yet hearty.*

1 Beat eggs until fluffy. For each egg, beat in 1 tbsp. milk or cream, a dash of salt, pepper. Pour into sizzling butter (1 tsp. per egg) in skillet over *low* heat.

2 Cook slowly . . . keeping heat low. As under-surface becomes set, start lifting it slightly with spatula to let uncooked portion flow underneath and cook.

3 To add herbs, cheese, meat, etc., sprinkle ½ tbsp. per egg over top of eggs.

4 As soon as all of mixture seems set, fold or roll it; serve immediately.

OMELET AUX FINES HERBES
On every menu in France.
Follow ✗ recipe above—*except* sprinkle with ½ tbsp. *each* minced *fresh* chives and parsley. Add a dash of other herbs (chervil, basil, thyme, sweet marjoram).

CHEESE OMELET
Follow ✗ recipe above—*except* add grated American cheese.

MUSHROOM OMELET
Fruit. Mushroom Omelet. Crisp bacon. Country Breakfast Muffins. Coffee or Milk. Perfect for a "company" breakfast!
Follow ✗ recipe above—*except* add sautéed sliced mushrooms (2 to 4 tbsp. for each egg).

TOMATO OMELET
Follow ✗ recipe above—*except* add 2 tbsp. sautéed cut-up fresh tomatoes for each egg.

INDIVIDUAL OMELETS (Roll-ups)
Clever egg maneuver from Mrs. Anthony Kennedy, Media, Pennsylvania.
Follow ✗ recipe above—*except* spread 1 egg beaten with 1 tbsp. milk over bottom of 10″ skillet. When egg is set, cut through center. Roll up each half (from end near you) as an individual omelet. Serve each with a small strip of crisp bacon.

JELLY OMELET
"Omelet filled with bright red currant jelly, hot popovers or corn bread, and coffee! What more delicious combination is there for luncheon or supper?" says Mary K. Ward of our company.
Follow ✗ recipe above—*except*, just before folding, spread with jelly.

BACON OR HAM OMELET
Follow ✗ recipe above—*except* sprinkle with 2 tbsp. broken crisp cooked bacon or flakes of cooked ham for each egg.

269

PUFFY OMELET (✐ Recipe) *A lovely main dish ... the cook's pride.*

2 Pour into sizzling butter (½ tbsp. per egg) in heavy skillet.

1 Beat egg whites until stiff. Beat egg yolks until thick and lemon-colored, beat in 1 tbsp. milk or cream per egg . . . salt and pepper. Fold into the beaten whites.

3 Turn heat to low. Cook slowly until light brown underneath (about 10 min.). (Bubbles will still appear through uncooked puffy top and mixture will look moist.)

4 Place skillet in mod. oven (350°). Bake until light brown on top and until, when touched lightly with finger, no imprint remains (about 10 to 15 min.).

5 Make ½" deep crease across omelet . . . half way between handle and opposite side. Slip turner under, tip skillet to loosen omelet, and fold in half without breaking.

6 Roll omelet top-side-down onto hot platter.

7 Garnish with hot sauce and serve at once.

HELPS TO HOLD UP PUFFY OMELETS

Soft Bread Crumbs: Use ½ tbsp. for each egg. Soak crumbs in the milk.

Medium White Sauce: Use ¼ cup for each egg. Blend into beaten yolks.

Cream of Tartar: Beat in with egg whites (¼ tsp. for 4 whites).

FAVORITE SAUCES

Delicious with Puffy Omelet or Scrambled Eggs.

Cheese Sauce	Creamed Chicken
Mushroom Sauce	Creamed Ham
Tomato Sauce	Creamed Asparagus

Any of these may be made as variations of Medium White Sauce (*p. 398*).

A Happily Chosen Main Dish
Makes The Meal

For a cozy fireside supper . . . bridge luncheon . . . club gathering . . . neighborhood buffet . . . or the homey evening meal with the family. Prepare one delicious main dish—and it's easy to complete the menu.

Betty Crocker

A FEW SUGGESTIONS FROM THIS CHAPTER

May start with:

meat or chicken
{ fresh
{ canned
{ leftover

fish or sea food
{ fresh
{ frozen
{ canned
{ leftover

cheese
{ grated or
{ shredded

And be combined with:

vegetables
{ fresh
{ frozen
{ canned
{ dried
{ leftover

rice

rolled oats
{ regular
{ quick-cooking

eggs
{ beaten
{ hard-cooked

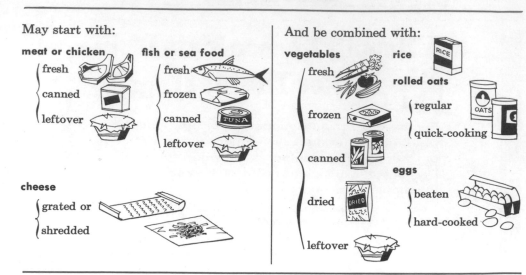

Or they may have a starchy foundation:

rice
{ regular
{ quick-cooking
{ wild rice

corn meal

beans
{ dried
{ canned

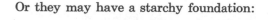

macaroni
{ elbow
{ long
{ shell

spaghetti
{ elbow
{ long
{ long
{ (Italian)

noodles
{ narrow
{ medium
{ wide
{ (lasagne)

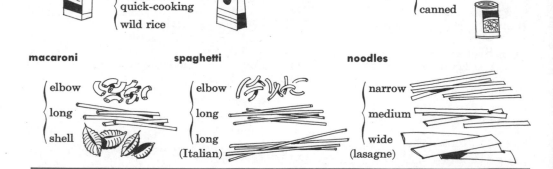

These starchy foods (*above*) may be combined with:

{ vegetables
{ cheese
{ sauces

{ soup
{ meat
{ cultured
{ sour cream

The meat, chicken, or fish combination dishes and starchy dishes may be held together with:

{ eggs
{ white sauce
{ soup

{ gravy
{ crumbs
{ gelatin

Meat, chicken, or fish dishes may be topped with a crust of:

{ biscuit dough
{ pastry
{ crumbs

Main dishes may also be interesting combinations placed between 2 slices of bread for a sandwich (hot or cold) which serves as the main part of the meal.

MAIN DISHES

Main Dishes are as American as apple pie or chocolate cake. Their origin may be a well known foreign dish, a modern product of imagination, or an exciting use of leftovers. Some main dishes in times past, when four or five course dinners were not uncommon, appeared as forerunners of the meat course. But the way main dishes are served today, as almost the entire luncheon or to take the place of the meat course at dinner, is typically American.

The planning and making of main dishes should be as carefully done as the dessert, salad, or any other part of the meal. Then the main dish truly becomes an interesting food adventure rather than a commonplace mixture of leftovers.

Poorly made main dishes have come to have a bad reputation, especially among men, as a substitute for meat. But a well seasoned, well cooked main dish can be as interesting and satisfying as a good steak.

Plan a main dish for lunch or for dinner, then choose other food to complement it. Oftentimes a good bread and dessert are all that are needed to make a satisfying, nutritious lunch. For dinner, a vegetable and salad in addition to the bread and dessert may make a dinner more complete.

SAVORY MEAT PIE

Glorifies leftover roast. Have mixture hot when topping goes on to insure a thoroughly baked top crust.

Sauté in hot fat . . .
> ¼ cup chopped onion
> 2 tbsp. chopped green pepper

Combine in 2-qt. baking dish with . . .
> 2 cups diced cooked meat (beef, lamb, veal from leftover roast)
> 2 cups diced cooked vegetables (fresh or leftover—such as carrots, celery, peas, corn, turnips, parsnips)
> 1½ to 2 cups well seasoned gravy thinned with milk or stock

Heat in hot oven (425°) 15 min.

Cover with . . .
> dough for Southern Biscuits (½ recipe) (p. 83) or Golden Pastry (p. 282)

Cut slits in top for steam to escape. Bake until golden brown.

TEMPERATURE: 425° (hot oven).

TIME: Bake about 20 min.

AMOUNT: 6 servings.

All you have to do—

For a different topping: make dough for Herb Biscuits (*p. 83*). Cut biscuits and place on top of hot mixture. *Or* use fluffy mashed potatoes for topping.

SKILLET MEAT LOAF

"My guests like this," says Helen Ayres Davis, who combines homemaking with an advertising career.

Mix thoroughly . . .
> 1¼ lb. ground beef
> ⅓ cup rolled oats
> ⅓ cup tomato purée
> 1 large onion, chopped fine (1 cup)
> 10 stuffed olives, sliced (⅔ cup)
> 1 tsp. salt
> ¼ tsp. pepper

Spread in heavy skillet. Arrange over top . . .
> 1 med. onion, sliced

Cover with . . .
> ¾ cup tomato purée

Bake. Baste occasionally with additional purée and a little water. During last 15 min., add . . .
> another ½ cup tomato purée

Continue baking. Cut in wedges to serve.

TEMPERATURE: 350° (mod. oven).

TIME: Bake 1 hr.

AMOUNT: 6 servings.

CRISPY BROWNED HASH

The secret of crispy browned hash is thorough browning before adding liquid.

Combine equal quantities of finely chopped cooked roast (beef is best) and diced cold cooked potatoes. Season with salt, pepper, and minced onion (also minced parsley, pimiento, or green pepper, if desired). Finish one of the following ways:

1. Brown in a skillet in small amount of fat over med. heat until crispy (about 30 min.); add liquid to moisten (milk or leftover gravy or a combination of both). Reheat or place in mod. oven (350°) 15 min.

2. Sprinkle small amount of cooking (salad) oil over mixture. Brown in a mod. oven (350°) about 1 hr. or until crispy; add liquid and return to oven for 15 min.

RED FLANNEL HASH: Use corned beef and add chopped cooked beets.

All you have to do—

To serve that Sunday roast deliciously another day: cut slices ¼″ thick, dip in beaten egg, then in fine dry bread crumbs. Fry in shallow fat in hot skillet.

MEAT CROQUETTES

Mix . . .
> 1 cup Thick White Sauce (p. 398)
> 1 tsp. *each* minced onion and parsley
> 2 cups coarsely ground or finely chopped cooked meat (beef, pork, ham, veal, lamb, or chicken)

Spread out on plate or pie pan. Chill thoroughly. Shape into cones or cylinders. Roll in flour, then dip in mixture of 1 egg, slightly beaten, and 2 tbsp. water, then in fine dry bread crumbs. Fry in deep hot fat (365°) until delicately browned (1½ to 2 min.). Be careful not to puncture during frying. Drain on absorbent paper in mod. oven (350°) until serving time. Serve with hot Mushroom Sauce (*p. 398*) or Tomato Sauce (*p. 283*).

AMOUNT: 8 croquettes (3x1″).

EGG CROQUETTES

Follow recipe for Meat Croquettes above —*except* use 6 hard-cooked eggs, chopped, in place of meat and add 2 tbsp. chopped pimiento and a dash of nutmeg.

HAM OR CHICKEN TIMBALES

Delicate individual molds.

Mix . . .

    4 eggs, slightly beaten
    1¼ cups milk
    1 tsp. each salt and onion juice
    ⅛ tsp. pepper
    ¼ tsp. paprika
    1½ to 2 cups chopped cooked ham or chicken

Spoon into buttered custard cups. Set in pan of water (1″ deep). Bake in mod. oven (350°) until firm (about 30 min.). Unmold. Serve with hot Béchamel Sauce (*p. 399*). *6 servings.*

MEAT OR CHICKEN SHORTCAKES

Split hot biscuits. Serve plenty of cut-up cooked meat or chicken in well seasoned gravy between and over top.

SOUTHERN HAM SHORTCAKES

Split hot cornbread squares. Place slivers or slices of baked ham between pieces. Cover with hot Mushroom Sauce (*p. 398*).

RED CINNAMON APPLES
WITH TINY PORK SAUSAGES

Beautifully colored apples with little sausages sticking out at perky angles. Marian South (now Mrs. Russell K. Johnson of Davenport, Iowa) perfected the recipe as a Christmas Eve Supper specialty when she was on our staff.

Boil together 5 min. . . . .

    1 cup sugar
    ½ cup water
    ⅓ cup small red cinnamon candies

Place peeled-side-down in the hot syrup and cook 5 min. . . . .

    6 cored firm apples (peeling removed from
        top halves)

Meanwhile, brown in skillet . . .

    18 little pork sausages

Remove apples from syrup and place peeled-side-up in individual custard or muffin cups or in 1 large baking pan. Place 3 browned sausages in center of each apple. Pour red cinnamon syrup over all. Bake until tender. Serve hot in leafy green wreaths of watercress or lettuce . . . accompanied by fluffy rice with hot Cheese Sauce (*p. 398*).

TEMPERATURE: 350° (mod. oven).

TIME: Bake 30 min.

AMOUNT: 6 servings.

PRESSED CHICKEN OR VEAL

Summertime luncheons are easy and delicious when this is prepared the day before.

Cook a 5-lb. chicken according to White Stock (*p. 412*) (or use 2-lb. veal and a veal knuckle in place of chicken). Cut up the cooked chicken or veal in small pieces (there should be about 4 cups). Cook stock down to 2 cups. Pour this layer of stock in 9x5x3″ loaf pan and chill in refrigerator until set. Make pattern of 1 hard-cooked egg, sliced, in the jellied layer. Alternate cooked meat in layers with . . .

    ½ cup minced parsley
    4 hard-cooked eggs, chopped

Pour stock over all. Place weight on top. Chill overnight. Unmold and slice. Serve cold, in slices, with mayonnaise (with chopped cucumber added, if desired).

AMOUNT: 10 to 12 servings.

HAM MOUSSE

Nell Nichols, magazine writer and epicure, was our guest for luncheon when we served this warm weather party dish.

Soften 1 envelope unflavored gelatin (1 tbsp.) in ¼ cup cold water and ¼ cup of vinegar. Dissolve over boiling water. Add 1 tsp. dry mustard. Cool. Stir in 2 cups chopped cooked ham, 1 cup finely diced celery and 1 tbsp. horse-radish. Fold in ½ cup heavy cream, whipped. Turn into mold and chill until set. Unmold and garnish with watercress. Serve with Cucumber Hollandaise (*p. 402*).

SYLTA (Scandinavian Pressed Meat)

Place in large kettle and cover with hot water . . .

    1 lb. veal shoulder
    1 lb. pork butt
    2 pork hocks or veal knuckles
    1 bay leaf
    1 small onion, sliced
    12 allspice
    4 whole black peppers
    2 tsp. salt

Simmer until meat is tender and separates from bones, about 2 hr. Remove meat, cut from bone, removing gristle and bone. Cut meat in ½″ pieces. Boil stock down to 1 cup. Place meat in 9x5x3″ loaf pan or empty no. 2½ can. Pour stock over meat until liquid appears. Chill several hours or overnight. Unmold or cut uncut end from can, push out. Slice and serve cold.

AMOUNT: 8 to 10 servings.

CEDRIC'S CASSEROLE

Cedric Adams, popular master of ceremonies and columnist, gave us this recipe—a favorite in his home.

Sauté . . .
  1 med. onion, chopped
in . . .
  3 tbsp. butter
Add, heating through but not browning . . .
  ½ lb. ground beef
  ¾ tsp. salt
  ⅛ tsp. pepper
Spread in 2-qt. baking dish . . .
  3 cups coarsely shredded cabbage
Cover with the meat mixture. Top with . . .
  3 more cups coarsely shredded cabbage
Pour over the top . . .
  10½-oz. can condensed tomato soup
Bake covered.

TEMPERATURE: 350° (mod. oven).
TIME: Bake 1 hr.
AMOUNT: 6 servings.

STUFFED GREEN PEPPERS

Cook in boiling water 5 min. . . .
  6 large green peppers (stem and seeds removed)
Drain. Mix . . .
  ½ lb. ground beef
  1 cup coarse dry bread or cracker crumbs
  1 tsp. salt
  ¼ tsp. pepper
  1 tbsp. chopped onion
Add . . .
  half of 10½-oz. can condensed tomato soup
Stuff peppers with meat mixture. Stand upright in small baking dish. Pour over remaining soup diluted with ½ soup can water. Bake covered 45 min., uncovered 15 min. longer.

TEMPERATURE: 350° (mod. oven).
TIME: Bake 1 hr.
AMOUNT: 6 servings.

SCALLOPED HAM AND POTATOES

Place slivers or pieces of baked ham (about 1½ cups) in layers when making Scalloped Potatoes (*p. 441*).

FULL OF BOLOGNA

Instead of ham (*above*), use cut-up pieces of bologna.

SPRINGTIME SKILLET DINNER

Mrs. Claude Stuart of Florin, California, originator of this dish, wrote: "It takes less time than regular stew . . . and tastes much better."

Brown in 2 tbsp. fat in 10" skillet . . .
  1 clove garlic, cut up
Remove garlic. Then add . . .
  1 cup finely diced onion
  ½ lb. ground beef
Cook until browned, stirring. Add . . .
  ½ cup uncooked rice
  5 to 6 cups water
Simmer uncovered over low heat 40 min.
Add . . .
  1 cup finely diced carrots
  1 cup finely diced potatoes
Continue simmering until tender (20 min.).
Season with . . .
  1 to 2 tsp. soy sauce
  1 tbsp. salt
  ⅛ tsp. pepper
Serve hot . . . garnished with parsley.
AMOUNT: 6 servings.

BEEF AND CORN CASSEROLE

A delicious Sunday supper dish from Isabel McGovern (Mrs. Wm. Kerr) of New York.

Sauté in 1 tbsp. fat until tender . . .
  ¼ cup chopped onion
  ¼ cup chopped green pepper
Add and cook until beef frizzles at edges . . .
  ¼ lb. cut-up dried beef
  1 cup sliced mushrooms
Meanwhile, blend together . . .
  2 cups Medium White Sauce (p. 398)
  2 egg yolks, beaten
  1 tsp. prepared mustard
  salt and pepper to taste
Combine with dried beef mixture. Add . . .
  2 cups kernel corn (no. 2 can), drained
Pour into greased 1½-qt. baking dish.
Sprinkle with . . .
  ½ cup grated sharp cheese (⅛ lb.)
  ¼ tsp. paprika
Bake. Serve hot.
TEMPERATURE: 350° (mod. oven).
TIME: Bake 30 min.
AMOUNT: 6 to 8 servings.

PIG IN A POKE

"Yorkshire Pudding" . . . baked with tasty little sausages in place of roast beef.

Arrange 1 lb. pork sausage links in 11x7" oblong pan. Heat in hot oven (425°) 10 min. Drain off most of fat. Pour Popover batter (*p. 78*) over sausages. Bake in hot oven (425°) 30 min. Cut in squares; loosen pieces with wide spatula. *6 servings.*

JULIUS LA ROSA'S SPITTINI

The popular singing star of television, radio, and stage, shares with us this recipe of true Italian origin given him by his mother.

Brown . . .

 2 onions, finely chopped

in . . .

 2 tbsp. olive oil

Add . . .

 6 tbsp. bread crumbs
 3 tbsp. grated Italian cheese
 2 tbsp. minced parsley
 8 raisins, chopped fine
 10 pieces pignolia (if available), chopped fine
 3 slices salami, chopped fine
 1 hard-cooked egg, chopped fine

Season to taste and add . . .

 3 or 4 tbsp. spaghetti sauce or meat sauce

Divide mixture into 6 servings and spread on . . .

 1½ lb. thinly sliced veal, cut in 6 serving-size pieces

Roll up and fasten with skewers. Dip in olive oil; roll in fine dry bread crumbs; brown in olive oil. Place in covered baking dish and bake until tender.

TEMPERATURE: 350° (mod. oven).
TIME: Bake 45 to 60 min.
AMOUNT: 6 servings.

RISË STEVENS' SZEGEDINER GULYAS

During her student days in Europe, preceding her operatic triumphs in America, the brilliant coloratura soprano of the Metropolitan Opera enjoyed this favorite Austrian dish.

Sauté in large heavy skillet . . .

 ⅓ cup finely chopped onion

in . . .

 2 tbsp. fat

Add . . .

 2 lb. mixed lean meat (beef, veal, pork), cut in 1″ pieces

Fry 30 min.

Stir in . . .

 two 1-lb. cans sauerkraut, drained
 1 bay leaf, crumbled

Simmer covered for 1½ hr., until meat and sauerkraut are tender. Season to taste with salt and pepper. Just before serving, stir in . . .

 1 cup cultured sour cream

AMOUNT: 4 to 6 servings.

CHILI CON CARNE

Zesty "south of the border" specialty.

Brown in 3 tbsp. hot fat . . .

 1 lb. ground beef
 1¼ cups minced onion

Add and cook 10 min. . . .

 2½ cups cooked kidney beans (no. 2 can)
 1⅓ cups condensed tomato soup

Make into a paste and blend in . . .

 1½ to 2 tbsp. chili powder
 1 tbsp. flour
 3 tbsp. water
 1 tsp. salt

Cook over low heat, stirring frequently, 45 min. Serve hot . . . with crackers or hot Fried Corn Meal Mush (*p. 293*).
AMOUNT: 4 servings.

SAUERBRATEN

Esther Hallock sent us this special recipe from a famous German restaurant in New York.

Place a 4 to 6-lb. pot roast (chuck or rump) in an earthenware bowl with . . .

 2 onions, sliced
 ½ parsnip, sliced
 2 carrots, sliced
 2 bay leaves
 6 whole cloves
 12 peppercorns
 12 juniper berries
 2 tsp. salt

Pour over this 1 qt. red wine vinegar that has been heated to boiling. Let marinate 3 days or more. Turn meat twice a day with 2 wooden spoons; never pierce with a fork. Keep in a cool place. When ready to cook, drain meat and brown it thoroughly on all sides in hot fat in heavy skillet. Add marinade with vegetables but not enough to cover the meat. Simmer slowly 3 to 4 hr. or until tender. Or cook for 1 hr. in pressure cooker at 10 lb. Serve with boiled potatoes and sweet-sour red cabbage.
AMOUNT: 8 to 10 servings.

Sauerbraten Gravy: Melt ¼ lb. butter, add 1 tbsp. sugar, and about ¼ cup flour to make roux. Let darken as much as possible, stirring constantly. Slowly add 1 cup of marinade, also ⅔ cup red wine and continue cooking until gravy is the consistency of heavy cream. Strain.

CREAMED CHICKEN (⚬ Recipe) *Helps master many delicious dinners.*

Melt...............................	6 tbsp. butter or chicken fat
Blend in...........................	{ 6 tbsp. GOLD MEDAL Flour
	1 tsp. salt
	⅛ tsp. pepper
Cook over low heat until smooth, bubbly.	
Remove from heat and stir in.............	{ 1½ cups well seasoned chicken stock
	1 cup cream or top milk
Bring to a boil and boil 1 min., stirring constantly. Stir in gently...................	1 cup cut-up stewed chicken (p. 329)
Just before serving, add if desired........	2 tbsp. sherry flavoring

Serve hot in patty shells, pastry cases, biscuit rings, or timbale cases; or over toast points, noodles, or fluffy rice.

AMOUNT: 6 servings.

CHICKEN À LA KING

At a shower for Hermina Kure (now Mrs. Harry Frederick), we served Chicken à la King with 1 cup cooked fresh peas and 1 hard-cooked egg added.

Follow ⚬ recipe above and, at the last, add 1 cup sautéed sliced mushrooms, ½ cup slivered green pepper, and ¼ cup slivered pimiento. Southerners substitute cooked ham for half the chicken.

RING AROUND THE CHICKEN

Enthusiastically received when served at a special luncheon for Katherine Fisher and Dorothy Marsh of Good Housekeeping Magazine.

Sift together into bowl . . .
    1½ cups *sifted* GOLD MEDAL Flour
    3 tsp. baking powder
    ¾ tsp. salt
    ½ to ¾ tsp. poultry seasoning
Cut in finely . . .
    ¼ cup shortening
Mix in thoroughly . . .
    ½ cup plus 2 tbsp. milk
Spoon into an 8″ ring mold. Bake in hot oven (450°) 15 min. Unmold on hot platter. Serve hot with hot Creamed Chicken (*above*) in center. *4 to 6 servings.*

SCALLOPED CHICKEN

Marjorie Child Husted says, "When I was in college, I used to prepare this simple dish for my mother's guests at Sunday suppers. It's easy and delicious."

Into greased 1½-qt. baking dish, place in alternate layers until all is used . . .
    2½ cups finely cut cooked chicken
    2½ cups rich chicken gravy
    1 cup fine dry bread crumbs
Dot with butter. Bake in mod. oven (350°) 20 to 30 min. Serve hot. *6 servings.*

SCALLOPED CHICKEN SUPREME

Contributed by Ethel M. Hughes, former member of our staff. Elegant enough for loveliest parties, yet not too fussy for a special treat for just the family.

Pour 1 cup chicken stock over . . .
    2 cups Boiled Rice (p. 290) (⅔ cup uncooked)
Place in alternate layers in greased 11x7″ oblong baking dish . . .
    cooked rice
    3 cups cooked cut-up chicken
    3 cups chicken gravy (p. 401) seasoned with celery salt or poultry seasoning
Sprinkle over each layer . . .
    toasted slivered almonds (½ cup in all)
    chopped pimiento (2 tbsp. in all)
    sautéed sliced mushrooms (1 cup in all)

Top with buttered bread crumbs or WHEATIES. Bake in mod. oven (350°) 45 min. *8 servings.*

CHICKEN CASSEROLE

Delicate, custardy consistency. Superb!

Sauté in 1 tbsp. butter . . .
    ¼ lb. sliced mushrooms (4-oz. can)
Mix with . . .
    3 cups soft bread crumbs
    1 cup milk
    1 cup chicken stock (well seasoned)
    2 eggs, beaten
    seasoning (salt, pepper, celery salt, paprika)
    2 tbsp. minced onion
    ¼ cup finely cut pimiento
    3 cups cut-up cooked chicken
Pour into greased 2-qt. baking dish. Set in pan of water (1″ deep). Bake in mod. oven (350°) about 1½ hr. Serve with Mushroom Sauce (p. 398).
AMOUNT: 6 servings.

CHICKEN PANCAKES VERSAILLES

The hot dish chosen for our special guest luncheons by Gertrude Jaeger (Mrs. Douglas T. Jaeger), now of Birmingham, Michigan, when she was on our staff.

Make French Pancakes (*p. 88*).

Make Chicken à la King (*p. 278*).

Spoon filling onto half of each pancake; fold over. Place in 11x7″ oblong baking dish. Cover with 1 cup White Sauce (*p. 398*) made with cream instead of milk. Sprinkle with ½ cup grated Swiss cheese. Brown in mod. oven (350°) until cheese melts.

CHICKEN CURRY

For a glamorous buffet … an East Indian dish.

7 little dishes of relishes around the platter of chicken, plate of sautéed bananas, and bowl of fluffy rice: sieved hard-cooked eggs, India relish, chopped salted peanuts, chutney, pickled onions, grated fresh coconut, crumbled crisp bacon.

Stew 4 to 5-lb. chicken until tender (*p. 329*). Remove tough skin, divide best pieces (breast and legs) in two or three pieces. Roll in flour, brown in butter, then remove to keep warm. To pan, add 2 tbsp. curry powder, a little minced garlic, 1 tbsp. chopped onion, and 1 cup diced apple. Add flour, seasonings, and milk to make gravy. Remove rest of chicken from bones and add to gravy with chicken pieces; heat through 30 min. to blend flavors.

To Serve: each guest goes around table, places a quarter of sautéed banana on his plate, a mound of rice, and spoons curried chicken on rice—then sprinkles a little of each relish over top.

MEAT CHOW MEIN

In Chicken Chow Mein (*right*) use thinly sliced cooked pork or veal in place of chicken, thinned gravy or chicken bouillon in place of stock.

CHICKEN ALMOND

As served in the Waikiki Room at Hotel Nicollet in Minneapolis, Minnesota.

In a small amount of cooking (salad) oil in a large skillet, sauté until lightly browned (about 10 min.) . . .

    2 cups cut-up cooked chicken

Add . . .

    ½ cup mushrooms, sliced
    ½ cup bamboo shoots, sliced very thin
    ½ cup sliced water chestnuts
    2 cups sliced celery
    ½ cup Chinese pea pods, if available
    1 tsp. salt

Sauté another 5 min.

Mix in saucepan . . .

    2 tbsp. cornstarch
    1 tsp. salt

Stir in gradually . . .

    2 cups chicken stock

Cook over med. heat, stirring constantly, until mixture thickens and boils. Boil 1 min. Add chicken stock to other ingredients; stir. Cover and simmer an additional 5 min. Serve with steaming mounds of fluffy rice and soy sauce. Sprinkle whole toasted almonds on each serving.

AMOUNT: 6 to 8 servings.

CHICKEN CHOW MEIN

Heat in deep skillet . . .

    ¼ cup cooking (salad) oil
    1 tsp. salt
    ¼ tsp. pepper

Add . . .

    2 cups sliced Chinese cabbage
    3 cups thinly sliced celery
    no. 303 can bean sprouts, drained
    4-oz. can water chestnuts, sliced (if desired)
    2 tsp. sugar

Stir in and cook about 10 min. . . .

    2 cups chicken stock or water

Blend . . .

    2½ tbsp. cornstarch
    ¼ cup cold water
    ¼ cup soy sauce

Add to vegetable mixture and stir until mixture thickens. Add . . .

    2 cups sliced cooked chicken, cut in thin slivers

Heat through. Serve over hot chow mein noodles.

AMOUNT: 4 servings.

HELEN TRAUBEL'S
CHICKEN EN CASSEROLE

For this elegant dish, perfect for informal dinners and suppers, we are indebted to Miss Helen Traubel, illustrious star of grand opera and one of America's most beloved entertainers.

Dip 4 to 5-lb. roasting chicken, cut up, in mixture of . . .

    1 cup GOLD MEDAL Flour
    2 tsp. salt
    1 tsp. pepper

Put in skillet over med. heat . . .

    ½ cup butter
    1 clove garlic, quartered

When butter bubbles, remove garlic. Brown chicken in butter . . . then transfer to 3-qt. baking dish. Sauté in same skillet until slightly brown . . .

    2 med. onions, sliced thin
    2 cups chopped celery
    3 small carrots, chopped
    ½ cup fresh mushrooms, sliced

Stir in . . .

    2 tbsp. minced parsley
    pinch thyme and marjoram
    dash Worcestershire sauce
    6 peppercorns, slightly bruised
    1 bay leaf, crumbled

Simmer a few minutes to blend flavors. Season with salt to taste; pour over chicken. Cover. Bake until tender. Serve hot.

TEMPERATURE: 350° (mod. oven).
TIME: Bake about 2½ hr.
AMOUNT: 6 to 8 servings.

CHICKEN DIVAN

As served in a popular French restaurant in New York, Divan Parisienne. Mrs. Albion Clapp, known for her beautiful and original entertaining, sometimes chooses it as the main luncheon or supper party dish in her antique-filled Wellesley Hills, Massachusetts home.

In a shallow baking pan or individual oven-proof casseroles, place large slices of cooked breast of chicken (or turkey). On top of each piece, place several pieces of cooked broccoli or asparagus and mushrooms.

Make Velouté Sauce (*p. 399*). Add ¼ cup grated Parmesan cheese and 1 tbsp. cooking sherry. Remove from heat; stir half the sauce into 1 egg yolk, slightly beaten; stir into remaining sauce. Bring just to boiling; pour over vegetable. Place under broiler until sauce is bubbly and slightly brown. Serve immediately.

BUFFET SUPPER CASSEROLE

Nice for entertaining as it can be prepared ahead of time.

Stew 4 to 5-lb. stewing chicken (*p. 329*), reserving 6 cups chicken stock. Remove meat from bones and cut into coarse pieces. Sauté in butter . . .

    ½ cup chopped onion
    ½ cup chopped green pepper
    4-oz. can mushrooms

Add liquid from mushrooms and from 8-oz. can ripe olives to stock. Bring to boiling and add . . .

    12 oz. noodles or macaroni (1½ pkg.)

Cook until tender. Add cut-up chicken, sautéed mixture and . . .

    3 to 4 tbsp. chopped pimiento
    1 cup chopped, pitted ripe olives (8-oz. can)
    12-oz. pkg. frozen peas, thawed
    celery salt, savory salt, salt and pepper to taste

Pour half the mixture into 3-qt. baking dish. Sprinkle with half of . . .

    1½ cups grated sharp Cheddar cheese

Pour in remaining mixture and top with remaining cheese. Bake covered. Uncover last 15 min. to brown. Serve hot.

TEMPERATURE: 325° (slow mod. oven).
TIME: Bake 1 hr.
AMOUNT: 8 to 10 servings.

CHICKEN TETRAZZINI

Perfect for buffet suppers. Often served by Genevieve Callahan and Lou Richardson of San Francisco in their apartment on Russian Hill where guests enjoy two charming hostesses, sprightly conversation, and the glorious view of bay and bridges.

Cook until brown and crisp . . .

    2 slices bacon, finely cut

Add and brown lightly in the bacon fat . . .

    ⅓ cup minced onion
    ½ cup minced green pepper

Add . . .

    2 cups grated American cheese (½ lb.)
    ¼ cup cut-up pimiento
    ¼ cup toasted shaved almonds
    1¾ cups cooked peas
    2 cups cut-up cooked chicken

Mix lightly with hot drained Boiled Macaroni (8 oz. uncooked) (*p. 294*). Heat . . . using chicken stock to moisten. Serve hot with tomato slices, parsley, and ripe olives.

AMOUNT: 8 servings.

SEA FOOD À LA NEWBURG

Delicious with shrimp, lobster, crabmeat, etc.

Mix carefully . . .

    2 cups hot Medium White Sauce (p. 398)

    2 egg yolks, beaten

Just before serving, stir in . . .

    1 tbsp. sherry flavoring or lemon juice

    2 cups cooked sea food, in large pieces

Serve hot over hot rich biscuits or toast points or in patty shells. Garnish with parsley and pimiento strips. *6 to 8 servings.*

SCALLOPED OYSTERS

Flavorful. Pleasing contrast of textures.

Into a greased 10x6″ oblong baking dish, place a layer of dry crumbs (¾ cup) (half bread, half cracker). Cover with a layer of oysters (½ pt. or 1 cup), minced parsley, and chopped celery. Season. Dot with butter. Repeat layers . . . one more of each. Pour over top ⅔ cup liquid (half oyster liquor, half milk or cream). Bake in hot oven (450°) about 30 min. *4 to 6 servings.*

CREOLE SHRIMP

Prize recipe from Mrs. R. E. Smith of Redgate Plantation, Jeanerette, Louisiana.

Sauté in 2 tbsp. butter . . .

    ½ cup minced onion

Blend in . . .

    2 tbsp. flour

    1 bay leaf, crushed

    ¼ cup diced celery

    1 tsp. minced parsley

    ½ cup minced green pepper

    dash of cayenne pepper

    ¼ tsp. pepper sauce

    ½ tsp. salt

    6¼-oz. can tomato paste

    3 cups water

Cook slowly, stirring occasionally, until thickened (30 min.). Stir in . . .

    2 cups cooked shrimp (two 7-oz. cans)

AMOUNT: 6 to 8 servings.

CURRIED SHRIMP

Especially elegant in a ring of Green Rice (p. 290).

Just before serving, blend 1½ tsp. lemon juice or sherry flavoring, 2 cups cooked shrimp (two 7-oz. cans) into 2 cups hot Curry Sauce (p. 398).

> **CAUTION:** *When using uncooked (green) shrimp, do not precook; cook in the sauce only until pink (10 min.).*

LOBSTER THERMIDOR

Rich creamed lobster, specially flavored, quickly baked in the original lobster shell or in individual shells.

Sauté in 2 tbsp. butter . . .

    2 tbsp. chopped onion

    ½ cup sliced button mushrooms

Blend in . . .

    2 tbsp. flour

    ¼ tsp. salt

    ⅛ tsp. pepper

    ⅛ tsp. paprika

Cook over low heat, stirring constantly until mixture is smooth and bubbly. Remove from heat and stir in . . .

    ½ cup cream or rich milk

    ½ cup chicken stock

    ½ tsp. Worcestershire sauce

Bring to boil; boil 1 min., stirring constantly. Add . . .

    1 egg yolk

    1 tbsp. sherry flavoring

    2 cups cooked lobster (in pieces)

Place mixture in shell of lobster or individual baking dishes and sprinkle with 3 tbsp. fine buttered cracker or dry bread crumbs. Parmesan cheese may be mixed with these crumbs, if desired. Bake.

TEMPERATURE: 450° (hot oven).

TIME: Bake 5 min.

AMOUNT: 6 servings.

DEVILED CRABMEAT

So easy and quick . . . once served on half hour's notice to wives of officers of our Company in Minneapolis from nearby Ferndale on a shopping trip just before Christmas.

Combine . . .

    1½ cups milk

    1½ cups soft bread crumbs

Gently stir in . . .

    2 cups flaked cooked crabmeat (two 7-oz. cans)

    whites of 5 hard-cooked eggs, finely sliced

Blend in . . .

    yolks of 5 hard-cooked eggs, mashed

    1½ tsp. salt

    ⅓ tsp. dry mustard

    ⅛ tsp. cayenne pepper

    ½ cup butter, melted

Pour into buttered 10x6″ oblong baking dish. Sprinkle with WHEATIES or buttered crumbs. Bake. Serve hot.

TEMPERATURE: 450° (hot oven).

TIME: Bake 15 min.

AMOUNT: 6 servings.

For main dish salads, see Baked Salads (*p. 391*) and Soufflé Salads (*p. 393*).

POMPANO EN PAPILLOTE

(Pompano in Paper Case) Reflects the glamor of old New Orleans. Worked out by Esther MacMillan of our staff after she enjoyed it in its famous setting. When Barrett Kiesling of Metro-Goldwyn-Mayer had luncheon with us he said, "It's even better than what they served me in New Orleans."

Cook pompano or white trout (2½ lb. for 6 servings) until firm in water with salt, bay leaves, onions in it. Prepare *Mushroom-Shrimp Sauce:* Make 3 cups Medium White Sauce (*p. 398*) with equal parts fish stock and milk . . . seasoning with celery salt, onion salt, bouillon cube, and sherry flavoring. Add 1½ cups sautéed sliced mushrooms (¾ lb.) and 1 cup quartered cooked shrimp (7-oz. can).

For each serving, cut a 10x6" oval out of parchment or heavy wrapping paper; butter both sides of paper. On half of oval, place 3 tbsp. Mushroom-Shrimp Sauce. Add 2 pieces boned cooked fish. Cover with more sauce. Fold other half of paper over. Close and seal by folding the 2 edges together (a double fold). Place on baking sheet. Bake in mod. oven (350°) 20 min. Cut slits in paper on top . . . and serve hot on supper plate.

TUNA SUPREME

"A perfectly grand dish for women's luncheons!" according to a former member of our staff, Ruby Nelson (Mrs. Charles W. Turner of Delmar, New York), who first made it in our test kitchen.

Arrange in alternate layers in buttered 1½-qt. baking dish . . .

    2 cups tuna (two 7-oz. cans), in large pieces
    2 cups crushed cheese crackers
    3 cups Medium White Sauce (p. 398)
    ¾ cup sliced ripe olives

Finish with a sprinkling of the crushed cheese crackers. Bake in mod. oven (350°) 35 min. Serve hot. *6 servings.*

TUNA-POTATO CHIP CASSEROLE

In Tuna Supreme, use crushed potato chips in place of crackers, sautéed mushrooms in place of olives.

EGGS FOO YUNG

Beat until very thick . . .
    6 eggs
Blend in . . .
    ½ cup diced cooked shrimp, pork, or ham
    ¼ cup shredded onions
    ¼ cup sliced water chestnuts, well drained
    1 cup bean sprouts, well drained
    1 tsp. soy sauce
    1 tsp. flavor extender
    salt and pepper to taste
Heat in heavy skillet . . .
    enough fat or oil to cover bottom

Pour batter from soup ladle or cup into skillet. When brown on one side, turn. Keep warm. Serve with Hot Soy Sauce (*below*).

AMOUNT: 10 to 12 patties.

HOT SOY SAUCE: Make paste of 2 tbsp. cornstarch and ¼ cup cold water. Stir into 2 cups boiling soup stock, bouillon, or consommé and 2 tbsp. soy sauce. Cook, stirring constantly, until clear and thickened.

CELLINI PIE

A sophisticated luncheon dish.

Cut rounds of Golden Pastry (*below*) 1½" larger than inverted 4" pie pans. Place loosely in pans; fold edge under to make stand-up collar. Spread over pastry a mixture of . . .
    1 small clove garlic, minced
    1 med. onion, minced
Cover with . . .
    4 thin slices Swiss cheese
Slice and dip in flour . . .
    4 small tomatoes
Place over cheese. Sprinkle with . . .
    12 anchovies, cut up
    capers
Pour over pies . . .
    1 cup heavy cream

Bake.

TEMPERATURE: 400° (mod. hot oven).
TIME: Bake 30 min.
AMOUNT: 4 servings.

GOLDEN PASTRY

Sift together 1 cup *sifted* GOLD MEDAL Flour, 1 tbsp. sugar, ½ tsp. salt. Cut in 6 tbsp. butter. Mix 1 egg yolk, 1½ tbsp. lemon juice, 1 tbsp. water. Blend into dry ingredients. Dough will be soft. Chill several hours or overnight in refrigerator. Roll out on lightly floured board.

CODFISH SOUFFLÉ

With lobster sauce, a delectable dish.

Separate into tiny pieces, leave in cold water 3 hr. (change water 3 times) . . .
    1 cup flaked codfish
Boil the freshened codfish with . . .
    2 cups cut-up raw potatoes
When potatoes are done, drain, mash, and beat until creamy. Beat in . . .
    1 tbsp. butter
    ½ cup milk or cream
    ½ tsp. salt
    ⅛ tsp. pepper
    4 egg yolks, well beaten
Fold in . . .
    4 egg whites, stiffly beaten

Pour into 12 buttered muffin cups, set in pan of water (1″ deep). Bake until set. Serve at once with hot lobster sauce (*see Sea Food Sauce, p. 398*).
TEMPERATURE: 350° (mod. oven).
TIME: Bake 30 min.
AMOUNT: 12 servings.

SHRIMP SUPREME

This rich, savory luncheon dish is often served by a very gracious hostess, Mrs. Richard Folsom Tickle, in her lovely home in Rolling Green, Minneapolis, Minnesota.

Sauté . . .
    1 lb. fresh mushrooms, sliced
in . . .
    2 tbsp. butter
Spread on bottom of 11x7″ oblong baking dish. Top with halves of . . .
    9 Deviled Eggs De Luxe (p. 265) made with mayonnaise and chopped pickle
Arrange on top of eggs . . .
    2 lb. fresh green shrimp, cooked and cleaned (p. 336) or two 4½-oz. cans shrimp
Make . . .
    2 cups Medium White Sauce (p. 398)
Fold in . . .
    1 cup grated mild Cheddar cheese
Pour sauce over and sprinkle with . . .
    1 cup grated mild Cheddar cheese
TEMPERATURE: 350° (mod. oven).
TIME: Bake 30 min.
AMOUNT: 6 to 8 servings.

SALMON MOUSSE

A handsome dainty pink mold to tempt the appetite on warm nights. Perfect for buffets on lawn or porch.

Follow recipe for Ham Mousse (*p. 275*)— *except* use 2 cups flaked salmon (1-lb. can) in place of ham, 1 tbsp. pickle relish in place of horse-radish, and 1¼ tsp. salt. Serve with Tomato-Cucumber Mayonnaise (*p. 380*).

SEA FOOD SYMPHONY

Flakes of white halibut, curls of pink shrimp . . . in tune with Rich Cheese Sauce.

Simmer until fish flakes with a fork . . .
    2 lb. halibut, fresh or frozen
in . . .
    small amount of water seasoned with several crumbled bay leaves, peppercorns, and 1 med. onion, cut up
While fish is cooking, prepare Rich Cheese Sauce (*below*). Drain fish well, break it up, and place in 11x7″ oblong baking dish. Spread over halibut . . .
    two 4½-oz. cans shrimp or 2 lb. fresh green shrimp

Cover the fish and shrimp with the cheese sauce and sprinkle lightly with paprika. Place baking dish under broiler until sauce bubbles and top browns.

AMOUNT: 6 to 8 servings.

RICH CHEESE SAUCE: To 2 cups Medium White Sauce (*p. 398*) add 2 cups cut-up or grated nippy American cheese, 2 tsp. dry mustard, 1 tsp. Worcestershire sauce, and 1 tbsp. cooking sherry. Stir until cheese is melted.

MINCED CLAM NEW-WAY SOUFFLÉ

Stir together until smooth . . .
    ½ cup mayonnaise
    ¼ cup GOLD MEDAL Flour
    ¼ tsp. salt
    ⅛ tsp. pepper
Stir in gradually . . .
    ¼ cup milk
Stir in . . .
    7-oz. can minced clams, drained
    1½ tsp. lemon juice
    1 tsp. grated onion
Fold mixture into . . .
    4 egg whites, stiffly beaten

Pour into 1½-qt. baking dish. Bake. Serve at once with Tomato Sauce (*below*).

TEMPERATURE: 325° (slow mod. oven).
TIME: 40 to 45 min.
AMOUNT: 4 to 6 servings.

TOMATO SAUCE: Brown 2 tsp. grated onion in 2 tbsp. butter; blend in 2 tbsp. flour and let bubble up. Add 1 cup tomato purée or tomato juice, dash of celery salt, ¼ tsp. Worcestershire sauce, salt and pepper to taste; cook until thick, stirring constantly.
AMOUNT: 1 cup sauce.

CHEESE SOUFFLÉ (✦ Recipe) *Flavorful and tempting*

Make Thick White Sauce (*p. 398*) adding ¼ tsp. mustard and a dash of cayenne pepper.

Stir into the hot white sauce . . .
 1 cup shredded sharp cheese (¼ lb.)

Remove from heat; stir in . . .
 3 egg yolks, well beaten

Beat until stiff . . .
 3 egg whites
 ¼ tsp. cream of tartar

Fold in . . .
 the cheese mixture

1 Stir cheese into sauce. **2** Stir in beaten egg yolks.

Pour into ungreased 1½-qt. baking dish. For High Hat Soufflé, make groove 1″ from edge. Set baking dish in pan of hot water (1″ deep). Bake until puffed and golden brown. Serve immediately . . . with crisp bacon or Mushroom Sauce (*p. 398*).

TEMPERATURE: 350° (mod. oven).

TIME: Bake 50 to 60 min.

AMOUNT: 4 servings.

3 Fold into beaten whites. **4** Make groove with spoon.

TOMATO-CHEESE SOUFFLÉ

A favorite at our guest luncheons served with creamed chicken or shrimp.

Follow ✦ recipe above—*except* use tomato juice in place of the milk.

CHEESE-AND-CORN SOUFFLÉ

Follow ✦ recipe above—*except* add, with seasonings, ¾ tsp. mustard and, with cheese, 1 cup drained cooked whole kernel corn and ½ cup soft bread crumbs.

TOMATO SOUFFLÉ RING

Simmer 20 min. 2 cups canned tomatoes, 1 bay leaf, crushed, 2 cloves, ½ large onion, cut up, 1 tsp. sugar. Strain. There should be 1 cup. Use instead of milk in Cheese Soufflé above. Pour into greased 8″ ring mold. Bake in pan of hot water (1″ deep) in mod. oven (350°) 30 to 40 min. Unmold and fill center with creamed chicken or tuna and mushrooms.

SALMON SOUFFLÉ

Follow ✦ recipe above—*except* use 1 cup flaked cooked salmon in place of cheese.

CHEESE-AND-HAM SOUFFLÉ

Follow ✦ recipe above—and add, with the cheese, ½ cup ground cooked ham.

MUSHROOM-CHEESE SOUFFLÉ

Follow ✦ recipe above—and fold 1 cup sautéed finely cut mushrooms into the Cheese Soufflé mixture at the last. Delicious with Sea Food Sauce (*p. 398*).

All you have to do—FOR SECOND SERVINGS: Bake Cheese Soufflé in two 5 to 6″ baking dishes . . . placing one in the oven 10 min. after the other. Bake only 30 to 35 min.

INDIVIDUAL CHEESE SOUFFLÉS

For Individual Cheese Soufflés, pour into custard cups. Bake 20 to 25 min.

WELSH RAREBIT (Welsh Rabbit) *See color picture, p. 289.*

The story goes that long ago in Wales the peasants, not allowed to hunt on the estates of noblemen, served melted cheese as a substitute for rabbit, popular prize of the hunt. It became a famous dish at Ye Olde Cheshire Inn, meeting place of England's illustrious penmen. There rare wits from Ben Jonson to Charles Dickens conversed copiously while enjoying this specialty of the house.

Melt over hot, *not boiling, water* . . . . 4 cups sliced nippy American cheese (1 lb.)
(*Never allow cheese to reach boiling point.*)

Gradually stir in . . . .
- ¾ cup cream
- ½ tsp. dry mustard
- ½ tsp. Worcestershire sauce
- ¼ tsp. salt
- dash of pepper

Serve at once on crisp crackers or toast, with pickles or relish on side. *6 servings.*

All you have to do —

To make Welsh Rarebit De Luxe: use ginger ale in place of cream.

For elegant supper dish: serve Welsh Rarebit on toast; top with tomato slice and anchovy fillet. Place 2 cooked sausage links on each serving. Garnish with parsley. See color picture, p. 289.

WELSH RAREBIT WITH KIDNEY BEANS

Hollywood supper party favorite in the home of Joan Crawford, Academy Award Winner of the movies.

Melt in chafing dish or top of double boiler over hot water 2 cups diced American cheese (½ lb.). Stir in 2½ cups heated cooked kidney beans with liquid (no. 2 can) and ½ cup diced green pepper. Keep hot. Serve on crisp toast or crackers.

CHEESE FONDUE

A simplified soufflé ... from a culinary artist, Marion Miller, whose mother used to plan it for the Minneapolis Woman's Club luncheons.

Melt in skillet . . .
- 3 tbsp. butter

Add and stir until lightly browned . . .
- 3 cups bread cubes (5 slices)

Place bread cubes in greased 1-qt. baking dish in alternate layers with . . .
- 1 cup shredded sharp American cheese (¼ lb.)

Mix and pour over bread and cheese . . .
- 1 large egg, beaten
- 1 cup milk
- ½ tsp. salt
- dash of pepper
- ⅛ tsp. dry mustard

Sprinkle with paprika. Set baking dish in pan of water (1″ deep). Bake. Serve hot.
TEMPERATURE: 350° (mod. oven).
TIME: Bake 40 min.
AMOUNT: 4 servings.

RUM TUM TIDDY (Pink Bunny)

Often served in the Boston Athletic Club. Inez-Muriel McLaughlin formerly of our staff (now Mrs. Byron McLaughlin) says, "This is a nice easy Sunday supper dish for busy mothers."

Heat 1¼ cups condensed tomato soup (or seasoned cooked tomatoes). Place over hot water and stir in 2 cups shredded American cheese (½ lb.). Remove from heat and blend in 1 egg, slightly beaten, ¼ tsp. dry mustard, ¼ tsp. Worcestershire sauce. Serve hot on toast points or crackers. Garnish with green pickles. *4 to 6 servings.*

NOTE: ½ cup minced onion cooked in butter may be added, if desired.

BRER RABBIT WITH CORN

Satisfying, quick party dish. Ideal for after skating on a cold night.

Make Rum Tum Tiddy (*above*)—*except* add 1 cup whole kernel corn with tomato and cheese.

CHEESE PIE

Rich in flavor, golden in color, satisfying with crisp salad and fruit dessert.

Make 8″ Baked Pie Shell (*p. 346*). Bake 5 min. Remove and reduce oven to 350° (mod.). Stir over hot water until cheese is melted: 1 lb. Cheddar cheese, grated, 3 eggs, well beaten, ½ tsp. salt, 3 tbsp. sugar. Pour into pie shell. Bake 15 to 20 min. *6 servings.*

MEXICAN ENCHILADAS

A Mexican dish consisting of large, thin, corn meal pancakes, spread with chili-flavored tomato sauce, and rolled up ... served hot with more of the spicy sauce on top.

Dip Tortillas (*below*) into melted fat (drippings, butter, or salad oil); then dip into Enchiladas Sauce (*below*). Place large spoonful of Tortilla Filling (*below*) on each and roll up. Arrange in serving dish or baking dish. Cover with remaining sauce, reheated, and sprinkle with remaining filling. Serve at once or reheat before serving in quick mod. oven (375°).

TORTILLAS

Combine in bowl ...
> 1 cup *sifted* GOLD MEDAL Flour
> ½ cup corn meal
> ¼ tsp. salt
> 1 egg
> 1½ cups cold water

Beat with rotary beater until smooth. Spoon 3 tbsp. batter onto a mod. hot ungreased griddle to make a very thin 6″ pancake. Turn tortillas when edges begin to look dry, not brown. Bake other side; keep warm in covered pan.
AMOUNT: 12 Tortillas.

TORTILLA FILLING

Mix thoroughly ...
> 2 cups grated sharp yellow cheese
> 1 cup minced onion
> ½ tsp. salt

ENCHILADAS SAUCE

Brown ...
> 2 tbsp. minced onion

in ...
> 2 tbsp. fat or drippings

Stir in ...
> 1 tbsp. flour

Then stir in ...
> 1 clove garlic, minced
> 2 tsp. chili powder
> no. 2 can tomatoes, drained
> 1 tsp. salt
> ¼ tsp. Tabasco sauce

Add about ½ cup tomato juice (drained from tomatoes) to make a sauce of med. thickness. Let simmer until thickened.

NOTE: Enchiladas fit perfectly in 11x7″ baking dish or 13x9″ pan. They may be kept hot in the oven for some time if covered with aluminum foil.

ITALIAN PIZZA

An excitingly flavored round, flat, tomato-topped bread of Neapolitan origin. Phyllis Dahl of our staff has happy memories of enjoying it in its native setting the summer she was in Rome.

DOUGH

Dissolve ...
> ¼ pkg. active dry yeast (½ tsp.)

in ...
> ¾ cup plus 2 tbsp. warm water (not hot—110 to 115°)

Blend in to make a stiff dough ...
> 3 to 3¼ cups *sifted* GOLD MEDAL Flour

Knead on lightly floured surface. Place in greased bowl, turn to grease top. Cover and let rise in warm place (about 85°) until doubled (about 1½ to 2 hr.). Roll dough into two 14x10″ rectangles or into two 14″ circles. Place on pizza pan, oblong pan with shallow sides, or a baking sheet. Roll edge to make stand-up ridge.

TOPPING

Combine and spread half over each pizza ...
> 3 cups tomato sauce (three 8-oz. cans)
> ½ tsp. oregano
> ½ tsp. rosemary
> ½ tsp. salt
> ¼ tsp. pepper

Sprinkle over each pizza ...
> 2 tbsp. cooking (salad) or olive oil

Sauté ...
> ⅔ cup chopped mushrooms (4 oz.)

in ...
> 1 tbsp. butter

Spread over each pizza, half of ...
> sautéed mushrooms
> ¼ cup grated Parmesan cheese
> 1 lb. Italian sausage, browned and drained or 2 links Pepperoni
> 1-oz. can anchovies, if desired
> 2 cups grated Mozzarella cheese

Bake. Cut in wedges or squares. Serve hot.

TEMPERATURE: 425° (hot oven).

TIME: Bake 25 to 30 min.

AMOUNT: 6 to 8 servings.

NOTE: May be made in round pizza pans.

BOSTON BAKED BEANS

Really "Indian" Baked Beans, as they were originated by the Indians 3 centuries ago ... baked in earthen pots as we bake them today. In early New England, they were traditional Saturday night fare.

Soak overnight in cold water ...
    2 cups navy or pea beans
Simmer in same water until tender (1 to 2 hr.). Drain, save liquor. Place in 2-qt. bean pot in layers ...
    the drained cooked beans
    ½ lb. salt pork (scalded, rind scraped)
    1 slice onion
Combine ...
    3 tbsp. molasses
    2 tsp. salt
    ⅛ tsp. pepper
    ¼ tsp. dry mustard

Pour over beans. Add just enough bean liquor to cover beans. Cover. Bake. Remove cover last half of baking, add a little boiling water if beans seem dry. Serve hot with hot Steamed Brown Bread (*p. 97*).

TEMPERATURE: 300° (slow oven).
TIME: Bake 8 hr.
AMOUNT: 6 servings.

COUNTRY-BAKED LIMAS

Wash thoroughly and soak overnight in 1 qt. cold water ...
    2 cups dried Lima beans
Simmer in same water about ½ hr. Drain, reserving liquor. Place in bean pot in layers ...
    the Lima beans
    ¼ lb. bacon, cut in small pieces
    1 med. onion, sliced
Combine ...
    ¼ cup light molasses
    2 tbsp. chili sauce
    1½ tbsp. brown sugar
    2 tsp. salt
    1 tsp. dry mustard
    1 cup tomato juice

Pour over beans, adding enough bean liquor to cover. Cover. Bake until tender. Uncover last ½ hr. to brown, if necessary.

TEMPERATURE: 250° (slow oven).
TIME: Bake 4 to 6 hr.
AMOUNT: 8 servings.

SPEEDY BAKED BEANS

Sauté until bacon is crisp and onion yellow ...
    4 strips bacon, diced
    1 large onion, minced
Stir in ...
    2 cans baked beans (with pork) (no. 2 can)
    1 tsp. prepared mustard
    ¼ cup chili sauce

Pour into greased 1½-qt. baking dish. Bake uncovered until beans are brown and bubbly. Serve hot.

TEMPERATURE: 350° (mod. oven).
TIME: Bake 45 min.
AMOUNT: 6 servings.

VEGETARIAN BAKED BEANS

This discovery of Adah E. M. Anderson of Knollwood, Hopkins, Minnesota, shows how tasty baked beans can be without meat.

Sauté until yellow in 2 tbsp. butter ...
    ⅓ cup minced onion
Stir in ...
    16-oz. can vegetarian baked beans
    2 tbsp. dark molasses
    ¼ cup catsup

Pour into 1-qt. baking dish. Bake.

TEMPERATURE: 350° (mod. oven).
TIME: Bake 25 min.
AMOUNT: 4 servings.

SPECIAL BAKED BEANS

Mrs. Nels I. Matson of Seattle, Washington, wrote, "This was given my husband by a man very fond of real baked beans. He offers it to all lovers of baked beans."

Soak overnight in cold water ...
    2 cups navy beans
In morning, drain. Save the bean liquor. Put through med. knife of food grinder ...
    ½ lb. salt pork (scalded, rind removed)
    6 sprigs parsley
    1 large onion
    1 clove garlic
    1 green pepper
    2 sweet red peppers
Mix above ingredients through beans with ...
    2 tbsp. maple syrup
    6 tbsp. catsup

Cover with fresh water. Simmer 2 hr. Put into 2-qt. bean pot; add just enough bean liquid to cover beans. Cover pot. Bake. Serve hot ... with hot Steamed Brown Bread (*p. 97*).

TEMPERATURE: 300° (slow oven).
TIME: Bake covered 2½ hr., remove cover, and bake 1½ hr. longer.
AMOUNT: 6 servings.

MAIN DISHES TO HIGHLIGHT A MEAL

Spaghetti with Meat Balls

Welsh Rarebit with Tomato Slices and Little Sausages

Chicken Almond   Fiesta Tamale Pie

Rice is sometimes called "the food of the ages" ... for it is as old as history. Twenty-eight hundred years before Christ, a Chinese emperor, Chin Nung, established a ceremonial custom of serving it. From Asia to Europe to America, rice cultivation has spread until rice rivals wheat as the world's most important food.

BOILED RICE ... WHITE OR BROWN 1 cup cooks to 3 or 4 cups.

1 Drop washed rice gradually into 2 qt. boiling (*keep it boiling*) salted water (1 tbsp. salt).

• To be sure of light, fluffy rice, always measure rice, salt, and water. Too much water makes rice soggy and gummy, too little lets it dry before it is cooked.

To Reheat Rice: heat over hot water 10 min. or until rice is hot and fluffy. Or sprinkle 1 tbsp. water over 2 cups cooked rice. Cover *tightly* and heat over low heat 5 to 8 min. . . . until hot and fluffy.

• To make rice extra white, add 2 tbsp. lemon juice to water before boiling it.

2 Boil rapidly (lift to prevent "sticking") until tender (15 to 20 min.). Kernels feel soft.

3 Drain; run boiling water through to separate kernels.

4 Cover with cloth, set over boiling water until fluffy.

HOW TO USE BOILED RICE: (1) in soups; (2) in place of potatoes; (3) in a main dish (*see following pages*); or (4) in desserts.

CURRIED RICE

With creamed shrimp, chicken, or ham, it's a highlight at buffet suppers.

Sauté 1 tbsp. minced onion in 2 tbsp. butter until yellow. Gently stir in 3 cups fluffy Boiled Rice (*above*), ¼ tsp. salt, ¼ tsp. pepper, 1 tsp. curry powder. Serve hot with any meat or sea food cooked in a sauce. *6 to 8 servings.*

BROWNED RICE (Risotto)

Distinctive and piquant flavor. Harold Hansen of Kentfield, California, likes to cook this for outdoor suppers, enjoyed by family and guests in the shadows of Mt. Tamalpais.

Cook until yellow in ¼ cup butter in heavy skillet: 1 cup uncooked rice. Stir in 4 cups Chicken Stock or Consommé (*p. 412*) (flavored with onion or garlic, herbs, salt, and paprika). Mr. Hansen adds diced Italian mushrooms soaked overnight. Cover. Simmer without stirring until rice is dry, flaky (25 min.). Serve hot as a meat accompaniment. *6 servings.*

GREEN RICE

One of the grand contributions of Abbie Reed Boutell (Mrs. R. E. Boutell). "Guests at our home in the country like it extra well with baked ham or chicken" she says.

Toss together . . .

    3 cups fluffy Boiled Rice (above) (1 cup uncooked)

    1 cup chopped spinach or parsley or combination

Mix . . .

    2 eggs, well beaten

    1 cup milk

    1 tsp. Worcestershire sauce

    1¼ tsp. salt

    ½ tbsp. grated onion or scant ¼ tsp. onion powder

Stir into rice mixture. Pour into 10x6" oblong baking dish or 2-qt. baking dish. Sprinkle over it . . .

    ¼ cup butter, melted

    ½ cup grated sharp cheese

Bake.

TEMPERATURE: 325° (slow mod. oven).

TIME: Bake about 30 to 40 min.

AMOUNT: 8 servings.

FRENCH PILAU

Old-time masterpiece from South Carolina.

Place in one kettle . . .
>   stewed 4 to 5-lb. chicken (p. 329)
>   1½ cups Chicken Stock (p. 412)

Place in another kettle . . .
>   about 6 cups Chicken Stock (p. 412)
>   1 cup washed uncooked rice

Boil slowly until rice is tender (p. 290). Drain. Save stock for chicken. Mix into rice . . .
>   1 cup Sultana (white) raisins
>   ½ cup toasted split blanched almonds
>   ½ tsp. curry powder
>   1 tsp. salt
>   ⅛ tsp. pepper

Place in large serving bowl. Place chicken, with well seasoned stock, in soup tureen or deep dish. Serve rice in shallow soup dishes. Ladle pieces of hot chicken with broth over rice.

AMOUNT: 8 servings.

SPANISH RICE

Fry until crisp . . .
>   4 slices bacon, cut up

Remove bacon to 1½-qt. baking dish; whisk around to grease dish.

Add to bacon fat . . .
>   ¼ cup finely chopped onion
>   ¼ cup finely chopped green pepper

Sauté until onion is yellow. Combine in baking dish with . . .
>   3 cups boiled rice (1 cup uncooked)
>   2 cups cooked tomatoes (no. 303 can)
>   1½ tsp. salt
>   ⅛ tsp. pepper

Sprinkle over top . . .
>   ¼ cup grated American cheese

Bake uncovered.

TEMPERATURE: 400° (mod. hot oven).
TIME: Bake 25 to 30 min.
AMOUNT: 4 to 6 servings.

FRANKFURTER SPANISH RICE

Use ½ lb. frankfurters (cut in pieces) in place of bacon. Brown in hot fat; remove. Add 1 clove garlic, chopped, 2 tsp. Worcestershire sauce, 1 tsp. chili powder, ¼ tsp. cloves, ½ tsp. cayenne pepper with other seasonings.

TEXAS HASH

One of the popular supper dishes served by Georgia Kelley of Boston. The recipe was given to her sister by a Texas friend, now a leading hostess of Washington, D. C.

Sauté until onions are yellow . . .
>   3 large onions, sliced
>   1 large green pepper, minced

in . . .
>   3 tbsp. fat

Add and fry until mixture falls apart . . .
>   1 lb. ground beef

Stir in . . .
>   2 cups cooked tomatoes (no. 303 can)
>   ½ cup washed uncooked rice (or 2 cups uncooked noodles)
>   1 tsp. chili powder
>   2 tsp. salt
>   ⅛ tsp. pepper

Pour into greased 2-qt. baking dish. Cover and bake . . . removing cover last 15 min. Serve hot.

TEMPERATURE: 350° (mod. oven).
TIME: Bake 1 hr.
AMOUNT: 6 servings.

All you have to do.

To make a Rice Ring: lightly press 2 cups fluffy Boiled Rice (⅔ cup uncooked) (p. 290) into well greased 10″ ring mold. Keep hot until time to serve. Unmold on hot platter and fill center with creamed sea food or chicken and mushrooms. Serve hot. 8 to 10 servings.

AMERICAN CHOP SUEY

Chinese favorite . . . United States style.

Brown in hot fat . . .
>   ½ to 1 lb. lean pork or veal, cut in small pieces
>   1 onion, sliced

Add . . .
>   2 cups cut-up celery
>   1 small green pepper, chopped
>   ¾ cup washed uncooked rice
>   5 cups meat stock (or 5 bouillon cubes dissolved in 5 cups boiling water)
>   1 to 2 tsp. salt
>   ⅛ tsp. pepper
>   1 to 2 tbsp. soy sauce

Cover, simmer 40 min. Uncover last 10 min. Serve hot . . . in shallow bowls.

AMOUNT: 6 servings.

Wild rice does not resemble cultivated rice, either white or brown. It is the seed of a shallow water grass . . . still harvested by Indians in the marshes of Minnesota. Its grains are long, spindly, grayish in color. A special delicacy with wild duck or pheasant . . . or as stuffing for pork . . . or as in dishes below.

BOILED WILD RICE 1 cup uncooked wild rice equals 3 cups cooked.

1 Place 1 cup wild rice in wire strainer under cold running water . . . lifting with fingers to wash thoroughly.

2 Soak 1 hr. in warm water to cover . . . to soften the bran coating (most of water will be absorbed).

3 Place with 2 cups boiling water, ¼ cup butter, 2 tsp. salt in top of double boiler. Cover, cook (about 2 hr.).

FLUFFY DRY WILD RICE Our thanks to Lelia McClelland, Minneapolis, for this method.

Cover 1 cup washed rice with 4 cups boiling water. Let stand covered 20 min. Drain and repeat 3 times, using fresh boiling water each time and adding 1 tbsp. salt the last time. Add generous amount of butter and season with salt and pepper. Keep warm in oven or in double boiler, covering if held longer than 5 min.

CURRANT-MINT SAUCE FOR WILD RICE

Combine and let stand 1 hr. . . . ¼ to ⅓ cup finely minced fresh mint leaves, 2 tbsp. grated orange rind, ¼ cup sugar. Mix in with fork 8 to 12-oz. jar currant jelly. Serve warm. (Jelly will not dissolve.)

NOTE: If fresh mint is not available, use 1 jar mint jelly. Add with currant jelly. Use only 2 tbsp. sugar.

KAEDJERE

American Indian version of a dish from far-away India.

Lightly toss together with fork . . .
    1 cup hot drained Boiled Wild Rice
    1 cup tuna (7-oz. can), flaked
    ½ cup sliced mushrooms, sautéed
    2 tbsp. minced green pepper
    2 tbsp. minced pimiento
    whites of 2 hard-cooked eggs, diced

Gently blend in . . .
    2 cups Curry Sauce (p. 398)

Pour into buttered 11x7″ oblong baking dish. Sprinkle with sieved yolks of 2 hard-cooked eggs. Bake in mod. oven (350°) 30 min. Just before serving, dribble melted butter over top. Sprinkle with split salted almonds. *6 servings.*

OYSTERS, HOLIDAY STYLE

A Christmas Eve favorite. And a tasty, sophisticated dish for any fall or winter supper. Perfected by Marguerite Truesdale (Mrs. Clark Truesdale) of Glencoe, Minnesota).

Brown lightly in ¼ cup butter . . .
    ½ cup minced onion
    2 cups chopped celery
Stir in . . .
    3 tbsp. flour
    ½ cup milk
    3 cups hot drained Boiled Wild Rice
    ½ tsp. salt
    ¼ tsp. sage
    ⅛ tsp. each thyme and pepper
Place in 11x7″ oblong baking dish. Dip in ¼ cup butter, melted . . .
    1 pt. well drained small oysters
Sprinkle with . . .
    ¼ cup cracker or dry bread crumbs

Arrange over top of rice. Sprinkle with remaining crumbs and butter. Place just low enough under broiler to keep crumbs from burning. Broil just until oysters curl (10 min.). Serve hot . . . with hot Mushroom Sauce (p. 398). *6 to 8 servings.*

 Christmas Eve Supper: Oysters, Holiday Style. Crusty Rolls. Fruit Salad Bowl. Fruitcake. Demitasse. Other Beverage.

PIONEER MACARONI AND CHEESE (⚲ Recipe) *The simplest kind of dish.*

{ 4 cups hot drained Boiled Macaroni (8 oz. uncooked)
(p. 294)
dots of butter (2 tbsp. in all)
1¼ cups cut-up sharp cheese (½" cubes) (⅓ lb.)
salt (1 tsp. in all)
pepper (¼ tsp. in all)

Combine and pour over . . . . { 2 eggs, beaten
3 cups milk

Sprinkle with. . . . . paprika

Bake until golden brown on top. Serve hot from baking dish . . . garnished, if desired, with parsley sprigs, pimiento strips, pepper rings, etc.

TEMPERATURE: 350° (mod. oven).

TIME: Bake 40 to 50 min.

AMOUNT: 6 to 8 servings.

CREAMY MACARONI AND CHEESE

Follow ⚲ recipe above—*except* use 3 cups Medium White Sauce (*p. 398*) in place of the milk and seasonings.

MACARONES CON JOCOQUI

Macaroni with cream . . . sour or sweet.

Follow ⚲ recipe above—*except* use 2½ cups cultured sour cream or sweet cream in place of eggs and milk. Bake 30 min.

MACARONI-TOMATO CASSEROLE

Follow ⚲ recipe above—*except* use 2 cups well seasoned cooked tomatoes in place of 2 cups of the milk.

MACARONI WITH FRIED TOMATOES

Mrs. William P. Duerre, of Lake City, Minnesota, often serves this delicious and picturesque dish in her charming home near the shores of Lake Pepin.

Dip firm tomato slices (¼" thick) into slightly beaten egg . . . then into fine cracker crumbs. Sprinkle with salt and pepper. Brown in melted butter. Remove slices and keep warm while making 2 cups Medium White Sauce (*p. 398*) in same skillet. Mix hot drained Boiled Macaroni (8 oz. uncooked) (*p. 294*) with the hot white sauce, ⅓ cup cut-up sharp cheese, and 1 tsp. salt. Heap onto hot platter, sprinkle with paprika. Surround with the pan-fried tomatoes. Add little parsley bouquets. Serve immediately.

MACARONI À LA CRÈME

A radio friend of Delta, Colorado, won a prize on this one-dish meal in our recipe contest.

Follow ⚲ recipe above—*except* use half as much macaroni (2 cups) and cook 2 large onions, finely minced, and 1 cup finely diced celery with it. In place of milk, use 2 cups hot Medium White Sauce (*p. 398*) and ½ cup tomato soup (undiluted). Sprinkle 2 slices bacon, cut up and fried until crisp, over top. Bake only 20 min.

MACARONI SAUTÉ

Bake in oven or cook on top of range.

Sauté over low heat . . .
  2 cups uncooked elbow macaroni
  ½ cup chopped onion
  ½ cup chopped green pepper
  1 clove garlic, crushed (if desired)

in . . .
  ½ cup fat or cooking (salad) oil
Stir occasionally until the macaroni turns slightly yellow.

Heat to boiling . . .
  no. 2 can tomato juice (2½ cups)

Add . . .
  1 tsp. salt
  ¼ tsp. pepper
  2 tbsp. Worcestershire sauce, if desired

Stir into macaroni mixture. Pour into 1½-qt. baking dish. Cover. Bake in mod. oven (350°) 30 to 40 min. Serve with fish or meat. *6 servings.*

To cook Macaroni Sauté on top of range: increase tomato juice to 3 cups; do not preheat. Bring just to boiling over high heat. Cover. Immediately reduce to lowest heat. Cook 20 min. without stirring.

RING OF PLENTY (⚡ Recipe) *The idea for this custardy one-dish meal came from Mrs. Frank J. Ebsen of Wisconsin Rapids, Wisconsin.*

Boil and drain (see p. 294).	8 oz. macaroni
	2 cups hot milk
	¼ cup butter
	2 cups shredded American cheese (½ lb.)
	2 cups soft bread crumbs
Combine with.	2 eggs, well beaten
	2 tbsp. each minced parsley, minced onion, and chopped pimiento
	2 tsp. salt
	¼ tsp. pepper

Pour into well greased 10″ ring mold, set in pan of water (1″ deep). Bake until set. Unmold on hot platter; fill center with creamed sea food, chicken, or vegetables.

TEMPERATURE: 350° (mod. oven).

TIME: Bake 30 to 35 min.

AMOUNT: 8 servings.

MACARONI LOAF

Ruth Kerker Smith, who developed many fine recipes when she was on our staff, likes to serve this for company luncheons.

Follow ⚡ recipe above. Bake in greased 9x5x3″ loaf pan 45 min. to 1 hr., or until set. Serve hot with Tomato Sauce (*p. 283*) or Mushroom Sauce (*p. 398*).

MACARONI MOUSSE

Follow ⚡ recipe above—*except* use only 4 oz. macaroni. Use 3 eggs, adding well beaten egg yolks to macaroni mixture. Fold in 3 egg whites, stiffly beaten. Bake in ungreased 2-qt. baking dish in mod. oven (350°) 1 hr. Serve with Mushroom Sauce (*p. 398*). *6 servings.*

Flavorful Meat Sauces add Zest!

Make sauce as directed in each recipe (*below*) and pour over hot drained Boiled Macaroni (8 oz. uncooked) (*p. 294*) on hot platter. Sprinkle with grated sharp American or Parmesan cheese. Serve immediately. *6 to 8 servings.*

YANKEE DOODLE MACARONI

About the time of our Revolutionary War, there was a group of young dandies in London who were called "Macaronis." They were the fops of that period, and adopted the title of "Macaroni" because it signified elegance. So when Yankee Doodle called his feather "Macaroni," he was assuring himself that it was elegant.

Sauté until onions are yellow in 3 tbsp. hot fat . . .
  2 cups minced onion
  2 cloves garlic, minced
  ¾ cup sliced mushrooms, if desired

Add and cook until brown . . .
  1 lb. ground beef

Add and cook slowly (about 45 min.) . . .
  3½ cups cooked tomatoes (no. 2½ can)
  1 tbsp. minced parsley
  1 tbsp. salt
  ⅛ tsp. pepper

HOME FRONT MACARONI

Makes a little meat go a long way.
Sauté until yellow in 1 tbsp. fat . . .
  1 cup minced onion

Add and cook until brown . . .
  ½ lb. bulk pork sausage or ground beef

Add and simmer 45 min. . . .
  2½ cups cooked tomatoes (no. 2 can)
  1 cup diced celery
  ¾ cup minced green pepper
  1 tsp. Worcestershire sauce
  2 tsp. salt
  ½ tsp. pepper

MONDAY MACARONI

Sunday leftovers in a delicious dish for Monday's dinner.
Sauté in 2 tbsp. butter and 1 tbsp. olive oil . . .
  2 onions, minced

Add and cook 5 min. . . .
  1 cup finely chopped cooked meat

Add and let simmer 15 min. . . .
  1 small can tomato purée or soup
  2 tsp. minced parsley
  bit of bay leaf

Add . . .
  1 cup cooked vegetables
  1 cup meat stock

Spaghetti, favorite food of Italy, differs from macaroni only in shape ... the tubes being much tinier. Travelers in Europe bring back memories of fascinating glimpses of great racks of spaghetti drying in the hot sun on the sandy shores of the Mediterranean between Naples and Amalfi. "They look almost like vineyards," one traveler said, "... row after row of wooden posts ... only with skeins of spaghetti wound 'round and 'round them."

MEATLESS ITALIAN SPAGHETTI
Simple. Satisfying. It doesn't take too much time ... just mix and stir, add, taste, and add a bit of something else, if desired.

Prepare............................. desired sauce, see Marinara Sauce or Spicy Tomato Sauce (*below*)

Pour over........................... hot drained Boiled Spaghetti (8 oz. uncooked) (p. 294) on hot platter

Sprinkle with....................... grated Parmesan or Roman Italian cheese

Serve immediately.

AMOUNT: 6 to 8 servings.

MARINARA SAUCE
Sauté until yellow in ¼ cup olive oil . . .
    1 clove garlic, minced
Add slowly a mixture of . . .
    2 tbsp. minced parsley
    1 tsp. salt
    ¼ tsp. pepper
    1 green pepper, minced
    3½ cups cooked tomatoes (no. 2½ can)
    ⅓ cup finely cut celery, if desired
Cover and simmer 30 min.

SAVORY SPAGHETTI
Spaghetti cooks in a savory sauce. Easy to do ahead of time and keep warm in slow oven.

Brown in small amount of fat in large skillet over med. heat . . .
    ½ lb. ground beef
    ¼ lb. ground pork
Add and cook 5 min. . . .
    1 small onion, chopped
    1 small green pepper, sliced
Add and mix lightly . . .
    ½ cup sliced ripe olives
    2-oz. can mushrooms, drained
    8-oz. can tomato sauce (1 cup)
Stir in a mixture of . . .
    no. 2 can tomatoes (2½ cups)
    2 cups water
    2 tsp. salt
    ¼ tsp. pepper
    1 tsp. Worcestershire sauce
    6 drops Tabasco sauce
Add and bring to boiling . . .
    4-oz. long spaghetti or noodles (uncooked)
Cover tightly, reduce heat and simmer 40 min., stirring occasionally. Uncover and simmer 15 min.
AMOUNT: 6 servings.

SPICY TOMATO SAUCE
Sauté until yellow in ¼ cup olive oil . . .
    1 cup minced onion
Add slowly a mixture of . . .
    2 tbsp. minced parsley
    1 tsp. salt
    ¼ tsp. pepper
    1 tsp. Worcestershire sauce
    8 drops Tabasco sauce
    8-oz. can tomato sauce
    4-oz. can tomato paste
Cover and simmer 30 min. Add water if necessary to thin during cooking.

In Restaurants in Florence, Italy
According to Margaret Spader formerly of our staff, "a pat of parsley butter is always placed on each individual serving of a macaroni or spaghetti dish the last thing. As the butter melts, it combines with the hot sauce to give a delicious blend of flavors."

SPAGHETTI VALHALLA
Sprinkle 2 cups grated sharp cheese over hot drained boiled spaghetti (8 oz. uncooked) in 11x7" oblong baking dish. On top, place alternately 1 lb. little pork sausages (parboiled 10 min., then browned) and 12 tomato slices. Season with salt and pepper. Pour ½ cup water over top. Bake in mod. oven (350°) 35 min. *6 servings.*

SPAGHETTI WITH MEAT BALLS

Buffet supper specialty . . . and feature of Marlon Brando's favorite menu, "From Sunny Italy," p. 52. See color picture, p. 289.

Prepare . . .

Tomato Sauce (*below*)

When sauce is partially done, mix lightly and shape into 1″ balls . . .

¾ lb. ground beef
¼ lb. ground pork
1 cup fine dry bread crumbs
½ cup grated Parmesan cheese
1 tbsp. minced parsley
1 clove garlic, cut fine
½ cup milk
2 eggs, beaten
1½ tsp. salt
⅛ tsp. pepper

Brown meat balls on all sides in hot fat. Pour off fat as it collects. Add to sauce 20 min. before sauce is done. Place hot drained Boiled Spaghetti (8 oz. uncooked) (*p. 294*) on warm platter. Top with sauce, surround with meat balls. Serve with grated Parmesan cheese.

AMOUNT: 4 to 6 servings.

TOMATO SAUCE

Sauté ½ cup chopped onion, 1 clove garlic, minced, in 3 tbsp. olive oil. Add 2 no. 2 cans tomatoes, rubbed through sieve, 8-oz. can tomato sauce, 6-oz. can tomato paste, 1 cup water, 1 tsp basil, 2 tbsp. minced parsley, 2 tsp. salt, ¼ tsp. pepper. Simmer over low heat 1 hr.

Every Italian dinner table — has its little sugar bowl-like dish of finely grated cheese.

SPAGHETTI, ITALIAN STYLE

From that picturesque land across the sea.

Cook until browned in 2 tbsp. hot olive oil . . .

1 lb. ground beef or beef and pork

Add and simmer slowly ½ to 1 hr. (long cooking improves flavor) . . .

3½ cups cooked tomatoes (no. 2½ can)
2 cloves garlic, finely cut
1 bay leaf, crumbled
1 tsp. salt
⅛ tsp. black pepper

Pour over hot drained Boiled Spaghetti (1 lb. uncooked) (*p. 294*) on hot platter. Sprinkle with grated Parmesan cheese.

AMOUNT: 12 servings.

HOLIDAY SPAGHETTI

From a famous movie star whose wife often serves it at their informal supper parties.

Sauté until onions are yellow . . .

1 cup minced onion
¾ cup minced green pepper
1 cup sliced mushrooms

in . . .

3 tbsp. hot drippings

Add and cook until browned . . .

1 lb. ground beef

Then add and heat . . .

2 tsp. salt
1 tsp. sugar
3½ cups cooked tomatoes (no. 2½ can)
hot drained Boiled Spaghetti (8 oz. uncooked) (p. 294)

Pour into well greased 2-qt. baking dish. Sprinkle with grated sharp cheese. Bake. Serve hot . . . garnished with crisp bacon and parsley bouquets.

TEMPERATURE: 350° (mod. oven).

TIME: Bake 30 min.

AMOUNT: 8 servings.

SPAGHETTI ORIENTAL

Cook until browned . . .

½ lb. ground beef
½ lb. ground pork

in . . .

1 tsp. hot drippings

Add and cook 10 min. . . .

1 small onion, minced
1 cup diced celery
1½ cups drained Chinese vegetables (sprouts, sweet peppers, mushrooms, bamboo shoots, and water chestnuts) (no. 2 can) or a mixture of chopped green peppers, mushrooms, and cooked kidney beans

Then mix with hot drained Boiled Spaghetti (4 oz. uncooked) (p. 294).

Add and simmer 30 min. . . .

10½-oz. can tomato soup
½ cup water or liquor drained from Chinese vegetables
¾ cup shredded sharp cheese
1½ tsp. salt

Or place in buttered 1½-qt. baking dish and bake. Serve hot.

TEMPERATURE: 350° (mod. oven).

TIME: Bake 45 min.

AMOUNT: 6 servings.

Noodles, the German version of macaroni, are made of a similar dough enriched with eggs or egg yolks. They are usually in the form of long, flat ribbons . . . or sometimes letters of the alphabet.

HOMEMADE NOODLES

Beat until very light . . .
    3 egg yolks
    1 whole egg
Beat in . . .
    3 tbsp. cold water
    1 tsp. salt
Stir in and work in with hands . . .
    2 cups *sifted* GOLD MEDAL Flour

Divide dough into 3 parts. Roll out each piece as *thin as possible* (paper thin) on lightly floured cloth-covered board. Place between 2 towels until dough is partially dry (like chamois skin). Roll up dough as for jelly roll. With a thin sharp knife cut into strips of desired widths (⅛" for fine noodles, up to ½" for broad noodles). Shake out the strips and allow to dry before using or storing. *6 cups or 10 oz.*

NOODLES WITH BROWNED CRUMBS

Handed down from the early German settlers of Pennsylvania who brought this recipe from the old country.

Heat ¼ cup butter in heavy skillet. Add and leave over low heat, stirring frequently, until lightly browned . . .
    1 cup fine dry bread crumbs

Add drained hot Boiled Noodles (5 to 6 oz. uncooked) (*p. 294*) . . . gently mixing crumbs through noodles. Heap on hot platter. Sprinkle with minced parsley. Serve piping hot . . . with pot roast and gravy, wieners and sauerkraut, or baked pork chops and gravy.

AMOUNT: 8 to 10 servings.

NOODLES ROMANOFF

Mix gently . . .
    1 cup cottage cheese
    1 cup cultured sour cream
    3 cups drained hot Boiled Noodles (5 to 6 oz. uncooked) (*p. 294*)

Season with minced onion, garlic, a little Worcestershire sauce, a dash of Tabasco sauce, ½ tsp. salt. Place in greased 2-qt. baking dish. Sprinkle with grated cheese. Bake in mod. oven (350°) 40 min. Serve hot. *6 servings.*

NOODLE RING

"My boys loved this filled with creamed chicken for Sunday supper for their friends!" says Mrs. Charles Poor of Bozeman, Montana.

Mix gently . . .
    3 eggs, slightly beaten
    1 tsp. salt
    ⅛ tsp. pepper
    ¾ cup milk
    1 tbsp. butter, melted
    drained hot Boiled Noodles (10 to 12 oz. uncooked) (*p. 294*)

Place in well buttered 10" ring mold. Set in pan of water (1" deep). Bake until silver knife stuck into center comes out clean. Unmold; fill center with hot creamed chicken or sea food, etc. Serve immediately.

TEMPERATURE: 350° (mod. oven).

TIME: Bake 45 min.

AMOUNT: 6 to 8 servings.

POPPY SEED NOODLES

Often served with Veal Paprika as the main dish of "a supper to remember" by Ruth M. Skinner of Chicago.

Melt in heavy skillet . . .
    1 tsp. butter

Add and stir over low heat until lightly browned . . .
    ½ cup blanched almonds, cut up

Add and stir gently until heated through . . .
    3 tbsp. butter
    drained hot Boiled Noodles (5 to 6 oz. uncooked) (*p. 294*)
    2 tsp. poppy seeds

Arrange around edge of serving platter and pour sea food or meat in gravy in center. Or serve with Veal Paprika (*below*). Garnish with parsley bouquets.

AMOUNT: 6 to 8 servings.

VEAL PAPRIKA

A gourmet dish of distinction . . . sent us by Mrs. W. H. Stutzman, Kirkwood, Missouri.

Roll individual servings of veal steak (2 lb. cut ½" thick) in Seasoned Flour (*p. 309*). Brown in hot fat in skillet rubbed with garlic. Add 1 cup hot water, cover, simmer 1½ hr. Arrange meat on hot platter around Poppy Seed Noodles. Into gravy left in pan, stir 1 cup cream; heat and pour over noodles. Sprinkle with paprika. *6 to 8 servings.*

299

AMERICAN LASAGNE

Donna Hosler (Mrs. James E. Hosler) brought us this easy version of the popular Italian Lasagne.

Brown in 1 tbsp. hot fat . . .

    1 lb. ground beef

    2 cloves garlic, chopped

Add . . .

    6-oz. can tomato paste

    no. 2 can tomatoes (2½ cups)

    1 tsp. salt

    ¾ tsp. pepper

    ½ tsp. oregano

Cover and simmer 20 min. Cook according to pkg. directions . . .

    8-oz. pkg. wide noodles

In 11x7″ oblong baking dish, alternate layers of . . .

    cooked noddles

    8 oz. Swiss cheese, cut-up (1½ cups)

    12-oz. carton cottage cheese

    the meat sauce (*above*)

Bake. Serve with grated Parmesan cheese.

TEMPERATURE: 350° (mod. oven).

TIME: Bake 20 to 30 min.

AMOUNT: 6 to 8 servings.

OLGA'S NOODLE CASSEROLE

Brown in Dutch oven or large heavy skillet . . .

    2 lb. cubed meat (pork and veal)

in . . .

    2 tbsp. hot fat

Add . . .

    1 large onion, chopped (1 cup)

    2 cups cut-up celery

    two cans condensed tomato soup diluted with 2 cans water or 2 no. 2 cans tomato juice

    1 tsp. salt

    ½ tsp. pepper

Simmer covered 1 hr. Meanwhile, cook in boiling salted water until tender . . .

    8 oz. pkg. broad noodles

Drain noodles, then add to meat mixture. Simmer 20 to 30 min. more.

AMOUNT: 10 to 12 servings.

NOTE: If desired, the meat-tomato sauce may be served separately over the cooked noodles.

SCALLOPED SALMON, ALMONDS, AND NOODLES

For years a delightful specialty in a famous tea room in Minneapolis.

Gently mix flaked salmon, toasted cut-up almonds, salt, and pepper with drained hot boiled noodles. Place in buttered baking dish. Cover with Medium White Sauce (*p. 398*). Sprinkle with WHEATIES. Bake in mod. oven (350°) 20 min. Serve hot.

LASAGNE

It is said that on Christmas Eve the grandmother in an Italian household measures the width of the children's mouths to know how wide to make the lasagne noodles.

Make Tomato Sauce (*p. 298*). Meanwhile, cook ½ lb. lasagne noodles according to directions on pkg. Drain. Prepare meat balls (*p. 298*). Brown in hot fat, add a small amount of water, cover and simmer 30 min. Place the following ingredients in layers in 13x9″ oblong pan in order listed, beginning and ending with the sauce. Repeat until all ingredients are used up.

    sauce

    single layer of noodles

    mixture of:

        ¾ lb. Ricotta cheese or cottage cheese

        1 tbsp. minced parsley

        1 tsp. oregano

    ¾ cup grated Parmesan cheese

    ¾ lb. Mozarella cheese, grated

Bake. Let stand 15 min., cut in squares and serve with meat balls.

TEMPERATURE: 350° (mod. oven).

TIME: Bake 30 min.

AMOUNT: 6 to 8 servings.

CORNED BEEF CASSEROLE

"This is one of those handy, happy, and hearty main dishes you can get ready the night before . . . refrigerate . . . then bake just before you want to serve it," says Mrs. Hugh Grove, delightful Minneapolis hostess.

Combine . . .

    12-oz. can corned beef, broken (about 1½ cups)

    ¼ lb. processed American cheese, chopped (about 1 cup)

    10½-oz. can condensed cream of chicken soup

    1 cup milk

    ½ cup chopped onion

Alternate in layers in greased 2-qt. baking dish with . . .

    8-oz. pkg. noodles, cooked and drained

Top with . . .

    ¾ cup buttered crumbs or WHEATIES

Bake until heated through. Garnish with minced parsley and sliced stuffed olives.

TEMPERATURE: 375° (quick mod. oven).

TIME: Bake 30 to 40 min.

AMOUNT: 6 to 8 servings.

BROILED TURKEY AND CHEESE SANDWICHES

For after the holiday feast.

Make sandwiches of toasted-on-one-side bread (buttered on untoasted side) and slices of roast turkey. Cover each sandwich with a thin slice of cheese. Place under broiler until cheese is melted. Serve hot with hot Mushroom Sauce (*p. 398*) over them.

HOT FRENCH TOASTED SANDWICHES

Make chicken, turkey, or ham sandwiches. Dip into beaten egg (or mixture of 1 beaten egg and ½ cup milk). Brown on both sides in butter in hot heavy skillet. Or bake on greased baking sheet in mod. hot oven (400°). Serve piping hot.

BROILED CRABMEAT OR SHRIMP SANDWICHES

Season mashed yolks of 4 hard-cooked eggs with 1 tsp. salt, ⅛ tsp. pepper, ¼ tsp. mustard, 1 tsp. minced chives. Blend in 2 tbsp. butter, melted, 1 egg yolk, ¼ cup thick cream, 1 cup flaked cooked crabmeat or shrimp (7-oz. can), and chopped whites of 4 hard-cooked eggs.

Spread over *un*toasted side of 8 slices toasted-on-one-side bread. Sprinkle with paprika and a little grated cheese, if desired. Place on baking sheet under broiler until mixture is delicately browned. Serve immediately. *8 servings.*

OPEN GRILLED CHEESE SANDWICHES

Kathryn Soth (Mrs. William H. Wisdom of "The Four Belles Farm," Grimes, Iowa), formerly of our staff, likes to make these to serve with coffee or tea for impromptu refreshments.

Cover lightly buttered untoasted side of bread slices (toasted on one side) with slices of American cheese. Place under broiler until cheese melts. Sprinkle with paprika, garnish with parsley, crisp pickles, and tomato wedges. Serve at once.

All you have to do—

To make Cheese Wafflettes: make *thin* cheese sandwiches. (Don't let cheese touch edges!) Bake in hot waffle iron until golden brown (2 min.). Serve hot . . . with crisp bacon and vegetable salad.

CLUB SANDWICH

Double-decker favorite.

Lightly toast 3 slices bread for each sandwich. Top first buttered slice with cold sliced chicken, top with second slice buttered on both sides, top second slice with lettuce leaf, sliced tomato, and 2 slices crisply fried bacon. Top with buttered third slice toast. Use mayonnaise on chicken layer, if desired. Secure corners with toothpicks or cut in halves or fourths.

TUNA BURGERS

Mix . . .
    7-oz. can tuna, flaked
    1 cup chopped celery
    1 small onion, minced
    ½ cup diced American cheese
    ½ cup chopped ripe olives
    ¼ cup mayonnaise
    salt and pepper to taste
Split and butter . . .
    6 hamburger buns

Fill buns with tuna mixture. Place in paper sandwich bags. Fold and fasten with paper clips. Just before serving, heat in oven.

TEMPERATURE: 350° (mod. oven).
TIME: Heat 15 to 20 min.
AMOUNT: 6 servings.

BACON-CHEESE SANDWICHES

Broil until crisp . . .
    8 slices bacon
Combine . . .
    1 egg, slightly beaten
    ¾ cup grated cheese
    ¼ tsp. paprika
    ½ tsp. Worcestershire sauce
Spread on untoasted side of . . .
    4 slices bread (toasted on one side)

Place under broiler until cheese melts. Serve hot with 2 strips of bacon on each slice. Garnish with tomato slices.
AMOUNT: 4 sandwiches.

CREOLE WIENERS

A new way of serving "hot dogs."

Pan-broil in heavy skillet until half done . . .
    8 thin slices bacon, cut in ½" squares
Drain off most of fat. Add and fry, stirring constantly, until golden brown . . .
    3 cups minced onions
Stir in . . .
    2½ cups cooked tomatoes (no. 2 can)
    ¾ tsp. salt
    ⅛ tsp. pepper
Place on top . . .
    8 to 10 wieners (1 lb.)

Cover and simmer gently, stirring occasionally, 45 min. Remove cover, and boil hard 5 to 10 min. to reduce liquid. Serve hot . . . a wiener and a spoonful of the hot sauce in each buttered bun.

AMOUNT: 8 to 10 wiener-filled buns.

BATTER FRANKS

Sift together . . .
    1 cup *sifted* GOLD MEDAL Flour
    1½ tsp. baking powder
    ½ tsp. salt
Mix in . . .
    2 tbsp. corn meal
Cut in . . .
    3 tbsp. shortening
Add and stir until blended . . .
    1 egg
    ¾ cup milk
Dip into batter . . .
    8 to 12 frankfurters

Fry in deep hot fat (365°) until brown, about 2 to 3 min. on each side. Drain on absorbent paper. Insert wooden skewer in end of each frankfurter. Serve with catsup.

AMOUNT: 8 to 12 servings.

BEEF-EGG SCRAMBLE

Similar to the well-known Denver sandwich.

Brown in 1 tbsp. hot fat . . .
    ¼ lb. ground beef
    ¼ cup chopped onion
    2 tbsp. chopped green pepper
Season with salt and pepper.
Beat slightly . . .
    3 eggs
with . . .
    1½ tbsp. cold water
Pour over cooked beef and vegetables and cook over low heat just until eggs are set. Serve hot between buttered, toasted bun halves. Serve with catsup, if desired.

AMOUNT: 4 to 6 servings.

BARBECUED HAMBURGERS

In a heavy skillet, brown in 2 tbsp. hot fat . . .
    1 lb. ground beef
    1 med. onion, grated
Season with . . .
    salt and pepper
Stir in . . .
    ½ cup chili sauce
    ½ cup sweet pickle relish

Stuff this mixture into hollowed-out large round buns. Put buns in covered roaster or any large covered pan. Heat.

TEMPERATURE: 300° (slow oven).

TIME: Heat about 20 min.

AMOUNT: 6 servings.

TOMATO CLUB SANDWICH

Place 2 slices fresh tomato on 1 thin piece of hot toast. Cover with second piece of toast. Lay 1 strip crisply fried bacon and 3 slices green pickle on top. Cover with third piece of toast. Pour hot Cheese Sauce (*p. 398*) over it. Serve immediately.

SAUCY SANDWICH ROLLS

Our good friend Cissy Gregg, charming and talented food editor of the Louisville Courier Journal, says this snack in a sack is fun for a backyard picnic or a cozy supper by the living-room fire.

Brown in 3 tbsp. hot bacon fat . . .
    1 lb. wieners, chopped or sliced
    1 med. onion, chopped fine
Remove from heat. Blend in . . .
    ¼ cup GOLD MEDAL Flour
    ¾ tsp. salt
    dash of pepper
    ½ tsp. each dry mustard, Worcestershire sauce
    ½ cup each catsup and water
    1 cup chopped celery
Cook about 5 min., until celery is tender, stirring constantly. Add . . .
    ½ cup grated cheese
Heat until cheese melts. Remove from heat. Remove some of soft centers from . . .
    12 hot dog buns

Fill pockets with mixture. Wrap in heavy waxed paper or aluminum foil, twisting ends tightly. Just before serving, heat in shallow pan.

TEMPERATURE: 350° (mod. oven).

TIME: Heat 10 to 15 min.

AMOUNT: 12 sandwich rolls.

The Importance of Knowing Our Meats

MEAT is like the star of the show ... the center around which the rest of the meal revolves. All the other foods are chosen on the basis of how well they go with the meat selected. Meat is also an expensive item in our food budget ... which makes it doubly important that we present this star performer to the best advantage.

— Betty Crocker

CHOOSE A MEAT TO FIT THE OCCASION

Listed below are but a few of the many meat recipes in this chapter.

TODAY'S MEAT, POULTRY AND FISH

Much of today's meat is pre-packaged by individual cuts in transparent cellophane, well displayed for you to make your choice. The label tells (1) the kind of meat, (2) the cut, (3) the weight, and (4) the price. Color and freshness are sealed in.

Poultry and fish, too, are wrapped and sealed in cellophane or plastic covering. Most meat cuts are stored in refrigerator cases; frozen meat, poultry, and fish in the frozen food cases. Keep frozen if to be placed in your home freezer.

CANNED MEATS

More and more meats, poultry, and fish are being canned. Some of the more successful are:

MEATS			POULTRY	FISH	
Stew	Corned Beef	Hamburgers	Boned Chicken	Salmon	Shrimp
Sausage	Dried Beef	in Sauce	Chicken Fricassee	Tuna	Crabmeat
Tongue	Meat Spreads	Cooked Meats	Whole Chicken	Fishflakes	Lobster
Ham	Luncheon Meat	for Children		Sardines	

FROZEN MEATS, POULTRY, AND FISH

HOME FREEZING OF MEATS, POULTRY, AND FISH

Choose products of high quality—freezing does not improve quality or make them more tender. For economy, buy large cuts, have them divided into meal-size cuts. Do not freeze cured meats (except ham). Freeze foods at home *only* if freezer maintains a temperature of 0°F. or below.

PREPARATION FOR FREEZING

Trim, remove excess bone and fat. Bone and cube meat for stew, grind meat for hamburger. Press ground meat together, place in freezer cartons or bags.

Place freezer paper between chops, steaks, ground beef patties. Wrap in moisture-vapor-proof material (*see p. 23*). (Never use ordinary waxed paper.) Exclude as much air as possible. Seal edges with freezer tape or fold ends over twice, tie securely.

Label with name of cut, weight or number of servings, date. Freeze immediately at 0° F., or below, on freezing plate of freezer, allowing room for air to circulate.

LENGTH OF STORING TIME

1 mo.	—combination meat dishes (soups, stews, etc.)
up to 2 mo.	—ham
2 to 3 mo.	—cooked meats
3 to 4 mo.	—fresh pork, veal, ground beef, variety meats, poultry, fish
6 to 7 mo.	—lamb
6 to 8 mo.	—beef

Do not freeze—bacon, pork sausage.

THAWING MEAT, POULTRY, AND FISH

Leave wrapped while thawing. Leave in main part of refrigerator or at room temperature (less loss of juices in refrigerator). Refrigerator defrosting takes 5 to 10 hr. per lb. Room temperature, 2 to 2½ hr. per lb. Partial defrosting takes half as long. Cook as soon as thawed and never re-freeze. Thawed products are cooked the same as fresh.

COOKING FROZEN MEAT, POULTRY, AND FISH

Roasting

In general, it is best to partially thaw roasts and poultry. If not thawed, add 20 min. per lb. to cooking time. Whether frozen or partially thawed, roast at same temperature as in recipe.

Most accurate way to determine doneness is with meat thermometer, inserted *after* meat is completely thawed in oven.

Broiling

Broiling of frozen thick steaks is not recommended as exterior overcooks before interior is cooked. Broil thinner frozen steaks or frozen fish fillets at reduced heat or farther from broiler unit.

Pan-broiling—rub skillet with fat, then brown quickly on both sides. Turn heat low; cook slowly so meat will thaw and brown at same time.

Braising

Allow pot roasts, Swiss steaks, etc. to thaw until flexible enough to touch pan and brown evenly. Proceed as usual.

Simmering

Cover meat with liquid and proceed as usual. Meat may be browned first.

MEATS

Meat has been the mainstay of man's diet from the beginning of time. Wild fowl and fish were devoured with the deer and wild boar which the cave man brought from the hunt. The great feasts of medieval times were made up of meat and very little else. It is not strange that food in those times was referred to merely as "meat."

Less than fifty years ago in our own country even, any dinner or banquet worthy of the name included a separate fish course, a main course usually referred to as "the roast," and following that "roast" an "entree" or made-dish such as creamed sweetbreads or chicken patties.

Today we are content with one serving of meat, fish, *or* poultry for dinner. Without one of these, many people feel the main meal of the day is not complete. Meat adds flavor and eating enjoyment; it is high in nutritional quality. All three—meat, fish, and poultry—provide large amounts of high quality protein and B-complex vitamins. Meat is also rich in iron and phosphorous, while fish contains Vitamin D and iodine.

In today's meal-planning, the meat course is usually decided first and the other foods chosen that best accompany and complement it. Certain vegetables "go with" certain meats, potatoes are best served in one way with roasts, another way with stews. Relishes, too, are chosen for the touch they add. You'll find menus built around various meats on pp. 44–48 in the chapter, Meal-planning.

4 DIFFERENT DISHES FROM 1 CUT OF LAMB

Lamb Curry

Roast Leg of Lamb   Broiled Lamb Steaks

Kabobs

Larger cuts are often cheaper per pound and sometimes special features. If you have thought these cuts were too big for your family or there would be too much for leftover meals, consider dividing them so you can make 2, 3, or even 4 different tasting fresh-cooked meat meals. Your meat man will make these cuts for you.

LEG OF LAMB

Especially recommended at the time of year when lamb legs run 7 to 9 lb. *See picture opposite page.*

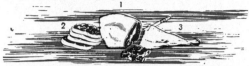

Meal 1: Roast Leg of Lamb (*p. 319*). For Sunday roast. Add partially cooked pared potatoes the last 30 min. Roll cooked onions in melted butter and minced parsley.

Meal 2: Broiled Lamb Steaks (*p. 319*). Add pear halves, brushed with melted butter and sprinkled with a little sugar, the last 10 min. Top with mint jelly.

Meal 3: Kabobs (*p. 320*). Cut meat from shank and cut into cubes. See recipe. Serve with fluffy rice.

BEEF CHUCK

Have a round-bone pot roast cut thick. Instead of pot roast Sunday and hash on Monday, try these meals:

Meal 1: Pot Roast (*p. 313*). Just right for one meal.

Meal 2: Old-fashioned Beef Stew (*p. 313*). Cut off a boneless piece to cut into cubes for beef stew.

Meal 3: Swiss Steak (*p. 311*). Split other end to make 2 Swiss Steaks.

PORK BUTT

The whole fresh pork shoulder butt weighs from 5 to 7 lb. and is nearly boneless. This piece can be divided at home.

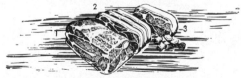

Meal 1: Pork Roast (*p. 316*). Use the piece with the bone for a roast.

Meal 2: Pork Steaks. Slice ½″ thick. Follow any of the pork chop recipes (*p. 316*).

Meal 3: American Chop Suey (*p. 291*). Cut remaining meat into cubes, use for chop suey or other casserole dishes.

PORK LOIN

In late fall and winter there are good buys in pork. And it's economical to buy half a loin.

Meal 1: Roast Pork (*p. 316*). A good sized piece for Sunday dinner.

Meal 2: Pork Chops (*p. 316*). Slice between ribs after backbone is removed.

Meal 3: Pork Tenderloin (*p. 316–317*). Strip out pork tenderloin with sharp knife, cut in 2″ pieces. Flatten with a cleaver.

Meal 4: Country Backbone. Have backbone sawed off, leaving 1″ layer of meat. Cook as you would spareribs (*p. 317*).

RIB ROAST

This cut is expensive but it becomes a better value when used as follows:

Meal 1: Roast Beef (*p. 311*). For Sunday dinner or company. Make Yorkshire Pudding (*p. 311*) for special treat.

Meal 2: Beef Short Ribs Jardiniere (*p. 313*). One of the most flavorful of beef cuts.

HALF A HAM

The shank halves of ham usually cost less. Be sure to buy a full shank.

Meal 1: Baked Ham (*p. 318*). Bake the piece with bone in.

Meal 2: Boiled Dinner. Use in place of corned beef in New England Boiled Dinner (*p. 314*).

Meal 3: Ham Slice (*p. 318*). Broil or Pan-fry.

Meal 4: Scalloped Ham and Potatoes (*p. 276*). Cut in cubes or slices for scalloped potatoes or other casserole dishes.

HOW TO COOK MEATS

We are indebted to Beth Bailey McLean (Martha Logan of Swift and Company) and Beth Peterson Campbell for helpful information and recipes from their book, "The Complete Meat Book."

METHODS OF MEAT COOKERY

DRY HEAT
(for tender cuts)

Roasting
Oven-broiling
Pan-broiling
Pan-frying

MOIST HEAT
(for less-tender cuts)

Braising
Stewing
Cooking in Water

HOW TO ROAST

Sturdy pan 2" deep may be used in place of a roaster.

The modern method of roasting meats at low temperatures does away with spattered ovens, cuts down shrinkage, and gives more and juicier servings per pound. Roasts may be cooked in frozen state but partial thawing is recommended as it cuts down cooking time.

1 Season meat with salt and pepper.

2 Place fat-side-up on rack in open roasting pan. For very lean cuts, such as veal, lay piece of pork or beef fat, strips of bacon or salt pork over top. Do not sear meat.

3 If you have one, insert meat thermometer through outside fat in thickest part of muscle so point does not rest on fat or bone.

4 Roast in preheated slow oven (325°) (325 to 350° for pork). Use this temperature throughout. Do not add water, do not cover, do not baste. A cover holds steam in so meat is steam-cooked and not really roasted. Steam-cooking changes flavor of the meat.

5 Remove when meat thermometer registers desired degree of doneness or follow time in recipe, allowing the longer time for smaller cuts of meat.

OVEN-BROWNED POTATOES

In open roasting pan, potatoes may become grease-soaked and hard. If desired, cook potatoes in water until almost done; drain, then add to roast the last 30 min. Turn to brown evenly.

GRAVY FROM ROASTS

Low meat temperatures do not produce as many brown drippings for gravy because juices stay in meat. For more gravy, add bouillon cubes or beef extract.

HOW TO BROIL

Meats may be broiled while still frozen or partially or completely thawed. Slash through outside fat 1" apart to keep cut from curling. Broiling is not recommended for any cut of veal. The only cuts of pork recommended for broiling are smoked ham steaks and bacon.

1 Set regulator at 550° or "broil."
2 Place meat on rack in broiler pan or in smaller shallow pan with rack in it. Place under broiler unit so the top surface is about 2" from heat (further for thicker cuts).
3 Broil with door closed in gas range, door slightly ajar in electric range.
4 Broil until meat is well browned; season with salt and pepper.
5 Turn and brown other side. Turn only once.
6 Serve immediately on hot platter as broiled meats cool quickly.

HOW TO PAN-BROIL

1 Preheat your heaviest cast aluminum or iron skillet or griddle. Do not add fat. If you like, rub skillet with piece of suet or grease lightly with other fat.

2 When skillet is very hot, put in meat and brown quickly on both sides. Do not cover.
3 Reduce heat and cook slowly until done. If fat collects, pour it off.
4 Season before serving.

HOW TO PAN-FRY

Pan-frying rather than pan-broiling is necessary when meat has very little fat or is floured or breaded. Add a little fat, then proceed just as for pan-broiling, using med. heat.

HOW TO BRAISE

Braising is sometimes called pot roasting. It is browning meat in a little hot fat, then cooking slowly in a *tightly* covered heavy aluminum or iron skillet with self-fitting lid, or in Dutch oven, with small amount of water.

1 Season with salt and pepper. Roll in flour for a richer brown. Or roll in Seasoned Flour.

Seasoned Flour means 1 tsp. salt, ¼ tsp. pepper, ¼ tsp. paprika (if desired) mixed with 1 cup GOLD MEDAL Flour.

2 Brown meat slowly and thoroughly on all sides in a little hot fat.

3 Add small amount of liquid (2 to 3 tbsp.). If liquid cooks away, more may be added.

4 Cover tightly. Cook over low heat at a simmering temperature on top of range or in slow mod. oven (325°) until meat is tender.

5 30 to 45 min. before meat is done, vegetables may be added. Continue cooking until meat and vegetables are tender.

6 Meat and vegetables may be removed to hot platter and kept warm and liquid thickened for gravy, if desired.

PRESSURE COOKING MEATS

Cuts of meat that require braising or cooking in water may be cooked in a pressure cooker at a saving of ⅓ to ½ the usual time. Pressure cooking is not recommended for the tender cuts of meat such as rib roasts of beef, leg of lamb, tender chops, and steaks. For best results, follow directions for your pressure cooker.

CUTS OF MEAT FOR BRAISING OR STEWING

Beef: Chuck, rump, heel of round, thick cuts of round, flank steak, short ribs, shank, brisket, oxtails, liver, heart.

Lamb: Shanks, riblets (neck slices), heart, breast, or stewing meat.

Veal: Loin or rib chops, Frenched cutlets, steak or cutlets, shank, or breast.

Pork: Rib or loin chops, shoulder steak, spareribs, heart, liver, cutlets.

HOW TO STEW

1 Have meat cut in uniform pieces 1 to 2″ square. Season with salt and pepper. Flour meat if you want deep brown color.

2 Brown on all sides in hot fat. Sliced or chopped onions may be browned in the fat first, removed, then placed on meat after it is browned.

3 Barely cover meat with water, stock, or other liquid. (Quick meat stock may be made from bouillon cube or beef extract in 1 cup of hot water.)

4 Cover kettle tightly and simmer slowly until meat is tender. Add more liquid if necessary.

5 Add vegetables long enough before meat is tender to be done but not over-cooked.

6 If desired, thicken liquid for gravy. Drain and add flour and water paste for desired thickness. Cook until thickened and serve separately.

HOW TO COOK IN WATER

This method is used for corned beef, fresh brisket, hocks, shank, and tongue. A deep kettle or a deep well in a range serves the purpose nicely.

1 Cover meat with hot water.

2 Season with salt and pepper (unless it is smoked, cured meat). Add onion, herbs, and spices, if desired.

3 Cover and cook over low heat at simmering temperature until done. See recipe.

4 Vegetables may be added 30 to 45 min. before meat is done.

CUTS OF MEAT FOR COOKING IN WATER

Beef: Corned brisket, tongue, sweetbreads.

Lamb: Heart, tongue.

Veal: Heart, tongue, sweetbreads.

Pork: Shoulder, tongue, heart, spareribs.

This method is also used in cooking meats for soups . . . brisket or plate, oxtails, hocks, etc.

"BUY MEAT WISELY . . . STORE IT CAREFULLY"

says Reba Staggs of the National Live Stock and Meat Board, Chicago, who contributed much of their good information to help us.

1 The lean and fat of all grades of meat have essentially the same nutritive value.

2 Select the grade best fitted to your pocketbook and the way you plan to cook it.

3 Insist on government-inspected meat. You can recognize it by this purple inspection stamp for wholesomeness on most fresh and cured meats. It is required for your protection on all meat shipped interstate.

U. S. Choice: Highest grade of beef, veal, lamb, or mutton normally found in retail stores . . . is well marbled with fat and has a moderately thick fat covering.

U. S. Good: Has a fat covering somewhat thinner and less marbling than the U. S. Choice.

U. S. Commercial and U. S. Utility: Lower grades with thin fat covering . . . for braising or cooking in liquid.

NOTE: Very little fresh pork is branded.

HOW TO STORE MEAT

2 Today's mild cured **Smoked Meats** . . . store the same as fresh.

1 Fresh Meat: Remove wrapping. Cover loosely with waxed paper, leaving ends open. Store in coldest part of refrigerator in meat compartment or drip tray under freezing unit. Use within 2 or 3 days.

3 Ground Meat: Darkens on standing and spoils more quickly than whole cuts. Unwrap, cover loosely with waxed paper. Store as for fresh meat. Cook within 24 hr. If kept longer, wrap each serving and freeze.

5 Variety Meats: Store the same as ground meat.

4 Frozen Meat: Store in freezing unit. Do not unwrap. Keep meat frozen until ready to use. It should be used promptly after thawing. *Do not refreeze.*

6 Cooked Meat: Cover tightly in dish or with foil to prevent drying, store in coldest part of refrigerator. Do not cut, grind, or slice until ready to use.

7 Poultry: Wrap loosely. Store in coldest part of refrigerator. Use whole birds within 2 to 3 days; cut-up birds within 24 hr. Store cooked poultry like cooked meat.

8 Fresh Fish: Wrap completely or place in tightly covered dish. Keep in coldest part of refrigerator. Cook within 24 hr. Store cooked fish like cooked meat.

All meat methods are used in cooking the various cuts of beef. Usually, only the rib (roasts) and loin (steaks) of high quality beef are aged. Aging increases tenderness but adds to the cost of the meat.

ROAST BEEF

Finest, most tender, and highest priced pieces of beef are rib roasts and loin steaks.

Allow ⅓ lb. with bone, or ¼ lb. rolled for each serving.

Choose:

Standing Rib   Rolled Rib

Rump (of prime or high quality) in piece or rolled may also be roasted.
Roast in slow mod. oven (325°). See p. 308 for How to Roast.

	Min. per Lb.	Meat Thermometer
Rare:	22 to 26	140°
Medium:	26 to 30	160°
Well done:	33 to 35	170°

For rolled roasts, add 10 min. per lb.
For frozen roasts, see p. 308.

YORKSHIRE PUDDING

In England, Yorkshire Pudding is a "must" with roast beef.

When roast is done, remove from oven and keep warm. Increase oven heat to 425°. Have batter for Popovers (*p. 78*) made. Drain off most of the fat in pan; pour in Popover batter. Bake 35 to 45 min. Serve immediately.

FILLET OF BEEF TENDERLOIN

This is an excellent roast for company dinner because it cooks in a short time, is easy to carve, sure to be tender, and there's no waste. It is best served crusty brown on the outside and rare inside.

Select a 4 to 6-lb. tenderloin with a little outside fat. Have it trimmed and larded. Place on rack in roasting pan; brush with melted butter or oil. Roast in hot to very hot oven (450 to 500°) 30 min. for rare; 40 min. for medium; 50 min. for well done. Extreme tenderness and lack of fat make high temperature preferable. If desired, cut small gashes in tenderloin and insert slices of garlic before roasting.
AMOUNT: 8 to 12 servings.

BROILED STEAK

Your choice is large.

Allow ⅓ to ¾ lb. with bone, or ⅓ to ½ lb. boneless for each serving.

Choose:

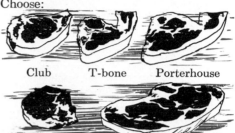

Club   T-bone   Porterhouse

Tenderloin (Filet Mignon)   Sirloin

Broil in oven. See p. 308 for How to Broil.

	Min. per Lb.	
	1″ thick	2″ thick
Rare:	5 min. each side	16 min. each side
Medium:	6 min. each side	18 min. each side
Well done:	8 min. each side	20 min. each side

Pan-broiling will take about same length of time. See p. 308 for How to Pan-broil. Steaks over 1″ thick should be oven-broiled or charcoal-grilled, not pan-broiled. (For frozen steaks, see p. 308.)

PLANKED STEAK

Choose: Large T-bone steak 1½″ thick. Broil steak 12 min. on one side; turn, broil 6 min. on second side. Place on oiled heated wooden plank. Pipe border of mashed potatoes around edge of plank; brush with beaten egg. Return to broiler until steak is done and potatoes browned. Arrange seasoned cooked vegetables of contrasting color and flavor between steak and potatoes—cauliflowerets, carrot sticks, fried tomatoes, mushrooms.

SWISS STEAK *Cooked by braising.*

Pound ½ cup Seasoned Flour (*p. 309*) into both sides of . . .
    3-lb. round steak (2″ thick)
Brown in hot fat in heavy skillet . . .
    2 onions, sliced
Remove onions and brown meat well on both sides. Top with onions. Add . . .
    2 cups cooked tomatoes (no. 303 can)
Cover tightly and cook slowly until tender (2½ to 3 hr.)
AMOUNT: 8 to 10 servings.

MAKING OLD-FASHIONED BEEF STEW

POT ROAST

Flavorful roasts of less tender beef braised with or without vegetables.

Allow ⅓ lb. with bone, or ¼ lb. boneless for each serving.

Choose:

Shoulder or Chuck

Blade-bone Round-bone

Boned Rump Sirloin Tip

Rub roast with ½ cup Seasoned Flour (*p. 309*). Brown in hot fat in heavy kettle 20 to 30 min. (A low rack or 3 jar lids punched with holes will keep meat from burning during cooking.) Add about 1 cup water and, if desired, other seasonings and ½ cup sliced onion. Cover tightly and simmer.

Weight	Thickness	Total Time
3 lb. (bone-in)	2"	2½ to 3 hr.
5 lb. (bone-in)	3"	3½ to 4 hr.

For large boneless roasts, allow 1 hr. more.

INDIVIDUAL POT ROASTS WITH NOODLES

Have 3-lb. pot roast cut into 6 pieces. Cook as above. Remove meat; make gravy with 3 tbsp. flour and 2 cups tomato juice. Season with ½ tsp. celery salt and 1 tsp. Worcestershire sauce. Cook 4-oz. pkg. noodles in 1 can bouillon (10½ oz.) diluted with 1 can water; serve with roast. AMOUNT: 6 servings.

POT ROAST AND VEGETABLES

Select 4 to 5-lb. pot roast. Follow recipe for Pot Roast (above) and omit onions. 45 min. before pot roast is done, add . . .

- 8 to 10 small onions
- 8 to 10 med. carrots
- 8 to 10 stalks celery, cut up
- 8 to 10 small potatoes or 4 large, quartered
- 1 tsp. salt

Remove meat and vegetables to hot platter. Thicken juice for gravy, if desired.

For special flavor and tenderness, spread browned meat with ½ cup horse-radish. AMOUNT: 8 servings.

GILDED POT ROAST

A good way to dress up a pot roast the second day.
Sauté . . .
- 1 onion, finely chopped
- ½ lb. mushrooms, sliced

in . . .
- 3 tbsp. butter

Stir in . . .
- 1 cup cream

Simmer 10 min. Season with salt and pepper. Pour out on large baking pan. Thinly slice leftover pot roast; arrange overlapping slices on mushroom mixture. Spread chopped leftover vegetables over meat. Pour over any meat juices. Cover with 1 cup grated Parmesan cheese. Place under broiler to brown slightly.

BEEF SHORT RIBS JARDINIERE

"The most flavorful cut of beef!" say many meat dealers.
Use 3 lb. short ribs (cut in serving pieces) in place of Pot Roast. 30 min. before time is up, add . . .
- 2 large carrots, cut up
- 1 green pepper, cut up
- 2 or 3 stalks of celery, cut up

Remove meat and vegetables. Thicken liquid for gravy.
AMOUNT: 6 servings.

OLD-FASHIONED BEEF STEW

"My husband worked with this recipe until he had just the right amounts of vegetables and seasonings," says Mrs. Edward Kruger of St. Louis, Missouri. See color picture opposite page.

Select 2-lb. chuck or bottom round (cut in 2" pieces). See p. 309 for How to Stew. Roll meat in Seasoned Flour (*p. 309*).

Brown thoroughly in . . .
- 1 tbsp. fat

Cover with . . .
- 1 qt. hot water

Simmer 2 hr., adding water if necessary. Add . . .
- 2 cups diced potatoes (3 med.)
- 1 cup diced turnips
- 1 cup diced carrots
- ½ cup diced parsnips
- 1 cup diced celery
- 1 green pepper, diced
- ½ cup diced onion (8 small), if desired
- 1 tbsp. salt
- 2 beef bouillon cubes

Cook until vegetables are tender, about 30 min. If desired, thicken liquid for gravy. The flavor of this stew gets better each time it is reheated.
AMOUNT: 12 servings.

COUNTRY-FRIED STEAK

Choose:

Bottom Round

Top Round

Steaks may also be cut from rump, shoulder, or sirloin tip.

Season with salt and other seasonings, if desired. Braise (*see p. 309 for How to Braise*). Cook slowly until tender, 45 min. to 2 hr., depending on thickness of steak.

ROUND STEAK ROYALE

Rub 1-lb. round steak (1″ thick) with cut clove of garlic. Cook as above 2 hr., topping with ¼ cup sliced onions and 4-oz. can mushrooms (sautéed in butter) after browning. Remove steak and add ½ cup cultured sour cream; thin to gravy consistency with water. Heat and serve with meat.

AMOUNT: 4 servings.

CHICKEN-FRIED STEAK

Have 1-lb. round steak cut in 4 pieces.

Dip in . . .

Seasoned Flour (p. 309)

then in . . .

1 egg and 2 tbsp. water, beaten together

Dip again in flour. Brown on both sides in hot fat. Cover and cook slowly 20 to 30 min. To make gravy, remove meat, add rest of Seasoned Flour mixed with 2 cups milk. Stir until gravy comes to a boil; boil 1 min.

AMOUNT: 4 servings.

CHICKEN-FRIED HAMBURGERS

Follow recipe above—*except* use 1 lb. ground beef shaped into 4 to 6 patties. Cook 10 to 15 min.

MINUTE STEAKS (Cube Steaks)

These less-tender steaks have been scored by a special machine to cut the fibers and make them more tender.

Brush heavy skillet with fat. Brown on one side, about 2 min. Turn and brown on other side.

FLANK STEAK

Flank steak is best when braised (*see p. 309 for How to Braise*). Have flank steak scored.

Spanish Style: After browning a 1½ to 2-lb. flank steak, cover with 1 med. onion, sliced, 2 cups cooked tomato, and 1 green pepper, sliced. Bake 2 hr. or until tender. If desired, combine ¾ tsp. chili powder and ¼ cup cold water and use to make gravy.

Stuffed Flank Steak: Season with salt; spread with Bread Stuffing (*p. 337*). Roll crosswise and fasten with metal skewers. Brown on all sides in hot fat in heavy skillet. Add 1 cup water. Cover and bake in mod. oven (350°) 2 hr. To serve, cut across roll in 1″ slices.

NEW ENGLAND BOILED DINNER

The favorite of many a man . . . woman, too.

Place in heavy kettle a 4 to 5-lb. corned brisket of beef. Cover with cold water; add herbs and seasonings, if desired, but no salt. Cover tightly and simmer about 3½ hr. Remove meat and keep warm.

Skim off excess fat and add . . .

8 small onions
8 whole carrots
4 potatoes, halved or quartered
2 turnips, cubed (if desired)

Cover and cook 20 min. Add . . .

1 green cabbage, cut in wedges

Continue cooking 25 min. Serve on hot platter, the vegetables around the corned beef.

AMOUNT: 8 servings.

BEEF BRISKET WITH HORSE-RADISH SAUCE

Streaked with fat, but very flavorful.

In a heavy kettle, place . . .

3-lb. fresh beef brisket

Cover with hot water.

Add . . .

2 tbsp. vinegar
2 tbsp. sugar
2 tsp. salt
4 whole cloves
1 bay leaf
1 clove garlic
2 stalks celery, sliced

Simmer covered 3 hr. Remove meat, slice, and serve with Horse-radish Sauce (*p. 399*), using stock from brisket.

FLUFFY MEAT LOAF (🖊 Recipe)

Mix thoroughly . . .
- 1 lb. ground beef or veal
- ½ lb. ground lean pork
- 3 med. slices soft bread, torn in pieces, and 1 cup milk *or* 1 cup dry bread crumbs and 1¼ cups milk
- 1 egg, beaten
- ¼ cup minced onion
- 1¼ tsp. salt
- ¼ tsp. *each* pepper, dry mustard, sage, celery salt, and garlic salt
- 1 tbsp. Worcestershire sauce

For better browning, shape into loaf on shallow baking pan. Bake until done. Serve hot or cold. For Catsup-topped Loaf, spread 3 tbsp. catsup on top before baking.
TEMPERATURE: 350° (mod. oven).
TIME: Bake 1½ hr.
AMOUNT: 8 servings.

All you have to do — For a Beef Loaf: use 1½ lb. ground beef for the meat in Fluffy Meat Loaf (*above*). In place of mustard and sage, use 1 tbsp. *each* horse-radish and catsup.

BARBECUED BEEFIES
(Individual Meat Loaves)

Jean Miller (now Mrs. Robert Lynum of Seattle, Washington) perfected these when she was on our staff.
Shape mixture for Fluffy Meat Loaf (*above*) into 8 individual loaves (1x2x3"). Place in greased shallow pan with thin slices of onion on each. Pour Texas Barbecue Sauce (*p. 317*) over all. Baste often.

LAYERED MEAT LOAF

To make dressing, brown in ¼ cup fat . . .
- 1 med. onion, chopped
- ¾ cup diced celery

Mix with . . .
- 3 cups soft bread cubes
- ½ cup water
- 2 eggs, beaten
- ⅓ cup diced green pepper
- 1 tbsp. salt
- ½ tsp. flavor extender

Add ½ of dressing to . . .
- 1 lb. pork butt and 1 lb. beef (ground together twice)

Pat out half of meat mixture in loaf pan, 10x5x3". Cover with rest of dressing; top with rest of meat mixture. Baste with . . .
- ½ cup tomato juice
- 2 tbsp. butter, melted

TEMPERATURE: 350° (mod. oven).
TIME: Bake 1¼ hr.
AMOUNT: 10 to 12 servings.

EMERGENCY STEAK

"T-bone," family style.
Mix . . .
- 1 lb. ground beef
- 1 tbsp. minced onion
- ½ cup milk
- 1 tsp. salt
- ¼ tsp. pepper
- 1 cup WHEATIES or ¼ cup dry bread crumbs

Place on lightly greased pan, pat into shape of T-bone steak (1" thick). Broil (*see p. 308 for How to Broil*). Serve immediately.
AMOUNT: 6 servings.

HAMBURGERS

The all-American favorite.
Ground beef and ground round steak are both sold for hamburger. Ground chuck contains more fat and makes a juicier hamburger.

Use 1 tsp. salt and ¼ tsp. pepper for each lb. ground beef.

For extra juicy hamburgers, add ½ cup water or evaporated milk per lb. of meat.

1 lb. makes 4 thick or 8 thin patties.

Fry in small amount of hot fat or broil on cold broiler pan 3" from heat, turning once.
Rare: 8 min.; **Medium:** 12 min.;
Well done: 16 min.

SWEDISH MEAT BALLS

Mix thoroughly . . .
- 1 lb. ground beef
- ½ lb. ground pork
- ½ cup minced onion
- ¾ cup fine dry bread crumbs
- 1 tbsp. minced parsley
- 1½ tsp. salt
- ⅛ tsp. pepper
- 1 tsp. Worcestershire sauce
- 1 egg
- ½ cup milk

Shape into balls the size of a walnut.
Brown in . . .
- ¼ cup hot fat or salad oil

Remove meat and stir into fat . . .
- ¼ cup GOLD MEDAL Flour
- 1 tsp. paprika
- ½ tsp. salt
- ⅛ tsp. pepper

Stir in . . .
- 2 cups boiling water
- ¾ cup sweet or cultured sour cream

Return meat to gravy; cook 15 to 20 min.
AMOUNT: 6 to 8 servings.

The flavor of pork is improved by browning the fat and by slow cooking. All pork should be thoroughly cooked. Pork may be roasted, braised, stewed, but never broiled.

ROAST PORK

Choose:

Pork Loin

Allow ⅓ to ½ lb. with bone or ¼ to ⅓ lb. boneless for each serving.

Loin End   Center Cut

Shoulder—fresh

Butt   Picnic   Fresh Ham

Any of the shoulder or leg cuts may also be sold as ham.

Roast in slow mod. to mod. oven (325 to 350°). *(See p. 308 for How to Roast.)*

	Min. per Lb.	Meat Thermometer
Loin	35 to 40	185°
Leg	25 to 40	185°
Shoulder,		
picnic	35 to 40	185°
butt	45 to 50	185°

The longer time is for smaller roasts.

 Frozen Meat: Thaw in refrigerator or add 15 to 20 min. per lb. to roasting time.

CURRIED PORK SLICES

Good way to use leftover roast.

Arrange slices of cooked pork roast in a baking dish. Top each with a cooked apricot half. Pour Curry Sauce *(p. 398)* over top, sprinkle with a little minced onion, if desired. Top with sautéed mushrooms. Heat in mod. oven (350°) 15 to 20 min.

STUFFED PORK TENDERLOIN

Larry Melander of our company said when he tasted it, "It's so nice to look at and so good to eat."

Split 2 tenderloins (¾ lb. each) almost in two. Season cut surface with salt and pepper. Spread one with Bread Stuffing *(p. 337)*; top with second tenderloin. Tie together with string. Lay pork fat or bacon strips over top. Roast *(see p. 308 for How to Roast)* in mod. oven (350°) 1¼ hr.

BRAISED PORK CHOPS

Chops from the loin are choicest . . . those from ribs or shoulder, most economical.

Allow ½ to ¾ lb. for each serving.

Trim excess fat from chops. Lightly grease hot skillet with fat edge of one chop. Brown chops slowly on both sides in heavy skillet. (Allow 3 min. on each side.) Add ¼ cup water; cover tightly and cook slowly on top of range or in mod. oven (350°) until tender and well done.

	Thickness	Min. per Lb.
Rib or loin chops	1″	30 to 35 min.
Rib or loin chops	½″	20 min.
Shoulder chops	½″	20 min.

Season after cooking.

NOTE: Thin chops need no added liquid—but a tight fitting cover and low heat are needed to keep moist.

PORK STEAKS (fresh ham): are cooked just like pork chops.

PORK CHOPS WITH APPLE RINGS

Cover browned seasoned pork chops with ¾″ thick rings of tart, raw apple. Sprinkle with a little brown sugar. Add a bit of water. Braise as above.

PORK CHOPS SUPREME

Top each browned seasoned pork chop with 1 thin onion slice and 1 thin lemon slice. Sprinkle with brown sugar. Top each chop with 1 tbsp. catsup. Braise as above.

STUFFED PORK CHOPS

Have pork chops cut double thick with a pocket on the bone side. Stuff pocket with well seasoned Bread Stuffing *(p. 337)*. Braise as above. Cover and cook slowly on top of range or in mod. oven (350°) 1½ hr.

CRANBERRY PORK CHOPS

Braise 4 pork chops as above. In place of water, pour over chops a mixture of 2 cups cleaned cranberries, ¼ cup water, ½ cup sugar, ¼ tsp. *each* ground cloves and nutmeg. Cover and bake in mod. oven (350°) 1½ hr.

ROAST SPARERIBS

Allow ¾ to 1 lb. ribs per person. Spareribs require very long, slow cooking because of the large amount of bone.

Place spareribs on rack in shallow baking pan. Season with salt, pepper, and crushed bay leaf. Roast in slow mod. oven (325°) until tender (about 1½ hr.). Serve.

BAKED STUFFED SPARERIBS

Brown bony side of 2 sets of ribs in roasting pan on top of range. Turn 1 set, brown side up, spread with Bread Stuffing or Apple Stuffing (*p. 337*). Cover with other set, brown side next to stuffing. Season with salt. Bake in mod. oven (350°) 1½ hr. If necessary, add ¼ cup water.

TEXAS BARBECUED SPARERIBS

Place on rack in shallow baking pan . . .
  3 lb. spare or loin ribs, cut in serving-size
    pieces
Do not cover. Do not add water.
On each piece, place . . .
  1 lemon slice
Sprinkle over all . . .
  ½ cup chopped onion

Bake in hot oven (450°) about 30 min. Pour over ribs Texas Barbecue Sauce (*below*). Continue baking in mod. oven (350°) 1½ to 2 hr.

Baste with sauce every 15 min. If sauce thickens, add a little hot water. To prevent ribs from browning too much, cover last 30 min. of baking.

TEXAS BARBECUE SAUCE

Mix in saucepan 2 tbsp. brown sugar, 1 tbsp. paprika, 1 tsp. salt, 1 tsp. dry mustard, ¼ tsp. chili powder, ⅛ tsp. cayenne pepper, 2 tbsp. Worcestershire sauce, ¼ cup vinegar, 1 cup tomato juice, ¼ cup catsup, ½ cup water. Simmer 15 min. or until slightly thickened.

PORK TENDERLOIN PATTIES

Pan-fry tenderloin patties (*see p. 308 for How to Pan-fry*). Add small amount of sour cream, tomato juice, or diluted cream of mushroom soup; cover, and simmer 20 to 30 min.

SAVORY PATTIES

Pan-fry 1 lb. tenderloin patties as above. Pour over **Savory Sauce** made of ½ cup cultured sour cream, 2 tbsp. orange juice, 1 tbsp. grated orange rind, and ¼ tsp. Worcestershire sauce. Cover and simmer 20 min.

AMOUNT: 4 servings.

SPARERIBS AND SAUERKRAUT

Choice of one of Hollywood's most exotic movie stars of all time.

Cut 2 lb. spareribs into 3 or 4-rib pieces. Season with salt and pepper. Brown over med. heat in heavy skillet. Add small amount of water; cover and cook slowly 1 hr. Empty no. 303 can sauerkraut (1¾ lb.) into kettle. Top with ribs using 3 tbsp. of the fat and ¼ cup water. Cook slowly 1 hr.

NOTE: For variety, add ½ tsp. caraway seeds, 3 tbsp. sugar, and 3 tbsp. chopped onion to sauerkraut. Or add ¼ cup brown sugar and 2 apples, cut in eighths.

PORK CUTLETS MORNAY

Boneless pieces of pork steak. Elegant for a party dish.

Flatten 1 lb. pork cutlets. Season and dip in beaten egg and bread crumbs. Braise (*see p. 309 for How to Braise*) until tender, about 30 min. Place on hot baking pan coated with tomato sauce. Cover with Sauce Mornay (*p. 399*). Sprinkle with ½ cup grated American cheese and paprika. Place under broiler until hot and bubbly.

AMOUNT: 6 servings.

PORK CUTLETS CREOLE

Dip in Seasoned Flour (p. 309) . . .
  1 lb. pork cutlets
Brown . . .
  ½ cup thinly sliced onions
in . . .
  1½ tbsp. fat or drippings
Add meat and brown thoroughly. Remove excess fat. Add . . .
  ½ cup chopped celery
  no. 2 can tomatoes (2½ cups)
  1 tsp. celery salt
  ½ to 1 tsp. chili powder, if desired

Cover tightly and simmer over low heat or bake in mod. oven (350°) until tender, about 1½ hr.

AMOUNT: 4 to 6 servings.

There are many kinds of cured and smoked ham. **Ready-to-eat** *means it is safe to eat without further cooking; but cooking will improve texture and flavor.* **Tenderized** *refers to a method of curing; it does not mean the ham has been cooked. Canned hams are ready to eat, or they may be reheated. Ham will vary greatly in price, the fully cooked or boned hams costing more and the center cuts even higher.*

BAKED HAM

Choose:

Shank

Leg
Butt

> Allow ½ to ¾ lb. uncooked with bone, ⅓ lb. boneless, ⅓ lb. cooked with bone, ⅛ to ¼ lb. boneless for each serving.

Shoulder or Picnic

Boneless Shoulder Butt

Follow directions for How to Roast (*p. 308*), omitting seasoning. Half an hour before ham is done, take from oven and remove rind. Score fat, add glaze, if desired, and return to a mod. hot oven (400°) for browning, 15 to 20 min.

	Minutes per Lb.	Meat Therm.
Whole ham, uncooked	18 to 20	160°
Whole ham, ready-to-eat	10	130°
Half ham, uncooked	22 to 25	160°
Half ham, ready-to-eat	10	130°
Picnic	30 to 35	170°
Boneless Butt	40 to 45	170°

Ham and picnics will carve more easily if allowed to rest out of oven 15 to 20 min. Add this time plus the 10 min. for scoring and glazing.

GLAZES FOR HAM

If desired, a whole clove may be inserted in each scored square.

1 1 cup brown sugar, 1 tbsp. dry mustard. ½ cup pickle juice or spiced fruit juice may be added.

2 1 cup brown sugar and ¾ cup crushed pineapple.

3 1 cup cranberry or currant jelly.

HAM "BOILED" BEFORE BAKING

Uncooked hams, picnics, or shoulder butts may be simmered in water. They will be milder in flavor than when baked the full time. A 12-lb. ham will take 3 hr.; a 6 to 8-lb. picnic, 3½ hr.; a boneless 2-lb. shoulder butt, 1¾ hr. After cooking in water, add glaze and brown in mod. hot oven (400°) 15 to 30 min.

BAKED HAM SLICE

Cut slashes in edge of a 1″ thick center cut slice of ham. Sprinkle with 1 tsp. dry mustard and ¼ cup brown sugar. Place in heavy skillet or baking pan. Pour on milk at side of ham slice until it barely reaches top. Bake uncovered in mod. oven (350°) 1¼ hr.

BROILED HAM SLICE

Cut slashes in edge of 1″ thick center cut slice of ham. Broil 10 min. 3″ from heat. Turn and broil on second side 10 min. For ready-to-eat ham, cut time in half.

PAN-BROILED HAM SLICE

Rub skillet lightly with fat. Place ¼ to ½″ slices of cured ham or Canadian bacon in skillet. Cook slowly until brown; turn and brown other side. Remove fat as it collects. For ready-to-eat or cooked ham, browning is all that is necessary.

HAM LOAF SUPERB

Grind together . . .
> ¾ lb. ham
> ½ lb. veal
> ¼ lb. pork

Mix in . . .
> 2 eggs, beaten
> ¾ cup soft bread crumbs
> ¾ cup milk
> dash of pepper

Pat mixture in 9x5x3″ loaf pan

Spread on top of loaf a mixture of . . .
> 2 tsp. prepared mustard
> ¼ cup brown sugar

Pour over loaf . . .
> ⅓ cup pineapple juice or pickled
>   peach juice

Baste loaf several times during baking. Serve with Easy Horse-radish Sauce (*p. 338*).

TEMPERATURE: 350° (mod. oven).
TIME: Bake 1½ hr.
AMOUNT: 5 to 6 servings.

BAKED CANADIAN BACON

Canadian bacon in the piece may be roasted like ham. Remove casing. For 2-lb. piece, roast 1½ hr.; for a 4-lb. piece, 2⅓ hr. or 170° for meat thermometer. Use glazes as for ham the last 15 min.

Lamb may be roasted or broiled, depending on the cut. A few of the less tender cuts are braised or made into stew. People are most familiar with lamb chops and leg of lamb. But there are many other cuts and delicious ways to prepare them.

ROAST LAMB

Choose:

French Leg

Allow ¼ to ½ lb. bone-in leg roast, ½ to ¾ lb. bone-in shoulder roast, ¼ to ⅓ lb. boneless for each serving.

Sirloin   Rib-crown Roast

SHOULDER

Square Cut   Cushion   Rolled

The "fell," a paper-like covering, may or may not be removed. Those who like a "lamby" taste prefer to leave the fell on. Season. Roast in slow mod. oven (325°). *See p. 308 for How to Roast.*

	Weight	Approx. Cook. Time	Meat Therm.
Leg (Medium)	6 lb.	3 hr.	175°
(Well done)		3½ hr.	182°
Crown	5 lb.	3¾ hr.	182°
Shoulder (bone-in)	4 lb.	2¼ hr.	182°
Shoulder (cushion)	4 lb.	2½ hr.	182°
Shoulder (rolled)	4 lb.	2½ hr.	182°

All you have to do —

For special seasoning: (1) cut slits in roast with tip of knife, insert slivers of garlic, (2) spread mint or currant jelly over roast, baste occasionally, (3) rub marjoram, thyme, or rosemary into surface before roasting.

STUFFED SHOULDER OF LAMB

Have shoulder of lamb cut "cushion style" with bone removed. Lace string across open side. Fill pocket with Bread Stuffing (*p. 337*) or Apple Stuffing (*p. 337*). Roast, following time above.

LAMB CHOPS AND STEAKS

Choose:

Sirloin Chop

Allow ½ to ¾ lb. chops for each serving; ⅓ to ½ lb. steaks for each serving.

Rib Chop   Loin Chop

Shoulder Chop   Shoulder Blade Chop   Leg Steak   English Chop

Broil in oven. *See p. 308 for How to Broil.*

		Time—each side	
	Thickness	Medium	Well done
Rib or Loin	1″	6 min.	7 min.
	1½″	9 min.	11 min.
Sirloin	1″	6 min.	7 min.
English Chop	2″	12 min.	15 min.
Shoulder Chops	1″		8 min.
Leg Steaks	1″		8 min.

Pan-broiling will take about same length of time. *See p. 308 for How to Pan-broil.* For extra flavor, rub surface of chops or steaks with cut clove of garlic or brush with French dressing.

ENGLISH LAMB CHOPS

Carol Schulz (Mrs. Rockwell Schulz) of our staff makes these often for her husband.

Season on both sides with salt . . .
    1″ thick loin or shoulder lamb chops, boned
Place in roasting pan. On each chop place . . .
    1 thin slice large onion
    1 thin slice process cheese (or sprinkle
        with grated cheese)
    1 tbsp. cultured sour cream

Bake uncovered in slow oven (300°) for ½ hr.; cover and bake 2½ hr. longer or until tender.

BAKED LAMB CHOPS

Brown on both sides 4 lamb shoulder chops (½″ thick). Place in shallow pan. Top with ½ recipe Apple Stuffing (*p. 337*), using fruit juice for liquid and adding 1 tbsp. minced mint leaves. Bake covered in a slow mod. oven (325°) 45 min. 4 servings.

319

KABOBS See color picture on p. 306.

Have 1½ lb. lamb shoulder or shank cut into 1″ cubes. Marinate in French dressing (with garlic) 1 hr. or overnight.

Cut in 1″ pieces . . .
 2 green peppers
 1 large onion
 2 firm tomatoes

Alternate meat cubes, pieces of pepper, onion, and tomato on metal skewers. Roll in salad oil. Broil 3″ from heat, allowing 30 min. Turn as meats and vegetables brown.

AMOUNT: 6 servings.

BRAISED LAMB SHANKS

Famous German dish.

Have bones cracked in 4 lamb shanks. Roll in flour. Brown thoroughly in hot fat.

Add . . .
 salt and pepper
 ¼ tsp. thyme
 ½ tsp. rosemary
 2 cups hot water

Cover and simmer 1½ hr.

Add . . .
 1 cup cut-up carrots
 1 cup cut-up potatoes
 ½ cup cut-up celery
 1 med. onion, chopped

Continue cooking 30 min. or until vegetables are tender.

AMOUNT: 4 servings.

IRISH STEW

Place in deep kettle . . .
 2 lb. lamb shoulder, cut in 2″ cubes

Add . . .
 4 cups hot water

Simmer covered about 2 hr. Then add . . .
 3 carrots, diced
 1 small turnip, diced
 1 onion, sliced
 2 cups cubed potatoes
 2 tsp. salt
 ¼ tsp. pepper
 1 bay leaf
 3 tbsp. minced parsley

Continue cooking until vegetables are tender (about ½ hr.). If desired, thicken broth with ¼ cup flour mixed with ½ cup cold water. Dumplings (*p. 97*) may be cooked on top of stew.

AMOUNT: 6 servings.

SCOTCH STEW

Some people prefer the flavor of browned meat.

In recipe for Irish Stew at left below, brown meat well in 1 tbsp. hot fat. Add ½ cup pearl barley with water. Omit potatoes.

LAMB CURRY

Sauté in butter until golden brown . . .
 3 large apples, pared, cored, and sliced
 1 onion, sliced
 1 clove garlic

Remove garlic.

Blend well and add . . .
 2 to 3 tbsp. flour
 1 tbsp. curry powder

Combine and stir in gradually . . .
 1 tbsp. lemon juice
 2 cups meat stock or bouillon
 1 tsp. gravy flavoring

Stir in . . .
 grated rind of ½ lemon
 ½ cup raisins
 3 whole cloves

Cover, simmer 30 min. Add . . .
 2 cups cubed leftover cooked lamb

Heat thoroughly. Serve with rice on a hot platter with a side dish of chutney.

AMOUNT: 6 servings.

SAVORY LAMB PATTIES

Ground lamb makes delicious "lamburgers."

Soak . . .
 2 cups soft bread crumbs

in . . .
 ¼ cup water

Add . . .
 1 egg
 1 lb. ground lamb
 1 tbsp. soft butter
 1½ tsp. salt
 ½ tsp. pepper
 2 tbsp. chopped onion
 1 small clove garlic, minced
 3 tbsp. minced parsley

Shape lightly into 8 patties. Dip in flour.

Cook 15 min. in . . .
 3 tbsp. hot fat

Turn to brown. Serve with catsup.

AMOUNT: 8 servings.

Veal is delicate in flavor and juicy when properly cooked. It combines well with other flavors. From the young beef, veal is lacking in fat and should not be broiled.

ROAST VEAL
Choose:

Loin

> Allow ⅓ to ½ lb. bone-in or ¼ to ⅓ lb. boneless for each serving. Roast should be at least 3 lb.

Leg

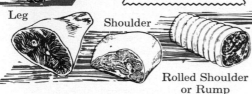

Shoulder

Rolled Shoulder or Rump

If roast lacks fat covering, cover with bacon or salt pork. Roast in slow mod. oven (325°) (*see p. 308 for How to Roast*).

	Weight	Cooking Time	Meat Therm.
Loin	5 lb.	3⅓ hr.	180°
Leg	3 lb.	2 hr.	180°
Shoulder	3 lb.	2 hr.	180°
Boned and rolled	4 lb.	2⅔ hr.	180°

Veal roasts may be covered or pot-roasted, if desired (*see p. 309 for How to Braise*). Vegetables may be cooked with roast same as for Pot Roast (*p. 313*). Veal roasts may be rubbed with cut clove of garlic, thyme, or crushed bay leaf before roasting.

VEAL DAUBÉ
An example of the superb French cuisine of New Orleans. Our staff said, "About the best seasoned meat we ever tasted!"

Rub with small piece of garlic . . .
>   4 to 5-lb. veal rump or shoulder roast

Rub well into meat a mixture of . . .
>   1 tsp. salt
>   ⅛ tsp. pepper
>   ¼ tsp. allspice
>   ½ tsp. each thyme and sage
>   2 bay leaves, crushed
>   ¼ cup GOLD MEDAL Flour

Brown in fat in deep heavy kettle. When well browned, remove from kettle.

Brown (in same kettle) . . .
>   1 onion, minced
>   4 carrots, sliced
>   2 stalks of celery, diced

Return browned roast to kettle and add . . .
>   1 cup boiling water

Cover and cook slowly until tender (2 to 2½ hr.). Thicken juice for gravy.

AMOUNT: 8 servings.

STUFFED BREAST OF VEAL
Follow directions for Stuffed Shoulder of Lamb (*p. 319*)—*except* use Sausage Stuffing or Apple Stuffing (*p. 337*).

VEAL CHOPS, STEAKS, CUTLETS
Choose:

> Allow ⅓ to ½ lb. bone-in or ¼ to ⅓ lb. boneless for each serving.

Rib Chop Loin Chop

| Shoulder Blade Chop or Steak | Shoulder or Leg Steak | Cutlet (Boneless pieces of Veal Steak) |

All veal chops and steaks are best when braised (*see p. 309 for How to Braise*). Dip in flour or corn meal, then in beaten egg, then in bread or cracker crumbs before browning in hot fat. The liquid used may be sweet or sour cream; cream of mushroom soup, cream of celery, chicken, or tomato soup; cooked tomatoes, or cooked fruits with juice.

	Thickness	Cooking Time after browning
Loin and rib chops	½ to ¾"	45 min.
Steaks or cutlets	½ to ¾"	1 hr.
Cutlets (Frenched)	¼ to ½"	25 min.

VEAL BIRDS
Cut into serving pieces (4x2") . . .
>   1-lb. veal steak (¼" thick)

Sprinkle with salt and pepper.
Combine . . .
>   1" cube salt pork, finely chopped
>   ½ cup fine dry bread crumbs
>   1 egg, slightly beaten
>   hot water to moisten

Or use ½ recipe Bread Stuffing (*p. 337*). Place stuffing on meat, roll up, and fasten with toothpicks. Roll in flour and brown in hot fat in heavy skillet. Turn to brown evenly.

Add . . .
>   1 cup cream or top milk
>   ¼ tsp. thyme

Cover and cook slowly about 1 hr. on top of range or in slow mod. oven (325°).

AMOUNT: 4 servings.

VEAL CUTLETS

Dip veal chops or slices of veal round in flour, then in beaten egg mixed with a little water, then in fine cracker or dry bread crumbs. Brown on both sides in hot fat. Season with salt and pepper. Add small amount of water; cover tightly. Cook slowly 1 hr. on top of range or in slow mod. oven (325°).

MADELON'S FRENCH VEAL

Brown in butter . . .
    2 lb. boneless veal, cut in bite-size pieces
Sprinkle over meat . . .
    2 tbsp. flour
    1 tsp. salt
    ¼ tsp. pepper
Brown again.
Add . . .
    2 1″ wide strips lemon peel
    1 cup boiling water
Cover. Simmer until tender (about 1 hr.).
Remove lemon peel. Stir in . . .
    1 cup heavy cream

Heat through. Serve over hot fluffy rice.
AMOUNT: 6 servings.

VEAL SUPREME

Popular at Sibley Tea House, near the home of an early Minnesota governor, at Mendota-on-the-Mississippi.

Roll in Seasoned Flour (p. 309) . . .
    1-lb. veal shoulder (cut in ½″ cubes)
Brown in hot fat.
Add and sauté . . .
    ½ cup sliced mushrooms
    ¼ cup finely chopped onion
Add . . .
    1 cup tomato juice
    ½ cup water
    pinch of chervil and rosemary
    ½ bay leaf, if desired
Simmer until meat is tender (about 25 min.).
Add . . .
    ¾ cup sweet or cultured sour cream
    1 cup diced celery

Cover and continue cooking 15 min. Serve in center of a ring of cooked noodles (use 2 cups uncooked noodles—4-oz. pkg.).
AMOUNT: 6 servings.

NOTE: The noodles may be added with the sour cream and all poured into a greased 10x6″ oblong pan. Garnish with blanched almonds. Bake in mod. oven (350°) 15 to 30 min.

VEAL CORDON BLEU

"The different ingredients make a rich, well seasoned dish," says Mrs. Leonard Strauss of St. Louis, Missouri.

Brown . . .
    1½ lb. veal, cut up for stew
in . . .
    2 tbsp. butter
Remove from pan. Blend in . . .
    2 tbsp. flour
Stir in . . .
    1 large tomato, sliced, or
        1 cup cooked tomatoes
    1 onion, minced
    3 fresh mushrooms, sliced, or
        3-oz. can mushrooms, drained
    1 tbsp. tomato paste (catsup may be used
        but will not give same flavor)
Stir in gradually . . .
    1½ cups beef bouillon
    1 bay leaf

Bring to boil; add browned meat. Season to taste with salt and pepper. Simmer until tender (about 1 hr.), adding more liquid, if necessary. Serve with rice or noodles.
AMOUNT: 4 servings.

SCHWEIZERSCHNITZEL

A member of our staff brought this recipe back from a European trip. She had this tasty dish in a small German restaurant near Munich.

Pound very thin . . .
    8 small veal cutlets (boneless)
Place on half of cutlets . . .
    thin slice ham
    thin slice cheese

Top with rest of cutlets. Roll in flour, then in beaten egg, and then in dry bread crumbs. Sauté quickly in hot fat to a golden brown on each side.
AMOUNT: 4 servings.

VEAL PARMESAN

With a reputation for years as a true gourmet, Susan Adams now shares her good recipes with her television audience.

Remove white fibers from veal cutlets or serving-size pieces of veal steak . . . and flatten. Sprinkle with salt, pepper, and paprika. Coat with grated Parmesan cheese. Sauté in hot fat until lightly browned (3 min. on each side). Serve hot with Poppy Seed Noodles (*p. 299*).

BACON

Bacon is sold in ½ and 1-lb. pkg. (16 to 20 slices per lb.) or in slabs (to be sliced as desired). Bacon squares are economical and are used for seasoning vegetables. Buy only enough bacon for 1 week. Flavor and aroma fade after that. Never freeze.

Pan-fry: Place slices in cold skillet. Heat slowly. As bacon heats, separate slices. Do not overcrowd. Turn to cook evenly. Drain on absorbent paper.

Broil: Place separated slices on broiling rack 3″ from heat. Turn once to brown evenly.

Bake: Place separated slices on rack in pan. Bake in mod. hot oven (400°) about 10 min. Do not turn.

BACON DRIPPINGS

Keep them in covered jar in cool place. Use for pan-frying, seasoning vegetables, or in making pancakes or waffles. Use within 2 weeks.

CANADIAN BACON (cured smoked boneless pork loin)

Comes sliced 22 to 26 slices per lb., or in a piece (for baking). See p. 318 for Baked Canadian Bacon. Allow 2 to 4 oz. for each serving. Pan-fry. Or broil as for Bacon (*above*).

FRANKFURTERS (in casings or skinless)

Completely cooked, they need only 5 min. heating in hot water, simmering in hot fat in skillet, or broiling (brush with oil and place 3″ from heat).

Good with potato salad, baked beans, sauerkraut, or in "hot dog bun" with chili sauce.

Quails: Split frankfurters lengthwise almost through. Place narrow stick of cheese in each. Wrap bacon slice spirally, fastening with toothpick at either end. Broil 3″ from heat until bacon is done, starting with split side down.

SAUSAGE

Sausage comes in bulk, or in casings as links. There are plain sausage links, Country Sausage, smoked coarse-ground Polish Sausage (smoked with garlic flavor) in large links or coils, Thuringer Sausage, and Swedish Sausage.

Pork Sausage Links: Place in skillet; add small amount of water. Cover and simmer 5 min. Drain. Pan-fry until brown. Never prick. Or bake in mod. hot oven (400°) 20 to 30 min.

Delicious served with scrambled eggs, applesauce, on top of a casserole of mashed sweet potatoes or corn, or with Spanish rice.

Pork Sausage Patties: Form bulk pork sausage into patties or cut from roll. Place in cold skillet; cook over low heat 12 to 15 min., or until brown. Pour off fat as it gathers. Or bake as for Pork Sausage Links (*above*).

Country Sausage and Polish Sausage: Cover with water; simmer 20 min. If desired, drain and brown slowly. Turn to brown evenly.

Extra good with hot potato salad.

Sausage and Hominy: Cook Country or Polish Sausage as above. After browning, add drained hominy and cook 5 min. Stir to brown evenly. Serve with sausage.

Sausage and Kraut: Place canned sauerkraut in skillet; top with Country or Polish Sausage. Cover. Bake in mod. oven (350°) 1 hr.

READY-TO-EAT SAUSAGE

Other sausages, such as bologna, liverwurst, and salami are usually served cold or in sandwiches.

Variety meats include liver, heart, sweetbreads, tongue, brains, and oxtails. Variety meats rate high nutritionally. They are often economical and lend variety to the menu.

LIVER (calf, lamb, beef, or pork)

Rich in iron.

Calf's liver is the most delicate, but young beef liver is often as tender. Do not soak or scald liver. Pre-cook only when it is to be ground. Avoid over-cooking. Allow ¼ lb. for each serving.

To Pan-fry (veal, beef, or lamb): Dip ½" slices in flour, brown in hot fat. Season. Reduce heat. Cook over low heat 10 to 15 min., turning once.

To Braise (older beef or pork liver): Cut into ½" slices. Roll in Seasoned Flour (*p. 309*). Brown in a little hot fat. Add a very little water. Cover and cook slowly on top of range or in mod. oven (350°) 1½ hr.

To Broil (veal or lamb): Slice ⅓ to ½" thick; brush well with melted butter. Broil 3 min. Turn once, broil 2 min.

Liver and Bacon: Pan-fry 2 slices bacon for each serving of liver. Remove and keep hot. Pan-fry flour-coated liver in the bacon fat.

Liver and Onions: Peel and slice sweet onions. Cook in bacon fat until golden. Cover and cook slowly until tender. Season. Pan-fry liver in another skillet. Serve topped with onions.

CALF'S LIVER SUPREME

Brown very thin slices of liver in bacon fat in skillet rubbed with garlic. Cook 1½ min. on each side over med. heat.

CRISPY FRIED LIVER

Leave 1 lb. baby beef liver in serving-size pieces or cut in strips, 4x¾". Dip in flour; then in milk and again in flour. Fry in hot fat until crispy brown, about 5 min. Turn and fry on other side. Season.

AMOUNT: 4 servings.

BRAISED LIVER WITH VEGETABLES

Braise liver (*opposite*)—*except* brown with the liver chopped onions, carrots, and celery. Season. Place in greased baking dish. Pour cooked tomatoes over all. Cover. Bake in mod. oven (350°) 1½ hr.

LIVER AND SCRAMBLED EGGS

Chop pan-fried liver and mix into scrambled eggs before cooking.

LIVER LOAF

Brown 1 lb. beef liver in hot fat. Put through food chopper with ½ lb. bulk pork sausage. Add 1½ cups soft bread crumbs, 2 tbsp. minced onion, 1 tsp. Worcestershire sauce, 1 tbsp. lemon juice, 1 tsp. salt, ⅛ tsp. pepper, 1 tsp. celery salt, 2 eggs, ½ cup bouillon. Top with 2 slices bacon. Bake in 9x5x3" loaf pan in mod. oven (350°) 45 min.

HEART (beef, lamb, veal, pork)

Delicious, nutritious, and economical.

To prepare: Trim off blood vessels and fat. Wash thoroughly by running water through it. Loosen and trim out small thread-like cords. Wipe with damp cloth.

CHICKEN-FRIED HEART

Slice heart in ¼" thick pieces. Dip in Seasoned Flour (*p. 309*). Brown on both sides in hot fat. Add a small amount of hot water. Cover and simmer 20 to 30 min.

STUFFED BEEF HEART

Fill cavity with well seasoned Bread Stuffing (*p. 337*). Fasten with skewers and string. Roll in Seasoned Flour (*p. 309*). Brown in hot fat. Add ½ cup hot water. Cover. Simmer until tender or bake in mod. oven (350°) about 2 hr.

OXTAIL STEW

Roll in Seasoned Flour (p. 309) . . .
  2 lb. disjointed oxtails
Brown thoroughly in hot fat.
Add . . .
  1 cup tomato juice
  ½ cup water
  1 cup chopped onion
  1 tsp. salt
  4 whole allspice
  1 bay leaf, crumbled
  1 clove garlic, minced
Cover and simmer 3 hr.
Remove allspice and bay leaf.
Add . . .
  2 tbsp. lemon juice
Serve with hot buttered noodles.
AMOUNT: 4 to 6 servings.

TONGUE (beef, lamb, veal, or pork)

Always a favorite, hot or cold. Sold fresh, smoked, cured, and pickled.

To Cook Fresh Tongue: Cover with cold water. Add 1 tbsp. salt, 1 small onion, few peppercorns, and 1 bay leaf. Simmer until tender (1 to 1½ hr. per lb.). Cool slightly; remove connective tissue, bones, and skin. Slice and serve hot or cold.

POPULAR COMBINATIONS

Hot tongue is good with buttered chopped spinach or Harvard beets.

Cold tongue is an excellent choice for the cold meat platter, with potato salad, or for sandwiches.

SPICED TONGUE

An inviting summertime supper dish. From Myrna Johnston, Food Editor of Better Homes and Gardens, who serves it at outdoor suppers in her own garden.

Add 1 lemon, sliced, 1 tsp. mixed pickling spices, and 2 tsp. salt to the hot water in which a 3-lb. beef tongue is to be simmered. Serve either hot or cold with Easy Horse-radish Sauce (*p. 338*).

SWEETBREADS

A very special delicacy. Always precook.

To precook: Drop into boiling salted water. Reduce heat and simmer 25 min. Drain. Plunge into cold water. Remove membranes. Store covered in refrigerator. Allow ¼ lb. for each serving.

PAN-FRIED SWEETBREADS

Dip cooked sweetbreads into melted butter. Pan-fry until brown (about 10 min.). Serve with Mushroom Sauce (*p. 398*).

CREAMED SWEETBREADS

Add cubed cooked sweetbreads to Medium White Sauce (*p. 398*) or to cream of mushroom soup. Serve in patty shells or on toast. May be combined with leftover ham, chicken, veal, peas, or mushrooms.

BAKED SWEETBREADS AND MUSHROOMS

Elegant company luncheon dish. We serve it frequently to guests.

Divide cooked sweetbreads into serving-size pieces. Roll in Seasoned Flour (*p. 309*) and pan-fry in butter until light brown. Place in baking dish. Sauté cut-up mushrooms in butter . . . then make Thin White Sauce (*p. 398*) in the pan. Pour over sweetbreads. Bake in mod. oven (350°) for 1 hr. Serve on rounds of toast or thin ham or Canadian bacon slices; garnish with watercress.

BRAINS

You'll never know how good they are unless you try them.

To precook: Soak 1 lb. brains in salted water 15 min. Drop into boiling water; add 1 tsp. salt; cover, and simmer 15 min. Drain, plunge into cold water, drain again. Remove membrane just before using.

Breaded Brains: Cut cooked brains in 1″ cubes. Mix 1 egg, 2 tbsp. milk, and 1 tsp. salt; pour over brains and stir with fork to coat. Roll in ½ cup fine cracker crumbs. Brown slowly in ¼ cup melted butter, turning carefully to avoid breaking. Serve hot with lemon slices or tart pickle relish. *4 servings.*

KIDNEY (beef, veal, lamb, or pork)

A real delicacy.

To prepare: Wash. Remove outer membrane. Split through center lengthwise. Remove fat and white tissue. Do not soak.

Broiled Kidney and Bacon: Wrap half a lamb kidney in half a slice of bacon; fasten with toothpick. Broil 3″ from heat 15 to 20 min., turning once. Serve 2 to a person.

Breaded Kidneys: Dip lamb or veal kidney into flour, then in slightly beaten egg, then in bread crumbs. Pan-fry 15 min. in hot fat. Serve with Piquant Brown Sauce (*p. 400*).

CHICKEN, TURKEY, DUCK, or GOOSE

The special flavor, texture, and shape make them adaptable to many interesting dishes. They must be selected with care and expertly prepared to be at their supreme best. Kathryn B. Niles of the Poultry and Egg National Board in Chicago very kindly gave us their latest information and pictures.

HOW SOLD? (Fresh or Frozen)

Dressed: feathers removed, head and feet on, but not drawn. Your meat dealer will draw and cut the bird for you.

Ready-to-Cook: fully drawn. Available whole, cut up, or by the piece.

Ready-to-cook bird weighs about ¼ less than dressed bird. Price per lb. will be more. Cut-up birds may be more per lb., as will the meaty pieces like breast and leg when sold by the piece.

COOKING FROZEN POULTRY

See p. 304.

WHAT KIND OF STUFFING?

See p. 337.

HOW TO CHOOSE (Ready-to-Cook Weight)

For Broiling: Under 2½ lb. Cut in half.

For Frying: 2 to 4 lb. Quarter small ones.

For Roasting: Plump and young—3 lb. or over. Capon—over 5 lb.

For Stewing: Big fat hen—3½ to 5 or 6 lb. Disjoint and cut up.

Young, tender birds are cooked by dry heat. Less tender ones, by moist heat. *See p. 310 for storing.*

WHAT TO DO WITH GIBLETS

Simmer the heart, gizzard, and neck in seasoned water until tender, 1 to 2 hr. Add the liver the last 5 to 15 min. Use meat and broth for gravy, soup, or stuffing.

PREPARING FOR ROASTING

Draw, singe, and remove pin feathers (use tweezer or strawberry huller). Remove leg tendons. Cut off head. Slit skin down back of neck and cut off neck. Cut out oil sac at base of tail. Wash inside and out. Dry. Sprinkle inside with salt. Just before roasting, stuff and truss. See p. 337 for choice of stuffings.

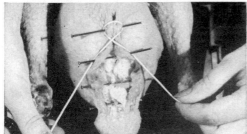

1 Stuff cavity well. *Do not pack.* (Stuffing will expand while cooking.) Fasten opening with skewers . . .then lace shut.

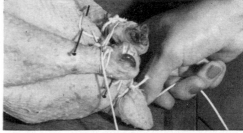

2 Tie leg ends to tail. Bring cord criss-cross over back, around base of wings. Tie. Insert stuffing in breast cavity, if desired.

3 Fasten neck skin to back with skewer. Lift wing tip up and over back for a natural brace when turned over. Tie in place.

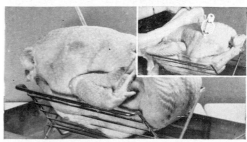

4 Brush entire bird with unsalted fat. Place on rack, breast side down. Cover parts that brown first with pieces of cloth dipped in melted fat. (*See Roast Chicken, p. 327.*)

ROAST TURKEY

Once traditional for the holiday feast. Now sold the year 'round.

Size or sex are not indications of age or tenderness. If you want a turkey between 8 and 15 lb., ask for a hen. If you want one between 16 and 25 lb., ask for a tom. Allow ½ to ¾ lb. ready-to-cook weight for each serving. The broad-breasted turkey has a larger proportion of white meat.

There are now broiler-fryer turkeys, specially grown, plump young birds weighing 4 to 8 lb. Roast as for other turkey or broil (*see Broiled Turkey below*).

Prepare turkey for roasting (*p. 326*). For time and temperature, follow chart at right below. Turn breast-side-up when ¾ done. Keep pieces of cloth moistened in melted fat or drippings.

Another test for doneness is if drumstick-thigh joint moves easily or breaks. Meat on drumstick should be soft when pressed with fingers. Do not pierce meat with fork.

HALF A TURKEY

Skewer skin to breast to prevent shrinkage. Roast as for whole turkey, cavity down, until half done (*see chart at right*). Remove from oven, place stuffing shaped to fill cavity on heavy paper on rack in pan. Place turkey over stuffing and continue roasting until done.

BROILED TURKEY

Choose young turkey (about 4 lb.). Have it split lengthwise. Snap joints to flatten. Skewer leg to body, fold wing under. Brush with melted fat, season, and place skin-side-down on broiler pan. Broil 7 to 10″ from heat. Regulate heat so turkey begins to brown in 10 min. Turn and brush with fat. Baste frequently. Allow about 60 min. cooking time.

PAN-FRIED TURKEY

Small young turkeys may be fried like chicken or oven-fried (*p. 328*). Brown thoroughly for 15 to 20 min. Cover and cook slowly until tender—45 min. for a 4-lb. bird; 50 to 60 min. for a 5-lb. bird. If skillet does not have tight fitting cover, add 1 or 2 tbsp. water. Uncover last 10 min. to recrisp skin.

A handsome bird all ready to be served.

ROAST CHICKEN

Prepare for Roasting as on p. 326. Turn breast-side-up when ¾ done. Follow time chart below.

ROAST GOOSE

Prepare for Roasting as on p. 326—*except* do not brush with fat, do not cover with cloth, and do not baste. Pour off fat as it accumulates. If very fat, parboil 20 min. Goose may be roasted in brown paper sack to eliminate fat splattering. Fasten end. When ⅔ done, puncture 6 to 8 holes in top of bag and turn. Excess fat drains into roasting pan.

ROAST DUCK

Follow directions above for Roast Goose. Some prefer to use an onion, quartered apple, and a few celery stalks in place of stuffing. Discard after roasting.

CHART FOR ROASTING POULTRY

*Ready-to-Cook Weight	Oven Temperature	**Total Cooking Time
TURKEY		
4 to 6 lb.	325°	3 to 3¾ hr.
6 to 8 lb.	325°	3¾ to 4½ hr.
8 to 12 lb.	325°	4 to 5 hr.
12 to 16 lb.	325°	5 to 6 hr.
16 to 20 lb.	325°	6 to 7½ hr.
20 to 24 lb.	325°	7½ to 9 hr.
CHICKEN		
4 to 5 lb.	325°	2½ to 3 hr.
over 5 lb.	325°	3 to 4 hr.
GOOSE		
6 to 8 lb.	325°	3 to 3½ hr.
10 to 12 lb.	325°	3¾ to 4¼ hr.
DUCK		
4 to 6 lb.	325°	1½ to 2 hr.

***Stuffed weight** of a bird is about the same as weight before it is drawn.

For **well done, add 5 to 10 min. per lb.

327

BROILED CHICKEN (⚭ Recipe)

Crisp and brown on the outside; tender, juicy, and perfectly done inside.

Select young chickens, not over 2 lb. in weight. Split in half lengthwise. Break joints to keep flat. Skewer wing and leg to body.

Place chicken on broiler pan (no rack). Season. Brush with melted fat. Broil 5 to 7″ from heat, skin-side-down. Broil slowly; regulate heat so chicken begins to brown in 10 min. Turn and brush with fat several times. Total time: Broil 35 to 50 min., or until tender.

DELMARVELOUS BROILED CHICKEN

Prize-winning recipe in a national chicken cooking contest in Salisbury, Maryland.

Place broiling chickens on broiler pan. Rub entire surface with cut lemon (squeezing to release juice). Coat with melted butter. Sprinkle with mixture of 1 tsp. *each* salt and sugar, ¼ tsp. paprika, and ⅛ tsp. pepper for each half. Follow ⚭ recipe for Broiled Chicken above.

BROILED SQUAB

Domesticated 4-week old pigeon. Often served at formal dinner parties.

Follow ⚭ recipe for Broiled Chicken above—*except* sprinkle a little lemon juice on the inside with the salt and pepper. One squab makes 1 generous or 2 small servings.

BROILED GUINEA HEN

Domesticated guinea hen with a slightly "gamey" flavor.

Follow ⚭ recipe for Broiled Chicken above. Allow ¾ to 1 lb. for each person. NOTE: Squab and guinea may be fried, braised, or roasted. Follow directions given on the following pages.

The method of frying chicken varies with the section of the country . . . each has a special characteristic and each is delicious in its own way. Be sure to select the right type of "Fryer" depending on the method you use (*see below*).

FRIED CHICKEN

Crisp on the outside, tender on the inside . . . according to the best Southern traditions.

Cut in halves, quarters, or pieces. Wash, dry, and flour by shaking several pieces at a time in a paper bag containing 1 cup GOLD MEDAL Flour, 2 tsp. salt, ¼ tsp. pepper, ½ tsp. celery salt, and 1 tsp. paprika.

Starting with meaty pieces, place in heavy skillet in ½″ hot fat (part butter, if you wish). Turn to brown evenly (15 to 20 min.). Reduce heat, cover tightly and cook slowly until tender, 20 to 40 min. If skillet cannot be covered tightly, add 1 to 2 tbsp. water. Uncover last 5 or 10 min. to recrisp.

MARYLAND FRIED CHICKEN

Dip chicken pieces in flour, then in beaten egg mixed with water, then in fine dry bread crumbs or cracker crumbs. Fry as above. Make Cream Gravy (*p. 401*) from drippings and serve over or with chicken.

EASY OVEN-FRIED CHICKEN

Melt ¼ cup fat (half butter) in shallow baking pan in mod. hot oven (400°).

Dip 2 ½-lb. frying chicken, cut in pieces, in Seasoned Flour (*p. 309*). Place in baking pan in single layer, skin-side-down. Bake 30 min. Turn skin-side-up and continue baking until tender, about 30 min.

AMOUNT: 6 servings.

CHICKEN FRIED IN BATTER

Encased in a delicious brown crust.

Cut larger fryer in serving-size pieces. Wash. Partially cook in boiling water, simmering 20 min. Drain. Sprinkle with a mixture of salt, celery salt, and pepper. Dip in Fritter Batter (*p. 96*). Drop into deep fat at 360° (cube of bread browns in 60 sec.). Fry until rich golden brown, 5 to 7 min. Serve immediately.

BARBECUED CHICKEN

Broil chicken as on p. 328; do not season. Broil until light brown on all sides. Spoon or brush Texas Barbecue Sauce (*p. 317*) over pieces; continue broiling until tender, 35 to 50 min.

To barbecue in oven, follow directions for Easy Oven-fried Chicken (*p. 328*), brushing Texas Barbecue Sauce (*p. 317*) over pieces after turning.

LEMON BARBECUED CHICKEN

Follow directions for Easy Oven-fried Chicken (*p. 328*). After turning pieces skin-side-up, pour over Lemon Barbecue Sauce (*below*). Continue baking 30 min. or until tender.

LEMON BARBECUE SAUCE

Mash 1 small clove garlic with ½ tsp. salt. Add and mix well ¼ cup cooking (salad) oil, ½ cup lemon juice (2 lemons), 2 tbsp. finely chopped onion, 1 tsp. black pepper, and ½ tsp. thyme.

BRAISED CHICKEN (✎ Recipe)

The fried chicken of the Middle West.

Prepare as for Fried Chicken (*p. 328*)—*except* use a larger fryer (3 to 4 lb.) and cut in serving-size pieces. After browning, add 3 tbsp. water. Cover. Cook over low heat on top of range, or bake in slow mod. oven (325°) until tender (45 to 60 min.). In either case, remove cover the last 10 min. to crisp crust.

SMOTHERED CHICKEN

Seasoned perfectly and cooked in cream.

Follow ✎ recipe for Braised Chicken above—*except* sprinkle remaining Seasoned Flour over chicken.

Pour over the browned chicken . . .
    2 cups hot sweet or cultured sour cream

Add more cream, if necessary, to half cover.

NOTE: Remove from oven as soon as tender. Cream will be less likely to separate.

All you have to do —

For an epicurean touch: some people drip a little white wine over the chicken while it is cooking to tenderize and flavor it.

STEWED CHICKEN

For dishes made with cooked chicken.

Singe, clean, and cut up . . .
    a stewing hen (4 to 5 lb.)
Place in kettle with just enough boiling water to cover, and add . . .
    2 sprigs parsley
    4 celery stalks with leaves, cut up
    1 carrot, sliced
    1 slice onion (2 slices if older hen)
    2 tsp. salt
    ⅛ tsp. pepper

Cover. Then simmer gently until tender (2 to 3 hr.). Add more water if necessary. Let cool in stock. Remove meat from bones in pieces as large as possible to use in chicken dishes.

NOTE: a 5-lb. chicken will give 4 cups of cut-up cooked chicken and 3 to 4 cups of chicken stock.

CHICKEN FRICASSEE (✎ Recipe)

Roll cut-up pieces of a 4½ to 5-lb. stewing chicken in Seasoned Flour (*p. 309*). Brown in thin layer of hot fat in deep heavy kettle. Drain off fat and save. Add 1 cup water and, if desired, chopped onion, lemon juice, or herbs such as rosemary or thyme. Cover tightly and cook slowly 2½ to 3½ hr. Add more water if needed. Remove chicken and make gravy using 1½ tbsp. of the saved fat and 1½ tbsp. flour to each cup of liquid. Serve with fluffy rice or mashed potatoes.

CHICKEN AND NOODLES

Follow ✎ recipe for Chicken Fricassee above—*except* cook Noodles (*p. 299*) before making the gravy. Serve in a divided dish . . . noodles on one side, Chicken Fricassee on the other.

CHICKEN FRICASSEE WITH DUMPLINGS

A fricassee without dumplings is like a wedding without a bride.

Follow ✎ recipe for Chicken Fricassee above—*except* make Dumplings (*p. 97*) before making the gravy. Arrange dumplings around the pieces of stewed chicken on hot platter. Serve hot . . . with gravy poured over chicken.

329

SOUTHERN BAKED HAM

OVEN-BAKED CHICKEN AND BISCUITS

BUTTER-KIST CHICKEN

"Even an old hen will be tender and taste like fried chicken when prepared in this way," says Hazel Smith who has given us ideas for many excellent dishes.

Melt ¼ cup butter in heavy skillet. Drop in chicken pieces. Cover skillet tightly. Simmer, turning pieces occasionally and sprinkling them with flavor extender and salt. As necessary, add small amounts of water (about 2 tbsp. at a time) to keep chicken from drying out and browning. When meat is tender (2 to 2½ hr.), remove skillet cover and let chicken brown. Remove chicken pieces to serving platter and make Cream Gravy (*p. 401*). Season to taste.

CHICKEN PIE

Of the type served at Wayside Inn, South Sudbury, Massachusetts.

Follow recipe for Stewed Chicken (*p. 329*). Make gravy, using 3 tbsp. chicken fat, 3 tbsp. flour, and 2 cups milk. Place the large pieces of boneless chicken in a 2-qt. baking dish. Pour over them the boiling gravy to about 1" of the top. Cover with dough for Southern Biscuits (*p. 83*), using chicken fat for shortening; or use pastry for crust. Roll about ¼" thick. Make slits in dough. Bake immediately in hot oven (450°) 15 min.
AMOUNT: 6 to 8 servings.

TURKEY OR CHICKEN CREAM PIE

Encore . . . leftovers take a bow!

Make Simplified Puff Pastry (*p. 348*). Pat into shallow baking dish to line sides.

Fill with alternate layers of . . .
   pieces of cold stuffing
   small slices of cooked turkey or chicken
   sautéed mushrooms

Pour a *generous* amount of leftover gravy over each layer (extend gravy with Medium White Sauce, p. 398, if necessary). (It takes 2 to 3 cups gravy to 1 cup meat, 1 cup stuffing.) Pat out remaining pastry to fit top. Cut slits in top. Place over filling. Brush pastry with slightly beaten egg. Bake in hot oven (425°) 25 to 30 min. Serve hot.

CHICKEN BREASTS BAKED IN CREAM

Brown in 3 tbsp. hot fat . . .
   3 lb. chicken breasts
Add . . .
   ½ cup chopped onion
   1 clove garlic, minced
   2 cups cream (20%)
   2 tsp. salt
   ⅛ tsp. pepper
   1 tbsp. Worcestershire sauce

Cover tightly. Bake until tender. Just before serving, remove chicken and keep warm while making gravy.

TEMPERATURE: 300° (slow oven).

TIME: Bake about 2 hr.

AMOUNT: 6 to 8 servings.

For the gravy, blend mixture of 2 tbsp. flour and ½ cup water into drippings in baking pan. Cook 2 to 3 min. If too thick, thin with milk.

OVEN-BAKED CHICKEN AND BISCUITS

Chicken fries in the oven and biscuits bake in the same pan. Flavored with peaches. See color picture on opposite page. To save time, make Drop Biscuits.

Heat oven to 425° (hot).

Mix in a paper bag . . .
   1 cup GOLD MEDAL Flour
   2 tsp. salt
   ¼ tsp. pepper
   2 tsp. paprika

Place ½ cup shortening (half butter) in 13x9" oblong pan and set in oven to melt. Shake 3 or 4 pieces of chicken at a time in bag to coat thoroughly. Place chicken, skin-side-down, in single layer in hot shortening. Bake 45 min; then turn.

Meanwhile, make dough for Biscuits (*p. 83*). Roll dough ¼" thick, cut into biscuits. Drain no. 2½ can cling peach halves and place a whole clove in each. Push chicken to one end in pan; place biscuits in single layer on other end. Place peach halves on top of chicken. Bake another 15 min., or until biscuits are lightly browned and chicken tender.

To make gravy: Remove chicken, peaches, and biscuits to serving platter. Add 2 tbsp. flour (saved from dredgings) to drippings in pan. Bring to boil. Add about 1½ cups hot milk. Boil 1 min.
AMOUNT: 4 servings.

Game includes all wild animals and fowl used for food. The method of preparing it is determined by the amount of "gamey" or "wild" flavor you wish to retain. All freshly killed game is tough. Stored from 2 to 4 days in a cool, dry place, it becomes more tender, firm, and better flavored. Venison requires about 2 weeks to "ripen." All game tends to be less tender and very lean. Cook it with that in mind. To reduce "wild" flavor, such as in ducks, soak in salt, soda, or onion water for about 1 hr.

PHEASANT AND PRAIRIE CHICKEN'

Similar . . . however, pheasant is more plentiful. Wells Wilbor, star hunter of General Mills, says: "Add white wine when you cook it as it tends to be dry."

Prepare like Chicken (any method). Especially delicious "smothered" . . . using sour cream. If "roasted," use Sausage Stuffing (*p. 337*).

POACHED PHEASANT

The epicurean way . . . as served at dinnertime by Mr. and Mrs. Edward Heum, formerly of Minneapolis, now of San Diego, California.

Poach sections of the breast of pheasant in hot butter in chafing dish at the table. Cook only until it loses its transparency (5 to 10 min.). The dark meat, legs, etc. can be served later in a main dish.

QUAIL AND RUFFED GROUSE

Called Bob White and Partridge (the most delicate of all game). Mostly breast meat.

Split in halves and pan-broil breast-side-down in lots of butter. Baste often. Or wrap in strips of bacon and bake in mod. oven (350°) 30 to 35 min.

VENISON (Deer, Moose, Elk)

Jack Andrews says: "It's an old wives' tale that venison must be cooked and cooked to remove wild taste and make it tender. My wife cooks it as she would a five dollar steak, and it's wonderful!"

Follow general directions for cooking Beef. It is usually well cooked. Most people feel that it is unappetizing when rare. Baste the roast with red wine for a special touch. Wild plum jelly is a natural with venison.

NOTE: If you like the "wild" flavor, cook a shorter time with simple seasonings. If you do not, increase cooking time and add more seasonings. *Never overcook! Venison becomes dry and unflavorful.* Braise if uncertain of age.

All you have to do –

To remove down from ducks: brush with melted paraffin. Cool and peel off.

SQUIRREL AND RABBIT

Best in the fall and early winter.

Prepare like Chicken. When roasting, truss the forelegs back and the hind legs forward. Fasten bacon over the shoulders and back. Baste with a mixture of ¼ cup butter and ½ cup boiling water. Turn several times. The stuffing is made as for Chicken. Garnish, when served, with lemon slices on watercress.

NOTE: Write to Betty Crocker for a folder of recipes for delicious Rabbit dishes.

ROAST WILD DUCK

Gourmets used to say: "Just heat the duck through. The red juice should follow every cut with the knife." Lewis Child, a crack-shot hunter, of Minneapolis, Minnesota, says they cook a large Mallard about an hour in a hot oven . . . basting it with wine.

Most of our hunters and their families say:

Prepare as for Roast Duck (*p. 327*). Place quartered apples, sliced orange, slices of onion, and celery leaves in the cavity (discard after roasting), or fill with the suggested vegetable stuffing below.

To Roast . . . for a brown crispy crust, roast uncovered in hot oven (425°). Baste several times with hot water at first, then with juices in pan or a wine, until moderately well done . . . tender and juicy (½ to 1 hr. depending on size and age of duck). If preferred, duck can be roasted longer in a mod. oven (350°).

To Glaze . . . the last few minutes and just before serving, brush with a mixture of orange juice and currant jelly.

To Garnish . . . use slices of orange topped with currant jelly.

For Stuffed Wild Duck . . . the experts say to use a mixture of equal parts of chopped carrots, onion, and celery sautéed in butter, and surround Duck with the vegetables—the flavor is extended in them.

We are grateful to Heloise Parker Broeg, popular radio and television star, Director of WEEI Food Fair, Boston, for her help and information on fish and sea food cookery.

HOW TO BUY

Fresh Fish: Have clear, bulging eyes; elastic, firm flesh; reddish pink gills; are free from strong odor. Buy fish stored and displayed on crushed ice . . . just before using. (The fresher the better.)

Frozen Fish: Available the year 'round (in steaks and fillets). For best results, thaw frozen fish (preferably in refrigerator) just before cooking. Never refreeze. Prepare as fresh fish. Have flavor and texture of fresh-caught fish.

AMOUNT TO BUY

Whole or round fish   1 lb. per serving.
Dressed fish. . . . . .   ½ lb. per serving.
Steaks, fillets, sticks.   ⅓ lb. per serving.
Shellfish . . . amount varies greatly according to the size portions desired. The meat dealer will help you select the amount.

Shellfish: Should be alive . . . such as crabs, lobster, turtles (move lively), clams, mussels, oysters (tight shells). Shrimp are not alive (headless), smell fresh, have green color, close fitting shell. Have soft-shelled crabs cleaned by dealer.

Shucked: Meat removed from shell of clams, oysters, and scallops. Must be refrigerated.

Cooked in Shell: Such as hard-shelled crabs, lobsters, shrimp. Must be refrigerated.

Cooked, Shell Removed: Such as lobster, crab, and shrimp. Must be refrigerated.

Canned: All shellfish are available. Some are smoked.

HOW TO IDENTIFY CUTS

Whole or Round
Exactly as caught.

Drawn
Entrails removed.

Dressed
Entrails, head, tail, fins removed.

Pan Dressed
Small sizes of dressed fish (such as crappie).

Fillets
Sides cut lengthwise. Usually boneless.

Butterfly Fillets
Double fillet held together by skin.

Steaks
Cross section slices of large dressed fish.

Sticks
Uniform pieces of fillets.

HOW TO COOK

Fat Fish: Have oil running through all the flesh and are generally best for broiling, baking, and planking. *Examples:*

Mackerel	Barracuda
Pompano	Tuna
Salmon	Shad
Lake Trout	Sturgeon
Rosefish	Whitefish
Herring	Catfish

Frozen Fish: See under HOW TO BUY Frozen Fish (*above*).

HOW TO FILLET FRESH FISH

Cut down the back of fish from head to tail on either side of and close to backbone. Cut the flesh free from the rib bones. Skin fish (if desired), beginning at tail end. (Fish with scales are scaled before filleting.)

Lean Fish: Have a drier flesh with the oil stored mainly in the liver and are generally best for boiling and steaming. When baking, add strips of bacon; when broiling, baste with melted fat. *Examples:*

Bass	Cod
Haddock	Buffalofish
Pike	Perch
Carp	Flounder
Red Snapper	Whiting
Halibut	Croaker

Both types good for pan or deep fat frying.

All you have to do —

To scale and clean fresh fish: hold fish by the tail. Scrape with a blunt knife (or fish scraper) from tail to head in short, firm strokes. Slit underside, remove entrails. Wipe out well.

FISH Seven standard methods of cooking fish.

- Wash—Dry
- Never overcook
- Serve at once
- Enjoy often

Swimming is easy—no tough muscles. Cook fish briefly (done when it flakes easily with fork).

Place fish on preheated platter. Garnish, serve immediately (becomes soggy on standing).

OVEN METHODS

Baking . . . suitable for any size or cut.

Place fish on aluminum foil in shallow baking-pan, or in greased shallow pan. Sprinkle with salt, pepper, melted butter. Bake. Serve with Egg Sauce (*p. 398*) or Anchovy Velouté Sauce (*p. 399*).

TEMPERATURE: 400° (mod. hot oven).

TIME: Bake 20 min. for fillets,
30 min. for steaks,
15 min. per lb. for whole fish.

Baked Fish with Stuffing:

For Whole Fish, fill cavity ⅔ full with Bread or Oyster Stuffing (*p. 337*) and sew shut.

For Fillets, place stuffing between 2 pieces of fish and hold sides secure with toothpicks. Bake as above except longer.

Planking . . . elegant for whole fish.

Place fish on hot greased plank (hickory, oak, or ash 1½" thick) or on heatproof glass. Sprinkle with salt, pepper, and melted butter. Bake as above. When fish is almost done, arrange a border of hot mashed potatoes around it. Brown under broiler. Surround with hot vegetables. Garnish. Serve on plank at table.

Broiling . . . for fillets, small whole fish.

Dip 4 or 6 fish fillets in oil and place (skin-side-down) on greased broiler pan or baking pan heated in a very hot oven (500°). Sprinkle with salt and paprika. Broil 2 to 3" from heat for 3 min. Remove and pour over 2 to 4 tbsp. chicken broth (or bouillon cube dissolved in water). Return to hot oven (450°) for 10 min. Pour 1 tsp. lemon juice and ¼ cup melted butter over fillets just before serving.

Smoked Fish . . . tantalizing flavor.

Skillfully smoked fish are delicious plain or very simply prepared (boiled, steamed, baked). Most popular are salmon, whitefish, finnan haddie.

TOP-OF-RANGE METHODS

Pan-Frying . . . especially for small game fish; trout, perch, sunfish, crappies.

Sprinkle fish with salt and pepper. Dip in flour or corn meal. Pan-fry in hot skillet with fat ⅛" deep (part butter gives superb flavor) over med. heat until golden brown. Turn carefully and brown other side (about 10 min. in all). Drain on absorbent paper. Serve hot.

Deep Fat Frying . . . perfect for fillets.

Heat fat in deep kettle until a cube of bread browns in 50 sec. (375°). Dip fish in flour, then in slightly beaten egg . . . then in bread or cracker crumbs, and drop into hot fat. Fry quickly until golden brown (3 to 6 min.). Drain on absorbent paper. Serve with lemon and Tartar Sauce (*p. 338*).

Boiling . . . for steaks and large pieces of fish.

Tie fish in cheesecloth. Lower into boiling water to which 1 sliced onion, carrot, several sprigs of parsley, 2 whole cloves, 1 bay leaf, 2 peppercorns, salt, and a little vinegar have been added. Simmer (6 to 10 min. per lb. depending on thickness). Serve with Egg Sauce (*p. 398*), or Mousseline Sauce (*p. 402*). Or flake and use in salads, creamed dishes, scalloped dishes, etc.

For Steamed Fish: Place fish in cheesecloth or cooking parchment on perforated rack or in wire basket directly above boiling water. Cover pot tightly. Cook until done (10 to 15 min. per lb. depending on thickness). Remove skin and bones. Season and serve immediately with sauces as for boiled fish.

Salted Cured Fish

Cod, mackerel, etc. require removing excess salt. Soak overnight in cold water. (Or soak for 2 hr. . . . then simmer in fresh water for 30 min.). Cook as desired.

CRISPY FRIED FISH

Cover fish fillets . . . pike, smelt, flounder, etc. with buttermilk. Sprinkle with salt (allow 1 tsp. salt for each lb.). Let stand about ½ hr. Drain. Dip each fillet in flour. Pan-fry. Serve with lemon.

FILETS ALMONDINE

Wonderful for fillets of sole, pike, whitefish.

Bake, broil, or pan-fry fish. Just before fish is done, add toasted, slivered, blanched almonds to butter. Pour over fish . . . season with salt and lemon juice. Serve immediately.

FISH À LA CREME

Delicately seasoned . . . baked in milk.

Place fish steaks (halibut, haddock, hake, etc.) in greased shallow baking dish. Scald milk (enough to cover) with bay leaf, parsley, onion, seasonings added. Pour over fish. Bake in mod. oven (350°) until fish tests done (about 40 min.). Brown top under broiler and serve.

GOLDEN BROILED STEAKS

Use shad, salmon, gar, cod, buffalofish, etc.

Arrange fish steaks (cut ¾" thick) on greased broiler rack. Spread with part of mixture of grated onion, soft butter, lemon juice, salt, pepper, and a little marjoram. Broil for 10 min. (2" under heat); turn, and spread with remaining mixture. Broil until golden brown. Serve hot with parsley garnish.

SCALLOP CASSEROLE

Arrange in greased 11x7" oblong baking dish . . .
 1 pt. scallops
Pour over part of . . .
 ½ to ¾ cup cream
Combine and sprinkle over scallops . . .
 3 cups soft bread crumbs
 ½ cup butter, melted
 1 tsp. salt
 ¼ tsp. pepper
 1 tbsp. celery seeds
Pour over remaining cream (it should come ¾ way up on scallops). Sprinkle with paprika. Bake.
TEMPERATURE: 375° (quick mod. oven).
TIME: Bake 30 to 40 min.
AMOUNT: 4 servings.

All you have to do —

To serve a Scandinavian holiday menu: have boiled lutefisk (cod treated in lye) with drawn butter, garnished with lingonberry sauce . . . with boiled potatoes, lefse, rice pudding, and sandbakkels.

FILET DE SOLE BONNE FEMME

Originally French, this recipe for preparing filet of sole in an unusually delicious way was brought to us from Scotland by Mrs. M. D. MacKenzie of Deland, Florida.

Mix 2 tbsp. melted butter, 2 to 3 tbsp. lemon juice (1 lemon), and ¼ cup finely chopped onion. Pour into an 11x7" oblong baking dish. Dip 1 lb. filet of sole or flounder in this mixture and turn to coat. Bake skin-side-up in mod. oven (350°) 20 to 30 min. Place on hot serving platter; pour over a thick fresh mushroom sauce thinned with the juices in which the fish was baked.

FISH TURBOT (pike, trout, bass, etc.)

Elegant dish from leftover cooked fish.

Arrange alternate layers of flaked cooked fish with Medium White Sauce (*p. 398*) (seasoned with onion salt, minced parsley, lemon juice, mace, and 1 egg yolk to each cup of sauce). Cover with buttered cracker crumbs and bake in mod. hot oven (400°) until browned on top (about 25 min.). Serve hot.

CODFISH BALLS

Favorite Sunday breakfast of New Englanders.

Cook together in boiling water until potatoes are tender . . .
 1 cup codfish (soaked and shredded)
 2 cups diced potatoes
Drain, shake over heat to dry, mash. Add . . .
 1 egg, beaten
 salt and pepper
 1 tsp. butter
Flour hands and roll mixture into balls the size of a small egg. Dip in flour; fry in deep fat (375°) until golden brown (3 to 5 min.). Serve with Egg Sauce (*p. 398*) or Tomato Sauce (*p. 283*).
AMOUNT: 8 servings.

SALMON LOAF

Flake and remove bones and skin . . .
 two 16-oz. cans salmon
Blend in . . .
 2 eggs
Stir in . . .
 liquid from salmon plus milk to make
  1½ cups
 3 cups coarse cracker crumbs
 2 tbsp. lemon juice
 2 tsp. chopped onion
 ¼ tsp. *each* salt and pepper
Spoon lightly into greased 9x5x3" loaf pan. Serve garnished with lemon wedges.
TEMPERATURE: 350° (mod. oven).
TIME: Bake 45 min.
AMOUNT: 8 servings.

HOW TO COOK SHELLFISH

Plunge live hard-shelled crab or shrimp into boiling water, well seasoned with lemon, parsley, celery leaves, etc. (Use plain salted boiling water for lobster.) Bring to boil, then simmer:

Shrimp: about 10 min. (shell turns pink).
Lobster: 10 min. per lb. for each.
Crab: about 20 min. (until red).

Drain. Let cool at room temperature.

HOW TO CLEAN SHRIMP

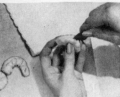

Peel off pink shells.   Remove black vein.
To serve: see "APPETIZERS," "MAIN DISHES."

TO SERVE LOBSTER

With sharp knife, split cooked lobster open from head to tail. Remove black vein, small sac back of head, and spongy lungs. Crack claws. Serve hot with melted butter, or chilled with mayonnaise. Or pry body meat and meat from claws loose with fork and use in hot dishes, salads, etc.

TO SERVE CRAB

Break off claws and legs from cooked crab; crack; remove meat. Break off tail or "apron." Force shell apart. Discard spongy material. Remove meat with nut pick; or if Dungeness Crab, tap crab against inside of dish. *6 crabs yield about 1 cup meat for salads, hot dishes, etc.*

BROILED LIVE LOBSTER

Place lobster on back; kill by cutting through head with a sharp knife or plunge into boiling water for 5 min. Split open, etc. as directed above. Place lobster, top shell-side-up, on broiler rack 4″ from heat. Cut tail crosswise twice (to help prevent curling). Brush with melted butter. Broil 6 to 8 min., turn over, and brush again with melted butter. Broil 4 to 6 min. until meat and shell are pink (or stuff as below and broil). Serve with side dish of melted butter and lemon.

BAKED STUFFED LOBSTER

To prepare stuffing: sauté the red roe and green liver in butter. Add finely crushed crackers. Season with onion juice, salt, pepper, minced parsley, and a bit of basil, marjoram, tarragon, and thyme. Stuff cavity of cleaned lobster lightly. Bake in hot oven (450°) for 12 to 15 min. Serve hot.

BROILED LOBSTER TAILS

Buy a 6 to 8-oz. lobster tail for each serving. Thaw frozen tails; cut away thin undershell with kitchen scissors. To keep tails from curling while they broil, bend each backward toward shell to crack. Place on broiler rack, shell-side-up, about 3″ from heat; broil 5 min. Turn flesh-side-up, brush with melted butter, sprinkle with paprika, broil 8 min. longer. Serve with melted butter and lemon wedges.

STEAMED CLAMS

Scrub clams under cold running water. Place in kettle with 1 cup water and 1 tsp. salt. Cover and steam about 8 min. or until shells begin to open. Serve in shells with individual dishes of melted butter and lemon juice. Serve strained broth in bouillon cups. *½ peck serves 4.*

FRENCH FRIED SEA FOOD

Oysters, Shrimp, Clams, Scallops.

Roll the sea food in Seasoned Flour (*p. 309*). Dip into egg, then into dry bread crumbs. Deep fat fry (*p. 334*). Drain on paper. Serve with catsup or Tartar Sauce (*p. 338*).

OLD-TIME FRIED CLAMS

Dip clams in Fritter Batter (*p. 96*) and deep fat fry (*p. 334*).

All you have to do –

To cook soft-shelled crabs: season prepared crabs. Roll in crumbs . . . beaten egg . . . and crumbs. Deep fat fry, broil, or pan-fry lightly.

FRIED OYSTERS

A wonderful suggestion from Harry Kleefisch of St. Louis.

Select large oysters. Dip in flour; then in 1 egg beaten with 2 tbsp. water; then in fine dry bread or cracker crumbs with salt and pepper added. Fry in deep fat (375°) until golden brown (2 to 5 min.). Drain on absorbent paper. Serve with lemon or hot Tartar Sauce (*p. 338*).

For other sea food recipes see MAIN DISHES (*pp. 281–283*).

STUFFING HINTS

2 to 4-day old bread is best for stuffing. Cut off crusts. Pull into ¼ or ½" crumbs, or cut in cubes.

A 1-lb. loaf of bread makes 8 cups loosely packed crumbs or cubes (2 qt.).

Plan a cup of stuffing for each pound of ready-to-cook weight.

Make dry or moist stuffing as desired.

Pack stuffing loosely into bird. Packing too tightly makes it heavy and soggy.

If the family has divided tastes about texture and seasoning of stuffing, pack some of each one in body cavity.

Bake extra stuffing separately in a pie pan during last 30 to 45 min. of roasting time.

Baste occasionally with poultry fat.

Stuff the bird just before roasting to avoid possibility of food poisoning. After the meal, remove stuffing from bird, place in separate dish, and chill.

BREAD STUFFING (Recipe)

	1 qt. for 4-lb. chicken	3 qt. for 12-lb. turkey
First, prepare coarse or fine crumbs or cubes, as desired................................	4 cups (1 qt.)	12 cups (3 qt.)
Melt in large heavy skillet................	⅓ cup butter	1 cup
Add and cook until yellow (stirring occasionally)...........................	¼ cup finely minced onion	¾ cup
Stir in some of bread crumbs. Heat, stirring to prevent excessive browning. Turn into deep bowl. Mix in lightly.....................	½ cup chopped celery (stalks and leaves)	1½ cups
	1 tsp. salt	1 tbsp. salt
	⅛ tsp. pepper	1 tsp. pepper
	1 tsp. dried sage, thyme, or marjoram	1 tbsp.
	poultry seasoning (to taste)	
	remaining crumbs	

For dry stuffing, add little or no liquid. For moist stuffing, mix in lightly with fork just enough hot water or broth to moisten dry crumbs. Cool and place stuffing in bird.

OYSTER STUFFING

The favorite of some for turkey.

Follow recipe above—*except* add 1 cup chopped drained oysters for each quart.

CHESTNUT STUFFING

Traditional with turkey.

Follow recipe above—*except* add 1 cup chopped boiled chestnuts for each quart.

APPLE STUFFING

Follow recipe above—*except* add 1 cup chopped apples for each quart.

ORANGE STUFFING

Nice with duck or goose.

Follow recipe above—*except* add 1 cup diced orange and 2 tsp. grated orange rind for each quart.

GIBLET STUFFING

Follow recipe above—*except* add chopped cooked giblets.

SAUSAGE STUFFING

Excellent for pheasant and veal.

Follow recipe above—*except* add ⅓ lb. bulk pack sausage, crumbled and browned, for each quart. Omit salt and use sausage fat as part of fat.

MUSHROOM-WILD RICE STUFFING

Elegant with roast pork or braised veal.

Melt in heavy skillet ½ cup butter or other fat. Add and cook for 5 min. 1 lb. sliced fresh mushrooms (or 8-oz. can). Remove mushrooms. Add ½ cup chopped onion, ½ cup minced parsley, 1 cup chopped celery. When onions turn yellow, add ⅓ cup water, 4 cups cooked wild rice, 1½ tsp. salt, ⅛ tsp. pepper. Add another ⅓ cup water and the cooked mushrooms. Simmer 15 min. Serve with roast.

AMOUNT: 8 servings.

WHOLE CRANBERRY SAUCE

Boil together 5 min. . . .
    2 cups water
    2 cups sugar
Add . . .
    4 cups cranberries
Boil together without stirring until all skins pop (about 5 min.). Cool.
AMOUNT: 4½ cups.

MOLDED CRANBERRY SAUCE

Boil Cranberry Sauce (*above*) until thick and cranberries are clear (15 min.). Pour into mold and chill.

CRANBERRY-ORANGE RELISH

Put through food chopper . . .
    rind and pulp of 1 large orange
    4 cups cranberries
Mix in and let stand several hours . . .
    2 cups sugar

ORANGE-CURRANT SAUCE

For roast duck, lamb, ham, or chicken.
Empty into bowl and break up with fork . . .
    ½ cup red currant jelly
Add . . .
    grated rind of 1 orange
    ⅛ tsp. *each* salt and cayenne pepper
    1 tbsp. prepared mustard dissolved in juice of 2 oranges
Beat well. Serve hot or cold.

TARTAR SAUCE

For fried or broiled fish, scallops, or shrimp.
Combine 1 cup mayonnaise, 1 tsp. grated onion, 2 tbsp. minced dill pickle, 1 tbsp. minced parsley, and 2 tsp. cut-up pimiento.
AMOUNT: 1 cup.

RED CINNAMON-APPLE RINGS

Cut cored, pared apples in ½″ rings or slices and cook until tender in syrup of 2 cups sugar, 1 cup water, ⅓ cup red cinnamon candies, and few drops red food coloring. Use as a garnish for meat.

BROILED FRUITS

For attractive garnishes around meats.
Drain canned pear, peach, or apricot halves, pineapple circles, or green gage plums. Place on absorbent paper to absorb excess juice. Brush with softened or melted butter. Then place under broiler a few minutes. Fill centers of pears, peaches, or apricots with red or green jelly.

RAISIN SAUCE

A perennial favorite for baked ham.
Melt over low heat in heavy saucepan . . .
    2 tbsp. butter
Blend in . . .
    2 tbsp. flour
Remove from heat, stir in . . .
    2 cups apple cider
    ½ cup seedless raisins
Bring to boil, stirring constantly. Boil 1 min. Remove from heat. Serve hot.
AMOUNT: 2 cups.

MINT SAUCE

A perennial favorite for roast lamb.
Dissolve . . .
    1½ tbsp. confectioners' sugar
in . . .
    3 tbsp. hot water
Cool and blend in . . .
    ⅓ cup finely minced mint leaves
    ½ cup very mild wine vinegar
Let stand ½ hr. Serve cool.
AMOUNT: 1 cup.

MAÎTRE D'HÔTEL BUTTER

Spread on steak or fish before serving.
Blend 3 tbsp. soft butter, 1 tbsp. lemon juice, 1 tbsp. minced parsley, ½ tsp. salt, ⅛ tsp. pepper.

EASY HORSE-RADISH SAUCE

Always welcome with ham loaf or tongue.
Fold 3 tbsp. well drained horse-radish and ½ tsp. salt into ½ cup whipping cream, whipped. For a different touch add ¼ cup tart applesauce.
AMOUNT: 1 cup.

TART APPLESAUCE

First choice with roast pork or duck.
Follow recipe for Old-fashioned Applesauce (*p. 226*) . . . using less sugar.

SPICED PEARS

Delicious with veal, lamb, or chicken.
Combine 1⅓ cups sugar, ⅓ cup water, ⅔ cup vinegar, 1½ sticks cinnamon, 12 whole cloves. Boil 20 min. Add 6 winter cooking pears (carefully pared). Cook until tender, 35 to 40 min. Stick 1 or 2 cloves in each pear. If desired, add red or green food coloring to tint pears.

PIE...A Symbol of Good Eating in a Good Land

If I were to design a coat of arms for our country, a pie would be the main symbol. It would appear with a background of wild berry bushes —and orchards. For pie is part of our history and tradition. By right of inheritance, adoption, and improvement, pies have become distinctively American. Every American home has its favorite pie.

Betty Crocker

PICK THE PIE THAT YOU PREFER
for a very special climax to your meal

Listed below are some of the many in this chapter.

BIRTHDAY SPECIAL

Make birthday dinner according to a menu requested by the guest of honor. For dessert, serve Birthday Pie (*p. 365*), complete with candles brightly lit.

PIES FOR SPECIAL HOLIDAYS

PIE IN A JIFFY

For the Crust

Use Betty Crocker Homogenized Pie Crust Mix for an easy-to-roll-out crust. No need to refrigerate it—you can keep it on your pantry shelf. It comes in sticks. And you can use 1 for a one-crust pie, or 2 for a two-crust pie.

For the Filling

Use pudding mixes—cooked or instant —for cream pies. But *never bake a meringue on an uncooked (instant) cream pie filling.* For fruit pies, try a prepared canned filling such as cherry, blueberry, apple, or pineapple.

PIE TOPPINGS

To make your pie pretty plus and to complement the flavor at the same time.

• **Sweetened Whipped Cream Topping:** See p. 222 for recipe. Spread on coconut, butterscotch, chocolate, or banana cream pie or on chiffon pies of various flavors. Or spoon onto individual pieces of fruit or berry pies. For variety, add chopped nuts or dates, finely crushed peanut brittle or peppermint candy, or grated orange rind.

Garnish plain whipped cream with toasted coconut, shaved chocolate, toasted slivered almonds, or chopped nuts.

For fancy swirls of whipped cream, use cooky press or canvas decorating bag with a large tip. Force whipped cream through onto pie.

• **Fruit Pie à la Mode:** Serve with topping of ice cream or Whipped Ice Cream (*p. 222*).

• **Crumb Topping:** When using a crumb crust, save some of the crumbs to sprinkle on top of the pie.

• **Fresh or Frozen Fruit Topping:** For vanilla cream or chiffon pie, spoon fruit over individual servings. Or pass a fruit sauce and let each person serve himself.

ACCOMPANIMENT OF CHEESE: Cut Cheddar or Swiss cheese in wedges or fancy shapes. Shape cream cheese into balls and roll in nuts, or whip it and scoop on individual pieces of pie.

FOR A LUNCHEON DESSERT

Chiffon pies are especially nice because they can be made in advance and chilled. Serve with salted nuts and pineapple cubes on sticks.

STORING LEFTOVER PIE

If there is any!

• **Fruit Pie:** Just cover with waxed paper or transparent wrap and place on a cupboard shelf. Freshen by heating a few minutes in a warm oven. *Or* cover with aluminum foil which may be left on when the pie is heated in a warm oven.

• **Cream, Custard, Chiffon, or Meringue Pie:** If kept several hours, store in the refrigerator. These pies cannot be freshened by heating.

FREEZING PIES AND PASTRY

Make several pies . . . freeze some!

 Fruit pies, pumpkin or sweet potato pie, mince pies, and chiffon pies may be frozen for 2 to 3 months. Baked and unbaked pie shells and graham cracker shells also freeze successfully. For more detailed information, see pp. 23–24.

NUMBER OF SERVINGS PER PIE

An 8″ pie cuts into 5 or 6 pieces. A 9″ pie cuts into 7 or 8 pieces.

VANILLA CREAM PARTY PIE

Quickly made using mixes.

Make . . .

    8 or 9″ Baked Pie Shell with Betty Crocker Homogenized Pie Crust Mix

Mix . . .

    1 pkg. vanilla pudding mix
    1 tsp. unflavored gelatin
    ¼ tsp. salt
    2 cups milk

Cook according to directions on pudding mix pkg. Cool covered until it begins to set.
Fold in half of . . .
    1 cup whipping cream, whipped stiff

Pour into baked pie shell. Spoon rest of whipped cream on top. Garnish gaily with fresh berries.

PIES AND PASTRIES

Pie is as American as the Fourth of July. Through those first lean and hungry years in New England and Virginia, courageous pioneer mothers contrived "pyes" out of the few simple foods at hand. They sliced the top off pumpkins, scooped out fiber and seeds, filled the pumpkins with milk, and set them to bake on the open hearth. Later, a greased pan sprinkled with rye meal was filled with pumpkin diluted with milk and spices. Still later, they added the pastry crust.

The "pyes" of old England were baked in a long deep dish called a coffin, and "pye receipts" up to Martha Washington's day directed colonial cooks to "first make your coffin." The first American pie pans were designed round to cut the corners, flat and shallow so pies would "go a long way." As orchards were planted and food became plentiful, pies gradually took on the "new world" look—large and richly crusted, lush with fruit and abundant fillings. Pies had become distinctively American, as glamorous and exciting as this thrilling new nation!

Step right up and take your choice! What a variety of pies you will find on the following pages! There are pies for every taste and for every occasion—delectable fillings encased in crisp, flaky, melt-in-the-mouth pastry. Some are brand new pies. Others are "tried-and-true" favorites.

The old expresssion "easy as pie" has now come true, for our staff has worked out new simplified methods. No guessing as to amount of water, no chilling of the pastry, no long, laborious preparation of fillings. The recipes are adjusted to your family and needs, to fit a 9″ pie pan or an 8″ pie pan. These new ways with pies will save you time, work, and worry. They mean satisfying adventures in good eating.

AMERICA'S CHOICE OF PIES

Apple   Lemon Meringue   Cherry

STANDARD PASTRY FOR TWO-CRUST PIE
Make with solid shortening. Always flaky and tender. Definite measurements give perfect results!

For 9″ Pie

2 cups *sifted* GOLD MEDAL Flour

1 tsp. salt

⅔ cup lard (or ⅔ cup plus 2 tbsp.
hydrogenated shortening such as Spry, Crisco, Swift'ning, or Snowdrift)

¼ cup water

For 8″ Pie

1½ cups *sifted* GOLD MEDAL Flour

¾ tsp. salt

½ cup lard (or ½ cup plus 2 tbsp.
hydrogenated shortening such as Spry, Crisco, Swift'ning, or Snowdrift)

3 tbsp. water

1 Measure flour into mixing bowl and mix salt through it. With pastry blender, cut in shortening until shortening particles are the size of giant peas.

2 Sprinkle with water, a tbsp. at a time . . . mixing lightly with a fork until all the flour is moistened.

3 Gather dough together with fingers so it cleans the bowl.

4 Press firmly into a ball. Then roll out, or keep in waxed paper in refrigerator.

GOOD TOOLS Use these for ease and success in pie making.

PASTRY BLENDER . . . cuts shortening into the flour. (Or use two knives in cutting motion.)

PIE TAPE (purchased in housewares departments of most stores) . . . or a 1½″ strip of aluminum foil or wet cloth . . . prevents edge of crust from becoming too brown. (*See step 12, p. 345.*)

CANVAS PASTRY CLOTH, STOCKINET COVERING FOR ROLLING PIN . . . will help avoid sticking of dough or having to add extra flour. (*See step 2, p. 344.*)

OVEN GLASS, ENAMEL, ALUMILITE, OR DULL METAL PIE PANS . . . absorb heat to give your pie crust a nice golden brown color. Shiny metal does not bake the undercrust as well because it reflects the heat. The pies in this book have been tested for pie pans 1¼″ deep. Measure from inside rim to inside rim, standard pans are 8 or 9″ across.

How to Make
A TWO-CRUST PIE Follow steps on p. 343—then

1 Divide dough about in half. Round up larger part on lightly floured cloth-covered board . . . the rolling pin covered with stockinet. Flour rubbed into covered board and covered rolling pin keeps dough from sticking . . . yet is not taken up by dough.

2 Flatten with hand, roll out not quite $\frac{1}{8}''$ thick. Roll lightly, being careful not to add extra flour as that makes pastry tough. Keep rounding edge of pastry. If it begins to break apart, pinch broken edges together immediately.

3 Keep pastry circular and roll it about 1″ larger around than inverted pie pan to line pan and allow for depth.

4 Fold pastry in half. Carefully transfer to pie pan.

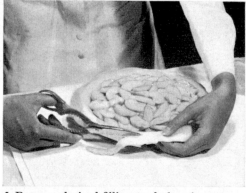

5 Unfold, and ease pastry loosely into pie pan, being careful not to stretch, for this will cause pastry to shrink during baking.

6 Prepare desired filling, and place in pastry-lined pie pan. Trim off over-hanging edges with scissors.

7 Roll out other part of dough for top crust large enough to extend 1″ beyond edge of pie pan. Measure by holding pie pan over rolled round of pastry.

8 Fold pastry for top crust in half. Make several slits near center to allow steam to escape or top crust will puff up leaving a hollow space underneath.

9 Moisten edge of bottom pastry with water. Carefully place folded pastry evenly on top of filling. Unfold. Leave a ½″ rim of pastry beyond edge of pan. Trim off any extra edges.

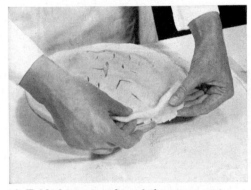

10 Fold the extra edge of the top pastry under the edge of the lower pastry. Seal thoroughly by pressing together with fingers on edge of pie pan.

11 Build up a high stand-up rim. Form a pretty fluted edge by firmly placing the right index finger on the inside of the rim, the left thumb and index finger around the pastry at that point. Pinch. Repeat all around the edge of the pie. Sharpen the points by pinching each one firmly.

12 To prevent edge of crust from becoming too brown, cover with a 1½″ strip of aluminum foil or wet pie tape or cloth. Bake pie as directed in each recipe. Remove aluminum foil about 15 min. before end of baking time or pie tape or cloth *immediately after* pie is taken from oven.

STANDARD PASTRY FOR ONE-CRUST PIE (8 or 9") Make with solid shortening. Pictures on making pastry on p. 343 show just how!

Mix	{ 1 cup *sifted* GOLD MEDAL Flour { ½ tsp. salt
Cut in with pastry blender	⅓ cup lard (or ⅓ cup plus 1 tbsp. hydrogenated shortening such as Spry, Crisco, Swift'ning, Snowdrift)
Sprinkle with	2 tbsp. water

Mix with fork until all the flour is moistened. Gather dough together and press firmly into a ball.

How to Make

A ONE-CRUST PIE in which filling and crust are baked together.

Make pastry following recipe above. Using whole ball of pastry, follow step pictures 1–5 on p. 344 for rolling and fitting. After pastry has been eased into pan, trim ragged edges with scissors, leaving ½″ overhanging edge of pan.

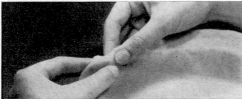

1 Fold extra pastry back and under, and build up a high fluted edge to hold a generous amount of filling.

2 Hook points of fluted edge under pan rim to help prevent shrinking during baking. *Do not prick pastry.* Pour most of filling into pastry-lined pie pan.

3 To prevent spilling, place pan on rack in oven. Pour in remaining filling. Bake. For baking temperature and time, see each recipe.

How to Make

A BAKED PIE SHELL to hold filling which is added later.

Follow directions for One-crust Pie (*opposite column*) through Step 1.

After building up fluted edge and hooking points of edge under pan rim, prick pastry thoroughly to prevent puffing during baking. (If pastry persists in puffing up, quickly reach in oven, prick again in a few places.) Bake until golden brown.

TEMPERATURE: 475° (very hot oven).
TIME: Bake 8 to 10 min.

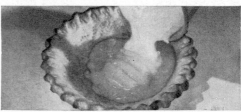

Finish pie according to each recipe. For *meringue pies*, pour in hot filling and top with Meringue (*p. 362*). For *chiffon pies*, pile filling into cooled shell and chill several hours until set.

STIR-N-ROLL PASTRY Tender, flaky, golden brown pastry that stays crisp and fresh even when refrigerated. Especially good for cream and chiffon pies.

TWO-CRUST PIE (8 or 9″)

Mix . . . . { 2 cups *sifted* GOLD MEDAL Flour
{ 1½ tsp. salt

Pour into measuring cup (but don't stir together) . . . . { ½ cup cooking (salad) oil
{ ¼ cup cold milk

1 Then pour oil and milk all at the same time into the flour.

2 Stir with fork until mixed. Dough looks moist, but isn't sticky. Press into smooth ball. Cut in halves; flatten halves slightly.

3 For BOTTOM CRUST: Place one half between 2 sheets of waxed paper (12″ square). Roll out gently to edges of paper. Dampen table top to prevent slipping. Peel off top paper. If dough tears, mend without moistening.

4 Lift paper and pastry by top corners. Place paper-side-up in pie pan. Peel off paper. Fit pastry into pan. Add filling. Trim crust even with rim.

ONE-CRUST PIE (8 or 9″) In which filling and crust are baked together.

Follow directions for Two-crust Pie above. But use:

{ 1⅓ cups *sifted* GOLD MEDAL Flour
{ 1 tsp. salt
{ ⅓ cup cooking (salad) oil
{ 3 tbsp. cold milk

Do not prick. After fitting pastry into pie pan, build up fluted edge. Pour in filling. Bake. For baking temperature and time, see each recipe.

BAKED PIE SHELL (8 or 9″) To hold filling which is added later.

Follow recipe above for pastry. Prick dough in pan thoroughly with fork. Bake until golden brown.

TEMPERATURE: 475° (very hot oven).

TIME: Bake 8 to 10 min.

5 For TOP CRUST: Roll as for bottom crust; place over filling. Trim to rim of pie pan. Seal by pressing gently with fork or by fluting edge. Cut 3 or 4 small slits near center to allow steam to escape during baking.

Bake until golden brown. For baking temperature and time, see each recipe.

SIMPLIFIED PUFF PASTRY Extra rich, extra flaky . . . for very special pies or fancy tarts.

Make Standard Pastry (*see pp. 343—346*). Roll out ⅛" thick.

1 Dot with bits of firm butter (use ⅓ cup). Too hard or soft butter breaks through.

2 Fold so two sides meet in center . . . seal by pressing side edges of pastry with fingers.

3 Fold ends to the center and seal. Then wrap in waxed paper and chill.

When ready to roll out, follow step pictures on pp. 344–345 for rolling and fitting. Or make into tart shells (*below*).

BAKED TART SHELLS Individual shells to fill as you like. Perfect for parties.

Make Standard Pastry for 8" Two-crust Pie (*p. 343*) or Simplified Puff Pastry (*above*). Divide pastry into 8 equal parts. Roll each part into 4" round or 4" square.

1 Fit pieces of pastry over backs of muffin cups or custard cups, making pleats so pastry will fit close. (Pastry may be rolled into rounds and fitted into individual pie pans or tart pans.)

2 Prick with fork to prevent puffing during baking. Place the pastry-covered or lined cups or pans on baking sheet. Bake in very hot oven (475°) 8 to 10 min.

3 When cool, remove from small cups or pans. Fill with any desired pie filling or special tart filling (*p. 370*). NOTE: If thinner tart shells are desired, divide pastry into 10 equal parts.

GRAHAM CRACKER CRUST
Good with refrigerated pies.

For 9″ Pie	**For 8″ Pie**

Blend thoroughly in pie pan . . .

1½ cups graham cracker crumbs (18 crackers)	1¼ cups (15 crackers)
3 tbsp. sugar	2 tbsp.
⅓ cup butter, melted	¼ cup

If desired, save ¼ cup blended mixture for topping. Press remaining mixture firmly in an even layer against bottom and sides of pie pan. Bake in mod. oven (350°) for 10 min. Cool. Fill with chiffon or cream-type filling (*pp. 364–368*).

COOKY CRUMB CRUSTS
Ginger, Chocolate, Vanilla.

Follow recipe for Graham Cracker Crust (*at left*)—*except* use gingersnaps, or chocolate or vanilla wafers in place of graham crackers, and omit sugar.

NUT CRUST
Delicious for cream pies.

Add ¼ cup finely chopped nuts to Standard or Stir-N-Roll Pastry for One-crust Pie.

ORANGE PASTRY
For lemon or orange pies.

Use orange juice in place of water in making pastry. Add ½ tsp. grated orange rind for one-crust pie.

EASY EDGES

FORK: Fold edge of pastry under. Use the sharp tines of a fork to press around the edge. To prevent sticking, dip your fork in flour every few times. For variety, press fork at intervals around edge of pie.

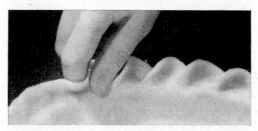

SHELL: Fold edge of pastry under and build up rim. Place thumb on edge of pie and press and twist the knuckle of the index finger toward the thumb.

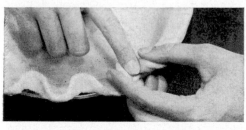

RUFFLE: Fold edge of pastry under and build up rim. Place left thumb and index finger ½" apart on outside of pastry rim. With right index finger, pull pastry between fingers. Repeat.

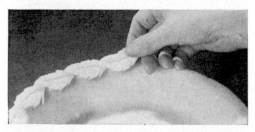

LEAF EDGE: Cut small pastry leaves. Dampen rim of pastry-lined pie pan; place leaves slightly overlapping. Press lightly to fasten.

GLAMOUR TOPS

LATTICE TOP

Line pie pan with half of pastry for Two-crust Pie. Trim, leaving 1" overhanging. Roll rest of pastry; cut into ½" strips. (Pastry wheel gives a pretty edge to the strips.) Moisten edge of bottom pastry with water. Lay half of pastry strips across filling 1" apart. Weave first cross strip through center. Add another cross strip, first folding back every other strip going the other way. Continue weaving until lattice is complete. Fold lower crust over pastry strips. Press firmly around edge to seal strips to the rim. Flute edge.

RIMLESS LATTICE TOP

Shown in picture on page 342.

Follow recipe for Lattice Top (*above*) but leave only ½" overhanging. Fold under. When lattice is completely woven, fold pastry strips under folded edge. Press to seal.

PASTRY CUTOUTS: Cut rolled pastry for top crust into appropriate shapes, such as pumpkins for Halloween, bells for Christmas. Brush them with water and sprinkle with sugar (colored, if desired). Bake on baking sheet. Cool. Then place on finished pie filling.

FOR A SHINY TOP: Brush the top crust with milk before baking.

FOR A SUGARY TOP: Using fingers, moisten the top crust with water; sprinkle evenly with granulated sugar before baking.

FOR A GLAZED TOP: Brush top crust lightly with beaten egg or with egg yolk mixed with a little water before baking.

APPLE PIE (✍ Recipe) From about 1630, Apple Pie was served almost daily in New England . . . when the newly planted orchards were bearing fruit. See color picture on p. 342.

Know your apples! Select tart, firm, juicy apples, such as Jonathans, Winesaps, Greenings, Duchess, Wealthies, or Roman Beauties. 1 lb. apples equals 3 med. apples or 3 cups sliced apples.

Peel apples, quarter them, remove cores, and slice ¼″ thick. If apples are dry, sprinkle with a little water. Use the smaller or larger amount of sugar according to sweetness of apples and desired taste. For more tartness, add a little lemon juice.

Make Pastry for Two-crust Pie of desired size. Line pie pan. (*See pp. 343–345, 347.*)

For the Filling	For 9″ Pie	For 8″ Pie
Mix	¾ to 1 cup sugar 1 tsp. cinnamon or nutmeg	½ to ¾ cup ¾ tsp.
Mix lightly through	6 to 7 cups sliced apples	4 to 5 cups
Heap up in pastry-lined pie pan.		
Dot with	1½ tbsp butter	1 tbsp.

Cover with top crust which has slits cut in it. Seal and flute. Bake until crust is nicely browned and apples are cooked through (*test with fork*). Serve warm or cold . . . may be topped with cream, whipped cream, or ice cream.

TEMPERATURE: 425° (hot oven).

TIME: Bake 50 to 60 min.

GREEN APPLE PIE

"When trees in apple orchards with fruit are bending down." Even 16th century English cook books refer to "pyes of greene apples."

Follow ✍ recipe above—*except* use about ½ cup more sugar for tart green apples and only ½ tsp. nutmeg (or cinnamon). If apples are extra juicy, mix about 2 tbsp. flour with the sugar to thicken the juice.

FRENCH APPLE PIE

From a famous Hollywood tearoom.

Make Pastry for One-crust Pie. Line pie pan. (*See pp. 346–347.*) Add filling as in ✍ recipe above—*except* use minimum amount of sugar. Sprinkle with

CRUMB TOPPING

For 9″ Pie	For 8″ Pie
Mix until crumbly . . .	
½ cup butter	⅓ cup
½ cup brown sugar (packed)	⅓ cup
1 cup GOLD MEDAL Flour	¾ cup

Bake in mod. hot oven (400°) 45 to 55 min. Serve warm with cream or ice cream.

All you have to do —

To save time and work . . . also vitamins and minerals: use unpeeled apples in pie. Adds color and flavor.

DEEP DISH APPLE PIE

Lots of apples .. no bottom crust.

13x9″ oblong pan	**9″ square pan**
Make pastry for . . .	
8″ Two-crust Pie (see pp. 343–345, 347)	One-crust Pie (see pp. 346–347)

Roll pastry about 1″ larger around than baking dish. Make several slits in crust for steam to escape during baking.

Follow ✍ recipe above for filling—*except* make . . .

double recipe for 9″ pie	double recipe for 8″ Pie

Place crust on filling, fold edge under and flute just inside edge of pan. Bake in hot oven (425°) about 50 min., until lightly browned.

DUTCH APPLE PIE

Rich sweet cream and apples. "Perfectly delicious!" says Blythe P. Thompson (Mrs. Roy Thompson) of our staff.

Follow ✍ recipe above—*except* make extra large slits in top crust. Then, 5 min. before baking time is up, remove pie from oven. Pour ½ cup heavy cream through slits in top crust. Return to oven and finish baking.

LITTLE PASTRIES

in sumptuous array . . . whirl the tray . . . take your pick!

Berry Basket Tarts of Glazed Strawberry, Grape, Blueberry.
Fluted Tarts of Peach, Lemon Fluff, Chocolate, Glazed Raspberry, Coconut.
Individual Pies of Pumpkin, Cherry, Lemon Meringue, French Strawberry.

FRESH BERRY PIE (⚲ Recipe) With thick, fruity juice bubbling through the crust.

Select ripe, juicy berries—blueberries, blackberries, raspberries, strawberries, loganberries, or boysenberries, etc. Berries picked at the height of the season are more flavorful, require less sugar, and make the most delicious pies.

1 Wash berries, drain well.   **2** Then pick them over.   **3** Remove stems and hulls.

Use the smaller or larger amount of sugar according to your taste and the sweetness of the fruit. Very tart fruit may require even more sugar (up to 1½ cups for 1 qt.).

Make Pastry for Two-crust Pie of desired size. Line pie pan. (*See pp. 343–345, 347.*)

For the Filling	For 9″ Pie	For 8″ Pie
Mix	1 to 1½ cups sugar ⅓ cup GOLD MEDAL Flour ½ tsp. cinnamon	⅔ to 1 cup ¼ cup ½ tsp.
Mix lightly through	4 cups fresh berries	3 cups
Pour berries into pastry-lined pie pan. Dot with	1½ tbsp. butter	1 tbsp.

Cover with top crust which has slits cut in it. Bake until crust is nicely browned and juice begins to bubble through slits in crust. Serve slightly warm, not hot.

TEMPERATURE: 425° (hot oven).

TIME: Bake 35 to 45 min.

RASPBERRY, BLACKBERRY, STRAWBERRY, LOGANBERRY, BOYSENBERRY, OR GOOSEBERRY PIE

Follow ⚲ recipe above using minimum amount of sugar. Halve large strawberries.

FRESH CHERRY PIE

The chosen dessert to top off a mountain trout luncheon at that charming, steeped-in-tradition resort, The Broadmoor, Colorado Springs, Colorado. See color picture on p. 342.

Follow ⚲ recipe above—*except* use pitted sour pie cherries in place of berries; increase sugar, add almond flavoring. Use:

For 9″ Pie	For 8″ Pie
1⅓ cups sugar	1 cup
4 drops almond flavoring	3 drops

BLUEBERRY PIE

"A summertime treat for us when wild blueberries are ripe in our north woods!" says Mrs. William Eades of Nisswa, Minnesota. "We like to serve it slightly warm . . . with either ice cream or whipped cream on top."

Follow ⚲ recipe above using minimum amount of sugar. For tart flavor, add 1 tbsp. lemon juice.

PEACH OR APRICOT PIE

Juicy with golden fruit. Mary McNaughton, now Mrs. Lou Taylor of Wausau, Wisconsin, when on our staff did much testing on these pies.

Follow ⚲ recipe above—*except* use sliced firm peaches or apricots instead of berries. Use minimum amount of sugar and 1 tbsp. less flour.

FRESH RHUBARB PIE (♪ Recipe)

Tart, refreshing, springtime delight. Mrs. Edward A. Cook of Wayzata, Minnesota, President of the National Council of Teachers of English, says, "One of the joys of living in the country comes in the spring. Then I pick my own rosy pink rhubarb and treat myself often to fresh rhubarb pie."

For mild flavor, choose early pink rhubarb. If tender and pink, do not peel. Cut into 1″ pieces (1 lb. makes 2 cups). Amount of sugar depends on tartness of rhubarb. Early rhubarb requires less sugar. Make your pie shallow.

Make Pastry for Two-crust Pie of desired size. Line pie pan. (*See pp. 343–345, 347.*)

For the Filling	For 9″ Pie	For 8″ Pie
Mix . . .	1⅓ to 2 cups sugar	1 to 1½ cups
	⅓ cup GOLD MEDAL Flour	¼ cup
Mix lightly through . . .	4 cups cut-up rhubarb	3 cups
Pour into pastry-lined pie pan.		
Dot with . . .	1½ tbsp. butter	1 tbsp.

Cover with top crust which has slits cut in it. Sprinkle with sugar. Bake until crust is nicely browned and juice begins to bubble through slits. Serve slightly warm.

TEMPERATURE: 425° (hot oven).

TIME: Bake 40 to 50 min.

RHUBARB CUSTARD PIE

Something special . . . the tart flavor of fresh rhubarb modified by sweet custard.

Make Pastry for Two-crust Pie of desired size. Line pie pan. (*See pp. 343–345, 347.*)

	For 9″ Pie	For 8″ Pie
Beat slightly . . .	3 eggs	2
Add . . .	3 tbsp. milk	2 tbsp.
Mix and stir in . . .	2 cups sugar	1½ cups
	¼ cup GOLD MEDAL Flour	3 tbsp.
	¾ tsp. nutmeg	½ tsp.
Mix in . . .	4 cups cut-up pink rhubarb	3 cups
Pour into pastry-lined pie pan.		
Dot with . . .	1 tbsp. butter	2 tsp.

Cover with a lattice top (*p. 349*). Bake until nicely browned. Serve slightly warm.

TEMPERATURE: 400° (mod. hot oven).

TIME: Bake 50 to 60 min.

All you have to do—

To keep fresh rhubarb fresh and crisp: wrap in wet towel in refrigerator. Save time by cutting up several stalks at once (*p. 31*).

STRAWBERRY OR BLUEBERRY-RHUBARB PIE

An inspiration of Mrs. Sherman Child, Minneapolis, Minnesota.

Follow ♪ recipe above—*except* substitute fresh strawberries or blueberries for half the rhubarb. Use the minimum amount of sugar.

PINEAPPLE-RHUBARB PIE

Follow ♪ recipe above—*except* substitute about 1 cup drained crushed pineapple for about 1 cup of the rhubarb. Use the minimum amount of sugar.

DEEP DISH FRUIT PIE

Fresh fruit baked with top crust only. Use rhubarb, berries, cherries, peaches, or apricots.

Make Pastry for One-crust Pie (*see pp. 346–347*). Roll into 10″ square; make several slits to allow steam to escape during baking. Follow ♪ recipe above or ♪ recipe on p. 352 for Berry, Cherry, Peach, or Apricot Pie—*except* make double amount of filling for 9″ pie. Place in 9″ square pan. Cover with pastry square. Fold edge of crust under; flute just inside edge of pan. Bake in hot oven (425°) until lightly browned, 40 to 50 min. Serve warm with whipped cream or ice cream.

FRESH FRUIT PIES Special favorites ... as homey as can be.

GRAPE PIE
Prize of the harvest season ... sweet, tart, juicy, fragrant with rich purple grapes. One of the many culinary secrets and recipes contributed by an ideal homemaker, Mrs. Philip Gearty of Minneapolis, Minnesota.

Make Pastry for Two-crust Pie of desired size. Line pie pan. (*See pp. 343–345, 347.*)

For the Filling	For 9″ Pie	For 8″ Pie
Remove and save skins from	5⅓ cups Concord grapes	4 cups
Put pulp into saucepan without water and bring to a rolling boil. While hot, rub through strainer to remove seeds. Mix strained pulp with skins.		
Mix lightly through grapes	1⅓ cups sugar / ¼ cup GOLD MEDAL Flour	1 cup / 3 tbsp.
Sprinkle with	1¼ tsp. lemon juice / ¼ tsp. salt	1 tsp. / ¼ tsp.
Pour grapes into pastry-lined pie pan. Dot with	1½ tbsp. butter	1 tbsp.

Cover with top crust which has slits cut in it. Bake until crust is nicely browned and juice begins to bubble through slits in crust. Serve cool or slightly warm, not hot.

TEMPERATURE: 425° (hot oven).

TIME: Bake 35 to 45 min.

CRANBERRY PIE
From down Cape Cod way.

Make Pastry for Two-crust Pie of desired size. Line pie pan. (*See pp. 343–345, 347.*)

For 9″ Pie	For 8″ Pie
Mix in saucepan . . .	
1½ to 2 cups sugar	1 to 1½ cups
¼ cup GOLD MEDAL Flour	3 tbsp.
¼ tsp. salt	¼ tsp.
Add . . .	
3 cups halved cranberries	2 cups
½ cup water	⅓ cup

Bring slowly to a boil, and boil gently 5 min., stirring constantly. Remove from heat and blend in . . .

½ tsp. almond flavoring	¼ tsp.

Pour into pastry-lined pie pan. Cover with top crust which has slits cut in it. Bake until crust is nicely browned. Serve slightly warm.

TEMPERATURE: 425° (hot oven).

TIME: Bake 30 to 40 min.

EARLY AMERICAN PEAR PIE
Delicately spiced and baked to a luscious glaze. Pear Pie vied in popularity with apple pie during the early days of our country.

Make Pastry for Two-crust Pie of desired size. Line pie pan. (*See pp. 343–345, 347.*)

For 9″ Pie	For 8″ Pie
Pare and slice firm pears. (1 pear makes about 1 cup sliced.)	
Mix . . .	
¾ cup sugar	½ cup
1 tsp. nutmeg or cinnamon	¾ tsp.
2 tbsp. flour	1½ tbsp.
Mix lightly through . . .	
6 cups sliced pears	4 cups
Pour into pastry-lined pie pan.	
Dot with . . .	
1½ tbsp. butter	1 tbsp.

Cover with top crust which has slits cut in it. Bake until nicely browned. Serve cool. If desired, garnish with cheese, whipped cream, or ice cream.

TEMPERATURE: 425° (hot oven).

TIME: Bake 35 to 45 min.

FRENCH STRAWBERRY GLACÉ PIE (⌀ Recipe) *An exciting and sparkling combination—flaky pastry, cream cheese, and ripe red berries.*

Make Baked Pie Shell of desired size (*pp. 346–347*).

For the Filling	For 9 or 8″ Pie
Wash, drain, and hull	1 qt. strawberries
Simmer together about 3 min.............	{ 1 cup strawberries ⅔ cup water
Blend and add to boiling mixture..........	{ 1 cup sugar 3 tbsp. cornstarch ⅓ cup water
Boil 1 min., stirring constantly. Cool. If desired, spread over bottom of cooled baked pie shell	3-oz. pkg. cream cheese, softened

Save out ½ cup choice berries; put remaining 2½ cups berries in baked pie shell. Cover with cooked mixture, and garnish with the ½ cup berries.

Refrigerate until firm—about 2 hr. Serve with Sweetened Whipped Cream (*p. 222*) or ice cream.

FRENCH RASPBERRY, BLACKBERRY, BLUEBERRY, OR CHERRY GLACÉ PIE

Follow ⌀ recipe above—*except*, in place of strawberries, use fresh raspberries, blackberries, blueberries, or pitted sweet cherries.

ARKANSAS APPLE PIE
Lattice-topped apple pie made with partially cooked apples ... the thickened syrup poured on the baked pie to give it a lovely glaze.

Make Pastry for 9″ Two-crust Pie (*pp. 343–345, 347*).

Slice thin with skins on ...
  8 to 10 cups tart red apples
Cook covered until tender ...
  the sliced apples
  1½ cups sugar
  ½ cup water
Drain apples, saving juice, and pile in pastry-lined pie pan. Sprinkle with ...
  1 tbsp. lemon juice
  ½ tsp. cinnamon
Dot with ...
  ¼ cup butter

Place wide strips of pastry across top of pie to make a lattice top (*p. 349*). Bake until nicely browned. Cook juice until it is thickened. Pour over top of baked pie as soon as it comes from the oven.

TEMPERATURE: 425° (hot oven).
TIME: Bake 30 to 35 min.

STREUSEL CREAM PEACH PIE
Custardy peach filling with rich crunchy topping . . . a pleasing contrast.

Make Pastry for 9″ One-crust Pie (*pp. 346–347*).

Arrange in pastry-lined pie pan ...
  4 cups quartered peeled peaches (8 to 10)
Sprinkle over peaches ...
  ½ cup sugar
  ½ tsp. nutmeg, if desired
Beat together, then pour over peaches and sugar ...
  1 egg
  2 tbsp. cream
Mix until crumbly ...
  ¼ cup brown sugar (packed)
  ½ cup GOLD MEDAL Flour
  ¼ cup soft butter

Sprinkle crumb mixture over fruit in pie pan. Bake until browned. Serve slightly warm. For an elegant garnish, pass a bowl of whipped ice cream or cultured sour cream.

TEMPERATURE: 425° (hot oven).
TIME: Bake 35 to 45 min.

CANNED CHERRY PIE (♪ Recipe) Overflowing with bright, sparkly fruit and juice.

Canned fruit pies require less fruit than those made with fresh fruit because the fruit has been precooked. To determine amount of sugar needed, look on label to see if fruit was packed in syrup. Use minimum sugar for fruit packed in syrup, maximum sugar for water-packed fruit. The proportion of fruit and juice in the same size can may vary with the brand. Because of this, we measure fruit and juice separately. There are approximately 1¾ cups cherries and 1 cup juice in a no. 2 can.

Make Pastry for Two-crust Pie of desired size. Line pie pan. (*See pp. 343–345, 347.*)

For the Filling	For 9" Pie	For 8" Pie
Mix in saucepan	¾ to 1 cup sugar ¼ cup GOLD MEDAL Flour ½ tsp. cinnamon ½ cup fruit juice	½ to ⅔ cup 2½ tbsp. ¼ tsp. ⅓ cup
Cook over med. heat, stirring constantly, until mixture thickens and boils. Pour hot thickened juice over.	3½ cups drained, pitted cherries	2⅓ cups
Mix lightly. Pour into pastry-lined pie pan. Dot with	1 tbsp. butter	1 tbsp.

Cover with top crust which has slits cut in it. Bake until nicely browned and juice begins to bubble through slits in crust Serve warm.

NOTE: In place of cinnamon, ¼ tsp. almond flavoring may be used in Canned Cherry Pie.

TEMPERATURE: 425° (hot oven).
TIME: Bake 35 to 45 min.

CANNED BLUEBERRY OR BOYSENBERRY PIE

Slightly tart . . . and oh so good.

Follow ♪ recipe above—*except* add lemon juice—2 tbsp. for 9" pie, 1 tbsp. for 8" pie—before pouring mixture into pastry-lined pie pan.

All you have to do —

To save pre-cooking fruit and juice before putting into pastry-lined shell: use tapioca instead of flour to thicken the filling. Omit flour. Using 2½ to 3 tbsp. quick-cooking tapioca for 9" pie, 1½ to 2 tbsp. for 8" pie, combine sugar, spices, tapioca. Mix through fruit and juice before pouring into pastry-lined pie pan.

FROZEN FRUIT PIE

Frozen fruit which retains its shape when thawed (such as cherries, blueberries, peaches, and apricots) may be substituted for canned fruit—*except* reduce sugar about ½ cup.

CANNED PEACH, APRICOT, OR PLUM PIE

Home canned fruit makes this super special.

Follow ♪ recipe above—*except* use canned sliced peaches, apricot halves, or plums and juice in place of cherries and juice.

PINEAPPLE PIE

"Very quick . . . and easy to prepare!" says Lynn Auten of our staff, who developed this recipe.

Make Pastry for Two-crust Pie of desired size. Line pie pan. (*See pp. 343–345, 347.*)

Mix in saucepan . . .
   1 cup sugar
   ¼ tsp. salt
   3 tbsp. cornstarch

Stir in . . .
   no. 2 can crushed pineapple and juice
   (2½ cups)

Cook over med. heat, stirring constantly, until mixture thickens and boils. Boil 1 min. Pour into pastry-lined pie pan. *Quickly* cover with top crust which has slits cut in it. Bake.

TEMPERATURE: 425° (hot oven).
TIME: Bake 25 to 30 min.

OLD-FASHIONED MINCE PIE *One of the earliest pies—meat and fruit minced for a rich, hearty filling. Mrs. Bruce Silcox, now of Alexandria, Virginia, made One-crust Mince Pies . . . topping the filling with beautiful Pastry Cutouts (p. 349) when she was on our staff.*

Make Pastry for Two-crust Pie of desired size. Line pie pan. *(See pp. 343–345, 347.)*

For the Filling		For 9″ Pie	For 8″ Pie
Mix	{	3 cups mincemeat (28 to 30-oz. jar)	2 cups (19-oz. jar)
		1½ cups chopped apple	1 cup

Pour into pastry-lined pie pan. Cover with top crust which has slits cut in it. Bake until crust is nicely browned. Serve slightly warm.

TEMPERATURE: 425° (hot oven).

TIME: Bake 40 to 45 min.

PACKAGED MINCEMEAT PIE

Follow directions on package for preparing the mincemeat for pie. One 9-oz. pkg. makes about 2 cups. Then follow recipe for Old-fashioned Mince Pie above.

SOUR CREAM RAISIN PIE

From covered wagon days. A favorite of men everywhere for its rich spicy custard.

Make Pastry for One-crust Pie of desired size. Line pie pan. *(See pp. 346–347.)*

For 9″ Pie	For 8″ Pie
Beat until very light and fluffy . . .	
3 eggs	2
Mix and blend in . . .	
1½ tbsp. flour	1 tbsp.
¾ cup sugar	½ cup
½ tsp. salt	¼ tsp.
3 tsp. cinnamon	2 tsp.
¾ tsp. cloves	½ tsp.
Fold in . . .	
1½ cups thick sour cream (20%) or cultured sour cream	1 cup
1½ cups seedless raisins	1 cup

Pour into pastry-lined pie pan. Bake until a silver knife inserted 1″ from side of filling comes out clean.

TEMPERATURE: 350° (mod. oven).

TIME: Bake 50 to 60 min.

MINCE PIE WITH BLACKBERRY SAUCE

"Different" . . . and elegant. Another prize-winning recipe . . . this one contributed by Miss Gertrude Mihm of Edwall, Washington.

Follow recipe for Old-fashioned Mince Pie above—*except* substitute well drained canned blackberries for ½ the mincemeat in the filling. Serve warm with

HOT BLACKBERRY SAUCE

Mix in saucepan . . .
   1 tbsp. sugar
   1 tbsp. cornstarch
   ¼ tsp. salt
Blend in . . .
   1 cup blackberry juice (drained
      from canned berries)
Bring to a boil, stirring constantly. Boil 1 min. Remove from heat. Stir in . . .
   1 tbsp. butter
   2 tbsp. lemon juice

RAISIN PIE

Called "Funeral Pie" by the Pennsylvania Dutch because it was always served when relatives and neighbors gathered from far and near to pay their "last respects."

Make Pastry for Two-crust Pie of desired size. Line pie pan. *(See pp. 343–345, 347.)*

For 9″ Pie	For 8″ Pie
Cook covered until tender (about 5 min.) . . .	
2 cups seedless raisins	1½ cups
2 cups boiling water	1½ cups
Stir in mixture of . . .	
½ cup sugar	⅓ cup
2 tbsp. flour	1½ tbsp.

Cook over med. heat, stirring constantly, until boiling. Boil 1 min. Remove from heat. Stir in . . .

½ cup chopped nuts	⅓ cup
2 tsp. grated lemon rind	1½ tsp.
3 tbsp. lemon juice	2⅓ tbsp.

Cover with top crust which has slits cut in it. Bake until nicely browned. Serve slightly warm.

TEMPERATURE: 425° (hot oven).

TIME: Bake 30 to 40 min.

357

CUSTARD PIE (✕ Recipe) Rich, satiny smooth custard baked right in the crust.

Make Pastry for One-crust Pie. Line pie pan. (*See pp. 346–347.*) Build up high fluted edge.

For the Filling	For 9″ Pie	For 8″ Pie
Beat slightly with rotary beater	4 eggs (or 8 egg yolks)	3 eggs (or 6 yolks)
Then beat in.	⅔ cup sugar ½ tsp. salt ¼ tsp. nutmeg *2⅔ cups scalding hot milk 1 tsp. vanilla, if desired	½ cup ¼ tsp. ¼ tsp. *2 cups ¾ tsp.

Pour into pastry-lined pie pan. Bake just until a silver knife inserted 1″ from side of filling comes out clean. The center may still look a bit soft but will set later. *Caution:* Too long baking makes custard "watery." Serve slightly warm or cold.

*Use part cream for an extra rich pie.

TEMPERATURE: 450° (hot oven) for 15 min., then 350° (mod. oven) to finish.
TIME: Bake 25 to 30 min.
NOTE: Can be baked at 425° for same time.

All you have to do—

To prevent soggy crust on custard pie—
Bake the custard alone—
The crust by itself,
And your custard pies
Won't stay on the shelf.

SLIP-SLIDE CUSTARD PIE

Certain-sure of a crisp undercrust every time.

Follow ✕ recipe above—*except* bake crust and filling separately. Pour filling directly into ungreased pie pan of *same* size as the one in which the crust is baked. Set pan in shallow pan of hot water. Bake just until a silver knife inserted 1″ from side of filling comes out clean. The center may still look a bit soft but will set later. When lukewarm, slip the baked filling into cooled Baked Pie Shell (*pp. 346–347*). Allow to settle a few minutes before serving.
TEMPERATURE: 350° (mod. oven).
TIME: Bake custard 30 to 35 min.

COCONUT CUSTARD PIE

Follow ✕ recipe above—*except* omit nutmeg, stir into custard moist shredded coconut (1 cup for 9″ pie, ¾ cup for 8″ pie). Sprinkle a little coconut over top. Bake.

FUDGE-TOPPED CUSTARD PIE

Follow ✕ recipe above. Just before serving, spread evenly over the cooled custard filling

FUDGE TOPPING

Mix ½ cup *sifted* confectioners' sugar, ⅛ tsp. salt, and 2 tbsp. cream. Blend in 1 sq. unsweetened chocolate (1 oz.), melted, and 2 tbsp. butter, melted.

SLIP-SLIDE PUMPKIN PIE

Follow directions for Pumpkin Pie (*p. 360*)—*except* bake crust and filling separately, using method for Slip-slide Custard Pie (*opposite*).

1 Loosen custard around edge of pan.

2 Shake pan gently to loosen completely.

3 Slip custard into shell, let settle.

4 The custard looks baked in the crust.

PECAN PIE (☞ Recipe) *Traditional recipe from Tidewater, Virginia. The choice among all desserts served at world renowned Williamsburg Inn in restored colonial Williamsburg.*

Make Pastry for One-crust Pie of desired size. Line pie pan. (*See pp. 346–347.*)

For the Filling	For 9″ Pie	For 8″ Pie
Beat together with rotary beater	3 eggs	2
	⅔ cup sugar	½ cup
	½ tsp. salt	¼ tsp.
	⅓ cup butter, melted	¼ cup
	1 cup dark corn syrup	¾ cup
Mix in	1 cup pecan halves	¾ cup

Pour into pastry-lined pie pan. Bake until set and pastry is nicely browned. Cool. Serve cold or slightly warm.

TEMPERATURE: 375° (quick mod. oven).

TIME: Bake 40 to 50 min.

SOUTHERN CHESS PIE

Originally from England, a delicacy of nuts and transparent custard.

Make Pastry for 8″ One-crust Pie (*pp. 346–347*).

Mix . . .
- 1 cup brown sugar (packed)
- ½ cup granulated sugar
- 1 tbsp. flour

Beat in thoroughly . . .
- 2 eggs
- 2 tbsp. milk
- 1 tsp. vanilla
- ½ cup butter, melted

Fold in . . .
- 1 cup pecans or walnuts

Pour into pastry-lined pie pan. Bake just until set. Serve slightly warm, plain or with whipped cream.

TEMPERATURE: 375° (quick mod. oven).

TIME: Bake 40 to 50 min.

SPICY WALNUT RAISIN PIE

Follow ☞ recipe above—*except* omit pecan halves and add:

	For 9″ Pie	For 8″ Pie
	½ tsp. cinnamon	¼ tsp.
	½ tsp. nutmeg	¼ tsp.
	½ tsp. cloves	¼ tsp.
	½ cup walnuts, chopped	⅓ cup
	½ cup seedless raisins	⅓ cup

CHOCOLATE BROWNIE PIE

Rich chocolatey version of Pecan Pie developed by Mary R. Jadwin of our staff.

Make Pastry for 9″ One-crust Pie (*pp. 346–347*).

Melt together over hot water . . .
- 2 sq. unsweetened chocolate (2 oz.)
- 2 tbsp. butter

Beat together with rotary beater . . .
- 3 eggs
- ½ cup sugar
- the chocolate mixture
- ¾ cup dark corn syrup

Mix in . . .
- ¾ cup pecan halves

Pour into pastry-lined pie pan. Bake just until set. Serve slightly warm or cold with ice cream, whipped cream, or Whipped Ice Cream (*p. 222*).

TEMPERATURE: 375° (quick mod. oven).

TIME: Bake 40 to 50 min.

359

PUMPKIN PIE (✒ Recipe) *Rich, brown, spicy.*

Pumpkins, or "pompions," were a standby of the early New England settlements. An old verse goes:
"For pottage, and puddings, and custards, and pies,
  Our pumpkins and parsnips are common supplies.
We have pumpkins at morning and pumpkins at noon;
  If it were not for pumpkins, we should be undoon."

Make Pastry for One-crust Pie. Line pie pan. (*See pp. 346–347.*) Build up high fluted edge.

For the Filling	For 9″ Pie	For 8″ Pie
	1¾ cups mashed cooked pumpkin (may be canned)	1¼ cups
	½ tsp. salt	¼ tsp.
	1¾ cups milk	1¼ cups
Beat together with rotary beater.........	3 eggs or 4 yolks	2 eggs or 3 yolks
	⅔ cup brown sugar (packed)	½ cup
	2 tbsp. granulated sugar	1½ tbsp.
	1¼ tsp. cinnamon	1 tsp.
	½ tsp. ginger	¼ tsp.
	½ tsp. nutmeg	¼ tsp.
	¼ tsp. cloves	¼ tsp.

Pour into pastry-lined pie pan. (For crispness, have bottom pastry a little thicker than ⅛″.) Bake just until a silver knife inserted 1″ from side of filling comes out clean. The center may still look soft but will set later. Serve slightly warm or cold.

TEMPERATURE: 425° (hot oven).

TIME: Bake 45 to 55 min.

NEW ENGLAND SQUASH PIE

Tastes like pumpkin pie, but because all white sugar and no cloves have been used, it has a lighter, milder flavor.

Follow ✒ recipe above for method. But use:

For 9″ Pie	For 8″ Pie
1¾ cups strained mashed cooked squash	1¼ cups
1 tsp. salt	¾ tsp.
1½ cups milk	1 cup plus 2 tbsp.
3 eggs	2
1 cup sugar	¾ cup
1 tsp. cinnamon	¾ tsp.
½ tsp. nutmeg	¼ tsp.
½ tsp. ginger	¼ tsp.
1 tbsp. butter, melted	2 tsp.

SOUTHERN SWEET POTATO OR YAM PIE

Follow recipe above for New England Squash Pie—*except* use mashed cooked sweet potatoes, strained, in place of squash.

AUTUMN PUMPKIN PIE

The golden pumpkin filling is made with condensed milk. See color picture on opposite page.

Make Pastry for 9″ One-crust Pie (*pp. 346–347*).

Beat together with rotary beater . . .
  1¾ cups mashed cooked pumpkin (may be canned)
  1⅓ cups sweetened condensed milk (15 oz.)
  1 egg
  ½ tsp. salt
  ½ tsp. cinnamon
  ¼ tsp. nutmeg
  ¼ tsp. ginger
  1 cup hot water

Pour into pastry-lined pie pan. Bake.
TEMPERATURE: 375° (quick mod. oven).
TIME: Bake 50 to 55 min.

PUMPKIN PIE WITH WHIPPED CREAM

Follow ✒ recipe above. Just before serving, cover cooled pie with a thin layer of Sweetened Whipped Cream (*p. 222*). Sprinkle chopped nuts over the top, if desired.

AUTUMN PUMPKIN PIE

In *meringue* pies (such as Lemon Meringue), a meringue is piled on top of the pie filling, and the pie with meringue baked according to directions below. In *chiffon* pies, an *unbaked* meringue is combined with the pie filling, and the pie is chilled (*pp. 366–368*).

PIE MERINGUE

Delicate, fluffy.

For 9″ Pie	For 8″ Pie
3 egg whites	2
*¼ tsp. cream of tartar	*¼ tsp.
6 tbsp. sugar	¼ cup
½ tsp. flavoring	¼ tsp.
(if desired)	

*1 tsp. lemon juice may be substituted for cream of tartar in meringue for Lemon, Lime, or Orange Meringue Pies.

1 Beat egg whites with cream of tartar until frothy. Gradually beat in sugar, a little at a time.

2 Continue beating until stiff and glossy. *Do not underbeat. Beat until sugar is dissolved.* Beat in flavoring.

3 Pile meringue onto *hot* pie filling, being careful to seal the meringue onto edge of crust to prevent shrinking and weeping.

4 Swirl or pull up points for decorative top. Bake until delicately browned.

TEMPERATURE: 400° (mod. hot oven).
TIME: Bake 8 to 10 min.

5 To cut meringue pie neatly, dip sharp knife into water, either warm or cold; shake off any excess drops; cut. Repeat the process between cuts.

FOR A PERFECT MERINGUE

Be sure you beat until all sugar is dissolved. You can test for this by tasting or rubbing a bit between your fingers to see if it is still "grainy."

Watch baking time carefully. The short baking time at a high temperature makes a tender meringue that cuts easily.

Cool gradually in a slightly warm place away from drafts.

LEMON MERINGUE PIE (🗝 Recipe) *Robert Taylor's favorite ... his mother's recipe, featured in our radio cooking school with an interview from this famous star. Its tangy, refreshing flavor makes it our favorite lemon pie, too.*

Make Baked Pie Shell of desired size (*pp. 346–347*).

	For 9″ Pie	For 8″ Pie
For the Filling		
Mix in saucepan......................	1½ cups sugar ⅓ cup cornstarch	1 cup plus 2 tbsp. ¼ cup
Stir in gradually......................	1½ cups water	1 cup plus 2 tbsp.
Cook over med. heat, stirring constantly, until mixture thickens and boils. Boil 1 min. Slowly stir at least half the hot mixture into	3 egg yolks, slightly beaten	2
Then blend into hot mixture in saucepan. Boil 1 min. longer, stirring constantly. Remove from heat. Continue stirring until smooth. Blend in..............................	3 tbsp. butter ¼ cup lemon juice 1 tbsp. grated lemon rind	2 tbsp. 3 tbsp. 1 tbsp.

Pour into baked pie shell. Cover with Pie Meringue (*p. 362*). Bake until a delicate brown. Serve as soon as cool.

TEMPERATURE: 400° (mod. hot oven).

TIME: Bake 8 to 10 min.

LEMON JUICE IN PIE MERINGUE

One med. lemon has 2 to 3 tbsp. juice. You may use extra lemon juice in place of cream of tartar for Pie Meringue. (Substitute 1 tsp. lemon juice for ¼ tsp. cream of tartar.)

All you have to do —

To save time: use frozen or bottled fruit juices.
To keep the fresh flavor of lemon or orange: grate just the thin colored rind (no white).

QUICK ORANGE MERINGUE PIE

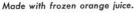

Made with frozen orange juice.

Follow 🗝 recipe above for method. But use:

- 1 cup sugar
- ¼ cup cornstarch
- 1⅓ cups frozen concentrate for orange juice (diluted according to directions on can)
- 2 egg yolks, slightly beaten
- 2 tbsp. butter

Omit grated rind. Pour into 8″ Baked Pie Shell (*pp. 346–347*). Top with Pie Meringue (*p. 362*).

LIME MERINGUE PIE

The idea for this pie with its cool sea green filling was brought from Florida by Jean Hall (Mrs. Myron Hall), formerly of our staff.

Follow 🗝 recipe above—*except*, in place of lemon, use lime and omit butter. Add a *few* drops of green food coloring for a delicate lime green color.

PINEAPPLE MERINGUE PIE

Delicate yellow filling with crushed pineapple. To Mildred Kranz, gracious hostess of our staff, this dessert recalls enchanting days and nights in the Hawaiian Islands.

Follow 🗝 recipe above for method—and blend in pineapple at the last. But use:

For 9″ Pie	For 8″ Pie
1 cup sugar	¾ cup
¼ cup cornstarch	3 tbsp.
½ cup water	⅓ cup
1 cup pineapple juice	¾ cup
3 egg yolks, slightly beaten	2
3 tbsp. butter	2 tbsp.
1 tbsp. lemon juice	2 tsp.
1¼ tsp. grated lemon rind	1 tsp.
1¼ cups well drained crushed pineapple	1 cup

VANILLA CREAM PIE (✒ Recipe)

Velvety smooth filling. Flavor perfect. For authentic gourmet's cream pie, substitute coffee cream for milk. So rich ... und so delicious!

Make Baked Pie Shell (with high fluted edge) of desired size (*pp. 346–347*).

For the Filling	For 9″ Pie	For 8″ Pie
Mix in saucepan	⅔ cup sugar 3 tbsp. cornstarch ½ tsp. salt	½ cup 2 tbsp. ½ tsp.
Stir in gradually	3 cups milk	2 cups
Cook over med. heat, stirring constantly, until mixture thickens and boils. Boil 1 min. Remove from heat. Gradually stir at least half of hot mixture into	3 egg yolks, slightly beaten	2

This...   Not this...

	For 9″ Pie	For 8″ Pie
Then blend into hot mixture in saucepan. Boil 1 min. more, stirring constantly. Remove from heat. Blend in	1 tbsp. butter 1½ tsp. vanilla	2 tsp. 1 tsp.

If pie is to be finished with Meringue (*p. 362*), pour immediately into baked pie shell. Spread meringue lightly on pie filling, sealing to edge of crust to prevent shrinking. Bake until delicately browned. Let cool at room temperature.

TEMPERATURE: 400° (mod. hot oven).
TIME: Bake 8 to 10 min.

WHIPPED CREAM FINISH

Instead of being finished with meringue, this pie may be chilled thoroughly (2 hr.) and topped with Sweetened Whipped Cream (*p. 222*).

CHOCOLATE CREAM PIE

Smooth, rich ... the kind to rave about.

Follow ✒ recipe above—*except* increase sugar and add cut-up unsweetened chocolate with the milk or cocoa with the sugar, cornstarch, and salt. Use:

For 9″ Pie	For 8″ Pie
1½ cups sugar	1 cup
3 sq. unsweetened choco- late (3 oz.), cut up or ½ cup cocoa	2 sq. (2 oz.) ⅓ cup

ALMOND CREAM PIE

Crunchy toasted almonds; smooth, soft, creamy custard in crispy pastry ... made famous by Mrs. Inez Norton Crawford, formerly of the lovely Boulevard Twins, Minneapolis, Minnesota, now of Phoenix, Arizona.

Follow ✒ recipe above—*except,* in place of vanilla, use ½ tsp. almond flavoring and add ½ cup toasted slivered blanched almonds to the cooled filling. Sprinkle a few toasted slivered almonds over whipped cream topping.

COCONUT CREAM PIE

"To me, this is the most delicious of all desserts!" says Genevieve Dziedzic, a career girl who combines skill with artistry.

Follow ✒ recipe above—*except* fold in ¾ cup moist shredded coconut just before filling baked pie shell. Sprinkle whipped cream or meringue topping with ¼ cup shredded coconut (toasted, if desired).

BANANA CREAM PIE

De luxe version.

Follow ✒ recipe above or recipe for Chocolate Cream Pie (*left*)—*except* cool filling. Arrange a layer of sliced bananas ½″ deep in pastry shell before pouring in cooled filling.

For 9″ Pie	For 8″ Pie
3 large bananas	2

If whipped cream topping is used, garnish with a ring of sliced bananas.

BUTTERSCOTCH CREAM PIE *Glossy smooth . . . with the true butterscotch flavor. Merriam Paulson of our staff thinks that "there is nothing better!"*

Make Baked Pie Shell of desired size (*pp. 346–347*).

For the Filling	For 9" Pie	For 8" Pie
Mix in saucepan......................	1 cup brown sugar (packed)	¾ cup
	¼ cup cornstarch	3 tbsp.
	½ tsp. salt	½ tsp.
Stir in gradually......................	1 cup water	¾ cup
	1⅔ cups milk	1¼ cups
Add..............................	⅓ cup butter	¼ cup
Cook over med. heat, stirring constantly, until mixture thickens and boils. Boil 1 min. Remove from heat. Gradually stir at least half of hot mixture into..........................	3 egg yolks, slightly beaten	2
Then blend into hot mixture in saucepan. Boil 1 min. more, stirring constantly. Remove from heat.		
Blend in............................	1½ tsp. vanilla	1 tsp.

If pie is to be finished with Meringue (*p. 362*), pour immediately into baked pie shell. Spread meringue lightly on top, sealing to edge of crust to prevent shrinking. Bake until delicately browned. Let cool at room temperature.
TEMPERATURE: 400° (mod. hot oven).
TIME: Bake 8 to 10 min.

WHIPPED CREAM FINISH

Instead of being finished with Meringue, this pie may be chilled thoroughly (2 hr.), and topped with Sweetened Whipped Cream (*p. 222*). Decorate with toasted nuts, if desired.

All you have to do –

For milder flavor and lighter color in Butterscotch Cream Pie: use all milk instead of milk and water. *For stronger flavor and darker color:* increase brown sugar 2 tbsp. or use dark brown sugar.

BIRTHDAY PIE

A happy substitute for a birthday cake . . . especially when you make the favorite pie of the one whose birthday it is. H. Eric Martin of Minneapolis chooses Lemon Meringue on August fourth.

Make cream pie of your choice. Drop Meringue (*p. 362*) on pie by spoonfuls with one for each candle. Bake. Insert candles (in holders) just before serving.

CHOCOLATE CHIP REFRIGERATOR PIE

Rich, creamy . . . to please your family and your guests.

Make 8" Baked Pie Shell (*pp. 346–347*).

Place in top of double boiler . . .
  ½ lb. marshmallows (about 32)
  ¾ cup milk
  ¼ tsp. salt

Heat over hot water until marshmallows melt. Cool thoroughly.

Fold in . . .
  1 cup whipping cream, whipped
  1 tsp. vanilla
  1 sq. unsweetened chocolate (1 oz.), grated
  ¼ cup chopped nuts

Pour into baked pie shell. Garnish top with ¼ cup grated coconut or shaved chocolate. Chill.

for best flavor

Remove chilled pies from refrigerator 20 min. before serving to make crust and filling taste their best.

LEMON CHIFFON PIE (⚿ Recipe) *Piquantly flavored . . . light and delicate.*

Make Baked Pie Shell of desired size (*pp. 346–347*).

For the Filling	For 9″ Pie	For 8″ Pie
	½ cup sugar	⅓ cup
	1 envelope unflavored gelatin (1 tbsp.)	2 tsp.
Blend thoroughly in saucepan	⅔ cup water	½ cup
Cook over med. heat, stirring constantly, *just* until mixture comes to a boil.	⅓ cup lemon juice	¼ cup
	4 egg yolks, slightly beaten	3
Stir in	1 tbsp. grated lemon rind	2 tsp.
Place pan in cold water; cool until mixture mounds slightly when dropped from a spoon.		
Fold into a Meringue made from . . . . (for method, see p. 362)	4 egg whites	3
	½ tsp. cream of tartar	¼ tsp.
	½ cup sugar	⅓ cup

Pile into cooled baked pie shell. Chill several hours until set. Serve with whipped cream, if desired.

LIME CHIFFON PIE

Follow ⚿ recipe above—*except* use lime juice and grated lime rind instead of lemon. Add a few drops green food coloring to intensify the color.

ORANGE CHIFFON PIE

Follow ⚿ recipe above—*except* use orange juice instead of lemon juice and water; orange rind instead of lemon rind.

PINEAPPLE CHIFFON PIE

Follow ⚿ recipe above—*except* use pineapple juice instead of lemon juice and water; instead of lemon rind, add ⅓ cup drained crushed pineapple for 9″ pie, and ¼ cup for 8″ pie.

pie fillings as desserts

Use filling for any of the Chiffon Pies (*pp. 366–368*), Meringue Pies (*p. 363*), or Cream Pies (*pp. 364–365*). Serve in sherbet glasses.

Or make squares as follows: Make recipe for 9″ Graham Cracker or Cooky Crumb Crust (*p. 348*), but reserve ½ cup of mixture for topping. Spread crumb mixture over bottom of 8 or 9″ square pan. Follow recipe for any Chiffon Pie filling or for Black Bottom Pie (*p. 368*). Spread over crumbs. Top with remaining crumbs. Chill several hours until set. Serve cut in squares. Top with whipped cream.

AMOUNT: 9 servings.

STRAWBERRY CHIFFON PIE

Make Baked Pie Shell of desired size (*pp. 346–347*).

For 9″ Pie	For 8″ Pie
Blend in saucepan and cook to a full rolling boil stirring constantly . . .	
⅔ cup sugar	½ cup
1 envelope unflavored gelatin (1 tbsp.)	2 tsp.
1 cup strawberries, thoroughly crushed	⅔ cup
Place pan in cold water; cool until mixture mounds slightly when dropped from a spoon.	
Then fold into a Meringue made from . . . (for method, see p. 362)	
3 egg whites	2
¼ tsp. cream of tartar	¼ tsp.
⅓ cup sugar	¼ cup
Carefully blend in . . .	
½ cup whipping cream, whipped	⅓ cup

Pile into cooled baked pie shell. Chill several hours until set. Serve cold, garnished with whole strawberries.

RASPBERRY CHIFFON PIE

Follow ⚿ recipe above—*except* use crushed raspberries in place of strawberries.

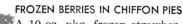

FROZEN BERRIES IN CHIFFON PIES A 10-oz. pkg. frozen strawberries or raspberries, thawed, may be used in place of fresh berries. Use ¼ cup sugar for 9″ pie, 3 tbsp. for 8″ pie.

CHOCOLATE CHIFFON PIE
Elegant, fluffy, delightful for a party dessert. First enjoyed at a patio supper at Mrs. Arch Vernon's home in Brentwood, California.

Make Baked Pie Shell of desired size (*pp. 346–347*) or Graham Cracker Crust (*p. 348*).

For the Filling	For 9″ Pie	For 8″ Pie
Blend thoroughly in saucepan............	1 envelope unflavored gelatin (1 tbsp.)	2 tsp.
	½ cup sugar	⅓ cup
	½ tsp. salt	¼ tsp.
	1⅓ cups water	1 cup
Add................................	2 sq. unsweetened chocolate (2 oz.), cut up	1½ sq. (1½ oz.)
Cook over med. heat, stirring constantly, until chocolate is melted. Remove from heat. Slowly stir all of mixture into................ Return to saucepan and cook over med. heat, stirring constantly, *just* until it begins to boil. Immediately remove from heat. Place pan in cold water. Cool until mixture mounds slightly when dropped from a spoon.	3 egg yolks, slightly beaten	2
Blend in............................	1 tsp. vanilla	¾ tsp.
Carefully fold in a Meringue of.......... (for method, *see p. 362*)	3 egg whites	2
	¼ tsp. cream of tartar	¼ tsp.
	½ cup sugar	⅓ cup
Gently fold in.......................	½ cup whipping cream, whipped stiff	⅓ cup

Pile into cooled baked pie shell or Graham Cracker Crust. Chill until set (about 2 hr.).

Top with sweetened whipped cream and sprinkle with shavings of dark chocolate.

EGGNOG CHIFFON PIE

"Perfect for holiday entertaining!" said Mabel Ross, formerly of our staff, whenever this pie was mentioned.

Make 9″ Baked Pie Shell (*pp. 346–347*) or Graham Cracker crust (*p. 348*).

Blend thoroughly in saucepan . . .
  2 tsp. unflavored gelatin
  ½ cup sugar
  2 tbsp. cornstarch
  ¼ tsp. salt

Stir in gradually . . .
  1 cup milk

Cook over med. heat, stirring constantly, until mixture thickens and boils. Boil 1 min. Remove from heat. Stir hot mixture into . . .
  3 egg yolks, slightly beaten

Return mixture to saucepan and bring *just* to boiling, stirring constantly. Remove from heat. Add . .
  1½ tsp. vanilla
  ¼ tsp. almond flavoring

Place pan in cold water. Cool until mixture mounds slightly when dropped from a spoon.

Fold in . . .
  1 cup whipping cream, whipped

Pour into cooled crust and sprinkle with nutmeg. Chill before serving.

PUMPKIN CHIFFON PIE

Modern version of the perennial favorite. Delicate. Smooth.

Make Baked Pie Shell (*pp. 346–347*) or Ginger Cooky Crust (*p. 348*).

For 9″ Pie	For 8″ Pie
Blend thoroughly in saucepan . . .	
1 envelope unflavored gelatin (1 tbsp.)	2 tsp.
⅔ cup brown sugar (packed)	½ cup
½ tsp. salt	¼ tsp.
½ tsp. cinnamon	¼ tsp.
½ tsp. nutmeg	¼ tsp.
½ tsp. ginger	¼ tsp.
1¼ cups mashed cooked pumpkin (may be canned)	¾ cup
3 egg yolks	2
½ cup milk	⅓ cup

Cook over med. heat, stirring constantly, until it boils. Remove from heat. Place pan in cold water. Cool until mixture mounds slightly when dropped from a spoon.

Carefully fold into a Meringue (for method, *see p. 362*) of . . .

3 egg whites	2
½ cup sugar	⅓ cup

Pour into cooled crust. Chill until set (2 hr.). Garnish with whipped cream.

WHITE CHRISTMAS PIE
Pure white heavenly concoction created by Ruby Livedalen Peterson (Mrs. Winton R. Peterson), formerly of our staff . . . from an idea brought by Dixie Willson of Mason City, Iowa.

Make Baked Pie Shell (with high fluted edge) of desired size (*pp. 346–347*).

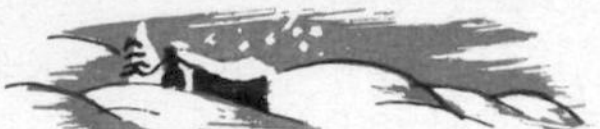

For the Filling	For 9" Pie	For 8" Pie
Blend thoroughly in saucepan............	½ cup sugar	⅓ cup
	¼ cup GOLD MEDAL Flour	3 tbsp.
	1 envelope unflavored gelatin (1 tbsp.)	2 tsp.
	½ tsp. salt	¼ tsp.
Stir in gradually.....................	1¾ cups milk	1⅓ cups

Cook over med. heat until mixture boils, stirring constantly. Boil 1 min. Place pan in cold water. Cool until mixture mounds slightly when dropped from spoon.

Blend in...........................	¾ tsp. vanilla	½ tsp.
	¼ tsp. almond flavoring	¼ tsp.
	3 egg whites	2
Carefully fold into a Meringue made of..... (for method, see p. 362)	¼ tsp. cream of tartar	¼ tsp.
	½ cup sugar	⅓ cup
Gently fold in........................	½ cup whipping cream, whipped	⅓ cup
Fold in.............................	1 cup moist shredded coconut	¾ cup

Pile into cooled baked pie shell. Sprinkle with moist shredded coconut.

Chill several hours until set. Serve cold. Delicious topped with crushed strawberries or raspberries.

BLACK BOTTOM PIE
Famous at the Hollywood Brown Derby. Creamy chocolate and rum-flavored layers in a Ginger Cooky Crust.

Make 9" Ginger Cooky Crust (*p. 348*).

Soften.............................	2 tsp. unflavored gelatin
in.................................	3 tbsp. cold water
Mix in saucepan......................	½ cup sugar
	2 tbsp. cornstarch
	½ tsp. salt
Stir in gradually......................	2 cups milk

Boil 1 min. on med. heat, stirring constantly. Remove from heat. Stir at least half of hot mixture into...................... 2 egg yolks, slightly beaten

Blend into hot mixture in saucepan. Boil 1 more min., stirring constantly. Remove from heat. Take out 1 cup of mixture. Stir softened gelatin into remaining hot mixture. Place pan in cold water to cool.

Add the 1 cup custard mixture to.......... 1 sq. unsweetened chocolate (1 oz.), melted

Blend well, pour into cooled 9" crust.

When custard-gelatin mixture is cool and mounds slightly when dropped from a spoon, blend in............................ 2 tsp. pure rum flavoring*

Then fold into a Meringue made of........ (for method, see p. 362)	2 egg whites
	¼ tsp. cream of tartar
	⅓ cup sugar

Pile on chocolate mixture in crust. Chill until firm. Spread with whipped cream. Sprinkle with shaved chocolate.

*If imitation rum flavoring is used, use only 1 tsp.

BAKED ALASKA PIE
May be made the night before serving and frozen uncovered just overnight. "Your guests will love this!" says Marylee Duehring of our staff.

Make 8″ Baked Pie Shell (*pp. 346–347*).

Wash, hull, halve, then chill	3 cups strawberries
Make	Meringue for 8″ pie (p. 362)
Place in the baked pie shell	2 cups of the berries
Spoon over the berries.	1 pt. firm bulk vanilla ice cream
Cover with	the remaining berries

Spread Meringue over pie, being careful to cover all parts. Bake until a delicate brown. Serve immediately.

NOTE: Fresh fruit in season . . . such as sliced peaches, Bing cherries, raspberries, or blueberries . . . may be used in place of strawberries.

TEMPERATURE: 500° (very hot oven).
TIME: Bake 3 to 5 min.

STRAWBERRY MINUTE PIE (✕ Recipe)
Easy to make pie with sparkling filling of frozen strawberries and strawberry gelatin.

Make 8″ Baked Pie Shell (*pp. 346–347*).

Dissolve . . .
    1 pkg. strawberry-flavored gelatin
in . . .
    1 cup hot water
Add . . .
    1 pkg. *unthawed* frozen sweetened sliced strawberries (16 oz.)

Break up frozen berries with a fork. As berries thaw, the gelatin thickens. When filling is partially set, pour into the cooled baked pie shell. Chill until completely set. Serve garnished with Sweetened Whipped Cream (*p. 222*).

RASPBERRY MINUTE PIE
Follow ✕ recipe above—*except* use raspberry-flavored gelatin in place of strawberry-flavored gelatin and frozen raspberries in place of frozen strawberries.

FROSTY FRUIT PIE (✕ Recipe)
Refreshing, fluffy, fruit-flavored pie.

Make 9″ Baked Pie Shell (*pp. 346–347*).

Bring to a boil . . .
    1 ¼ cups crushed pineapple, applesauce, apple juice, orange juice, grape juice, prune juice, apricot nectar, or pineapple juice
Stir in until dissolved . . .
    1 pkg. lemon-flavored gelatin
Mix in . . .
    ¾ to 1 cup sugar (depending on sweetness of fruit)
Cool until almost stiff.
Whip until stiff . . .
    *1 cup chilled evaporated milk
with . . .
    1 tbsp. lemon juice

Pour on top of gelatin mixture. Beat in slowly with rotary beater or electric mixer (on low speed). Pour into cooled baked pie shell. Chill several hours until firm. Garnish with whipped cream, if desired.

*Evaporated milk must be thoroughly chilled before it will whip. For quick chilling, pour into refrigerator tray and freeze until crystals form around the outside edge.

LEMON OR LIME FROSTY FRUIT PIE
Follow ✕ recipe above—*except* use 1 cup boiling water and ¼ cup lime or lemon juice (fresh or bottled). Lime or lemon-flavored gelatin may be used.

369

FILLED TART SHELLS *Flaky little shells holding the filling of your choice.*

Bake Tart Shells according to recipe on p. 348. Cool. Then fill with fruit, cream, or chiffon filling, and top with whipped cream or a sprinkling of nuts. Or use one of the suggestions below.

FAVORITE COCONUT TARTS

A delectable use for extra egg yolks.

Make 8 Baked Tart Shells (*p. 348*).

Mix in saucepan . . .

 1 cup sugar
 2 tbsp. cornstarch
 ½ tsp. salt

Stir in gradually . . .

 1 cup water

Cook over med. heat, stirring constantly, until mixture boils. Boil 1 min. Remove from heat. Stir at least half of hot mixture into . . .

 3 egg yolks, slightly beaten

Then beat into hot mixture in saucepan. Boil 1 min. longer, stirring constantly. Remove from heat. Continue beating until smooth. Stir in . . .

 ¼ cup butter
 1 tsp. vanilla
 2 tsp. lemon juice
 1 cup moist shredded coconut
 ¼ cup cut-up filberts

Pour into cooled baked tart shells.

Sprinkle over top . . .

 ¼ cup toasted coconut

Serve cool or slightly warm.

CRUSTY BAKED APPLES

Apples baked in a jacket of flaky pastry.

Make Standard Pastry for Two-crust Pie (*p. 343*). Round into ball. Divide into 6 parts. Roll each part into an 8″ round on lightly floured board. Place med. apple, pared and cored, on each round; fold pastry over apple. Place on baking sheet, sealed-side-down. Cut slits in top. Brush with milk and sprinkle with sugar. Bake in hot oven (425°) for 30 to 35 min. Serve warm with Fluffy Sauce (*below*) or Vanilla Sauce (*make ½ recipe on p. 233*).

FLUFFY SAUCE

Beat with electric mixer or rotary beater . . .

 ¼ cup soft butter
 1 cup *sifted* confectioners' sugar
 1 egg
 1 tsp. vanilla

LEFTOVER PASTRY DAINTIES

Roll out trimmings from pie crust. Sprinkle with grated cheese, or with sugar and cinnamon, mixed. Cut into fancy shapes. Bake as for tarts. Serve with salads, tea.

GLACÉ FRUIT TARTS

With your choice of fresh fruit.

Line Baked Tart Shells (*p. 348*) with cream cheese beaten with a little milk or pineapple or orange juice. Fill with fresh or frozen berries, sliced peaches, or other fruits. Top with glaze made by melting currant or other bright jelly.

SOUTHERN CHESS TARTS

Elegant little tarts to serve for teas or fancy occasions.

Make Pastry for 8″ Two-crust Pie (*p. 343*). Divide pastry into 24 equal parts and roll each into circle 3½ to 4″ in diameter. Line 24 tiny tart pans with pastry.

Mix . . .

 ½ cup brown sugar (packed)
 ¼ cup granulated sugar
 ½ tbsp. flour

Beat in thoroughly . . .

 1 egg
 1 tbsp. milk
 ½ tsp. vanilla
 ¼ cup butter, melted

Fold in . . .

 ½ cup pecans or walnuts

Put a scant tablespoon of mixture in each tart. Bake until set.

TEMPERATURE: 425° (hot oven).
TIME: Bake 15 to 20 min.

SUNDAE TARTS

Fill cooled Baked Tart Shells (*p. 348*) with ice cream. Top with chocolate or butterscotch sauce, fresh or frozen fruit. Or sprinkle ice cream with chopped nuts, shaved chocolate, or coconut.

COVENTRY TARTLETS

Cooks used to stand in the tavern doorways in old Coventry crying their goodies from the oven to the passerby. Today's adaptations of these tarts make delicious hors d'oeuvres or tea accompaniments.

Make Pastry for 8″ Two-crust Pie (*p. 343*). Line 24 tiny tart pans (about 2″ in diameter) with pastry. Prick. Bake in very hot oven (475°) 8 to 10 min.

Blend . . .

    ½ lb. soft sharp flavored cheese
      (Old English type)
    ¼ cup soft butter
    ½ cup sugar
    2 egg yolks
    ¼ tsp. nutmeg
    1 tbsp. orange juice

Fill baked tart shells ⅔ full. Bake in hot oven (425°) until puffed and golden brown, 12 to 15 min. Top each tart with a teaspoon of currant jelly. Serve warm.

JOSEPHINES

Like Napoleons, but daintier and not so rich. Tiny pastry sandwich delicacies, put together with cream filling and topped with frosting and nuts.

Make Pastry for 9″ Two-crust Pie (*p. 343*). Roll ⅛″ thick and cut into 3x2″ oblongs (makes 24). Place on baking sheet, prick. Bake in very hot oven (475°) until delicately browned, 8 to 10 min.

Just before serving, spread tops of half the oblongs with Easy-Creamy Icing (*p. 188*), then sprinkle with chopped nuts. Put oblongs together in pairs with chilled Vanilla Cream Filling (*p. 364*) between. (Make amount of filling for 8″ pie.)

AMOUNT: 12 Josephines.

SIMPLIFIED TARTS

Do not require tart pans. Make pastry and filling ahead of time and put together shortly before serving.

Roll pastry ⅛″ thick. Cut with cooky cutter into 3″ rounds. Place on ungreased baking sheet. Prick with fork. Bake in very hot oven (475°) until delicately browned, 8 to 10 min. Top with softened cream cheese, then with sweetened or glazed fruit; or top with chocolate or other cream pie filling, then with whipped cream, nuts, etc.

BANBURY TARTS

Specialty of the famous Banbury Cross region near London. A favorite with Charles II.

Make Pastry for One-crust Pie (*p. 346*). Roll into large square 12x12″. Cut into nine 4″ squares.

Mix . . .

    ½ cup raisins, chopped
    ½ cup sugar
    1½ tbsp. fine cracker crumbs
    1 egg yolk
    ½ tbsp. soft butter
    dash of salt
    1 tbsp. lemon juice
    1 tbsp. grated lemon rind
    2 tbsp. chopped walnuts

Spread filling over half of each square. Moisten edges, fold into triangles, and press edges together with tines of fork. Prick tops. Bake in hot oven (450°) until delicately browned, 12 to 15 min.

FANCY TARTS

Made in a variety of shapes.

Cut rolled pastry into squares, crescents, or diamonds, making two pieces alike for each tart. Spread desired filling on each lower piece. Cover with matching top piece. Press edges together. Cut slits in top crust. Bake in very hot oven (475°) 8 to 10 min., until golden brown.

IN-A-JIFFY PASTRY SHELLS

Make ahead of time and freeze.

Cut rolled pastry into 5″ circles. Prick with fork; stack with waxed paper between circles. Place in plastic bag or wrap in aluminum foil and freeze. When ready to use, heat oven to 475° (very hot). Place frozen circles over inverted custard cups on baking sheet or over inverted muffin cups. Bake 8 to 10 min.

Simple Tarts for Dessert Luncheons.

371

APPLE DUMPLINGS (✗ Recipe) *Packages of luscious fruit encrusted with sugar.*

"Apple, Apple Dumpling,
My first choice,"
Cry all the husbands
With one voice.

"Apple for the Filling,
Sugar and spice,
Wrap it up in pastry,
Count me twice!"

Make Pastry (*pp. 343–345*) for number of dumplings desired. (Pastry for 9" Two-crust Pie makes 6 dumplings, for 8" Two-crust Pie, 4 dumplings.) Roll out pastry a little less than ⅛" thick, and cut into 7" squares. Pare and core a med. tart, juicy apple for each dumpling. Then prepare a syrup.

	For 6 Dumplings	For 4 Dumplings
Boil together for 3 min . . .		
1 cup sugar		⅔ cup
2 cups water		1½ cups
3 tbsp. butter		2 tbsp.
¼ tsp. cinnamon		¼ tsp.
Fill cavities of apples with mixture of . . .		
½ cup sugar		⅓ cup
1½ tsp. cinnamon		1 tsp.
Dot with . . .		
1 tbsp. butter		2 tsp.

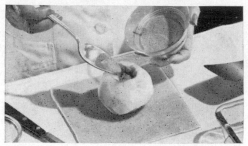

1 Place apple on each square of pastry. Fill core cavity with sugar and cinnamon mixture . . . dot with butter.

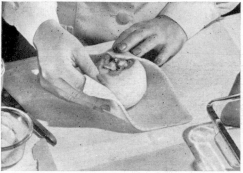

2 Bring opposite points of pastry up over the apple. Overlap, moisten, and seal.

3 Lift carefully, place a little apart in baking dish. Pour hot syrup *around* dumplings.

Bake immediately until crust is nicely browned and apples are cooked through (*test with fork*). Serve warm with the syrup and with cream or whipped cream.

TEMPERATURE: 425° (hot oven).

TIME: Bake 40 to 45 min.

PEACH DUMPLINGS

Follow ✗ recipe above—*except* use 8 pared fresh peaches instead of 6 apples and smaller squares of pastry to fit. Cut a segment out of each peach. Remove the pit. Fill the hollow with jam or jelly (or the sugar, cinnamon, and butter, as for Apple Dumplings). Replace segment. Wrap in pastry. Bake. (Good juicy peaches do not require the syrup.) Serve warm with cream.

APPLE TURNOVERS

Make Simplified Puff Pastry (*p. 348*). Roll out ⅛" thick, cut into 5" squares. Place drained cooked apple slices in center of each. Sprinkle with sugar, cinnamon, and lemon juice. Dot with butter. Moisten edges with cold water. Fold into triangle and seal well. Cut slits in top. Brush with milk, sprinkle with sugar. Bake in very hot oven (475°) until delicately browned, 15 to 20 min.

A Salad a Day

Salads are refreshing, lovely . . . like coming upon a woodland spring, clear and cool. Beauty will be the reward of your understanding touch. And health benefits will abundantly bless your table through the precious vitamins and minerals of crisp, sparkling salad ingredients. Salads are the delightful way to ensure those prescribed raw vegetables and fruits every day.

Betty Crocker

THERE'S A SALAD FOR EVERY OCCASION
Below are listed a few suggestions from the many in this chapter.

SALAD BUFFET
Miroton of Sea Food (p. 390)
Pickle Plate
(Each lettuce cup holds 1 kind of pickle: gherkins, dill pickles, ripe olives, and pimiento-stuffed olives.)
Buttered Assorted Breads
Fresh Fruit   Cheese   Crisp Crackers
Coffee

A SALAD LUNCHEON
Oven Chicken Salad (p. 391)
Corn Sticks (p. 92)   Crisp Relishes
Strawberry Shortcake (p. 235)
Coffee

Q. *Where should individual salads be placed?*

A. First course salads should be in the center of each place . . . on a large plate for formal serving. Main course salads should be placed at left of dinner plate . . . or, if table is crowded, directly above forks and the bread-and-butter plate omitted.

Q. *Should dressing always be passed?*

A. Some salads are served without dressing so that their beauty of arrangement will not be marred; these require the passing of dressing.

Q. *May salad be on the table at the beginning of a meal?*

A. Yes, it may be placed on table just before guests are seated.

Q. *May a salad be cut with the knife?*

A. Yes, if one is unable to do so with the fork.

Q. *Where does the salad fork appear in the table setting?*

A. This depends on when in the meal the salad is served. If for the first course, the fork is at the extreme left. If with the main course or following it, the fork is inside the dinner fork just at left of the dinner plate.

Q. *How should I serve a bowl of mixed salad or a platter of salad?*

A. It may be passed; but the individual servings should be easy to remove. Or the hostess may serve it onto salad plates and pass them around the table.

Q. *Should one eat the salad green?*

A. Yes, it is part of the salad and is intended to be eaten.

Q. *Is a salad fork always necessary?*

A. A dinner salad may be eaten with the same fork as the main course.

LOW CALORIE SALADS FOR WEIGHT-WATCHERS

Cottage Cheese Ring: Season cottage cheese with salt, pepper, chives, and parsley. Spoon into ring mold. Invert onto salad greens. Fill center with tomato and cucumber slices or fruit.

Cooked Vegetable Salad: Spinach, string beans, or asparagus topped with slices of hard-cooked egg. Sprinkle with salt, pepper, and salad herbs.

Tossed Green Salad: A glamorous Hollywood star says: "Break several salad greens into bowl. Toss with minced anchovies, lemon juice, and freshly ground pepper."

1-2-3 Fruit Dressing: No oil. See p. 381..

TO PREVENT DISCOLORATION OF FRUIT

Slice fruit with stainless steel knife at the last moment. Or sprinkle with lemon juice or powdered ascorbic or citric acid preparations (may be purchased in drug store), and store in refrigerator until serving time.

HAVE YOU TRIED . . .

TAKING SALADS ON A PICNIC

Carry the dressing in a closed jar and the greens wrapped in a damp cloth. Mix just before eating.

BOWLS OR PANS FOR SALAD MOLDS

Round bowls, cake pans, or pie pans may be used for molds instead of the regular salad molds. Cut the jellied salad into squares or wedges for individual servings.

A TOMATO SUBSTITUTE

Cut chilled Tomato Aspic (p. 394) into cubes or slices and add to green salads.

WILTED LETTUCE

Fry 4 slices bacon, cut up, until crisp. Add ¼ cup vinegar, 2 tbsp. water. Heat. Pour over 1 qt. shredded lettuce tossed with 2 green onions, chopped, 1 tsp. salt, pepper. Sprinkle 1 chopped hard-cooked egg over top.

Wilted Greens: Use spinach, endive, romaine, or a combination, in place of lettuce.

TO PREPARE SOME FRESH FRUITS AND VEGETABLES FOR SALADS, see pp. 32, 55.

SALADS

Here is a Custom from Ancient Days. "Roman emperors," we read, "dined on dressed lettuce, and ordered served on plates of gold, radishes so thin that the gold gleamed through." From Italy and early Greece, the custom of mixing greens with oils and herbs traveled to Spain and France where the people lovingly adopted it. When Catharine of Aragon went to England as the bride of Henry the Eighth, it was necessary for the royal household to send abroad to get greens to please her accustomed taste. In time, the French and Spaniards introduced salads to America.

Salads have become increasingly popular throughout the years until now they occupy a place of prominence in our menus. They appear in dinners and luncheons . . . and as smart party refreshments. They are important for balanced meals.

Choose the Right Salad. Salads may be classified according to the place they occupy in a meal: *Appetizer Salads* . . . served as a first course. *Dinner or With-the-Meal Salads* . . . served as an accompaniment to or just after the meat course. *Main Dish or Salad Plates* . . . served as the main course for luncheons or suppers or as the main dish at parties. *Dessert Salads* . . . served as the dessert course and often accompanied by cheese and crackers.

Just as an artist combines colors on a canvas to make a beautiful painting, a culinary artist combines ingredients of varying forms and colors to make a salad that is a picture.

Once you have mastered the making of the few basic types of salad, there is no end to the varieties you can serve. For almost any fruits or vegetables may be combined with salad greens. We have included suggestions for many of the most popular combinations. On the following pages, too, are little hints for attaining the refreshing salads that help make a luncheon or dinner or special party a memorable affair.

A DIFFERENT SALAD EVERY DAY
MAKES YOUR MEALS HEALTHFUL AND GAY

(1) Soufflé Salad with Fruit   (2) Chicken Salad   (3) Palace Court Salad
(4) Grapefruit-cherry Salad   (5) Tomato stuffed with Perfection Salad   (6) Cantaloupe Ring
(7) Avocado-grapefruit-tomato Salad   (8) Orange-and-Bermuda Onion Salad
(9) Melon Boat Salad   (10) Artichoke Hearts, Celery, Anchovy Salad
(11) Avocado stuffed with Crabmeat Salad   (12) Plum Tomato, Deviled Egg, etc.
on Romaine Leaves   (13) Pineapple Fruit Plate

A SALAD CENTER

For speed and ease in making salads, arrange a salad center with the staple ingredients (oil, vinegar, herbs, seasonings) and the necessary utensils together. Cupboard and working space for salads near the refrigerator make an ideal place.

HOW TO MAKE A GOOD SALAD

1 Choose the right type salad.
Light salad with hearty meal.
Tart salad with fish.
Hearty or hot salad for main course.
Fruit salad as appetizer, dessert, or meat accompaniment.

2 Choose pleasing combinations with contrasts in color, texture, form, and flavor.

3 Prepare Salad Greens with care.
As soon as salad greens are delivered from market or gathered from the garden, trim off inedible leaves. Store unwashed in tightly covered container or plastic bag in refrigerator. Wash as needed to avoid "rusting."
Head Lettuce: Do not wash . . . just pull off the outer leaves. (Leaves must be thoroughly dry to insure crispness.)
Leaf Lettuce, Endive, Spinach, etc.: Swish in water, washing each leaf separately. Lukewarm water is best. Allow water to drain off. Roll up in clean towel to absorb excess moisture. Store, wrapped, in refrigerator until ready to use.

4 Choose correct dressing. (*See suggestions under each salad dressing recipe.*)

5 Toss ingredients lightly. Do not bruise or crush greens. Use a minimum amount of dressing . . . too much makes a limp salad.

6 Arrange attractively but avoid a "fixed" appearance. Salads must be simple and casual. Use a large enough plate so salad does not extend over edge.

7 COLD . . . CRISP . . . COLD: Assemble the salad ingredients, prepared in advance, from the refrigerator just before eating. Chill plates or bowls in warm weather.

A VARIETY OF GREENS GIVES INTEREST TO SALADS

Use one alone or combine several.

Head Lettuce

Boston or Bibb Lettuce

Chicory

Escarole

Romaine or Cos Lettuce

Beet Greens

Nasturtium Leaves

Mint

Curly Endive

Oak Leaf Lettuce

French Endive

Dandelion Greens

Spinach

Mustard Greens

Cabbage

Watercress

Bronze Lettuce

CHOOSE FROM THESE SALAD BASES

Mound of shredded greens.

Slice of head lettuce.

Lettuce Cup (slit leaf part way and overlap). Use one or more leaves. Illustrated.——>

Bibb lettuce arranged petal fashion (*see also Individual Salads, p. 386*).

Avocado half on salad greens.

Tomato Flower Cup (*p. 390*) on salad greens.

Orange cup on salad greens.

Ring of watercress. ——>

HERBS ADD THE GOURMET TOUCH

Dried herbs are available packaged in jars. Tarragon, sweet basil, chervil, and rosemary are first choice for salads. Learn to develop extra zest in salads with a dash of such herbs as dill, mustard, curry powder, or poppy seeds.

FRENCH DRESSING (American version)

(For Classic French Dressing, see Best Tossed Salad, p. 383.)

The dressing for simple green salads. Also the foundation of many delightful variations. Harry J. Kleefisch, St. Louis, Missouri, known to many as "Enrique," learned special food secrets from a former chef of the King of Italy. He says: "Add some grated lemon rind to a French Dressing for real zesty flavor." In this recipe he uses a mild vinegar.

Beat together with rotary beater or shake well in tightly covered jar . . .

> 1 cup olive oil, salad oil, or combination
> ¼ cup vinegar
> ¼ cup lemon juice
> 1 tsp. salt
> ½ tsp. dry mustard
> ½ tsp. paprika

Keep in covered jar in refrigerator. Shake again to mix before using; it separates after standing.

AMOUNT: 1½ cups dressing.

SWEET FRENCH DRESSING

For fruit salads.

To ½ cup French Dressing (*above*), add 2 tbsp. *sifted* confectioners' sugar or honey. (In place of vinegar, you may use orange, pineapple, or maraschino cherry juice.)

PIQUANT DRESSING

Superb on a vegetable salad. A favorite combination, too, with broken lettuce, seeded Tokay grapes, and sliced fresh pears.

To ½ cup French Dressing (*above*), add 2 tbsp. sugar, ½ tsp. *each* celery seeds and grated onion. Let 1 clove garlic, cut crosswise, stand in dressing 1 hr.

VINAIGRETTE DRESSING

For vegetables cold or hot. Especially good on cooked cold asparagus. For Tomatoes Vinaigrette, see p. 386.

To ½ cup French Dressing (*above*), add 3 green olives, chopped fine; 1 small dill pickle, chopped fine; ½ tbsp. minced chives; ½ tbsp. minced pimiento; 1 hard-cooked egg, chopped fine. Mix. Chill.

ROQUEFORT DRESSING

Sophisticated touch for vegetable salads.

Mash ¼ cup Roquefort cheese with ⅛ tsp. Worcestershire sauce. Blend in ½ cup French Dressing (*above*).

SPECIAL SALAD ACCOMPANIMENTS
Hot Cheese Puffs (*p. 65*)
Savory Crackers (*p. 58*)
Crackers with Cheese Spreads (*p. 66*)

Cheese Straws: Roll grated sharp cheese into pastry dough. Cut into strips. Bake in very hot oven (475°) until lightly browned.

GARLIC FRENCH DRESSING

For a tossed green salad with Italian food. And, according to Margaret Wolfe, there is nothing better for Orange-Bermuda Onion Salad (p. 387), her favorite.

Crush 1 clove garlic into fine paste. Mix in some freshly ground pepper and ½ cup French Dressing (*at left above*).

CHIFFONADE DRESSING

Good with hearts of lettuce, cabbage, and tomato.

To ½ cup French Dressing (*at left above*), add 1 tbsp. shredded ripe olives, 1 tbsp. shredded green pepper, 1 hard-cooked egg (white sieved, yolk mashed), and 1 tbsp. finely cut chives.

LORENZO DRESSING

For fruit or vegetable salads.

To ½ cup French Dressing (*at left above*), add 1 tbsp. chili sauce.

WATERCRESS DRESSING

Elegant with pear salads.

To ½ cup French Dressing (*at left above*), add 2 tbsp. *each* minced watercress and chili sauce and 1 tbsp. currant jelly.

HERB DRESSING

Especially good with greens.

To ½ cup French Dressing (*at left above*), add 2 tsp. minced parsley, ⅛ tsp. powdered thyme, ½ tsp. oregano.

CURRY DRESSING

Try this on salads of greens, meats, and fish.

To ½ cup French Dressing (*at left above*), add ⅛ tsp. curry powder.

CATSUP DRESSING

Good on wedges of lettuce.

To ½ cup French Dressing (*at left above*), add ½ cup catsup.

MAYONNAISE (Recipe)

The foundation of a myriad of intriguing salad dressings.

Beat together with rotary beater . . .
    1 egg yolk
    1 tsp. mustard
    1 tsp. confectioners' sugar
    ¼ tsp. salt
    dash of cayenne pepper
    1 tbsp. lemon juice or vinegar
Continue beating while adding, at first drop by drop, gradually increasing amount as mixture thickens until all is used . . .
    1 cup salad oil
Slowly add . . .
    1 more tbsp. lemon juice or vinegar

Beat well. Chill before serving. When using, modify as desired with heavy or whipped cream.

AMOUNT: 1½ cups dressing.

FRUIT SALAD MAYONNAISE

For fruit combinations, single fruits, and Waldorf Salad.

Into ½ cup Mayonnaise, fold ¼ cup whipping cream, whipped stiff.

PRINCESS MAYONNAISE

A dainty pink dressing for fruits.

Into ½ cup Mayonnaise, blend 1 tbsp. maraschino cherry juice and 4 chopped maraschino cherries. Mix well. Fold in ¼ cup whipping cream, whipped stiff.

TOMATO-CUCUMBER MAYONNAISE

Excellent on sea food salads.

To 1 cup Mayonnaise, add ½ cup *each* drained diced tomato and cucumber, 1 tsp. minced onion, salt.

THOUSAND ISLAND DRESSING

Popularly used on just wedges of lettuce.

Mix ½ cup Mayonnaise; 1 tbsp. chili sauce; 1 tbsp. chopped stuffed olives; 1 tsp. minced chives; 1 hard-cooked egg, chopped; ¼ tsp. paprika, and additional salt and pepper to taste.

RUSSIAN DRESSING

With salad greens alone, it makes a perfect dinner salad.

To ½ cup Mayonnaise, add ¼ cup thick chili sauce and a few drops of onion juice. An additional teaspoon lemon juice may be added, if desired.

COOKED MAYONNAISE

Uses those "extra" egg yolks.

Mix in saucepan . . .
    ⅓ cup GOLD MEDAL Flour
    1 tsp. sugar
    1 tsp. salt
    1 tsp. dry mustard
Add gradually . . .
    ¾ cup water
    ¼ cup mild vinegar or lemon juice

Cook over low heat, stirring constantly, until mixture boils. Boil 1 min. Remove from heat. Pour into bowl. Beat in with rotary beater . . .
    4 egg yolks (or 2 whole eggs)
Continue beating . . . adding a little at a time . . .
    1 cup salad oil

Chill before serving. When using, modify as desired with heavy or whipped cream.

AMOUNT: 2 cups dressing.

COOKED SALAD DRESSING

Also called "boiled" dressing. For potato, cabbage, and other hearty salads.

Mix in saucepan . . .
    ½ cup *sifted* GOLD MEDAL Flour
    ½ cup sugar
    2 tsp. salt
    2 tsp. dry mustard
    ⅛ tsp. paprika
Blend in gradually . . .
    1 cup water
    ¾ cup mild vinegar or lemon juice

Cook over direct low heat, stirring constantly, until mixture thickens and boils. Boil 1 min. Stir at least half of mixture into . . .
    4 egg yolks (or 2 whole eggs), slightly beaten.
Then stir into hot mixture in saucepan. Bring to boil, stirring constantly. Boil 1 min. Remove from heat. Add . . .
    1 tbsp. butter

Cool. When using, modify as desired with heavy sweet cream or cultured sour cream.

AMOUNT: 2½ cups dressing.

SOUR CREAM MAYONNAISE

Ideal with mixed chopped garden vegetables: cucumber, tomato, tender spinach, or lettuce and carrots.

To ¼ cup Mayonnaise, Cooked Mayonnaise, or Cooked Salad Dressing, add ¼ cup plain or whipped sour cream, 2 tsp. minced chives, and a dash of coarse black pepper.

1-2-3 FRUIT DRESSING

No oil. Tart and refreshing. Whipped cream may be folded in for some types of salads.

Combine in saucepan . . .
    juice and grated rind of 1 lemon, lime, and orange
    1 egg, well beaten
    1 cup sugar

Cook over med. heat, stirring constantly, until boiling. Boil 1 min. Remove from heat. Cool.

LIME OR LEMONADE DRESSING

Fresh, zesty . . . so good on fruit.

Combine in small bowl . . .
    1/3 cup undiluted frozen concentrate for lime-ade or lemonade
    1/3 cup honey
    1/3 cup salad oil
    1 tsp. celery seed

Beat with rotary beater until smooth.

OLD-FASHIONED FRUIT DRESSING

Use this for 24-hour Salad (p. 387).

Beat together with rotary beater . . .
    2 eggs
    2 tbsp. sugar
    2 tbsp. vinegar or lemon juice
    2 tbsp. pineapple juice
    1 tbsp. butter
    dash of salt

Cook in saucepan over low heat, stirring constantly, just to boiling. Remove from heat. Cool. Fold in . . .
    1 cup whipping cream, whipped

RUBY RED DRESSING

On oranges and citrus things,
It makes a feast that's fit for kings.

Beat with fork until smooth . . .
    1/2 cup currant jelly

Add and beat until smooth . . .
    1/4 cup salad oil
    2 tbsp. lemon juice
    dash of salt
    few drops onion juice

SOUR CREAM DRESSING

Spoon over baked potatoes, sliced cucumbers, tender young leaf lettuce, or hot or cold sea food.

Mix 1 cup cultured sour cream, 3 tbsp. minced chives or onion, 2 tbsp. lemon juice, salt and pepper to taste.

GREEN GODDESS SALAD DRESSING

The most popular at a large San Francisco hotel. Especially delicious on salad greens or sea food. For a milder fla-vored, thicker dressing, omit vinegar.

Combine thoroughly . . .
    1 clove garlic, crushed or grated
    3 tbsp. finely minced chives or onions
    1/3 cup finely minced parsley
    3 tbsp. anchovy paste or finely minced anchovies
    1 tbsp. lemon juice
    3 tbsp. tarragon wine vinegar
    1/2 cup cultured sour cream
    1 cup mayonnaise
    salt and freshly ground pepper to taste

Chill thoroughly; it mellows and thickens on standing.

AMOUNT: 2 cups dressing.

Rancho Roquefort Dressing: omit parsley, anchovies, and vinegar. Stir in 1/2 cup crumbled Roquefort or Bleu cheese.

LIME-HONEY DRESSING

Delicious with fruit salads, such as Waldorf, orange, or a combination of cut-up pineapple, bananas, Tokay grapes, and dates. Good, too, over molded gelatins.

Mix thoroughly in saucepan . . .
    2 to 3 tbsp. lime juice (or lemon)
    1/2 cup honey
    2 eggs, well beaten

Cook over med. heat until thickened (mixture becomes clear), stirring constantly. Cool. Just before serving, fold in . . .
    1/2 cup whipping cream, whipped stiff

AMOUNT: 1 1/2 cups dressing.

TOMATO SOUP DRESSING

Serve on shredded greens. This recipe came from the pop-ular cook book, "Our Favorite Recipes," published in connection with the New Ulm Centennial. It was contributed by Mrs. E. A. Nierengarten of New Ulm, Minnesota.

Combine in quart jar . . .
    1 tbsp. sugar
    1 tbsp. Worcestershire sauce
    1 tsp. *each* dry mustard, paprika, salt
    10 1/2-oz. can condensed tomato soup
    1 cup *each* salad oil and vinegar
    1 clove garlic, pressed or grated
    1 small onion, grated

Cover. Shake well. Store in refrigerator.

AMOUNT: 3 1/2 cups dressing.

HOW TO MAKE THE EASIEST, QUICKEST GREEN SALAD

1 For a faint whisper of garlic flavor, rub chilled bowl with garlic bud.

2 Break up in bowl crisp, dry, cold salad greens (lettuce, endive, spinach, etc.).

3 Add attractive sized pieces (to retain identity) of fruits, sea foods, vegetables, etc.

4 Just before serving, add dressing . . . only enough to make leaves of greens glisten.

6 Add juicy tomato sections at the last.

5 Gently toss ingredients so that every piece is coated with dressing.

7 Serve in large bowl or in individual bowls or on individual salad plates.

BEST TOSSED SALAD

with Classic French Dressing

Janette Kelley, director of our staff, has this as her basic salad favorite to which she adds either canned artichoke hearts or a few thinly sliced uncooked mushrooms or fresh water chestnuts.

Tear into bite-size pieces (do not cut) . . .
- 1 large head lettuce
- 1 bunch leaf lettuce
- ½ small bunch endive (1 cup)
- ½ small bag spinach (2 cups)

Toss with salad oil until leaves glisten. Then toss with a mixture of . . .
- 2 tbsp. white tarragon wine vinegar
- 1½ tsp. salt
- 1 clove garlic, pressed or minced
- ground fresh pepper
- dash of flavor extender

Toss again and serve immediately.

AMOUNT: 6 to 8 servings.

CHEF'S SALAD

Julienne strips of meat with mixed greens make a hearty main dish salad.

Follow method for Mixed Green Salad (*opposite page*)—except use:
- 1 head lettuce
- ½ bunch romaine or endive
- ½ cup chopped green onion
- ½ cup sliced celery
- 1 cup match-like sticks of Swiss cheese
- 1 cup match-like strips of cold cooked meat (such as beef, ham, tongue, chicken)
- 2-oz. flat can fillets of anchovy, if desired

Toss, just before serving, with ½ cup mayonnaise and ¼ cup French Dressing (*p. 379*). Garnish with strips of meat and cheese, olives, and hard-cooked eggs.

AMOUNT: 4 servings.

Russian Salad: Add some or all: ½ cup *each* diced cooked beets, kidney beans, sauerkraut, 1 to 2 tbsp. minced sardines or anchovies, 1 med. potato, diced, ¼ cup *each* diced cucumber and sweet pickles. Garnish with sieved hard-cooked egg and caviar.

GRANDMA'S LETTUCE SALAD

"Many happy childhood memories are recalled each time I serve this," says Mrs. Burt C. Sloate, Billings, Montana.

Cut or tear into large bowl 4 cups crisp cold leaf lettuce. Toss with a mixture of ½ cup cream, 1 to 1½ tbsp. sugar, ¼ tsp. salt, and 3 to 4 tbsp. vinegar. *6 servings.*

PALACE COURT SALAD

A luncheon specialty at the Palace Hotel in San Francisco.

Arrange a mound of finely shredded lettuce on salad plate. On top, place a thick large tomato slice. On tomato, place one large cooked artichoke heart (or 3 small). Cover this with pieces of cooked crab, shrimp, or chicken. Garnish around edge of lettuce with sieved hard-cooked egg. Serve with Russian Dressing (p. 380).

FRESH SPINACH SALAD

Toss together lightly . . .
- ½ lb. washed, dried spinach, torn in shreds (4 cups)
- 1 small Bermuda onion, sliced
- ¼ cup diced celery
- 4 hard-cooked eggs, sliced
- salt and pepper to taste

Chill. Before serving, toss lightly with

LEMON SALAD DRESSING

Blend 1 tbsp. salad oil, 2 tbsp. flour, and ½ cup water. Bring to boil, stirring constantly. Boil 1 min. Remove from heat. Blend in 1 egg yolk, ½ tsp. salt, ½ tsp. dry mustard, ¼ tsp. paprika, 2 tbsp. lemon juice, and ½ cup salad oil. Beat until smooth.

WESTERN WAY SALAD

Sometimes called Caesar's Salad. A connoisseur's salad, made for our staff by a delightful visitor, famous home economist, Essie L. Elliott of California.

In advance: Cover ½ clove garlic with 2 tbsp. salad oil; let stand. Also, prepare 2 cups Croutons (*p. 30*).

Place 3 qt. dry, cold, crisp salad greens in large bowl. Add ⅓ cup *each* salad oil, grated dry cheese, and crumbled Bleu cheese. Salt and pepper to taste. Break 1 raw egg over greens. Squeeze juice of 2 lemons over egg. Toss well.

Just before serving: Remove garlic from oil; combine oil and croutons, and sprinkle over top of salad. *8 servings.*

SOME VEGETABLE SALAD FAVORITES

Serve on salad greens with your favorite dressing.

- Cooked asparagus tips sprinkled with grated cheese on thick tomato slices.

- Grated raw carrots and diced celery mixed with raisins or nuts.

- Halves of peeled chilled tomatoes sprinkled with minced parsley or chives. After dressing is added, sprinkle with basil or oregano.

- Little red cherry tomatoes, yellow plum tomatoes with unpared cucumber slices, and sliced spring onions.

- Overlapping slices of tomato, unpared cucumber slices, and onion rings or slices.

- Sliced cucumbers and minced parsley.

- Green pepper rings, onion rings, and sliced water chestnuts or raw mushrooms.

- Raw cauliflowerets, thinly sliced radishes, wafer thin slices of raw turnips with mixed salad greens.

- Sprigs of young spinach leaves or bib lettuce, raw cauliflowerets, thinly sliced raw mushrooms, bits of crisp bacon, and sieved hard-cooked eggs.

- Finely shredded raw baby beets, red cabbage, and raw parsnips, topped with thin cucumber slices and onion rings.

- Small tomatoes stuffed with cottage cheese sprinkled with minced chives, parsley, or toasted almonds. Or stuffed with grated cabbage and minced mint. Or stuffed with cream cheese mixed with minced onion, green pepper, and stuffed olives.

- Mound of cottage cheese with diced green or red pepper, cucumber, and onions.

SOME FRUIT SALAD COMBINATIONS

Serve on salad greens with your favorite dressing.

- Avocado cubes or slices and melon balls.

- Honeydew melon slices with balls of cantaloupe and watermelon.

- Cut-up apples, oranges, bananas, grapes, marshmallows, and nuts blended with mayonnaise and whipped cream.

- Cream cheese balls rolled in chopped pistachio nuts on apricot, peach, or pear halves.

- Pineapple slices or peach or pear halves topped with cottage or cream cheese.

- Fresh or canned pineapple spears, strawberries, and halves of blue plums.

- Pear halves stuck with salted almonds or salted peanuts.

- Cantaloupe balls, Bing cherries, halved sweet green or Tokay grapes (seeded).

- Pineapple chunks, canned or fresh Bing cherries, and pecans.

- Prunes or apricots stuffed with cream or cottage cheese or peanut butter.

- Orange or grapefruit sections, avocado slices, unpared red apples.

- Sliced fresh pears and halved Tokay grapes (seeded).

- Halved sweet green grapes or cherries in hollow of pear or peach halves.

- Banana slices rolled in chopped peanuts.

- Pear or peach halves with mayonnaise in hollow, topped with grated yellow cheese.

- Fresh peach slices, small green grapes, and peanuts.

- Avocado slices, grapefruit sections, and a sprinkling of pomegranate seeds.

- Diced fresh pineapple, strawberries, and a sprinkling of finely minced mint.

SEASONAL SALAD BOWLS

WINTER: Carrot Curls, Golden Orange Slices, Spinach, Lettuce, and Celery Leaves.

AUTUMN: Red Apple Slices, Diced Green Celery, Lettuce Hearts, Sprigs of Parsley.

SUMMER: Cauliflowerets, Tomato Sections, Sprigs of Mint, Head Lettuce.

SPRING: Radishes, Bermuda Onion Rings, Cucumber, Endive, Nasturtium Leaves.

HOLIDAY SEASON: Green Grapes, Pomegranate Seeds, Cucumber, Watercress, Endive.

PLATTER OF CONTRASTING ROWS OF SALAD VEGETABLES

Arrange desired cut-up vegetables (cold and crisp) in rows . . . with an eye to color and pattern. (Tomato slices, cucumber slices, latticed carrots, asparagus stalks, etc.)

PLATTER OF SALAD GREENS

Cooling shades of dark and light.

Arrange a variety of different salad greens on a platter, such as: curly endive around the outside, inner leaves of lettuce next, then watercress sprigs, and in the center artichoke hearts. Sprinkle sliced shallots and finely minced St. Mary's herbs over all. Pass French Dressing (*p. 379*).

INDIVIDUAL SALADS IN LETTUCE CUPS

Katharine Eustis of Minneapolis, known among other things for her beautiful salads, lines her lettuce cups with darker green leaves of Bibb lettuce.

Prepare enough Lettuce Cups (*p. 378*) to serve number desired. Fill with cut-up fruits or chilled vegetables mixed with just enough French Dressing (*p. 379*) to glisten . . . or place individual molded gelatin salad in each. Arrange on platter or tray and chill again. Serve on individual salad plates, or pass platter or tray for each guest to serve himself.

BOUQUET OF SALADS

With hot rolls, beverage, and dessert, a plate luncheon . . . as served at a famous eating place in Silver Springs, Maryland.

Circle 4 small servings of individual salads in Lettuce Cups (*p. 378*) on each dinner-sized plate. Fill center with sprigs of watercress, top with a fresh flower. Plan a variety of salads that will harmonize: (1) appetizer salad: tomato mixture; (2) hearty salad: chicken or sea food; (3) green vegetable salad: avocado, asparagus, or tossed garden; (4) dessert salad: fruit or fruit aspic.

SALAD BAR

"As pretty as a bouquet of vari-colored flowers. Perfect for a buffet supper or a big crowd!" says Eileen Kueffner (Mrs. William Kueffner) of Red Wing, Minnesota.

Marinate by tossing separately with ½ tbsp. French Dressing (each in separate bowl) and letting stand in refrigerator about 1 hr . . .
   1 cup each finely shredded cabbage,
      chopped radishes,
      watercress sprigs,
      coarsely grated carrots,
      cut-up fringed cucumber slices
Pile each vegetable high in a triangle . . . the point at center of plate and radiating out to edge. 2 or 3 pieces of cardboard held at angles to each other keep vegetables separate until placed. Serve cold . . . pass French Dressing (*p. 379*).
AMOUNT: 8 servings.

PINEAPPLE FRUIT PLATE

Helen Holloway Hallbert of our staff, co-founder with her husband of a famous line of salad dressings, often serves this salad at supper parties. See color picture, p. 377.

Cut top from fresh pineapple, cut pineapple in two crosswise, and scoop out inside; cut pineapple in cubes, removing core. Toss pineapple cubes together with other fresh fruits (halved Tokay or sweet green grapes, Bing cherries, orange sections, cut-up sweet plums, apricot halves, pear sticks) and Sweet French Dressing (*p. 379*). Refill pineapple shell with the fruit salad mixture. Serve on large chop plate surrounded by sprigs of watercress or endive or by Lettuce Cups (*p. 378*) filled, if desired, with additional fruit.

TOMATOES VINAIGRETTE

Serve on luncheon or dinner plate with or without greens.

Arrange in 8 or 9″ square pan . . .
   8 or 9 thick tomato slices or smaller
      whole tomatoes (with tops cut off)
Spoon over tomatoes mixture of: 2 cloves garlic (pressed or minced), 1 tsp. salt, ½ tsp. pepper, 2 tsp. oregano, ½ tsp. dry mustard, ⅓ cup wine vinegar, 1 cup olive oil. Cover. Refrigerate 2 to 3 hr., basting occasionally. To serve, sprinkle with minced onion and parsley and some of dressing. *8 servings.*

ORANGE OR GRAPEFRUIT SALADS

See p. 32 for How to Prepare special fruits for salads (grapefruit, pineapple, melon balls, avocado).

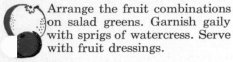 Arrange the fruit combinations on salad greens. Garnish gaily with sprigs of watercress. Serve with fruit dressings.

Grapefruit-Orange Salad: Alternate sections of orange and grapefruit.

Apple-Avocado-Orange-Grape Salad: Alternate slices of unpared apple, orange sections, and peeled avocado with a sprinkling of halved little green or Tokay grapes.

Grapefruit-Pomegranate Salad: Arrange grapefruit sections in petal fashion. Sprinkle with pomegranate seeds.

Avocado-Grapefruit-Orange Salad: Arrange thin slices of peeled avocado between sections of grapefruit and orange.

Avocado-Grapefruit-Tomato Salad: Place Tomato Flower Cups (*p. 390*) on lettuce leaves. Arrange around each tomato, sections of grapefruit and slices of orange. Insert thin slices of avocado here and there to resemble leaves. Bit of mayonnaise in center.

 Orange-Bermuda Onion Salad (especially good with wild game): Alternate slices of orange with rings of Bermuda onion. Garnish with sprigs of watercress and chopped fresh mint.

Grapefruit-Avocado-Persimmon Salad: Alternate slices of avocado and persimmon with sections of grapefruit. Garnish with watercress.

Grapefruit-Cherry Salad: Put sections of grapefruit together with softened cream cheese between. Top with a few large Bing or Royal Ann cherries.

24-HOUR SALAD

No longer takes 24 hours, but is as good as ever. Make Old-fashioned Fruit Dressing (p. 381).

Toss together . . .
    2 cups drained, pitted, canned white or Bing cherries
    2 cups drained pineapple bits or chunks
    2 oranges, peeled, sectioned, and cut up
    24 marshmallows, cut in fourths

Blend in the dressing. Chill several hours. Serve in large bowl with or without salad greens or in individual Lettuce Cups (*p. 378*). Garnish with orange sections and maraschino cherries.

AMOUNT: 8 servings.

MELON SALADS

One of these is often a feature of the dinners served at her beautifully appointed table by Mrs. Richard Eldred of Riverside, Illinois. Sometimes a little ball of cream cheese rolled in shaved pistachio nuts is an attractive garnish.

Combine watermelon, cantaloupe, or honeydew melon balls, cubes, or slices. Or use 1 variety combined with other fruits. Serve on greens with a sweet fruit dressing.

Cantaloupe Ring: See color picture, p. 376. Place ¾" thick slice of cantaloupe (rind removed) on bed of salad greens. Fill center with seasonal fruits (melon balls, sweet green grapes, cherries, strips of pears, blackberries, etc.). Serve with fruit dressing.

Melon Boat Salad: See color picture, p. 376. Place boat-shaped section of cantaloupe (rind removed) on bed of salad greens. Fill boat with seasonal fruits as in Cantaloupe Ring (*above*). Garnish ends of boat with tiny garden flowers.

Melon-Plum-Peach-Grape Salad: Alternate slices of melon, red plums, fresh peaches. Add a few small green grapes.

WALDORF SALAD

Lightly mix diced apple (red skin on) with half as much diced celery and a few broken nuts. Toss with mayonnaise or Cooked Salad Dressing (*p. 380*) combined with cream. Serve in Lettuce Cups (*p. 378*). Garnish each with a maraschino cherry.

FROZEN FRUIT SALAD

Serve on lettuce with hot buttered breads or tiny broiled cheese sandwiches.

Soften . . .
    1 envelope unflavored gelatin (1 tbsp.)
in . . .
    1 cup cold water
Dissolve over hot water. Blend into . . .
    ⅓ cup mild mayonnaise
    1 cup whipping cream, whipped
Fold in . . .
    1 cup drained canned pineapple chunks
    1 cup sliced bananas
    1 cup cut-up orange
    ½ cup halved maraschino cherries, dates, nuts, or combination
    2 tbsp. lemon juice

Pour into refrigerator tray; freeze until firm.

AMOUNT: 8 servings.

CABBAGE SALAD

Probably one of the earliest in America. And it has so many variations.

Place in vegetable crisper or covered dish in re-frigerator 2 or more hr. . . .

>2½ cups finely shredded, chopped, or grated cabbage

Then sprinkle with . . .

>1 tsp. salt

Moisten with . . .

>Cooked Salad Dressing (p. 380) or mayon-naise mixed with a little cream

Add, if desired . . .

>1½ to 2 cups cut-up fruits, vegetables, or nuts (*see below*)

Toss lightly with fork. Serve immediately.

delicious additions

- Cut-up red apple, celery, and nuts.
- Drained pineapple, cut-up marshmallows, halved small green grapes or seeded Tokay grapes.
- Grated raw carrots, dill, chopped green pepper.
- Raisins, grated carrots, celery seeds.
- Cut-up red apple, sliced bananas, and salted peanuts.
- Grated turnip, minced onion, and pimiento.
- Cut-up tomato and cucumber, summer savory.
- Minced green pepper, onion, and pimiento, cut-up celery, sprinkle of celery seeds.
- Equal parts of cut-up cucumber and minced green onions, sprinkle of celery seeds.

WINTER SALAD BOWL

We first tasted this salad at the home of Mrs. Verne D. Whitaker. Eleanor Combs Halderman makes a variation . . . adding grated rind and sections of 1 orange in place of the olives, raw carrots cut in strips for part of the parsnips.

Marinate in ¼ cup French Dressing (p. 379) . . .

>1½ cups grated raw parsnips (3 med.)
>⅓ cup chopped sweet onion
>¾ cup chopped celery (2 stalks)
>12 pimiento-stuffed olives, chopped
>½ tsp. salt
>dash of pepper

Just before serving, add . . .

>1 med. head lettuce, torn into bite-size pieces

Toss lightly with . . .

>¼ cup mayonnaise

AMOUNT: 6 to 8 servings.

YEHUDI MENUHIN'S BEET SALAD

The world-famous violinist recommends that for this salad only organically grown beets and almonds with unpasteurized cream be used.

Mix grated raw beets and finely grated almonds. Stir in cream and lemon juice to right consistency. Serve in individual nests of butter lettuce with olive oil and lemon dressing on only the lettuce.

OLD-FASHIONED COLE SLAW

"Cole" is the Old English word for cabbage. The dressing may vary from heavy sweet cream to vinegar and sugar.

Follow recipe for Cabbage Salad (*at left*)— except add 1 tbsp. sugar, 1 tsp. scraped onion, 1 tbsp. vinegar, 6 tbsp. cream, and 1 tbsp. mustardy salad dressing.

Delicate Cole Slaw: Omit onion and mustardy salad dressing. Add drained pineapple cubes or a few green grapes.

HOT CABBAGE SLAW See p. 430.

NEW NETHERLANDS COLE SLAW
(Hot Cabbage Salad)

First introduced to America by the Holland Dutch when they settled in New York in 1624. They called it "Kool-slaa." It was their "great sallad dressed with vinegar."

Heat to boiling in saucepan . . .

>¼ cup mild vinegar
>1 tbsp. sugar
>1 tsp. salt
>¼ tsp. pepper
>½ tsp. dry mustard
>1 tbsp. butter

Add at least half of hot mixture to . . .

>1 egg, slightly beaten

Then stir into the hot vinegar in saucepan. Cook until mixture thickens and boils. Remove from heat. Beat in . . .

>2 tbsp. cream

Pour while hot over . . .

>4 cups finely shredded cabbage

Serve hot or cold.

AMOUNT: 6 servings.

To serve hot, place in pan over low heat *just* until heated through.

POTATO SALAD

A good potato salad is the mark of a good cook.

Place in bowl . . .
>4 cups cubed cold boiled potatoes
>1 tbsp. finely chopped onion

Sprinkle with . . .
>½ tsp. salt
>dash of pepper

Mix lightly with . . .
>¼ cup French Dressing (p. 379)

Chill an hour or two. Toss lightly with . . .
>½ cup Cooked Salad Dressing (p. 380) or mayonnaise

Blend in carefully . . .
>2 cut-up large hard-cooked eggs

Mix in a little minced pimiento and parsley for color. Add extra seasoning and dressing to taste. Serve in bowl or on platter surrounded with salad greens, tomato sections, slices or wedges of hard-cooked eggs, cucumber sticks, etc. Garnish with paprika.

AMOUNT: 6 servings.

Special Potato Salad: Add 1 cup chopped celery; 1 cucumber, diced; 1 tsp. celery seeds; 1 cup grated carrots.

Meat-and-Potato Salad: Add strips of cooked lean meat such as beef, ham, veal, or chicken.

Gourmet Potato Salad: Use only 3 cups potatoes. Omit both dressings. Remove the yolks from the hard-cooked eggs. Dice the whites and add to the potatoes. *For the dressing,* mash the yolks and mix into ⅔ cup cultured sour cream. Stir in 2 tbsp. vinegar, 1 tsp. prepared mustard, ½ tsp. celery seeds, 2 tbsp. mayonnaise, and ⅓ cup sweet relish. Pour over potato mixture and toss lightly.

BEAN SALAD

Mrs. Charles Kuoni, Jr. of Glen Ellyn, Illinois, likes to serve this at impromptu luncheons in her suburban home.

Mix . . .
>2 cups drained cooked kidney beans (no. 2 can)
>¼ cup diced celery
>3 chopped pickles (dill or sweet)
>1 small onion, minced
>2 hard-cooked eggs, sliced
>½ tsp. salt
>⅛ tsp. pepper

Mix lightly with . . .
>about ¼ cup mayonnaise or cultured sour cream

Chill thoroughly. Serve on salad greens. Garnish with grated cheese.

AMOUNT: 6 servings.

HOT GERMAN POTATO SALAD

Mrs. Joseph Teynor, New Ulm, Minnesota, serves this with baked or boiled ham, baked spareribs, or frankfurters.

Boil 6 med. potatoes in their jackets. Peel and slice thinly.

Fry slowly in skillet, then drain on paper . . .
>6 slices bacon

Sauté in bacon fat until golden brown . . .
>¾ cup chopped onion

Blend in . . .
>2 tbsp. flour
>1 to 2 tbsp. sugar
>1½ tsp. salt
>½ tsp. celery seeds
>dash of pepper

Cook over low heat, stirring until smooth and bubbly. Remove from heat. Stir in . . .
>¾ cup water
>⅓ cup vinegar

Bring to boil, stirring constantly. Boil 1 min. Stir in carefully the potatoes and the crumbled bits of bacon. Remove from heat, cover, and let stand until ready to serve.

AMOUNT: 6 to 8 servings.

HOT CABBAGE SALAD

See New Netherlands Cole Slaw (*p. 388*), Hot Cabbage Slaw (*p. 430*).

HEARTY MACARONI SALAD

Church gatherings, Granger meetings, and family reunions find this an old standby.

Combine in bowl . . .
>3 cups chilled cooked macaroni (1½ cups uncooked)
>½ lb. liver sausage, cubed, or bits of crisp bacon
>½ cup chilled cooked peas
>½ lb. Cheddar cheese, cubed
>1 cup chopped celery (about 2 stalks)
>2 tbsp. minced onion
>2 tbsp. minced parsley
>¼ cup minced green pepper, if desired
>salt and pepper to taste

Toss together with mayonnaise mixed with a little cream. Serve on crisp lettuce or other salad greens garnished with chopped hard-cooked eggs.

AMOUNT: 6 to 8 servings.

Macaroni-Salmon or Tuna Salad: Omit liver sausage or bacon. Add 8-oz. can salmon or tuna, flaked, and 1 cup diced cucumber.

Macaroni-Chicken or Veal Salad: Omit liver sausage or bacon. Add 1½ cups diced cooled cooked chicken or veal.

CHICKEN SALAD (✎ Recipe) An All-American favorite.

Toss together . . .
2 cups cut-up cold cooked chicken
(large chunks)
1 cup cut-up celery (½" pieces)
1 tbsp. lemon juice
salt and pepper to taste

Mix in . . .
½ cup mayonnaise

Carefully fold in . . .
2 or 3 hard-cooked eggs, cut up

Chill thoroughly. Arrange a mound in each Lettuce Cup (*p. 378*) and garnish with olives or little sweet pickles and parsley.
AMOUNT: 6 servings.

Tomato Flower Cups: Cut tomatoes almost through into 6 sections so they will open like flowers. Fill with Chicken Salad. Garnish with sieved hard-cooked eggs.

CHICKEN-FRUIT PARTY SALAD

Follow ✎ recipe above—*except* omit hard-cooked eggs. Add 1 cup halved sweet green grapes or drained cut-up pineapple. Sprinkle with ½ cup salted almonds.

CHICKEN AND BACON-OR-ALMOND SALAD

Follow ✎ recipe above—*except* sprinkle with ½ cup finely broken *crisp* bacon or salted almonds, halved.

All you have to do —

For a different service for entertaining: serve chicken or sea food salad in peeled avocado halves or on drained round slices of canned pineapple on crisp lettuce. Garnish with sprigs of watercress. Dainty finger sandwiches of rye or brown bread make a pleasing accompaniment.

SEA FOOD SALAD

Delicious made with crabmeat, shrimp, lobster, tuna, or salmon. Attractive served in center of ring of Tomato Aspic (p. 394).

Mix lightly in order . . .
1 cup flaked cooked sea food
1 tsp. lemon juice
1 tsp. finely minced onion
salt and paprika to taste
1 cup diced celery
1 cup lettuce hearts in small pieces

Chill thoroughly. Just before serving, drain and toss together with mayonnaise to moisten. Serve on crisp lettuce. Garnish with tomato sections, wedges of lemon, slices of hard-cooked egg, and shiny ripe olives.
AMOUNT: 4 servings.

CHICKEN-CRANBERRY SALAD

Recommended as "something special" by Janet Crawford Taylor (Mrs. Jack Taylor) of Plymouth, Massachusetts, and the National Cranberry Association.

Follow ✎ recipe above—*except* omit hard-cooked eggs and substitute 1 cup cubed cranberry jelly for 1 cup of the chicken.

MOCK CHICKEN SALAD

A delicious and economical substitution for the real thing . . . when chicken is high and veal not so expensive.

Follow ✎ recipe above—*except*, in place of the chicken, use cut-up cooked veal.

MIROTON OF SEA FOOD

Potato and sea food salads combined. An impressive main dish for the buffet table . . and for years a favorite at our big community cooking schools.

Marinate by tossing separately with 2 tbsp. French Dressing (each in separate bowl) and letting stand in refrigerator about 1 hr. . . .
2 cups cubed cold boiled potatoes
2 cups flaked cooked tuna, salmon, crabmeat, shrimp, or lobster

Mix lightly with . . .
3 tbsp. capers or chopped crisp pickles
mayonnaise to moisten

Heap in a high mound on serving platter. Sprinkle top with paprika and finely minced parsley. Garnish with wedges of hard-cooked eggs. Surround with crisp Lettuce Cups (*p. 378*). Place sections of tomatoes and shiny black olives in lettuce to be served with each portion.
AMOUNT: 6 to 8 servings.

APPETIZER SALADS
For a dramatic first course.

Plum tomato (its center sprinkled with sieved hard-cooked egg yolk), a deviled egg half (sprinkled with finely cut chives) at either side . . . on salad greens. Garnish of shiny ripe olives.

Artichoke hearts, diced celery, tomato sections, and anchovies, Piquant French Dressing (*p. 379*) . . . in Lettuce Cup. Garnish of strips of green pickles, large green olives.

Avocado half, stuffed with crabmeat, highly seasoned mayonnaise . . . in Lettuce Cup. Garnish of sieved hard-cooked egg, watercress, radish roses, large ripe olives.

Avocado half, drenched with lemon juice, seed cavity filled with a little mayonnaise (thinned with lemon juice). Then a spoonful of lemon or cranberry ice. Serve on a bed of watercress.

BAKED SALADS
Fascinating main dishes for luncheons and suppers.

OVEN CHICKEN SALAD (Recipe)
Bake in individual casseroles or ramekins for easy serving.

Combine . . .
    2 cups cubed cooked chicken
    2 cups thinly sliced celery
    1 cup toasted bread cubes
    ½ cup chopped toasted almonds
    ½ tsp. salt
    2 tsp. grated onion
    1 cup mayonnaise
    2 tbsp. lemon juice
Pile lightly into individual baking dishes. Sprinkle with . . .
    ½ cup grated cheese
    1 cup toasted bread cubes

Bake until bubbly.

TEMPERATURE: 450° (hot oven).

TIME: Bake 10 to 15 min.

AMOUNT: 6 servings.

HOT TUNA SALAD
Sea food shells can be used for attractive individual servings.

Make either chicken salad on this page—*except* omit chicken and use tuna. Garnish with slice of lemon, twisted.

BAKED AVOCADO SALAD
Cut 5 avocados in halves, remove stones, and heat in quick mod. oven (375°) for 10 min. Remove avocados and turn oven down to 350°. Fill with any of the above mixtures. Bake until avocados are tender and filling bubbles. Serve immediately.

TEMPERATURE: 350° (mod. oven).

TIME: Bake 10 to 15 min.

AMOUNT: 10 servings.

HOT CRABMEAT SALAD
Serve in casseroles or spooned out hot on tomato slices in lettuce cups. Unusual, elegant variation of a recipe sent to us by a very clever cateress, Mrs. O. Schultz, of Minneapolis, Minnesota.

Melt in saucepan . . .
    ¼ cup butter
Blend in . . .
    ½ cup *sifted* GOLD MEDAL Flour
    1 tsp. dry mustard
    ⅛ tsp. paprika
    1 tsp. salt
Cook over low heat until mixture is smooth, bubbly. Remove from heat. Stir in . . .
    1 cup milk
Bring to boil; boil 1 min., stirring constantly. Remove from heat. Stir into . . .
    2 egg yolks, slightly beaten
Marinate . . .
    2 cups flaked cooked crabmeat
    1 cup chopped celery
    ⅓ green pepper, chopped
    1 large pimiento, chopped
    ⅓ cup chopped blanched almonds
in . . .
    ¼ cup mild vinegar
Combine the white sauce and marinated mixture. Pile lightly into 8 individual casseroles or oblong baking dish, 12x8″. Bake until bubbly.

TEMPERATURE: 425° (hot oven).

TIME: Bake 12 to 15 min.

AMOUNT: 8 servings.

HOT CHICKEN-CHIP SALAD
Follow recipe at left above—*except* omit bread cubes. Sprinkle 1 cup potato chips over top before baking.

HOW TO MAKE A MOLDED SALAD for example:
STRAWBERRY OR RASPBERRY SALAD GLACÉ

First, prepare the gelatin: Pour 2 cups hot water over 2 pkg. raspberry or strawberry-flavored gelatin. Stir well to completely dissolve the gelatin. Add 2 cups cold water.

Prepare the garnish: Soften 8-oz. pkg. cream cheese with cream. Shape into balls, using 1 level tsp. for each. Roll in ½ cup finely chopped nuts.

1 Place some of the cheese balls evenly spaced in 9″ ring mold.

2 Cover with alternate layers of lightly sugared strawberries (use strawberries with strawberry gelatin, raspberries with raspberry gelatin) and cheese balls.

3 Pour the cooled raspberry or strawberry-flavored gelatin over the cheese balls and berries. Chill until the gelatin is set.

4 Unmold on large serving plate: tip to let in air at one side; loosen with spatula thrust in around edge; turn upside-down onto plate.

5 Garnish with watercress sprigs or lettuce frills and large perfect berries. (For a special dessert, fill center with pineapple sherbet.)

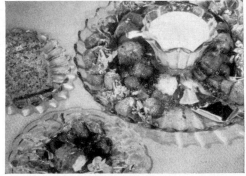

6 Serve on individual plates ... topped with mayonnaise with whipped cream added or with Sweet French Dressing (p. 379).

MOLDED GELATIN SALAD (⚹ Recipe) Made with flavored gelatin. Choose flavor to make an interesting combination with the fruits or vegetables, etc. you add.

Double the recipe to fill 9″ ring mold for 12 servings.

Prepare according to directions on pkg...... 1 pkg. flavored gelatin
Add........................... 2 tbsp. lemon juice (or vinegar)
Chill, and when partially set (mixture
mounds off spoon), add............. 1½ to 2½ cups well drained
and cut-up fresh or canned
fruit, vegetables, or sea food, etc.

When partially set again, pour into 6 or 8 individual molds. Chill until firm. Unmold on large chop plate or individual salad plates. Garnish with crisp lettuce, curly endive, or lacy watercress.

NOTE: Serve with appropriate dressing: Mayonnaise with whipped cream for mild salads ... or Tomato-Cucumber Mayonnaise for vegetable and sea food salads. AMOUNT: 6 to 8 servings.

JELLIED FRUIT MEDLEYS

With toasted cheese sandwiches, one of these sparkling salads is a specialty at Sunday night candlelight suppers in the enchanting southern Colonial home of Roy and Eleanor Larsen, overlooking Mirror Lake, in the suburbs of Minneapolis.

Follow ⚹ recipe above—except omit lemon juice, and use whole or cut-up fruit. (See combinations of fruit on pp. 384, 387.)

JELLIED VEGETABLE-FRUIT SALADS

Follow ⚹ recipe above—using lemon or lime-flavored gelatin and special combinations of cut-up vegetables and fruits:

Complexion Salad: 1½ cups grated raw carrots, 1¼ cups well drained canned crushed pineapple. For **Hartley Salad**, add thin cucumber slices in place of grated carrots.

Carrot-Grape Salad: 1¼ cups each finely diced raw carrots, halved sweet green grapes.

Cottage Cheese Salad: add ½ tsp. salt, 1 tbsp. minced onion, 1 tbsp. minced green pepper, 2 tbsp. chopped celery, 1 cup cottage cheese.

Very good on molded vegetable salads

Goldenrod Mayonnaise: to 1 cup mayonnaise, add finely chopped egg whites from 2 hard-cooked eggs. Top the salad with the sieved egg yolks.

Cheese-Olive Dressing: mix 3-oz. pkg. cream cheese, ¼ cup cream, and ¼ cup chopped ripe olives.

PERFECTION SALAD

Molded version of an old church supper favorite of the Gay Nineties.

Follow ⚹ recipe above using lemon-flavored gelatin, 1 cup *finely* shredded cabbage, 1 cup finely diced celery, 2 finely chopped pimientos, and 6 chopped sweet pickles. Add 1 tsp. salt.

MOLDED GARDEN SALAD

Delicately refreshing.

Follow ⚹ recipe above using lemon-flavored gelatin, ¼ cup finely sliced green onions, ½ cup diced cucumber, ½ cup *each* thinly sliced radishes, celery, and raw cauliflowerets. Add 1 tsp. salt.

SEA FOOD SALAD MOLD

Follow ⚹ recipe above using lemon-flavored gelatin. Add 1 extra tbsp. lemon juice; ½ tsp. prepared mustard; dash of salt; paprika; 1 cup flaked drained cooked lobster, crabmeat, shrimp, tuna, or salmon, and ½ cup thinly sliced celery.

SOUFFLÉ SALAD

Follow ⚹ recipe above—using either lime or lemon-flavored gelatin and omit ½ cup water. Blend in with rotary beater 3 tbsp. vinegar or lemon juice, ½ cup mayonnaise, ¼ tsp. salt, dash of pepper. Pour into refrigerator tray. Freeze 15 to 20 min. or until firm around edge but soft in center. Turn into bowl; whip until fluffy. Fold in fruit, vegetables, cheese, chicken, or sea food. (See combination possibilities on this page.) Chill until firm.

Chicken-Almond Soufflé Salad: fold in 1 cup diced cooked chicken, ½ cup sweet green grapes, ⅓ cup toasted slivered almonds.

TOMATO ASPIC

Colorful, piquant, refreshing. Double the recipe to fill a 9" ring mold for 12 servings.

Soften . . .
    2 envelopes unflavored gelatin (2 tbsp.)
in . . .
    ½ cup cold water
Meanwhile, simmer together 15 min. . . .
    2 cups tomato juice
    1 tsp. salt
    1 tsp. confectioners' sugar
    dash of cayenne pepper and celery salt
    1 bay leaf
    1 small onion, cut up
    a few celery leaves

Strain, and add softened gelatin and 1 tbsp. lemon juice, stirring until dissolved. Cool, then pour into 6 to 8 individual molds. Chill until firm. Unmold on salad greens and serve with mayonnaise.

AMOUNT: 6 to 8 servings.

Chicken-Tomato Aspic: add 1 cup diced cooked chicken before chilling.

Holiday-Tomato Aspic: add 1 cup diced celery and ½ cup chopped bread-and-butter pickles before chilling.

FESTIVE DEVILED EGG SALAD MOLD

First made for a guest luncheon in our Early American dining room one hot summer day by Marion Knowlton of our staff (now Mrs. C. W. Loomer of Madison, Wisconsin).

Make double the recipe for Tomato Aspic (*above*). Press 10 deviled egg halves, stuffed-side-down, around bottom of 9" ring mold. Cover with slightly thickened Tomato Aspic. Chill. Unmold on greens; serve with desired dressing.

LIME PARTY SALAD

Melt in top of double boiler . . .
    ¼ lb. marshmallows (about 16)
    1 cup milk
Pour hot mixture over . . .
    1 pkg. lime-flavored gelatin
Stir until dissolved; then stir in . . .
    two 3-oz. pkg. cream cheese
Stir until cheese dissolves. Add . . .
    no. 2 can undrained crushed pineapple
Cool. Blend in . . .
    1 cup whipping cream, whipped
    ⅔ cup mayonnaise

Chill until firm.

AMOUNT: 12 servings.

CRANBERRY-GRAPE SALAD

For holiday entertaining. Delicious with tiny hot rolls for parties.

Cook gently until skins break . . .
    4 cups cranberries
in . . .
    2 cups water
Rub through sieve. To pulp, add . . .
    1½ cups sugar
Boil slowly 5 min. Take off heat. Soften . . .
    2 envelopes unflavored gelatin (2 tbsp.)
in . . .
    ¼ cup cold water
Blend into hot cranberry mixture. Let cool until mixture mounds slightly when dropped from spoon. Add . . .
    1 cup Tokay grapes (seeded and quartered)
    1 cup diced canned pineapple (drained)
    ½ cup broken walnuts, if desired

Pour into molds (9" ring mold or 8 individual molds) and chill. When set, unmold and serve on salad greens with mayonnaise or Cooked Salad Dressing (*p. 380*) mixed with whipped cream.

AMOUNT: 8 to 12 servings.

CRANBERRY-APPLE SALAD

Cranberries and salad in one.

Follow recipe above—*except*, in place of the Tokay grapes, pineapple, and walnuts, use 1 cup cut-up celery, 1 cup cut-up apples, and ½ cup chopped salted peanuts.

BEET SALAD RING

Attractive zesty-flavored red salad with diced beets and crisp celery.

Cook until tender . . .
    about ¾ lb. fresh beets
Dissolve . . .
    2 pkg. lemon-flavored gelatin
in . . .
    3 cups boiling beet liquid
Add . . .
    ⅓ cup vinegar
    1 tsp. grated onion
    2½ tbsp. horse-radish
Chill until mixture mounds slightly when dropped from spoon. Add . . .
    1½ cups diced cooked beets
    1 cup diced celery

Pour into 1½-qt. ring mold (9"). Place in refrigerator until firm. Unmold on platter and surround with chicory or other lacy greens. Place bowl of mayonnaise in the center.

AMOUNT: 8 servings.

The Sauce Can Make The Dish

Sauces are the accessories—those last touches that can turn the plain and basic into something fine and fancy. Once you realize how much a special sauce can do to enhance everyday foods you will be using all the recipes on these pages.

Betty Crocker

THERE'S A SAUCE FOR EVERY OCCASION

To give you inspiration, a few from the many in this chapter are listed below.

395

WHEN TIME IS SHORT

You can let your can opener help you make the zesty sauces below out of cans and jars. Then use your imagination for others and see what good things you can concoct.

FROM A CAN

QUICK BROWN SAUCE: To 1 can beef gravy, add 1 tsp. gravy flavoring, 1 tbsp. tomato catsup.

DEVIL SAUCE: To 1 can tomato sauce, add 1 beef bouillon cube, 1 tsp. prepared mustard, ¼ cup vinegar.

QUICK CREAM SAUCE: To 1 can condensed cream of chicken soup add ½ soup can cream. Heat. Season with nutmeg.

MINTED PINEAPPLE SAUCE: To 1 can crushed pineapple add a few drops of mint flavoring and green food coloring.

FROM A BAG OF CANDIES

PEANUT CRUNCH CREAM: Fold ¼ cup crushed peanut brittle into 1 cup whipping cream, whipped.

MARSHMALLOW SAUCE: Melt 1½ doz. marshmallows in ½ cup cream over hot water. Serve warm.

CHOCOLATE MINT SAUCE: Melt over hot water 10 large chocolate-covered peppermint cream wafers. Blend in 3 tbsp. cream.

CARAMEL CREAM SAUCE: Combine and heat over hot water ½ lb. caramels and 1 cup evaporated milk.

FROM A JAR OR BOTTLE

SIMPLE HOLLANDAISE SAUCE: Heat gently ½ cup cultured sour cream with 2 tbsp. soft butter, 2 tbsp. bottled lemon juice.

HONEY PEANUT BUTTER SAUCE: Combine and heat 1 cup honey and ¼ to ½ cup peanut butter.

EGGNOG SAUCE: Add rum or brandy flavoring to bottled eggnog. Then fold in beaten egg whites, 1 to each cup of eggnog.

MINCEMEAT SAUCE: Thin mincemeat with pineapple juice. Serve over vanilla ice cream.

FROM A PACKAGE

QUICK CUSTARD SAUCE: Take 1 package vanilla pudding mix and use 1½ times as much milk as the package directions call for. The same can be done with lemon, chocolate, butterscotch, coconut cream, and strawberry pudding mixes.

For a delicious Chocolate Fudge, Chocolate Malt, or Peanut Creme Sauce, follow directions on Betty Crocker Frosting Mix package.

WHEN TIME IS EVEN SHORTER, TAKE YOUR PICK OF SAUCES ALL READY TO USE

Buy them in jars at your grocer's or delicatessen shop.

Or make up your favorite fussy sauce when you have the time; then freeze it for later use.

Butterscotch	Caramel	
	Chocolate	
Pineapple	Cheese	Tomato

ANYTHING GOES FOR SAUCES WHEN YOU SERVE THEM

You don't need a special sauceboat. It's fun to be different. And any of these will give your sauce a fillip.

Pitcher	Big Cup and Saucer	Butter Warmer
Amusing Pottery Duck		An Antique Glass Bowl
A Chocolate Pot		Paper Nut Cup for Individual Servings

SAUCES

Sauces for meat and game were such an important part of medieval feasts that every palace and wealthy home had a *saucier* whose sole business it was to preside over that part of the menu. Old paintings of banquets of those days show this saucier at work with his two assistants at an elaborately equipped side table.

Today we have sauces for vegetables and desserts as well as meat, fish, and poultry. Modern chefs classify them all as "pick-ups" . . . their term for a finishing touch that literally lifts a dish up . . . glamorizes and gives it distinction.

This "picking-up" is accomplished by contrasts. First, a color contrast to make a dish *look* tempting. Like crushed strawberries served over white ice cream. Then when we taste this dessert, the strawberry flavor and texture add a great deal to our enjoyment of the ice cream.

A sauce does not need to be complicated and tricky. A little lemon added to the salt and pepper used in seasoning a baked fish becomes a sauce. It's as simple as that. The important point is learning to combine flavors.

A world famous chef has advised women to be daring and experiment with herbs and other seasonings. Better yet, you can have a wonderful time trying sauces others have found add to the enjoyment of desserts, vegetables, and meats. In these pages we have tried to give you a wide variety of the best known tried and true sauces. We know you will have fun serving them . . . and that your family will be very proud of your new skill.

WHITE SAUCE (⌀ Recipe) The start of creamed dishes and many other sauces. "White Sauce is a good beginning for the small cook," says Virginia Hathaway, Child Psychologist with the Minneapolis Public Schools.

1 Melt butter over low heat in a heavy saucepan. Wooden spoon for stirring is a help.

2 Blend in flour, seasonings. Cook over low heat, stirring until mixture is smooth, bubbly.

3 Remove from heat. Stir in milk. Bring to boil, stirring constantly. Boil 1 min.

Thin	Medium	Thick
Like coffee cream. For creamed vegetables, soup base.	Like thick cream. For creamed and scalloped dishes.	Like batter. For croquettes, soufflés.
1 tbsp. butter	2 tbsp.	¼ cup
*½ to 1 tbsp. flour	2 tbsp.	¼ cup
¼ tsp. salt	¼ tsp.	¼ tsp.
⅛ tsp. pepper	⅛ tsp.	⅛ tsp.
1 cup milk	1 cup	1 cup

*Use smaller amount with starchy vegetables (peas, potatoes), larger with non-starchy (cream of tomato soup).

> **THREE RULES**
> **FOR**
> **PERFECT WHITE SAUCE**
>
> 1. To eliminate raw, starchy taste, bubble flour and butter about 1 min.
> 2. For easier, smoother blending, remove from heat when adding milk.
> 3. For smooth, velvety texture, keep stirring until thickened.

Medium White Sauce is usually preferred in the following variations, although some prefer the Thin White Sauce.

CHEESE SAUCE

For vegetable, rice, macaroni, and egg dishes.

Follow ⌀ recipe above—*except* add ¼ tsp. dry mustard with the seasonings. Blend in ½ cup nippy American cheese (cut up or grated). Stir until cheese is melted.

MUSHROOM SAUCE

A general favorite with many supper dishes.

Follow ⌀ recipe above—*except* sauté 1 cup sliced mushrooms and 1 tsp. grated onion in the butter 5 min. before adding flour.

SEA FOOD SAUCE

Elegant with shrimp, lobster, or crabmeat . . . good with salmon or tuna.

Follow ⌀ recipe above—*except* carefully stir into sauce ½ to 1 cup cooked shrimp or pieces of other sea food.

RED SAUCE

Good on chicken or eggs.

Follow ⌀ recipe above—*except* stir in 3 tbsp. tomato puree.

CURRY SAUCE

Combines perfectly with chicken, lamb, shrimp, and rice.

Follow ⌀ recipe above—*except* sauté ½ tsp. curry powder in the butter before adding flour and other seasonings.

EGG SAUCE

A pleasant addition to salmon and other fish.

Follow ⌀ recipe above—*except* carefully stir in 2 diced hard-cooked eggs. Season.

CUCUMBER SAUCE

Refreshing with salmon and other fish.

Follow ⌀ recipe above—*except* add ½ cup cucumber, grated or thinly sliced, and a dash of cayenne pepper. Simmer 10 min.

DILL SAUCE

An ideal mate for bland meat or fish.

Follow ⌀ recipe above—*except*, with the seasonings, add 1 tsp. minced fresh dill or ½ tsp. dried dill and a dash of nutmeg. Simmer 2 or 3 min.

VELOUTÉ SAUCE (Velvet Sauce) (✒ Recipe) *As elegant and French as Paris.*

Melt over low heat......................	2 tbsp. butter
Stir in until well blended..................	2 tbsp. flour
Cook over low heat, stirring until mixture is smooth, bubbly. Remove from heat. Gradually stir in................................	1 cup chicken or veal or fish stock
Bring to boil, stirring constantly. Boil 1 min.	
Blend in..............................	{ salt to taste dash of white pepper ⅛ tsp. nutmeg

Serve hot with croquettes, baked or steamed fish, and use as a base for special sauces.

AMOUNT: 1 cup.

BÉCHAMEL SAUCE

Named for Louis de Béchamel, steward to King Louis XIV of France.

Follow ✒ recipe above—*except* blend in ½ tsp. salt, ⅛ tsp. pepper, ¼ tsp. paprika. Then fold in ½ cup cream.

HORSE-RADISH SAUCE

A nippy touch for canned beef, boiled beef, lamb, or ham.

Follow ✒ recipe above—*except* stir in 1 tbsp. well drained prepared horse-radish and 1 tsp. prepared mustard.

ENGLISH PARSLEY SAUCE

Adds color and flavor to new potatoes, green beans, or fresh peas.

Follow ✒ recipe above—*except* stir in ¼ cup finely minced parsley and 2 well beaten egg yolks.

ALMOND VELVET SAUCE

A typical French touch when used to dress up leftover veal or chicken. Also a delicious accompaniment to sea food.

Follow ✒ recipe above—*except* stir in ¼ cup toasted slivered blanched almonds just before serving.

SAUCE MORNAY

A rich cheese sauce. Chefs glamorize meats, hash, eggs, and vegetables with it.

Follow ✒ recipe above—*except* stir in 1 cup cream and ⅛ tsp. cayenne. Heat, stirring constantly. Stir in 1 cup cut-up sharp American, Parmesan, or Swiss cheese.

NORMANDY SAUCE

For fish mousse, timbales, or soufflé.

Follow ✒ recipe above—*except* use fish stock. Beat at least half of hot sauce into 2 egg yolks, and beat into remaining sauce. Blend in ...
  1 tbsp. lemon juice
  salt, pepper, and cayenne pepper to taste

ANCHOVY VELOUTÉ SAUCE

For boiled or baked fish.

Follow ✒ recipe above—*except* blend 1½ tsp. anchovy paste into the flour and butter paste. Omit salt, and use fish stock instead of veal or chicken stock. Just before serving, add 1 tbsp. minced parsley.

to glamorize leftovers

ALLEMANDE SAUCE

Turns yesterday's cabbage into a delight.

Follow ✒ recipe above—*except* stir in 1 slightly beaten egg yolk, 1 tsp. lemon juice, and 2 tbsp. cream.

RAVIGOTE SAUCE

Makes any leftover taste like new.

Follow ✒ recipe above—*except* stir in 2 tbsp. lemon juice, 1 tbsp. minced onion, 1 tsp. *each* finely minced chervil, tarragon, and chives.

HOT TARTARE SAUCE

Especially liked by our friend Helen Clapesattle, Director of the University Press and author of "The Doctors Mayo," when she lunched with us in our Early American dining room. We served it on broccoli.

Follow ✒ recipe above—*except* stir in ½ cup mayonnaise, 1 tsp. minced onion, 1 tsp. lemon juice, 1 tbsp. *each* finely chopped sweet pickles, stuffed olives, green pepper, and parsley.

BROWN SAUCE (Sauce Espagnole) (⚡ Recipe) *Basic dark sauce with a full, rich flavor.*

Heat in small heavy skillet over low heat until browned..........................	2 tbsp. butter or drippings
Add and sauté until light brown...........	½ slice onion
Remove onion. Stir in until well blended.....	2 tbsp. flour
Cook over low heat, stirring constantly, until flour is a deep mahogany brown. Remove from heat. Gradually stir in...................	1 cup beef stock
Bring to boil, stirring constantly. Boil 1 min.	
Stir in............................	salt and pepper to taste
Strain, if desired.	AMOUNT: 1 cup.

BORDELAISE SAUCE

It's fun to play around with herbs and this is a good beginning. Try it with steaks and chops.

Follow ⚡ recipe above—*except* add ½ tsp. *each* finely minced parsley, thyme, bay leaf, onion.

PROVENCALE SAUCE

A real treat for garlic lovers. Use with meat, spaghetti or noodles, and vegetables.

Follow ⚡ recipe above—*except* stir in 1 tomato, chopped, and 1 clove garlic, crushed.

PIQUANT BROWN SAUCE

For tongue, beef, veal, or fish.

Simmer together 5 min. ½ tbsp. *each* minced onion and chopped capers, 2 tbsp. vinegar, ½ tsp. sugar, dash of paprika and salt. Stir into Brown Sauce (*follow ⚡ recipe above*). Then stir into 2 tbsp. thick chili sauce or chopped sweet pickle.

MUSHROOM BROWN SAUCE

Adds zest to fish, meat, or omelets.

Follow ⚡ recipe above—*except* add 1 cup sliced mushrooms to the butter or drippings; brown slowly before adding flour. Stir in a few drops Worcestershire sauce.

ROBERT SAUCE

Glorifies the humble hamburger.

Follow ⚡ recipe above—*except* stir in 1 tbsp. vinegar, 1 tbsp. minced onion, 3 tbsp. sliced sour pickles, and 2 tsp. prepared mustard.

BROWN DEVIL SAUCE

Hot and zippy on steak or meat loaf.

Follow ⚡ recipe above—*except* stir in 1 tsp. Worcestershire sauce, 1 tsp. vinegar, and 1 tbsp. minced parsley.

DILL SAUCE

A natural for fish, lamb, or veal.

Follow ⚡ recipe above—*except* stir in 2 tbsp. vinegar and dill to taste.

MEXICAN SAUCE

Edwin Ford of the University of Minnesota tells us he would rather cook than teach. He admits to flipping a mean omelet and tops it with this sauce.

Follow ⚡ recipe above—*except* stir in ½ tsp. gravy flavoring, ½ cup tomato catsup, 1 tbsp. *each* minced onion and green pepper sautéed in butter. Season to taste with salt, paprika, and celery salt.

TOMATO-MUSHROOM SAUCE *Easy and delicious for quick spaghetti, Spanish omelet, leftover chicken or turkey, cheese soufflé.*

Sauté................................	1 diced strip bacon
Blend into bacon fat.....................	1 tbsp. flour 1½ tsp. sugar ⅛ tsp. salt
Cook until smooth and bubbly. Remove from heat. Gradually stir in...................	1 cup tomato juice or strained juice from canned tomatoes
Bring to boil, stirring constantly. Boil 1 min.	
Brown...............................	*2-oz. can broken pieces and stems of mushrooms (about ½ cup), drained
in.................................	1 tbsp. butter
Add mushrooms to sauce with.............	2 tbsp. chopped ripe olives
AMOUNT: 1⅓ cups.	*¼ lb. fresh mushrooms may be used.

PAN GRAVY

Pan Gravy is a rich gravy that makes use of the natural meat fats in the pan after cooking roasts, steaks, chops, and fried chicken.

For Each Cup of
Medium Gravy
- 2 tbsp. fat
- 2 tbsp. flour
- 1 cup liquid (water, meat stock, or bouillon-cube broth)

Thin Gravy
- 1 tbsp. fat
- 1 tbsp. flour
- 1 cup liquid

Thick Gravy
- 3 tbsp. fat
- 3 tbsp. flour
- 1 cup liquid

1. Remove meat to warm place. Pour off fat; measure amount needed back into pan. *Measure accurately ... too little fat makes gravy lumpy.*

2. Add *level* tablespoons of flour. Stir fat and flour together until smooth, then cook over low heat, stirring steadily, until it's all bubbly and brown. *Measure flour accurately so your gravy is never greasy.*

3. Stir in liquid, taking pan off heat to avoid lumps. Always measure liquid—too much weakens flavor. Return pan to heat, stirring and scraping in the rich drippings. Boil 1 min., season, and serve.

All you have to do—

For improved flavor in Pan Gravy: cook meat with bay leaf, peppercorns, onion, garlic, or celery salt, or any favorite seasoning.

CREAMY PAN GRAVY FOR CHICKEN, CHOPS

Use milk for part of liquid in Pan Gravy.

MUSHROOM GRAVY

For beef, veal, or chicken.

Brown a drained small can mushrooms in fat before adding flour in making Pan Gravy. Use mushroom liquor as part of liquid. Blend in ½ tsp. Worcestershire Sauce.

GIBLET GRAVY

Cook gizzard, heart, and neck of fowl in 4 cups salted water until tender ... 1 to 2 hr. Add liver last half hour. Remove neck, chop giblets into small pieces, return to cooking water. Use as part or all of liquid in making Pan Gravy.

KETTLE GRAVY

Kettle Gravy is made from the liquid in which pot roasts and stews have been simmered. Remember, the less liquid you use, the richer the flavor of the broth.

For Each Cup of
Medium Gravy
- 1 cup meat broth
- ¼ cup cold water
- 2 tbsp. flour

Thin Gravy
- 1 cup meat broth
- ¼ cup cold water
- 1 tbsp. flour

Thick Gravy
- 1 cup meat broth
- ¼ cup cold water
- 3 tbsp. flour

1. Remove meat to platter. Keep warm. Skim excess fat from meat broth and store for future use. Pour off broth, measure amount needed, and return to kettle.

2. Shake water and flour together in covered jar. Remember, *put water in first, flour on top, for a smooth mixture.*

3. Stir flour and water slowly into hot broth. Bring to boil. Boil 1 min. Season, and serve.

CREAM GRAVY FOR CHICKEN, PORK, HAM

Use milk in place of water in making Kettle Gravy (*above*).

HELPFUL HINTS

• The broth will be tastier if you flour meat and brown *slowly* on all sides for about 30 min. before simmering.

• For extra richness and flavor, mix paprika with flour when you coat meat for browning.

• If there is less than a cup of meat stock (juice) in the pan, add extra liquid to make 1 cup or the amount wanted.

• Potato water or water drained from cooked mild vegetables may be used for part or all of the liquid. Or use consommé, sour cream, tomato or vegetable juice as gravy liquid.

• Bouillon cubes may be added to increase flavor, or dissolved in water to increase stock.

• Remember gravy contains some of the precious vitamins and minerals from the meat. Bread and gravy is a nutritious dish we can profitably enjoy.

HOLLANDAISE SAUCE

Who said Hollandaise was tricky? It's different, because it's not thickened with flour. But it's easy when made this way—always smooth and creamy. Just follow the two rules.

1. Keep heat low.
2. Stir briskly all the time.

HOLLANDAISE SAUCE (Recipe)

The humblest vegetable, the blandest fish will be company food when served with this aristocrat of sauces. A favorite of Dr. Reynold A. Jensen, Professor of Child Psychiatry at the University of Minnesota, one of those inspired cooks whose wife, Lil, really likes to have him in the kitchen.

In a small saucepan, stir with wooden spoon.. { 2 egg yolks
{ 3 tbsp. lemon juice

Add................................ ¼ cup very cold butter (½ stick or ⅛ lb.)

Stir over very low heat until butter is melted.

Add .... another ¼ cup cold butter (½ stick or ⅛ lb.)

Continue stirring until butter is melted and sauce thickened. Be sure butter melts slowly as this gives eggs time to cook and thicken the sauce without curdling.

Serve hot or at room temperature. Any sauce left over will keep in refrigerator. To serve, stir in a little hot water.

AMOUNT: 1 cup.

CUCUMBER HOLLANDAISE

Party fare over sliced tomatoes, along with roast beef and browned potatoes.

Follow recipe above—*except* stir in 1 cup drained chopped cucumber.

ROSY HOLLANDAISE

Just the right touch with cold meats.

Follow recipe above—*except* stir in 3 tbsp. tomato purée, 1 tbsp. minced parsley, and a dash of cayenne pepper.

CALIFORNIA HOLLANDAISE

Turns asparagus or broccoli into an adventure.

Follow recipe above—*except* stir in 2 tbsp. orange juice and 1 tsp. grated orange rind.

EASY HOLLANDAISE SAUCE

A thrifty substitute for the above.

See recipe on p. 425.

BEARNAISE SAUCE

A highly flavored Hollandaise.

Follow recipe above—*except* stir in 1 tbsp. minced parsley, ½ tsp. dried tarragon, and 1 tbsp. tarragon vinegar.

MOUSSELINE SAUCE

Does something wonderful for boiled fish, eggs, artichokes, broccoli, cauliflower, or spinach.

Follow recipe above—*except*, when ready to serve, blend in stiffly whipped cream (whip ¼ cup). Serve warm.

SIMPLE BUTTER SAUCES to glorify vegetables, fish or eggs, and pasta.

DUTCH POPPY SEED SAUCE

For cooked asparagus, broccoli, cauliflower, almost any vegetable.

Melt in saucepan . . .
    ¼ cup butter
Stir in . . .
    juice of ½ lemon (about 2 tbsp.)
    1 tsp. poppy seeds
    dash of cayenne pepper

IRISH BUTTER SAUCE

With boiled onions or tiny new potatoes.

Cream ¼ cup butter. Blend in 6 tbsp. tomato catsup, salt, pepper, and a pinch of nutmeg.

BLACK BUTTER SAUCE

Gives zip to plain fried eggs.

Let ⅓ cup butter bubble in small saucepan until it's a golden brown. Pour in 1 tbsp. vinegar or lemon juice and let foam up. Add a dash of salt and pepper and serve at once.

GREEN SAUCE

Try it for a change on spaghetti or noodles, with grated Parmesan cheese on the side.

Melt ¼ lb. butter; add 1 clove garlic, minced or squeezed through garlic press. Toss in 1 bunch parsley, minced.

BROILED MAYONNAISE

Something new and different for asparagus, Brussels sprouts, string beans, broccoli, and spinach.

Beat 1 egg white until stiff but not dry; fold in 1 cup mayonnaise. Pour to 1½" depth in shallow baking dish; place 4 to 5" under very hot broiler until delicately browned, about 1 min. Pass separately.

AMOUNT: 1 cup.

HOT THOUSAND ISLAND DRESSING

Creates new interest in fresh, frozen, or canned vegetables such as broccoli, cauliflower, or Lima beans.

Melt . . .
    ¼ cup butter
Blend in . . .
    ¼ cup GOLD MEDAL Flour
    ½ tsp. salt
    ¼ tsp. pepper
Cook over low heat, stirring until mixture is smooth, bubbly. Remove from heat.
Stir in . . .
    2 cups milk
Bring to boil over direct heat, stirring constantly. Boil 1 min.
Blend in . . .
    ½ cup mayonnaise
    ½ cup chili sauce

Heat through.

AMOUNT: 3 cups.

DRAWN BUTTER SAUCE

A transparent sauce that gives a fillip to bland vegetables . . . green and wax beans, shredded beets or carrots, cooked celery.

Melt . . .
    2 tbsp. butter
Blend in . . .
    2 tbsp. flour
Cook over low heat, stirring until mixture is smooth, bubbly. Remove from heat.
Stir in gradually . . .
    1 cup water
Cook until thickened. Season with . . .
    ¼ tsp. salt
    dash pepper
    ¼ tsp. paprika
    1 tsp. Worcestershire sauce
Just before taking from heat, add . . .
    1 tbsp. butter, in small pieces

AMOUNT: 1 cup.

SAUCE SUPREME

A simple addition turns Drawn Butter Sauce into party fare . . . smooth and subtle.

Fold into Drawn Butter Sauce (*above*) ½ cup whipping cream, whipped stiff.

POLONAISE SAUCE

Unpretentious carrots, green beans, or cauliflower go places when dressed up with this sauce.

Brown in saucepan . . .
    1½ tbsp. butter
Add . . .
    1 tbsp. flour
    ¼ tsp. salt
Stir in . . .
    1 cup canned consommé
Stir constantly until mixture boils. Blend at least half of mixture into . . .
    2 egg yolks, slightly beaten
Blend into rest of hot mixture. Cook and stir on low heat 1 min.
Stir in . . .
    1 tbsp. lemon juice
    dash paprika

AMOUNT: 1 cup.

BOHEMIAN SAUCE

For an elegant party, serve over sliced hearts of palm (they come in cans). For everyday, it makes the same old beets utterly different and delicious.

Mix . . .
    1¼ cups sour cream
    2 tbsp. prepared mustard
    1 tsp. salt
    1 tsp. cracked pepper
    3 tbsp. lemon juice

Keeps a week or more in refrigerator.

AMOUNT: 1¼ cups.

CRUMB SAUCE

A buttery, crisp topping for cauliflower, asparagus, or other vegetables.

Heat until golden brown . . .
    ½ cup dry bread crumbs
in . . .
    ¼ cup butter

CREAMY MINT SAUCE

Creates a subtle difference in peas, carrots, or the two combined.

Stir 1 tbsp. lemon juice and 3 tbsp. finely chopped fresh mint into 1 cup hot Medium White Sauce (*p. 398*). Cover tightly and let stand for about 5 min. Do not cook.

CHANTILLY SAUCE

This cool sauce folded into hot peas, asparagus, or spinach, makes an interesting combination of temperatures and flavors.

Equal quantities of mayonnaise and whipped cream.

All you have to do — *To turn sliced tomatoes or cold asparagus into a refreshing salad:* arrange them on a salad plate and dribble over them a few spoonfuls of Vinaigrette Dressing (*p. 379*).

FOR ICE CREAM AND ELEGANT FROZEN DESSERTS

BUTTERSCOTCH SAUCE

True butterscotch flavor, super-smooth. "It's the best butterscotch sauce in the world!" says Frances Ohm of Los Angeles. "We like to serve it hot over ice cream when we come in from the beach. Sometimes we sprinkle salted almonds over the top."

Mix in saucepan . . .
- ¾ cup sugar
- ½ cup light corn syrup
- ¼ tsp. salt
- ¼ cup butter
- ½ cup cream

Cook over low heat, stirring, to soft ball stage (234°). Stir in additional . . .
- ½ cup cream

Cook to thick, smooth consistency (228°). Remove from heat. Stir in . . .
- ½ tsp. vanilla

Serve hot or cold.

AMOUNT: 2 cups.

HOLIDAY SAUCE

Rich and fruity—worthy of the most festive occasion.

Combine and let stand several hours . . .
- 1 cup dates, chopped
- two 4-oz. jars maraschino cherries and juice
- 1 cup figs, diced

Add . . .
- ¼ lb. blanched almonds, coarsely chopped and toasted, or salted almonds
- pinch of salt

Boil 5 min. . . .
- ½ cup sugar
- ½ cup water

Add to fruit mixture. Chill.

KENTUCKY SAUCE

A novel blend of flavors.

Cook together for 5 min. . . .
- 1 cup granulated sugar
- 1 cup brown sugar (packed)
- ½ cup water

Mix in thoroughly . . .
- 1 cup strawberry jam
- 1 cup orange marmalade
- 1 cup pecans, cut up
- 1 lemon (juice and rind, chopped fine)
- 1 orange (juice and rind, chopped fine)

Let sauce ripen in a glass jar in refrigerator for 2 weeks before using. Will keep indefinitely in refrigerator.

three chocolate sauces

RICH CHOCOLATE SAUCE

"Mother makes chocolate sauce by the quart for our family of six," says Margaret Kemp from Mankato, Minnesota. "This one is her favorite for parties."

Melt over hot water . . .
- ½ lb. German sweet chocolate

with . . .
- ¼ cup water
- ¼ cup sugar

Stir until smooth. Take from heat. Blend in . . .
- ¼ cup cream

Serve hot or cold.

AMOUNT: 1 cup.

QUICK CHOCOLATE SAUCE

Melt over hot water . . .
- 6-oz. pkg. semi-sweet chocolate pieces

Beat in . . .
- 5½-oz. can evaporated milk
- ⅛ tsp. salt

Blend in . . .
- *½ tsp. peppermint flavoring, if desired

Serve hot or cold.

*Be sure to use peppermint flavoring as oil of peppermint is much stronger.

GLOSSY CHOCOLATE SAUCE

Rich and fudgey. But made without sugar. Created during World War II, when sugar was at a premium.

Melt over hot water . . .
- 2 sq. unsweetened chocolate (2 oz.)

Mix in and heat slowly, stirring constantly . . .
- 1 cup light corn syrup

Remove from heat *immediately* and stir in . . .
- ½ tsp. vanilla
- 1 tbsp. butter

AMOUNT: 1 cup.

PEPPERMINT CANDY SAUCE

Karyl Wilson (Mrs. Lawrence W. Wilson), a charming young homemaker friend, thinks nothing of entertaining 24 guests for supper, and often serves this refreshing and colorful ice cream sauce at her parties.

Mix 1½ cups coarsely chopped peppermint stick candy and ½ cup water in small saucepan. Cover. Bring to boil, cook over low heat until candy is melted, about 18 min. Remove from heat. Chill until mixture thickens. Stir in 2 tbsp. coarsely chopped peppermint stick candy.

AMOUNT: 1 cup.

FOR STEAMED PUDDINGS, COTTAGE PUDDING, SHORTCAKE, FRESH-FROM-THE-OVEN CAKES

BEST SAUCE

"And so it is," says 83-year-old Mrs. Walter B. Kelley, who brought the recipe from Maine to Minnesota when she was a bride. Her family likes it best on a luscious steamed chocolate pudding.

Beat until smooth and creamy . . .
  1 cup *sifted* confectioners' sugar
  1 cup soft butter
Whip . . .
  1 cup whipping cream

Heat with the above and then boil till foamy. Serve immediately.

ALMOND CREAM SAUCE

Almost too good to be true.

Mix in saucepan . . .
  ½ cup sugar
  ½ tsp. salt
  2 tbsp. cornstarch
Stir in gradually . . .
  2 cups milk
Cook over med. heat, stirring constantly, until mixture thickens and boils. Boil 1 min. Remove from heat. Slowly stir at least half of hot mixture into . . .
  2 egg yolks, slightly beaten
Blend into remaining hot mixture in saucepan. Boil 1 min. more, stirring constantly. Remove from heat. Blend in . . .
  2 tsp. butter
  1 tsp. vanilla
  ½ tsp. almond flavoring
Cool. Fold in . . .
  1 cup whipping cream, whipped

AMBER SAUCE

Very sweet and butterscotchy.

Mix in saucepan 1 cup brown sugar (packed), ½ cup light corn syrup, ¼ cup soft butter, and ½ cup cream. Cook over low heat, stirring to blend well (5 min.). Serve warm.

AMOUNT: 2 cups.

TAFFY SAUCE

Tastes like old-fashioned butterscotch taffy.

Blend in saucepan 2 tbsp. flour and 1 cup brown sugar (packed). Add 2 tbsp. butter and ½ cup water. Bring to boil. Boil 1 min. Serve hot.

AMOUNT: About 1 cup.

CREAMY SAUCE (see p. 239)

Rich and smooth; some like it even better than Hard Sauce with steamed puddings.

OLD-FASHIONED LEMON SAUCE

It's a real find that came to us from the Old South.

Combine in saucepan ½ cup butter, 1 cup sugar, ¼ cup water, 1 egg, well beaten, 3 tbsp. lemon juice (1 lemon), and grated rind of 1 lemon. Cook over med. heat, stirring constantly, just until mixture comes to a boil.

AMOUNT: 1⅓ cups.

SATIN SAUCE

Beat until foamy in saucepan 1 egg and 1 tbsp. water. Stir in ¾ cup sugar and ¼ tsp. salt. Cook over low heat 1 min., stirring constantly. Remove from heat and stir in 2 tbsp. lemon juice and 1 tsp. vanilla. Serve hot.

AMOUNT: 1½ cups.

CLEAR ORANGE SAUCE

Mrs. J. King Ross, of Northridge, California, makes this delicious sauce often. "When you live in California," she says, "you find yourself using oranges in some way at almost every meal."

Mix in saucepan 1 cup sugar, ¼ tsp. salt, and 2 tbsp. cornstarch. Stir in 1 cup orange juice, ¼ cup lemon juice, and ¾ cup boiling water. Boil 1 min., stirring constantly. Remove from heat. Stir in 1 tbsp. butter and 1 tsp. *each* grated orange and lemon rind. Serve hot on cottage pudding or warm cake.

AMOUNT: 2 cups.

RASPBERRY SAUCE

Elegant topping for Raspberry Shortcake (p. 235).

Melt in saucepan . . .
  ½ cup butter
Stir in . . .
  1 cup sugar
  1 cup fresh raspberries, mashed
Blend in . . .
  1 tbsp. cornstarch, dissolved in 1 tbsp. cold water
Boil 1 min., stirring constantly; cool. Fold in . . .
  1 egg white, stiffly beaten

AMOUNT: 6 servings.

HARD SAUCE

The egg white makes it fluffy.

Cream until soft ½ cup butter (¼ lb.). Gradually blend in 1 cup *sifted* confectioners' sugar. Then beat in 1 unbeaten egg white. Stir in ½ tsp. vanilla. Put in serving dish, sprinkle with nutmeg, and chill in refrigerator about an hour.

405

FOR FRUITS—FRESH, FROZEN, AND CANNED

MOCK DEVONSHIRE CREAM

Out of this world over fresh strawberries, raspberries, peaches, or warm apple pie.

Mash two 3-oz. pkg. cream cheese. Blend in 1 cup cream and 1 tbsp. sugar.

RASPBERRY-CURRANT SAUCE

Barbara Beck of our staff says, "For a luscious dessert, pour this over sliced peaches or ice cream."

Mash, blend, and bring to boil . . .
 10-oz. pkg. frozen raspberries
 ½ cup currant jelly
Make paste of . . .
 1 tbsp. cold water
 ½ tbsp. cornstarch

Stir into boiling mixture. Boil 1 min., stirring constantly. Cool and strain.

AMOUNT: 1⅓ cups.

IRENE'S CARAMEL SAUCE

Irene Danielson, who gave us this recipe, uses it on cottage pudding. But we think it makes an epicurean dish out of plain canned peaches or baked apples.

Mix . . .
 2 egg yolks
 ½ cup brown sugar (packed)
 ½ cup granulated sugar
 ½ cup water
 ¼ cup butter
 1 tsp. vanilla

Cook over hot water, stirring, until thick.

BILL'S EASY CARAMEL SAUCE

Bill Kelley of Lake Minnetonka is renowned among his friends for his oatmeal bread. But he calls this sauce his greatest triumph, when it complements those crisp little sweet green grapes.

Mix . . .
 ¼ to ½ cup brown sugar (packed)
 1 cup cultured sour cream

Pour over seedless green grapes, sliced peaches, or fresh strawberries.

FRESH MINT FOAMY SAUCE

Refreshing and different served over fresh fruit, especially pears or strawberries.

Cream together . . .
 ¼ cup soft butter
 1 cup *sifted* confectioners' sugar
Blend in . . .
 1 egg, well beaten
 ¼ cup fruit juice
Beat until fluffy. Mix . . .
 2 tbsp. minced fresh mint leaves
 1 tbsp. sugar

Let stand an hour or more. Just before serving, blend the mint leaves into sauce.

AMOUNT: 2 cups.

GOLDEN EGGNOG SAUCE

For hot baked pears or peaches.

Mix . . .
 2 egg yolks
 ¼ cup sugar
 1 tsp. vanilla
Fold sauce into . . .
 1 cup whipping cream, whipped stiff

BUTTER CUSTARD SAUCE

Elegant over poached fruits.

Combine . . .
 1 cup sugar
 1 cup light cream
 ¼ cup butter
Cook over med. heat, stirring constantly, 3 to 4 min. Stir at least half of hot mixture into . . .
 1 egg yolk, beaten
Return to saucepan. Cook 1 min., stirring constantly. Remove from heat. Blend in . . .
 1 tsp. vanilla

SOFT CUSTARD See p. 230.

SPEEDY CUSTARD SAUCE See p. 222.

EASY CUSTARD SAUCE See p. 230.

FROZEN CREAM

Pour 2 cups heavy cream into freezing tray of refrigerator. Leave without stirring until almost frozen through (¾ to 1 hr.). Should be crystallized but not quite stiff. At dessert time, scrape out into a small bowl and serve with hot fruit.

COCONUT CREAM SAUCE

With baked bananas.

Cut 4-oz. can moist coconut into shorter shreds. Combine with 1 cup cream and let mellow in refrigerator an hour or so.

AMOUNT: 6 to 8 servings.

Soups for Satisfaction

Few foods can warm the cockles of the heart and produce such completely blissful satisfaction as a bowl of steaming, fragrant, flavorful soup.

Betty Crocker

THERE'S A SOUP FOR EVERY OCCASION

Listed below are a few suggestions from the many in this chapter.

AN ELEGANT SUPPER— YET SO SIMPLE

Cream of Carrot Soup (p. 418)
English Muffins
(split, spread with garlic butter and broiled)
Tossed Salad
(Bibb lettuce, fresh pear cubes, and cucumber slices)
Lemon Cake Pudding (p. 237)

COZY SATURDAY NIGHT SUPPER

Reminiscent of the Deep South.

Ellen's Shrimp Gumbo (p. 414)
Hot Buttered French Bread (p. 105)
Best Tossed Salad (p. 383)
Fresh Pineapple Spears
Camembert Cheese   Salty Crackers
Black Coffee

SOUP IN A HURRY

Start with a can, an envelope, or a cube. In jig time you'll have a cheery appetizer or a one-bowl meal.

SOUP MATES

A can of each. Dilute with 1½ cups milk or water.

Purée Mongole: Tomato Soup and Green Pea Soup. Heat them separately and swirl them together in the bowl.

Celery Noodle Soup: Cream of Celery Soup and Chicken Noodle Soup.

Scotch Chowder: Cream of Mushroom Soup and Scotch Broth.

Bean-Pea Soup: Bean with Bacon Soup and Green Pea Soup.

Tomato-Clam Chowder: Tomato Soup and Clam Chowder.

Vegetable-Green Pea Soup: Green Pea Soup and Vegetable Soup.

Cream of Mushroom-Tomato Soup: Tomato Soup and Cream of Mushroom Soup.

Cream of Chicken-Mushroom Soup: Cream of Chicken Soup and Cream of Mushroom Soup.

SOUP TRICKS

With a pinch of your personality added.

Soup Shakes: Cream soups whipped with milk and served chilled, garnished with sprig of mint or slice of cucumber.

Soup Nogs: Cream soups whipped with egg and milk. Serve cold or heat slowly over low heat.

Hot Buttered Soup: Seasoned butter dropped into soup just before serving.

Hot Soup Cocktail: Tomato soup thinned out with bottled clam juice and spiked with Worcestershire sauce.

Frozen Vegetables Cooked in Soup: Chopped Spinach in Cream of Mushroom Soup. Corn in Cream of Chicken Soup.

Leftovers Cooked in Soup: Bits of ham and sliced potatoes escalloped in Cream of Mushroom Soup.

Shrimp and rice baked with Cream of Celery Soup.

QUICK PICK-ME-UPS FOR HOT WEATHER

Soup on the Rocks: Clear Consommé poured over ice cubes in a low glass bowl.

Chilled Black Bean Soup: Black Bean Soup, Consommé, sherry, water, and lemon slices.

Vichyssoise: Cream of Chicken Soup, onion, butter, potatoes, salt, pepper, water, light cream, milk, and chives.

Chicken-Curry Glacé: Cream of Chicken Soup, curry powder, and milk.

FREEZER SHORTCUTS

 Make twice as much soup as you need. Freeze half in bread pans. Turn out of pans, wrap the frozen blocks of soup, and store in freezer.

For a quick soup base, freeze extra meat or chicken stock the same way.

Keep several cans of frozen soup on hand.

EASIER WAYS TO MAKE SOUP HEARTIER

Just add:

· A can of crabmeat to Pea Soup.
  Tiny cooked meat balls to Vegetable Soup.
  A can of shrimp to Cream of Mushroom Soup.
  Bits of ham or bacon to Cream of Chicken Soup.

FESTIVE SOUP SUPPER

Start in living room with Chilled Fruit Juice Cocktail (p. 63). Canapé Bases (p. 65) and Spreads (p. 66).

Then in the dining room serve Old-time Vegetable Soup (p. 413). Herb Bread (p. 108). Celery Hearts. Frozen or Fresh Strawberries with Individual Baked Custards (p. 230). Cookies.

ENJOY SUPPER ON THE PORCH

Fruit Cup (p. 62). Mulligatawny Soup (p. 415). Finger Sandwiches of Bread and Butter. Platter of Crisp Relishes. Chocolate Bavarian Cream (p. 229).

COOL OFF ON A HOT NIGHT

Vichyssoise (p. 418). Bean Salad (p. 389). Deviled Ham Sandwiches. Peach Melba (p. 257).

SOUPS

Soup is as old as the art of cooking. In fact, it goes back to ages before cooking was an art at all—the days when the aborigines threw whatever flesh food they had into a kettle to cook over an open fire. Later, ingenious souls discovered, perhaps by accident, that a few herbs made the food taste better. The French *pot au feu* is a survival of these primitive soups. It's the soup always simmering on the stove, into which the French housewife throws herbs, vegetable tag ends, and meat bones. All the flavors are extracted and blended during the long slow cooking while the kettle smiles and chuckles, but *never* laughs outright in a full rollicking boil.

La Soupe is the name given the evening meal in parts of rural France today. The time for enjoying the steaming, savory contents of that smiling, simmering kettle. We have taken the word *supper* from this. But we have left behind the soup that made the meal.

Each nation has its own special soups, rich in chunks of meat, hearty with vegetables and barley, rice, or macaroni. Such soups have long been celebrated in song and story. Some even as cures for various ailments, like the soup called "*Restaurant*" which was popular in 16th Century France. People believed it had "restorative" powers. A chef printed the name over his door to tell all that he was serving it. In time, "*restaurant*" came to mean a place where all kinds of foods were served.

Today, soup serves a double purpose. It stimulates the appetite and provides wholesome nourishment. We choose our soup with an eye on the rest of the meal. If this is to be rich and hearty, we decide on a thin clear soup with an aroma and flavor that will flag the appetite to attention. With less hearty food to follow, the soup can be richer . . . perhaps one of our delicious cream soups that help us maintain our daily milk quota. And, of course, there are still many grand soups that are meals in themselves. You will find them all here.

"SOUP OF THE EVENING ... BEAUTIFUL SOUP"
—Alice in Wonderland

Jellied Madrilene
Eddie Fisher's Lima Bean Soup

Onion Soup Au Gratin
Consommé

Cream of Spinach Soup

Enhance Your Soup in an Interesting Dish

THESE ARE PROPER FOR SOUP

At formal dinners, soup plates and soup spoons are high style for any type of soup.

Thin soups in bouillon cups with bouillon spoons or teaspoons.

Cream soups and chowders in cream soup cups or pottery bowls with either bouillon or soup spoons.

Hearty one-dish meal soups in pottery bowls or earthenware casseroles with soup spoons.

If you don't have the traditional dishes, it's fun to be unconventional and use what you have, with an eye for color, design, and appetite appeal as we did in the color picture on the opposite page.

The Jellied Madrilene is refreshingly unorthodox in a charming blue footed saucedish of Early American pressed glass. Next to it, the Onion Soup Au Gratin is in the typical pottery bowl. Also traditional is the tureen from which Eddie Fisher's Lima Bean Soup is served into the classic wide soup plate. For the Consommé, we have used an antique cup and saucer; these first Early American cups didn't have handles. We are formal and correct again, serving Cream of Spinach Soup in a two-handled cream soup cup.

SPECIALS FOR SOUP

Rye bread with Eddie Fisher's Lima Bean Soup; Italian Bread Sticks with Italian Minestrone; Hard-crusted French Rolls with Onion Soup Au Gratin; Buttered Toast with Clam Chowder; Assorted Plain Rolls with Split Pea Soup.

to go with

Savory Crackers: Brush crackers with soft butter; sprinkle with poppy seeds, celery seeds, onion salt, or paprika. Brown under broiler or heat in mod. oven (350°) until lightly browned.

Cheese Paprika Toast: Sprinkle toasted bread strips or triangles with grated American cheese and paprika. Place under broiler or in mod. oven (350°) until cheese is melted.

to go in

Egg Rivels: Work 1 unbeaten egg into 1 cup sifted GOLD MEDAL Flour and ¼ tsp. salt, sifted together, until mixture looks like corn meal. Drop into boiling hot soup in kettle. Then cover tightly, and cook gently 10 min.

Butter Rivels: Make same as Egg Rivels—*except* use ⅓ cup butter instead of egg. Work until mixture is completely blended. Shape into ½" balls. Drop into boiling soup. Cover, cook gently 10 min. Rivels will separate, look like rice.

to go on

Clear Soup: Thin slice of lemon, cucumber, radish, or avocado. Minced parsley or chives.

Cream Soup: Slivered salted almonds or cashews. Garlic croutons. Salted whipped cream. Popcorn. Crisp ready-to-eat cereal. Minced parsley or chives.

Jellied Soup: Chopped olives. Sprigs of parsley or watercress. Sprinkle of herbs. Lemon slice.

Thick Soup: Slice of hard-cooked egg. Slices of sausage. Crisp bacon bits. Crumbled potato chips. Sprinkle of grated cheese. Thin celery rings or olive slices.

Stock is to soup what flour is to cake.

THREE RULES FOR GOOD SOUP STOCK

1 Good bones—a beef shin for brown stock, a veal knuckle or chicken for white stock. Two-thirds meat, one-third bone.

2 A big kettle with a tight lid.

3 Long, slow cooking. The test of good soup stock—when cool, it jells.

STOCK FOR SOUP *Your kitchen will be warm and cozy, and smell so good. See color picture on p. 410.*

	Brown Stock (Bouillon)	White Stock OR Chicken Stock (Consommé)
Scrape marrow from.....................	1 to 2 lb. marrow bones, cracked	
Melt in large kettle over low heat.		
Add and brown in the marrow fat.......... (Do not brown the meat for White Stock. Add all the meat with water at once.)	half of 4 lb. shin of beef, cut in small pieces	5 lb. veal knuckle or chicken with bones (or 2½ lb. each)
Add remaining meat, bones, and.......... Cover and bring slowly to boil. Remove scum.	3 qt. cold water	3 qt.
Add....................................	3 sprigs parsley, minced	2 sprigs
	¼ tsp. thyme	¼ tsp.
	¼ tsp. marjoram	
	1 small bay leaf, crumbled	½ leaf
	½ cup diced carrots	⅓ cup
	½ cup chopped onion	⅓ cup
	½ cup diced celery (with leaves)	½ cup
	10 peppercorns	6
	5 cloves	2
	1 tbsp. salt	1 tbsp.

Choose the right kettle

Clarifying stock is easy

A large soup pot with a tight-fitting cover is essential, whether it be a regular kettle or Dutch oven. Slow, gentle simmering over low heat brings out the flavors, helps keep meat tender, and prevents stock boiling away.

Egg white and egg shells clarify stock— 1 egg white blended with 1 tbsp. cold water added to stock with pieces of shell. Stir until stock boils. Boil 2 min. Let stand off heat 20 min. Strain through double cheesecloth.

Cover and simmer gently 4 hr. Remove scum occasionally. Strain and cool quickly. Store in covered jars in refrigerator. The layer of fat on top helps preserve the stock, but must be skimmed off before use in soups and sauces. Clarify stock to use as Bouillon or Consommé (*see left*).

AMOUNT: 2½ qt.

All you have to do—

To get fat off soup quickly: pour into refrigerator tray. Return to refrigerator. Skim fat off when firm.

MADRILENE
Heat together equal amounts Consommé or Bouillon, Chicken Broth, and tomato juice. Garnish with lemon slice, serve.

Jellied Madrilene (color picture on p. 410):
Thoroughly chill Madrilene. It will jell. Break up slightly with fork and serve as for Jellied Bouillon (*at right*).

TOMATO BOUILLON
Heat together equal amounts Bouillon and tomato juice with 3 or 4 whole cloves in it. Garnish with lemon slices.

JELLIED BOUILLON (or Consommé)
Thoroughly chill homemade Bouillon or Consommé (it will jell). The canned bouillon or consommé will usually jell if chilled overnight. To make it go further, heat 1 can bouillon or consommé with slice of onion and ½ tsp. celery salt. Strain through fine strainer or cheesecloth. Then add 1¼ tsp. gelatin (softened in 1 tbsp. cold water). Add 1 cup water, ⅛ tsp. salt, and 1 tbsp. lemon juice. Chill thoroughly. Break up slightly with fork and pile in bouillon cups. Top with lemon slice.

OLD-TIME VEGETABLE SOUP

Add 3 cups finely diced vegetables (celery, onions, carrots or turnips, cabbage, or any desired combination) to 1½ qt. (6 cups) Brown Stock (*p. 412*). Cook about 30 min. *6 servings.*

VEGETABLE NOODLE SOUP

To Old-time Vegetable Soup (*above*), add 1½ cups noodles and cook with the vegetables for the last 15 min.

CHICKEN NOODLE SOUP

To 1 qt. Chicken Stock (*p. 412*), add 1 cup noodles and cook 10 to 15 min.

All you have to do —

For clear noodle soups: cook the noodles separately, drain, and add them (hot) when serving soup.

OXTAIL SOUP

"My first experience in using oxtails was in this soup. It's a wonderfully flavorful and delicious dish . . . so satisfying!" says Mrs. John F. Lynch.

Brown well in a little hot fat in kettle . . .
  1½ lb. oxtail, cut into 2" pieces
Add . . .
  1½ qt. water
  1 tbsp. salt (3 tsp.)
Simmer covered about 3¼ hr. Remove meat from bones. Return meat to soup. Add . . .
  ½ cup diced onion
  ¾ cup diced raw carrot
  ½ cup diced raw celery
  2 tbsp. white rice
Cover, simmer 30 min. Skim off fat. Add . . .
  1 cup cooked tomatoes

Heat and serve.
AMOUNT: 6 servings.

MUTTON BROTH

Cut in small pieces . . .
  3 lb. mutton (from neck)
Put in kettle . . .
  meat and bones
Cover with . . .
  2 qt. cold water
Heat to boiling and skim. Season with . . .
  1 tsp. salt
  4 peppercorns
Simmer until meat is tender (about 2 hr.). Strain and remove fat and bones. Bring to boil. Add . . .
  3 tbsp. barley
Simmer until barley is cooked (about 2 hr.). Before serving, add some of meat.

CONSOMMÉ JULIENNE

To each serving of Consommé (*p. 412*), add 1 tbsp. finely shredded vegetables (carrots, beans, leeks, celery, onions). Cook 5 min.

CONSOMMÉ ANGLAISE

To each serving of Consommé (*p. 412*), add 1 tbsp. finely chopped cooked chicken and 1 tbsp. chopped toasted blanched almonds.

PEARL SOUP

Delightful "before dinner" soup served in the home of Caroline Crosby of Minneapolis.

Bring 1 qt. (4 cups) Consommé (*p. 412*) to boil and add ¼ cup quick-cooking tapioca. Cook 10 min., stirring occasionally. Combine 1 egg yolk, well beaten, and 1 cup milk. Stir into Consommé. Bring to boil; season to taste with salt. Sprinkle minced parsley on each serving.

SPICY TOMATO SOUP

Often served as "first course" at guest luncheons by our staff. Mrs. W. H. Bussey of Minneapolis served it at a lovely luncheon.

Place in kettle . . .
  1½ qt. tomato juice (6 cups)
  1¼ cups tomato puree (no. 1 can)
  3 tbsp. sugar
  5 cloves and a dash of ground cloves
  1 slice onion
  2 cups Brown Stock (Bouillon) (p. 412)
  1¼ tsp. salt
  1 bay leaf, crumbled
  ⅛ tsp. mixed herbs (marjoram, thyme)

Bring to boil, stirring occasionally. Simmer 5 min. Serve with lemon slice.
AMOUNT: 8 servings.

CHICKEN OR TURKEY SOUP

Curtain call of the holiday bird.

Remove meat from carcass of chicken, turkey, or duck and set aside. Crack bones. Place the bones in kettle, add skin, several stalks of celery, 1 carrot, 1 onion, 6 peppercorns, tip of 1 bay leaf, 4 cloves. Cover with water. Simmer 2 hr. Cool slightly, strain. Return meat to stock. Chill, skim off fat. Add salt to taste. Simmer 15 min.

413

SPLIT PEA SOUP

Navy beans, black turtle beans, black-eyed peas, or other dried peas or beans may be used instead of split peas. (Quick-cooking dried peas and beans do not require overnight soaking.)

Soak overnight in large kettle . . .
>2 cups dried split peas (1 lb.)

in . . .
>3 qt. water

Then add . . .
>1 ham bone or small shank end of ham
>1 large onion, minced
>3 stalks celery (with tops), chopped fine
>1 sprig parsley

Heat to boiling. Cover. Simmer 4 to 5 hr. until peas are tender and liquid partially cooked down. Season to taste with . . .
>salt and pepper

For a smoother soup, put through a sieve.
AMOUNT: 8 servings.

AMERICAN POTAGE

A quick, savory, meat-and-vegetable soup.

Brown slowly in a little hot fat in a heavy kettle . . .
>1 lb. ground beef

Add and cook 5 min. more . . .
>1 cup chopped onions

Add . . .
>4 cups hot water (1 qt.)
>1 cup *each* cut-up carrots, celery, potatoes
>2 tsp. salt
>½ tsp. pepper
>1 tsp. meat extract
>1 bay leaf, crumbled
>pinch basil

Mix thoroughly, loosening the brown crustiness from bottom of kettle. Bring to boil, cover, then simmer 20 min. Add . . .
>6 whole fresh tomatoes, stems removed

Cover and simmer 10 min. longer. Serve.
AMOUNT: 6 servings.

EASY CHICKEN GUMBO

Tastes like the old-time Creole favorite.

Simmer in kettle until soft . . .
>¼ cup chopped green pepper
>1½ cups canned okra, cut in ½" pieces
>¼ cup chopped onion

in . . .
>3 tbsp. butter

Stir in . . .
>1 qt. Consommé or Chicken Stock (p. 412)
>2½ cups cooked tomatoes (no. 2 can)
>1 small piece bay leaf, crumbled

Boil gently 15 min. Season to taste. Add . . .
>1 tbsp. minced parsley
>1 cup finely diced cooked chicken

AMOUNT: 6 servings.

EDDIE FISHER'S LIMA BEAN SOUP

When the popular singing star comes home for a visit this is the first treat his mother makes for him. See color picture on p. 410.

Place in large stewing pan . . .
>3½ to 4-lb. stewing chicken, cut up

Cover with water.
Cook 1 hr. Lower heat. Add . . .
>1 lb. large dried Lima beans
>2 whole carrots
>1 small stalk celery, cut up
>soup greens, such as spinach, endive, parsley
>salt and pepper to taste

Simmer until Lima beans are tender, about 2 hr. Remove chicken from bones and serve in the soup.
AMOUNT: 10 servings.

ELLEN'S SHRIMP GUMBO

From Ellen Connelly, former member of our staff, now an associate editor of Good Housekeeping magazine . . . in whose new cook book this recipe for a delicious Southern dish also appears.

Sauté in large heavy kettle . . .
>2 cloves garlic, minced
>2 onions, sliced
>½ green pepper, thinly sliced

in . . .
>¼ cup butter

Stir in . . .
>2 tbsp. flour

Cook over low heat until vegetables are tender. Then add . . .
>2½ cups tomatoes (no. 2 can)
>no. 2 can okra, drained, or 1 pkg. frozen whole okra
>⅔ cup tomato paste (6-oz. can)
>3 beef bouillon cubes
>4 tsp. Worcestershire sauce
>⅛ tsp. ground cloves
>½ tsp. chili powder
>pinch dried basil
>1 bay leaf
>1½ tbsp. salt
>¼ tsp. pepper
>3 cups water

Simmer 45 min. Just before serving, add to the simmering tomato mixture . . .
>1½ lb. deveined shelled raw shrimp

Simmer covered 5 min., or until shrimp are pink and tender. Toss together . . .
>3 cups hot Boiled Rice (p. 290)
>¼ cup minced parsley

Serve in shallow plates; add "island" of rice and parsley at side of each plate.
AMOUNT: 8 servings.

"Of soup and love, the first is best!" said Thomas Fuller back in 1732.

ITALIAN MINESTRONE

There's a version for every town in Italy.

Cook together in kettle (3 to 4 hr.) . . .
　1 cup dried kidney beans or white beans
　2 cups Brown Stock (Bouillon) (*p. 412*)
　6 cups water

Sauté . . .
　1 large onion, chopped
　1 clove garlic, minced
　3 large carrots, finely diced
　3 stalks celery (with leaves), diced
　1 cup diced raw potatoes

in . . .
　2 tbsp. olive oil

Add sautéed vegetables to beans in kettle. Cover, cook slowly 30 min., stirring often.
Add . . .
　1 cup cooked macaroni in ½″ pieces (½ cup
　　uncooked)
　1 tbsp. salt
　¼ tsp. pepper
　1 cup cooked tomatoes

Simmer 15 min. If a thinner consistency is desired, thin with water or Brown Stock (*p. 412*).

AMOUNT: 10 servings.

MULLIGATAWNY SOUP

East Indian curry soup—popular in England.

Sauté in deep kettle or Dutch oven . . .
　1 med. onion, peeled and sliced

in . . .
　¼ cup butter

Add . . .
　1 med. carrot, diced
　1 stalk celery, diced
　1 green pepper, seeded and diced
　1 med. apple, pared, cored,
　　and sliced
　1 cup cut-up cooked chicken

Stir in gradually . . .
　⅓ cup GOLD MEDAL Flour
　1 tsp. curry powder
　⅛ tsp. mace
　2 whole cloves
　1 sprig parsley, minced
　2 cups White Stock (Consommé) (*p. 412*)
　1 cup cooked tomatoes
　salt and pepper to taste

Simmer covered ½ hr. Serve hot.

AMOUNT: 6 servings.

ONION SOUP AU GRATIN

As served at boulevard cafés in France. "C'est trés bon!" says our friend, Ed Sylvestre, with gusto. See color picture on p. 410.

Brown until tender . . .
　4 large onions, sliced very thin

in . . .
　2 tbsp. butter

Add . . .
　1 qt. (4 cups) Brown Stock (Bouillon) (*p. 412*)
　1 tsp. Worcestershire sauce
　½ tsp. salt
　⅛ tsp. pepper

Bring to boil and place in large or individual baking dishes. Arrange over top of soup . . .
　2 French rolls, sliced and toasted

Sprinkle with ½ cup grated Parmesan cheese. Place under broiler to brown. Serve immediately.

AMOUNT: 6 servings.

BORSCH

Russian beet soup with especially fine flavor. Also a native of Poland. Can be served hot or cold, so that it's good for cold or hot weather.

Shred on medium-fine grater and set aside . . .
　5 large beets, well scrubbed but not peeled
　¼ med. head cabbage
　2 carrots

Sauté in large soup kettle . . .
　2 large yellow onions, chopped
　2 stalks celery (with leaves), diced

in . . .
　¼ cup butter

Add . . .
　2 qt. Beef Stock (or Bouillon) (*p. 412*)

Bring to boil. Add shredded vegetables.
Boil 10 min. Add . . .
　¾ cup catsup
　¼ cup light corn syrup

Keep warm until ready to serve, but do not boil. Garnish each serving with sour cream, top with chopped ripe olives.

AMOUNT: 6 to 8 generous servings.

NOTE: For added flavor, add ½ cup dry red wine.

415

SEA FOOD CHOWDER (✎ Recipe)

New England contribution to the international soup pot. The "makins" for Clam Chowder were always available in early New England. Everybody or his neighbor had a cow, raised potatoes and onions, and could get "quahogs" for the digging.

Sauté in large kettle....................
- ¼ cup finely cut salt pork or bacon
- ¼ cup minced onion

Add.................................
- liquor from two 7-oz. cans minced or whole clams, lobster, or other sea food
- 2 cups finely diced raw potatoes
- ½ cup water

Cook until potatoes are tender (10 min.).
- clams or other sea food from two 7-oz. cans

Just before serving, add..................
- 2 cups milk
- 1 tsp. salt
- ⅛ tsp. pepper

NOTE: Butter may be used in place of pork or bacon.

Heat to boiling, stirring occasionally. Serve immediately.

AMOUNT: 6 servings.

MANHATTAN CLAM CHOWDER

The New Yorker's version . . . not historical.

Follow ✎ recipe above—using bacon. Use cooked tomatoes (no. 303 can) instead of milk. Increase water to 1 cup and add ⅓ cup diced celery with clam liquor. Add ¼ tsp. thyme and 2 tsp. minced parsley.

VEGETABLE CHOWDER

Follow ✎ recipe above—*except* add 2 tbsp. minced green pepper with the onion. Add ¼ cup *each* diced carrots and celery, and ½ cup peas with the potatoes; increase water to 1 cup. Add broken soda crackers and 1 tbsp. butter just before serving.

CHICKEN AND CORN CHOWDER

Norman E. Dewes of our company enjoyed this chowder so much in Lancaster, Pennsylvania, that he begged the recipe for us.

Place the neck, wings, back pieces, and giblets of a fat hen in a kettle with . . .
- 1½ qt. boiling water
- 1 onion, sliced
- 3 stalks celery (with leaves), chopped fine
- 1 carrot, diced
- 1 tbsp. salt

Cover and simmer until tender (about 1½ hr.). Slip meat from bones, cut it up fine, and return to broth. Add . . .
- 2 cups cream style corn (no. 303 can)

Simmer 10 min., then add . . .
- 2 hard-cooked eggs, chopped fine

Drop Rivels (*p. 411*) into soup, simmer 10 min.

AMOUNT: 6 servings.

CORN CHOWDER

Follow ✎ recipe above—*except* use only 2 tbsp. onion, omit liquor from sea food. Use 1 cup boiling water with potato and add 1 cup finely cut celery and carrots. In place of clams or other sea food, use 2 cups cream style corn (no. 303 can).

POTATO SOUP

For just the right finishing touch before serving, sprinkle with grated cheese and pop under the broiler to brown.

Sauté gently . . .
- 1 tbsp. chopped onion

in . . .
- 2 tbsp. butter

Add . . .
- 1 tsp. salt
- ¼ tsp. celery salt
- ⅛ tsp. pepper
- 1 cup mashed or boiled potatoes, put through a coarse sieve

Stir in . . .
- 2 cups hot milk

Simmer slowly for about 5 min., stirring occasionally.

AMOUNT: 6 servings.

SOUP SUPPER: Cream of Potato Soup, Sea Food Salad in Lettuce Cups, Hot Rolls, Bowl of Fruit, Coffee.

CREAM OF VEGETABLE SOUP (✗ Recipe) *Delicious, nutritious, delicate.*

Sauté............................	1 tsp. finely chopped onion
in...............................	2 tbsp. butter
Blend in..........................	{ 2 to 3 tbsp. flour 1 tsp. salt ⅛ tsp. pepper
Stir over med. heat until smooth and bubbly. Stir in..............................	1 cup puréed cooked vegetables (asparagus, peas, broccoli, or other vegetables)
Bring to boil, boil 1 min., stirring constantly. Remove from heat. Gradually stir in.......	4 cups milk (part consommé or vegetable water may be used)

Heat to serving temperature.   AMOUNT: 6 servings.

A HELPFUL HINT

For a cream soup that is light and fluffy like whipped cream, use an electric blender at end.

Use 2 tbsp. flour with starchy vegetables; 3 tbsp. flour with non-starchy vegetables.

CREAM OF CELERY DE LUXE

Follow ✗ recipe above—*except* use 2 cups rich milk, 2 cups Chicken Stock (*p. 412*), and 1 cup diced or puréed cooked celery.

CREAM OF SPINACH DE LUXE

Follow ✗ recipe above—*except* instead of puréed vegetables, stir in 1 lb. finely chopped washed fresh spinach (or 10-oz. pkg. frozen chopped spinach). Cook 3 to 5 min., stirring constantly, before adding liquid—2 cups milk, and 2 cups Chicken Stock (*p. 412*).

CREAM OF CHICKEN SOUP

Follow ✗ recipe above—*except* use chicken fat instead of butter. Use 3 cups Chicken Stock (*p. 412*), and 1 cup top milk or cream. Blend in ½ cup diced cooked chicken instead of puréed vegetables. Sprinkle each serving with minced chives.

CREAM OF MUSHROOM SOUP

Follow ✗ recipe above—*except* use 2 cups rich milk and 2 cups Chicken Stock (*p. 412*). Sauté 1 cup (¼ lb. fresh) chopped mushrooms in butter before flour is added. Omit vegetable purée. Add paprika and onion salt to taste.

CREAM OF CORN SOUP

Follow ✗ recipe above—*except* use 2 cups cream style corn (no. 303 can) instead of puréed vegetables.

CREAM OF TOMATO SOUP

Sauté . . .
   1 tsp. finely chopped onion
in . . .
   2 tbsp. butter
Stir in . . .
   3 tbsp. flour
   2 tsp. sugar
   1 tsp. salt
   ⅛ tsp. pepper
Cook until smooth and bubbly, stirring constantly. Remove from heat. Gradually stir in . . .
   2 cups tomato juice
Bring to a boil, stirring constantly. Boil 1 min. Stir HOT tomato mixture gradually into . . .
   2 cups COLD milk

Heat rapidly to serving temperature. Serve immediately.

AMOUNT: 4 servings.

CHEDDAR CHEESE SOUP

Given to us by Will Jones, the popular columnist of the Minneapolis Tribune.

Simmer together in covered pan until vegetables are tender (about 10 min.) . . .
   1½ cups diced potato (1 large)
   1 cup chopped onion (1 large)
   1 cup water
Purée vegetable mixture and blend in . . .
   2 cups consommé
   ¼ lb. grated Cheddar cheese
   ½ cup cream

Heat to serving temperature.

CLAM BISQUE (✒ Recipe)

Unusually delicious and so easy to make.

Sauté . . .
>   1 tsp. grated onion

in . . .
>   1 tbsp. butter

Stir in . . .
>   1 tbsp. flour
>   1 tsp. salt
>   ⅛ tsp. pepper
>   ⅛ tsp. celery salt
>   2 tsp. finely minced parsley

Cook until smooth and bubbly.
Remove from heat.
Stir in gradually . . .
>   1 cup water
>   2 cups milk

Bring to boil. Boil 1 min. Blend in . . .
>   7-oz. can minced clams and liquor

Heat to serving temperature. Serve sprinkled with minced parsley.

AMOUNT: 8 servings.

OYSTER BISQUE

Follow ✒ recipe above—*except*, instead of clams and clam liquor, use ½ pt. oysters, chopped, and liquor from oysters.

CRAB, LOBSTER, OR SHRIMP BISQUE

Follow ✒ recipe above—*except*, in place of clams and clam liquor, use 7-oz. can crabmeat, lobster, or shrimp (cut in fine pieces) and liquor from sea food.

QUICK CRAB BISQUE

Sauté about 1 cup crabmeat in butter and season to taste with salt and cayenne. Blend into 3 cups cream of pea soup (*see Cream of Vegetable Soup, p. 417*). Heat thoroughly. Serve at once.

AMOUNT: 6 servings.

OYSTER STEW

Old-time favorite for sleighride parties.

Heat to scalding . . .
>   1 pt. milk
>   ½ cup cream

Just before serving, melt in saucepan . . .
>   ¼ cup butter

Add . . .
>   1 pt. oysters (with the liquor)

Cook gently *just* until oyster edges curl. Add to scalded milk and cream. Season with . . .
>   1 tsp. salt
>   dash of pepper

Serve immediately . . . offer oyster crackers.

CREAM OF CARROT SOUP

Called Potage Crème Nivernaise by Mrs. E. H. Andreson when she served it at a gourmet luncheon with French bread, green salad, and white wine.

Simmer in covered saucepan until tender (15 to 20 min.) . . .
>   2 cups thinly sliced carrots (5 med.)
>   2 tbsp. butter
>   1 tsp. sugar
>   ½ tsp. salt
>   ½ cup water

While carrots are cooking, melt in another saucepan . . .
>   2 tbsp. butter

Blend in . . .
>   2 tbsp. flour
>   ½ tsp. salt
>   dash of pepper

Stir over med. heat until smooth and bubbly. Remove from heat and stir in . . .
>   2¼ cups milk

Bring to boil, boil 1 min., stirring constantly. Combine contents of both saucepans and put through an electric blender or very fine sieve. Blend in . . .
>   ½ cup cream (20%)

Heat and serve.

VICHYSSOISE (Chilled)

Gertrude McGee of Minneapolis suggests the faint flavor of nutmeg that gives distinction to this popular summertime soup.

Brown . . .
>   2 med. onions, sliced

in . . .
>   1 tbsp. butter

Add . . .
>   3 med. potatoes, thinly sliced
>   ½ cup chopped celery
>   2 cups veal or Chicken Stock (p. 412)
>   ½ tsp. salt

Cover and simmer ½ hr. or until vegetables are soft. Press through a fine sieve, forcing through as much of the pulp as possible. To this mixture, add . . .
>   1 cup hot milk
>   1 cup hot cream (20%)
>   ⅛ tsp. pepper
>   1 tsp. salt
>   ¼ tsp. nutmeg

Bring to boil. Chill thoroughly (preferably overnight). When ready to serve, thin with 30% cream (3 cups or less). Serve in chilled soup cups. Garnish with chopped chives and paprika.

AMOUNT: 10 to 12 servings.

Vegetables...a source of Color, Beauty, and Health

THE "VEGETABLE KINGDOM" is worth exploring. It offers mineral and vitamin riches galore. And you will find in it the Humble and Haughty, the Strong and the Mild . . . the Brilliant and Pale. They need recognition, however, to keep them from hiding their light under a bushel. Let's enjoy all the wealth, beauty, and color of this wonderful kingdom.

Betty Crocker

METHODS FOR COOKING FRESH VEGETABLES

See p. 423.

Boil (Simmer)   Steam
Bake   Braise
Fry   Broil

Pressure Cook

FROZEN VEGETABLES ... HOW TO USE THEM

See p. 424.

HOW TO USE CANNED VEGETABLES

See p. 424.

GLAMOROUS WAYS TO SERVE VEGETABLES

See p. 425.

Buttered   Scalloped
Creamed   Au Gratin

. . . with Glorified Butters
. . . with Sauces
. . . with Garnishes
. . . with Herbs (*p. 424*)

For IDEAS FOR SERVING VEGETABLES

See suggestions under each vegetable.

VEGETABLES TO COMPLIMENT THE MEAT

See Menus for Everyday Dinners (*pp. 45–48*).

SOMETHING SPECIAL FOR ENTERTAINING

VEGETABLES FOR A LUNCHEON MAIN DISH

VEGETABLES WITH A FOREIGN FLAVOR

1 Salad Maker shreds vegetables 2 Slicer for potatoes, cucumbers 3 Wooden Bowl and Chopper 4 Graters in three sizes for grating and shredding 5 Nutmeg Grater; also grates lemon rind 6 French Chef's Knife and Cutting Board 7 Food Chopper with three movable blades 8 Parer makes quick work of paring potatoes, carrots 9 Paring Knife 10 Bean Slicer makes cutting French-style beans easy

To purée or rice for soups and soufflés, choose: 11 Electric Blender 12 Food Mill or 13 Ricer. *To rice, mash or whip vegetables, choose:* 13 Ricer 14 Electric Mixer or 15 Masher.

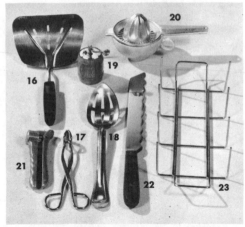

To lift vegetables: 16 Lifter 17 Tongs or Slotted Spoon. *For flavor distinction:* 19 Pepper Mill 20 Juicer and 21 Garlic Press. 22 Frozen Food Saw. 23 Rack for baking potatoes saves oven space, speeds baking.

Be utensil-wise. Choose the right pan for the use. Select those of good quality.

Tight covers mean less water, more food value: 24 Saucepan 25 Baby Saucepan for melting butter 26 Skillet for sautéing, frying, braising 27 Minute-minder Timer prevents overcooking 28 Pressure Saucepan for speed 29 Double Boiler for reheating vegetables and cooking in milk or cream

VEGETABLES

Vegetables have family trees that go back to the dawn of history. Even long before the Christian era, the Greeks and Romans were eating peas and spinach. In the early days of our own country, vegetables were "garden sauce" or just "sass" to go with meat. Beets and carrots sometimes were referred to as "long sauce," while onions and potatoes were "short sauce." A vendor who sold vegetables from door to door was a "sauce man."

We no longer depend on a sauce man plus our own kitchen gardens for vegetables. Thanks to modern agriculture, we not only have bigger, juicier vegetables than our grandmothers or the old Greeks and Romans ever knew, but because of modern transportation and refrigeration, we enjoy vegetables from all over the country the year around.

These fine, handsome vegetables add a bright note to our meals. Just think how drab and monotonous our food would be without the cheery gold of carrots, the refreshing green of peas and beans, or the rich reds of beets and tomatoes! We've learned to cook them, too, so they will keep their bright colors. For vegetables are like people. By treating them with sympathy and understanding, they give us their best in color, nutrients, and flavor. Indifferent treatment, however, makes them drab and lifeless, their precious minerals and vitamins lost. Like people whose fine talents are wasted.

Fortunately there's more than one way to cook vegetables so they will look bright, taste delicious, and reward us with their full bounty of health-giving minerals and vitamins. You'll find all these methods in these pages . . . making it possible for you and your family to enjoy vegetables in all sorts of interesting ways. There are both top-of-the-range and oven methods to fit in with the rest of the meal you may be planning. So pick your pets from among fresh, canned, or frozen vegetables . . . and see how many delightful ways there are for serving them.

pleasing combinations in
PLATE DINNERS 'ROUND THE YEAR
Spring   Summer   Autumn   Winter

See menus on p. 52.

PLATE DINNERS

It's smart to serve vegetables on the same plate with the meat. In Grandma's day, a flotilla of little boat-shaped dishes used to surround each dinner plate. Today we place the vegetables on the main dinner plate. Their bright colors enhance the appearance of the meat. Each plate becomes a picture to tempt reluctant appetites. And there are fewer dishes to wash after the meal.

HOW TO COOK FRESH VEGETABLES

If their colors are bright, you are cooking them right. If their colors are faded, you are not getting the most out of your vegetables in flavor and health-giving vitamins and minerals.

DO cook them in as little water as possible (*see recipes*) for the shortest possible time. DO NOT drown them in liquid. DO NOT overcook! DO NOT add soda.

BOIL (SIMMER) covered in ½ to 1″ boiling salted water (*see recipes*). Use high heat until steam appears, then *reduce* heat and simmer gently until tender.

STEAM preserves color and the nutritional value of vegetables to a very high degree. Place vegetables in perforated compartment of a steamer or deep well cooker. Cover. Steam *over* rapidly boiling water. Steaming takes 5 to 15 min. longer than boiling in most cases.

BAKE directly on rack or in shallow pan or on baking sheet (*see recipes for baking time and temperature*). Allow about 3 times more time than for boiling.

OVEN STEAM, when baking oven meals, in covered casserole with small amount of water. In mod. oven (350°), allow about 3 times more cooking time than for boiled vegetables.

FRY in hot fat over med. heat in heavy skillet. **SAUTÉ** in small amount of fat. Or **SHALLOW FRY** in ½ to 2″ hot fat. Do not allow fat to smoke.

BRAISE in covered pan or skillet with about 2 tbsp. butter or meat drippings and 1 to 2 tbsp. water. These are sometimes called **PANNED** Vegetables.

FRENCH FRY in hot fat deep enough to cover or float the vegetables. Allow 360 to 375° for raw vegetables, 390° for cooked vegetables. Do not crowd the pan . . . cook in small amounts. (*See recipes.*)

BROIL tender raw vegetables, such as eggplant, cut into strips, or tomato slices. (*See recipes.*) Cooked vegetables may be brushed lightly with butter or oil and reheated this way.

PRESSURE COOK vegetables to save time. Follow manufacturer's directions carefully. DO NOT OVERCOOK.

Did you know . . . "strong vegetables" are strong only when you let the sulphur they contain break loose? When cabbage and Brussels sprouts begin to smell their presence, it means they are being overcooked. Color is your guide. Eat vegetables when they are still green . . . for easier digestion, better flavor.

423

Seasonal vegetables are all-season-long now—thanks to the vast scientific growth in our canning and frozen foods industries! Each day new ones appear; the variety is endless.

HOW TO BUY CANNED VEGETABLES

All grades have the same nutritive value. Let your guide be the amount of money you have to spend and the way you intend to cook the vegetables.

Be sure to check the labels on canned vegetables. Most of them state size, net weight, and cup measurement.

HOW TO COOK CANNED VEGETABLES

To preserve their fresh flavor and food value, drain liquid into saucepan, boil quickly to reduce amount ½, add vegetable, and heat quickly—do not boil. Season to taste. Or drain and save extra liquid for use in soups, gravies, and white sauces.

Serve attractively (*see Ways of Serving, p. 425*) for appetite appeal.

HOW TO COOK FROZEN VEGETABLES

Most vegetables are not thawed before cooking, but there are some exceptions to the rule. Follow package directions carefully.

Cook the exact time specified on the package. Start counting the minutes when the frozen block of vegetables is broken up and the water starts boiling again. Use high heat until steam appears, then reduce heat and simmer gently until tender.

TO "BUTTER BOIL" FROZEN VEGETABLES

Place frozen block of vegetables into pan with ⅛″ water, salt, and 1 to 2 tbsp. butter. Cover tightly. Use high heat until steam appears, then reduce heat and simmer gently until tender.

TO OVEN-BAKE FROZEN VEGETABLES

Directions are on each package. Follow them carefully. Frozen vegetables may be baked in the oven with the rest of the meal.

TO USE PART OF A FROZEN PACKAGE

Use a special saw-toothed knife or saw (*p. 420*) to cut frozen blocks of vegetables.

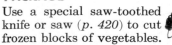

OVEN-ROASTED CORN ON COB

See p. 433.

FROZEN PEAS IN CREAM See p. 439.

TO LIFT VEGETABLES OUT OF PAN

Use the right tools. Tongs (*p. 420*), a flat wire whip, or slotted spoon are a help in lifting such vegetables as corn on cob, asparagus, broccoli, cauliflower out of boiling water.

TO COOK 2 PACKAGES AT THE SAME TIME

For faster, more even cooking, use a pan large enough so the frozen blocks may be placed side by side on bottom of pan—not one on top of the other.

HERB CHART FOR VEGETABLES

The soul of a dish lies in its seasonings. Add the seasonings sparingly . . . to bring out the natural flavor of the vegetables—to enhance but not to destroy it.

Thyme	Basil	Bay Leaf	Marjoram	Oregano	Dill Weed	Mint	Rosemary	Sage	Savory
Beets	Onions	In water	Mushrooms	Tomatoes	Green Beans	Carrots	Mushrooms	Onions	Salsify
Onions	Eggplant	when cooking	Zucchini	Cabbage	Greens	New Potatoes	Peas	Tomatoes	Mushrooms
Carrots	Squash	Potatoes	Peas	Lentils	Cucumbers	Spinach	Spinach	Eggplant	Peas
Green	Tomatoes	Carrots	Spinach	Broccoli	New Potatoes	Peas	Squash	Lima Beans	Green Beans
Beans	Beets	Stewed To-	Green		Asparagus				Beets
		matoes	Beans						

BUTTERED VEGETABLES

Most frequently used method of serving.

Add butter, salt, pepper, and other desired seasonings to hot cooked vegetables. Use 1 to 3 tbsp. butter to 2 cups vegetables. Meat drippings are good with some vegetables, such as corn, beans.

GLORIFIED BUTTERS FOR VEGETABLES

6 to 8 servings

Pass Glorified Butter in a small pitcher.

To ¼ cup butter heated to golden brown

For	Add
Celery Butter.........	1 tsp. celery seeds
Cheese Butter.........	2 tbsp. grated Swiss or Parmesan cheese
Garlic Butter..........	1 small garlic bud, peeled and cut in 2 (remove before serving)
Horse-radish Butter.....	1 tbsp. horse-radish
Lemon Butter..........	2 tbsp. lemon juice 1 tsp. grated lemon rind
Lemon Chive Butter.....	1 tbsp. minced chives in Lemon Butter
Mustard Butter........	¼ tsp. dried or prepared mustard 1 tsp. lemon juice dash of sugar dash of salt
Scallion Butter........	2 tbsp. sliced scallions

EASY HOLLANDAISE SAUCE

Place 2 slightly beaten egg yolks, 2 to 3 tbsp. lemon juice, and 1 stick ice cold butter (¼ lb.) in saucepan. Cook over low heat, stirring constantly, until sauce is slightly thick. Season to taste with salt. *Makes 1 cup.*

HONEY BUTTER

Beat together until fluffy: ½ cup honey, ½ cup soft butter, 1 tsp. grated orange rind, if desired. Good over carrots or beets.

ALMOND OR CASHEW SAUCE

In ¼ cup butter, slowly sauté ¼ cup almonds or cashew nuts until golden. Add ¼ tsp. salt, 2 tsp. lemon juice. Pour over hot vegetables (asparagus, green beans).

CREAMED VEGETABLES

"Creaming" makes them go further and adds a sauce. Use one vegetable, or two or three in combination.

For 6 servings, add at least 1 cup hot Medium White Sauce (*p. 398*) to 2 cups hot cooked vegetables. Serve plain, on toast or hot biscuits, or in a rice or noodle ring.

OTHER SAUCES FOR VEGETABLES

A gourmet's touch ... to mix with vegetables or spoon on top.

Black Butter Sauce. `. . . . . .p. 402
Cheese Sauce. . . . . .p. 398
Crumb Sauce (Buttered Crumbs) . p. 403
Egg Sauce. .p. 398
English Parsley Sauce . . . . .p. 399
Hollandaise Sauce. . . . . .p. 402
Hot Tartare Sauce . . . . .p. 399
Mushroom Sauce. . . . . .p. 398

SCALLOPED VEGETABLES

Originally baked in scallop shells.

Place Creamed Vegetables in greased casserole, or arrange vegetables and White Sauce (*p. 398*) in alternate layers. Top with Crumb Sauce (*p. 403*). Bake in mod. oven (350°) 20 min. or until browned.

VEGETABLES AU GRATIN

Follow recipe above—*except* sprinkle layers with grated cheese . . . or cover with Cheese Sauce (*p. 398*) and top with Buttered Crumbs (*p. 403*).

CHOOSE A GARNISH

To make your vegetables attractively tempting, try pairing them with one of these garnishes:

- Paprika
- Parsley
- Minced green onion tops or chives
- Sieved hard-cooked eggs or yolks
- Quartered or sliced hard-cooked eggs
- Crumb Sauce (*p. 403*)
- Croutons (*p. 30*)
- Pimiento strips
- Green pepper rings or strips (*p. 55*)
- Grated cheese (broil until melted)
- Thin lemon slices or wedges
- Chopped toasted almonds, peanuts, cashews
- Crumbled potato chips, crisp ready-to-eat cereals, cheese crackers, etc.
- French fried onions (crisp, canned variety)
- Crumbled crisp bacon bits

ARTICHOKES (French or Globe) *Adventures in food are fun, and artichokes are a real adventure. There is a little trick to eating them but that, too, is part of the fun.*

1 lb. **serves 1**

Break off stems to about ½". Remove outer lower leaves and thorny leaf tips. Tie with string to keep leaves in place.

Cook covered in 1" boiling salted water (seasoned with 1 clove garlic, crushed, 1 tbsp. salad oil, 1 slice lemon for each artichoke) 30 to 45 min. until leaf pulls away easily. Remove carefully; trim stem; serve upright on plates.

JERUSALEM ARTICHOKES

Cousins in name only, they look like knobby potatoes and are served mashed, creamed, fried, scalloped, or sliced cold in salad.

Graceful Artichoke Eating

Pull off leaf; dip wide end into melted butter mixed with a little lemon juice or Hollandaise Sauce (*p. 402*); or into mayonnaise mixed with lemon juice and prepared mustard. Scrape soft pulp from base with teeth. Discard the rest. With knife and fork, remove and discard "choke." Dip cut-up "hearts" into sauce.

ARTICHOKE CASSEROLE SUPREME

Heat in baking dish in mod. oven (350°) alternate layers of cooked artichoke hearts; cut-up cooked sea food, chicken or turkey; and Medium White Sauce (*p. 398*) . . . sprinkled with grated cheese or Crumb Sauce (*p. 403*).

ASPARAGUS *From the volcanic slopes of Mount Vesuvius in Italy came the first tender stalks. Charles Lamb thought this "vegetable orchid" brought gentle thoughts. And Madam DuBarry inspired Louis XV of France to create the first asparagus omelet.*

2 lb. **serves 4**

Break off stalks as far down as they snap easily. Wash well. Leave whole or break into 1" lengths.

Tie whole stalks in bunches with string and cook upright in narrow deep pan or coffeepot. Catch string with fork when lifting out.

Cook covered in 1" boiling salted water— whole, 10 to 20 min.; pieces, 10 to 15 min.; tips, 5 to 10 min.

If cut in pieces, drop lower stems in water first, tips last 5 min.

ASPARAGUS IN AMBUSH

Roll cooked stalks of asparagus in thin slices of boiled ham or dried beef. Broil. Serve with Cheese Sauce or White Sauce (*p. 398*).

Ideas for serving...

• Serve with butter, salt, and pepper. Vary with dash of lemon juice, minced onion, grated nutmeg, or prepared mustard.
• Add Black Butter Sauce (*p. 402*), Lemon Butter, Almond or Cashew Sauce, or Crumb Sauce (*pp. 403, 425*).
• Spoon Cheese, Egg, Mushroom, or Hollandaise Sauce (*pp. 398, 402*) over asparagus spears.

ASPARAGUS AND ALMONDS

Alternate layers of drained cooked asparagus with Cheese or White Sauce (*p. 398*) and chopped, toasted almonds in baking dish. Bake in mod. oven (350°) 15 to 20 min. Sprinkle with minced parsley.

ASPARAGUS PARMESAN

Top toast squares or Croutons (*p. 30*) with cooked asparagus, sliced hard-cooked eggs, White Sauce (*p. 398*). Sprinkle with grated Parmesan cheese, crisp bacon. Baked tomatoes go well with this!

CREAMED ASPARAGUS

See Creamed Vegetables (*p. 425*). A little nutmeg added to seasonings in the white sauce gives a delicious flavor.

BEANS (Green or Wax)

BEANS (Green or Wax) *String beans go back to ancient Roman times. The Indians grew them when Miles Standish courted Priscilla. Now, through the miracle of modern times, they are mostly stringless.*

1½ lb. serves 4

Wash. Snip off ends. Leave whole, cut into 1″ lengths, or sliver lengthwise (French style).

Cook covered in ½ to 1″ boiling salted water—whole, 15 to 20 min.; 1″ lengths, 15 to 20 min.; strips, 10 min.

To "French" beans, cut into 2 strips.

Then cut each strip into 2 narrow strips.
To Save Time: Use a bean slicer (*p. 420*).

Ideas for serving...

* Season with butter, salt, pepper. Sprinkle very lightly with one of these herbs: dill weed, basil, savory, thyme, or marjoram. Add a dash of lemon juice.
* Sprinkle buttered beans with grated nutmeg, chili or curry powder, or dried mustard.
* Serve with Black Butter Sauce, Lemon Butter, or Crumb Sauce (*pp. 402–403, 425*).
* Add Cheese, White, Mushroom, or Hollandaise Sauce (*pp. 398, 402*).
* Combine with tiny green onion rings and diced celery, raw or sautéed in butter.
* Serve with sautéed mushrooms, or mushrooms sautéed and then simmered in milk or cream which has been seasoned with salt, sugar, and nutmeg.
* Toss with thin strips of boiled ham, bologna, or anchovies just before serving.

EASY BAKED GREEN BEANS

Partially cook 2 pkg. frozen French-style green beans. Mix with 1 can undiluted cream of mushroom soup in 1½-qt. baking dish. Top with buttered crumbs or crisp French fried onions (canned). Bake in quick mod. oven (375°) 15 to 20 min. until beans are tender. *6 to 8 servings.*

PUERTO RICAN GREEN BEANS

Toss together lightly 1 pkg. frozen green beans, cooked, 3 tbsp. butter, 1 tbsp. minced onion, 1 tbsp. chopped green pepper, 1 to 2 tsp. lemon or lime juice, salt, pepper. *4 servings.*

HUNGARIAN GREEN BEANS

Spread in 2-qt. baking dish . . .
    2 no. 303 cans green beans, drained (4 cups)
Mix . . .
    2 cups Medium White Sauce (p. 398)
    1 small onion, chopped
    2 tbsp. minced parsley
    ¼ tsp. paprika
    salt, pepper to taste
    2 egg yolks, slightly beaten
    4-oz. can mushrooms and liquid
Pour over beans. Top with buttered crumbs. Bake.
TEMPERATURE: 350° (mod. oven).
TIME: Bake 30 min.
AMOUNT: 6 servings.

GREEN BEANS WITH CASHEW NUTS

Sauté ¼ cup cut-up cashew nuts and 2 tbsp. minced onion in 2 tbsp. butter. Toss lightly with 1 pkg. frozen green beans, French style, cooked. *4 servings.*
Green Beans Almondine: Use almonds in place of cashew nuts.

TANGY GREEN BEANS

Combine . . .
    2 tbsp. prepared mustard
    2 tbsp. sugar
    ⅓ cup butter
    ½ tsp. salt
Heat slowly, stirring constantly. Stir in . . .
    2 tbsp. lemon juice
    2 tbsp. vinegar
Pour over . . .
    3 cups hot cooked green beans
Heat thoroughly.
AMOUNT: 6 servings.

BEANS (Green Lima) Indians planted them with corn to choke out the weeds; then taught the Pilgrims to make Succotash, the first truly American dish.

<table>
<tr><td>*3 lb.
serves 4</td></tr>
</table>

(in the pod) or 1 pt. *(shelled)*

Cut off outer rim or rounded side of pods. Shell like peas.

Cook covered in ½ to 1″ boiling salted water 20 to 25 min.

 Ideas for serving...

• Add butter, salt, pepper, and milk or cream, if desired.
• Combine with sautéed mushrooms, celery, carrots, or tomatoes.
• Mound buttered Lima beans in hollows of baked squash. Season with salt and pepper.

SAVORY BABY GREEN LIMAS

Mix and cook until tender 1 pkg. frozen or 2 cups fresh baby Lima beans, 1 tsp. dry mustard, 1 tsp. sugar, ¼ tsp. salt. Drain. Add 2 tbsp. melted butter, 1 tsp. lemon juice. Garnish with a half slice of lemon. *4 servings.*

GREEN LIMAS BAKED IN CREAM

To 1 pkg. frozen green Lima beans, add ½ cup cream, 1 tsp. salt, dash of pepper. Bake in covered baking dish in mod. oven (350°) 50 to 60 min.

LIMA BEANS IN SOUR CREAM

To 2 cups hot cooked Lima beans, add 2 tbsp. finely chopped onion, 2 tbsp. chopped pimiento, 2 tbsp. butter, ½ cup cultured sour cream, salt and pepper to taste. Heat through. *6 servings.*

SPICY LIMA BEANS

Mix cooked Lima beans with condensed cream of tomato soup, tomato paste or purée, catsup or chili sauce. Heat and serve.

EASY FROZEN SUCCOTASH

Combine 1 pkg. *each* frozen corn niblets and baby Limas, 2 to 4 tbsp. butter, ½ to ¾ cup cream, 1 tsp. salt, pepper. Bake in covered baking dish in mod. oven (350°) or simmer over hot water 50 to 60 min.

BEETS The name Beet comes from the Greeks. When they paid homage to Apollo, they served him beet roots on a silver platter.

<table>
<tr><td>1 lb.
serves 4</td></tr>
</table>

Cut off all but 2″ of tops. Wash. Save tops of young beets to serve as greens. Do not peel beets to be cooked whole; after cooking, run cold water over them and slip off skins. For *quick cooking,* pare, then dice, slice, or shred on coarse grater.

Cook covered in ½ to 1″ boiling salted water—whole, 30 to 45 min.; sliced, 15 to 20 min.; shredded, 8 min.

Or, season with dash of sugar, vinegar, salt, and, if desired, few whole cloves or crumbled bay leaf. Bake covered in mod. oven (350°) in ¼″ water 40 to 60 min. (20 min. for shredded).

 Ideas for serving...

• Serve with butter, salt, pepper. Vary with touch of grated orange or lemon rind, cinnamon, nutmeg, or with herbs (see Herb Chart, p. 424).
• See Borsch (*p. 415*).

HARVARD BEETS

Heat together . . .
   3 cups diced cooked beets
   1 cup liquid (beet juice and water)
Mix . . .
   3 tbsp. flour or 1½ tbsp. cornstarch
   2 tbsp. sugar
   1 tsp. salt
   dash of pepper
   ¼ to ⅓ cup vinegar

Stir into beets. Cook, stirring constantly, until smoothly blended and thickened.
AMOUNT: 6 servings.

QUICK PICKLED BEETS

Drain into saucepan juice from no. 2 or no. 303 can sliced beets. Add ¼ cup vinegar, 1 tsp. salt, ¼ tsp. cinnamon, ⅛ tsp. cloves, dash of pepper. Bring to boiling. Pour over beets. Chill.

ZIPPY BEETS

Cook 3 cups shredded beets. Add ⅓ cup cream, 2½ tsp. horse-radish, 1 tsp. salt.

SAVORY BEETS

To no. 2 or no. 303 can drained tiny beets, add ½ tsp. basil, ½ tsp. savory, 2 tbsp. butter, salt, and pepper. Heat in double boiler about 30 min., stirring occasionally. Heating slowly over hot water blends in the flavor of the herbs. *4 servings.*

BEETS WITH ORANGE SAUCE

To 3 cups sliced cooked beets, add a mixture of 2 tbsp. flour, ¼ cup sugar, ½ tsp. salt, ½ cup orange juice, and 2 tbsp. butter. Bake in covered pan in mod. oven (350°) 15 min. Sprinkle with grated orange rind, if desired. Serve with roast pork, roast duck, pork or veal chops, etc. *6 servings.*

CHRYSANTHEMUM BEETS

Shred raw beets on coarse grater. Cook 8 to 10 min. Serve buttered and seasoned in fluffy mass.

POLISH BEETS

Blend into 2 tbsp. melted butter . . .
   2 tsp. flour
Cook until bubbly, remove from heat. Add . . .
   2 tbsp. vinegar
   1 tbsp. sugar
   ¼ tsp. salt
   ⅛ tsp. pepper
   ¼ tsp. dill weed
Stir in . . .
   no. 303 can tiny whole beets, drained
Heat through slowly. Add . . .
   ½ cup cultured sour cream

Heat, but do not boil. Serve immediately. AMOUNT: 4 servings.

GLAZED BEETS

Add 2½ cups drained cooked tiny beets to 3 tbsp. melted butter in saucepan. Shake pan to coat beets with butter. Cook over low heat about 3 min. Sprinkle with 1 tbsp. sugar and again shake pan.

BROCCOLI *Sometimes called Italian Asparagus, broccoli was known to the Romans before Pompeii. It is best when cooked quickly and "on its feet," like asparagus.*

| 1½ lb.
serves 4 | Wash. Trim tips of stems. Make 3 to 4 gashes through stems. Set upright in pan. Cook covered in 1″ boiling |

salted water 10 to 15 min.

BROCCOLI SOUFFLÉ

Cook 1 lb. fresh or frozen broccoli until almost tender but not soft (3 to 5 min.). Chop into small pieces.

Make . . .
   1 cup Thick White Sauce (*p. 398*)
Stir gradually at least half of hot sauce into . . .
   4 egg yolks, slightly beaten
Then mix into rest of hot sauce. Add . . .
   1 tsp. lemon juice
   ⅛ tsp. nutmeg
   cooked broccoli
Remove from heat.
Beat until soft peaks form . . .
   4 egg whites
   ¼ tsp. cream of tartar

Fold into sauce. Pour into 1½-qt. baking dish set in pan of hot water (1″ deep). Bake until puffed and golden brown. Serve immediately.

TEMPERATURE: 350° (mod. oven).
TIME: Bake 45 to 50 min.
AMOUNT: 6 servings.

Ideas for serving...

- Serve with butter, salt, pepper. Vary as for Asparagus (Ideas for serving, *p. 426*).
- Serve Creamed (*p. 425*). With Hollandaise Sauce (*p. 402*). With grated cheese.

BROCCOLI-MUSHROOM CASSEROLE

Cook 1 to 1½ lb. broccoli until tender but not soft (3 to 5 min.). Drain. Spread in greased 9″ square pan or 1-qt. baking dish.

Make . . .
   2 cups Medium White Sauce (*p. 398*)
Add . . .
   1 cup grated or cubed cheese
     (reserve ¼ cup for top)
   ½ lb. mushrooms (1 to 1½ cups),
     sliced and sautéed in butter
   2 tbsp. chopped green pepper

Pour sauce over broccoli. Sprinkle with cheese and paprika. Bake until tender and golden brown.

TEMPERATURE: 350° (mod. oven).
TIME: Bake 15 to 20 min.
AMOUNT: 4 servings.

BRUSSELS SPROUTS
Known as Tom Thumb Cabbages during the days of that famous circus midget, these miniature cabbages grew first in Brussels, Belgium.

1½ lb. serves 4	Remove loose or discolored leaves. Trim tips of stems. Wash. Cook covered in 1″ boiling salted water 8 to 10 min.

For ways to serve, see Ideas for Serving under CABBAGE (*below*).

BRUSSELS SPROUTS PIQUANT

Pour over cooked Brussels sprouts, condensed cream of tomato soup, catsup, or chili sauce. Sprinkle generously with grated cheese and heat in oven or under broiler until cheese melts.

CABBAGE
Many people don't know how delicious cabbage can be. For the most appetizing flavor, texture and color, it must be cooked briefly and quickly.

*1 head serves 4	Wash. Cut into wedges or shred.

*(1½ to 2 lb.)

1 For "coarsely" shredded cabbage, use a knife. **2** For finely shredded cabbage, use a grater.

Cook covered—wedges or slices, in ½ to 1″ boiling salted water, 10 to 15 min.; shredded, in ¼″ water, 5 to 8 min. For red cabbage, lemon juice or vinegar in water helps to keep color bright. Cabbage is especially mild-flavored when simmered in milk.

 Ideas for serving...

- Serve with butter, salt, pepper. Vary with dash of lemon or lime juice, caraway seeds, chopped mint, or parsley.
- Pour Black Butter Sauce, Lemon Butter, Mustard Butter, or Crumb Sauce (*pp. 402–403, 425*) over cabbage.
- Serve Creamed (*p. 425*) or with Hollandaise or Cheese Sauce (*pp. 398, 402*). Sprinkle with crisp bacon or chopped, toasted nuts.

PANNED CABBAGE

Melt in skillet 2 tbsp. fat, 1 tsp. beef extract or 1 bouillon cube, ⅛ tsp. salt. Add 3 cups shredded cabbage. Cover. Cook 10 min. until tender. *4 servings.*

BOHEMIAN CABBAGE

Mix lightly in skillet: 5 to 6 cups finely shredded cabbage, ¼ cup water, 1 tbsp. minced onion, 1 tsp. salt, ¼ tsp. pepper, ½ tsp. caraway seeds (if desired). Cover. Cook over low heat 5 min. Stir in ½ cup cultured sour cream. Heat through. *6 servings.*

SCALLOPED CABBAGE

Mix lightly 2 cups Medium White Sauce (p. 398) and 5 cups shredded raw cabbage in 1½-qt. baking dish. Top with 1 cup grated cheese and 2 tbsp. fine crumbs. Bake in mod. hot oven (400°) 20 min., until tender. *6 servings.*

HOT CABBAGE SLAW

Mix in deep pan or skillet . . .
- 2 tbsp. butter
- 2 eggs, slightly beaten
- ¼ cup vinegar
- ½ cup milk
- ¼ tsp. dry mustard
- 1½ to 2 tbsp. sugar
- ½ tsp. salt
- ⅛ tsp. paprika
- dash of pepper

Cook over low heat until slightly thickened, stirring constantly. Add . . .
- 5 cups shredded raw cabbage

Heat but do not cook. Serve immediately. AMOUNT: 6 servings.

GOLDEN CABBAGE

Cook 8 cups shredded cabbage. Drain. Stir in 1 egg, slightly beaten, 2 tbsp. butter, 1 tbsp. lemon juice. *6 servings.*

CELERY CABBAGE (Chinese)

Shred. Cook covered in ¼″ boiling salted water 4 to 5 min. Serve buttered or with light cream.

CARROTS *They don't make your hair curl, but do help protect your health. Formerly raised as fodder . . . now a colorful addition to our meals.*

| **1 to 2 lb.** **serves 4** | Remove tops. Scrub well or pare thin. Leave whole, cut into slices or strips, or shred. |

Cook covered in ½ to 1″ boiling salted water (¼″ for shredded)—whole, 15 to 20 min.; sliced or strips, 10 to 20 min.; shredded, 5 min. Add a pinch of sugar, a bit of orange or lemon peel, or slice of apple for extra flavor. Or bake covered with ¼″ water in mod. oven (350°) 45 to 60 min.

 Ideas for serving...

- Serve with butter, salt, pepper. Vary with dash of lemon juice, minced chives, chopped mint or parsley, thyme, nutmeg, or cinnamon.
- Serve with Black Butter Sauce or Lemon Butter (*pp. 402, 425*).
- Add White Sauce, Egg Sauce, or Mint Sauce (*pp. 398, 403*).
- Combine with cooked peas, celery, or little green onions. Serve with Lemon Butter (*p. 425*).
- Mash and add cream, sugar, salt, and pepper.
- Add marshmallows and heat over hot water until marshmallows melt. For something different, add a pinch of candied ginger.
- Combine equal amounts mashed carrots and turnips. Add cream and sugar.
- Use leftover Hard Sauce (*p. 405*) from steamed puddings. Spoon a little over hot carrots. Sprinkle with grated orange rind.
- Serve whole buttered or glazed carrots with a sprig of parsley thrust in the end of each. They look like fresh carrots!

CARROTS IN CREAM
Heat until thickened 1 cup cream combined with 1 egg yolk, 2 tbsp. butter, ½ tsp. sugar, ⅛ tsp. nutmeg. Add to 2 cups hot cooked carrot slices. Sprinkle with minced parsley. *4 servings.*

CARROTS AMBROSIA
Glaze 12 whole small cooked carrots with butter and sugar as in Mint-glazed carrots (*at right*). Add 2 oranges, sliced. Heat thoroughly. *4 servings.*

CARROT RING
Mix . . .
> 2 cups mashed cooked carrots
> 2 tbsp. butter
> 3 egg yolks
> ½ cup dry bread or cracker crumbs
> 1 cup milk
> ¼ cup finely chopped onion
> ⅛ tsp. pepper
> 1 tsp. salt
> dash of Worcestershire Sauce or paprika, if desired
> 3 egg whites, stiffly beaten

Pour into greased 1½-qt. ring mold set in pan of hot water (1″ deep). Bake in mod. oven (350°) 40 to 45 min. Delicious with cooked peas and sautéed mushrooms or cooked baby Lima beans in the center. Serve with Egg Sauce (*p. 398*).

ZESTY CARROTS
Spread 6 to 8 cooked carrots (cut in lengthwise strips) in shallow baking dish. Mix and pour over carrots . . .
> ¼ cup water or liquid from carrots
> 2 tbsp. grated onion
> 2 tbsp. horse-radish
> ½ cup mayonnaise
> ½ tsp. salt
> ¼ tsp. pepper

Top with mixture of . . .
> ¼ cup fine bread or cracker crumbs
> 1 tbsp. butter
> dash of paprika

Bake in quick mod. oven (375°) 15 to 20 min. Garnish with minced parsley. *6 servings.*

MINT-GLAZED CARROTS
Simmer 2 cups cooked carrot strips with ¼ cup butter, ¼ cup sugar, 1 tbsp. mint jelly until soft and glazed. *4 servings.*

NIPPY CARROTS
Simmer until bubbly 2 tbsp. butter, ¼ cup brown sugar, 2 tbsp. prepared mustard, 1 tsp. salt. Pour over 2 to 3 cups hot cooked carrot slices. *4 servings.*

BAKED SHREDDED CARROTS
Heap shredded carrots lightly in baking dish with 2 to 4 tbsp. water, salt, pepper, sugar, a little orange rind. Bake covered until tender in mod. oven (350°) 15 to 20 min.

CAULIFLOWER Queen of the cabbage family. For delicate flavor, treat gently. Cook quickly!

> ***1 head**
> **serves 4**
>
> **(about 3 lb.)*

Wash well. Remove green stalks. Leave head whole with 1" of stem, or separate into flowerets.

Cook covered in ½ to 1" boiling unsalted water—whole, 20 to 30 min.; flowerets, 8 to 15 min. Whole head can be set upright in deep pan. Sugar, lemon, or milk added will keep color white. Salt darkens, so add later.

Ideas for serving...

* Add butter, salt, pepper. Or serve with a sauce: Cheese, Egg, or Hollandaise Sauce (*pp. 398, 402*).
* For Blushing Cauliflower, simmer in tomato purée and seasonings.
* For Christmas Cauliflower, serve with strips of pimiento and green pepper in a cheese or white sauce.
* For cauliflower au beurre noir, toss together or top with browned buttered crumbs.
* Arrange raw cauliflowerets around a bowl of your favorite cheese or cocktail dip.

CAULIFLOWER PORCUPINE

Tuck toasted salted almonds or cashew nuts into whole cooked head of cauliflower. Serve with White Sauce (*p. 398*).

CAULIFLOWER WITH CHEESE

Tuck cubes of cheese into whole cooked head of cauliflower. Place in baking dish with a little cream. Sprinkle with buttered crumbs and crisp bacon bits. Bake in mod. oven (350°) 15 to 20 min., until cheese melts.

CAULIFLOWER CASSEROLE

Pour 2 cups Medium White Sauce (*p. 398*) over 1 head cauliflower (whole or in flowerets) in baking dish. Sprinkle with ½ to 1 cup grated sharp cheese. Bake 20 min., or until cheese melts and sauce is bubbly, in mod. oven (350°). *4 servings.*

HUNGARIAN CAULIFLOWER

In baking dish, pour about 1 cup cultured sour cream over head of cooked seasoned cauliflower coated with fine crumbs. Brown in mod. oven (350°).

CELERY Dutch gardeners of Kalamazoo, Michigan, grew it first in America and sold it on the trains that passed through town.

> ***1 stalk**
> **serves 4**
>
> **(medium)*

Remove leaves; trim roots. Wash well. Reserve inner stalks to serve raw. Dice or slice outer stalks.

Cook covered in ½ to 1" boiling salted water 10 to 20 min. Add bouillon cube for extra flavor.

Ideas for serving...

* Serve with butter, salt, pepper. Vary with chopped onion or chives, mint, parsley.
* Black Butter Sauce or Lemon Butter (*pp. 402, 425*). Combine with other vegetables and add to meat dishes.
* Serve Creamed (*p. 425*) or Braised (*p. 423*) in meat drippings. Sprinkle with celery seeds.
* Combine buttered cooked celery and carrots. Sprinkle with finely chopped mint.

CHINESE CELERY

Steam Pascal (green) celery in oil or butter with very little water (2 to 4 tbsp.). If desired, add onion, sliced unpeeled zucchini squash, Chinese green peas, bean sprouts, or frozen mixed vegetables. Season with salt, pepper, soy sauce. Cook just until tender but still crisp.

CREOLE CELERY

Sauté in 2 tbsp. butter until golden ½ cup chopped onion, ½ cup chopped green pepper. Add 2 to 2½ cups cooked tomatoes (may be canned), 2 cups diced celery, 1 tsp. salt. Cook gently until tender. *6 servings.*

CELERY WITH WATER CHESTNUTS

Cook diced celery in chicken broth until just tender. Add sliced canned water chestnuts and slivered almonds; thicken sauce if desired. Sprinkle with paprika or parsley. Almonds may be toasted and sprinkled over celery before serving.

CORN *Surrounded by mystery and legend, American Indians believed it was the gift of the Great Spirit. Though known in other countries, corn is still typically American.*

> **2 ears
> serve 1**

Corn is best when eaten as soon after picking as possible. Just before cooking, remove inner husks and silks.

Cook covered in ½ to 1″ boiling unsalted water 3 to 6 min. Salt toughens, so add later. You may line bottom of pan with some of inner husks, place corn on top, or put it in alternate layers. Sugar helps flavor of older corn.

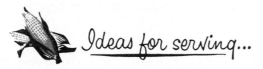 *Ideas for serving...*

- *On the Cob:* Serve with butter, salt, pepper.
- *Off the Cob:* Add seasoned cream, butter. Or combine with White Sauce (*p. 398*). Sprinkle with crisp bacon bits or chopped green pepper.

MEXICAN CORN SAUTÉ

Mix in skillet . . .
    3 tbsp. butter, melted
    no. 303 can whole kernel corn (about 2 cups fresh), drained
    1 tbsp. *each* chopped green pepper and pimiento
    ½ tsp. salt
    ½ tsp. chili powder
Cover. Simmer 10 to 15 min., stirring occasionally. *4 servings.*

CORN PATTIES (Mock Oysters)

Combine 2 beaten egg yolks, 1½ cups cooked whole kernel corn, 2 tsp. flour, 1 tsp. butter, 2 tsp. cream, ½ tsp. salt, dash of pepper. Fold in 2 stiffly beaten egg whites. Drop by teaspoonfuls onto hot greased griddle. Cook until brown on each side. Serve with meat and fish. *Makes 24 patties.*

OVEN-ROASTED CORN ON COB, FROZEN

Thaw corn. Brush with salted melted butter. Roast in hot oven (400°) 15 to 20 min., or until tender and golden brown.

CORN CUSTARD (Corn Pudding)

Combine 3 eggs, slightly beaten, 1 tsp. salt, ⅛ tsp. pepper, 1 tbsp. sugar, no. 303 can whole kernel corn, drained (about 2 cups fresh), 2 tbsp. butter melted in 2 cups scalded milk. Pour into 1½-qt. baking dish set in pan of hot water (1″ deep). Bake in mod. oven (350°) 35 to 40 min. until silver knife inserted near center comes out clean. *6 servings.*

SCALLOPED CORN

Sauté until golden . . .
    ¼ cup *each* chopped onion, green pepper
in . . .
    2 tbsp. butter
Blend in, and cook until bubbly . . .
    2 tbsp. flour
    1 tsp. salt
    ½ tsp. paprika
    ¼ tsp. dry mustard
    dash of pepper
Remove from heat. Add gradually . . .
    ¾ cup milk
Bring to boiling; boil 1 min., stirring constantly. Remove from heat. Add . . .
    no. 303 can whole kernel corn, drained (about 2 cups fresh)
    1 egg, slightly beaten
Pour into 1-qt. baking dish. Top with buttered crumbs. Bake in mod. oven (350°) 20 to 30 min. *4 servings.*

CORN-TOMATO CASSEROLE

Combine in 1-qt. baking dish, 2½ cups cooked whole kernel corn, 2½ cups tomatoes, ¼ cup chopped green pepper, ½ cup cracker crumbs, 2 tbsp. butter, 1½ tsp. salt, 1 tsp. sugar, dash of pepper. Sprinkle with grated cheese and cracker crumbs. Dot with butter, if desired. Bake in mod. hot oven (400°) 25 to 30 min. *8 servings.*

CORN SOUFFLÉ

Put no. 303 can whole kernel corn, drained (about 1⅔ cups), through food grinder or blender. Combine with 1 cup rich cream, 1 tsp. salt, and 5 beaten egg whites. Bake in 1½-qt. baking dish set in pan of hot water (1″ deep) in mod. oven (350°) 50 to 60 min. *4 to 6 servings.*

433

CUCUMBERS Ancient Chinese and Romans ate them three hundred years ago, one Roman emperor had them on his table every day of the year. Usually eaten raw, they are delicious cooked.

2 serves 4

Leave skins on, or pare thinly. Cut into thick slices, lengthwise quarters, or cubes. Not desirable to soak in salted water.

Cook covered in ¼″ boiling salted water 10 to 15 min.

 Ideas for serving...

• Serve with butter, salt, pepper, and a dash of garlic salt, dill weed, or chili powder, if desired.
• Combine with a little minced onion, chives, or parsley.
• Toss sliced scored cucumbers with Sour Cream Dressing (*p. 381*).

CUCUMBERS IN SOUR CREAM CONSOMMÉ

Melt 1 tbsp. butter in skillet. Blend in 1 tbsp. flour. Cook over low heat, stirring until mixture is smooth, bubbly. Remove from heat. Stir in ½ cup consommé or bouillon, 3 tbsp. cultured sour cream, 1 tbsp. lemon juice, 1 clove garlic, minced, 1 large cucumber, cut in thick slices, salt, and pepper. Cover. Simmer 8 to 10 min. *4 servings.*

BAKED CUCUMBERS WITH CREAM

Spread thick slices of cucumber in baking dish. Season with salt, pepper, and chopped parsley or chives. Bake in quick mod. oven (375°) 10 to 12 min. When almost done, add enough sour cream to make a sauce.

EGGPLANT The Ancients called it "mad apple" because they thought it was poisonous. Its delicate flavor blends well with herbs and other vegetables.

*1 med. serves 4

about 1½ lb.

Wash; do not soak. Paring not necessary unless skin is tough. Slice, cube, or cut in strips. Cook covered in ½″ boiling salted water 10 to 15 min. For added flavor, add a few peppercorns, chopped parsley, green onions, crushed garlic, or crumbled bay leaf.

 Ideas for serving...

• Combine in Scalloped and Au Gratin (*p. 425*) dishes with tomatoes, cheese.
• Serve with tomato sauce, catsup, or chili sauce.
• Sprinkle with minced chives, parsley, or grated Parmesan cheese.

FRIED EGGPLANT

Dip strips or slices of eggplant in flour or dry crumbs, egg, crumbs. Sauté in small amount of hot fat 5 to 10 min. or French fry in hot fat (375°) to float 2 to 4 min. on each side until tender and golden brown. Season with salt and pepper.

BROILED EGGPLANT

Make same as Fried Eggplant above—*except* broil slowly 5 to 10 min. on each side until tender and golden brown.

SPANISH EGGPLANT

Fry 4 slices bacon until crisp; remove and save for top. Chop fine 1 med. onion and 1 green pepper; sauté until golden. Add 1 cubed pared eggplant, 2 tsp. salt, ¼ tsp. pepper, 6 to 10-oz. can tomato purée, 1 cup water. Cook covered 5 to 10 min. until almost tender. Pour into 1½-qt. baking dish. Top with 1 cup grated cheese, Crumb Sauce (*p. 403*), and crumbled bacon bits. Bake uncovered in mod. oven (350°) 20 to 30 min. until tender. *6 to 8 servings.*

STUFFED EGGPLANT

Cut large lengthwise slice off med. eggplant. Remove from shell and cut in cubes. Cook in small amount of boiling salted water for 10 min. While eggplant is cooking, brown ¾ cup sliced mushrooms, 2 tbsp. chopped onion, 1 clove garlic, chopped, in 2 tbsp. butter. When partially browned, add drained eggplant. Then add salt and pepper to taste, ½ cup cream. Simmer 10 to 15 min. until soft. Fill eggplant shell with mixture and top with 1 slice bacon, chopped. Bake in mod. oven (350°) 45 min. *4 servings.*

Delicious Supper Dish: Barbecued Hamburger (*p. 302*) or Beef-Egg Scramble (*p. 302*) on strips of Fried or Broiled Eggplant (*at left*).

GREENS *Great grandmother never heard of vitamins, but she knew that greens were good for her family. So she gathered the wild greens and planted the seeds of many others.*

| 1 to 2 lb. serves 4 | For sketches of some greens, see p. 378. |

Chicory   Mustard Greens
Collards   Romaine
Dandelion Greens   Spinach
Escarole   Swiss Chard
Lettuce   Watercress

Tops of Beet, Radish, Kale, Kohlrabi, Turnip.

Trim root ends and damaged leaves. Wash well by lifting in and out of cool water about 3 times. Or use a salad basket (*p. 420*) for washing. Sand will sink to the bottom. Save tender young greens to add raw in salads!

Cook covered, using only the water that clings to the leaves after washing, 3 to 10 min., or just until tender. Older greens will take longer than younger ones. Kale will take longer than spinach.

 Ideas for serving...

• Serve with butter, salt, pepper. Vary with dash of vinegar or lemon juice.
• Minced onion or garlic, grated nutmeg, prepared mustard, or horse-radish may be added during cooking, together with oil, butter, or bacon drippings.
• Add bacon or salt pork to dandelion and turnip greens. Just before serving, add a little brown sugar and vinegar and garnish with slices of hard-cooked eggs.
• To collard greens, add clove of garlic, celery salt, pepper, sugar, pod of red pepper during cooking time.
• Serve with wedges of lemon or slices of hard-cooked eggs.
• Serve as Cuban greens—cooked chopped greens seasoned with salt, pepper, onion juice, horse-radish, served on toast squares and topped with crisp bacon and chopped dill pickle.

PEPPER SAUCE is typically southern, made by pouring vinegar over red hot peppers and allowing to stand until spicy hot. Served at the table, it is added to greens a drop at a time!

SPINACH TIMBALES

Cook 1½ to 2 lb. fresh or 1 pkg. frozen spinach 1 to 3 min., or until tender but still crisp. Drain; chop fine. Add to . . .

     3 eggs, slightly beaten
     1 cup milk
     1 tsp. salt
     ¼ tsp. pepper
     2 tsp. vinegar
     1 tsp. grated onion

Pour into greased custard cups (¾ full). Set in pan of hot water. Bake in mod. oven (350°) 25 to 30 min. until firm. Serve with Hollandaise, White, Egg, or Cheese Sauce (*pp. 398, 402*). *8 servings.*

For a more substantial main dish, place tomato slices on rounds of toast; place under broiler a few minutes. Top with Spinach Timbales and sauce. Sprinkle with paprika and minced parsley.

SPINACH SPRITE

Cook 1 lb. spinach just until tender, crisp, and still green, 3 to 5 min. Toss lightly with 1 tbsp. butter, 2 tsp. horse-radish, ¼ cup cream, rich milk, or cultured sour cream. *4 servings.*

EASY CREAMED SPINACH

Partially thaw and break apart 1 pkg. frozen chopped spinach. Make 1 cup Thick White Sauce (*p. 398*) in top of double boiler; add spinach, ⅛ tsp. nutmeg. Cover and cook over boiling water 15 min. or until tender, stirring occasionally. *4 servings.*

SPINACH PROVENCALE

To ¼ cup hot olive or salad oil or butter, add . . .

     2 lb. spinach, washed and well drained
     1 tsp. salt
     ¼ tsp. pepper
     ½ cup chopped onion
     1 clove garlic, minced

Cover; cook until spinach sinks down in pan. Remove cover and cook quickly until juices evaporate. Remove from heat; stir in . . .

     2 eggs, slightly beaten

Pour into 1-qt. baking dish. Top with buttered bread or cracker crumbs, grated Parmesan cheese. Bake in mod. oven (350°) 15 to 20 min. *4 servings.*

KOHLRABI Sometimes called an educated turnip. The small ones are more tender and delicate in flavor.

1 serves 1

Wash. Trim off root and stems. Leaves may be served as greens. Pare and cut into slices or cubes.

Cook covered in boiling salted water 25 to 30 min. Or bake, steam, or fry, the same as potatoes. When frying, avoid having fat too hot (too hot fat makes kohlrabi shrivel).

Ideas for serving...

- Serve with butter, salt, pepper. Vary with sauces and seasonings as given for asparagus, potatoes, turnips.
- Young kohlrabi is delicious eaten raw.

MUSHROOMS Once called "food of the gods" by ancient Egyptians, mushrooms were believed to have magic powers because they grew overnight. They are so tender that a few minutes of cooking is enough.

1 lb. serves 4

Wash. Do not peel. Leave whole, cut in slices, or chop stems and leave caps whole.

Sauté in about ¼ cup butter over low heat 8 to 10 min. (*See p. 31 for "How to Prepare Fresh Mushrooms."*) Or place ½ tsp. butter in hollow of each mushroom cap in shallow baking pan. Sprinkle with salt and pepper. Broil 5 to 8 min.

STUFFED MUSHROOMS IN CREAM

Place 12 large mushroom caps hollow-side-up in shallow baking dish. Chop stems finely; mix with 2 tbsp. *each* chopped celery, parsley; 1 tbsp. chopped onion or chives; ½ tsp. salt; dash of marjoram and pepper. Sauté in 3 tbsp. fat until golden. Mix in ½ cup fine dry bread crumbs. Spoon into mushroom caps. Pour ½ cup cream over. Bake in quick mod. oven (375°) 10 to 15 min. Serve as garnish over a main dish. *6 servings.*

Ideas for serving...

- Serve with meat as a garnish, or in sauces or soups.
- Combine with other vegetables, such as peas or beans.
- Serve in cream or creamed on toast (*see Mushroom Sauce, p. 398*). If desired, add an egg yolk, dash of sherry flavoring, or lemon juice.
- Add minced green onions, pinch of thyme, parsley, bay leaf, and/or garlic to butter when sautéing mushrooms.
- Save the liquor or juice from cooked or canned mushrooms for sauces, hot dishes, and soups.
- Toss sliced raw mushrooms with greens or other cut-up raw vegetables when making vegetable salads.

OKRA A southern belle in the vegetable kingdom. Fried, it tastes surprisingly like oysters.

1 lb. serves 4

Wash. Cut off stems. Leave small pods whole and cut large pods into ½" slices.

Cook covered in ½ to 1" boiling salted water 10 to 15 min., or steam in colander over hot water just until tender.

Or fry. Beat 1 egg with 2 tbsp. water. Pour over okra slices; drain slightly. Roll in corn meal, flour, or fine crumbs. Sauté in small amount of hot fat 2 to 6 min. *Or* French fry in hot fat (375°) deep enough to float 2 to 4 min. Sprinkle with salt. Serve hot.

Ideas for serving...

- Serve boiled or steamed okra with butter, salt, pepper. Vary with dash of vinegar or lemon juice, or minced onion or garlic.
- Sauté sliced or chopped green pepper and onion in hot fat until golden. Add sliced okra, fresh or canned tomatoes, salt, pepper, garlic if desired, parsley. Cook just until tender. Add corn and dash of chili powder, too, if desired.

DRAMATIC VEGETABLE PLATTERS

Cauliflower surrounded by Shredded Beets in
Spinach Nests and Glazed Onions

Stuffed Eggplant on Bed of Celery Cabbage . . .
and Glazed Carrots with Parsley Tops

ONIONS Related to the lily, it is quite a family as you can see below. Egyptian laborers building the pyramids ate onions for strength, soldiers ate them for courage.

	DRY	GREEN	LEEKS	GARLIC
***½ lb. dry serves 4**	White Bermudas Yellow Spanish (sweet) Real Domestic (small, hot)	Scallions Scallots Chives		

*(or 2 bunches green onions)

Wash and peel dry onions. Leave whole, chop, or cut in slices or rings. Trim all but about 2″ of tops of green onions and leeks.

Cook dry onions covered in 1 to 2″ boiling salted water—whole, 30 to 35 min.; tiny whole or sliced, 15 to 20 min. Green onions and leeks in ½ to 1″ boiling salted water 8 to 15 min., or bake in mod. oven (350°) 50 to 60 min.

 Ideas for serving...

• Serve with butter, salt, and pepper, or with Black Butter, Lemon Butter, or Crumb Sauce (*pp. 402, 403, 425*).

• Serve creamed (*p. 425*) or in well seasoned cream with butter.

• Add Cheese, Egg, or Hollandaise Sauce (*pp. 398, 403*).

• Combine with other vegetables or meats in hot dishes.

• Use green onion tops and chives in salads and for seasoning or garnishing.

EASY CREAMED ONIONS

Pour enough cream to almost cover canned small onions in baking dish. Dot with butter. Season with salt, pepper, dash of sugar. Bake covered in mod. oven (350°) 15 to 20 min., or until cream is bubbly.

ESCALLOPED ONIONS AND CHEESE

Add 1 tsp. mustard, ½ cup cut-up cheese to 2 cups Medium White Sauce (*p. 398*). Pour over 2 cups whole small cooked and drained onions in 1½-qt. baking dish. Bake in mod. oven (350°) 15 to 20 min. *4 to 6 servings.*

> **ONION IN BROWNED POTATO**
> **for flavor**
> Carve into each pared potato a little cavity just large enough to hold a baby onion. Press in the onion. Proceed as for Browned Potatoes (*p. 440*).

FRENCH FRIED ONIONS

Dip onion rings into milk, then into flour seasoned with salt; or into a batter made from beating together 1 egg, ¾ cup GOLD MEDAL Flour, ½ tsp. salt, ½ cup milk (for 4 to 5 onions). Lower into hot fat (375°) to float. Fry until brown . . . about 2 min. Drain on absorbent paper.

SAUTÉED ONIONS

Put sliced onion rings into skillet with just enough water for steam (1 to 4 tbsp.). Dot generously with butter, sprinkle with salt (to glaze, sprinkle with sugar). Cover. Cook 5 to 10 min. until tender. Remove cover and finish cooking until tender, shiny, and golden, stirring occasionally.

CARAMEL CREAM ONIONS

Cook tiny fresh or canned onions with a whole clove in each end. In skillet, sauté onions gently in butter. Sprinkle with brown sugar. Turn frequently. When golden and slightly caramelized, stir in enough cream to make a sauce. Heat and serve. (Allow 2 tbsp. butter, 2 tbsp. sugar, and ¼ cup cream for 6 tiny onions.)

GLAZED ONIONS

Cook onions as for Caramel Cream Onions, using twice as much sugar (granulated or brown) as butter. Omit cream.

SWEET-SOUR ONIONS are onions cooked with seasonings and enough vinegar and sugar added to suit one's taste. Serve with generous dabs of butter.

STUFFED BAKED ONIONS

Cook large whole onions until slightly tender. Drain; cool. Cut thin slices from root end. Hollow out centers—leaving ½″ shell. Chop centers and combine with Mushroom or Cheese Sauce (*p. 398*), or a creamed meat mixture. Fill hollows; top with crumbs. Bake in mod. hot oven (400°) about 1 hr.

PARSNIPS
An old gardening book says "parsnips are not sweet 'til bit by frost." That is because frost changes the starch to sugar which greatly improves the taste.

1½ lb.
serves 4

Scrape, pare, or scrub with brush. Leave whole or cut into cubes, slices, or strips.

Cook covered in ½ to 1" boiling salted water (a little sugar improves flavor)—whole, 25 to 30 min.; sliced or cubed, 10 to 15 min.

- Or bake in mod. oven (350°) 30 to 45 min.
- Or season with salt, pepper; sauté in small amount of hot fat 5 to 10 min.
- Or French fry in hot fat (375°) to cover, 3 to 6 min.

JANETTE'S PARSNIPS
Cook whole parsnips in their jackets 15 min. or until almost tender. Pare. (Waxed parsnips are pared before cooking.) Cut in strips or slices. Dip in flour. Sauté slowly in butter until golden brown. Season.

GLAZED BAKED PARSNIPS
Peel and slice parsnips into a greased baking dish. Add a few tablespoons water for steam; sprinkle with brown or granulated sugar. Dot with butter and a sprig of orange peel or a little orange juice. Bake covered in mod. oven (350°) about 1 hr. or until tender.

PEAS (Green)
One of the most popular of all vegetables. They are not only delicious to eat, but a bright, refreshing color contrast on the dinner plate.

*3 lb.
serves 4

*(unshelled)

Shell just before cooking. Save a few of the pods to add flavor in cooking.

Cook covered in ½ to 1" boiling salted water (if desired, add sugar and pods for flavor) 8 to 12 min.

FRENCH STYLE GREEN PEAS
Line bottom and sides of saucepan with washed lettuce leaves. Add peas, sprinkle with salt, pepper, sugar, nutmeg. Add 2 to 4 tbsp. butter. Cover with lettuce leaves. Cook covered over low heat until tender, about 20 min. Discard leaves. Serve.

FROZEN PEAS IN CREAM
Cook 1 pkg. frozen peas just until well thawed; drain. Heat ½ to 1 cup cream seasoned with salt, pepper, sugar, butter. Add peas. Cook covered over boiling water 15 to 30 min., until tender. *4 servings.*

Ideas for serving...

- Serve with butter, salt, pepper, and a dash of lemon or lime juice, minced onion, or melted mint jelly.
- Serve Creamed (*p. 425*), or in seasoned cream with butter, or with Hollandaise or Cheese Sauce (*pp. 402, 398*).
- Combine with other vegetables . . . celery or sautéed mushrooms and pimiento, carrots, or little green onions. Cook separately or together.

BLACK-EYED PEAS
Favorite of the south.

To Dr. James E. Curtis, a true southerner, this dish brings back memories of happy boyhood days in his farm home in Arkansas.

2 lb.
serves 4

Shell as for peas (green). Cook covered in ½ to 1" boiling salted water (to which ham hock or bacon drippings or salt pork, and ½ tsp. sugar have been added) 30 to 40 min. until tender.

PEPPERS (Sweet Green)
Do not confuse with the "hot" variety called Chili peppers.

Wash. Remove seeds, stem, ribs. Leave whole or cut in half for baking.

Stuff (see *Stuffed Green Peppers, p. 276*).

All you have to do to keep peppers in shape while baking: put in muffin pan or individual muffin cups.

SAUTÉED GREEN PEPPERS
Chop peppers or cut in strips. Sauté in fat seasoned with salt, garlic, or oregano. Serve as meat accompaniment.

Green Pepper Rings, for garnishing salads and hot dishes. **Minced Green Pepper,** for flavoring same. See p. 55 for *"How to Prepare."*

POTATOES (White) *Though we call them Irish, they came from Peru where, instead of being cooked, they were cured by frost and then dried. Now we cook them dozens of ways and eat them almost every day.*

2 lb. serves 4

Native of America. Called "Irish potatoes" because they once sustained people during a famine in Ireland. Potatoes with their Vitamin C saved the sailors of old from dying of scurvy on long voyages. In Civil War days, the women packed potatoes in barrels of brine, and sent them to prison camps to save lives of the undernourished prisoners.

Wash. Leave skins on whenever possible. Scrub with brush. Or pare thin. Leave whole or cut in large pieces or slices.

Cook covered in 1″ boiling salted water— whole, 30 to 40 min.; cut-up or whole tiny new potatoes, 20 to 25 min.; or bake in mod. hot oven (400°) 1 hr.

BOILED (cooked) POTATOES

Follow directions above. Shake over low heat to dry. Serve with butter, salt, and pepper.

PARSLEYED POTATOES

New potatoes are usually used for these.

Melt ¼ cup butter. Remove from heat. Mix in ¼ cup minced parsley. Toss 6 boiled potatoes in mixture until coated.

CREAMED POTATOES

Combine Thin or Medium White Sauce (*p. 398*) with boiled potatoes. Allow at least 1 cup sauce for 4 med. or 8 small potatoes. Season with salt, pepper. Sprinkle with paprika or minced parsley or chives.

AU GRATIN POTATOES

Follow above recipe for Creamed Potatoes but use Cheese Sauce (*p. 398*). Top with grated cheese.

LEMON-BUTTERED NEW POTATOES

To ¼ cup butter, melted, add grated rind of 1 lemon, 2 tbsp. lemon juice, 1 tbsp. minced chives, salt, pepper, dash of nutmeg. Pour over 6 servings hot boiled potatoes.

BROWNED POTATOES (Franconia)

Add pared potatoes around roast in roasting pan. Turn occasionally to brown on all sides. Or cook pared potatoes until almost tender. Drain; add to roast last 30 min. Turn to brown.

Fan-Tan Potatoes: Slice *almost* through the pared raw potatoes (⅛″ gashes). Dribble with meat juices or butter. Bake as for Browned Potatoes.

BROILED POTATOES

Cut cooked potatoes lengthwise in slices about ¼″ thick. Dip into melted butter, then sprinkle with salt and pepper. Broil until a golden brown on both sides.

COTTAGE FRIED POTATOES (Fried Cooked)

Slice boiled potatoes. Heap slices lightly into skillet coated generously with heated butter or bacon drippings. Sprinkle with salt, pepper. Brown slowly until crisp, turning as sections brown.

LYONNAISE POTATOES

Follow recipe for Cottage Fried Potatoes (*above*)—*except* add sautéed onion slices to the potatoes before frying.

POTATOES ANNA (Fried Raw)

Melt 2 tbsp. butter in heavy skillet. Arrange *thinly* sliced or grated raw potatoes in 2 or 3 layers. Sprinkle each layer with salt, pepper; dot generously with butter. Cover; steam 15 min. Uncover; cook until tender and crispy brown on the bottom. Invert on serving plate. *4 to 6 servings.*

HASHED BROWNED POTATOES

Melt 3 tbsp. fat in heavy skillet. Mix 3 cups chopped or grated boiled potatoes with 3 tbsp. flour, 1 tbsp. minced onion, ¼ cup top milk, 1 tsp. salt, ⅛ tsp. pepper. Pack potatoes firmly in skillet. Brown over low heat on underside (20 min.). Fold over like omelet. *4 servings.*

SAUTÉED POTATO BALLS

In hot melted butter or salad oil in skillet, sauté whole little cooked new potatoes. Cook until golden, tossing occasionally. Season to taste.

POTATO PANCAKES

Grate 3 med. potatoes. Add and blend thoroughly 1 beaten egg, 1 tsp. salt. Shape into patties and fry in greased skillet, about 2 min. on each side, until tender and brown. *4 to 6 servings.*

FRENCH FRIED POTATOES

Cut pared potatoes into 3/8" lengthwise strips. If potatoes are pared and cut ahead of time, let stand in cold water. Drain and dry thoroughly. Drop strips into hot fat (375°) deep enough to float. Do not crowd pan but fry small amounts at a time. Fry until tender, crisp, and golden brown (5 to 7 min.). Drain on paper. Sprinkle with salt. Serve hot.

POTATO CHIPS

Follow recipe for French Fried Potatoes (*above*)—*except* cut potatoes in thin slices.

BAKED FRENCH POTATOES

Arrange thin strips of raw potato (pared or unpared) in single layer in shallow baking pan in which fat (about 1 tbsp. per potato) has been melted. Brush with more melted fat. Bake in hot oven (425°) 30 to 40 min., until tender. Turn occasionally to brown evenly. Season with salt and pepper.

MASHED POTATOES

Cook potatoes until done but not mushy. Heat milk—*at least* 1/2 cup for 8 potatoes. Drain potatoes, shake over heat to "dry." Mash slightly, add butter, seasonings, milk. Whip vigorously until light and fluffy. Sprinkle with paprika, minced parsley, or chives. To keep potatoes hot and fluffy, set covered pan in hot water.

MASHED POTATO CAKES

Shape seasoned mashed potatoes into little cakes. Or form into a roll; wrap in waxed paper; chill; slice. Dip cakes or slices into flour. Fry slowly in hot fat until brown. For "special" cakes, add beaten egg, chopped parsley, celery seeds, or grated onion.

POTATO PUFF

To 4 cups seasoned mashed potatoes, add 2 eggs, separated and beaten (fold in whites last), 1/2 cup cream, and 2 tbsp. butter. Heap lightly into 1 1/2-qt. baking dish. Bake in mod. oven (350°) 30 min., until puffed and brown. *6 to 8 servings.*

DUCHESS POTATOES

Make Mashed Potatoes and beat in beaten eggs (2 eggs for 3 cups potatoes). Spoon into mounds; or with pastry bag and tube form rosettes on a greased baking sheet; or pipe in a border around planked meat or fish. Brush with butter. Brown in hot oven (425°).

BAKED POTATOES

Choose baking potatoes of med. size. Scrub with a brush. Rub with fat for soft skin. Prick skin with fork to let steam escape during baking. Cut large potatoes in half; place cut side down in baking pan. Bake until potatoes "squeeze" soft in mod. hot oven (400°) 1 hr., or in mod. oven (350°) 1 1/2 hr. *For oven meals in which other foods are being baked, use the temperature given for the other foods, adjusting the length of baking time for potatoes accordingly.*

After baking, cut criss-cross gash on potato top; squeeze until potato pops up through opening. Into opening, tuck butter, sweet or sour cream, or cheese (heat in oven to melt cheese).

PUFFED POTATOES IN THE HALF-SHELL

Cut baked potatoes in halves lengthwise. Scoop out potato; whip until fluffy with butter, milk, seasonings. Mound back into shells. Sprinkle with paprika or grated cheese. Heat in mod. hot oven (400°) until golden brown and cheese has melted.

SPECIAL PUFFED POTATOES IN THE HALF-SHELL

Follow recipe above—*except* add for each potato:

2 tbsp. bits of cooked ham or tuna, 1 tbsp. minced onion, 1 tsp. minced parsley or

2 tbsp. cultured sour cream, 2 tbsp. crisp bacon bits, 1 tbsp. minced onion, dash of nutmeg or

2 tbsp. cottage cheese, 2 tbsp. crisp bacon bits or cooked ham, 1 tbsp. chopped chives

SCALLOPED POTATOES

Arrange layers of thinly sliced or coarsely grated raw potatoes in greased baking dish. Sprinkle each layer with salt, pepper, minced onion, or desired seasonings; dot with butter. Pour *hot* milk over, 1/2 to 3/4" from top of potatoes. Bake uncovered in mod. oven (350°) about 1 1/4 hr., or until tender.

GLORIFIED SCALLOPED POTATOES

Dice potatoes (very small) and use juice from drained canned mushrooms and canned consommé or bouillon for the liquid. When sprinkling layers of potatoes with salt and pepper, add mushrooms (sautéed in butter), too.

SHIRRED POTATOES

Make 3 cups Thin White Sauce (p. 398). Drop 3 cups grated raw potato *immediately* into the hot sauce. Season to taste with salt, pepper, minced onion. Pour into *shallow* baking dish. Dot with 1 to 2 tbsp. butter. Bake uncovered in slow mod. oven (325°) about 2 hr., until tender and crunchy brown on top. *4 to 6 servings.*

OVEN-CREAMED NEW POTATOES

In baking dish, pour cream or a Thin White Sauce (p. 398) over tiny new raw potatoes (leave in their jackets, if desired). Sprinkle with salt, pepper, and salad herbs for a different touch. Dot with butter. Bake covered in mod. oven (350°) about 1 hr., until tender.

SO-EASY CREAMED POTATOES

Heat 1 cup cream in top of double boiler. Add 3 cups coarsely grated raw potato, 1 tsp. salt, dash of pepper. Cook covered over boiling water about 45 min., until tender. If potatoes become thick, add more cream. *4 servings.*

BUFFET POTATOES

Pare and cut into strips 4 med. baking potatoes. Mix in 1½-qt. baking dish, with 2 tsp. salt, pepper, 3 tbsp. minced parsley, ½ cup grated *sharp* cheese. Dot with 3 tbsp. butter and pour ½ cup cream over. Sprinkle with 1 tbsp. minced parsley. Bake in mod. oven (350°) 1½ to 2 hr. Remove cover last 20 min. of baking to brown. *4 servings.*

SWEET POTATOES

Jersey sweets are dry and pale yellow; yams are moist and orange. They are cooked the same way—baked, mashed, candied, sautéed, or French fried.

2 lb. serves 4

Wash and cut off woody portion. Do not pare. Cook same as potatoes. Remove skins after cooking. To mash, bake, sauté, or French fry follow same directions as for potatoes.

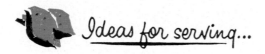

Ideas for serving...

• To mashed sweet potatoes, add cream or whipped cream and a dash of nutmeg or cinnamon.

• Or add orange juice and grated orange rind, spiced apple or peach juice, or crushed pineapple to mashed sweet potatoes.

• Sprinkle French fried sweet potatoes with confectioners' sugar before serving.

• Tuck marshmallows into mashed sweet potatoes for a special treat. Bake until marshmallows melt.

• To "candy-easy," use canned butterscotch sundae sauce.

• Bake together yams, apple slices, lemon slices, butter, and brown sugar.

All you have to do —

To make Candied Sweet Potatoes extra "caramelly": bake them in a shallow baking dish.

BAKED CANDIED SWEET POTATOES

Slice 6 cooked sweet potatoes into baking dish. Pour over syrup made by bringing to boil 1 cup brown sugar (packed), ¼ cup *each* butter, water, ½ tsp. salt. Bake in mod. oven (350°) about 30 min., basting occasionally. *6 servings.*

SKILLET CANDIED SWEET POTATOES

Follow recipe above—except mix butter, sugar, and water in heavy skillet. Cook until mixture bubbles. Add potatoes and cook slowly, turning occasionally until potatoes get caramelly (about 20 min.). *6 servings.*

SWEET POTATO APPLES

Shape seasoned mashed baked Jersey sweet potatoes around a marshmallow to form an apple. Place a clove in 1 end for a stem. Brush with beaten egg yolk mixed with water, then paprika. Place on greased pan. Heat in mod. oven (350°) 12 min.

BANANA MERINGUE SWEET POTATO PUFF

Whip 2 cups cooked sweet potato with 1 egg yolk, 2 tbsp. butter, ½ tsp. salt. Pile lightly into buttered 1-qt. baking dish. Top with 1 banana, sliced, and a meringue made from the egg white and 2 tbsp. sugar. Bake in mod. oven (350°) 30 min. *4 servings.*

PUMPKIN

Cut, seed, trim off stringy portions. Cook like potatoes until tender. To mash, follow recipe for Mashed Sweet Potatoes (*p. 442*). To bake, follow recipe for baked squash (*below*).

SALSIFY

Prepare and serve like parsnips, carrots. Plunge into cold water with a little lemon juice to prevent darkening after paring.

RUTABAGAS See Turnips and Rutabagas (*p. 444*).

SAUERKRAUT Fresh or canned, long cooking is unnecessary. Heat *through* slowly in covered saucepan or in covered baking dish in mod. oven (350°). Brown first in butter or meat drippings (add minced onion, if desired) . . . or dot top with butter or meat drippings. Raw apple or potato, grated, improves flavor. Sprinkle with celery seed or caraway seed.

SPARERIBS AND SAUERKRAUT
See p. 317.

SPINACH See Greens (*p. 435*).

SQUASH The Northern American Indians called it "Askutasquash." We have many names for the dozen or more varieties grown now.

SUMMER SQUASH
Skins are soft.

| 2 lb. serves 4 | Wash, do not pare. Remove stem and blossom ends. Cut into ½ to ¾" slices or cubes. |

Cook covered in a very small amount of water (2 to 4 tbsp.), 1 to 2 tbsp. salad oil or butter, salt, pepper, and clove of garlic or bouillon cube, if desired, for 10 to 15 min., until *just* tender.

Or sauté or French fry as for Parsnips (*p. 439*).

Serve with butter, salt, pepper, and sprinkling of Parmesan cheese or paprika. Vary with dash of catsup, tomato, or chili sauce. Pour Black Butter Sauce (*p. 402*) or Lemon Butter (*p. 425*) over.

SUMMER SQUASH CALIFORNIAN

In baking dish, spread layers of sliced squash, cottage or cheddar cheese, tomatoes, salt, pepper, garlic salt, if desired. Bake covered in mod. oven (350°) 30 to 45 min. or until tender. Sprinkle with minced parsley.

ZUCCHINI PROVENCALE

In skillet, sauté 1 med. onion, sliced, and 1 clove garlic, minced, in ¼ cup salad oil. Add 2 lb. sliced zucchini squash, 4 cut-up tomatoes, 1 chopped green pepper, salt and pepper to taste. Cook until tender. Sprinkle with minced parsley and Parmesan cheese before serving. *8 servings.*

WINTER SQUASH
Skins are hard.

| 3 lb. serves 4 | Wash. Cut into halves or individual servings; remove seeds. Bake cut portions uncovered for crusty top, covered |

in baking dish or wrapped in aluminum foil for moist top, 30 to 60 min. in mod. (350°) to mod. hot oven (400°). Time and temperature vary with size of squash. Brush with butter and season before or after baking. Or place halves cut-side-down in shallow pan. Bake 25 to 30 min. Turn up; brush with butter and seasonings. Bake 25 to 30 min. or until tender. Hubbard squash may be removed from shell and cooked as for potatoes.

Ideas for serving...

• Spoon brown sugar, cut-up marshmallows, or cranberry sauce with dash of nutmeg into hollows for last 15 to 30 min. of baking.

• Fill hollows with sausage or ground beef patties. Little link sausages are good, too.

• Scoop out and mash with cream and nutmeg or candied ginger, or with orange juice and grated orange rind.

• For Glazed Squash, follow recipe for Skillet Candied Sweet Potatoes (*p. 442*).

TOMATOES *Once known as "love apples" and considered poisonous. Call it "tomay-to" or "tomah-to," the tomato is still one of the best liked of all our vegetables.*

2 lb. serves 4

Wash. Peel, if desired. (Dip first into hot water 30 seconds; then in cold water. Or hold on fork over direct heat until skin splits. Or stroke skin lightly with back of knife; then slip off skin.) Leave whole, or cut into quarters or slices. Cook covered with no water added, 8 to 10 min.

STEWED TOMATOES

Cook as above 2½ cups tomatoes seasoned with 1 tsp. minced onion, ½ tbsp. sugar, dash of salt, pepper, 2 tbsp. butter, and ½ cup soft bread crumbs. Or omit bread crumbs and sprinkle with crumbs or croutons sautéed in garlic butter just before serving. *4 servings.*

BROILED TOMATOES

Dot tomato halves or thick slices of tomato with butter. Sprinkle with salt, pepper, sweet basil or savory. Broil under low heat 3 to 5 min., just until heated.

FRIED TOMATOES WITH CREAM

Sauté thick tomato slices slowly in butter until golden brown on each side. Remove from pan. Stir in ½ to ¾ cup sweet or cultured sour cream and let bubble slowly over low heat until brown. Serve over tomatoes. Sprinkle with sweet basil, if desired.

BAKED TOMATOES

Bake whole or cut tomatoes in shallow baking dish in mod. oven (350°) 20 to 30 min. If desired, pour Brown Sauce (*p. 400*) over for last 10 min. of baking.

OTHER TOPPINGS FOR BAKED TOMATOES

Dots of butter, thin slice of onion, crushed cracker crumbs

Grated cheese

Minced chives mixed with crumbs, butter

Thin slice onion, dash of prepared mustard

STUFFED TOMATOES

Cut slice from top of 6 unpeeled tomatoes. Scoop out centers and mix pulp with . . .

½ cup crumbled crisp bacon bits (about 6 slices)

¼ cup chopped celery

1 small onion, finely chopped

1 cup soft bread crumbs

½ tsp. salt

half of ½ cup grated cheese

Fill centers. Sprinkle with rest of grated cheese; dot with butter. Bake in greased muffin cups or baking dish.

TEMPERATURE: 350° (mod. oven).
TIME: Bake about 30 min.
AMOUNT: 6 servings.

TURNIPS AND RUTABAGAS *Yellow they are rutabagas; white they are turnips, a little more delicate in flavor. Both are cooked and served the same way.*

2 lb. serves 4

Firm heavy ones are best; lightweights are woody, strong flavored. Pare; slice, dice, or leave small ones whole. (Rutabagas usually have waxed covering to preserve them during shipping.)

Cook covered in ½ to 1″ boiling salted water (a little sugar improves flavor)—turnips, 20 to 30 min.; rutabagas 25 to 40 min. Or sauté as for Janette's Parsnips (*p. 439*).

TURNIP OR RUTABAGA PUFF: Follow recipe for Potato Puff (*p. 441*)—*except* use mashed turnips or rutabagas in place of potatoes.

 Ideas for serving...

• Serve with butter, salt, and pepper.

• Mash with cream or whipped cream and nutmeg.

• Combine with a White Sauce (*p. 398*). Add a few tbsp. minced onion or chives and a dash of Worcestershire sauce.

GLAZED TURNIPS OR RUTABAGAS

Cook, slice, and sauté slowly in butter . . . sprinkling lightly with sugar . . . continuing to add sugar until turnips or rutabagas are well glazed. Turn occasionally.

Index

INDEX (cont.)

INDEX

453

T